Cantor/Choir Resource

for

CELEBRATING THE EUCHARIST

and

SACRED SONG

LITURGICAL PRESS
Collegeville, Minnesota

www.litpress.org

This *Cantor/Choir Edition* is a publication of Liturgical Press, Saint John's Abbey, P.O. Box 7500, Collegeville, Minnesota 56321-7500, © 2009 Order of Saint Benedict, Collegeville, Minnesota. All rights reserved under United States copyright law. No part of this publication may be reproduced or transmitted in any form or by any means, electronic or mechanical, including photocopying, recording, or by any information storage and retrieval system, without permission in writing from the appropriate copyright owner/administrator. The index of this edition contains contact information for publishers and copyright holders/administrators.

The English translation of various Psalm Responses, Lenten Gospel Acclamations, and Alleluia and Gospel Verses from *Lectionary for Mass* © 1969, 1981, 1997, International Committee on English in the Liturgy, Inc. (ICEL); excerpts from the English translation of the *Rite of Baptism for Children* © 1969, ICEL; excerpts from the English translation of *Rite of Holy Week* © 1972, ICEL; excerpts from the English translation of *The Roman Missal* © 1973, ICEL; excerpts from the English translation of *The Liturgy of the Hours* © 1974, ICEL; excerpts from the English translation of *Eucharistic Prayer for Masses with Children* © 1975, ICEL; excerpts from the English translation of *Rite of Dedication of a Church and an Altar* © 1978, ICEL; the music of the Gospel Acclamation by Sr. Theophane Hytrek, O.S.F., the Lenten Gospel Acclamation by Howard Hughes, S.M. and the text of "Our Father, We Have Wandered" from *Resource Collection of Hymns and Service Music for the Liturgy* © 1981, ICEL; excerpts from the English translation of *Order of Christian Funerals* © 1985, ICEL; excerpts from the English translation of *Rite of Christian Initiation of Adults* © 1985, ICEL; the text and music of Psalm 85 "God is Speaking Peace" from *Psalms for All Seasons* © 1987, ICEL. All rights reserved. Used with permission.

Excerpts from the *Lectionary for Mass for Use in the Dioceses of the United States* © 2001, 1998, 1997, and 1970 Confraternity of Christian Doctrine, Inc., Washington, DC. Used with permission. All rights reserved. No portion of this text may be reproduced without permission in writing from the copyright holder.

The *Prayer for the Blessing of Liturgical Music* written by Michael Kwatera, OSB, © 2004, Order of Saint Benedict, Collegeville, MN 56321. All right reserved.

Cover design by Ann Blattner.

Printed in the United States of America.

ISBN 978-0-8146-3079-2

Contents

HYMNS & SONGS 1–480

SERVICE & RITUAL MUSIC

    Jubilation Mass *(James J. Chepponis)* 481

    New Plainsong Mass *(David Hurd)* 491

    Mass of Creation *(Marty Haugen)* 494

    Mass of the Angels and Saints *(Steven R. Janco)* 505

    Land of Rest Mass *(Marcia Pruner and Richard Proulx)* 516

    Community Mass *(Richard Proulx)* 521

    Saint Benedict Mass *(Robert LeBlanc)* 525

    Cantus Missae 533

    Additional Service and Ritual Music 546

INDEXES

    Index of Gospel Acclamation Verses 600

    Index of Tune Names 601

    Index of Metrical Tunes 602

    Liturgical Index 603

    Index of Service Music 604

    Index of First Lines and Common Titles 605

Prayer for the Blessing of Liturgical Music

We give you thanks, God of all times and places,
for sending your Son, Jesus Christ, to be our Savior.
He brought to this world
the song of your praise
that fills the halls of heaven.

Let the ministry of poets, composers, and musicians
help us to give pleasing worship to you
in this holy house
and generous service to our sisters and brothers
in the world outside.

Be powerfully present in every word and note
we sing or play or hear
as you were present in the heart's melody
of your holy martyr Cecilia,
whom the Church honors
as the patron saint of music.

In company with her,
and with the Blessed Virgin Mary,
who sang of your mercy and justice,
we praise and glorify you,
both now and for ever. Amen.

Hymns and Songs

1 A Hymn of Glory Let Us Sing

A Hymn of Glory Let Us Sing, pg. 2

Text: *Hymnum canamus gloria;* Venerable Bede, 673–735; tr. *Lutheran Book of Worship,* ©1978, administered by Augsburg Fortress. All rights reserved. Used with permission.
Music: LASST UNS ERFREUEN, LM 88 44 88 with alleluias, *Geistliche Kirchengesange,* Cologne, 1623;
Harmony: Christine Manderfeld, OSB, © 2009, the Sisters of Saint Benedict, St. Joseph, MN. Administered by Liturgical Press, Collegeville, MN. All rights reserved.
Descant: Eugene Martin Lindusky, 1924–2005, © Mary C. Lindusky. All rights reserved. Used with permission.

A Mighty Fortress Is Our God

A New Heaven and Earth

Text and music: Marty Haugen, b. 1950, © 2002, GIA Publications, Inc. All rights reserved. Used with permission.

A Nuptial Blessing

A Nuptial Blessing, pg. 2

Text: Vicki Klima, b. 1952; adapt. by Michael Joncas, b. 1951, and George Szews, b. 1951. Music: Michael Joncas, b. 1951.
Text and music: © 1989, GIA Publications, Inc. All rights reserved. Used with permission.

A Prayer for the Elect

Text: Omer Westendorf, 1916–1997, © 1989, World Library Publications, 3708 River Road, Franklin Park, IL 60131. www.wlpmusic.com All rights reserved. Used with permission.
Music: WINCHESTER NEW, LM, adapt. from *Musikalischers Handbach,* Hamburg, 1690.
Descant: Christine Manderfeld, OSB, © 2009, the Sisters of Saint Benedict, St. Joseph, MN. Administered by Liturgical Press, Collegeville, MN. All rights reserved.

Adeste Fideles / O Come, All Ye Faithful

Adoramus te Christe

We adore You, O Christ, and we bless You, because by your Holy Cross You have redeemed the world.

Adapt. from antiphon of Good Friday Liturgy, Th. Dubois, d. 1924.

Adoro Te Devote

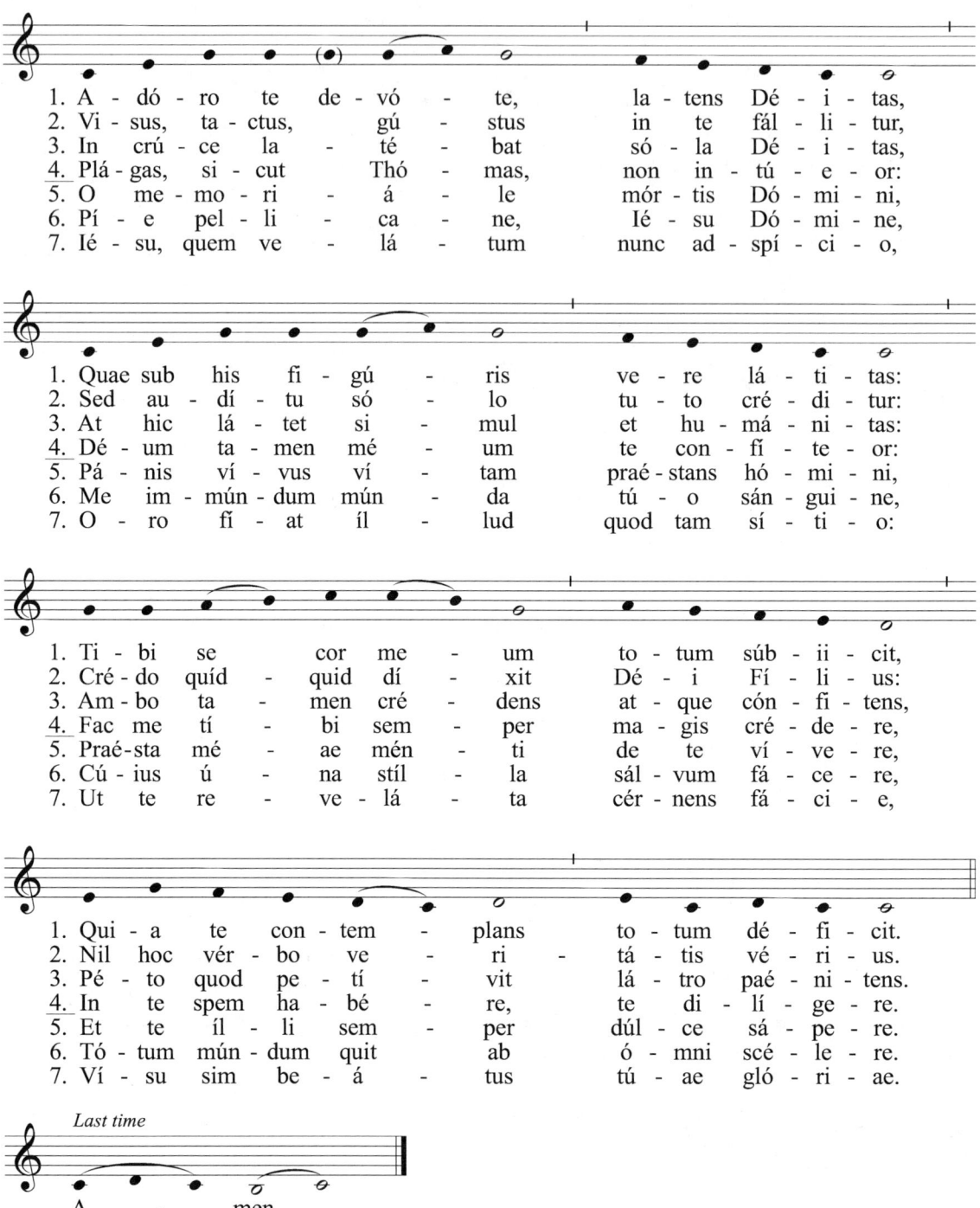

Text: Saint Thomas Aquinas, OP, ca. 1225–1274. Music: ADORO TE DEVOTE, irregular, Plainchant, Mode V.

Advent Gathering Song: Come, Come Emmanuel

Text and music: James J. Chepponis, b. 1956, © 1995, GIA Publications, Inc. All rights reserved. Used with permission.

Again We Keep This Solemn Fast

1. Again we keep this solemn fast A gift of faith from ages past, This Lent which binds us lovingly To faith and hope and charity.
2. The law and prophets from of old In figured ways this Lent foretold, Which Christ, all ages' Lord and Guide, In these last days has sanctified.
3. More sparing, therefore, let us make The words we speak, the food we take, Our sleep, our laughter, ev'ry sense; Learn peace through holy penitence.
4. Let us avoid each harmful way That lures the careless mind astray; By watchful prayer our spirits free From scheming of the Enemy.
5. We pray, O blessed Three in One, Our God while endless ages run, That this, our Lent of forty days, May bring us growth and give you praise.

Text: *Ex more docti mystico;* ascr. to Gregory the Great, c. 540–604; tr. Peter J. Scagnelli, b. 1949, © 1973, Peter J. Scagnelli. All rights reserved. Used with permission.
Music: ERHALT UNS HERR, LM; Klug's *Geistliche Lieder,* 1543; harm. J. S. Bach, 1685–1750.
Descant: Randall Sensmeier, © 1992, GIA Publications, Inc. All rights reserved. Used with permission.

All Are Welcome

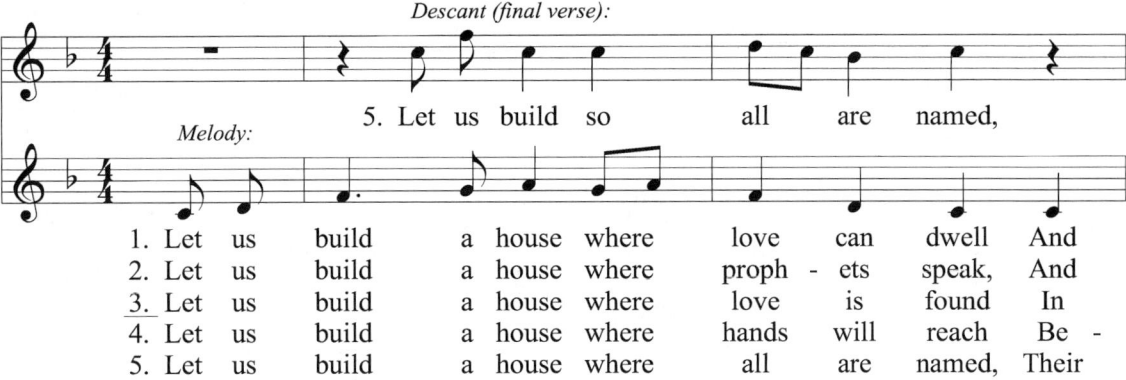
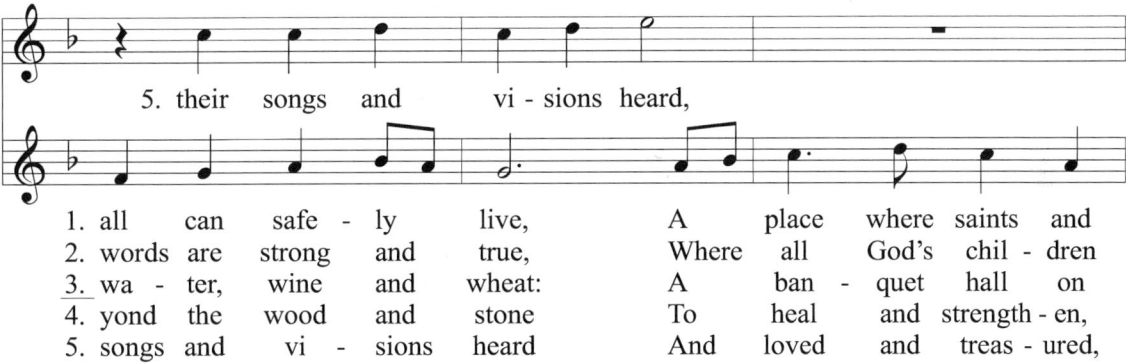

All Are Welcome, pg. 2

Text: Marty Haugen, b. 1950. Music: TWO OAKS, 9 6 8 6 8 7 10 with refrain; Marty Haugen, b. 1950.
Text and music: © 1994, GIA Publications, Inc. All rights reserved. Used with permission.

All Creatures of Our God and King

All Creatures of Our God and King, pg. 2

Text: St. Francis of Assisi, c. 1182–1226; tr. William Henry Draper, 1855–1933.
Music: LASST UNS ERFREUEN, LM 88 44 88 with alleluias, *Geistliche Kirchengesange,* Cologne, 1623.
Harmony: Christine Manderfeld, OSB, © 2009, the Sisters of Saint Benedict, St. Joseph, MN. Administered by Liturgical Press, Collegeville, MN. All rights reserved.
Descant: Eugene Martin Lindusky, 1924–2005, © Mary C. Lindusky. All rights reserved. Used with permission.

All Glory Is Yours

13

All Glory, Laud, and Honor

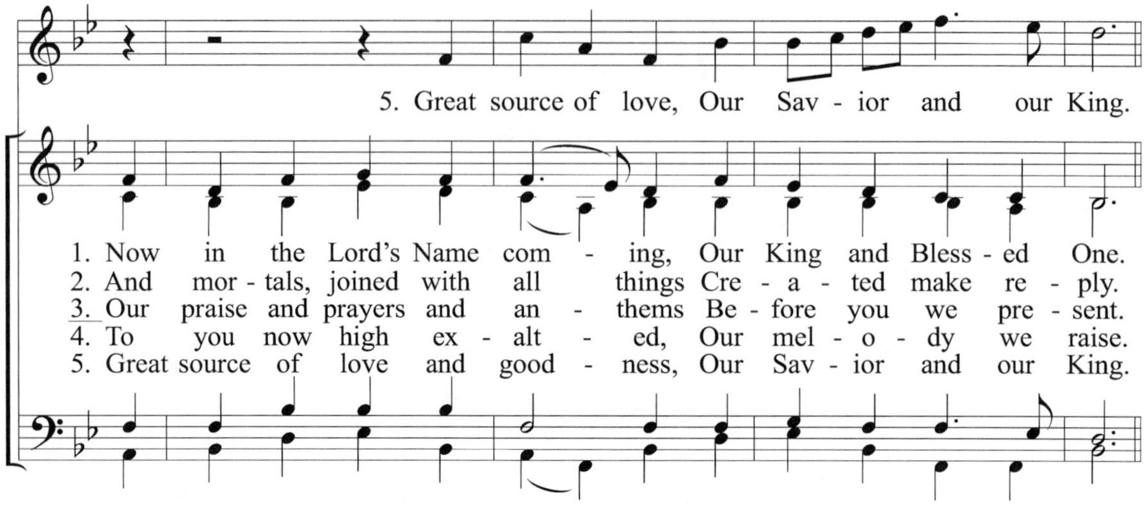

All Glory, Laud, and Honor, pg. 2

1. Now in the Lord's Name com — ing, Our King and Bless — ed One.
2. And mor — tals, joined with all things Cre — a — ted make re — ply.
3. Our praise and prayers and an — thems Be — fore you we pre — sent.
4. To you now high ex — alt — ed, Our mel — o — dy we raise.
5. Great source of love and good — ness, Our Sav — ior and our King.

Descant: 5. Great source of love, Our Sav — ior and our King.

Text: *Gloria, laus et honor,* Theodulph of Orleans, c. 760–821; tr. John M. Neale, 1818–1866, alt. Music: ST. THEODULPH, 76 76 D, Melchior Teschner, 1584–1635.
Descant: Christine Manderfeld, OSB, b. 1938, © 2009, the Sisters of Saint Benedict, St. Joseph, MN. Administered by Liturgical Press, Collegeville, MN. All rights reserved.

15   All Hail, Adored Trinity

Descant (final verse):
3. O Trin — i — ty, O U — ni — ty, Be pres — ent as we wor — ship thee; And to the an — gels'

1. All hail, a — dor — ed Trin — i — ty; All praise, e — ter — nal U — ni — ty: O God the Fa — ther,
2. Three Per — sons praise we ev — er — more, One on — ly God our hearts a — dore: In your sure mer — cy
3. O Trin — i — ty, O U — ni — ty, Be pres — ent as we wor — ship thee; And to the an — gels'

All Hail, Adored Trinity, pg. 2

Text: Latin, c. 11th cent.; tr. John Chandler, 1806–1876. Music: OLD HUNDREDTH, LM, Louis Bourgeois, c. 1510–1561.
Descant: Christine Manderfeld, OSB, b. 1938, © 2009, the Sisters of Saint Benedict, St. Joseph, MN. Administered by Liturgical Press, Collegeville, MN. All rights reserved.

All Hail the Power of Jesus' Name 16

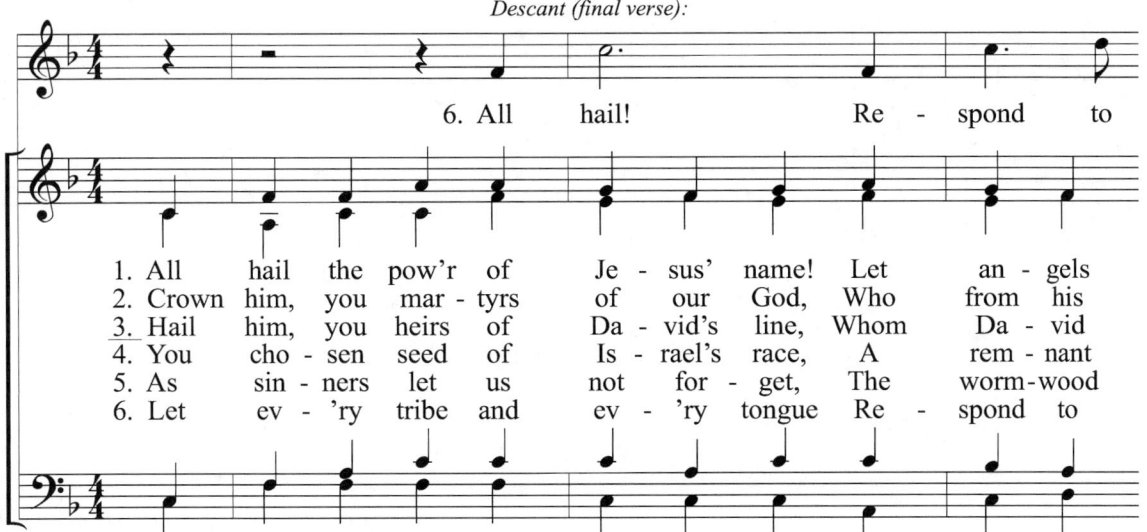

All Hail the Power of Jesus' Name, pg. 2

Text: Edward Perronet, 1726–1792; tr. John Rippon, 1751–1836, alt. Music: CORONATION, 86 86 86, Oliver Holden, 1765–1844.
Descant: Craig Westendorf, © 1980, GIA Publications, Inc. All rights reserved. Used with permission.

All People That on Earth Do Dwell / Praise God from Whom All Blessings Flow

All People That on Earth Do Dwell / Praise God from Whom All Blessings Flow, pg. 2

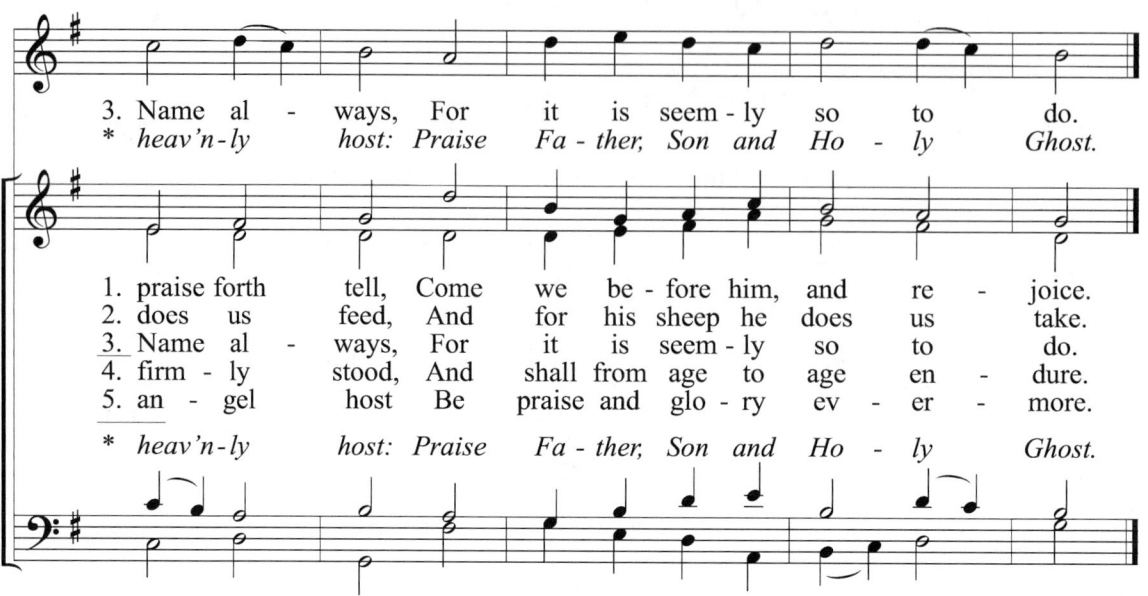

* *This stanza may be sung alone or used as an alternate to stanza 5.*

Text: Psalm (99) 100; William Kethe, d.c. 1593; Doxology, Thomas Ken, 1637–1711. Music: OLD HUNDREDTH, LM, Louis Bourgeois, c. 1510–1561.
Descant: Christine Manderfeld, OSB, b. 1938, © 2009, the Sisters of Saint Benedict, St. Joseph, MN. Administered by Liturgical Press, Collegeville, MN. All rights reserved.

18   All the Wonder That Surrounds Us

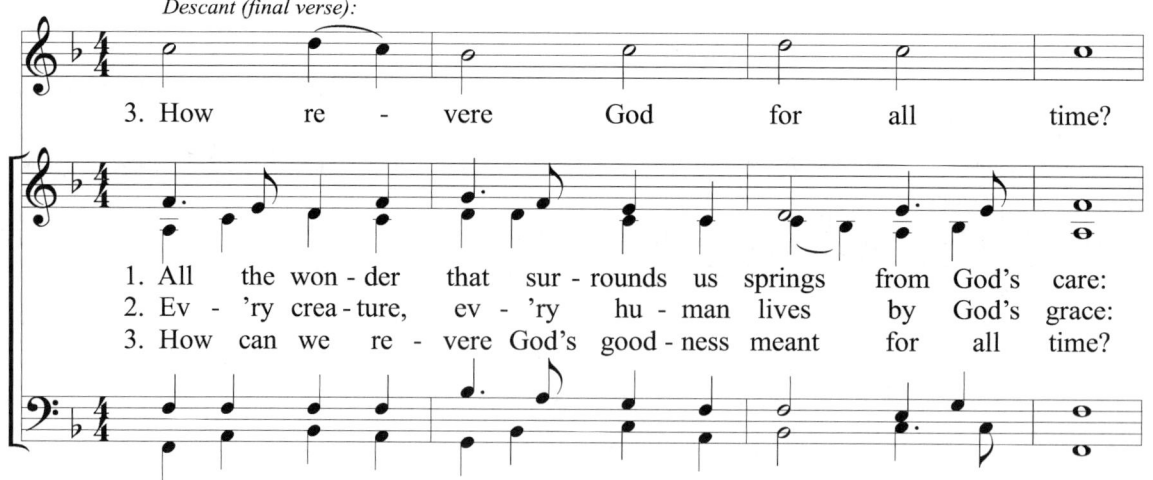

All the Wonder That Surrounds Us, pg. 2

Text: John L. Bell, © 2002, WGRG, Iona Community, Glasgow, Scotland. All rights reserved. GIA Publications, Inc., North American agent. Used with permission.
Music: AR HYD Y NOS, 84 84 88 84, traditional Welsh melody.
Descant: Christine Manderfeld, OSB, b. 1938, © 2009, the Sisters of Saint Benedict, St. Joseph, MN. Administered by Liturgical Press, Collegeville, MN. All rights reserved.

All Who Hunger, Gather Gladly

Text: Sylvia G. Dunstan, 1955–1993, © 1991, GIA Publications, Inc. All rights reserved. Used with permission.
Music: HOLY MANNA, 87 87 D, William Moore, 1835.
Descant: Robert Hobby, © 1992, GIA Publications, Inc. All rights reserved. Used with permission.

Alleluia! Alleluia! Let the Holy Anthem Rise   20

1. Alleluia! Alleluia! Let the holy anthem rise,
And the choirs of heaven chant it In the temple of the skies;
Let the mountains skip with gladness And the joyful valleys ring,
With Hosannas in the highest To our Savior and our King.

2. Alleluia! Alleluia! Like the sun from out the wave
He has risen up in triumph From the darkness of the grave,
He's the splendor of the nations, He's the lamp of endless day;
He's the very Lord of glory Who is risen up today.

3. Alleluia! Alleluia! Blessed Jesus, make us rise
From the life of this coruption To the life that never dies.
May your glory be our portion, When the days of time are past,
And the dead shall be awakened By the trumpet's mighty blast.

Text: Edward Caswall, 1814–1878. Music: HOLY ANTHEM, 87 87 D, traditional melody.

Alleluia! Sing to Jesus

Alleluia! Sing to Jesus, pg. 2

Text: William Chatterton Dix, 1837–1898, alt. Music: HYFRYDOL, 87 87 D, Rowland H. Prichard, 1811–1887.
Descant: Christine Manderfeld, OSB, b. 1938, © 2009, the Sisters of Saint Benedict, St. Joseph, MN. Administered by Liturgical Press, Collegeville, MN. All rights reserved.

Alma Redemptoris Mater / O Gracious Mother

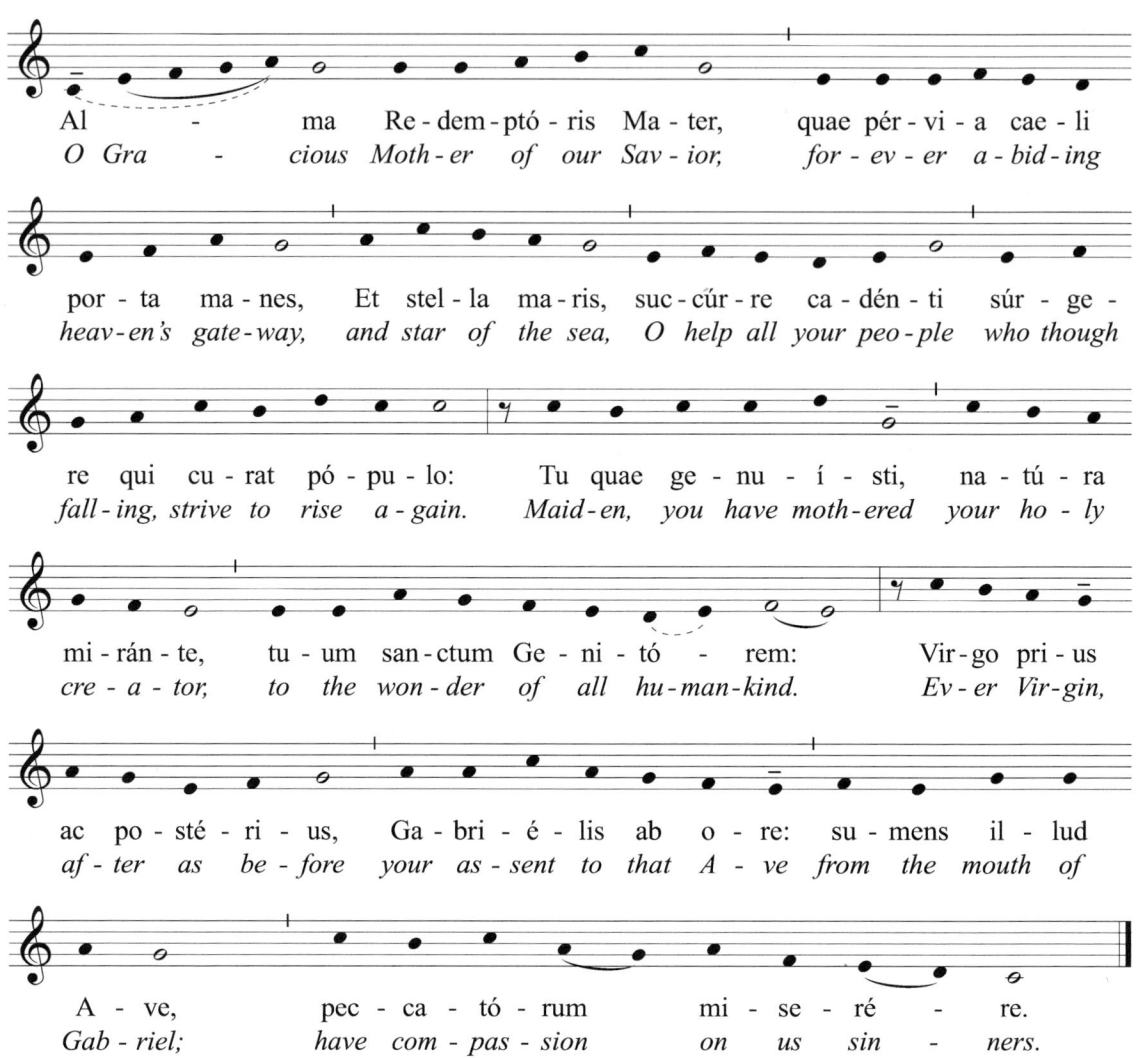

Alma Redemptóris Mater, quae pérvia caeli porta manes, Et stella maris, succúrre cadénti súrgere qui curat pópulo: Tu quae genuísti, natúra miránte, tuum sanctum Genitórem: Virgo prius ac postérius, Gabriélis ab ore: sumens illud Ave, peccatórum miserére.

O Gracious Mother of our Savior, forever abiding heaven's gateway, and star of the sea, O help all your people who though falling, strive to rise again. Maiden, you have mothered your holy creator, to the wonder of all humankind. Ever Virgin, after as before your assent to that A-ve from the mouth of Gabriel; have compassion on us sinners.

Text: Ascr. to Hermannus Contractus, 1013–1054; tr. by Cecile Gertken, OSB, 1902–2001, © 1990, the Sisters of Saint Benedict. Administered by Liturgical Press, Collegeville, MN. All rights reserved.
Music: Plainchant, Mode V.

Amazing Grace

*This phrase has been restored to respect the author's original text. An alternate text is provided in *italic*.

Text: John Newton, 1725–1807, alt. vv. 1–4; John Rees, fl. 1859, v. 5, attr. Music: NEW BRITAIN, 86 86, early American melody, 1831; adapt. Edwin Othello Excell, 1851–1921. Descant: Craig Westendorf, © 1980, GIA Publications, Inc. All rights reserved. Used with permission.

America (My Country, 'Tis of Thee)

America (My Country, 'Tis of Thee), pg. 2

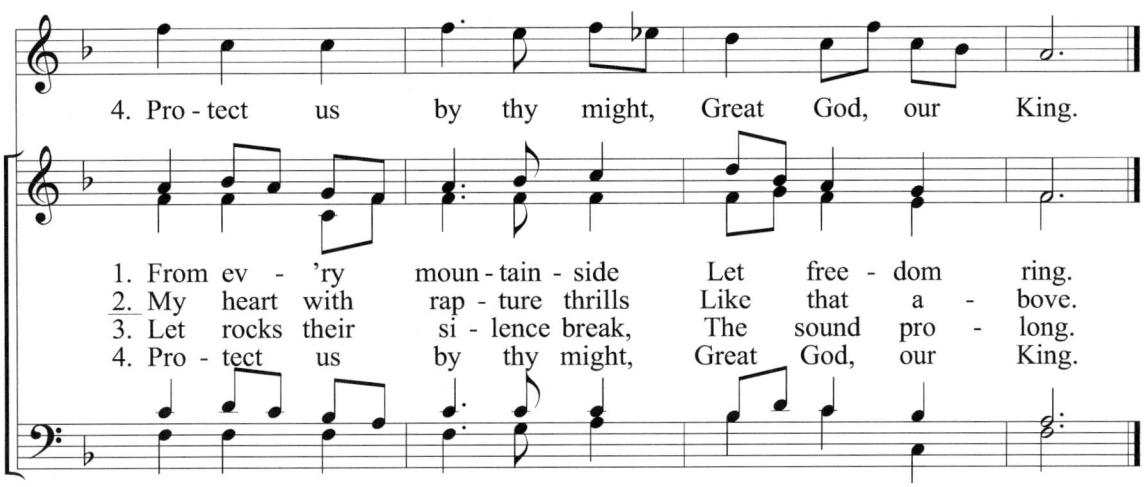

Text: Samuel Francis Smith, 1805–1895. Music: AMERICA, 664 6664, *Thesaurus Musicus,* 1744.
Descant: Austin Lovelace, © 1992, GIA Publications, Inc. All rights reserved. Used with permission.

America the Beautiful 25

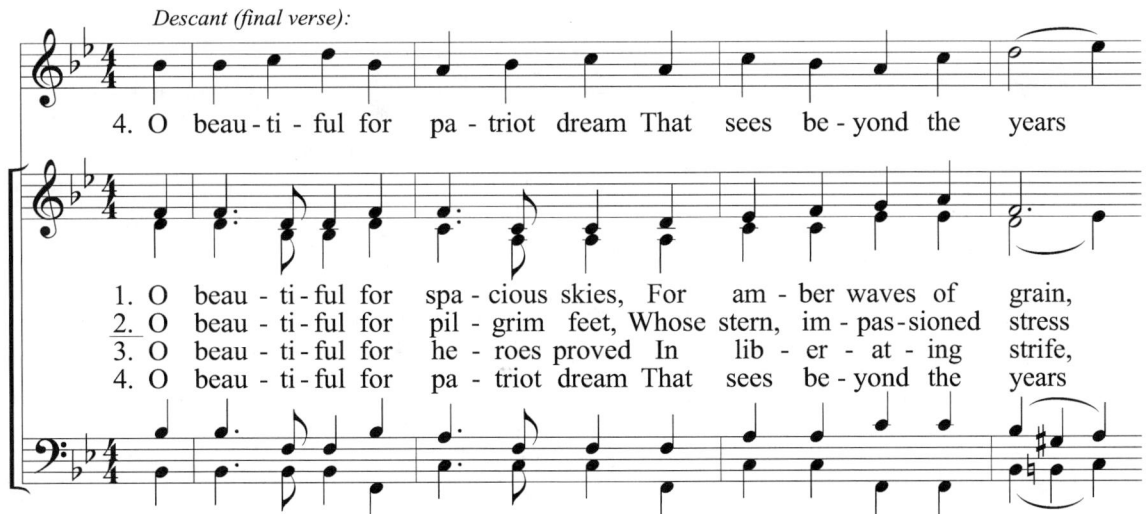

Angels, from the Realms of Glory

26

Angels, from the Realms of Glory, pg. 2

Text: James Montgomery, 1771–1854, vv. 1–3; *Christmas Box,* 1825, v. 4. Music: REGENT SQUARE, 87 87 87; Henry Smart, 1813–1879.
Descant: Delores Dufner, OSB, b. 1939, © 2009, the Sisters of Saint Benedict, St. Joseph, MN. Administered by Liturgical Press, Collegeville, MN. All rights reserved.

27   Angels We Have Heard on High

Verses

1. Angels we have heard on high Sweetly singing o'er the plains, And the mountains in reply Echo back their joyous strains.
2. Shepherds, why this jubilee? Why your joyous strains prolong? Say what may the tidings be, Which inspire your heav'nly song.
3. Come to Bethlehem and see Him whose birth the angels sing; Come adore, on bended knee, Christ, the Lord, the newborn King.
4. See him in a manger laid, Whom the choirs of angels praise; Mary, Joseph, lend your aid, While our hearts in love we raise.

Text: Traditional French carol, tr. James Chadwick, 1813–1882, in *Crown of Jesus,* 1862, alt. Music: GLORIA, 77 77 with refrain, traditional French carol.
Descant: Christine Manderfeld, OSB, b. 1938, © 2009, the Sisters of Saint Benedict, St. Joseph, MN. Administered by Liturgical Press, Collegeville, MN. All rights reserved.

Around This Table, Altar Blest

1. A-round this table, altar blest, we feast with Christ, our host and guest. God's banquet here for all is spread: refreshing cup and living bread.

2. In you, O Christ, we find our rest, our troubled hearts, God's comfort blest. So we give thanks, our praise declare for God's great love, whose gifts we share.

3. As we to you, O Lord, process, your people clothe in holiness. With beauty fashioned by your art adorn our lives and ev'ry heart.

4. O King of glory, heaven's light, make all our earthly darkness bright. Let your good Spirit fill us here to make our vision new and clear.

5. How lovely, Lord, your dwelling place, your presence shown in time and space. On us your blessing here bestow; grant us your saving love to know.

Text: Michael Kwatera, OSB, b. 1950, © 2005, Order of Saint Benedict, Collegeville, MN. Administered by Liturgical Press, Collegeville, MN. All rights reserved.
Music: PROSPECT 88 88; William Walker's *Southern Harmony*; arr. by Marty Haugen, b. 1950, © 1991, GIA Publications, Inc. All rights reserved. Used with permission.

As Grain on Scattered Hillsides

29

As Grain on Scattered Hillsides, pg. 2

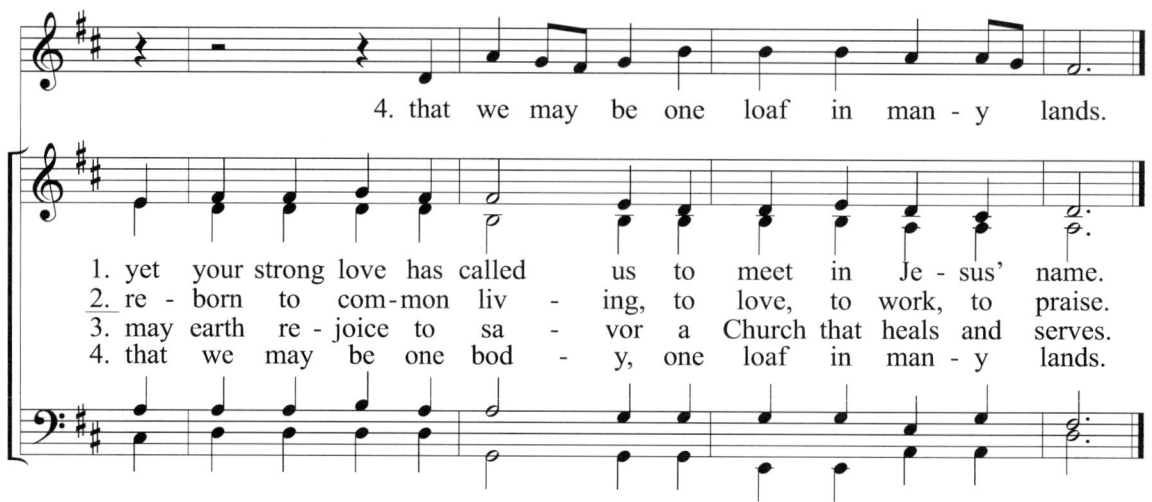

Text: Ruth Duck, b. 1947, © 1986, 1990, 1992, GIA Publications, Inc. All rights reserved. Used with permission.
Music: AURELIA, 76 76 D, Samuel S. Wesley, 1810–1876.
Descant: Christine Manderfeld, OSB, b. 1938, © 2009, the Sisters of Saint Benedict, St. Joseph, MN. Administered by Liturgical Press, Collegeville, MN. All rights reserved.

30 As We Gather at Your Table

Descant (final verse):

3. Al - le - lu - ia, al - le - lu - ia.

1. As we gath-er at your Ta-ble, As we lis-ten to your Word,
2. Turn our wor-ship in-to wit-ness In the sac-ra-ment of life;
3. Gra-cious Spir-it, help us sum-mon Oth-er guests to share that feast

3. Al - le - lu - ia, al - le - lu - ia.

1. Help us know, O God, your pres-ence: Let our hearts and minds be stirred.
2. Send us forth to love and serve you, Bring-ing peace where there is strife.
3. Where tri-um-phant Love will wel-come Those who had been last and least.

As We Gather at Your Table, pg. 2

1. Nourish us with sacred story Till we claim it as our own;
Teach us through this holy banquet How to make Love's victory known.
2. Give us, Christ, your great compassion To forgive as you forgave;
May we still behold your image In the world you died to save.
3. There no more will envy blind us Nor will pride our peace destroy,
As we join with saints and angels To repeat the sounding joy.
Alleluia, alleluia.

Text: Carl P. Daw, b. 1944, © 1989, Hope Publishing Co., Carol Stream, IL 60188. All rights reserved. Used with permission.
Tune: NETTLETON 87 87 D; Wyeth's *Repository of Sacred Music,* Part II, 1813.
Descant: Christine Manderfeld, OSB, b. 1938, © 2009, the Sisters of Saint Benedict, St. Joseph, MN. Administered by Liturgical Press, Collegeville, MN. All rights reserved.

As with Gladness Men of Old 31

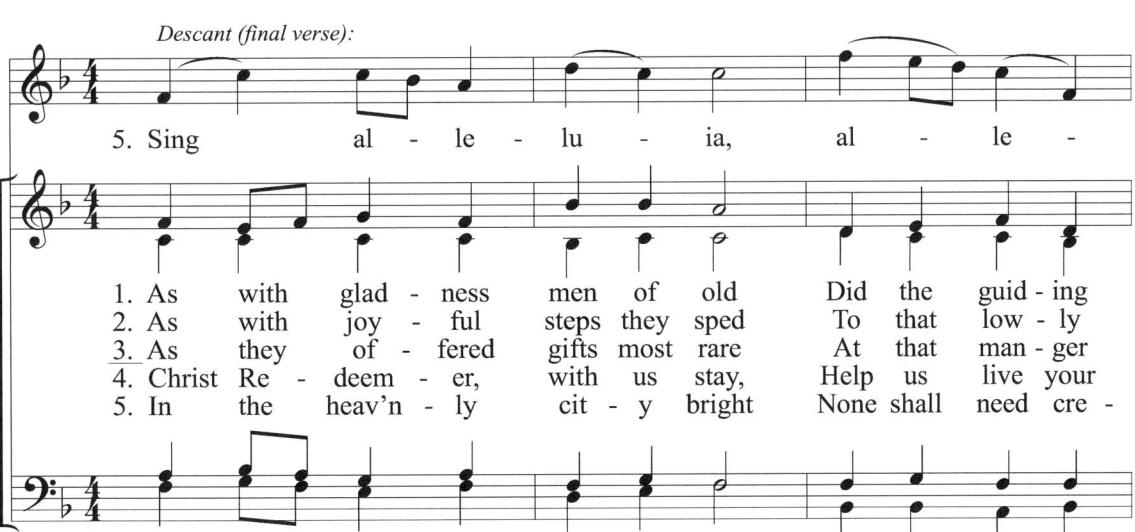

Descant (final verse):
5. Sing alleluia, alle-

1. As with gladness men of old Did the guiding
2. As with joyful steps they sped To that lowly
3. As they offered gifts most rare At that manger
4. Christ Redeemer, with us stay, Help us live your
5. In the heav'nly city bright None shall need cre-

At That First Eucharist 32

1. At that first Eucharist before you died, O Lord, you prayed that all be one in you; At this our Eucharist again preside, And in our hearts your law of love renew.
   Thus may we all one bread, one body be, Through this blest sacrament of unity.

2. For all your Church, O Lord, we intercede; O make our lack of charity to cease; Draw us the nearer each to each, we plead, By drawing all to you, O Prince of Peace.
   Thus may we all one bread, one body be, Through this blest sacrament of unity.

3. So, Lord, at length when sacraments shall cease, May we be one with all your Church above, One with your saints in one unending peace, One with your saints in one unbounded love.
   Thus may we all one bread, one body be, Through this blest sacrament of unity.

Text: William Harry Turton, 1856–1938, alt. Music: UNDE ET MEMORES, 10 10 10 10, with refrain, William Henry Monk, 1823–1889, alt.

At the Cross Her Station Keeping

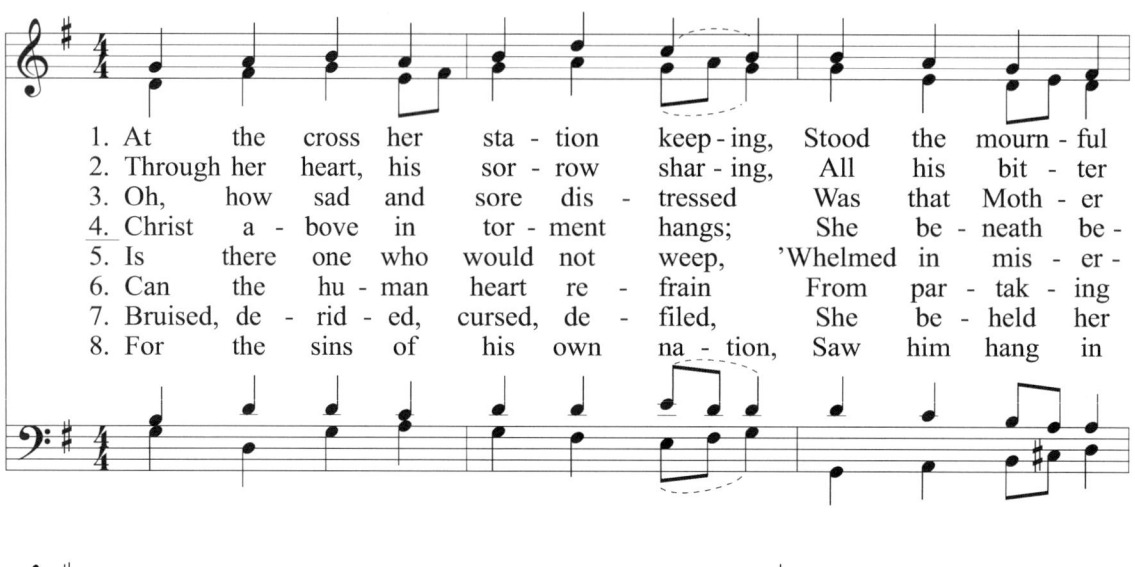

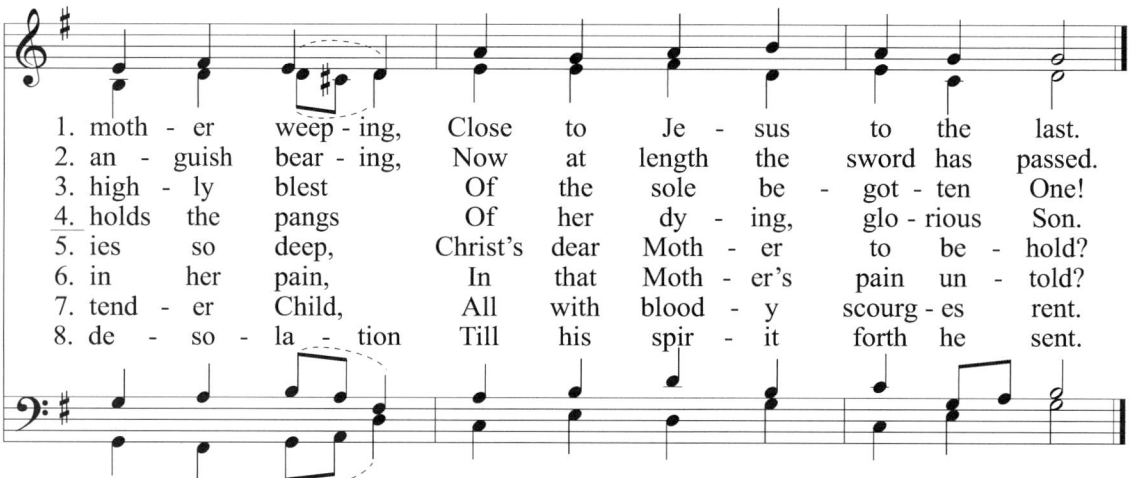

1. At the cross her station keeping, Stood the mournful mother weeping, Close to Jesus to the last.
2. Through her heart, his sorrow sharing, All his bitter anguish bearing, Now at length the sword has passed.
3. Oh, how sad and sore distressed Was that Mother highly blest Of the sole begotten One!
4. Christ above in torment hangs; She beneath beholds the pangs Of her dying, glorious Son.
5. Is there one who would not weep, 'Whelmed in miseries so deep, Christ's dear Mother to behold?
6. Can the human heart refrain From partaking in her pain, In that Mother's pain untold?
7. Bruised, derided, cursed, defiled, She beheld her tender Child, All with bloody scourges rent.
8. For the sins of his own nation, Saw him hang in desolation Till his spirit forth he sent.

9.
O sweet Mother! fount of love,
Touch my spirit from above,
Make my heart with yours accord.

10.
Make me feel as you have felt;
Make my soul to glow and melt
With the love of Christ, my Lord.

11.
Holy Mother, pierce me through,
In my heart each wound renew
Of my Savior crucified.

12.
Let me share with you his pain,
Who for all our sins was slain,
Who for me in torments died.

13.
Let me mingle tears with thee,
Mourning him who mourned for me,
All the days that I may live:

14.
By the cross with you to stay,
There with you to weep and pray
This I ask of you to give.

Text: Ascr. to Jacopone da Todi, 1230–1306; tr. Edward Cassall, 1814–1878, alt.
Music: STABAT MATER, 88 7, *Maintzisch Gesangbuch,* 1661; harm. by Richard Proulx, b. 1937, © 1986, GIA Publications, Inc. All rights reserved. Used with permission.

At the Lamb's High Feast We Sing 34

Text: *Ad regias agni dapes;* Latin, 4th C.; tr. Robert Campbell, 1814–1868. Music: SALZBURG, 77 77 D, Jacob Hintze, 1622–1702; adapt. by J. S. Bach, 1685–1750. Descant: Christine Manderfeld, OSB, b. 1938, © 2009, the Sisters of Saint Benedict, St. Joseph, MN. Administered by Liturgical Press, Collegeville, MN. All rights reserved.

Attende, Domine / Hear Our Entreaties, Lord 35

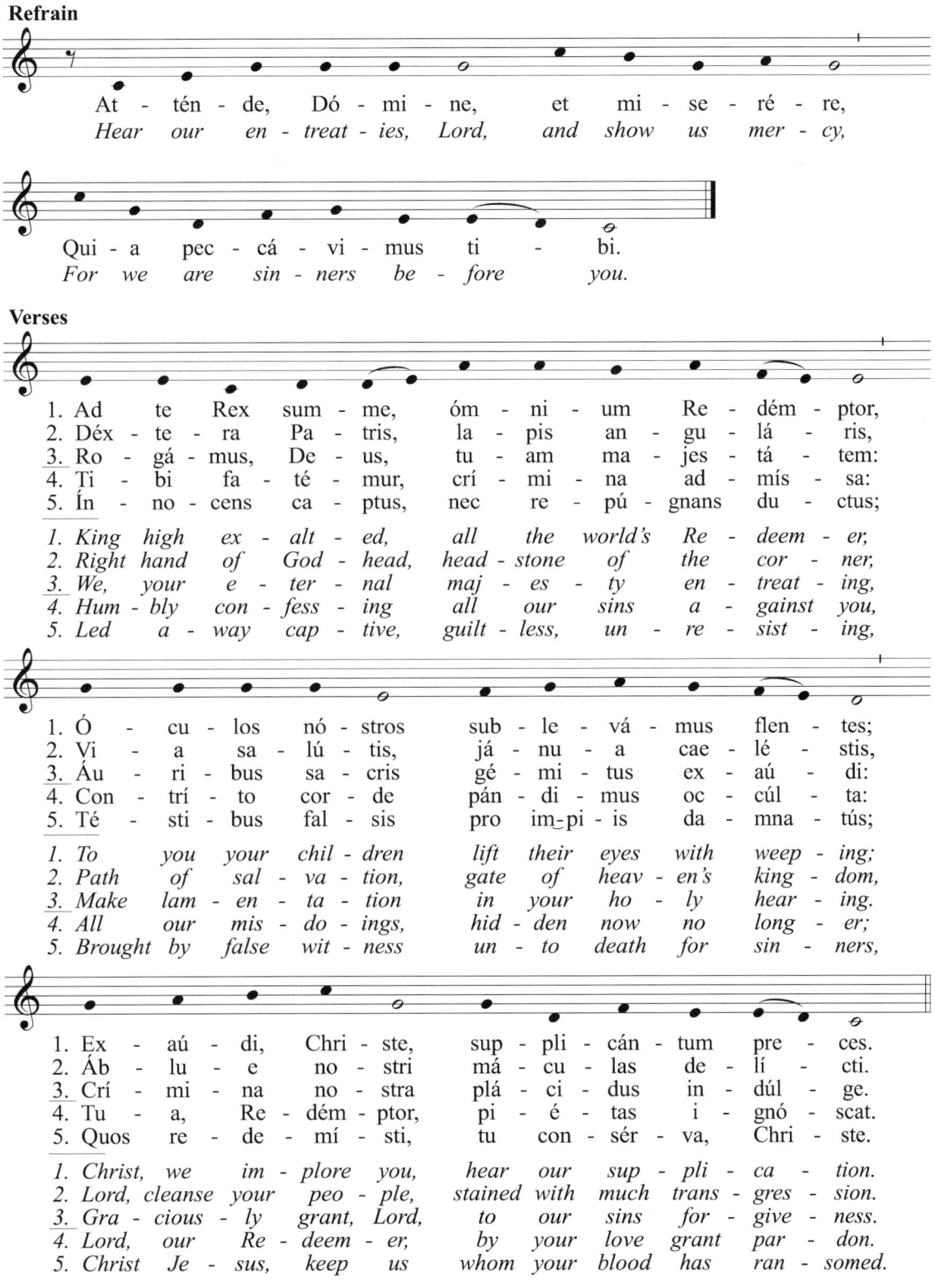

Text: Ancient Mozarabic Litany; tr. Irvin Udulutsch, OFM, Cap, b. 1920, © 1959, 1977, Order of Saint Benedict, Collegeville, MN.
Administered by Liturgical Press, Collegeville, MN. All rights reserved. Music: ATTENDE DOMINE, 11 11 11 with refrain, Mode V.

Ave Maria

*The cantor or solo voice sings the first phrase.

Text: Luke 1:26-37. Music: AVE MARIA, irregular, Plainchant, Mode I.

Ave Maria, God Is with You

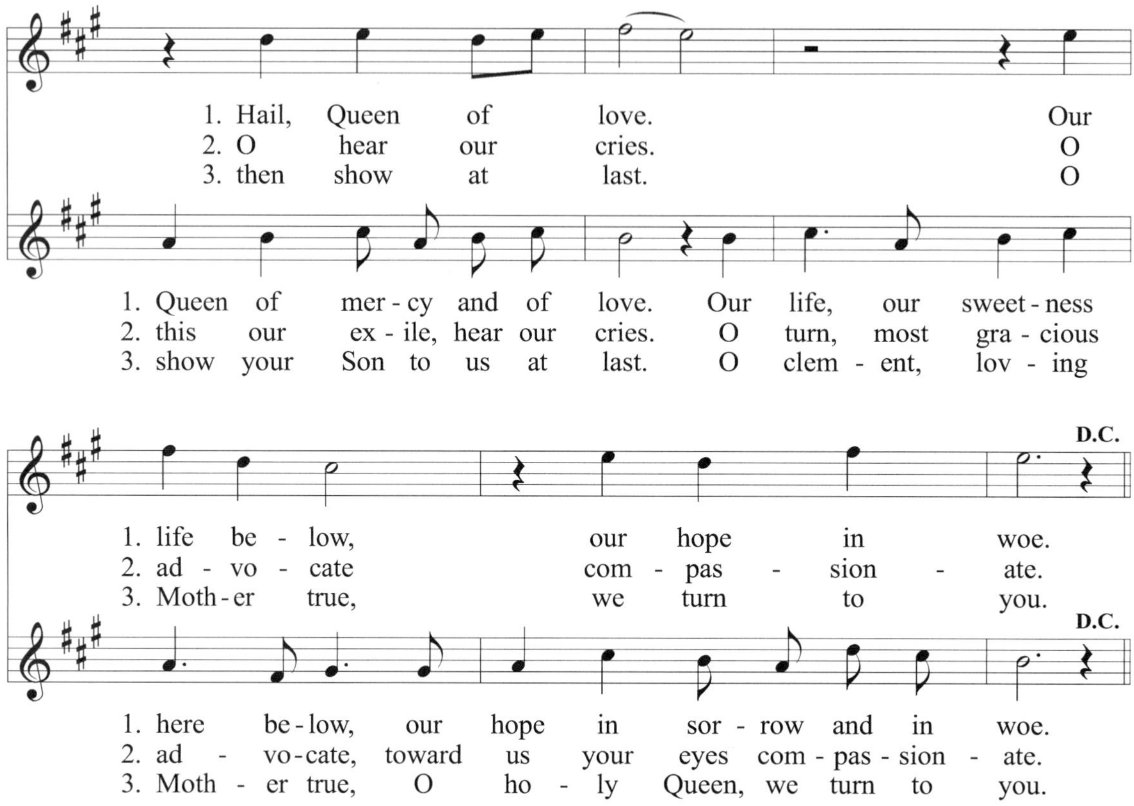

Ave Maria, God Is with You, pg. 2

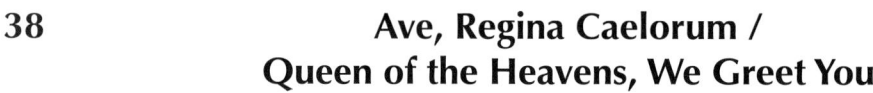

1. Hail, Queen of love. Our
2. O hear our cries. O
3. then show at last. O

1. Queen of mer-cy and of love. Our life, our sweet-ness
2. this our ex-ile, hear our cries. O turn, most gra-cious
3. show your Son to us at last. O clem-ent, lov-ing

1. life be-low, our hope in woe.
2. ad-vo-cate com-pas-sion-ate.
3. Moth-er true, we turn to you.

1. here be-low, our hope in sor-row and in woe.
2. ad-vo-cate, toward us your eyes com-pas-sion-ate.
3. Moth-er true, O ho-ly Queen, we turn to you.

Text: Based on *Salve Regina*, ca. 1080; adapt. by James J. Chepponis, b. 1956. Music: James J. Chepponis, b. 1956.
Text and music: © 1993, GIA Publications, Inc. All rights reserved. Used with permission.

38 Ave, Regina Caelorum / Queen of the Heavens, We Greet You

A-ve, Re-gí-na cae-ló-rum, A-ve Dó-mi-na an-ge-ló-rum:
Queen of the heav-ens, we greet you, gra-cious La-dy of all the an-gels,

Sal-ve ra-dix, sal-ve por-ta, Ex qua mun-do lux est or-ta:
you are dawn and door of morn-ing, whence the world's true light is ris-en.

Gau-de Vir-go glo-ri-ó-sa, Su-per o-mnes spe-ci-ó-sa:
Joy to you, O maid-en glo-rious, beau-ti-ful be-yond all oth-ers.

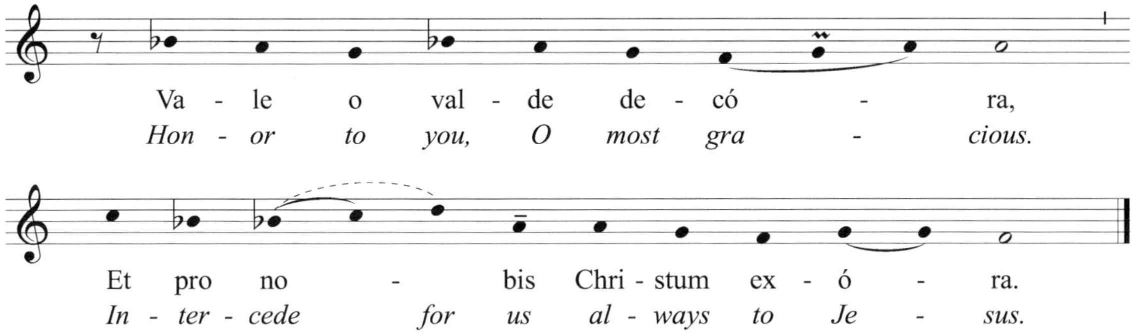

Ave, Regina Caelorum / Queen of the Heavens, We Greet You, pg. 2

Va - le o val - de de - có - ra,
Hon - or to you, O most gra - cious.

Et pro no - bis Chri - stum ex - ó - ra.
In - ter - cede for us al - ways to Je - sus.

Text: *Ave, Regina caelorum*; tr. by Cecile Gertken, OSB, 1902–2001, © 1990, the Sisters of Saint Benedict, St. Joseph, MN.
Administered by Liturgical Press, Collegeville, MN. All rights reserved.
Music: Plainchant, Mode VI.

Ave Verum Corpus   39

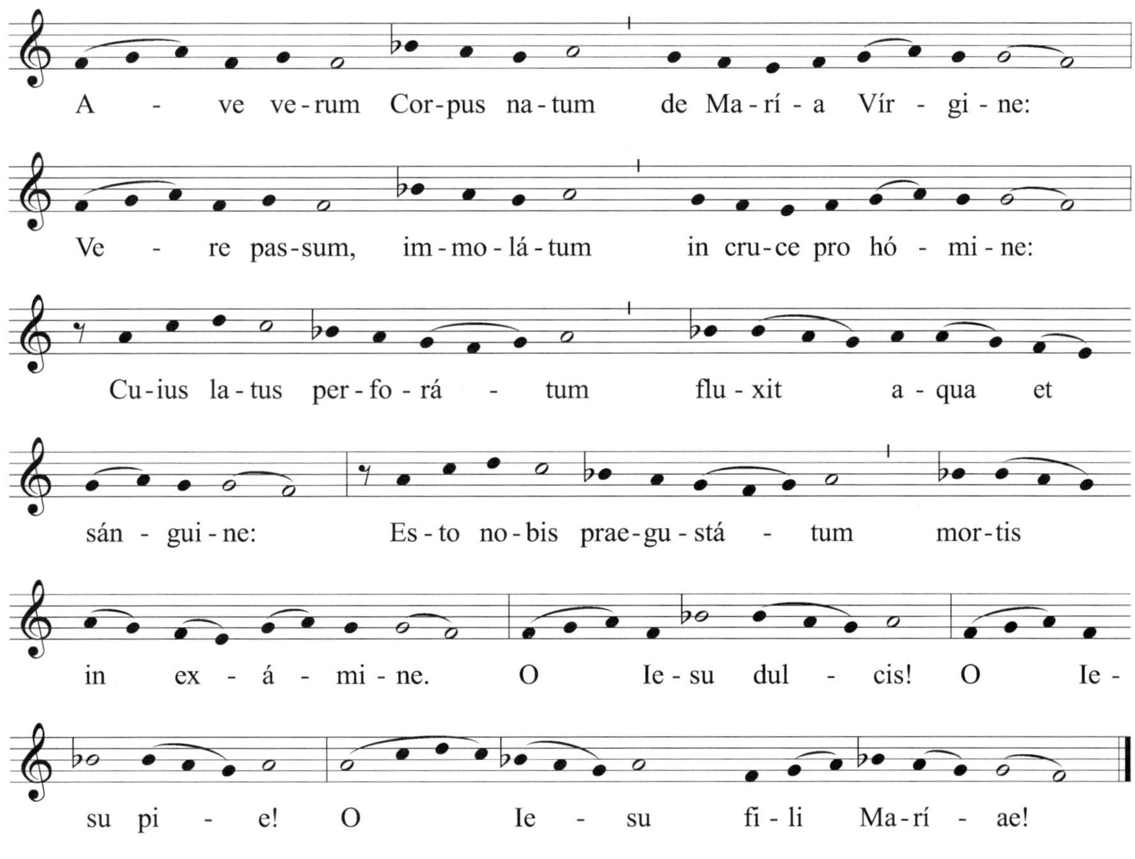

A - ve ve - rum Cor - pus na - tum de Ma - rí - a Vír - gi - ne:

Ve - re pas - sum, im - mo - lá - tum in cru - ce pro hó - mi - ne:

Cu - ius la - tus per - fo - rá - tum flu - xit a - qua et

sán - gui - ne: Es - to no - bis prae - gu - stá - tum mor - tis

in ex - á - mi - ne. O Ie - su dul - cis! O Ie -

su pi - e! O Ie - su fi - li Ma - rí - ae!

Text: Ascr. to Innocent VI, d. 1362. Music: AVE VERUM, Plainchant, Mode VI.

Awake! Awake, and Greet the New Morn

1. A-wake! a-wake, and greet the new morn, For angels herald its dawning, Sing out your joy, for now* he is born, Behold! the Child of our longing. Come as a baby weak and poor, To bring all hearts to-

2. To us, to all in sorrow and fear, Emmanuel comes a-singing, His humble song is quiet and near, Yet fills the earth with its ringing; Music to heal the broken soul And hymns of loving

3. In darkest night his coming shall be, When all the world is despairing, As morning light so quiet and free, So warm and gentle and caring. Then shall the mute break forth in song, The lame shall leap in

4. Rejoice, rejoice, take heart in the night, Though dark the winter and cheerless, The rising sun shall crown you with light, Be strong and loving and fearless; Love be our song and love our prayer, And love, our endless

*During Advent: "soon"

Awake! Awake, and Greet the New Morn, pg. 2

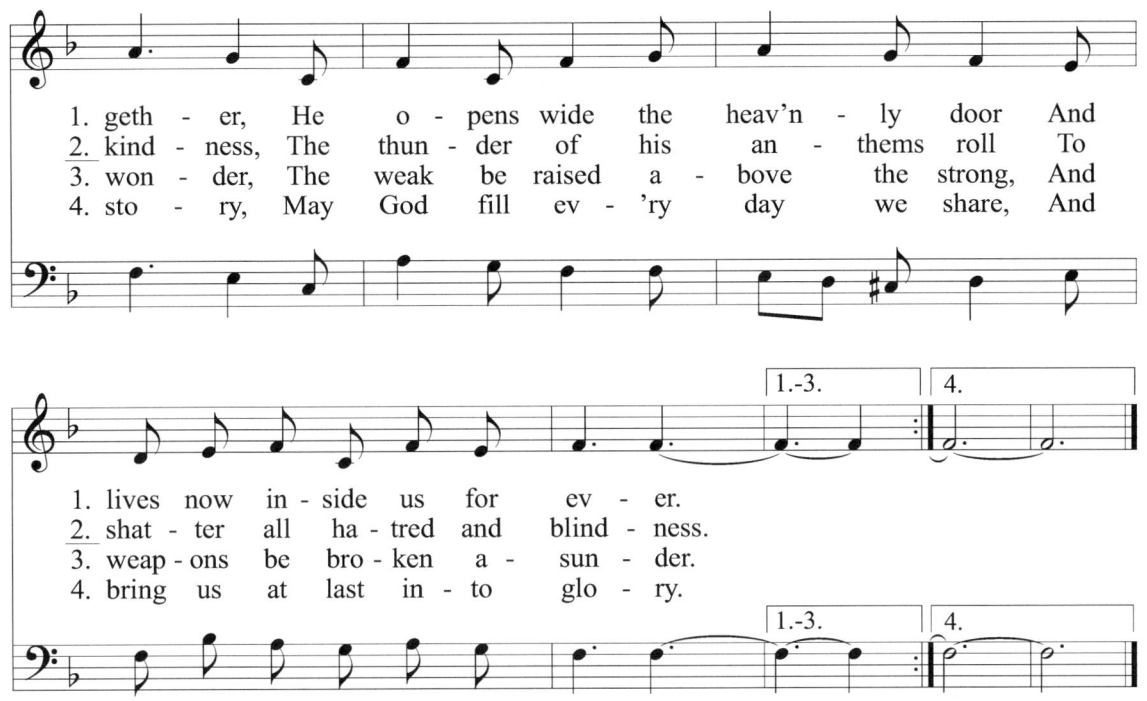

1. geth-er, He o-pens wide the heav'n-ly door And
2. kind-ness, The thun-der of his an-thems roll To
3. won-der, The weak be raised a-bove the strong, And
4. sto-ry, May God fill ev-'ry day we share, And

1. lives now in-side us for ev - er.
2. shat-ter all ha-tred and blind-ness.
3. weap-ons be bro-ken a-sun-der.
4. bring us at last in-to glo - ry.

Text: Marty Haugen, b. 1950. Music: REJOICE, REJOICE, 9 8 9 8 8 7 8 9, Marty Haugen, b. 1950.
Text and music © 1983, GIA Publications, Inc. All rights reserved. Used with permission.

Away in a Manger   41

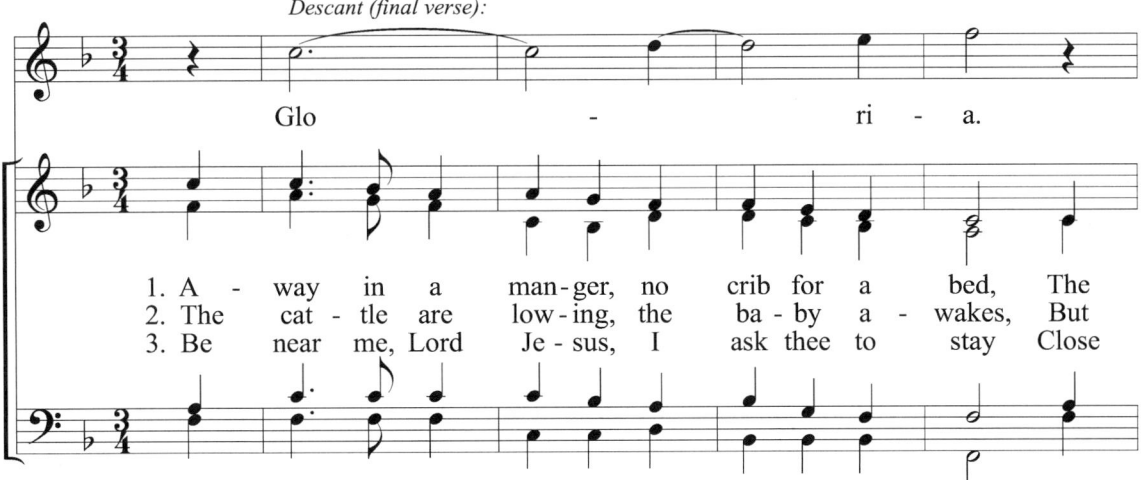

Descant (final verse): Glo - ri - a.

1. A-way in a man-ger, no crib for a bed, The
2. The cat-tle are low-ing, the ba-by a-wakes, But
3. Be near me, Lord Je-sus, I ask thee to stay Close

Baptized in Water 42

Text: Michael Saward, b. 1932, © 1982, Jubilate Hymns, Ltd. All rights reserved. Administered by Hope Publishing Co., Carol Stream, IL 60188. Used with permission.
Music: BUNESSAN, 5 5 5 4 D; traditional Gaelic melody. Descant: Donald Busarow, © 1992, GIA Publications. All rights reserved. Used with permission.

Be Joyful, Mary

1. Be joyful, Mary, heav'nly Queen, be joyful, Mary! Your grief is changed to joy serene, Alleluia! Rejoice, rejoice, O Mary.
2. The Son you bore by heaven's grace, be joyful, Mary! Did by his death our guilt erase, Alleluia! Rejoice, rejoice, O Mary.
3. The Lord has risen from the dead, be joyful, Mary! He rose in glory as he said, Alleluia! Rejoice, rejoice, O Mary.
4. Then pray to God, O Virgin fair, be joyful, Mary! That he our souls to heaven bear, Alleluia! Rejoice, rejoice, O Mary.

Text: *Regina caeli, jubila;* Latin, 17th C.: tr. anon. in *Psallite,* 1901. Music: REGINA CAELI, 8 5 8 4 7, Leisentritt's *Gesangbuch,* 1584, alt.

Text and music: Bob Dufford, SJ, b. 1943.
Text and music: © 1975, Robert J. Dufford, SJ, and OCP Publications. All rights reserved. Used with permission.

Be Patient, God's People 45

Text: Based on James 5; adapt. by Bob Moore, b. 1962. Music: Bob Moore, b. 1962. Text and music: © 1993, GIA Publications, Inc. All rights reserved. Used with permission.

Be Thou My Vision

Text: Dallan Forgaill, attr.; tr. Mary E. Byrne, 1880–1931; versified by Eleanor H. Hull, 1860–1935, alt. Music: SLANE, 10 10 9 10, Irish ballad melody; harm. David Evans, 1874–1948, adapt. *The Church Hymnary*, 1972, © Oxford University Press. All rights reserved. Used with permission.
Descant: Christine Manderfeld, OSB, b. 1938, © 2009, the Sisters of Saint Benedict, St. Joseph, MN. Administered by Liturgical Press, Collegeville, MN. All rights reserved.

Beloved Son and Daughter Dear

47

Beloved Son and Daughter Dear, pg. 2

3. With love may we re-spond to Love, and fol-low where Love leads.
1. who knows our pain and heals our wounds, whose gift is life re-stored.
2. more lav-ish than the green-ing spring, our God who saves and frees!
3. With love may we re-spond to Love, and fol-low where Love leads.

Text: Delores Dufner, OSB, b. 1939, © 1983, 1992, 2006, the Sisters of Saint Benedict, St. Joseph, MN. Administered by Liturgical Press, Collegeville, MN. All rights reserved.
Music: KINGSFOLD, CMD, English tune; harm. Ralph Vaughan Williams, 1872–1958.
Descant: Christine Manderfeld, OSB, b. 1938, © 2009, the Sisters of Saint Benedict, St. Joseph, MN. Administered by Liturgical Press, Collegeville, MN. All rights reserved.

48 Beneath the Tree of Life / En el Árbol de la Vida

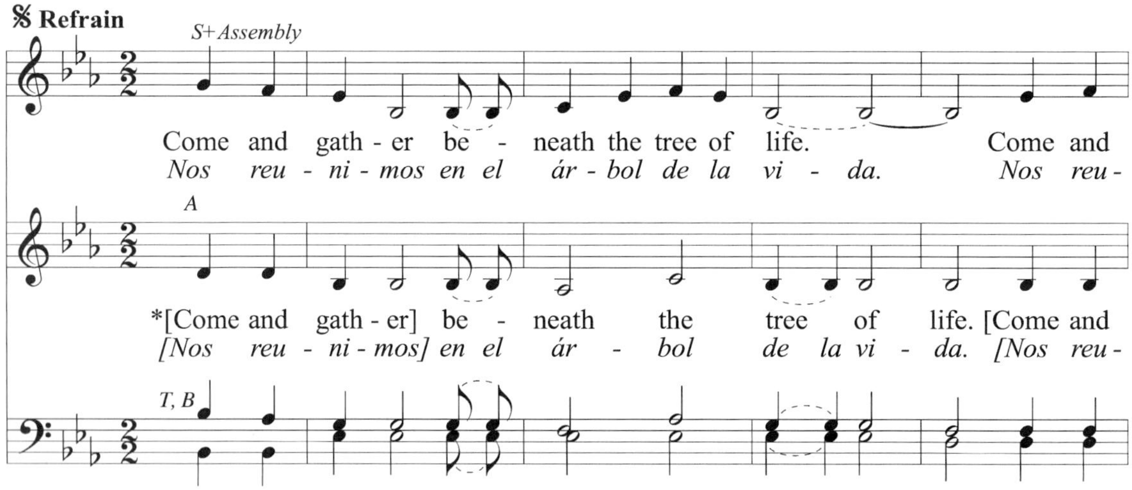

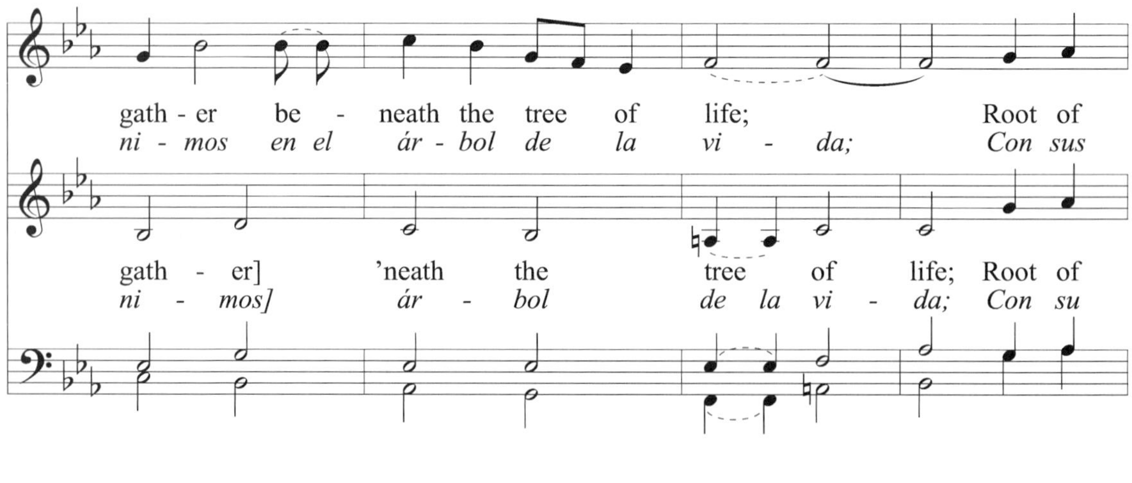

Refrain

Come and gath-er be-neath the tree of life. Come and
Nos reu-ni-mos en el ár-bol de la vi-da. Nos reu-

*[Come and gath-er] be-neath the tree of life. [Come and
[Nos reu-ni-mos] en el ár-bol de la vi-da. [Nos reu-*

gath-er be-neath the tree of life; Root of
ni-mos en el ár-bol de la vi-da; Con sus

gath-er] 'neath the tree of life; Root of
ni-mos] ár-bol de la vi-da; Con su

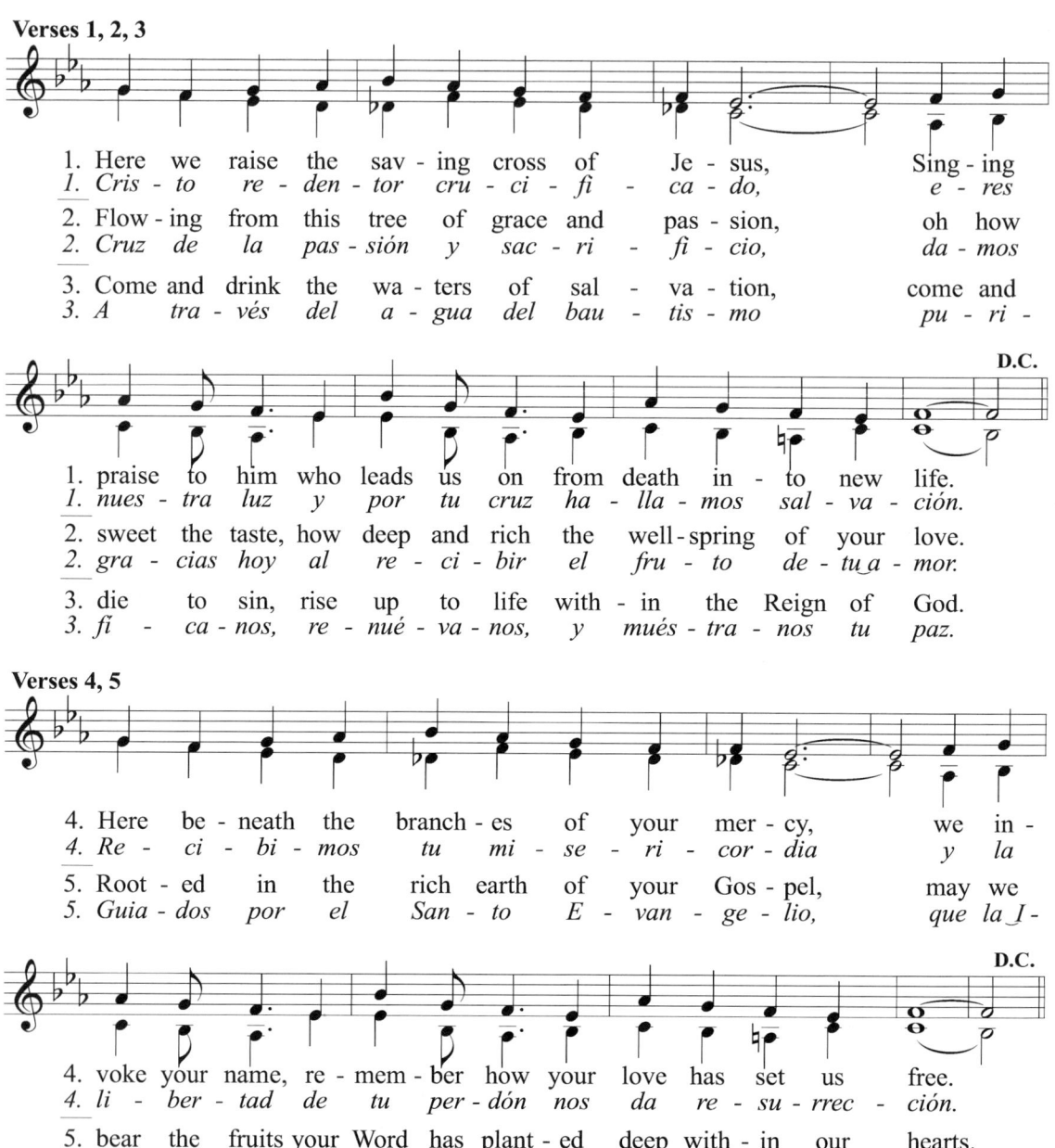

Bless the Lord

49

*Choose either part

Blessed Be the God of Israel

50

Text: Canticle of Zachary, adapt. by Marty Haugen, b. 1950, © 2000, GIA Publications, Inc.
Music: LAND OF REST, CM, traditional American folk melody; harm. by Richard Proulx, b. 1937, © 1975, GIA Publications, Inc. All rights reserved. Used with permission.
Descant: Christine Manderfeld, OSB, b. 1938, © 2009, the Sisters of Saint Benedict, St. Joseph, MN. Administered by Liturgical Press, Collegeville, MN. All rights reserved.

51 Blessed Jesus, at Thy Word

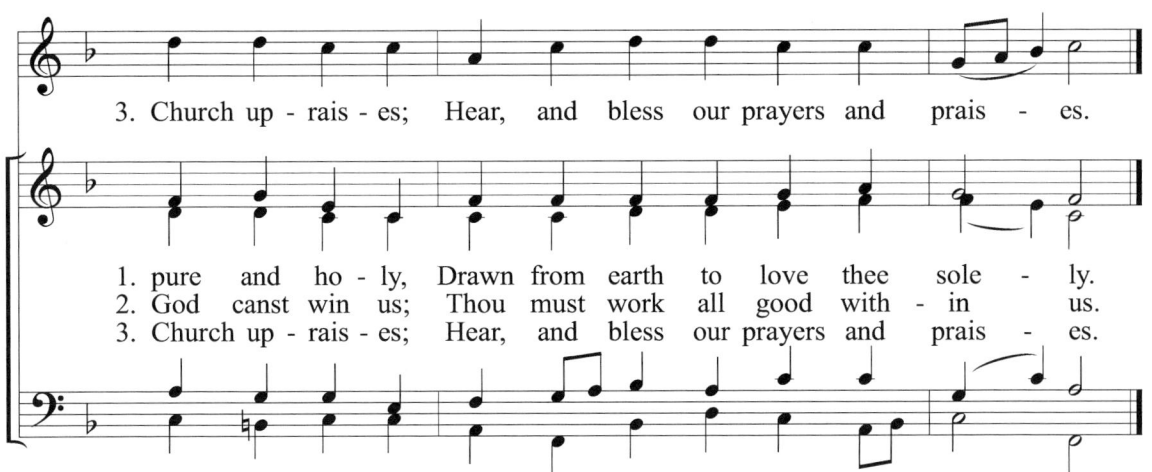

Text: Benjamin Schmolck, 1672–1737; tr. Catherine Winkworth, 1827–1878, alt.
Music: LIEBSTER JESU, 78 78 88, Johann R. Ahle, 1625–1673; arr. George H. Palmer, 1846–1926.
Descant: Christine Manderfeld, OSB, b. 1938, © 2009, the Sisters of Saint Benedict, St. Joseph, MN. Administered by Liturgical Press, Collegeville, MN. All rights reserved.

52 — Blest Are the Pure in Heart

Text: John Keble, 1792–1866, vv. 1 & 3; William John Hall, 1793–1861, vv. 2 & 4.
Music: FRANCONIA, 66 86, Johann B. Konig, 1691–1758, from his *Chorale;* adapt. and harm. by William Henry Havergal, 1793–1870.
Descant: Christine Manderfeld, OSB, b. 1938, © 2009, the Sisters of Saint Benedict, St. Joseph, MN. Administered by Liturgical Press, Collegeville, MN. All rights reserved.

Blest Are They

53

Text: Based on Matthew 5:3–12; adapt. by David Haas, b. 1957. Music: David Haas, b. 1957; arr. by Michael Joncas, b. 1951.
Text and music: © 1985, GIA Publications, Inc. All rights reserved. Used with permission.

Bread of Life / Pan de Vida

Refrain

Bread of life from heav-en, your blood and body giv-en, we eat this bread and drink this cup un-til you come a-gain.
Pan de vi-da e-ter-na, nos das tu cuer-po y san-gre. Has-ta que vuel-vas tú, Se-ñor, co-me-mos en tu a-mor.

Verses

1. Break now the bread of Christ's sac-ri-fice; Giv-ing thanks,
2. Seek not the food that will pass a-way; Set your hearts
3. Love as the One who, in love for you, Gave him-self
4. Take in the light that will nev-er dim, Taste the life
5. Dwell in the One who now dwells in you; Make your home
6. Drink of this cup and de-clare his death; Eat this bread

7. *Ven y com-par-te el di-vi-no pan; De-mos gra-*
8. *Es-te mis-te-rio es el máx-i-mo sa-cri-fi-*
9. *Ven a la me-sa de com-pa-sión, re-cor-de-*
10. *Hoy que co-me-mos del pan de a-mor so-mos u-*
11. *Ce-na que nos re-pre-sen-ta hoy la vi-da, muer-*

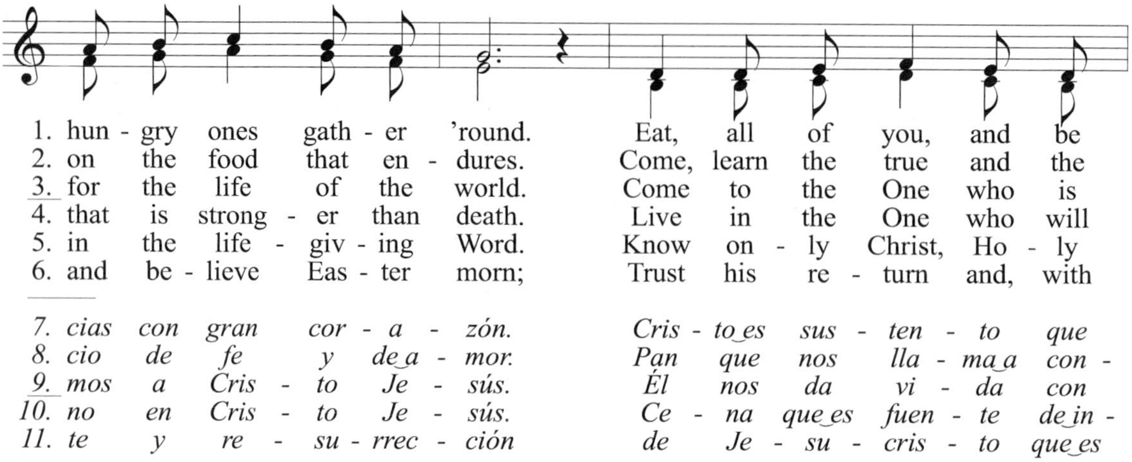

Bread of Life / Pan de Vida, pg. 2

1. hun-gry ones gath-er 'round. Eat, all of you, and be
2. on the food that en-dures. Come, learn the true and the
3. for the life of the world. Come to the One who is
4. that is strong-er than death. Live in the One who will
5. in the life-giv-ing Word. Know on-ly Christ, Ho-ly
6. and be-lieve Eas-ter morn; Trust his re-turn and, with

7. cias con gran cor-a-zón. Cris-to es sus-ten-to que
8. cio de fe y de a-mor. Pan que nos lla-ma a con-
9. mos a Cris-to Je-sús. Él nos da vi-da con
10. no en Cris-to Je-sús. Ce-na que es fuen-te de in-
11. te y re-su-rrec-ción de Je-su-cris-to que es

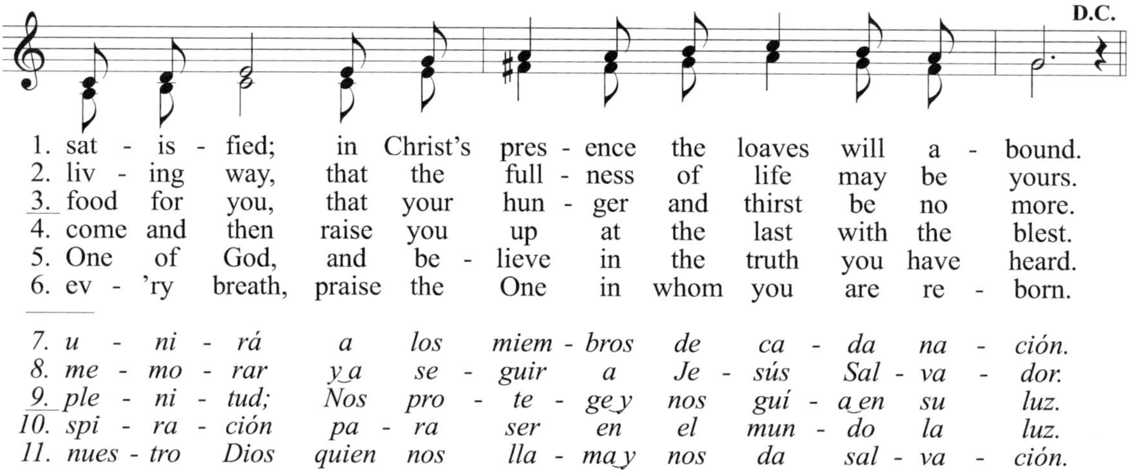

D.C.

1. sat-is-fied; in Christ's pres-ence the loaves will a-bound.
2. liv-ing way, that the full-ness of life may be yours.
3. food for you, that your hun-ger and thirst be no more.
4. come and then raise you up at the last with the blest.
5. One of God, and be-lieve in the truth you have heard.
6. ev-'ry breath, praise the One in whom you are re-born.

7. u-ni-rá a los miem-bros de ca-da na-ción.
8. me-mo-rar y a se-guir a Je-sús Sal-va-dor.
9. ple-ni-tud; Nos pro-te-ge y nos guí-a en su luz.
10. spi-ra-ción pa-ra ser en el mun-do la luz.
11. nues-tro Dios quien nos lla-ma y nos da sal-va-ción.

Text: Based on John 6; adapt. by Susan R. Briehl, b. 1952; Spanish by Jaime Cortez, b. 1963. Music: Argentine folk melody; adapt. and verses by Marty Haugen, b. 1950.
Text and music: © 2001, GIA Publications, Inc. All rights reserved. Used with permission.

55 By All Your Saints Still Striving

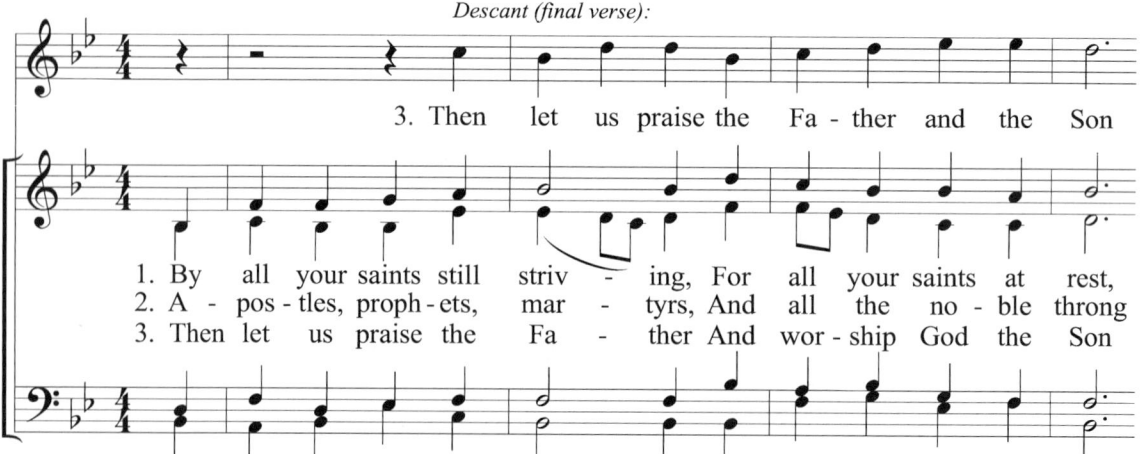

Descant (final verse):
3. Then let us praise the Fa-ther and the Son

1. By all your saints still striv-ing, For all your saints at rest,
2. A-pos-tles, proph-ets, mar-tyrs, And all the no-ble throng
3. Then let us praise the Fa-ther And wor-ship God the Son

By All Your Saints Still Striving, pg. 2

Text: Based on *From All Thy Saints in Warfare* by Horatio Bolton Nelson, 1823–1913;
Jerry D. Godwin, b. 1944, © 1985, The Church Pension Fund. All rights reserved. Used with permission of Church Publishing, Inc., New York.
Music: ST. THEODULPH, 76 76 D, Melchior Teschner, 1584–1635.
Descant: Christine Manderfeld, OSB, b. 1938, © 2009, the Sisters of Saint Benedict, St. Joseph, MN. Administered by Liturgical Press, Collegeville, MN. All rights reserved.

56   By Your Hand, You Feed Your People

Text: Susan R. Briehl, b. 1952; Music: CAMROSE, 87 87 D, Marty Haugen, b. 1950. Text and music: © 2002, GIA Publications, Inc. All rights reserved. Used with permission.

Called and Gathered by the Spirit

57

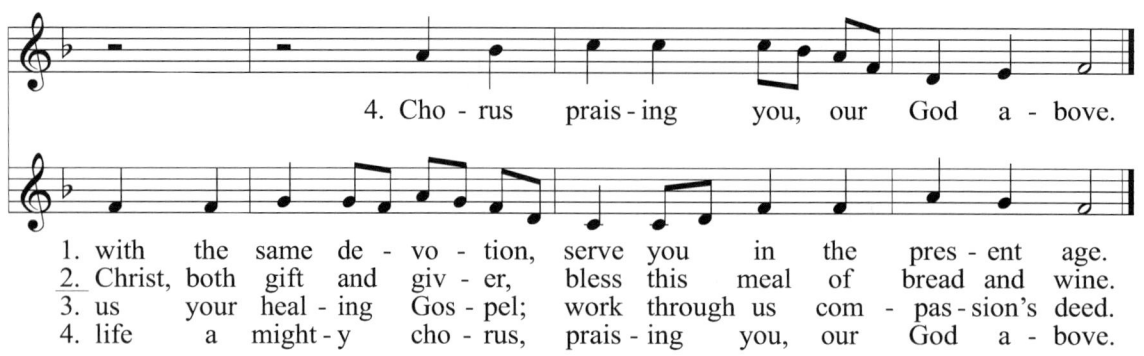

Can God a Lavish Table Spread?   58

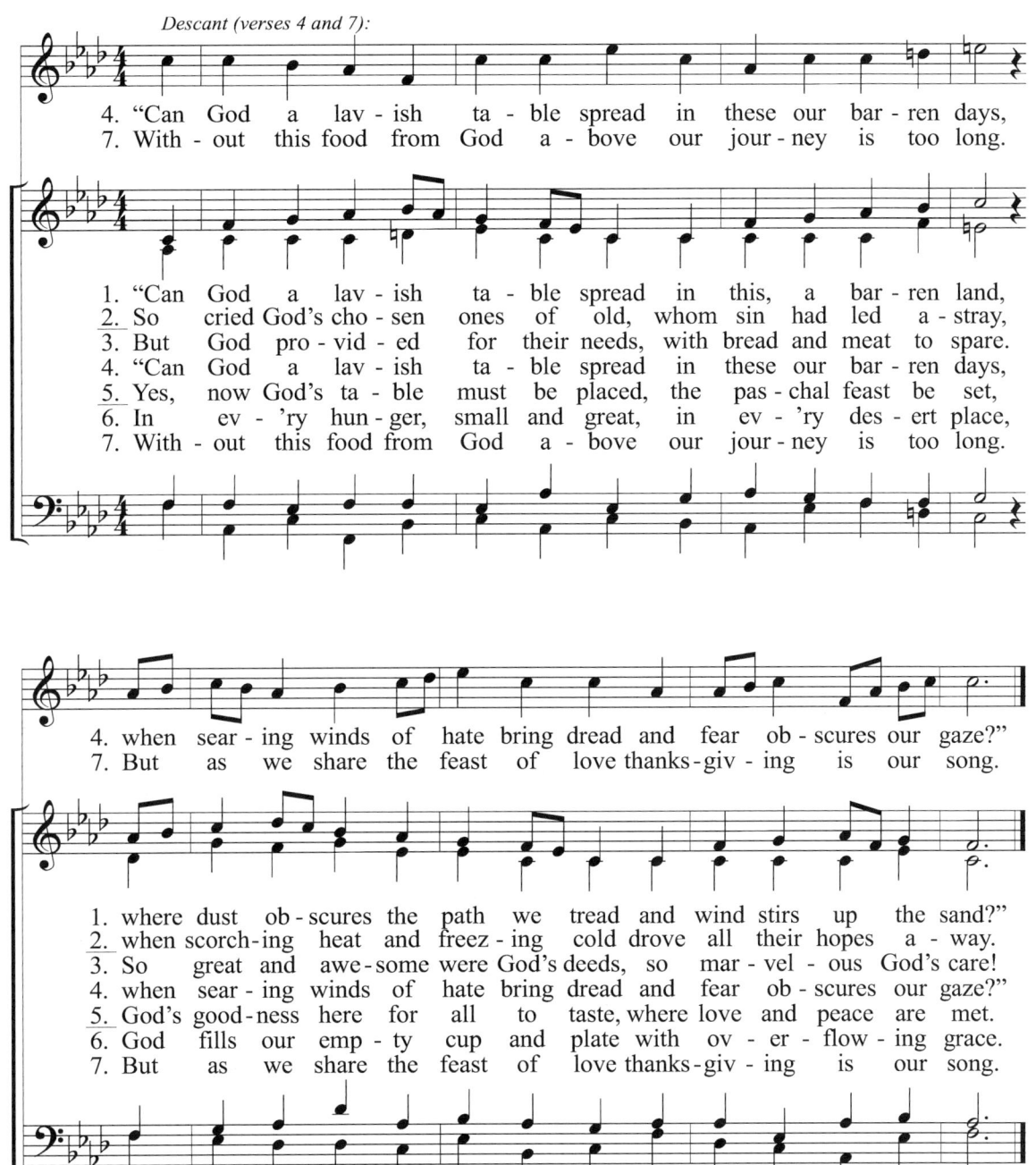

Descant (verses 4 and 7):

4. "Can God a lavish table spread in these our barren days,
7. Without this food from God above our journey is too long.

1. "Can God a lavish table spread in this, a barren land,
2. So cried God's chosen ones of old, whom sin had led astray,
3. But God provided for their needs, with bread and meat to spare.
4. "Can God a lavish table spread in these our barren days,
5. Yes, now God's table must be placed, the paschal feast be set,
6. In ev-'ry hunger, small and great, in ev-'ry desert place,
7. Without this food from God above our journey is too long.

4. when searing winds of hate bring dread and fear obscures our gaze?"
7. But as we share the feast of love thanksgiving is our song.

1. where dust obscures the path we tread and wind stirs up the sand?"
2. when scorching heat and freezing cold drove all their hopes away.
3. So great and awesome were God's deeds, so marvelous God's care!
4. when searing winds of hate bring dread and fear obscures our gaze?"
5. God's goodness here for all to taste, where love and peace are met.
6. God fills our empty cup and plate with overflowing grace.
7. But as we share the feast of love thanksgiving is our song.

Text: Michael Kwatera, OSB, b. 1950, vv. 1-3 based on Psalm 78:18-29, © 2003, Order of Saint Benedict, Collegeville, MN.
Administered by Liturgical Press, Collegeville, MN. All rights reserved.
Music: MORNING SONG, 86 86, *Kentucky Harmony,* 1816.
Descant: Christine Manderfeld, OSB, b. 1938, © 2009, the Sisters of Saint Benedict, St. Joseph, MN. Administered by Liturgical Press, Collegeville, MN. All rights reserved.

59 Canticle of the Sun

Canticle of the Sun, pg. 2

of the Lord.

Verses

1. Praise for the sun, the bring-er of day, He car-ries the light of the Lord in his rays; The moon and the stars who light up the way Un-to your throne.
2. Praise for the wind that blows through the trees, The seas' might-y storms, the gen-tl-est breeze; They blow where they will, they blow where they please To please the Lord.
3. Praise for the rain that wa-ters our fields, And bless-es our crops so all the earth yields; From death un-to life her mys-t'ry re-vealed Springs forth in joy.
4. Praise for the fire who gives us his light, The warmth of the sun to bright-en our night; He danc-es with joy, his spir-it so bright, He sings of you.
5. Praise for the earth who makes life to grow, The crea-tures you made to let your life show; The flow-ers and trees that help us to know The heart of love.
6. Praise for our death that makes our life real, The knowl-edge of loss that helps us to feel; The gift of your-self, your pres-ence re-vealed To lead us home.

D.C.

Text and music: Marty Haugen, b. 1950, © 1980, GIA Publications, Inc. All rights reserved. Used with permission.

Child of Mercy

Child of Mercy, pg. 2

1. those who dwell in fear, a light has shone!
2. on his shoul - der glo - ry rests!
3. Ho - ly One for ev - er: Prince of peace!
4. you is born a sav - ior: Christ the Lord!

Text: Based on Isaiah 9:1, 5; adapt. by David Haas, b. 1957. Music: David Haas, b. 1957, © 1991, GIA Publications, Inc. All rights reserved. Used with permission.

Christ, Be Our Light   61

1. Long - ing for light, we wait in dark - ness. Long - ing for
2. Long - ing for peace, our world is trou - bled. Long - ing for
3. Long - ing for food, man - y are hun - gry. Long - ing for
4. Long - ing for shel - ter, man - y are home - less. Long - ing for
5. Man - y the gifts, man - y the peo - ple, man - y the

1. truth, we turn to you. Make us your own,
2. hope, man - y de - spair. Your word a - lone
3. wa - ter, man - y still thirst. Make us your bread,
4. warmth, man - y are cold. Make us your build - ing,
5. hearts that yearn to be - long. Let us be ser - vants

1. your ho - ly peo - ple, light for the world to see.
2. has pow'r to save us. Make us your liv - ing voice.
3. bro - ken for oth - ers, shared un - til all are fed.
4. shel - ter - ing oth - ers, walls made of liv - ing stone.
5. to one an - oth - er, mak - ing your king - dom come.

Christ, by Whose Death

62

Text: Herman G. Stuempfle, Jr., 1923–2007, © 1993, 1997, GIA Publications, Inc. All rights reserved. Used with permission.
Music: SINE NOMINE, 10 10 10 with alleluias; Ralph Vaughan Williams, 1872–1958.
Descant: Michael Young, © 1979, GIA Publications, Inc. All rights reserved. Used with permission.

Christ Is Alive

1. Christ is a-live! Let Christians sing. The cross stands empty to the sky. Let streets and homes with praises ring. Love, drowned in death, shall nev-er die.

2. Christ is a-live! No long-er bound To distant years in Pal-es-tine, but saving, heal-ing here and now, and touch-ing ev-'ry place and time.

3. In ev-'ry in-sult, rift, and war, where col-or, scorn or wealth di-vide, Christ suf-fers still, yet loves the more, And lives, where ev-en hope has died.

4. Wo-men and men, in age and youth, can feel the Spir-it, hear the call, and find the way, the life, the truth, re-vealed in Je-sus, freed for all.

5. Christ is a-live, and comes to bring good news to this and ev-'ry age, till earth and sky and o-cean ring with joy, with jus-tice, love and praise.

Text: Brian A. Wren, b. 1936, © 1975, 1995, Hope Publishing Co., Carol Stream, IL 60188. All rights reserved. Used with permission.
Music: TRURO, 88 88, *Psalmodia Evangelica*, Part II, 1789; harm. Lowell Mason, 1792–1872, alt.
Descant: Richard Proulx, © 1979, GIA Publications, Inc. All rights reserved. Used with permission.

Christ Is Born
64

1. Christ is born! Now all the angels join to praise the Rising Sun. Word made flesh, God's self incarnate, Mystery of love begun. Chant aloud in awe and wonder, "Peace on earth to ev'ryone!"

2. Christ is born! A child is given. Shepherds coming from the night rapt in glory, tell a story, stars and songs and signs and sight; find a stable, manger, baby—revelation dawning bright.

3. Christ is born! O Love Eternal, born within my waiting heart, let my soul become a stable, and obedience be my part; majesty within, in a manger, here salvation's work must start.

4. Christ is born! Let all creation shout in joyous hope today. Christ is born! O Jesus, Savior, God with us now and always. Christ is born! To God be glory honor, blessing, thanks and praise.

Text: Sylvia Dunstan, 1955–1993, © 1991, GIA Publications, Inc. All rights reserved. Used with permission.
Music: UNSER HERRSCHER, 87 87 87, Joachim Neander, 1650–1680.

Christ Is Made the Sure Foundation

Christ Is Made the Sure Foundation, pg. 2

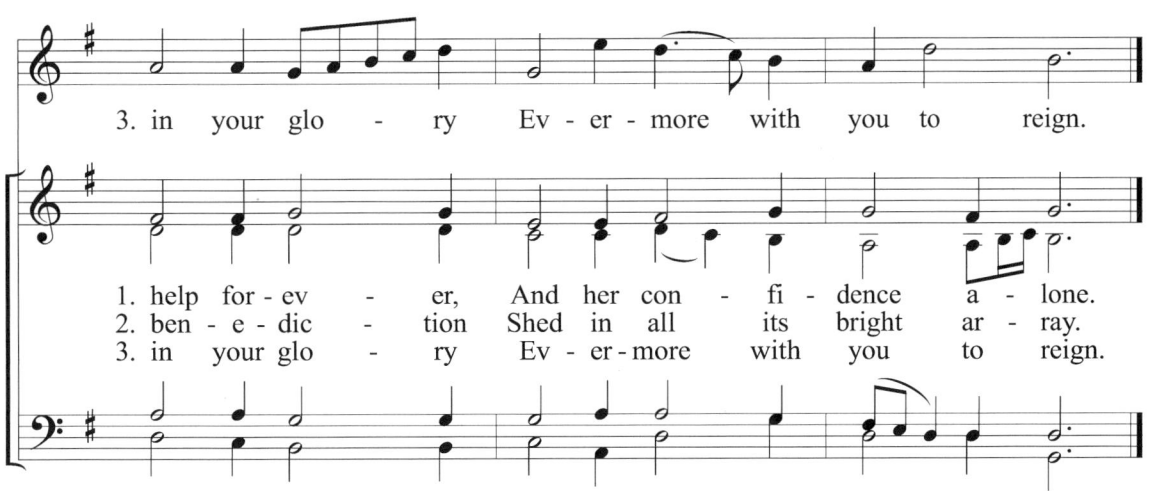

Text: Latin, 7th cent.; tr. John Mason Neale, 1818–1866, alt.
Music: WESTMINSTER ABBEY, 87 87 87, Henry Purcell, 1659–1695, adapt.
Descant: James Gillespie, © 1982, Church Society, London; alt. All rights reserved. Used with permission.

Christ Is Risen! Shout Hosanna!   66

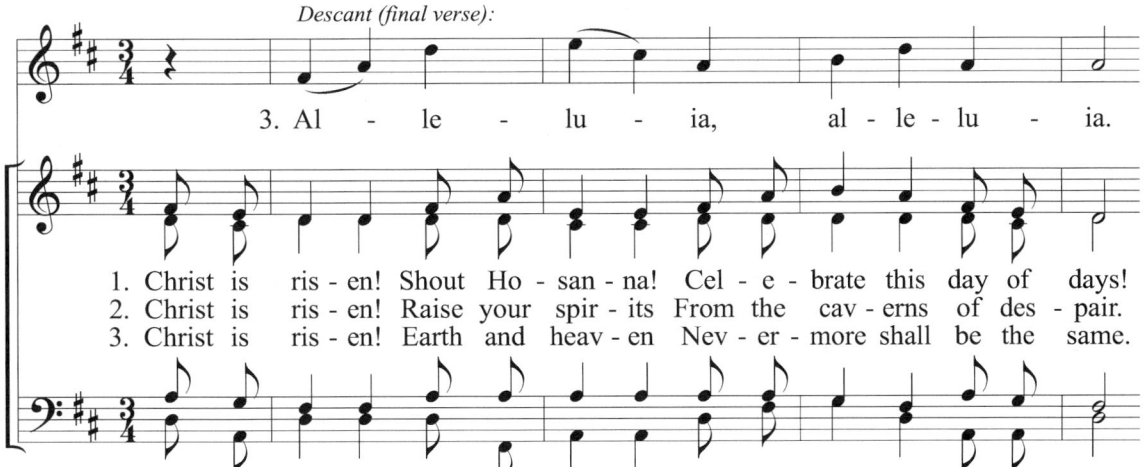

Text: Brian A. Wren, b. 1936, © 1986, Hope Publishing Co., Carol Stream, IL 60188. All rights reserved. Used with permission.
Music: NETTLETON 87 87 D; Wyeth's *Repository of Sacred Music,* Part II, 1813.
Descant: Christine Manderfeld, OSB, b. 1938, © 2009, the Sisters of Saint Benedict, St. Joseph, MN. Administered by Liturgical Press, Collegeville, MN. All rights reserved.

Christ Is the King 67

Christ Is the King, pg. 2

Al - le - lu - ia, al - le - lu - ia, al - le - lu - ia.

Al - le - lu - ia, al - le - lu - ia, al - le - lu - ia.

Text: George K. A. Bell, 1883–1958, alt., © Oxford University Press. All rights reserved. Used with permission.
Music: GELOBT SEI GOTT, 888 with alleluias, Melchior Vulpius, c. 1560–1616.
Descant: Christine Manderfeld, OSB, b. 1938, © 2009, the Sisters of Saint Benedict, St. Joseph, MN. Administered by Liturgical Press, Collegeville, MN. All rights reserved.

68 Christ the Lord Is Risen Today

Descant:

Al - le - lu - ia, al - le - lu - ia! Al - le - lu - ia,

1. Christ the Lord is ris'n to-day; Chris-tians, haste your vows to pay; Of - fer now your prais - es meet
2. Christ, the vic - tim un - de - filed, God and sin - ners rec - on - ciled; When in strange and aw - ful strife
3. Say, O wond-'ring Mar - y, say What you saw a - long the way. "I be - held, where Christ had lain,
4. Christ, who once for sin - ners bled, Now the first - born from the dead, Throned in end - less might and pow'r,

Christ the Lord Is Risen Today, pg. 2

Text: Wipo of Burgundy, c. 10th cent., attr.; tr. Jane Elizabeth Leeson, 1808–1881. Music: VICTIMAE PASCHALI, 77 77 D, Wurth's *Katholisches Gesangbuch*, 1859.
Descant: Christine Manderfeld, OSB, b. 1938, © 2009, the Sisters of Saint Benedict, St. Joseph, MN. Administered by Liturgical Press, Collegeville, MN. All rights reserved.

69 Christ, the Word Before Creation

1. Christ, the Word before creation; Christ, the Lord of time and space; Christ, who came for our salvation; Christ, incarnate truth and grace: Fill the Church, your
2. Christ, who walked among the lowly; Christ, who with the outcast dined; Christ, who sought the lost and lonely; Christ, who healed the sick, the blind: Send your Church with
3. Christ, upon the cross suspended; Christ, your body tombed in stone; Christ, alive, to God ascended; Christ, forever with your own: Help your Church in
4. Christ, whose Word brings hope and gladness; Christ, the name in which we pray; Christ, whose comfort conquers sadness; Christ, our Life, our Truth, our Way: Through your Church's

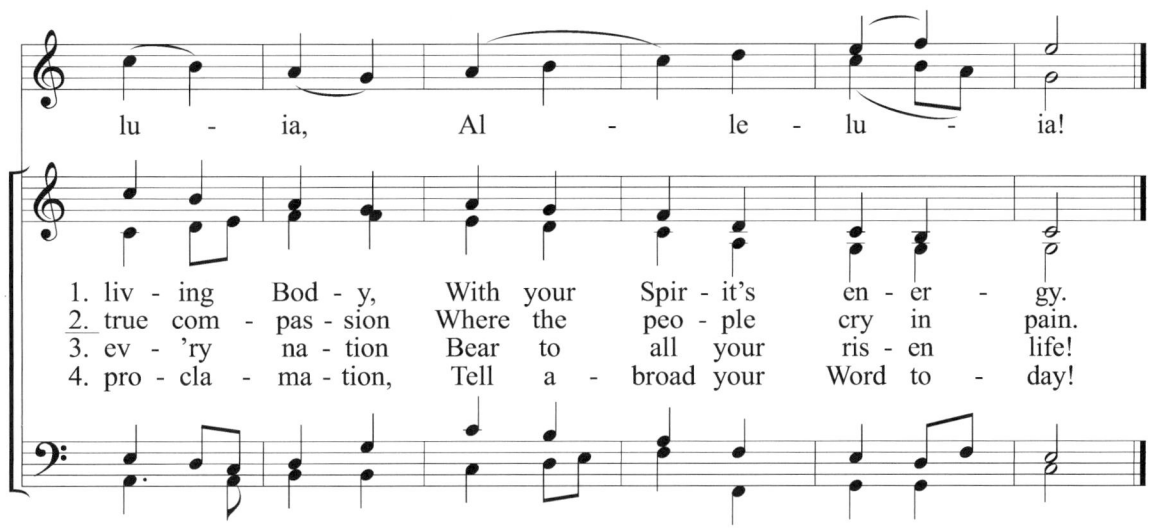

Text: Herman G. Stuempfle, Jr., 1923–2007, © 1997, World Library Publications, Inc., 3708 River Road, Franklin Park, IL 60131. www.wlpmusic.com
All rights reserved. Used with permission.
Music: LAUDA ANIMA, 87 87 87, John Goss, 1800–1880.
Descant: Christine Manderfeld, OSB, b. 1938, © 2009, the Sisters of Saint Benedict, St. Joseph, MN. Administered by Liturgical Press, Collegeville, MN. All rights reserved.

Christ Was Born on Christmas Day 70

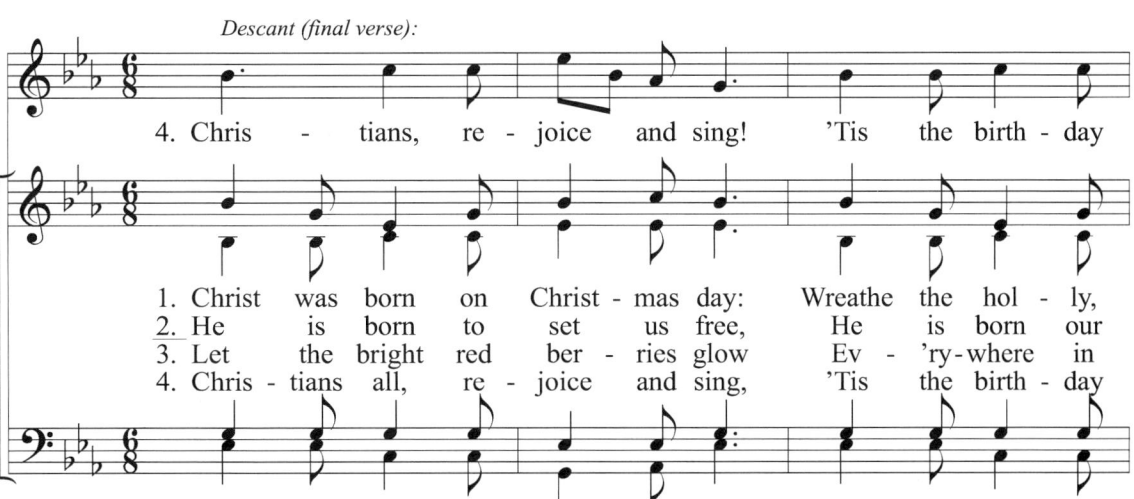

Christ Was Born on Christmas Day, pg. 2

Text: Traditional. Music: RESONET IN LAUDIBUS, 7 7 7 11; German, 16th cent.; harm. by Ralph Vaughan Williams, 1872–1958.
Descant: Christine Manderfeld, OSB, b. 1938, © 2009, the Sisters of Saint Benedict, St. Joseph, MN. Administered by Liturgical Press, Collegeville, MN. All rights reserved.

71   Christ, You Formed the Church, Your Body

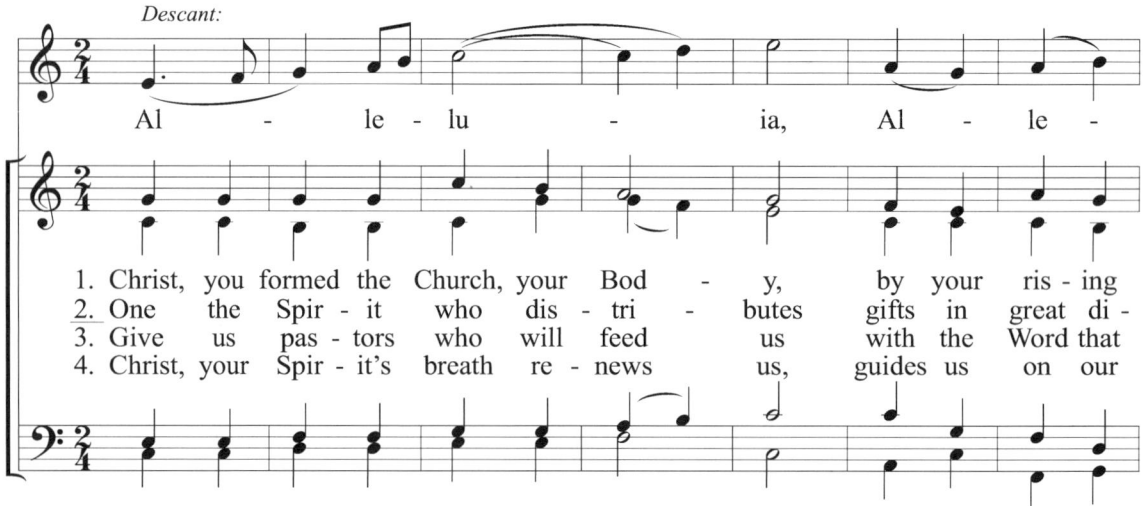

72 Christ's Church Shall Glory in His Power

Christ's Church Shall Glory in His Power, pg. 2

Text: Christopher Idle, b. 1938, © 1982, Jubilate Hymns, Ltd. (admin. by Hope Publishing Company, Carol Stream, IL 60188). All rights reserved. Used with permission.
Music: EIN' FESTE BURG, 87 87 66 66 7; Martin Luther, 1483–1546; harm. by J. S. Bach, 1685–1750.
Descant: Scott Withrow, © 1980, GIA Publications, Inc. All rights reserved. Used with permission.

Church of God, Elect and Glorious

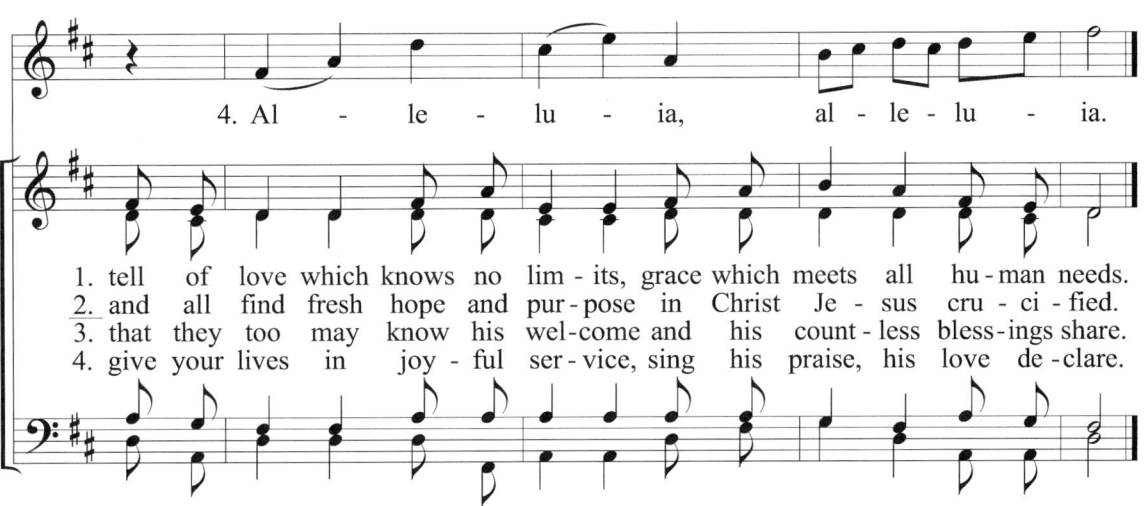

Church of God, Elect and Glorious, pg. 2

1. tell of love which knows no lim- its, grace which meets all hu-man needs.
2. and all find fresh hope and pur-pose in Christ Je- sus cru- ci- fied.
3. that they too may know his wel-come and his count-less bless-ings share.
4. give your lives in joy- ful ser-vice, sing his praise, his love de-clare.

Text: James Siddon, © 1982, Jubilate Hymns, Ltd. (admin. by Hope Publishing Co., Carol Stream, IL 60188). All rights reserved. Used with permission.
Music: NETTLETON 87 87 D; from Wyeth's *Repository of Sacred Music,* Part II, 1813.
Descant: Christine Manderfeld, OSB, b. 1938, © 2009, the Sisters of Saint Benedict, St. Joseph, MN. Administered by Liturgical Press, Collegeville, MN. All rights reserved.

74 — Come and Eat This Bread

Come and Eat This Bread, pg. 2

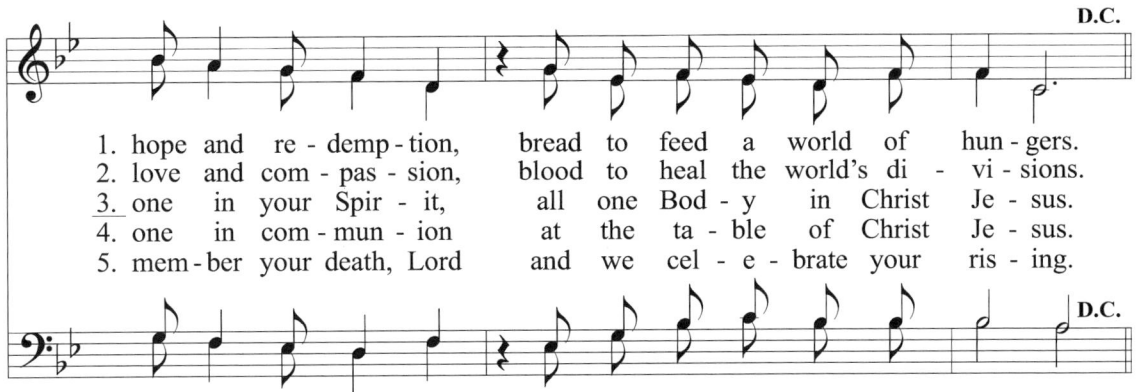

1. hope and re-demp-tion, bread to feed a world of hun-gers.
2. love and com-pas-sion, blood to heal the world's di-vi-sions.
3. one in your Spir-it, all one Bod-y in Christ Je-sus.
4. one in com-mun-ion at the ta-ble of Christ Je-sus.
5. mem-ber your death, Lord and we cel-e-brate your ris-ing.

Text and music: Marty Haugen, b. 1950, © 1997, GIA Publications, Inc. All rights reserved. Used with permission.

Come, Gather at the Table   75

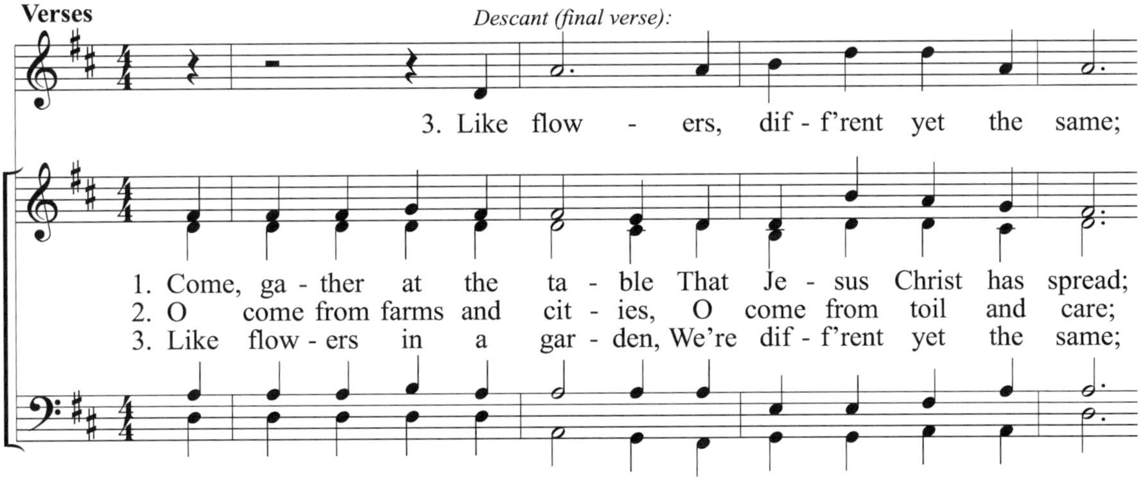

Verses

Descant (final verse):

3. Like flow-ers, dif-f'rent yet the same;

1. Come, ga-ther at the ta-ble That Jesus Christ has spread;
2. O come from farms and cit-ies, O come from toil and care;
3. Like flow-ers in a gar-den, We're dif-f'rent yet the same;

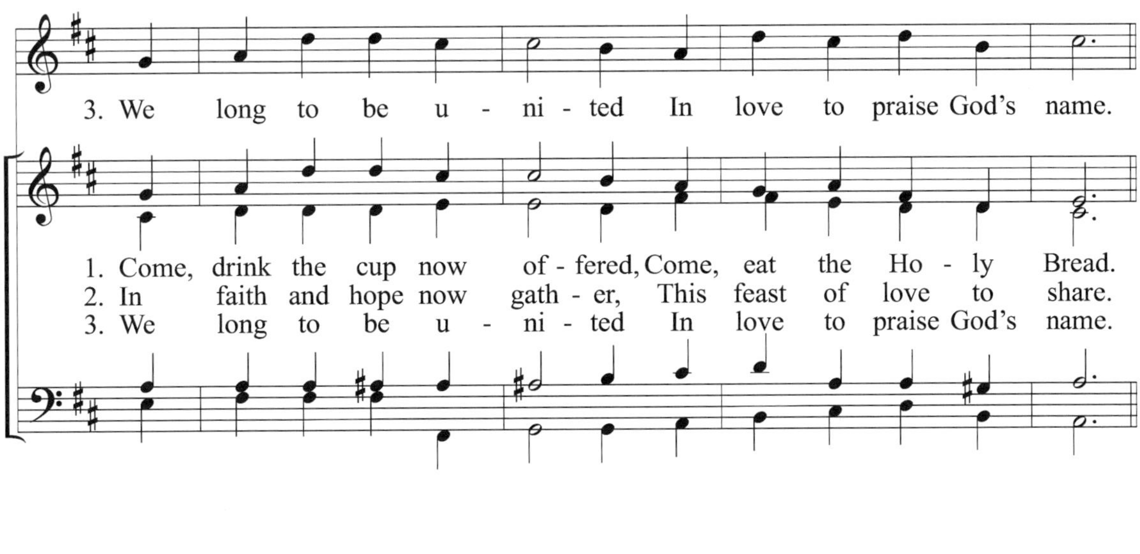

3. We long to be u-ni-ted In love to praise God's name.

1. Come, drink the cup now of-fered, Come, eat the Ho-ly Bread.
2. In faith and hope now gath-er, This feast of love to share.
3. We long to be u-ni-ted In love to praise God's name.

Come, Gather at the Table, pg. 2

Text: Jane Klimisch, OSB, © 1989, Sacred Heart Convent, Yankton, SD. Administered by Liturgical Press, Collegeville, MN. All rights reserved.
Music: AURELIA, 76 76 D, Samuel S. Wesley, 1810–1876.
Descant: Christine Manderfeld, OSB, b. 1938, © 2009, the Sisters of Saint Benedict, St. Joseph, MN. Administered by Liturgical Press, Collegeville, MN. All rights reserved.

Come, Gracious Spirit, Heavenly Dove

76

1. Come, gracious Spirit, heav'nly dove, With light and comfort from above. Come, be our guardian and our guide; O'er ev'ry thought and step preside.
2. The light of truth to us display And make us know and choose your way; Plant holy fear in ev'ry heart, That we from God may ne'er depart.
3. Lead us to Christ, the living way, Nor let us from his pastures stray; Lead us to holiness, the road That we must take to dwell with God.
4. Lead us to heav'n, that we may share Fullness of joy forever there; Lead us to our eternal rest, To be with God forever blest.

Text: Simon Browne, 1680–1732, alt. Music: WAREHAM, 88 88, William Knapp, 1698–1768.
Descant: Sydney Hugo Nicholson, 1875–1987, © 1982, Royal School of Church Music. All rights reserved. Used with permission.

Come, Let Us Sing for Joy

Text: Psalm 95, adapt. Marty Haugen, b. 1950; Music: Marty Haugen, b. 1950, © 2000, 2001, GIA Publications, Inc. All rights reserved. Used with permission.

Come, My Way, My Truth, My Life 79

1. Come, my Way, my Truth, my Life: Such a way as gives us breath; Such a truth as ends all strife; Such a life as killeth death.
2. Come, my Light, my Feast, my Strength: Such a light as shows a feast; Such a feast as mends in length; Such a strength as makes his guest.
3. Come, my Joy, my Love, my Heart: Such a joy as none can move; Such a love as none can part; Such a heart as joys in love.

Text: George Herbert, 1593–1632. Music: THE CALL, 77 77, Ralph Vaughan Williams, 1872–1958.

Come, O Spirit

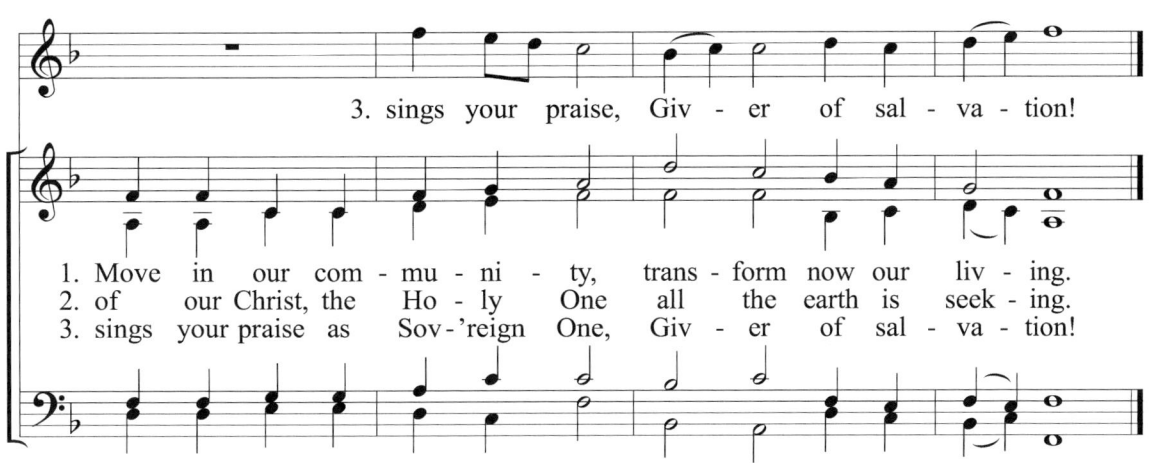

Text: John A. Dalles, 1983, © 2000, GIA Publications, Inc. All rights reserved. Used with permission. Music: GAUDEAMUS PARITER, 76 76 D, Johann Horn, c. 1495–1547.
Descant: Christine Manderfeld, OSB, b. 1938, © 2009, the Sisters of Saint Benedict, St. Joseph, MN. Administered by Liturgical Press, Collegeville, MN. All rights reserved.

Come, Our Almighty King

Text: Anon., c. 1757, alt. Music: ITALIAN HYMN, 66 4 666 4, Felice de Giardini, 1716–1796.
Descant: Christine Manderfeld, OSB, b. 1938, © 2009, the Sisters of Saint Benedict, St. Joseph, MN. Administered by Liturgical Press, Collegeville, MN. All rights reserved.

83 Come, Spirit, Come

Text: Based on Psalm 104; adapt. by Paul F. Page. Music: Paul F. Page.
Text and music: © 1998, World Library Publications, 3708 River Road, Franklin Park, IL 60131. www.wlpmusic.com All rights reserved. Used with permission.

Come, Thou Long Expected Savior 84

Text: Charles Wesley, 1707–1788.
Music: STUTTGART, 87 87, Christian Friedrich Witt, 1660–1716; adapt. and harm. William Henry Havergal, 1793–1870, alt.
Descant: Christine Manderfeld, OSB, © 2009, the Sisters of Saint Benedict, St. Joseph, MN. Administered by Liturgical Press, Collegeville, MN. All rights reserved.

85 Come to Me, All Pilgrims Thirsty

Text: Delores Dufner, OSB, b. 1939, © 1992, 1996, the Sisters of Saint Benedict, St. Joseph, MN. Administered by Liturgical Press, Collegeville, MN. All rights reserved.
Music: BEACH SPRING, 87 87 D; *The Sacred Harp*, 1844.
Descant: Christine Manderfeld, OSB, b. 1938, © 2009, the Sisters of Saint Benedict, St. Joseph, MN. Administered by Liturgical Press, Collegeville, MN. All rights reserved.

Come to Me and Live   86

*For a two-part version, use the melody (soprano part) and descant only.

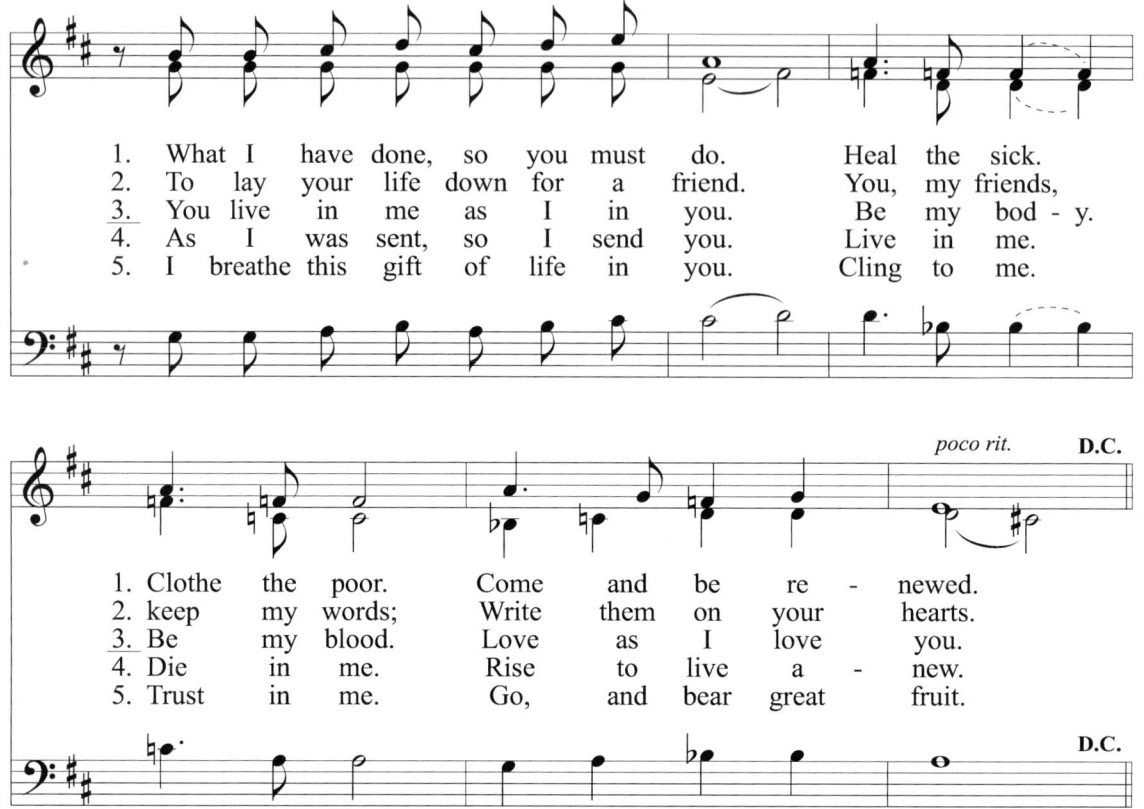

Text: Based on John 15, adapt. by Francis Patrick O'Brien, b. 1958. Music: Francis Patrick O'Brien, b. 1958.
Text and music: © 1996, GIA Publications, Inc. All rights reserved. Used with permission.

Come to the Banquet

87

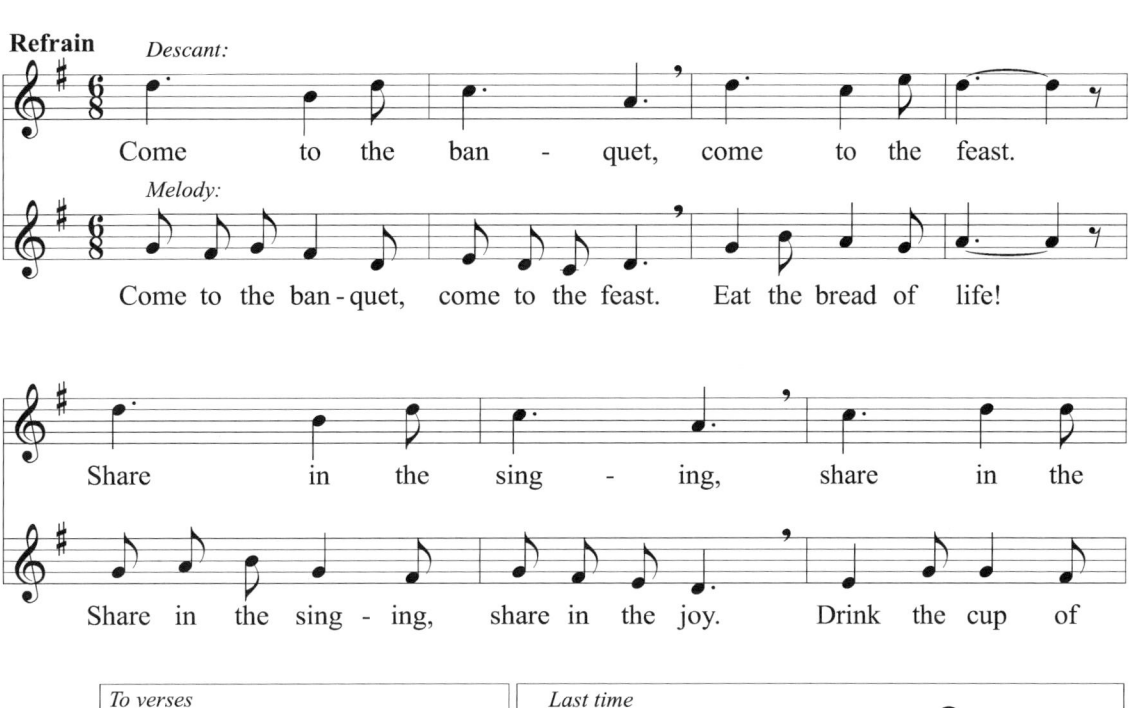

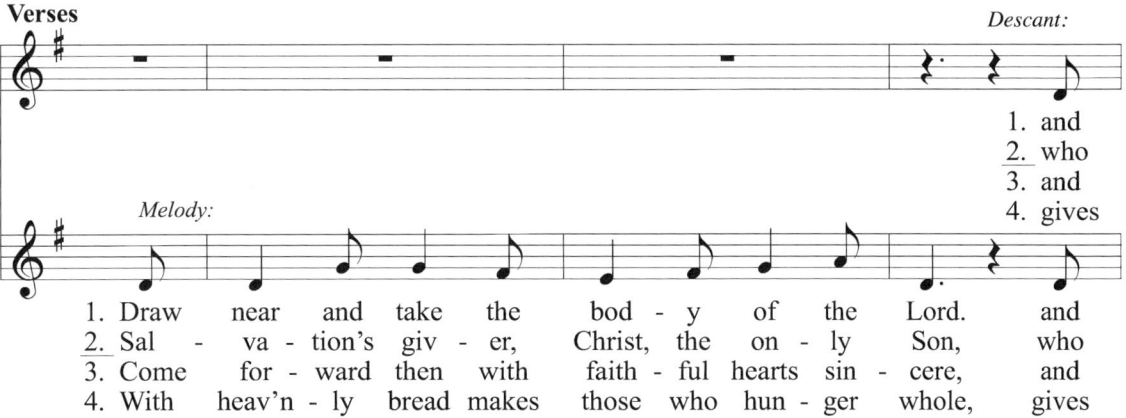

Come, You Faithful, Raise the Strain

88

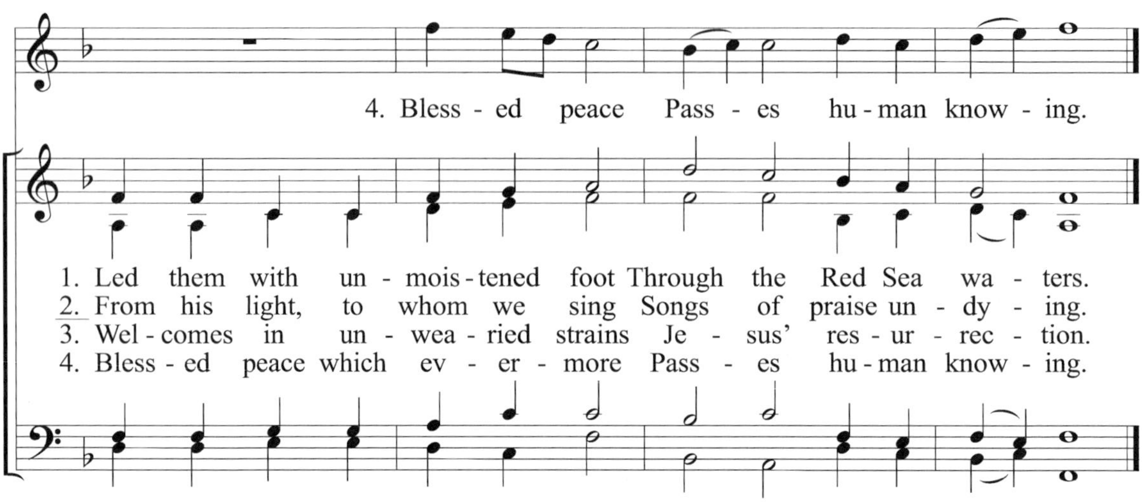

Come, You Faithful, Raise the Strain, pg. 2

4. Bless-ed peace Pass-es hu-man know-ing.

1. Led them with un-mois-tened foot Through the Red Sea wa-ters.
2. From his light, to whom we sing Songs of praise un-dy-ing.
3. Wel-comes in un-wea-ried strains Je-sus' res-ur-rec-tion.
4. Bless-ed peace which ev-er-more Pass-es hu-man know-ing.

Text: St. John of Damascus, 8th cent.; tr. John Mason Neale, 1818–1866, alt. Music: GAUDEAMUS PARITUR, 76 76 D, Johann Horn, c. 1495–1547.
Descant: Christine Manderfeld, OSB, b. 1938, © 2009, the Sisters of Saint Benedict, St. Joseph, MN. Administered by Liturgical Press, Collegeville, MN. All rights reserved.

89 Come, You Thankful People, Come

Descant (final verse):

4. E-ven so, Lord, quick-ly come To your fi-nal

1. Come, you thank-ful peo-ple, come, Raise the song of
2. All the world is God's own field, Fruit un-to his
3. For the Lord our God shall come, And shall take his
4. E-ven so, Lord, quick-ly come To your fi-nal

4. har-vest home; Gath-er all your peo-ple in, Free from

1. har-vest home: All is safe-ly gath-ered in, Ere the
2. praise to yield; Wheat and tares to-geth-er sown, Un-to
3. har-vest home; From his field shall in that day All of-
4. har-vest-home; Gath-er all your peo-ple in, Free from

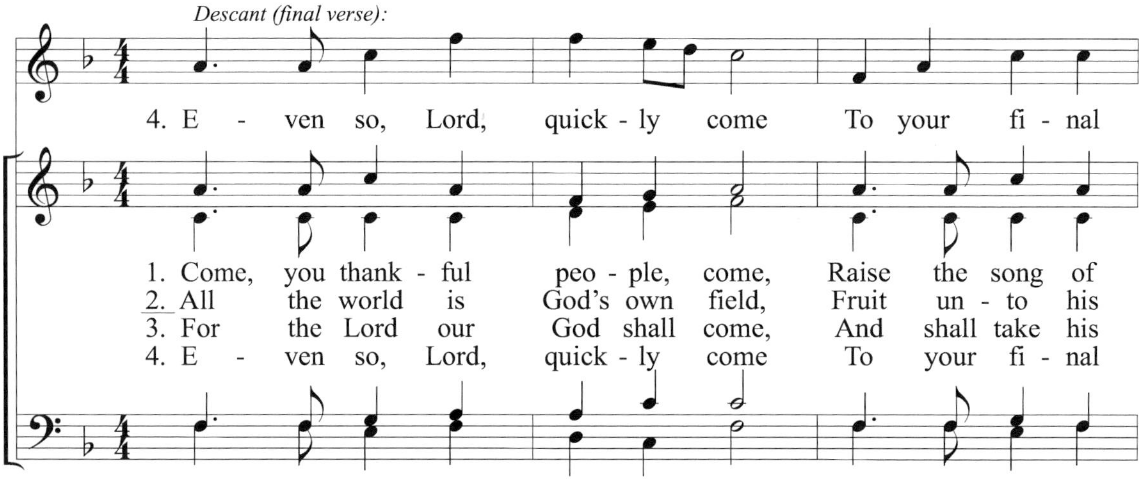

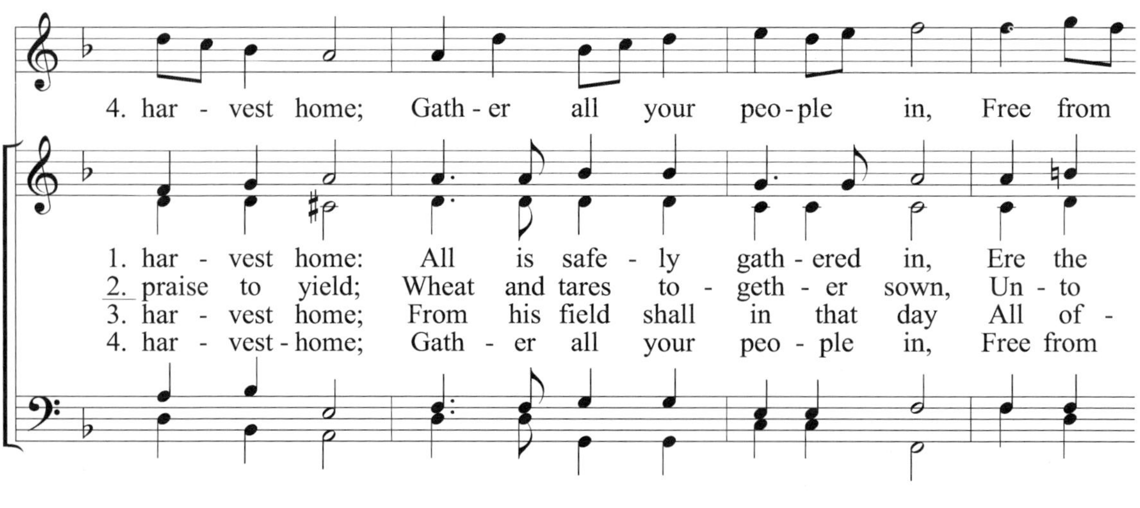

Come, You Thankful People, Come, pg. 2

Text: Henry Alford, 1810–1871. Music: ST GEORGE'S WINDSOR, 77 77 D, George Elvey, 1816–1893.
Descant: Christine Manderfeld, OSB, b. 1938, © 2009, the Sisters of Saint Benedict, St. Joseph, MN. Administered by Liturgical Press, Collegeville, MN. All rights reserved.

Comfort, Comfort, Ye My People

1. Com-fort, com-fort, ye my peo-ple, Speak ye peace, thus says our God:
   Com-fort those who sit in dark-ness Bowed be-neath their sor-row's load;
   Speak ye to Je-ru-sa-lem Of the peace that waits for them:
   Tell her that her sins I cov-er, And her war-fare now is o-ver.

2. For the her-ald's voice is cry-ing In the des-ert far and near,
   Bid-ding all to seek re-pen-tance Since the king-dom now is near.
   O that warn-ing cry o-bey! Now pre-pare for God a way;
   Let the val-leys rise to meet him, And the hills bow down to greet him.

3. Make ye straight what long was crook-ed, Make the rough-er plac-es plain:
   Let your hearts be true and hum-ble As be-fits his ho-ly reign;
   For the glo-ry of the Lord Now o'er earth is shed a-broad,
   And all flesh shall see the to-ken That his word is nev-er bro-ken.

Text: Johannes Gottfried Olearius, 1611–1684; tr. Catherine Winkworth, 1827–1878. Music: BOURGEOIS, 87 87 77 88, Louis Bourgeois, 1510–1561.

Conditor Alme Siderum / Creator of the Stars of Night   91

1. Cónditor alme síderum, aetérna lux credéntium, Christe, redémptor ómnium, exáudi preces súpplicum.

2. Qui cóndolens intéritu, mortis periclitantium, salvásti mundum lánguidum, donans reis remédium.

3. Vergénte mundi véspere, uti sponsus de thálamo, egréssus honestíssima, Vírginis matris cláusula.

4. Cuius forti poténtiae, genu curvántur ómnia; caeléstia, terréstria, nutu faténtur súbdita.

5. Te, Sancte, fide quaésumus, ventúre iudex saéculi, consérva nos in témpore, hostis a telo pérfidi.

6. Sit, Christe, rex piíssime, tibi Patríque glória, cum Spíritu Parácilo, in sempitérna saécula.

---

1. Creator of the stars of night, Your people's everlasting light, Lord Jesus, Savior of us all, Now hear your servants when they call.

2. Our Father heard the helpless cry Of all creation doomed to die, And saved our lost and guilty race By healing gifts of heav'nly grace.

3. When earth was near its ev'ning hour, You did, in love's redeeming pow'r, Like bridegroom from his chamber, come Forth from a maiden mother's womb.

4. At your great name, exalted now, All knees should bend, all heads should bow, All things in heav'n and earth adore, And praise you, King forevermore.

5. To you, O Holy One, we pray, Our judge in that tremendous day, Ward off, while yet we dwell below, The weapons of our crafty foe.

6. To God the Father, God the Son, And God the Spirit, three in one, Praise, honor, might and glory be From age to age eternally.

Text: Latin, 9th cent.; tr. John Mason Neale, 1818–1866, alt. Music: CONDITOR ALME SIDERUM, 88 88, Plainchant, Mode IV.

92 Confitemini Domino / Come and Fill

Ostinato Refrain

Text: Based on Psalm 137, Taizé Community, 1982; Music: Jacques Berthier, 1923–1994, © 1982, 1991, Les Presses de Taizé, GIA Publications, Inc., North American agent. All rights reserved. Used with permission.

Crown Him with Many Crowns 93

Crown Him with Many Crowns, pg. 2

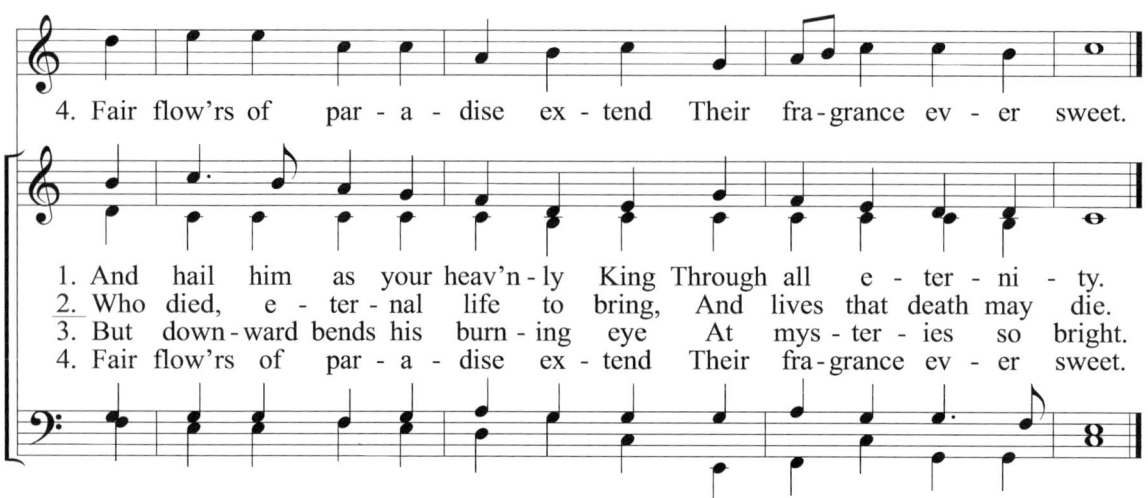

4. Fair flow'rs of par-a-dise ex-tend Their fra-grance ev-er sweet.

1. And hail him as your heav'n-ly King Through all e-ter-ni-ty.
2. Who died, e-ter-nal life to bring, And lives that death may die.
3. But down-ward bends his burn-ing eye At mys-ter-ies so bright.
4. Fair flow'rs of par-a-dise ex-tend Their fra-grance ev-er sweet.

Text: Matthew Bridges, 1800–1894, vv. 1, 3, 4; Godfrey Thring, 1823–1903, v. 2. Music: DIADEMATA, 66 86 D, George Job Elvey, 1816–1893.
Descant: Christine Manderfeld, OSB, b. 1938, © 2009, the Sisters of Saint Benedict, St. Joseph, MN. Administered by Liturgical Press, Collegeville, MN. All rights reserved.

94 Daily, Daily Sing to Mary

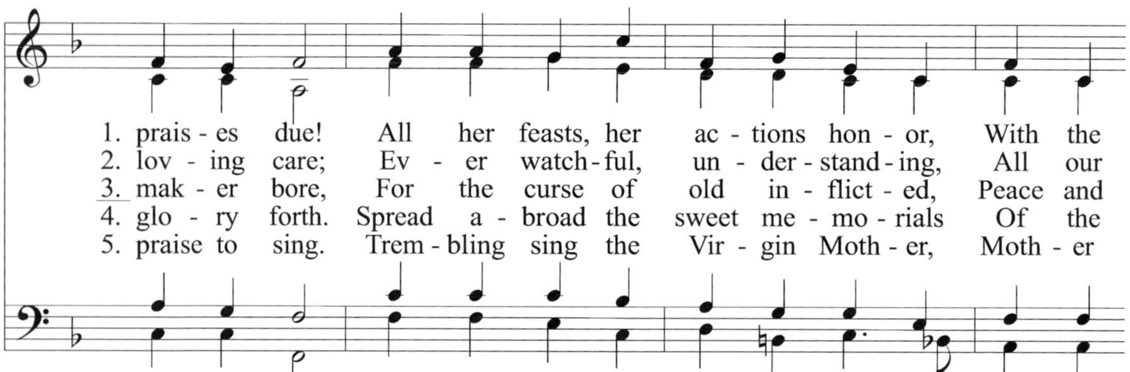

1. Dai-ly, dai-ly sing to Mar-y, Sing with joy her prais-es due! All her feasts, her ac-tions hon-or, With the
2. She is might-y in her plead-ing, Ten-der in her lov-ing care; Ev-er watch-ful, un-der-stand-ing, All our
3. Sing my tongue, the Vir-gin's hon-ors, Who for us her mak-er bore, For the curse of old in-flict-ed, Peace and
4. All my sens-es, heart, af-fec-tions, Strive to sound her glo-ry forth. Spread a-broad the sweet me-mo-rials Of the
5. All our joys do flow from Mar-y All then join her praise to sing. Trem-bling sing the Vir-gin Moth-er, Moth-er

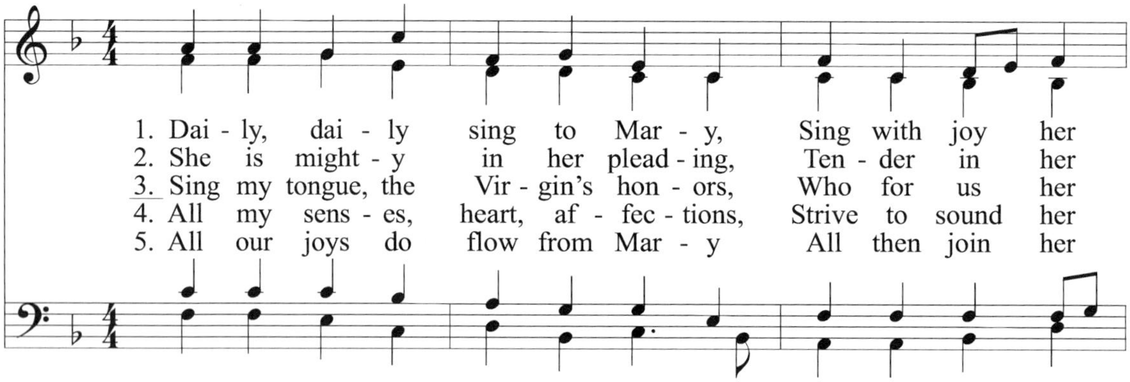

Daily, Daily Sing to Mary, pg. 2

Text: St. Bernard of Cluny, c. 1150, attr.; Henry Bittleston, 1818–1886; alt. Irvin Udulutsch, OFM, Cap, b. 1920.
Music: ALLE TAGE SING UND SAGE, 87 87 D, traditional German melody; harm. Mary Teresine Haban, OSF, b. 1914.
Text and harm.: © 1959, 1977, Order of Saint Benedict, Collegeville, MN. Administered by Liturgical Press, Collegeville, MN. All rights reserved.

95 Day Is Done

Descant (final verse):
3. Eyes will close, but you keep watch;
   Death may come— still we abide. God of love, all evil quelling, sin forgiving, fear dispelling,

1. Day is done, but love unfailing dwells ever here;
   shadows fall, but hope, prevailing, calms ev'ry fear. God, our Maker, none forsaking, take our hearts, of love's own making,
2. Dark descends, but light unending shines through our night;
   you are with us, ever lending new strength to sight: One in love, your truth confessing, one in hope of heaven's blessing,
3. Eyes will close, but you unsleeping watch by our side;
   death may come, in love's safe keeping still we abide. God of love, all evil quelling, sin forgiving, fear dispelling,

Day Is Done, pg. 2

3. stay with us this e - ven - tide.

1. watch our sleep-ing, guard our wak-ing, be al-ways near.
2. may we see, in love's pos-sess-ing, love's end-less light.
3. stay with us, our hearts in-dwell-ing, this e-ven-tide.

Text: James Quinn, SJ, b. 1919, © 1969, James Quinn, SJ, Selah Publishing Co. Inc., North American agent. All rights reserved. Used with permission.
Music: AR HYD Y NOS, 84 84 88 84, traditional Welsh melody.
Descant: Christine Manderfeld, OSB, b. 1938, © 2009, the Sisters of Saint Benedict, St. Joseph, MN. Administered by Liturgical Press, Collegeville, MN. All rights reserved.

Draw Near and Take the Body of Your Lord   97

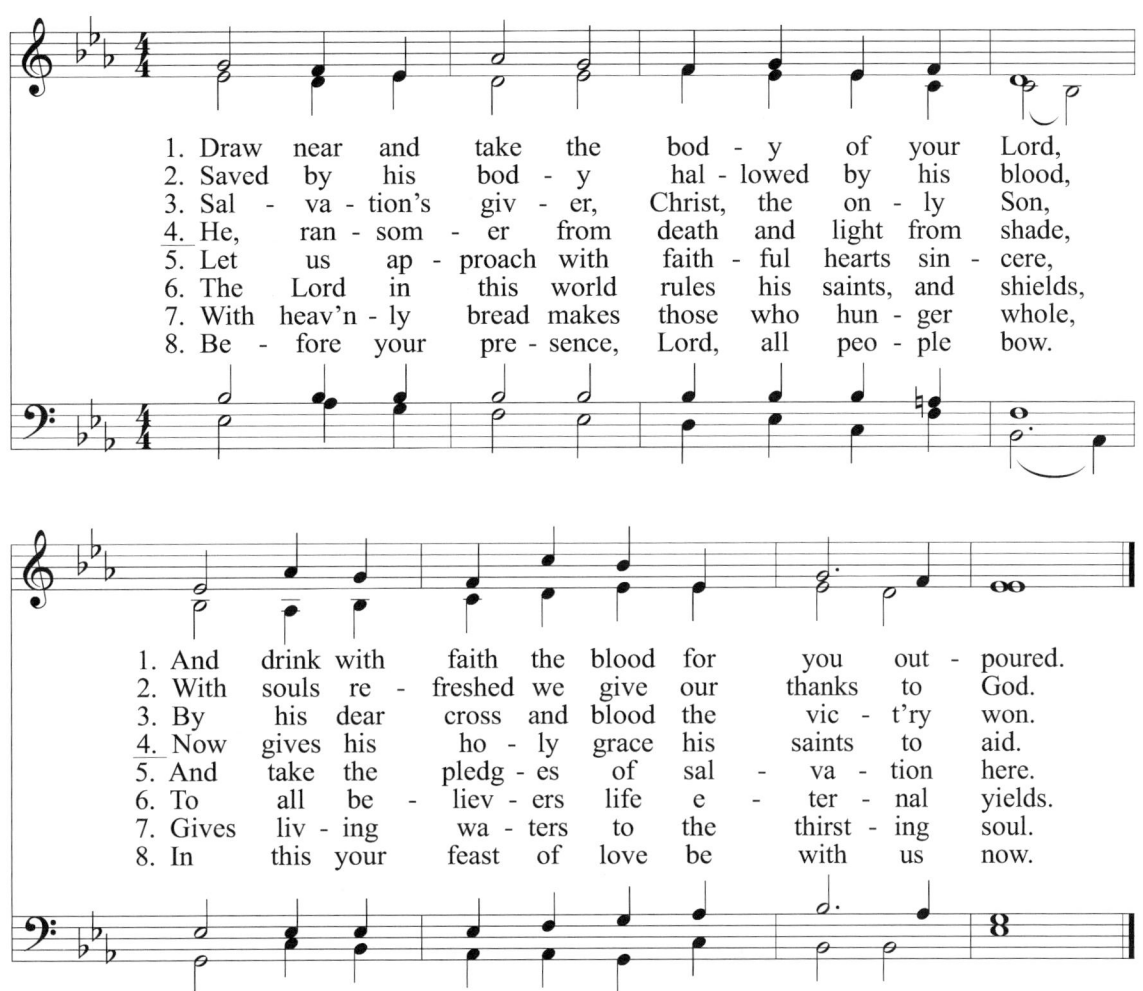

1. Draw near and take the body of your Lord,
And drink with faith the blood for you outpoured.
2. Saved by his body hallowed by his blood,
With souls refreshed we give our thanks to God.
3. Salvation's giver, Christ, the only Son,
By his dear cross and blood the vict'ry won.
4. He, ransomer from death and light from shade,
Now gives his holy grace his saints to aid.
5. Let us approach with faithful hearts sincere,
And take the pledges of salvation here.
6. The Lord in this world rules his saints, and shields,
To all believers life eternal yields.
7. With heav'nly bread makes those who hunger whole,
Gives living waters to the thirsting soul.
8. Before your presence, Lord, all people bow.
In this your feast of love be with us now.

Text: Latin hymn, 7th cent.; tr. John M. Neale, 1818–1866, alt.
Music: COENA DOMINI, 10 10, Arthur S. Sullivan, 1842–1900.

98   Drinking Earth's Pure Water

1. Drinking earth's pure water, nature springs alive.
2. O'er the flood's deep waters, Noah rode secure.
3. In the Red Sea waters, Pharaoh's hosts were slain.
4. Saved from death's dark waters, Christ the Lord now lives.
5. In this sacred water, Christians come to birth.

1. Sprinkled with this water, weary souls revive.
2. Sailing on this water, ours a passage sure.
3. Drowned now in this water, pow'r of sin is vain.
4. Baptized in this water, ours the life he gives.
5. Blest now with this water, ours a godly worth.

1. We share anew God's goodness from above:
2. We share anew God's favor from above:
3. We share anew God's freedom from above:
4. We share anew God's likeness from above:
5. We share anew God's glory from above:

1.–5. Christ has won salvation, everlasting love!

Text: Michael Kwatera, OSB, b. 1950, and David Klingeman, OSB, b. 1955, © 1991, Order of Saint Benedict, Collegeville, MN.
Administered by Liturgical Press, Collegeville, MN. All rights reserved.
Music: NOEL NOUVELET, 11 10 10 11, French carol; harm. by Marty Haugen, b. 1950, © 1987, GIA Publications, Inc. All rights reserved. Used with permission.

Dulcis Iesu Memoria / O Jesus, Joy of Loving Hearts

1. Dulcis Iesu memória, dans vera cordi gáudia, sed super mel et ómnia eius dulcis praeséntia.
2. Nil cánitur suávius, audítur nil iucúndius, nil cogitátur dúlcius quam Iesus Dei Fílius.
3. Iesu, dulcédo córdium, fons veri, lumen méntium, excédis omne gáudium et omne desidérium.
4. Quando cor nostrum vísitas, tunc lucet ei véritas, mundi viléscit vánitas et intus fervet cáritas.
5. Da nobis largus véniam, amóris tui cópiam; da nobis per praeséntiam tu am vidére glóriam.
6. Laudes tibi nos pángimus, diléctus es qui Fílius, quem Patris atque Spíritus splendor revélat ínclitus.

1. O Jesus, joy of loving hearts, the fount of life and our true light, we seek the peace your love imparts and stand rejoicing in your sight.
2. Your truth unchanged has ever stood; you save all those who heed your call; to those who seek you, you are good, to those who find you all in all.
3. We taste you, Lord, our living bread, and long to feast upon you still; we drink of you, the fountainhead, our thirsting souls to quench and fill.
4. For you our restless spirits yearn where'er our changing lot is cast; glad, when your presence we discern, blest, when our faith can hold you fast.
5. O Jesus, ever with us stay; make all our moments calm and bright; oh, chase the night of sin away, shed o'er the world your holy light.
6. To God the Father and the Son, to Holy Spirit, three-in-one. May praise and honor, glory be to you, eternal Trinity.

Text: Ascr. to Saint Bernard of Clairvaux, 1091–1153; tr. Ray Palmer, 1808–1887, alt.
Music: JESU DULCIS MEMORIA, LM, Mode I.

Dust and Ashes

Text: Brian Wren, b. 1936, © 1989, Hope Publishing Co., Carol Stream, IL 60188. All rights reserved. Used with permission.
Music: David Haas, b. 1957, © 1991, GIA Publications, Inc. All rights reserved. Used with permission.

101 Dwellers in the Holy City

Dwellers in the Holy City, pg. 2

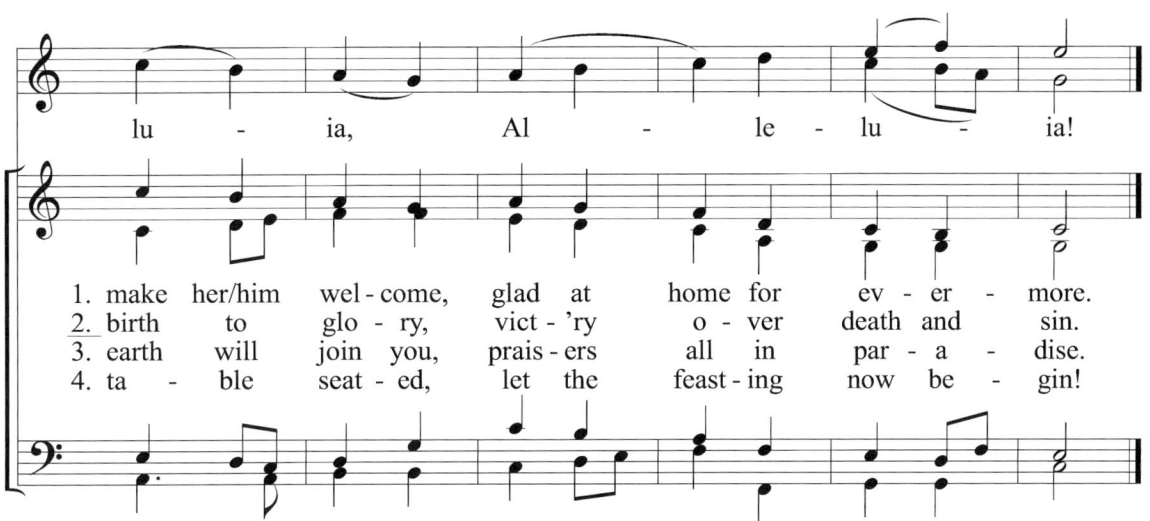

Text: Delores Dufner, OSB, b. 1939, © 2002, the Sisters of Saint Benedict, St. Joseph, MN. Administered by Liturgical Press, Collegeville, MN 56321. All rights reserved.
Music: LAUDA ANIMA, 87 87 87, John Goss, 1800–1880.
Descant: Christine Manderfeld, OSB, b. 1938, © 2009, the Sisters of Saint Benedict, St. Joseph, MN. Administered by Liturgical Press, Collegeville, MN. All rights reserved.

Earth, Earth, Awake! 102

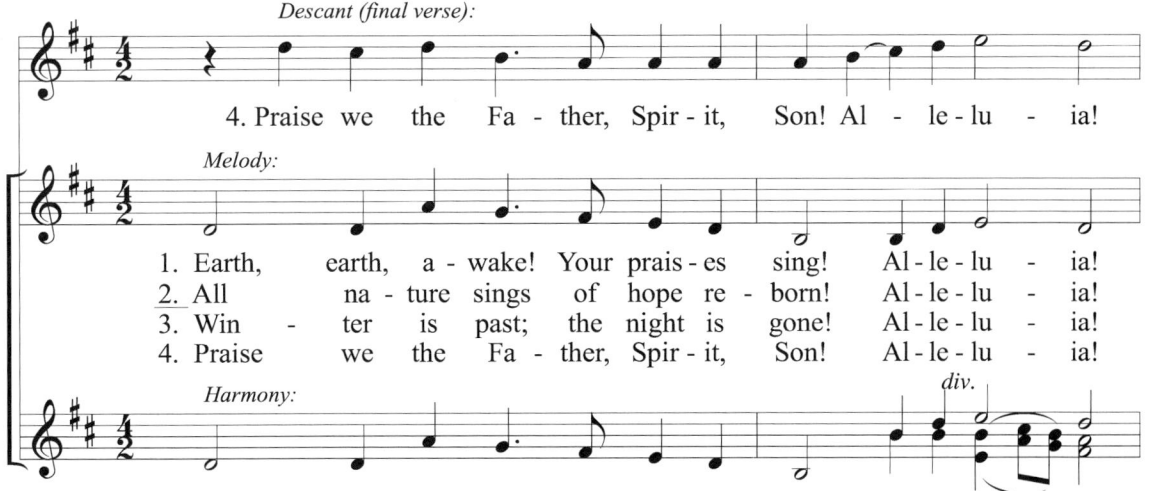

Earth Has Many a Noble City 103

Text: Aurelius Clemens Prudentius, 348–413; tr. by Edward Caswall, 1814–1878.
Music: STUTTGART, 87 87, Christian Friedrich Witt, 1660–1716; adapt. and harm. William Henry Havergal, 1793–1870, alt.
Descant: Christine Manderfeld, OSB, © 2009, the Sisters of Saint Benedict, St. Joseph, MN. Administered by Liturgical Press, Collegeville, MN. All rights reserved.

Easter Alleluia

Refrain: Alleluia, alleluia, alleluia! alleluia!

Verses:
1. Glory to God who does wondrous things, Let all the people God's praises now sing, All of creation in splendor shall ring: Alleluia!
2. See how salvation for all has been won, Up from the grave our new life has begun, Life now perfected in Jesus, the Son:
3. Now in our presence the Lord will appear, Shine in the faces of all of us here, Fill us with joy and cast out all our fear:
4. Call us, Good Shepherd, we listen for you, Wanting to see you in all that we do, We would the gate of salvation pass through:
5. Lord, we are open to all that you say, Ready to listen and follow your way, You are the potter and we are the clay:
6. If we have love, then we dwell in the Lord, God will protect us from fire and sword, Fill us with love and the peace of his word:

Text: Marty Haugen, b. 1950. Music: O FILII ET FILIAE, 10 10 10 with alleluias; adapt. by Marty Haugen, b. 1950.
Text and arrangement: © 1986, GIA Publications, Inc. All rights reserved. Used with permission.

Eat the Bread of Thanksgiving   105

Eat the Bread of Thanksgiving, pg. 2

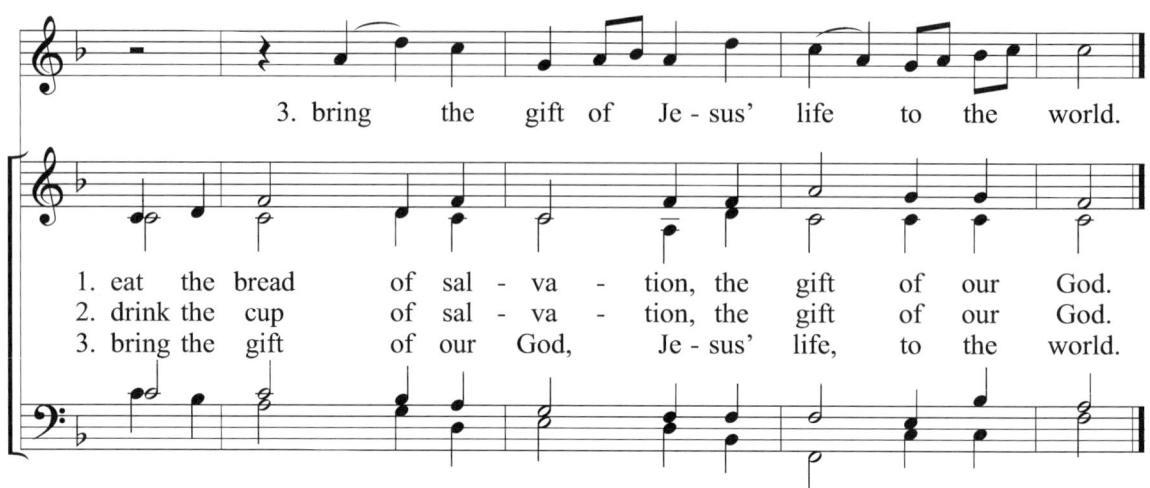

Text: Delores Dufner, OSB, b. 1939, © 1997, the Sisters of Saint Benedict, St. Joseph, MN. Administered by Liturgical Press, Collegeville, MN. All rights reserved.
Music: FOUNDATION, 11 11 11 11, Funk's *Compilation of Genuine Church Music,* 1832; arr. Charles Russell Woollen, 1923–1994.
Descant: Christine Manderfeld, OSB, b. 1938, © 2009, the Sisters of Saint Benedict, St. Joseph, MN. Administered by Liturgical Press, Collegeville, MN. All rights reserved.

106   Eat This Bread / Jesus Christ, Bread of Life

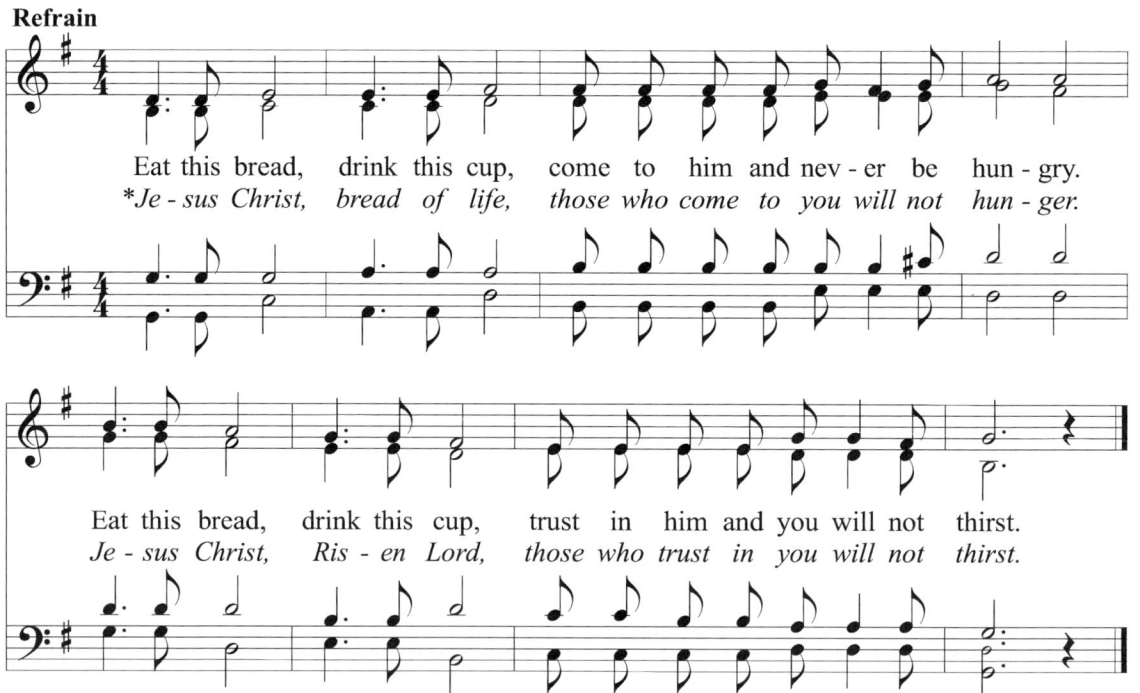

107 Epiphany Carol

1. Ev-'ry nation sees the glory Of a star that pierced the night.
2. Ev-'ry tongue shall sing the praises Of his birth in deepest night.
3. Once again may we discover Word made flesh sent from above,
4. Gather, God, the world together In the brightness of your day.

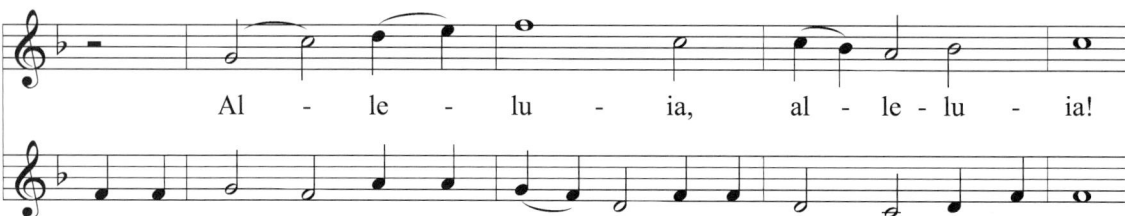

1. As we tell the wondrous story We are bathed in radiant light.
2. He is healing for the ages; He is Christ, our God's delight.
3. In our neighbor, sister, brother, In the lonely and unloved.
4. Fill our hearts with joy forever; Help us walk the holy way.

1. Star sent forth from highest heaven, Dancing light of God's design,
2. He proclaims within his being All our hopes, our great desires.
3. May we touch him, may we hold him, May we cradle him with care
4. May your justice rule the nations; May all people live as one.

Sing: Alleluia, alleluia!

1. Shine upon the gift that's given: Word made flesh now born in time.
2. He shall die to rise, redeeming All who follow with their lives.
3. As we learn to love each other, Bringing hope from out despair.
4. Now we see our true salvation In the glory of your Son.

Text: Francis Patrick O'Brien, b. 1958, © 2002, GIA Publications, Inc. All rights reserved. Used with permission.
Music: BEACH SPRING, 87 87 D; *The Sacred Harp*, 1844.
Descant: Christine Manderfeld, OSB, b. 1938, © 2009, the Sisters of Saint Benedict, St. Joseph, MN. Administered by Liturgical Press, Collegeville, MN. All rights reserved.

Eternal Father, Strong to Save

108

Text: William Whiting, 1825–1878, alt., vv. 1, 4; Robert Nelson Spencer, 1877–1961, vv. 2, 3. Music: MELITA, 88 88 88, John Bacchus Dykes, 1823–1876.
Descant: Irving Lauf, © 1980, GIA Publications, Inc. All rights reserved. Used with permission.

Text: Delores Dufner, OSB, b. 1939, © 1991, 2003, GIA Publications, Inc. All rights reserved. Used with permission.
Music: HYMN TO JOY, 87 87 D, Ludwig van Beethoven, 1770–1827, adapt. Edward Hodges, 1796–1867.
Descant: Christine Manderfeld, OSB, b. 1938, © 2009, the Sisters of Saint Benedict, St. Joseph, MN. Administered by Liturgical Press, Collegeville, MN. All rights reserved.

Exultate, Justi 110

Text: Based on 1 Corinthians 2:9-10; Marty Haugen, b. 1950. Music: Marty Haugen, b. 1950.
Text and music: © 1982, GIA Publications, Inc. All rights reserved. Used with permission.

Fairest Lord Jesus 112

Text: German composite; tr. Joseph August Seiss, 1823–1904.
Music: ST. ELIZABETH, 11 8 10 8, melody from *Schlesische Volkslieder*, 1842; harm. Thomas Tertius Noble, 1867–1953.
Descant: Christine Manderfeld, OSB, b. 1938, © 2009, the Sisters of Saint Benedict, St. Joseph, MN. Administered by Liturgical Press, Collegeville, MN. All rights reserved.

Faith of Our Fathers

Text: Frederick William Faber, 1814–1868, alt.
Music: ST. CATHERINE (TYNEMOUTH), 88 88 88, Henry Frederick Hemy, 1818–1888; adapt. and arr. James George Walton, 1821–1905.
Descant: Hal Hopson, © 1979, GIA Publications, Inc. All rights reserved. Used with permission.

Father, We Thank Thee Who Hast Planted

Father, We Thank Thee Who Hast Planted, pg. 2

Text: *Didache*, c. 110, tr. F. Bland Tucker, 1859–1984, rev.; © 1940, The Church Pension Fund.
All rights reserved. Used by permission of Church Publishing, Inc., New York.
Music: RENDEZ À DIEU, 98 98 D, *Genevan Psalter,* 1551; attr. to Louis Bourgeois, c. 1510–1561.
Descant: Christine Manderfeld, OSB, b. 1938, © 2009, the Sisters of Saint Benedict, St. Joseph, MN. Administered by Liturgical Press, Collegeville, MN. All rights reserved.

Fire of God, Undying Flame

1. Fire of God, undying flame, Spirit who in splendor came, Let your heat my soul refine, Till it glows with love divine.
2. Breath of God, that swept in pow'r In the Pentecostal hour, Holy breath, be now in me Source of vital energy.
3. Strength of God, your might within Conquers sorrow, pain and sin; Fortify from evil art All the gateways of my heart.
4. Truth of God, your piercing rays Penetrate my secret ways, May the light that shames my sin Guide me holier paths to win.
5. Love of God, your grace profound Knows not either age or bound; Come, my heart's own guest to be, Dwell for evermore in me.

Text: Albert F. Bayly, 1901–1984, alt., © Oxford University Press. All rights reserved. Used with permission.
Music: NUN KOMM DER HEIDEN HEILAND, 77 77, *Geistliche Gesangbüchlein,* Wittenberg, 1524; harm. by Melchior Vulpius, 1560–1616.
Descant: Christine Manderfeld, OSB, b. 1938, © 2009, the Sisters of Saint Benedict, St. Joseph, MN. Administered by Liturgical Press, Collegeville, MN. All rights reserved.

For All the Blessings of the Year   116

Text: Albert H. Hutchinson. Music: JUST AS I AM, 888 6; Joseph Barnby, 1838–1896.

117. For All the Faithful Women

Descant (final verse):
6. We praise her, Who came at Easter dawn / And near the tomb did tarry, But found her Lord was gone. / And then with joy she saw him In resurrection light.

1. For all the faithful women Who served in days of old, / To you shall thanks be given; To all, their story told. / They served with strength and gladness In tasks your wisdom gave.

2. We praise your name for Miriam Who sang triumphantly / While Pharoah's vaunted army Lay drowned beneath the sea. / As Israel marched to freedom, Her chains of bondage gone,

3. All praise for that brave warrior Who fought at your command; / You made her Israel's savior When foes oppressed the land. / As Deborah stood with valor Upon the battlefield,

4. To Hannah, praying childless Before the throne of grace, / You gave a son whose service Would be before your face. / Grant us her perseverance; Lord, teach us how to pray,

5. We sing of Mary, mother, Fair maiden, throne of grace, / She bore the Christ, our brother, Who came to save our race. / May we, with her, surrender Ourselves to your command

6. We praise the other Mary Who came at Easter dawn / And near the tomb did tarry, But found her Lord was gone. / And then with joy she saw him In resurrection light.

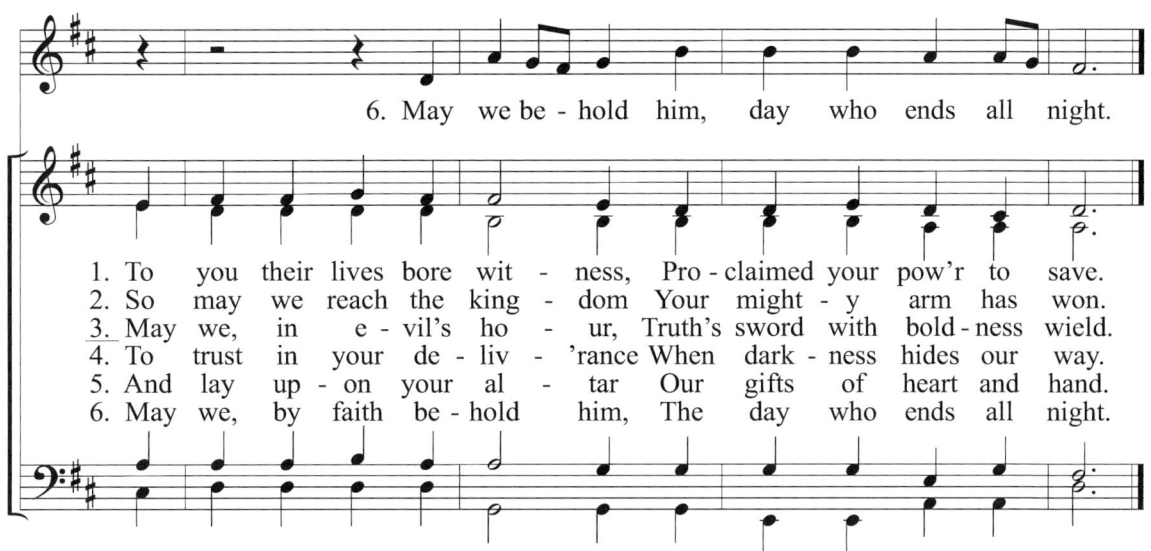

Text: Herman Stuempfle, 1920–2007, © 1993, GIA Publications, Inc. All rights reserved. Used with permission.
Music: AURELIA, 76 76 D, Samuel S. Wesley, 1810–1876.
Descant: Christine Manderfeld, OSB, b. 1938, © 2009, the Sisters of Saint Benedict, St. Joseph, MN. Administered by Liturgical Press, Collegeville, MN. All rights reserved.

For All the Saints — 118

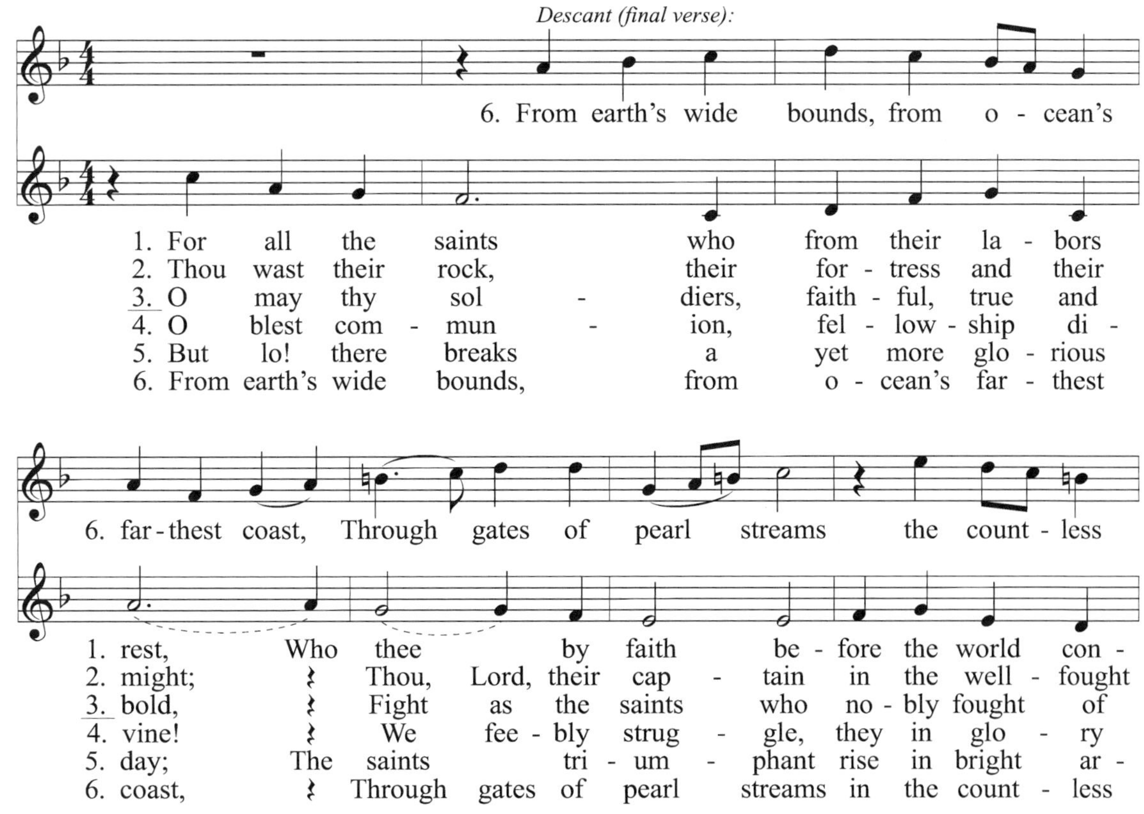

Descant (final verse):
6. From earth's wide bounds, from o - cean's far-thest coast, Through gates of pearl streams the count-less

1. For all the saints who from their la - bors rest, Who thee by faith be - fore the world con -
2. Thou wast their rock, their for - tress and their might; Thou, Lord, their cap - tain in the well - fought
3. O may thy sol - diers, faith - ful, true and bold, Fight as the saints who no - bly fought of
4. O blest com - mun - ion, fel - low-ship di - vine! We fee - bly strug - gle, they in glo - ry
5. But lo! there breaks a yet more glo - rious day; The saints tri - um - phant rise in bright ar -
6. From earth's wide bounds, from o - cean's far - thest coast, Through gates of pearl streams in the count - less

For All the Saints, pg. 2

Text: William Walsham How, 1823–1897. Music: SINE NOMINE, 10 10 10 with alleluias, Ralph Vaughan Williams, 1872–1958.
Descant: Michael Young, © 1979, GIA Publications, Inc. All rights reserved. Used with permission.

119   For the Beauty of the Earth

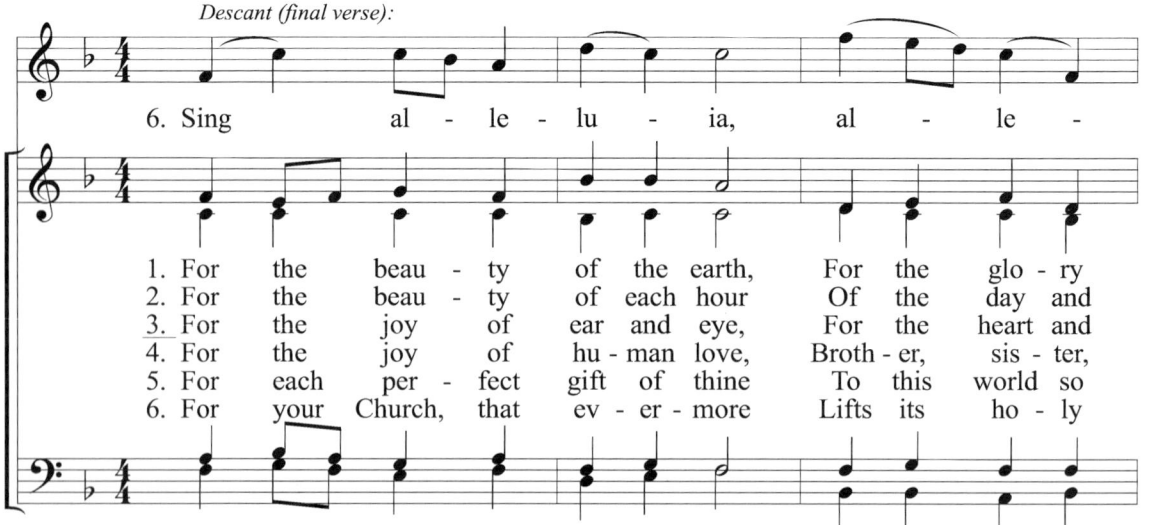

120 — For the Coming of the Savior

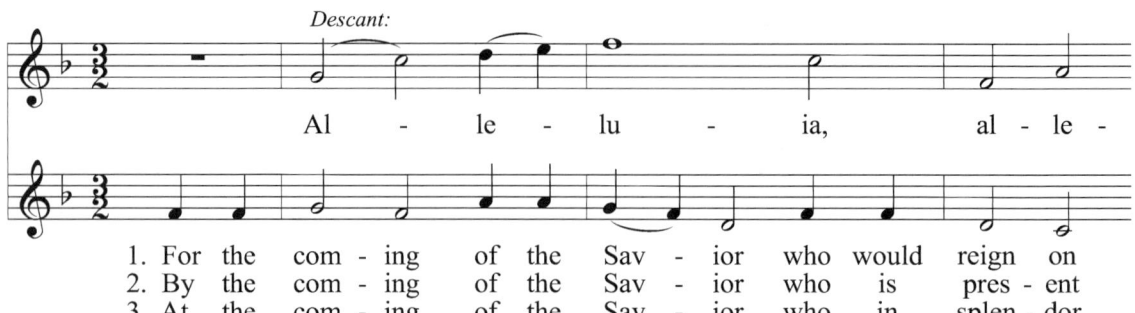

Descant: Alleluia, alle-

1. For the coming of the Savior who would reign on
2. By the coming of the Savior who is present
3. At the coming of the Savior who in splendor

-luia! Alleluia,

1. David's throne, free God's people from oppression, and restore their heritage; Israel looked with expectation
2. with his own in the sacraments and scripture, and the bidden calm of prayer; Christians still this truth discover
3. will be known when he vanquishes Death's legions, and return to reign in might; all the world at last shall witness

alleluia! Allelu-

-ia, alleluia! Sing: Al-

1. for the dawning of that age, and we share their
2. and a timeless blessing share greater than sheer
3. how God's judgment can unite truth with mercy,

For the Coming of the Savior, pg. 2

le - lu - ia, al - le - lu - ia!
1. sense of long-ing: in their hope, we see our own.
2. thought can fa-thom: for by faith is Christ made known.
3. peace with jus-tice: joined in love through Christ a-lone.

Text: Carl P. Daw, b. 1944, © 1990, Hope Publishing Co., Carol Stream, IL 60188. All rights reserved. Used with permission.
Music: BEACH SPRING, 87 87 D; *The Sacred Harp,* 1844.
Descant: Christine Manderfeld, OSB, b. 1938, © 2009, the Sisters of Saint Benedict, St. Joseph, MN. Administered by Liturgical Press, Collegeville, MN. All rights reserved.

For the Fruits of All Creation   121

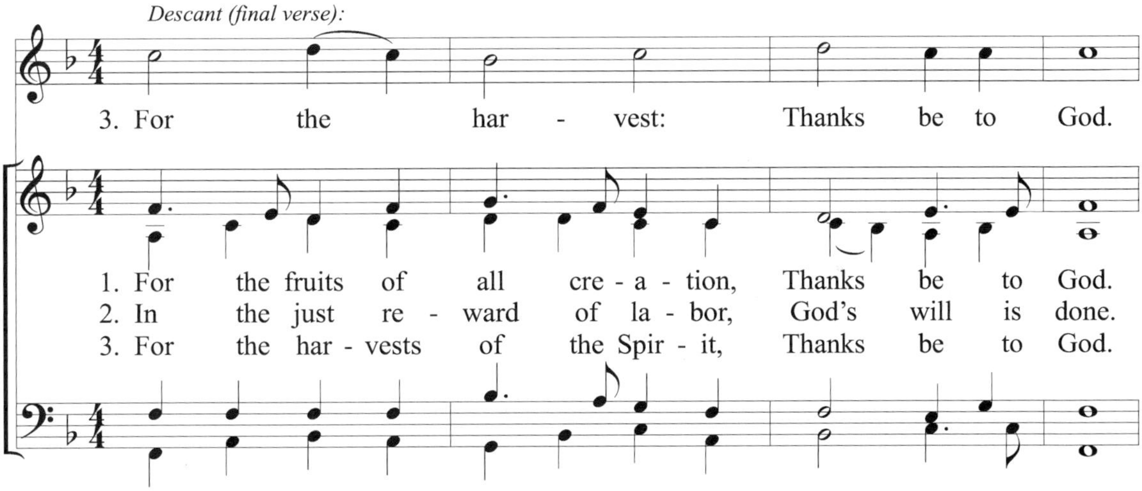

Descant (final verse):
3. For the har - vest: Thanks be to God.

1. For the fruits of all cre-a-tion, Thanks be to God.
2. In the just re-ward of la-bor, God's will is done.
3. For the har-vests of the Spir-it, Thanks be to God.

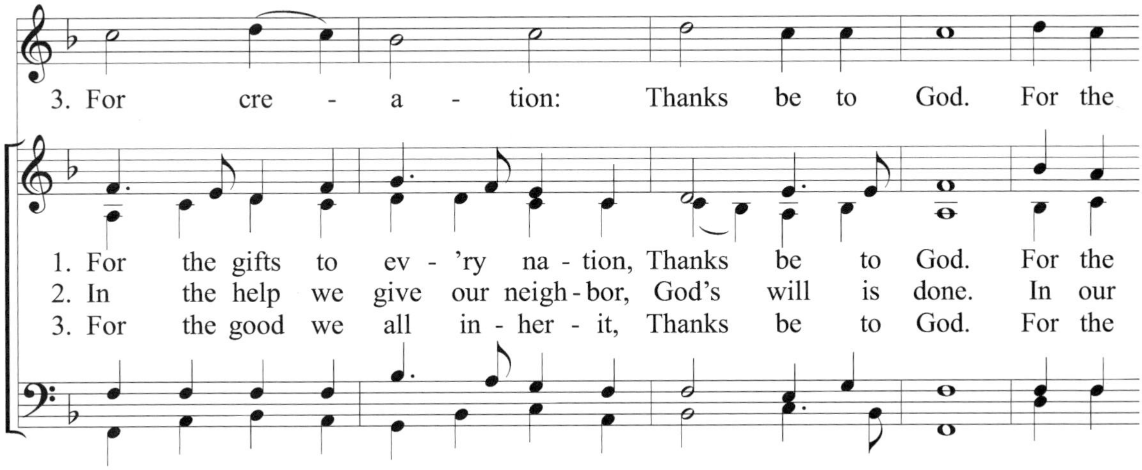

3. For cre - a - tion: Thanks be to God. For the

1. For the gifts to ev-'ry na-tion, Thanks be to God. For the
2. In the help we give our neigh-bor, God's will is done. In our
3. For the good we all in-her-it, Thanks be to God. For the

For the Fruits of All Creation, pg. 2

Text: Fred Pratt Green, 1903–2000, © 1970, Hope Publishing Co., Carol Stream, IL 60188. All rights reserved. Used with permission.
Music: AR HYD Y NOS, 84 84 88 84, traditional Welsh melody.
Descant: Christine Manderfeld, OSB, b. 1938, © 2009, the Sisters of Saint Benedict, St. Joseph, MN. Administered by Liturgical Press, Collegeville, MN. All rights reserved.

Forgive Our Sins 122

Text: Rosamund E. Herklots, 1905–1987, alt., © 1969, Oxford University Press. All rights reserved. Used with permission.
Music: MORNING SONG, 86 86, *Kentucky Harmony*, 1816.
Descant: Christine Manderfeld, OSB, b. 1938, © 2009, the Sisters of Saint Benedict, St. Joseph, MN. Administered by Liturgical Press, Collegeville, MN. All rights reserved.

From All That Dwell Below the Skies 124

1. From all that dwell below the skies, Let the Creator's praise arise; Let the Redeemer's name be sung, Through ev'ry land, by ev'ry tongue.
2. Eternal are your mercies, Lord; Eternal truth attends your Word: Your praise shall sound from shore to shore, Till suns shall rise and set no more.
3. Your lofty themes, all mortals bring; In songs of praise divinely sing; The great salvation loud proclaim, And shout for joy the Savior's name.
4. In ev'ry land begin the song; To ev'ry land the strains belong; In cheerful sounds all voices raise, And fill the world with loudest praise.

Text: Isaac Watts, 1674–1748, vv. 1 & 2; anon., v. 3; Robert Spence, v. 4; para. Psalm 117. Music: DUKE STREET, 88 88, John Hatton, c. 1710–1793.
Descant: Christine Manderfeld, OSB, b. 1938, © 2009, the Sisters of Saint Benedict, St. Joseph, MN. Administered by Liturgical Press, Collegeville, MN. All rights reserved.

125   From Ashes to the Living Font

Descant (final verse):

4. From ashes to the living font Your Church must journey still,

1. From ashes to the living font Your Church must journey, Lord,
2. Through fasting, prayer, and charity Your voice speaks deep within,
3. *(Sing verse below appropriate to the Sunday.)*
4. From ashes to the living font Your Church must journey still,

4. Through cross and tomb to Easter joy, In Spirit-fire fulfilled.

1. Baptized in grace, in grace renewed By your most holy word.
2. Returning us to ways of truth And turning us from sin.
3.
4. Through cross and tomb to Easter joy, In Spirit-fire fulfilled.

Verse 3:

1st and 2nd Sundays of Lent
From desert to the mountaintop
In Christ our way we see,
So, tempered by temptation's might
We might transfigured be.

3rd Sunday of Lent
For thirsting hearts let waters flow,
Our fainting souls revive;
And at the well your waters give
Our everlasting life.

4th Sunday of Lent
We sit beside the road and plead,
"Come, save us, David's son!"
Now with your vision heal our eyes,
The world's true Light alone.

5th Sunday of Lent
Our graves split open, bring us back,
Your promise to proclaim;
To darkened tombs call out, "Arise!"
And glorify your name.

Text: Alan J. Hommerding, b. 1956, © 1994, World Library Publications, Inc., 3708 River Road, Franklin Park, IL 60131. www.wlpmusic.com
All rights reserved. Used with permission.
Music: ST. FLAVIAN, CM; *John's Day Psalter*, 1562; harm. based on the original faux-bourdon setting.
Descant: Christine Manderfeld, OSB, b. 1938, © 2009, the Sisters of Saint Benedict, St. Joseph, MN. Administered by Liturgical Press, Collegeville, MN. All rights reserved.

Gather Us In, pg. 2

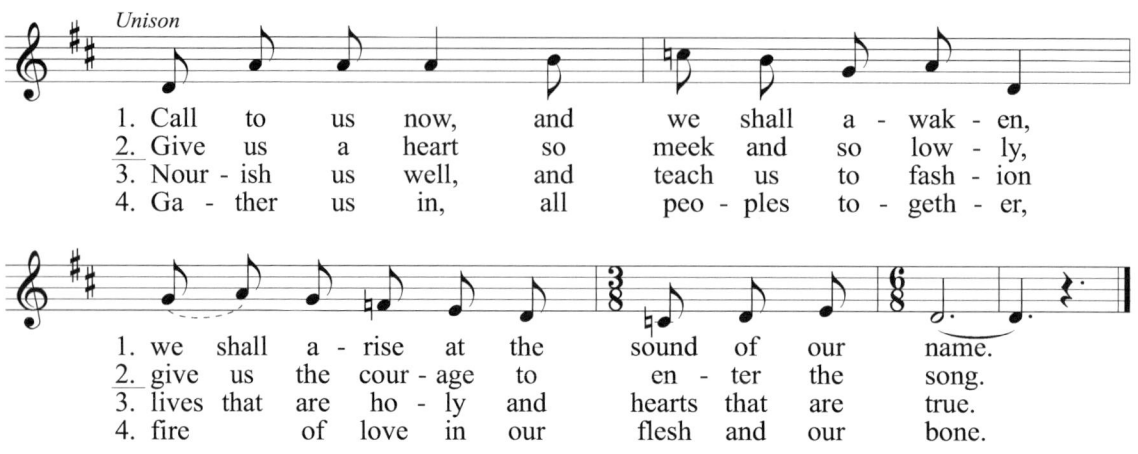

Text and music: Marty Haugen, b. 1950, © 1982, GIA Publications, Inc. All rights reserved. Used with permission.

127 Gathered Now

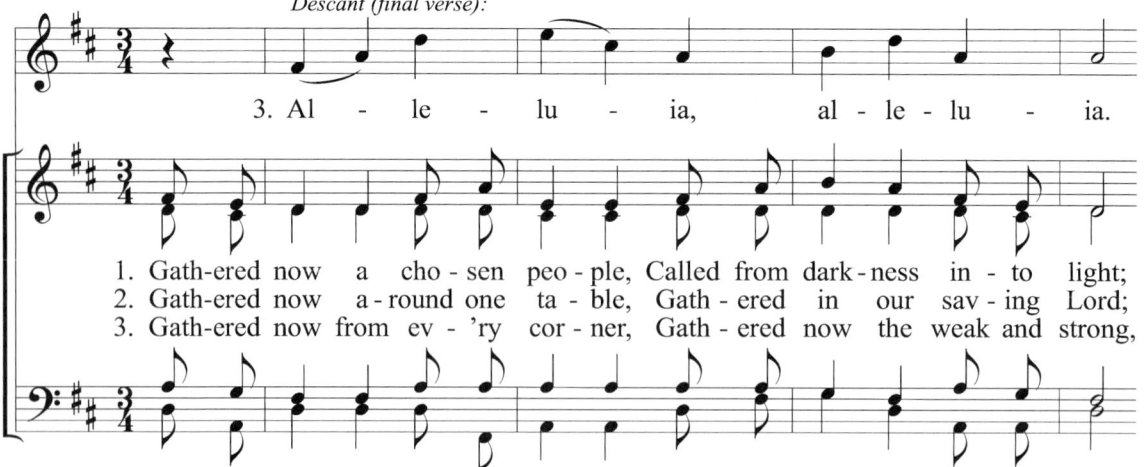

128 Gift of Finest Wheat

Text: Omer Westendorf, 1916–1997. Music: BICENTENNIAL, CM, with refrain, Robert E. Kreutz, 1922–1996.
Text and music: © 1977, Archdiocese of Philadelphia. All rights reserved. Used with permission.
Descant: Christine Manderfeld, OSB, b. 1938, © 2009, the Sisters of Saint Benedict, St. Joseph, MN. Administered by Liturgical Press, Collegeville, MN. All rights reserved.

129. Gift of God / Come to Us

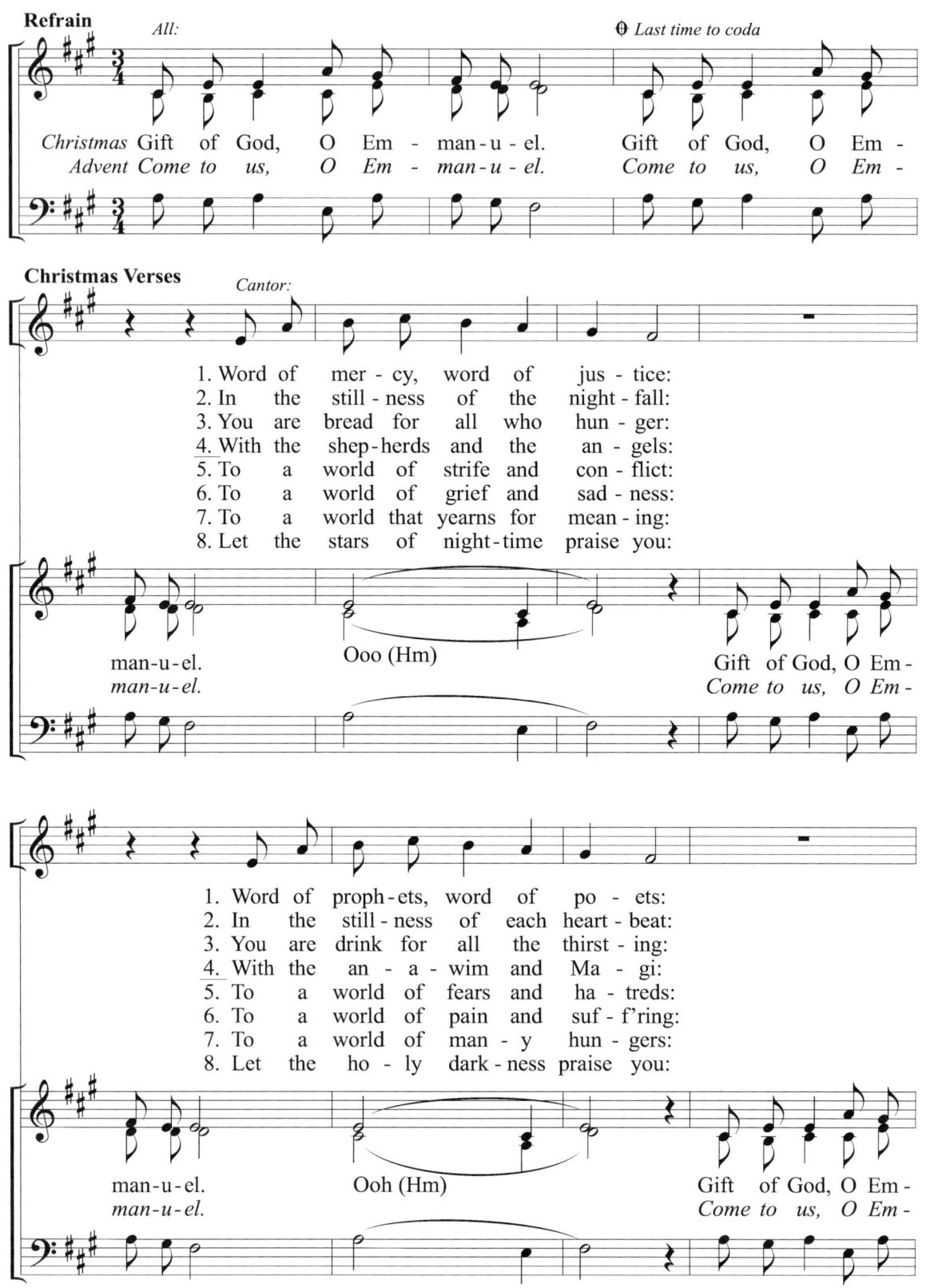

130 Go, Be Justice

Al - le - lu - ia, al - le - lu - ia!

1. Go, be jus-tice to God's peo-ple; Teach the hard-ened heart to learn.
2. Go, be heal-ing to God's peo-ple; Seek and share the sav-ing call.
3. Go, be mer-cy to God's peo-ple In for-give-ness free-ly shown;

Al - le - lu - ia, al - le - lu - ia!

1. Break the bread of true com-mun-ion, Pour the cup of true con-cern.
2. Be the touch of Christ for oth-ers, Be the voice of Christ for all.
3. Find the strang-er, call her kind-red, Find the ex-ile, call him home.

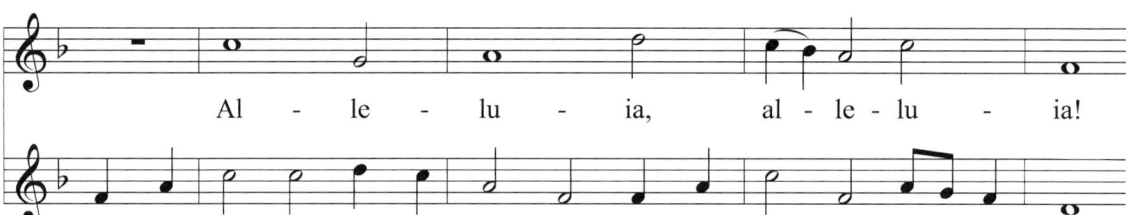

Al - le - lu - ia, al - le - lu - ia!

1. Feed the hun-gry, house the home-less, Catch the ty-rants in their lies;
2. Lives are bro-ken all a-round you, and Christ has no hands but yours;
3. Age to age God's mer-cy wel-comes With a love that will not cease;

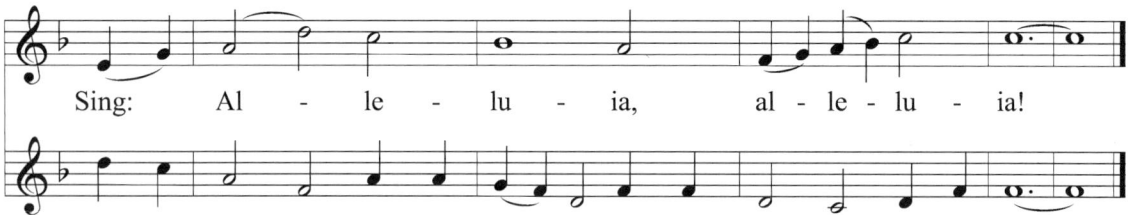

Sing: Al - le - lu - ia, al - le - lu - ia!

1. Be the Lord's a-noint-ed ser-vant So God's jus-tice nev-er dies.
2. Hold in them the ones who suf-fer So Christ's heal-ing love en-dures.
3. Go, be Christ-light to God's peo-ple, Be an in-stru-ment of peace.

Text: Martin Willett, © 2001, World Library Publications, Inc., 3708 River Road, Franklin Park, IL 60131. www.wlpmusic.com All rights reserved. Used with permission.
Music: BEACH SPRING, 87 87 D; *The Sacred Harp*, 1844.
Descant: Christine Manderfeld, OSB, b. 1938, © 2009, the Sisters of Saint Benedict, St. Joseph, MN. Administered by Liturgical Press, Collegeville, MN. All rights reserved.

Go Tell It on the Mountain 131

Go Tell It on the Mountain, pg. 2

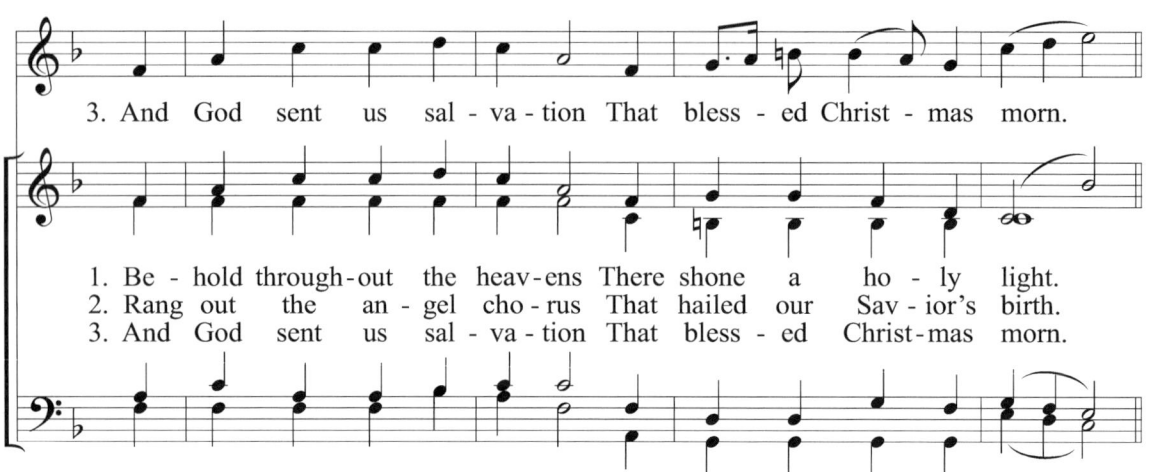

Text: African-American spiritual, 19th cent.; adapt. by John W. Work, Jr., 1871–1925, alt.
Music: GO TELL IT ON THE MOUNTAIN, 76 76 with refrain, African-American spiritual; harm. by John W. Work III, 1901–1967.
Descant: Christine Manderfeld, OSB, b. 1938, © 2009, the Sisters of Saint Benedict, St. Joseph, MN. Administered by Liturgical Press, Collegeville, MN. All rights reserved.

132 Go to the World

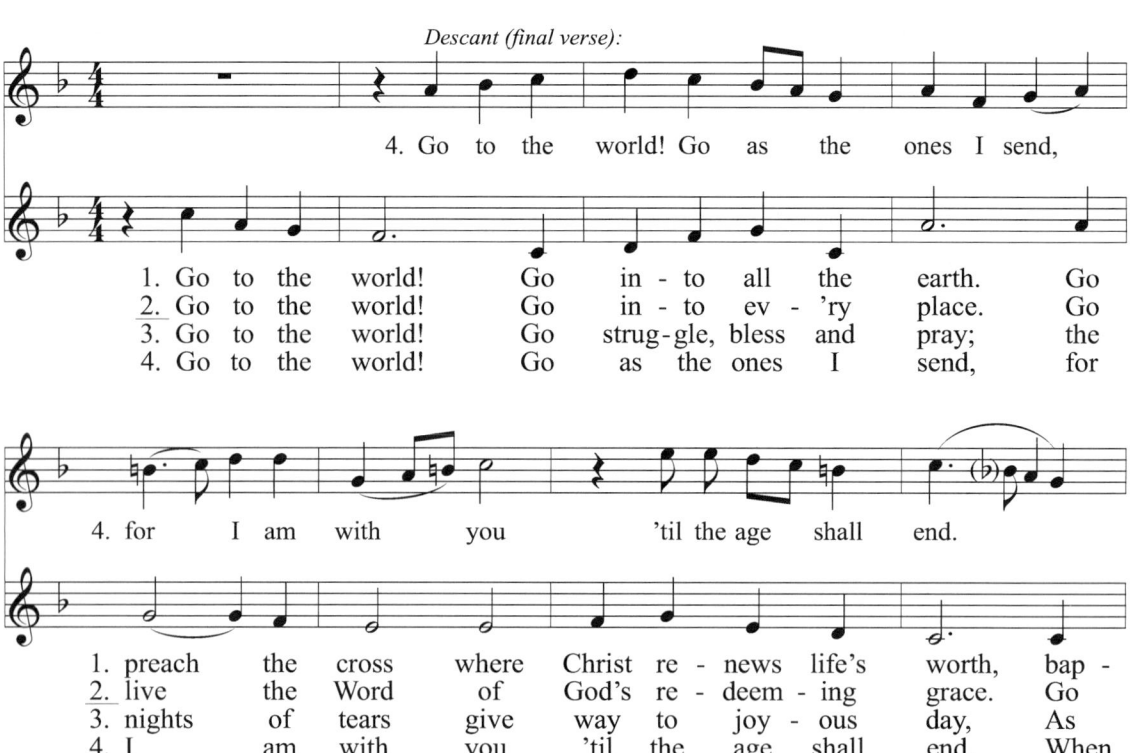

Go to the World, pg. 2

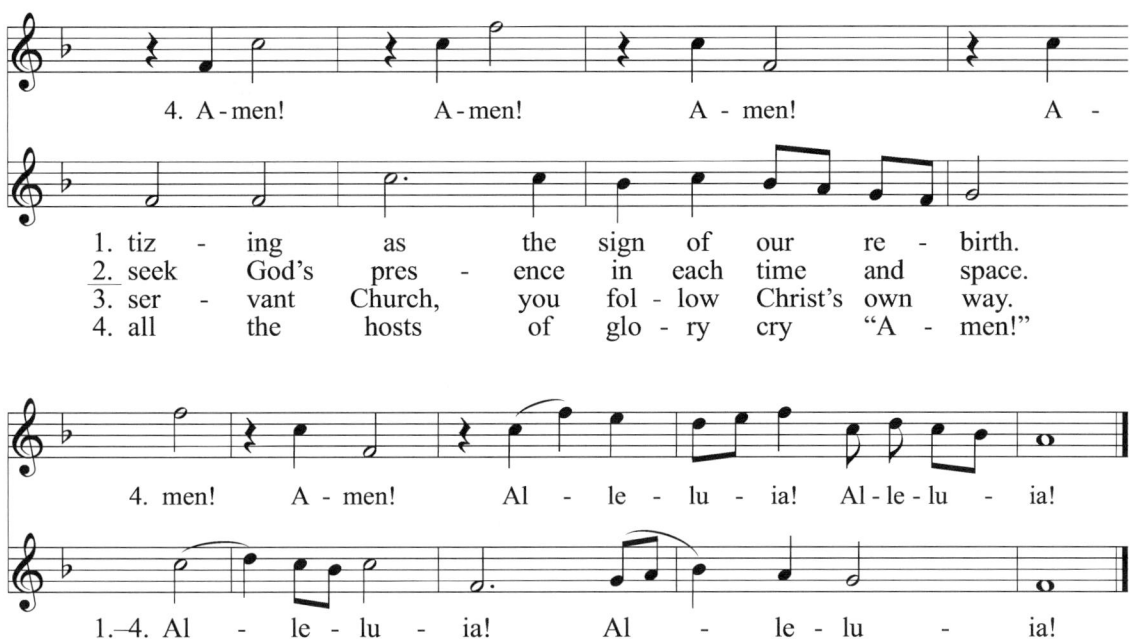

Text: Sylvia G. Dunstan, 1955–1993, © 1991, GIA Publications, Inc. All rights reserved. Used with permission.
Music: SINE NOMINE, 10 10 10 with alleluias, Ralph Vaughan Williams, 1872–1958.
Descant: Michael Young, © 1979, GIA Publications, Inc. All rights reserved. Used with permission.

God in the Planning 133

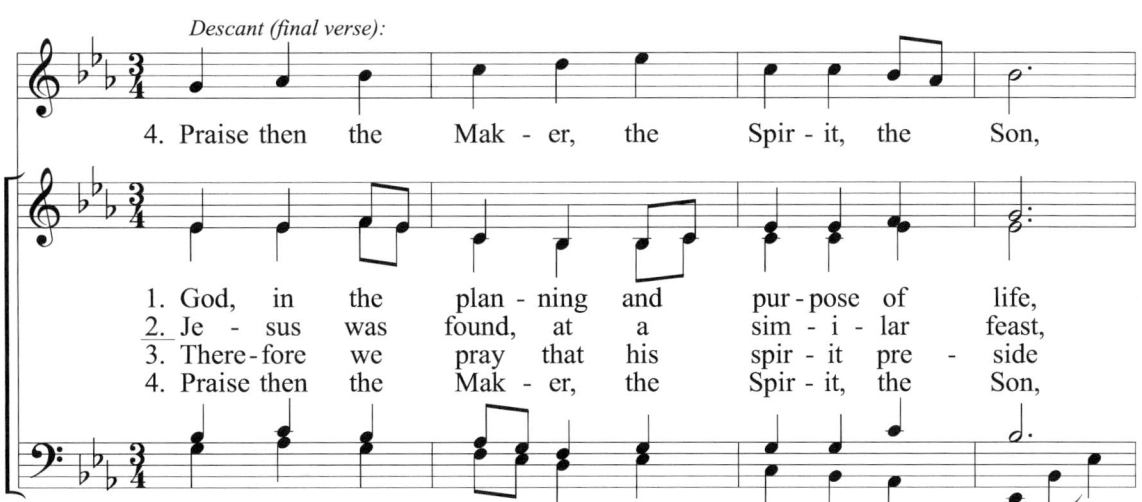

God in the Planning, pg. 2

Text: John L. Bell, b. 1949, © 1989, Iona Community, GIA Publications, Inc., North American agent. All rights reserved. Used with permission.
Music: SLANE, 10 10 9 10, Irish ballad melody; harm. David Evans, 1874–1948, © Oxford University Press. All rights reserved. Used with permission.
Descant: Christine Manderfeld, OSB, b. 1938, © 2009, the Sisters of Saint Benedict, St. Joseph, MN. Administered by Liturgical Press, Collegeville, MN. All rights reserved.

God Is Here! As We His People 134

1. God is here! As we his peo-ple Meet to of-fer praise and prayer,
2. Here are sym-bols to re-mind us Of our life-long need of grace;
3. Here our chil-dren find a wel-come In the Shep-herd's flock and fold;
4. Lord of all, of Church and king-dom, In an age of change and doubt,

1. May we find in ful-ler meas-ure What it is in Christ we share:
2. Here are ta-ble, font and pul-pit, Here the cross has cen-tral place:
3. Here, in sa-cred food par-tak-en, Christ sus-tains us as of old:
4. Keep us faith-ful to the gos-pel, Help us work your pur-pose out:

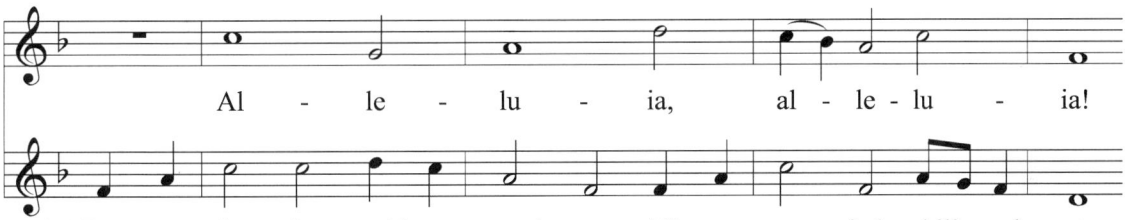

1. Here, as in the world a-round us, All our var-ied skills and arts
2. Here in hon-es-ty of preach-ing, Here in si-lence as in speech,
3. Here the ser-vants of the Ser-vant Seek in wor-ship to ex-plore
4. Here, in this day's ded-i-ca-tion, All we have to give, re-ceive;

Sing: Al - le - lu - ia, al - le - lu - ia!

1. Wait the com-ing of his Spir-it In-to o-pen minds and hearts.
2. Here in new-ness and re-new-al God the Spir-it comes to each.
3. What it means in dai-ly liv-ing To be-lieve and to a-dore.
4. We who can-not live with-out you, We a-dore you! We be-lieve!

Text: Fred Pratt Green, b. 1903–2000, © 1979, Hope Publishing Co., Carol Stream, IL 60188. All rights reserved. Used with permission.
Music: BEACH SPRING, 87 87 D; *The Sacred Harp*, 1844.
Descant: Christine Manderfeld, OSB, b. 1938, © 2009, the Sisters of Saint Benedict, St. Joseph, MN. Administered by Liturgical Press, Collegeville, MN. All rights reserved.

135. God Is Love

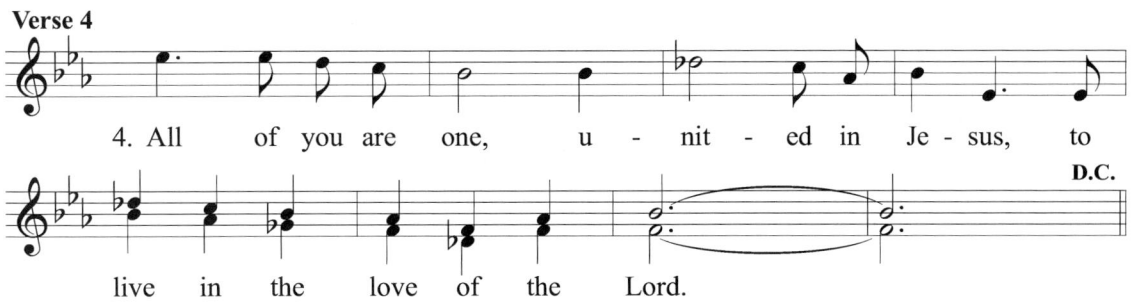

Verse 4

4. All of you are one, u - nit - ed in Je - sus, to live in the love of the Lord.

D.C.

Text and music: David Haas, b. 1957, © 1987, GIA Publications, Inc. All rights reserved. Used with permission.

136 God of All People

1. God of all places: present, unseen; Voice in our silence, song in our midst. We are your people, knowing, unsure. Come, Lord Jesus, come!
2. God of all dreaming, near and yet far. Vision unheard of, wake us to rest. We are your presence, sent forth afraid. Come, Lord Jesus, come!
3. God of all people, dust and the clay. Breath of a new wind, fire in our hearts. Light born of heaven, peace on the earth. Come, Lord Jesus, come! Come, Lord Jesus, come!

Text: David Haas, b. 1957. Music: KINGDOM, 9 9 9 5; David Haas, b. 1957.
Text and music: © 1988, GIA Publications, Inc. All rights reserved. Used with permission.

God of Day and God of Darkness 137

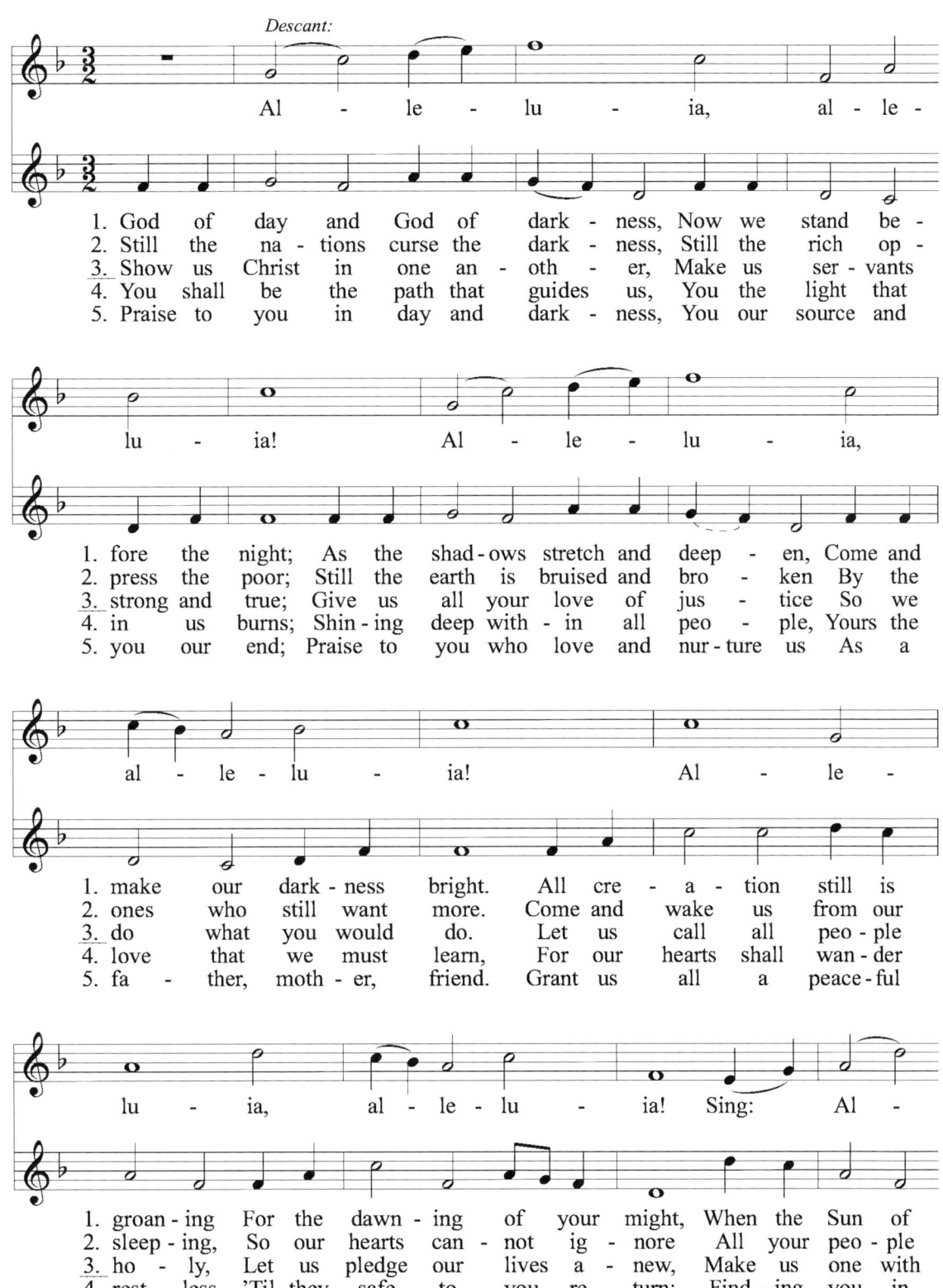

God of Day and God of Darkness, pg. 2

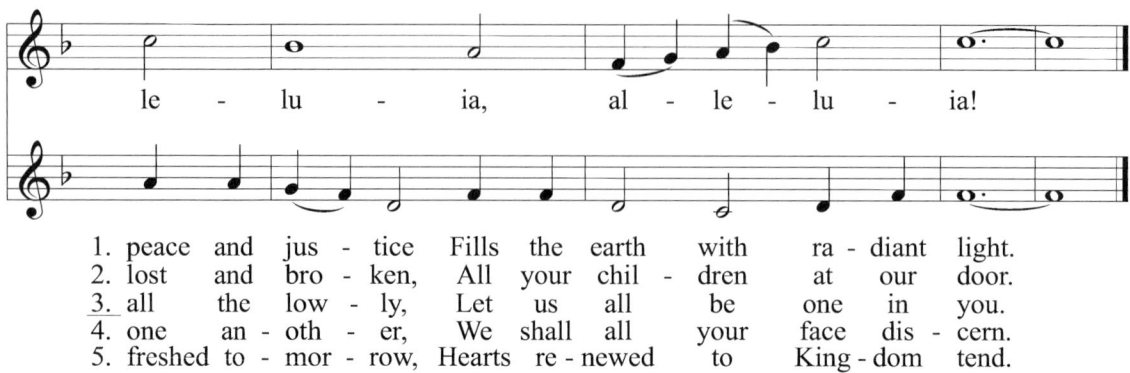

1. peace and jus - tice Fills the earth with ra - diant light.
2. lost and bro - ken, All your chil - dren at our door.
3. all the low - ly, Let us all be one in you.
4. one an - oth - er, We shall all your face dis - cern.
5. freshed to - mor - row, Hearts re - newed to King - dom tend.

Text: Marty Haugen, b. 1950, © 1985, 1994, GIA Publications, Inc. Music: BEACH SPRING, 87 87 D; *The Sacred Harp,* 1844.
Descant: Christine Manderfeld, OSB, b. 1938, © 2009, the Sisters of Saint Benedict, St. Joseph, MN. Administered by Liturgical Press, Collegeville, MN. All rights reserved.

138   God of Love

1. God of love, whose mer - cies dai - ly Like the morn - ing
2. Christ, who lived through earth - ly suf - f'ring, Loss, be - tray - al,
3. Ho - ly Spir - it, whose in - dwell - ing Makes a tem - ple
4. God of mer - cy, love and mem - 'ry, Give us strength to

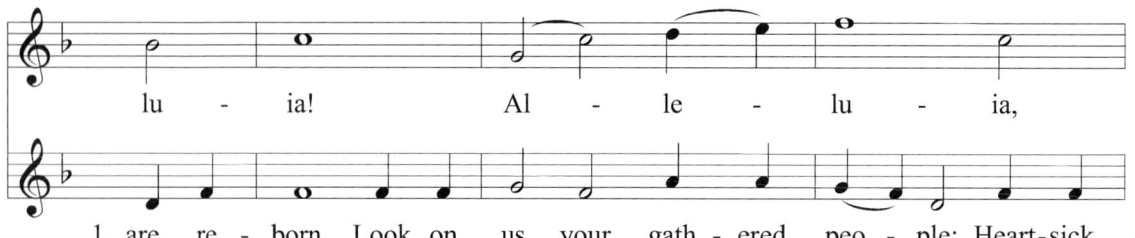

1. are re - born, Look on us, your gath - ered peo - ple: Heart-sick,
2. fear and death, Ev - er - faith - ful to your call - ing, Serv - ing
3. of each heart, Par - a - clete of strength-'ning pow - er, Be with
4. fol - low you; Let us trust that our de - part - ed, Now at

139 — God of Mercy and Compassion

Verses

1. God of mercy and compassion, Lord of life and blinding light.
2. God most holy and forgiving, Penetrate our pride and sloth;
3. Lord, who out of love consented To the worst that we could do;

1. Truth whom creatures would refashion, Place on us the gift of sight.
2. On a people partly living, Place the gift of life and growth.
3. Lord, abandoned and tormented, Let us love and suffer too.

Refrain

Truth insistent and demanding, Love resented and ignored, Life beyond all understanding, Give us peace and pardon, Lord.

Text: Michael Hodgetts, alt.
Music: AU SANG QU'UN DIEU, 87 87 D, traditional French melody; arr. Rev. Percy Jones, © Allens Publishing Company, Ltd. All rights reserved. Used with permission.

141 God Rest You Merry, Gentlemen

God Rest You Merry, Gentlemen, pg. 2

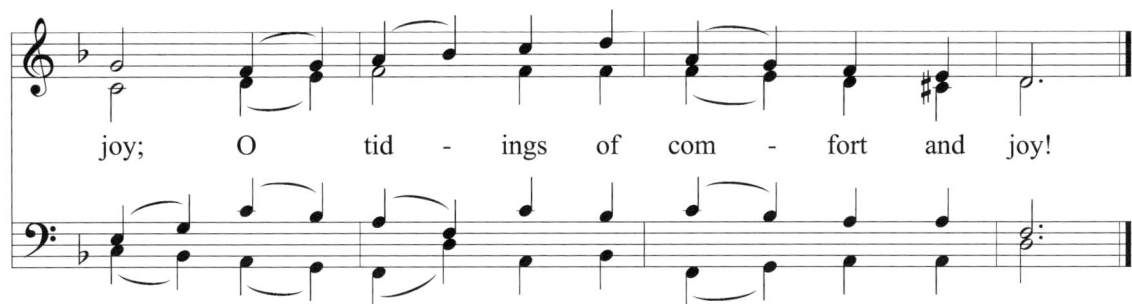

Text: 18th cent. English carol, alt.
Music: GOD REST YOU MERRY, 76 76 86 with refrain, 18th cent. English carol; harm. John Stainer, 1840–1901.

God, We Praise You! 142

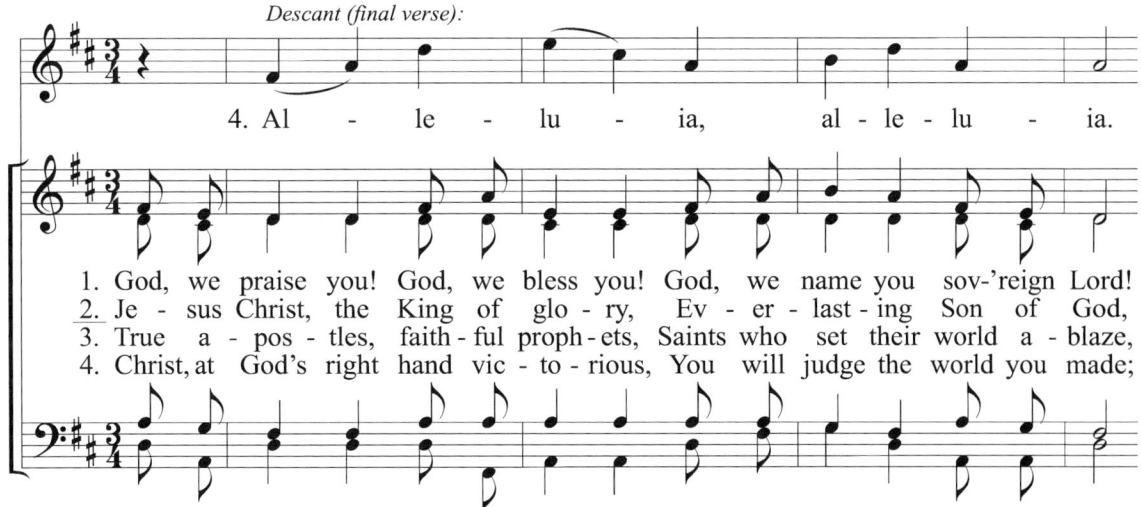

God, We Praise You!, pg. 2

Text: Based on the *Te deum,* Christopher Idle, b. 1938, © 1982, Jubilate Hymns (admin. by Hope Publishing Co., Carol Stream, IL 60188). All rights reserved. Used with permission.
Music: NETTLETON 87 87 D; Wyeth's *Repository of Sacred Music,* Part II, 1813.
Descant: Christine Manderfeld, OSB, b. 1938, © 2009, the Sisters of Saint Benedict, St. Joseph, MN. Administered by Liturgical Press, Collegeville, MN. All rights reserved.

God, You Made the Earth and Heavens 143

God, You Made the Earth and Heavens, pg. 2

[Musical score with lyrics:]

3. give - ness and peace be theirs.

1. lov - ing - ly did breathe and brood, life on earth be-
2. new - ly made be - fore you stood— man and wom - an,
3. peace and pa - tient gen - tle - ness; may their un - ion,

3. May their un - ion mir - ror your own faith - ful - ness.

1. gan to quick - en, and you saw that it was good.
2. in your im - age— you pro - nounced them ver - y good.
3. ev - er faith - ful, mir - ror your own faith - ful - ness.

Text: St. 1, adapted from an anonymous text; St. 2–3, Delores Dufner, OSB, b. 1939, © 1993, 2003, GIA Publications, Inc. All rights reserved. Used with permission.
Music: HYMN TO JOY, 87 87 D, Ludwig van Beethoven, 1770–1827, adapt. Edward Hodges, 1796–1867.
Descant: Christine Manderfeld, OSB, b. 1938, © 2009, the Sisters of Saint Benedict, St. Joseph, MN. Administered by Liturgical Press, Collegeville, MN. All rights reserved.

144 Good Christian Friends, Rejoice

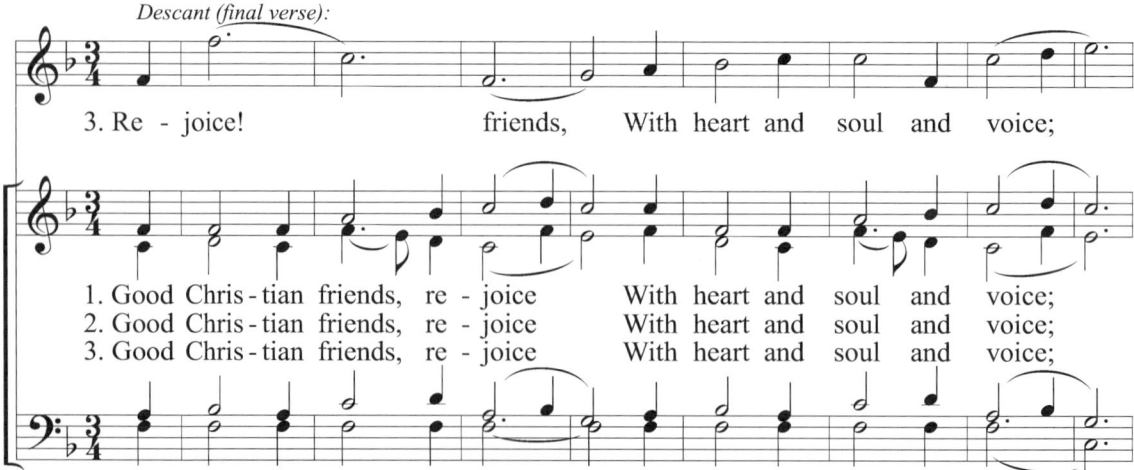

Descant (final verse):
3. Re - joice! friends, With heart and soul and voice;

1. Good Chris - tian friends, re - joice With heart and soul and voice;
2. Good Chris - tian friends, re - joice With heart and soul and voice;
3. Good Chris - tian friends, re - joice With heart and soul and voice;

Good Christian Friends, Rejoice, pg. 2

Text: *In dulci jubilo;* Latin and German, 14th c.; tr. John M. Neale, 1818–1866.
Music: IN DULCI JUBILO, 66 77 78 55; Klug's *Geistliche Lieder,* Wittenberg, 1535; harm. by Robert L. Pearsall, 1795–1856.
Descant: Christine Manderfeld, OSB, b. 1938, © 2009, the Sisters of Saint Benedict, St. Joseph, MN. Administered by Liturgical Press, Collegeville, MN. All rights reserved.

145 — Good Christians All, Rejoice and Sing!

Descant (final verse):
4. Your Name we bless, ris-en Lord,
4. And sing with one ac-cord
4. The life laid down and re-stored:

1. Good Christians all, re - joice and sing!
2. The Lord of life is ris'n to - day!
3. Praise we in songs of vic - to - ry
4. Your Name we bless, O ris - en Lord,

1. Now is the tri - umph of our King!
2. Sing songs of praise a - long the way;
3. That love, that life which can - not die,
4. And sing to - day with one ac - cord

1. To all the world glad news we bring:
2. Let all the earth re - joice and say:
3. And sing with hearts up - lift - ed high:
4. The life laid down, the life re - stored:

Good Christians All, Rejoice and Sing!, pg. 2

Text: Cyril A. Arlington, 1872–1955, alt., © 1958, 1986, Hope Publishing Co., Carol Stream IL 60188. All rights reserved. Used with permission.
Music: GELOBT SEI GOTT, 888 with alleluias, Melchior Vulpius, 1560–1616.
Descant: Christine Manderfeld, OSB, b. 1938, © 2009, the Sisters of Saint Benedict, St. Joseph, MN. Administered by Liturgical Press, Collegeville, MN. All rights reserved.

146   Gospel Responses for Advent—Year A

Text: Delores Dufner, OSB, b. 1939, © 1997, 2003, GIA Publications, Inc. All rights reserved. Used with permission.
Music: STUTTGART, 87 87, Christian Friedrich Witt, 1660–1716; adapt. and harm. William Henry Havergal, 1793–1870, alt.
Descant: Christine Manderfeld, OSB, © 2009, the Sisters of Saint Benedict, St. Joseph, MN. Administered by Liturgical Press, Collegeville, MN. All rights reserved.

Gospel Responses for Advent—Year B

Text: Delores Dufner, OSB, b. 1939, © 1997, 2003, GIA Publications, Inc. All rights reserved. Used with permission.
Music: STUTTGART, 87 87, Christian Friedrich Witt, 1660–1716; adapt. and harm. William Henry Havergal, 1793–1870, alt.
Descant: Christine Manderfeld, OSB, © 2009, the Sisters of Saint Benedict, St. Joseph, MN. Administered by Liturgical Press, Collegeville, MN. All rights reserved.

148   Gospel Responses for Advent—Year C

Text: Delores Dufner, OSB, b. 1939, © 1997, 2003, GIA Publications, Inc. All rights reserved. Used with permission.
Music: STUTTGART, 87 87, Christian Friedrich Witt, 1660–1716; adapt. and harm. William Henry Havergal, 1793–1870, alt.
Descant: Christine Manderfeld, OSB, © 2009, the Sisters of Saint Benedict, St. Joseph, MN. Administered by Liturgical Press, Collegeville, MN. All rights reserved.

Hail, Holy Queen Enthroned Above   149

Hail, Holy Queen Enthroned Above, pg. 2

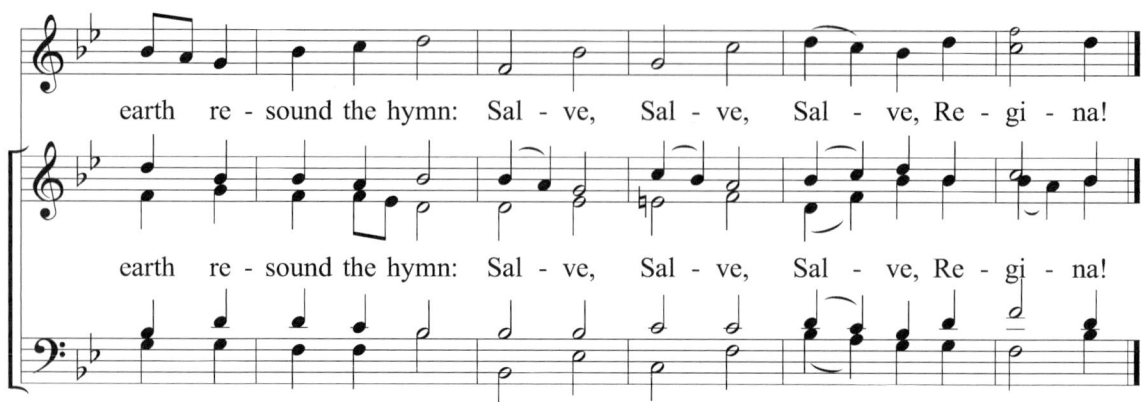

Text: Hermanus Contractus, 1013–1054, attr.; vv. 1, 2, 5, and refrain tr. anon., c. 1884, alt.; vv. 3, 4, 6 para. by editors of *Collegeville Hymnal*, © 1990, Order of Saint Benedict, Collegeville, MN. Administered by Liturgical Press, Collegeville, MN. All rights reserved.
Music: SALVE REGINA COELITUM, 8 4 8 4 777 4 5.
Descant: Christine Manderfeld, OSB, © 2009, the Sisters of Saint Benedict, St. Joseph, MN. Administered by Liturgical Press, Collegeville, MN. All rights reserved.

Hail, Redeemer, King Most Blest! 150

Hail the Day That Sees Him Rise 151

Hail the Day That Sees Him Rise, pg. 2

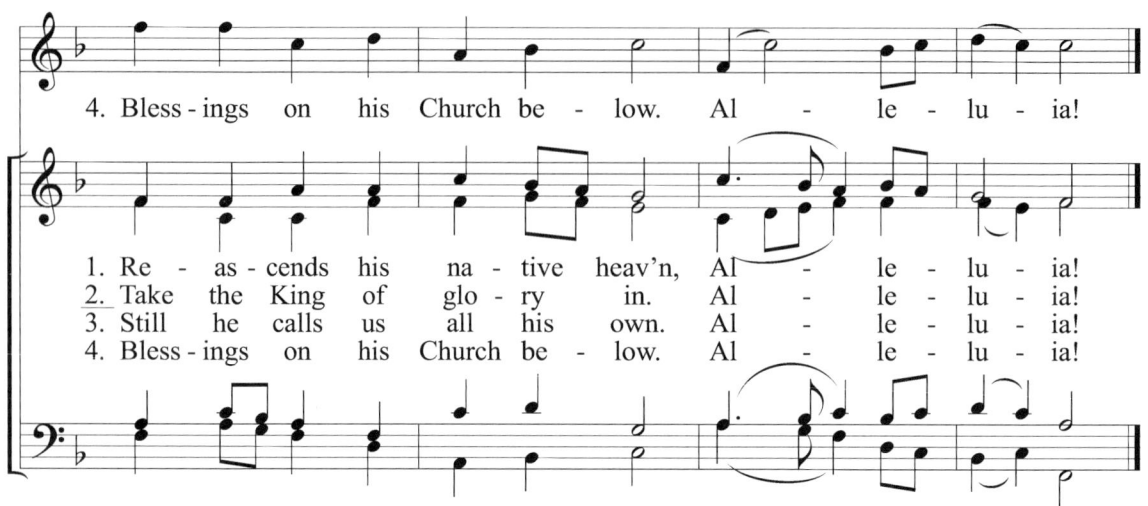

1. Re-ascends his native heav'n, Alleluia!
2. Take the King of glory in. Alleluia!
3. Still he calls us all his own. Alleluia!
4. Blessings on his Church below. Alleluia!

Text: Charles Wesley, 1707–1788. Music: LLANFAIR, 77 77 with alleluias, Robert Williams, 1781–1821; harm. John Roberts, 1822–1877.
Descant: Christine Manderfeld, OSB, b. 1938, © 2009, the Sisters of Saint Benedict, St. Joseph, MN. Administered by Liturgical Press, Collegeville, MN. All rights reserved.

152 Hail Thee, Festival Day!

Refrain

Descant:

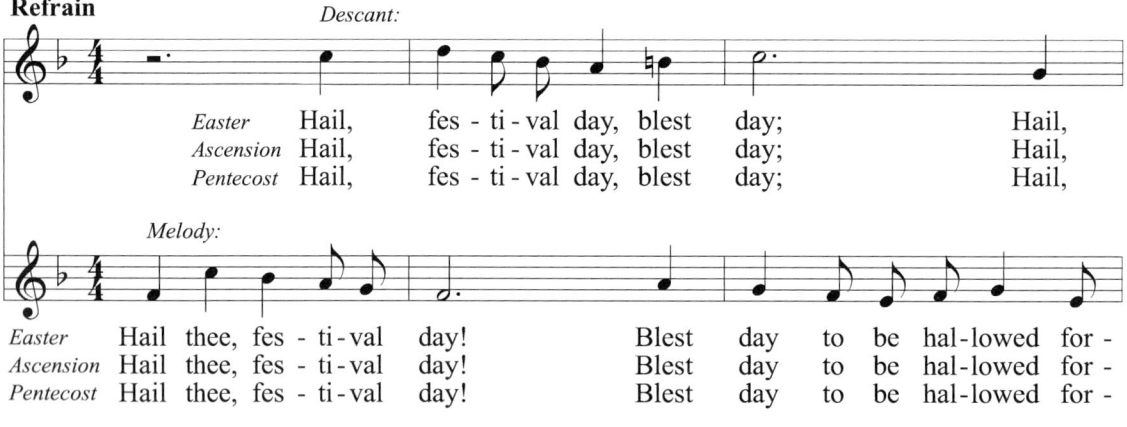

Easter — Hail, fes-ti-val day, blest day; Hail,
Ascension — Hail, fes-ti-val day, blest day; Hail,
Pentecost — Hail, fes-ti-val day, blest day; Hail,

Melody:

Easter — Hail thee, fes-ti-val day! Blest day to be hal-lowed for-
Ascension — Hail thee, fes-ti-val day! Blest day to be hal-lowed for-
Pentecost — Hail thee, fes-ti-val day! Blest day to be hal-lowed for-

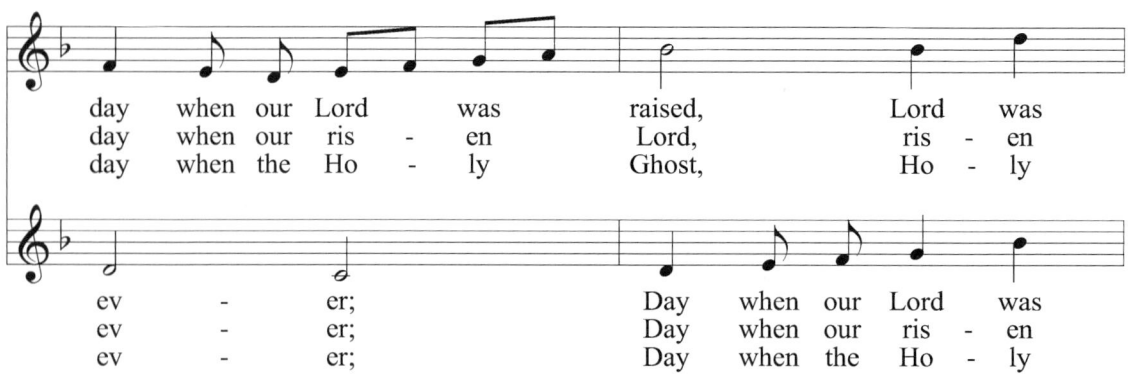

day when our Lord was raised, Lord was
day when our ris-en Lord, ris-en
day when the Ho-ly Ghost, Ho-ly

ev-er; Day when our Lord was
ev-er; Day when our ris-en
ev-er; Day when the Ho-ly

Hail Thee, Festival Day!, pg. 2

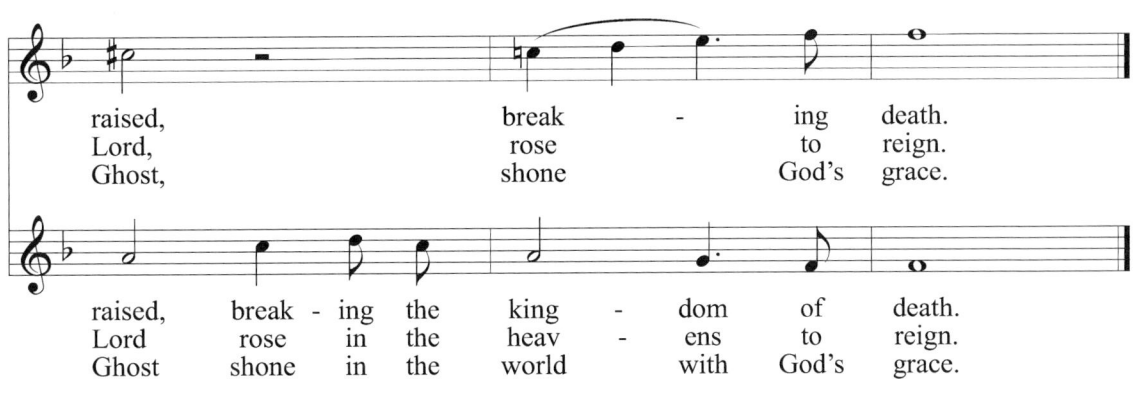

Verses 1, 3, 5 (1a = Easter, 1b = Ascension, 1c = Pentecost)

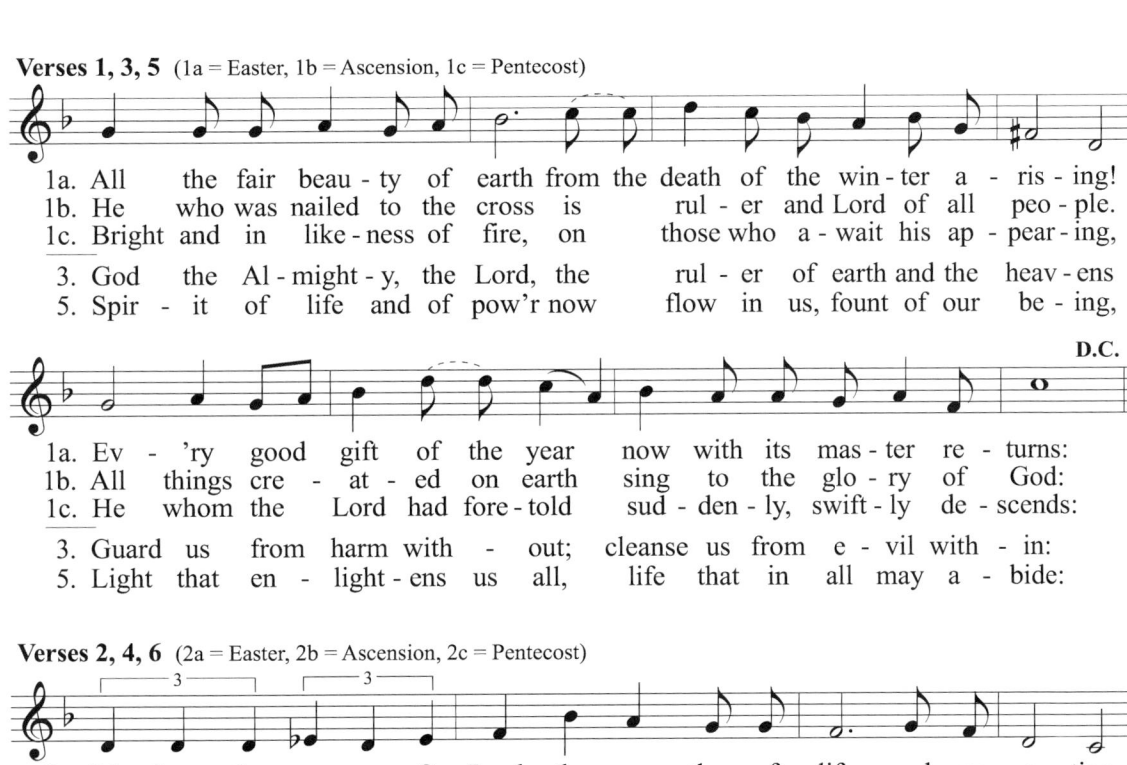

Verses 2, 4, 6 (2a = Easter, 2b = Ascension, 2c = Pentecost)

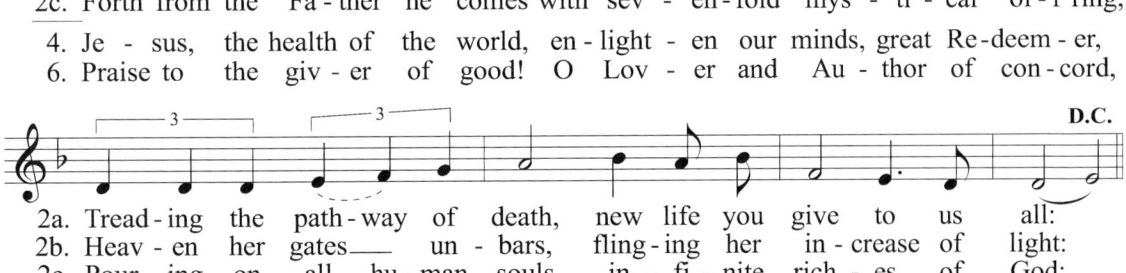

Text: Venantius Fortunatus, c. 530–609; tr. *English Hymnal*, 1906, alt. Music: SALVE, FESTA DIES, irregular with refrain, Ralph Vaughan Williams, 1872–1958.
Descant: Scott S. Withrow, © 1980, GIA Publications, Inc. All rights reserved. Used with permission.

153. Hail to the Lord's Anointed

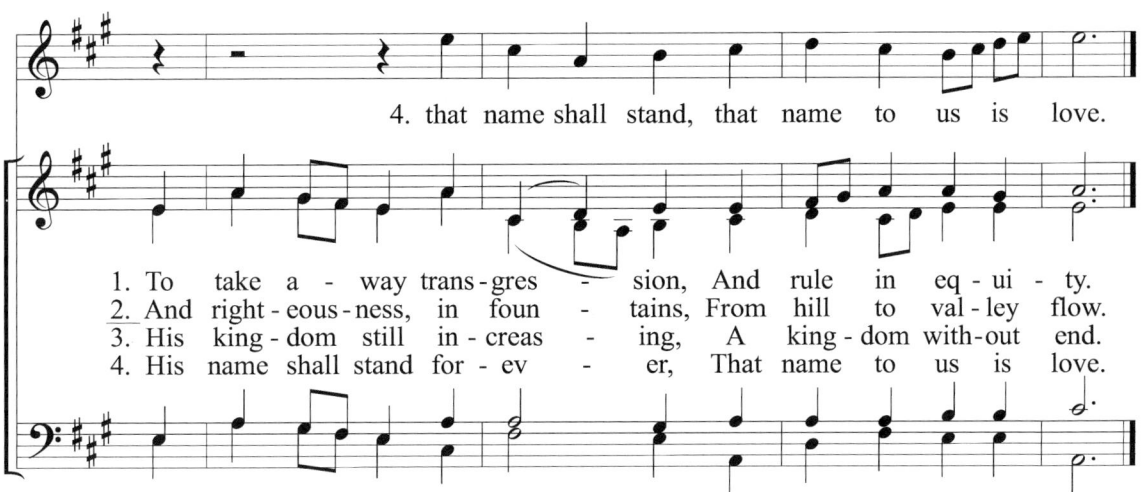

Text: James Montgomery, 1771–1854; Psalm 72. Music: ELLACOMBE, 76 76 D, *Gesangbuch der Herzogl,* 1784, adapt. 1863; harm. William Henry Monk, 1823–1889.
Descant: Christine Manderfeld, OSB, b. 1938, © 2009, the Sisters of Saint Benedict, St. Joseph, MN. Administered by Liturgical Press, Collegeville, MN. All rights reserved.

Hands of Healing

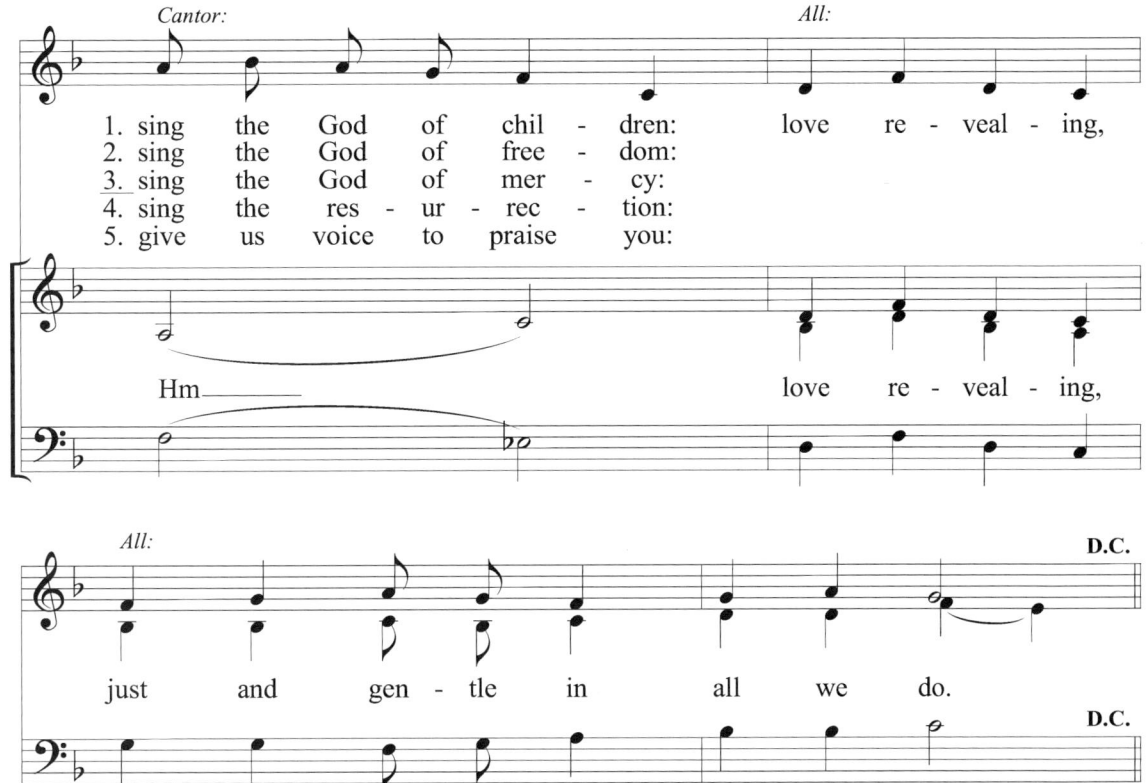

Text and music: Marty Haugen, b. 1950, © 1999, GIA Publications, Inc. All rights reserved. Used with permission.

155   Hark! A Thrilling Voice Is Sounding

1. Hark! a thrilling voice is sounding! "Christ is nigh," it seems to say. "Cast away the works of darkness, O ye children of the day!"
2. Wakened by the solemn warning, from earth's bondage let us rise; Christ, our sun, all ill dispelling, shines upon the morning skies.
3. See the Lamb, so long expected, comes with pardon down from heaven; let us haste, with tears of sorrow, one and all to be forgiv'n;
4. So, when next he comes with glory and the world is wrapped in fear, may he with his mercy shield us, and with words of love draw near.
5. Honor, glory, might, and blessing to the Father and the Son, with the everlasting Spirit while unending ages run.

Text: Latin, ca. 6th cent.; tr. Edward Caswall, 1814–1878., and others. Music: MERTON, 87 87, William Henry Monk, 1823–1889.

Hark! The Herald Angels Sing 156

Hark! The Herald Angels Sing, pg. 2

Text: Charles Wesley, 1707–1788, alt. Music: MENDELSSOHN, 77 77 D and refrain, Felix Mendelssohn, 1808–1847; adapt. William H. Cummings, 1831–1915.
Descant: Christine Manderfeld, OSB, b. 1938, © 2009, the Sisters of Saint Benedict, St. Joseph, MN. Administered by Liturgical Press, Collegeville, MN. All rights reserved.

Have Mercy, Lord, on Us 157

1. Have mercy, Lord, on us, For you are ever kind; Though we have sinned before you, Lord, Your mercy let us find.
2. Lord, wash away our guilt, And cleanse us from our sin; For we confess our wrongs and see How great our guilt has been.
3. The joy your grace can give, Let us again obtain; And may your Spirit's firm support Our spirits then sustain.
4. To God the Father, Son, And Spirit glory be, Who was and is and shall be so For all eternity.

Text: Nahum Tate, 1652–1715, and Nicholas Brady, 1659–1726. Music: SOUTHWELL, 66 86, William Damon, c. 1550–1593.
Descant: Christine Manderfeld, OSB, b. 1938, © 2009, the Sisters of Saint Benedict, St. Joseph, MN. Administered by Liturgical Press, Collegeville, MN. All rights reserved.

158. He Is Risen, He Is Risen

1. He is risen, he is risen! Tell it out with joyful voice; He has burst his three days' prison; Let the whole wide earth rejoice: Death is conquered, we are free, Christ has won the victory.

2. Come, ye sad and fearful-hearted, With glad smile and radiant brow! Death's long shadows have departed; Jesus' woes are over now, And the passion that he bore Sin and pain can vex no more.

3. Come, with high and holy hymning, Hail our Lord's triumphant day; Not one darksome cloud is dimming Yonder glorious morning ray, Breaking o'er the purple east, Symbol of our Easter feast.

4. He is risen, he is risen! He hath opened heaven's gate: We are free from sin's dark prison, Risen to a holier state; And a brighter Easter beam On our longing eyes shall stream.

Text: Cecil Francis Alexander, 1818–1895, alt. Music: UNSER HERRSCHER, 87 87 77, Joachim Neander, 1650–1680.

Hear Us Now, Our God and Father   159

Hear Us Now, Our God and Father, pg. 2

Text: Henry N. Huxhold, b. 1922, vv. 1 & 2; John Newton, 1725–1807, v. 3, alt.; vv. 1 & 2, © 1978, *Lutheran Book of Worship,* admin. by Augsburg Publishing House. All rights reserved. Used with permission.
Music: HYMN TO JOY, 87 87 D, Ludwig van Beethoven, 1770–1827, adapt. Edward Hodges, 1796–1867.
Descant: Christine Manderfeld, OSB, b. 1938, © 2009, the Sisters of Saint Benedict, St. Joseph, MN. Administered by Liturgical Press, Collegeville, MN. All rights reserved.

Here I Am, Lord 160

Text: Based on *Isaiah 6;* Dan Schutte, b. 1947. Music: Dan Schutte, b. 1947; arr. by Michael Pope. SJ, and John Weissrock.
Text and music © 1981, OCP Publications. All rights reserved. Used with permission.

Holy God, We Praise Thy Name 161

Holy God, We Praise Thy Name, pg. 2

Text: Ignaz Franz, 1719–1790, attr.; tr. Clarence Augustus Walworth, 1820–1900.
Music: TE DEUM (GROSSER GOTT), 78 78 77 77, *Katholisches Gesangbuch,* 1686; alt. *Cantate,* 1851.
Descant: Christine Manderfeld, OSB, © 2009, the Sisters of Saint Benedict, St. Joseph, MN. Administered by Liturgical Press, Collegeville, MN. All rights reserved.

Holy, Holy, Holy! 162

Holy, Holy, Holy!, pg. 2

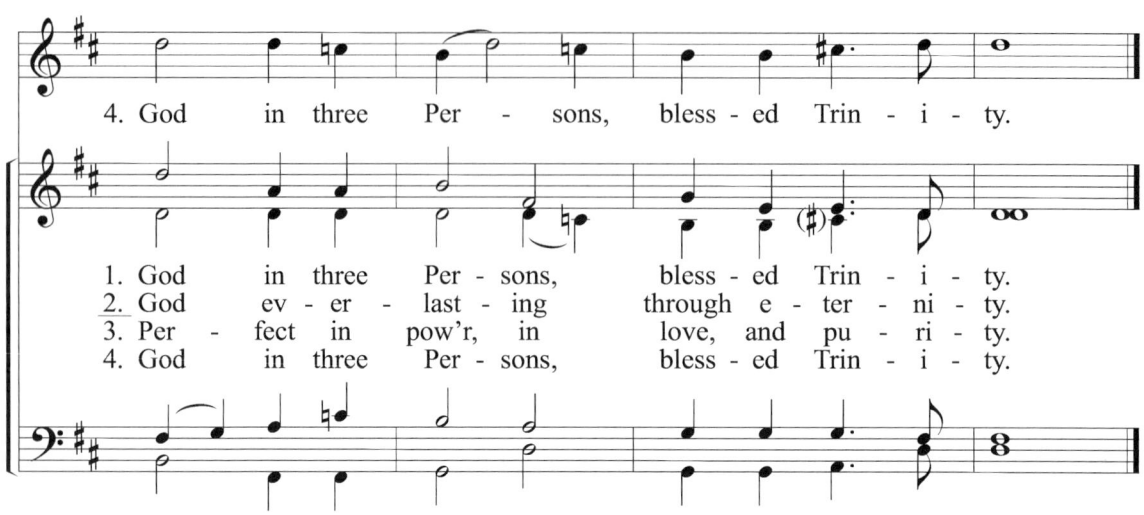

Text: Reginald Heber, 1783–1826, alt. Music: NICAEA, 11 12 12 10, John Bacchus Dykes, 1823–1876.
Descant: Hal Hopson, © 1979, GIA Publications, Inc. All rights reserved. Used with permission.

163 Holy Spirit, Come to Us

Ostinato Refrain

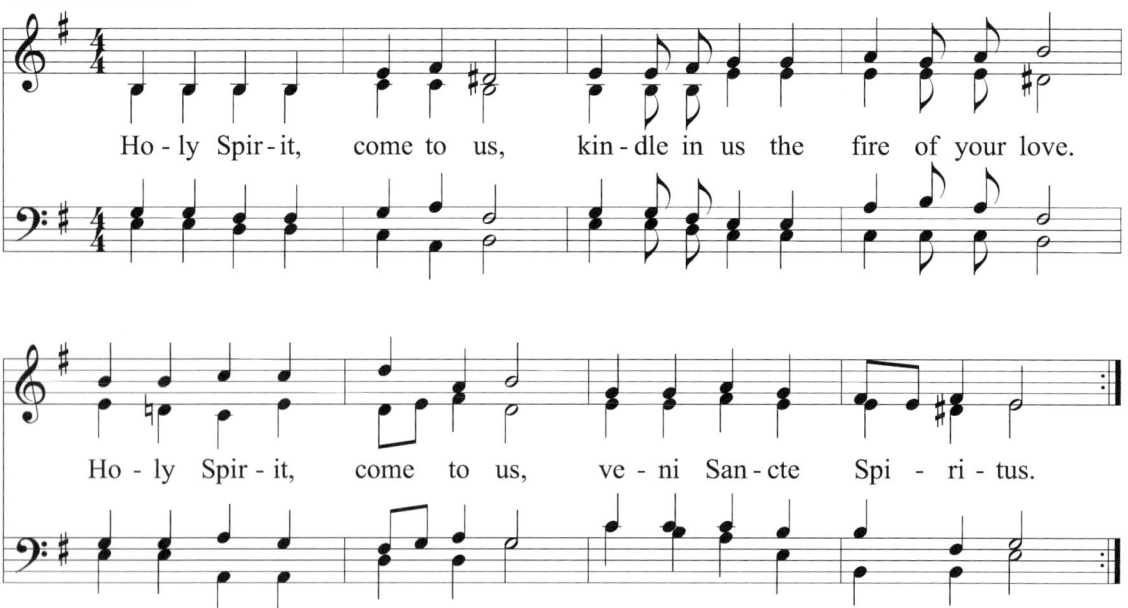

Holy Spirit, Come to Us, pg. 2

Verses *(superimposed on Ostinato Refrain)*

1. Jesus said, "I give you a new commandment: Love one another just as I have loved you."
2. Jesus said, "It is by your love for one another, that ev'ryone will recognize you as my disciples."
3. Jesus said, "No one has greater love than this: to lay down one's life for those one loves."
4. We know love by this, that Christ laid down his life for us.
5. This is love: it is not we who have loved God but God who loved us.
6. God is love, and those who abide in love abide in God and God in them.

* *Choose either part*

Text: Based on John 13:35, 15:12-13; 1 John 3:16, 4:10, 16. Music: Jacques Berthier, 1923–1994,
© 1998, Les Presses de Taizé, GIA Publications, Inc., North American agent. All rights reserved. Used with permission.

164 Hosanna!

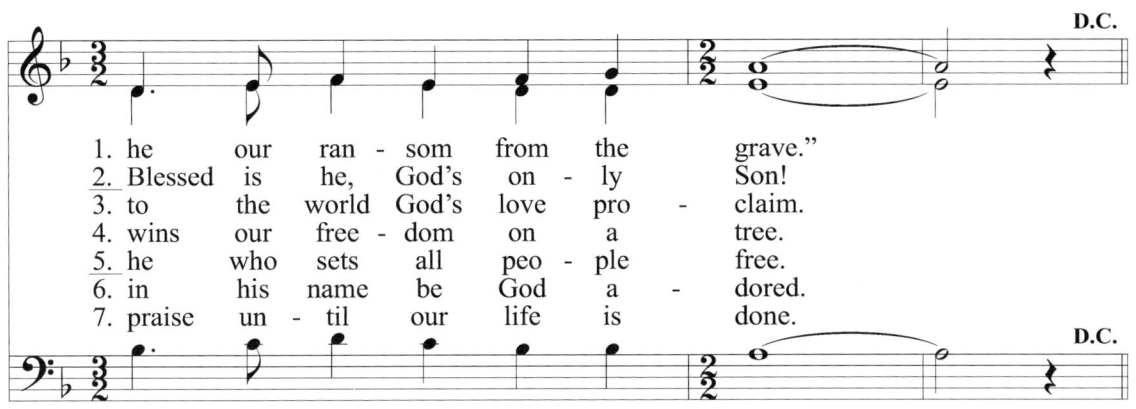

How Can I Keep from Singing?   166

How Can I Keep from Singing?, pg. 2

Text: Robert Lowry, 1826–1899. Music: ENDLESS SONG, traditional Quaker melody, 87 87 with refrain, Robert Lowry, 1826–1899.
Descant: Christine Manderfeld, OSB, b. 1938, © 2009, the Sisters of Saint Benedict, St. Joseph, MN. Administered by Liturgical Press, Collegeville, MN. All rights reserved.

167 How Firm a Foundation

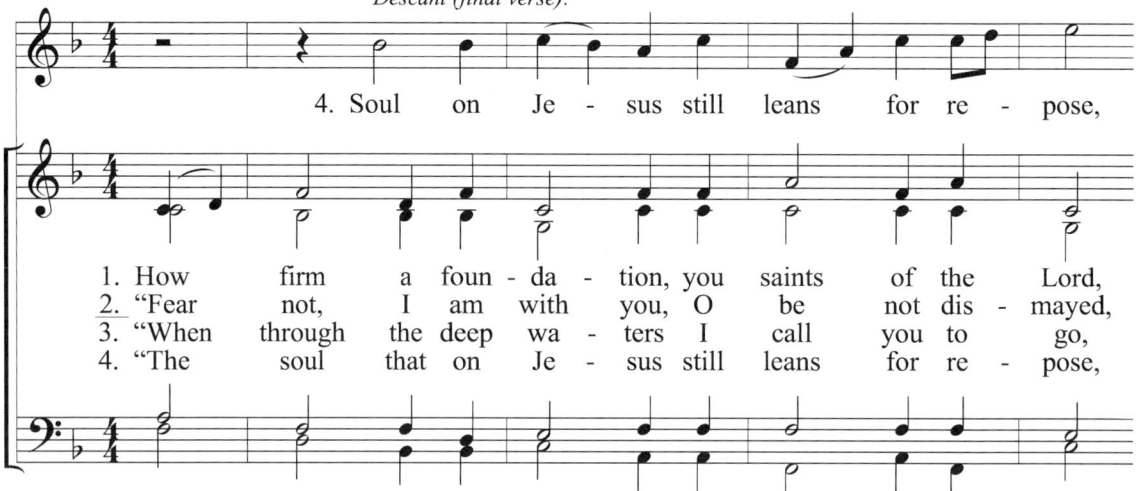

Text: "K" in Rippon's *A Selection of Hymns,* 1787.
Music: FOUNDATION, 11 11 11 11, Funk's *Compilation of Genuine Church Music,* 1832; arr. Charles Russell Woollen, 1923–1994.
Descant: Christine Manderfeld, OSB, b. 1938, © 2009, the Sisters of Saint Benedict, St. Joseph, MN. Administered by Liturgical Press, Collegeville, MN. All rights reserved.

168 How Good It Is

1. How good it is, what pleasure comes, when people live as one. When peace and justice light the way the will of God is done.
2. True friendship then like fragrant oil surrounds us with delight; and blessings shine like morning dew upon the mountain height.
3. How good it is when walls of fear come tumbling to the ground. When swords are changed to farming tools, the fruits of life abound.
4. What quiet joy can bloom and grow when people work for peace, when hands and voices join as one that hate and war may cease.

Text: Ruth Duck, b. 1947, © 1991, 1992, GIA Publications, Inc. All rights reserved. Used with permission.
Music: LAND OF REST, CM, traditional American folk melody; harm. by Richard Proulx, b. 1937, © 1975, GIA Publications, Inc. All rights reserved. Used with permission.
Descant: Christine Manderfeld, OSB, b. 1938, © 2009, the Sisters of Saint Benedict, St. Joseph, MN. Administered by Liturgical Press, Collegeville, MN. All rights reserved.

How Great Thou Art 169

*Author's original words are "works" and "mighty."

Text and music: Stuart K. Hine, 1899–1989, © 1953, Stuart K. Hine. Renewed 1981.
Administered by Manna Music, Inc., 35255 Brooten Road, Pacific City, OR 97135. All rights reserved. Used with permission.

How Lovely Is Your Dwelling Place 170

1. How lovely is your dwelling place, O God, I long to see your face. My soul into your courts would wing and, in your presence, gladly sing.
2. As yearns the sparrow for her nest, so yearns my heart to find its rest before your altar, there to stay and make my home through night and day.
3. How rich the joy to live with you, and sing your praise my whole life through, how happy those who travel here to find their God is ever near.
4. How blessed are those who trust your care, the path to you is sweet and fair; to pilgrim ears the desert sings, dry ground is laced with cool, clear springs.
5. Oh hear my call, great God of might, as now I stand within your sight, this pilgrim in your holy place, oh look, and see your servant's face.
6. One day with you I hold more dear than thousands spent away from here. If I could stand before your door and serve you well, I'd want no more.
7. My sun, my shield, my heart, my grace, my blessing sure, my dwelling place, unfailing light to pilgrims' feet who journey forth, their God to meet.

Text: Based on Psalm 84, adapt. by Marty Haugen, b. 1950, © 2001 GIA Publications, Inc.,
Music: PROSPECT, 88 88; William Walker's *Southern Harmony*; arr. by Marty Haugen, b. 1950, © 1991, GIA Publications, Inc.
All rights reserved. Used with permission.

171. How Wonderful the Three in One

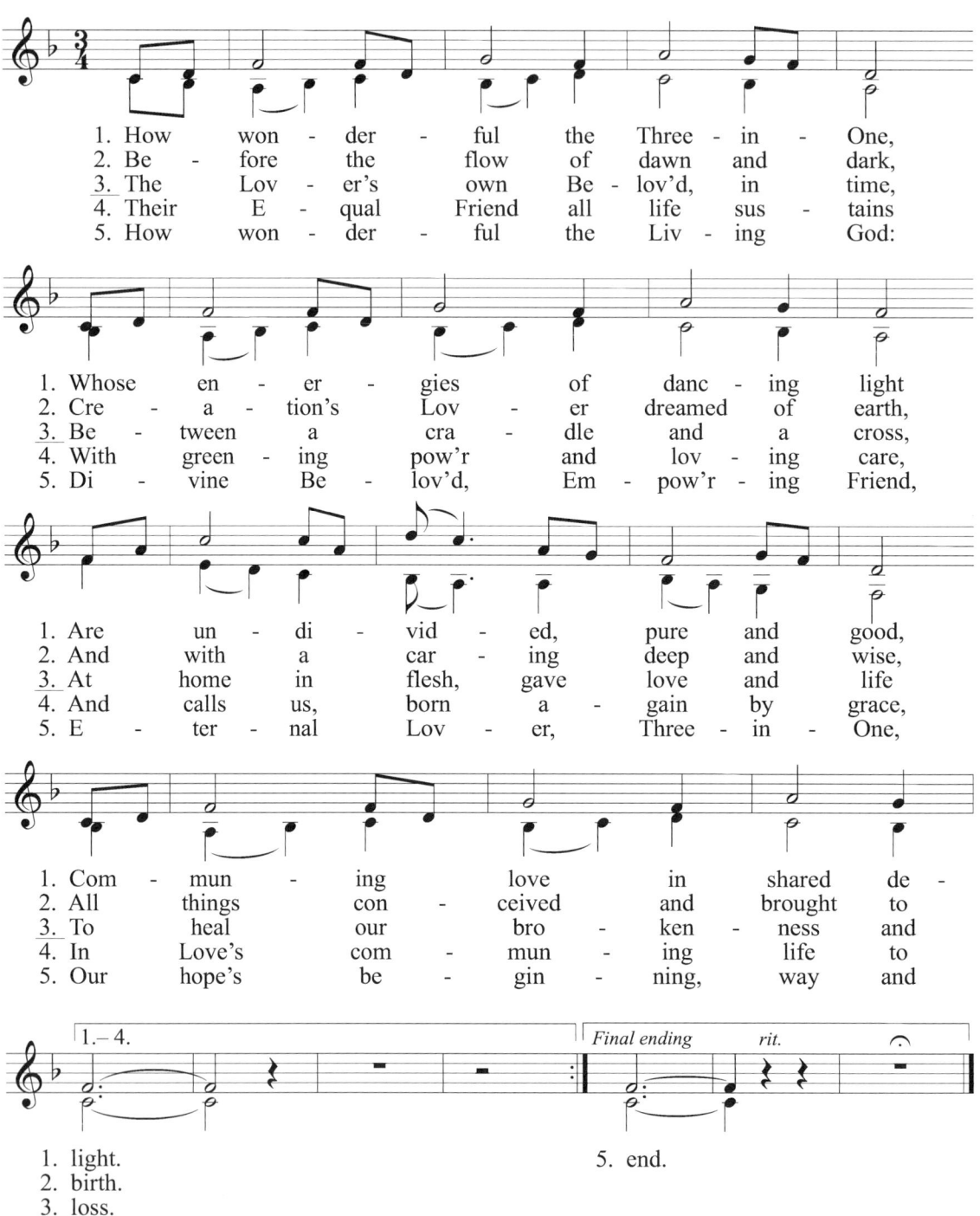

1. How wonderful the Three-in-One,
   Whose energies of dancing light
   Are undivided, pure and good,
   Communing love in shared delight.

2. Before the flow of dawn and dark,
   Creation's Lover dreamed of earth,
   And with a caring deep and wise,
   All things conceived and brought to birth.

3. The Lover's own Belov'd, in time,
   Between a cradle and a cross,
   At home in flesh, gave love and life
   To heal our brokenness and loss.

4. Their Equal Friend all life sustains
   With greening pow'r and loving care,
   And calls us, born again by grace,
   In Love's communing life to share.

5. How wonderful the Living God:
   Divine Belov'd, Empow'ring Friend,
   Eternal Lover, Three-in-One,
   Our hope's beginning, way and end.

Text: Brian Wren, b. 1936, © 1989, Hope Publishing Co., Carol Stream, IL 60188. All rights reserved. Used with permission.
Music: PROSPECT 88 88; William Walker's *Southern Harmony*; arr. by Marty Haugen, b. 1950, © 1991, GIA Publications, Inc. All rights reserved. Used with permission.

I Am the Bread of Life / Yo Soy el Pan de Vida 172

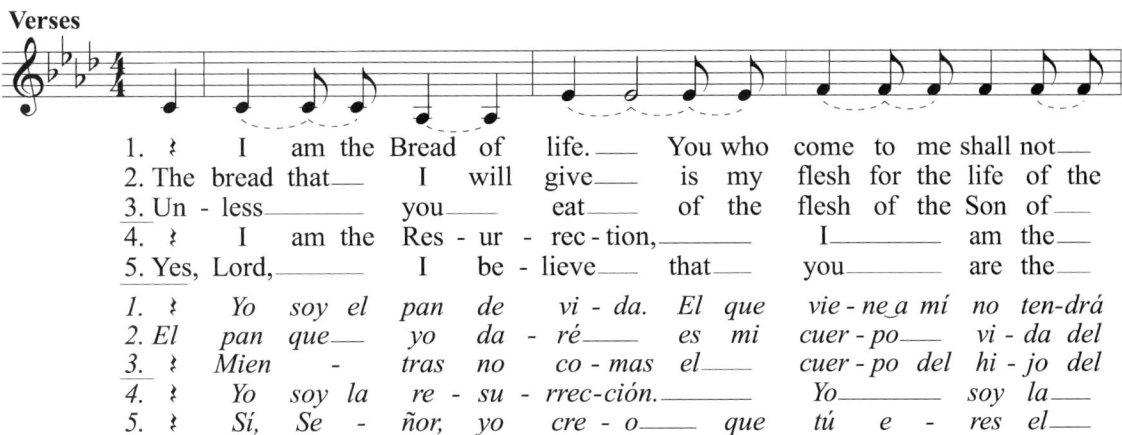

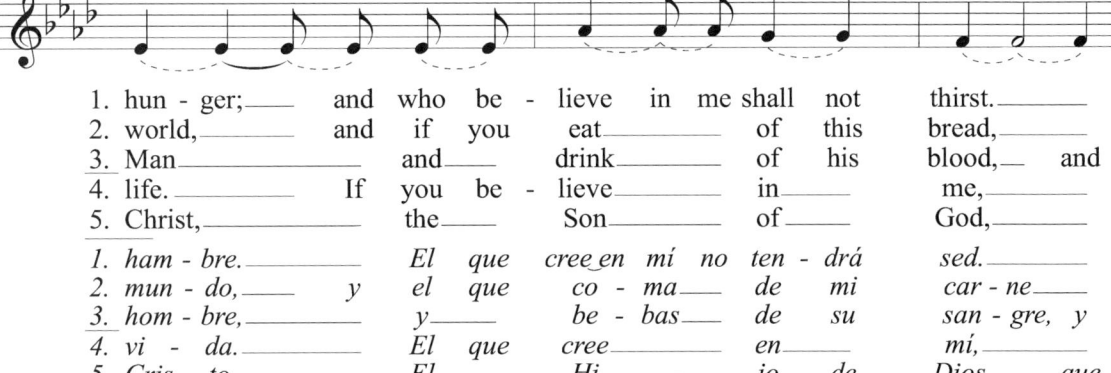

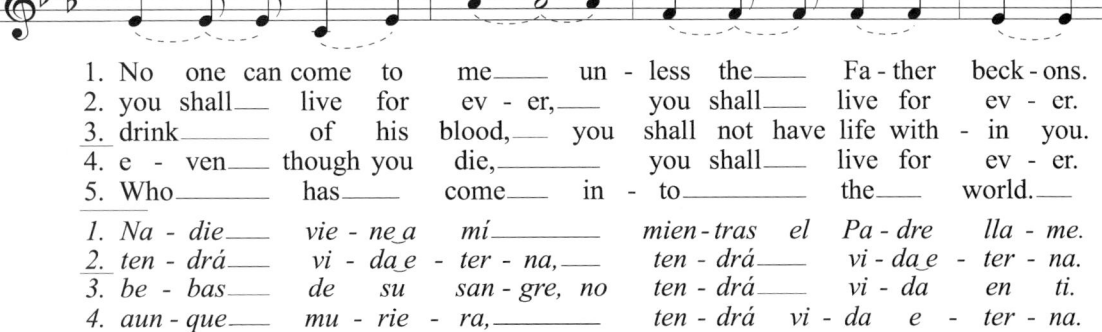

Text: Based on John 6; Suzanne Toolan, SM, b. 1927 Music: BREAD OF LIFE, irregular with refrain; Suzanne Toolan, SM, b. 1927
Text and music: © 1966, 1970, 1986, 1993, GIA Publications, Inc. All rights reserved. Used with permission.

I Call You to My Father's House 173

1. I call you to my Father's house, a lovely dwelling place. He comes to meet you on the road, arms ready to embrace.
2. Lay down your sorrow, calm your fear; the Father bids you come. With open arms he welcomes you to your eternal home.
3. Although the way be hard and long into the promised land, be not afraid to walk with me: I hold you by the hand.
4. I have prepared a wedding feast of finest food and wine. O join us at this banquet where my friends, the saints, now dine.
5. I call you to my Father's house, a lovely dwelling place. Be not afraid to travel there and meet him face to face.

Text: Delores Dufner, OSB, b. 1939, © 1983, 2003, GIA Publications, Inc. All rights reserved. Used with permission.
Music: LAND OF REST, CM, traditional American folk melody; harm. by Richard Proulx, b. 1937, © 1975, GIA Publications, Inc. All rights reserved. Used with permission.
Descant: Christine Manderfeld, OSB, b. 1938, © 2009, the Sisters of Saint Benedict, St. Joseph, MN. Administered by Liturgical Press, Collegeville, MN. All rights reserved.

174 I Come with Joy

Text: Brian Wren, b. 1936, © 1971, 1995, Hope Publishing Co., Carol Stream, IL 60188. All rights reserved. Used with permission.
Music: LAND OF REST, CM, traditional American folk melody; harm. by Richard Proulx, b. 1937, © 1975, GIA Publications, Inc. All rights reserved. Used with permission.
Descant: Christine Manderfeld, OSB, b. 1938, © 2009, the Sisters of Saint Benedict, St. Joseph, MN. Administered by Liturgical Press, Collegeville, MN. All rights reserved.

I Heard the Voice of Jesus Say 175

I Heard the Voice of Jesus Say, pg. 2

Text: Horatius Bonar, 1808–1889. Music: KINGSFOLD, CMD, English tune; harm. Ralph Vaughan Williams, 1872–1958.
Descant: Christine Manderfeld, OSB, b. 1938, © 2009, the Sisters of Saint Benedict, St. Joseph, MN. Administered by Liturgical Press, Collegeville, MN. All rights reserved.

I Know That My Redeemer Lives 176

Text: Samuel Medley, 1738–1799. Music: DUKE STREET, LM, John Hatton, c. 1710–1793.
Descant: Christine Manderfeld, OSB, b. 1938, © 2009, the Sisters of Saint Benedict, St. Joseph, MN. Administered by Liturgical Press, Collegeville, MN. All rights reserved.

177 I Received the Living God

Text: Anon.; v. 2, Alan J. Hommerding, b. 1956, © 1994, World Library Publications, 3708 River Road, Franklin Park, IL 60131. www.wlpmusic.com
All rights reserved. Used with permission. Music: LIVING GOD, 77 77 with refrain, anon.
Antiphon descant: Christine Manderfeld, OSB, © 2009, the Sisters of Saint Benedict, St. Joseph, MN. Administered by Liturgical Press, Collegeville, MN. All rights reserved.
Verse harmony: Richard Proulx, b. 1937, © 1986, GIA Publications, Inc. All rights reserved. Used with permission.

I Sing the Almighty Power of God   178

I Sing the Almighty Power of God, pg. 2

Text: Isaac Watts, 1674–1748, alt. Music: FOREST GREEN, 86 86 D, English; harm. by Ralph Vaughan Williams, 1872–1958.
Descant: Christine Manderfeld, OSB, b. 1938, © 2009, the Sisters of Saint Benedict, St. Joseph, MN. Administered by Liturgical Press, Collegeville, MN. All rights reserved.

I Want to Walk as a Child of the Light   179

Text: Based on Ephesians 5:8-10, Revelation 21:23, John 12:46, 1 John 1:5, Hebrews 12:1; Kathleen Thomerson, b. 1934, © 1970, 1975, Celebration.
Music: HOUSTON, 10 7 10 8 9 9 10 7; Kathleen Thomerson, b. 1934, © 1970, 1975, Celebration; harm. by Robert J. Batastini, b. 1942.
All rights reserved. Used with permission.

I Will Be the Vine

180

Immaculate Mary 181

Immaculate Mary, pg. 2

Text: Anon.; tr. Irwin Udulutsch, OFM, Cap, b. 1920.
Music: LOURDES (MASSABIELLE), 65 65 with refrain, *Grenoble,* 1882; harm. Irwin Udulutsch, OFM, Cap, b. 1920, alt..
Text and harmonization: © 1959, 1977, Order of Saint Benedict, Collegeville, MN. Administered by Liturgical Press, Collegeville, MN. All rights reserved.
Descant: Christine Manderfeld, OSB, b. 1938, © 2009, the Sisters of Saint Benedict, St. Joseph, MN. Administered by Liturgical Press, Collegeville, MN. All rights reserved.

182   Immortal, Invisible, God Only Wise

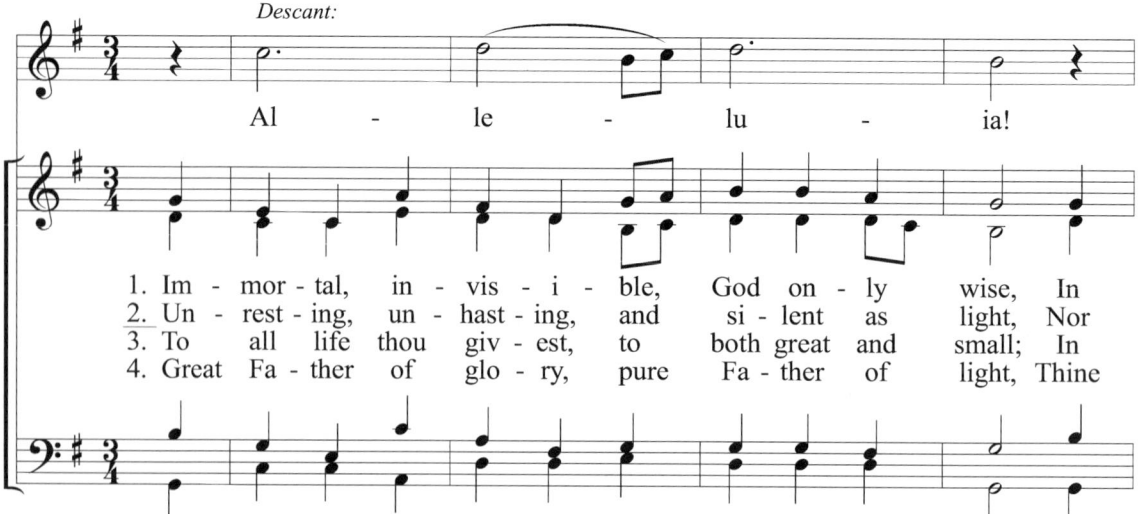

Immortal, Invisible, God Only Wise, pg. 2

Text: Walter Chalmers Smith, 1824–1908. Music: ST. DENIO, 11 11 11 11, Welsh melody, John Roberts, 1822–1877.
Descant: Christine Manderfeld, OSB, b. 1938, © 2009, the Sisters of Saint Benedict, St. Joseph, MN. Administered by Liturgical Press, Collegeville, MN. All rights reserved.

183 In Christ There Is No East or West

Text: John Oxenham, 1852–1941. Music: MCKEE, 86 86, African-American spiritual; adapt. Harry T. Burleigh, 1866–1949.
Descant: Christine Manderfeld, OSB, b. 1938, © 2009, the Sisters of Saint Benedict, St. Joseph, MN. Administered by Liturgical Press, Collegeville, MN. All rights reserved.

In Paradisum / May Choirs of Angels 184

Text: *In Paradisum*, tr. © 1986, GIA Publications, Inc., All rights reserved. Used with permission.
Music: Mode VII.

185 In the Cross of Christ

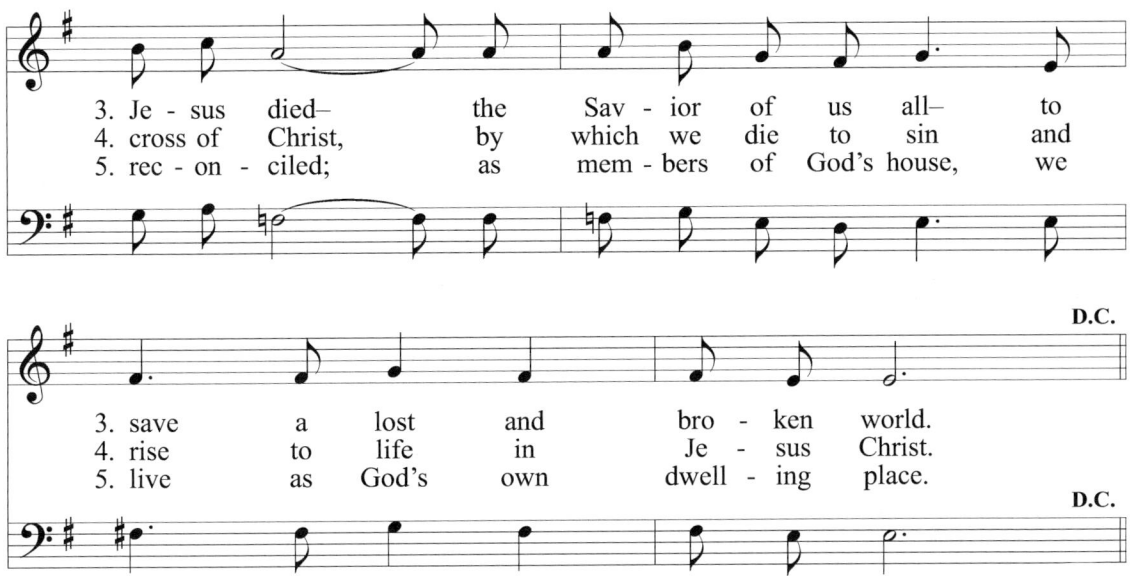

Text: Based on Philippians 2:5-8; Ephesians 2:12-13; Galatians 6:14; adapt. by Marty Haugen, b. 1950. Music: Marty Haugen, b. 1950.
Text and music: © 1997, GIA Publications, Inc. All rights reserved. Used with permission.

186 In the Cross of Christ I Glory

Text: Sir J. Bowring, 1792–1872.
Music: RICHARD'S SHOP, 87 87, Henry Bryan Hays, OSB, b. 1920, © 1989, Order of Saint Benedict, Collegeville, MN.
Administered by Liturgical Press, Collegeville, MN. All rights reserved.

In the Lord I'll Be Ever Thankful   187

Text: Taizé Community. Music: Jacques Berthier, 1923–1994, © 1986, 1991, Les Presses de Taizé, GIA Publications, North American agent. All rights reserved. Used with permission.

188 Infant Holy, Infant Lowly

Text: Polish carol; para. by Edith M. G. Reed, 1885–1993.
Music: W ZLOBIE LEZY, 44 7 44 7 4444 7; Polish Carol; harm. by A. E. Rusbridge, 1917–1969, © Bristol Churches Housing Assoc. Ltd.
Descant: Randall Sensmeier, © 1992, GIA Publications, Inc. All rights reserved. Used with permission.

189 Infant Wrapped in God's Own Light

Descant (final verse):

4. Radiance of the Father's face, Shine his love in ev'ry place. Splendor of God's glory bright, Lead us to eternal light!

1. Infant wrapped in God's own light, Savior sent to conquer night, King before whom kings bowed low, Let a star before us go.
2. Light of all the nations, shine! Show to us who wait a sign. God on earth, our host and guest, Be in flesh made manifest.
3. Servant Savior, chosen one, You are God's beloved Son. Let your Spirit on us rest; Be in us made manifest.
4. Radiance of the Father's face, Shine his love in ev'ry place. Splendor of God's glory bright, Lead us to eternal light!

Text: Delores Dufner, OSB, b. 1939, © 1984, 2003, GIA Publications, Inc. All rights reserved. Used with permission.
Music: NUN KOMM DER HEIDEN HEILAND, 77 77, *Geistliche Gesangbüchlein*, Wittenberg, 1524; harm. by Melchior Vulpius, 1560–1616.
Descant: Christine Manderfeld, OSB, b. 1938, © 2009, the Sisters of Saint Benedict, St. Joseph, MN. Administered by Liturgical Press, Collegeville, MN. All rights reserved.

It Came Upon the Midnight Clear

190

It Came Upon the Midnight Clear, pg. 2

Text: Edmund Hamilton Sears, 1810–1876, alt. Music: CAROL, 86 86 D, Richard S. Willis, 1819–1900.
Descant: Robert J. Powell, © 1982, GIA Publications, Inc. All rights reserved. Used with permission.

Jerusalem, My Destiny

191

Jerusalem, My Happy Home 192

Text: F.B.P., London, ca. 16th cent., alt.
Music: LAND OF REST, CM, traditional American folk melody; harm. by Richard Proulx, b. 1937, © 1975, GIA Publications, Inc. All rights reserved. Used with permission.
Descant: Christine Manderfeld, OSB, b. 1938, © 2009, the Sisters of Saint Benedict, St. Joseph, MN. Administered by Liturgical Press, Collegeville, MN. All rights reserved.

193 Jesu, Jesu, Fill Us with Your Love

Je - su, (Je-su,) Je - su, (Je-su,) fill us with your love, show us how to serve the neigh-bors we have from you.

Verses

1. Kneels at the feet of his friends, si - lent - ly wash - es their feet, Mas - ter who acts as a slave to them.
2. Neigh - bors are rich and poor, neigh-bors are black and white, neigh - bors are near - by and far a - way.
3. These are the ones we should serve, these are the ones we should love. All are neigh - bors to us and you.
4. Lov - ing puts us on our knees, serv - ing as though we were slaves; this is the way we should live with you.

Text: Ghana folk song based on John 13:3-5; tr. Tom Colvin, b. 1925, © 1969, Hope Publishing Co., Carol Stream, IL 60188.
Music: CHEREPONI, irregular, Ghana folk song; acc. Charles H. Webb, b. 1933, © 1989, Hope Publishing Co., Carol Stream, IL 60188.
All rights reserved. Used with permission.

Jesus at the Jordan Baptized 194

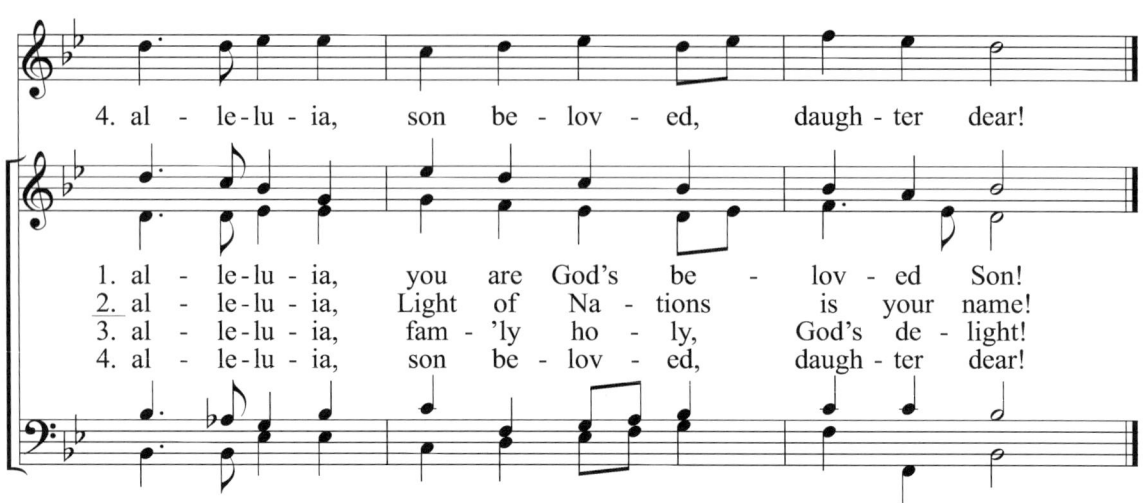

Text: Delores Dufner, OSB, b. 1939, © 1983, 1992, 2006, the Sisters of Saint Benedict, St. Joseph, MN. Administered by Liturgical Press, Collegeville, MN. All rights reserved.
Music: REGENT SQUARE, 87 87 87; Henry Smart, 1813–1879.
Descant: Delores Dufner, OSB, b. 1939, © 2009, the Sisters of Saint Benedict, St. Joseph, MN. Administered by Liturgical Press, Collegeville, MN. All rights reserved.

195   Jesus Christ Is Risen Today

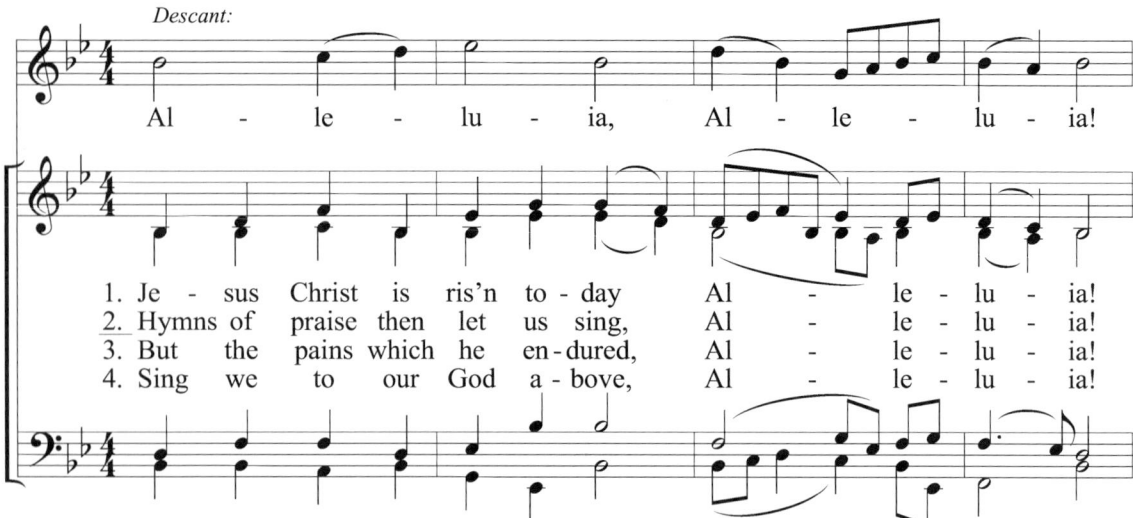

196   Jesus Christ, Yesterday, Today and For Ever

Jesus Christ, Yesterday, Today and For Ever, pg. 2

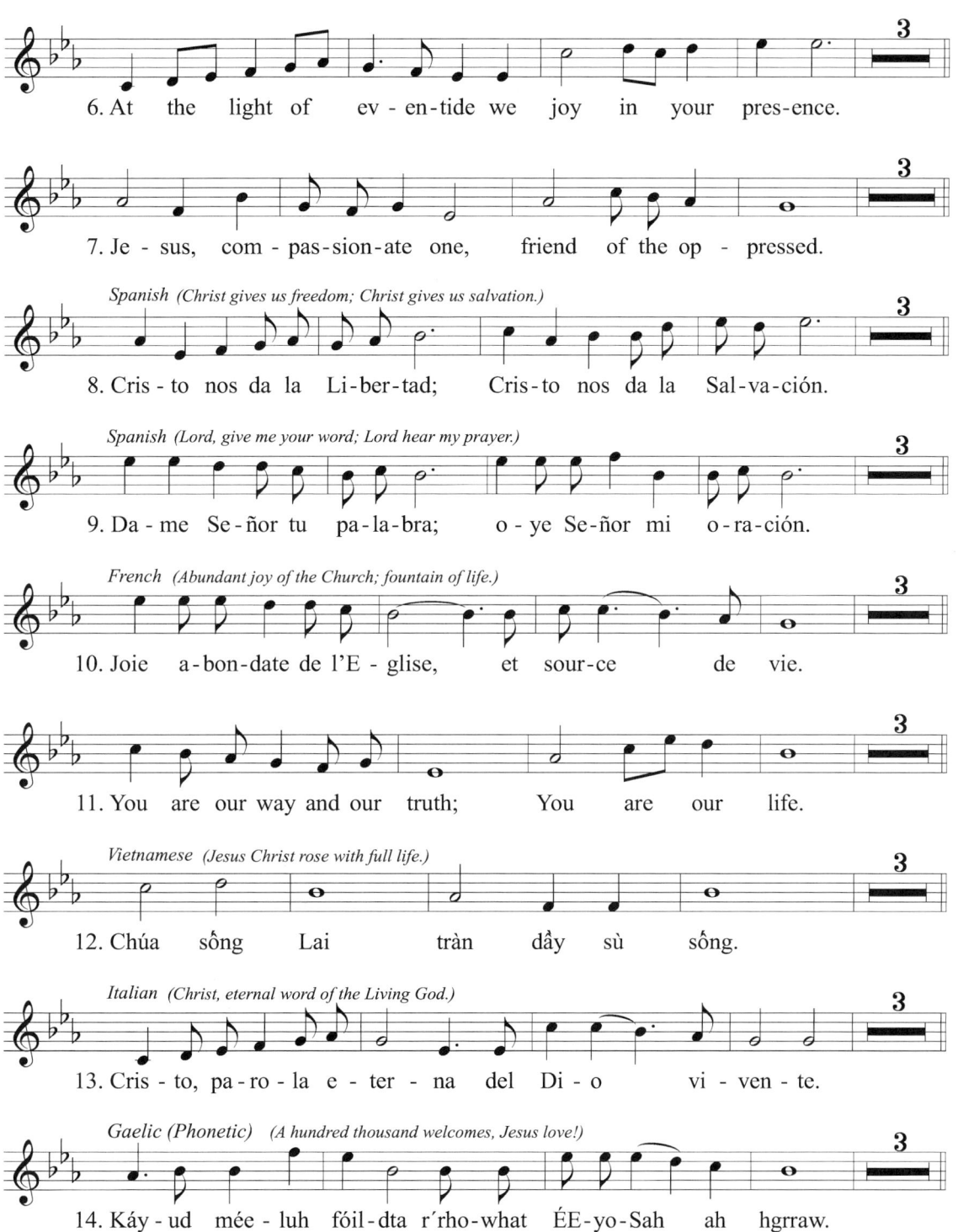

Text and music: Suzanne Toolan, SM, b. 1927, © 1988, GIA Publications, Inc. All rights reserved. Used with permission.

197   Jesus, My Lord, My God, My All

1. Jesus, my Lord, my God, my all, How can I love you as I ought? And how revere this wondrous gift So far surpassing hope or thought?

2. Had I but Mary's sinless heart, How I would love you, dearest King! O with what bursts of fervent praise Your goodness, Jesus, would I sing!

Refrain
O God of love, whom we adore, O make us love you more and more; O make us love you more and more!

Text: Frederick W. Faber, 1814–1863, adapt. Music: SWEET SACRAMENT, 88 88 with refrain; *Romischkatholisches Gesangbuchlein,* 1826.

Jesus, Remember Me

198

Ostinato Refrain

Jesus, remember me when you come into your Kingdom.

Jesus, remember me when you come into your Kingdom.

Text: Based on Luke 23:42; Taizé Community, 1981. Music: Jacques Berthier, 1923–1994, © 1981, Les Presses de Taizé, GIA Publications, Inc., North American agent. All rights reserved. Used with permission.

199   Jesus Shall Reign

Text: Isaac Watts, 1674–1748. Music: DUKE STREET, 88 88, John Hatton, c. 1710–1793.
Descant: Christine Manderfeld, OSB, b. 1938, © 2009, the Sisters of Saint Benedict, St. Joseph, MN. Administered by Liturgical Press, Collegeville, MN. All rights reserved.

Jesus Took a Towel
200

Joy to the World

201

Joy to the World, pg. 2

Joyful, Joyful, We Adore Thee 202

Joyful, Joyful, We Adore Thee, pg. 2

Text: Henry van Dyke, 1852–1933, alt.
Music: HYMN TO JOY, 87 87 D, Ludwig van Beethoven, 1770–1827, adapt. Edward Hodges, 1796–1867.
Descant: Christine Manderfeld, OSB, b. 1938, © 2009, the Sisters of Saint Benedict, St. Joseph, MN. Administered by Liturgical Press, Collegeville, MN. All rights reserved.

Jubilate Servite
203

Canon – *2 voices*

Ju - bi - la - te De - o om - nis ter - ra.
Raise a song of glad-ness peo-ples of the earth.

Ser - vi - te Do - mi - no in lae - ti - ti - a.
Christ has come, bring-ing peace, joy to ev - 'ry heart.

Al - le - lu - ia, al - le - lu - ia, in lae - ti - ti - a.
Al - le - lu - ia, al - le - lu - ia, joy to ev - 'ry heart!

Al - le - lu - ia, al - le - lu - ia, in lae - ti - ti - a!
Al - le - lu - ia, al - le - lu - ia, joy to ev - 'ry heart!

Text: Based on Psalm 100, Taizé Community, 1978; Music: Jacques Berthier, 1923–1994. © 1979, Les Presses de Taizé, GIA Publications, Inc., North American agent. All rights reserved. Used with permission.

204 Keep In Mind

Refrain
Keep in mind that Jesus Christ has died for us and is risen from the dead. He is our saving Lord, he is joy for all ages.

Verse 1
1. If we die with the Lord, we shall live with the Lord.
   If we endure with the Lord, we shall reign with the Lord.

Verses 2, 3
2. In Christ all our sorrow, in Christ all our joy.
   In him hope of glory, in him all our love.
3. In Christ our redemption, in Christ all our grace.
   In him our salvation, in him all our peace.

Text and music: Lucien Deiss, 1921–2007, © 1965, 1966, World Library Publications,
3708 River Road, Franklin Park, IL 60131. www.wlpmusic.com All rights reserved. Used with permission.

Laudate Dominum 205

Text: Based on Psalm 117; adapt. by the Taizé Community, 1980. Music: Jacques Berthier, 1923–1994.
Text and music: © 1980, Les Presses de Taizé, GIA Publications, Inc., North American agent. All rights reserved. Used with permission.

206 Let All Mortal Flesh Keep Silence

Text: Liturgy of St. James; tr. Gerard Moultrie, 1829–1885. Music: PICARDY, 87 87 87, French carol, 17th cent.
Descant: Randall Sensmeier, © 1992, GIA Publications, Inc. All rights reserved. Used with permission.

Let All Things Now Living
207

Descant: Sing, Alleluia! Sing, Alleluia! Sing, Alleluia! Sing, Alleluia!

1. Let all things now living a song of thanksgiving to God our Creator triumphantly raise; Who fashioned and made us, protected and stayed us, by guiding us on to the end of our days.
2. His law he enforces, the stars in their courses, the sun in its orbit obediently shine, The hills and the mountains, the rivers and fountains, the depths of the ocean proclaim God divine.

Let All Things Now Living, pg. 2

Text: Katherine K. Davis, 1892–1980, © 1939, E.C. Schirmer Music Co. All rights reserved. Used with permission.
Music: ASH GROVE, 66 11 66 11 D, traditional Welsh; harm. by Gerald H. Knight, 1908–1979, © The Royal School of Church Music. All rights reserved. Used with permission.
Descant: Christine Manderfeld, OSB, b. 1938, © 2009, the Sisters of Saint Benedict, St. Joseph, MN. Administered by Liturgical Press, Collegeville, MN. All rights reserved.

Let Desert Wasteland Now Rejoice   208

Text: Delores Dufner, OSB, b. 1939, © 1982, 2003, GIA Publications, Inc. All rights reserved. Used with permission.
Music: LOBT GOTT IN SEINEM HEILIGTUM; Heinrich Schütz, 1585–1672.
Descant: Christine Manderfeld, OSB, b. 1938, © 2009, the Sisters of Saint Benedict, St. Joseph, MN. Administered by Liturgical Press, Collegeville, MN. All rights reserved.

209. Let Hymns of Joy to Grief Succeed

Text: *Aurora caelum purpurat;* tr. R. Campbell, 1868, alt.
Music: LASST UNS ERFREUEN, LM 88 44 88 with alleluias, *Geistliche Kirchengesange,* Cologne, 1623.
Harmony: Christine Manderfeld, OSB, b. 1938, © 2009, the Sisters of Saint Benedict, St. Joseph, MN. Administered by Liturgical Press, Collegeville, MN. All rights reserved.
Descant: Eugene Martin Lindusky, 1924–2005, © Mary C. Lindusky. All rights reserved. Used with permission.

Let There Be Peace on Earth

Let There Be Peace on Earth, pg. 2

Text and music: Sy Miller, 1908–1971, and Jill Jackson, 1913–1995; arr. by Dennis Richardson, b. 1947.
Text and music: © 1955, 1982, renewed 1983, 1997, Jan-Lee Music. All rights reserved. Used with permission.

Lift High the Cross 212

Text: George W. Kitchin, 1827–1912, and Michael R. Newbolt, 1874–1956, alt., © 1974, Hope Publishing Co., Carol Stream, IL 60188.
Music: CRUCIFER, 10 10 with refrain, Sydney H. Nicholson, 1875–1947, © 1947, Hope Publishing Co.
Descant: George Carthage and the Cathedral of Saint Mary, St. Cloud, MN, © 2003, Hope Publishing Co.
All rights reserved. Used with permission.

213 Lift Up Your Heads, You Mighty Gates

Text: Based on Psalm 24, Georg Weissel, 1590–1635, tr. Catherine Winkworth, 1827–1878.
Music: TRURO, LM, *Psalmodia Evangelica*, 1789.
Descant: Richard Proulx, © 1979, GIA Publications, Inc. All rights reserved. Used with permission.

Lo, How a Rose E'er Blooming 214

1. Lo, how a Rose e'er bloom-ing From ten-der stem hath sprung! Of Jes-se's lin-eage com-ing, As proph-ets long have sung. It came, a flow'r-et bright, A-mid the cold of win-ter, When half-spent was the night.
2. I-sa-iah 'twas fore-told it, The Rose I have in mind; With Ma-ry we be-hold it, The Vir-gin Moth-er kind. To show God's love a-right, She bore the world a Sav-ior, When half-spent was the night.
3. O Flow'r, whose fra-grance ten-der With sweet-ness fills the air, Dis-pel with glo-ri-ous splen-dor The dark-ness ev-'ry-where. True Man, yet ver-y God, From sin and death now save us And light-en ev-'ry load.

Text: Based on Isaiah 11:1; trad. German carol, 15th cent.; tr. Theodore Baker, 1851–1934.
Music: ES IST EIN ROS' ENTSPRUNGEN, 76 76 676, German, 16th cent.; *Speierischen Gesangbuch,* Cologne, 1599; harm. by Michael Praetorius, 1571–1621.

Lord and God, Devoutly You I Now Adore   216

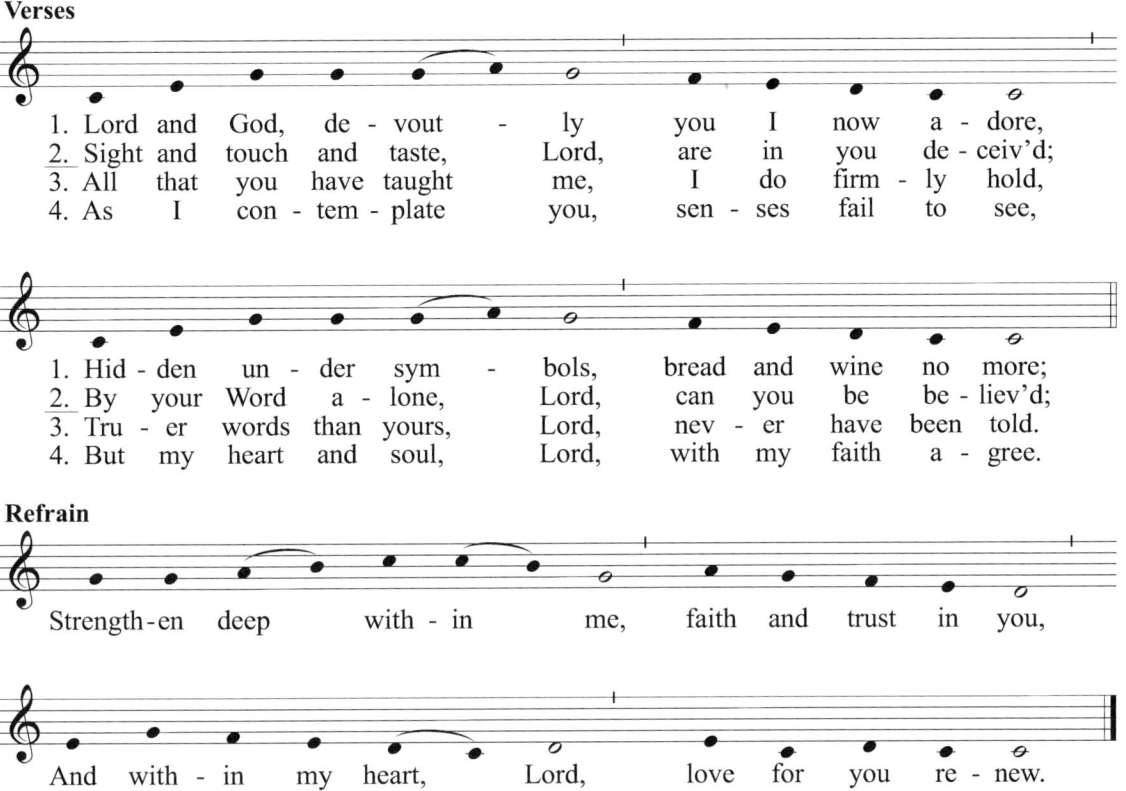

Verses

1. Lord and God, devout - ly you I now adore,
2. Sight and touch and taste, Lord, are in you deceiv'd;
3. All that you have taught me, I do firm - ly hold,
4. As I con - tem - plate you, sen - ses fail to see,

1. Hid - den un - der sym - bols, bread and wine no more;
2. By your Word a - lone, Lord, can you be be - liev'd;
3. Tru - er words than yours, Lord, nev - er have been told.
4. But my heart and soul, Lord, with my faith a - gree.

Refrain

Strength-en deep with - in me, faith and trust in you,

And with - in my heart, Lord, love for you re - new.

Text: Tr. Roger Schoenbechler, OSB, © 1977, Order of Saint Benedict, Collegeville, MN. Administered by Liturgical Press, Collegeville, MN. All rights reserved.
Music: ADORO TE DEVOTE, irregular.

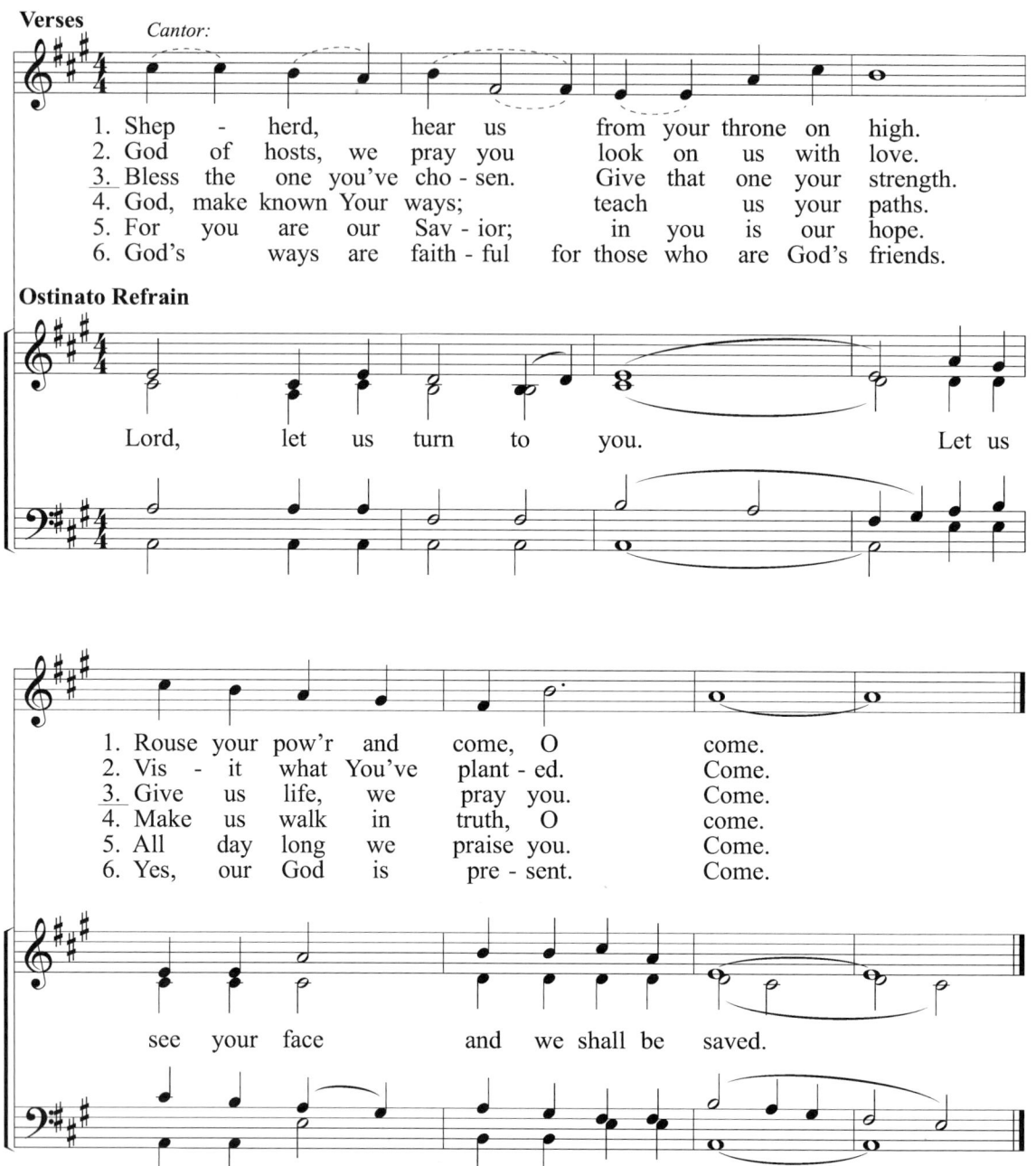

Lord, Help Us Walk Your Servant Way

218

Descant (final verse):

5. Lord, help us walk your servant way wherever love may lead and, bending low, forgetting self, each serve the other's need.

1. Lord, help us walk your servant way wherever love may lead and, bending low, forgetting self, each serve the other's need.
2. You came to earth, O Christ, as Lord, but pow'r you laid aside. You lived your years in servanthood, in lowliness you died.
3. No golden scepter but a tow'l you place within the hands of those who seek to follow you and live by your commands.
4. You bid us bend our human pride nor count ourselves above the lowest place, the meanest task that waits the gift of love.
5. Lord, help us walk your servant way wherever love may lead and, bending low, forgetting self, each serve the other's need.

Text: Herman G. Stuempfle, Jr., 1923–2007, © 1994, 1997, GIA Publications, Inc. All rights reserved. Used with permission.
Music: MORNING SONG, 86 86, *Kentucky Harmony*, 1816.
Descant: Christine Manderfeld, OSB, b. 1938, © 2009, the Sisters of Saint Benedict, St. Joseph, MN. Administered by Liturgical Press, Collegeville, MN. All rights reserved.

219   Lord Jesus, as We Turn from Sin

1. Lord Jesus, as we turn from sin With strength and hope restored, Receive the homage that we bring To you, our risen Lord.
2. We call on you whose living word Has made the Father known; O Shepherd, we have wandered far. Find us and lead us home.
3. Your glance at Peter helped him know The love he had desired. Now gaze on us and heal us, Lord, Of selfishness and pride.
4. Reach out and touch with healing pow'r The wounds we have received, That in forgiveness we may love And may no longer grieve.
5. Then stay with us when evening comes And darkness makes us blind, O stay until the light of dawn May fill both heart and mind.

Text: Ralph Wright, OSB, b. 1938, © 1980, ICEL. All rights reserved. Used with permission.
Music: GRAEFENBERG, 86 86, Johann Cruger, 1598–1662.
Descant: James Chepponis, b. 1956, © 1980, GIA Publications, Inc. All rights reserved. Used with permission.

Lord of All Hopefulness

Lord of All Hopefulness, pg. 2

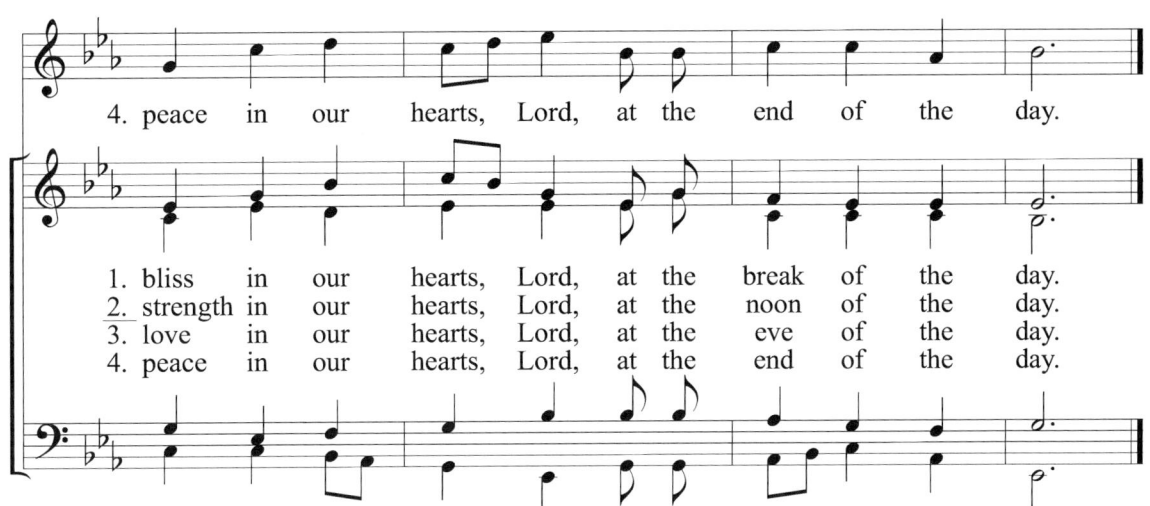

Text: Jan Struther (Joyce Placzeh, neé Torrens), 1901–1953, © Oxford University Press. All rights reserved. Used with permission.
Music: SLANE, 10 10 9 10, Irish ballad melody; harm. David Evans, 1874–1948, © Oxford University Press. All rights reserved. Used with permission.
Descant: Christine Manderfeld, OSB, b. 1938, © 2009, the Sisters of Saint Benedict, St. Joseph, MN. Administered by Liturgical Press, Collegeville, MN. All rights reserved.

222 Lord, Teach Us How to Pray Aright

1. Lord, teach us how to pray aright With reverence and with fear;
Though dust and ashes in thy sight, We may, we must draw near.
We perish if we cease from prayer; O grant us power to pray;
And when to meet thee we prepare, Lord, meet us by the way.

2. God of all grace, we come to thee With broken contrite hearts;
Give, what thine eye delights to see, Truth in the inward parts;
Faith in the only sacrifice That can for sin atone;
To cast our hopes, to fix our eyes, On Christ, on Christ alone.

3. Patience to watch, and wait, and weep, Though mercy long delay;
Courage our fainting souls to keep, And trust thee though thou slay.
Give these, and then thy will be done; Thus strengthened with all might,
We, through thy Spirit and thy Son, Shall pray, and pray aright.

Text: J. Montgomery, 1771–1854.
Music: ELKHORN TAVERN, 86 86 D, Henry Bryan Hayes, OSB, b. 1920, © 1981, Order of Saint Benedict, Collegeville, MN.
Administered by Liturgical Press, Collegeville, MN. All rights reserved.

Lord, When You Came / Pescador de Hombres 223

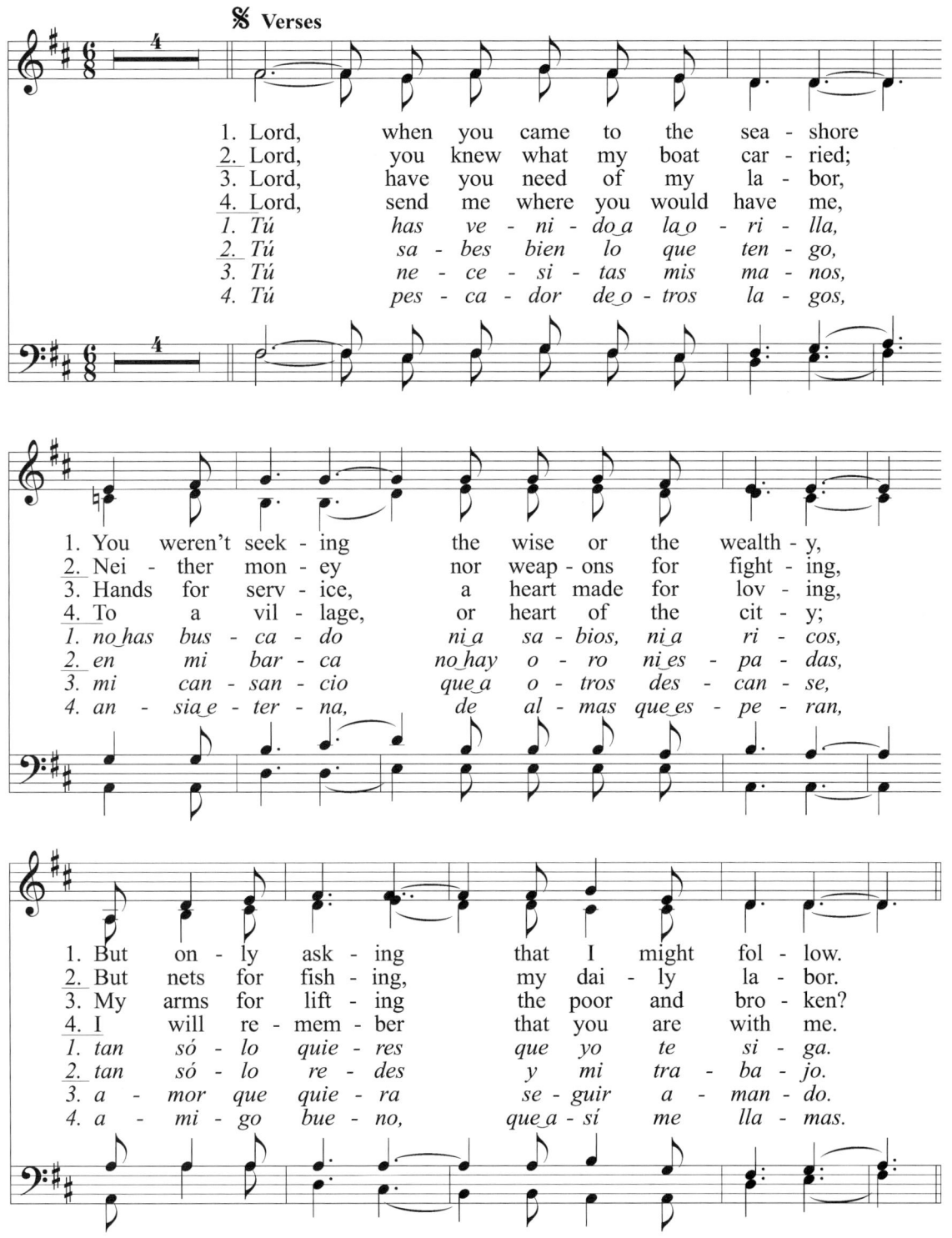

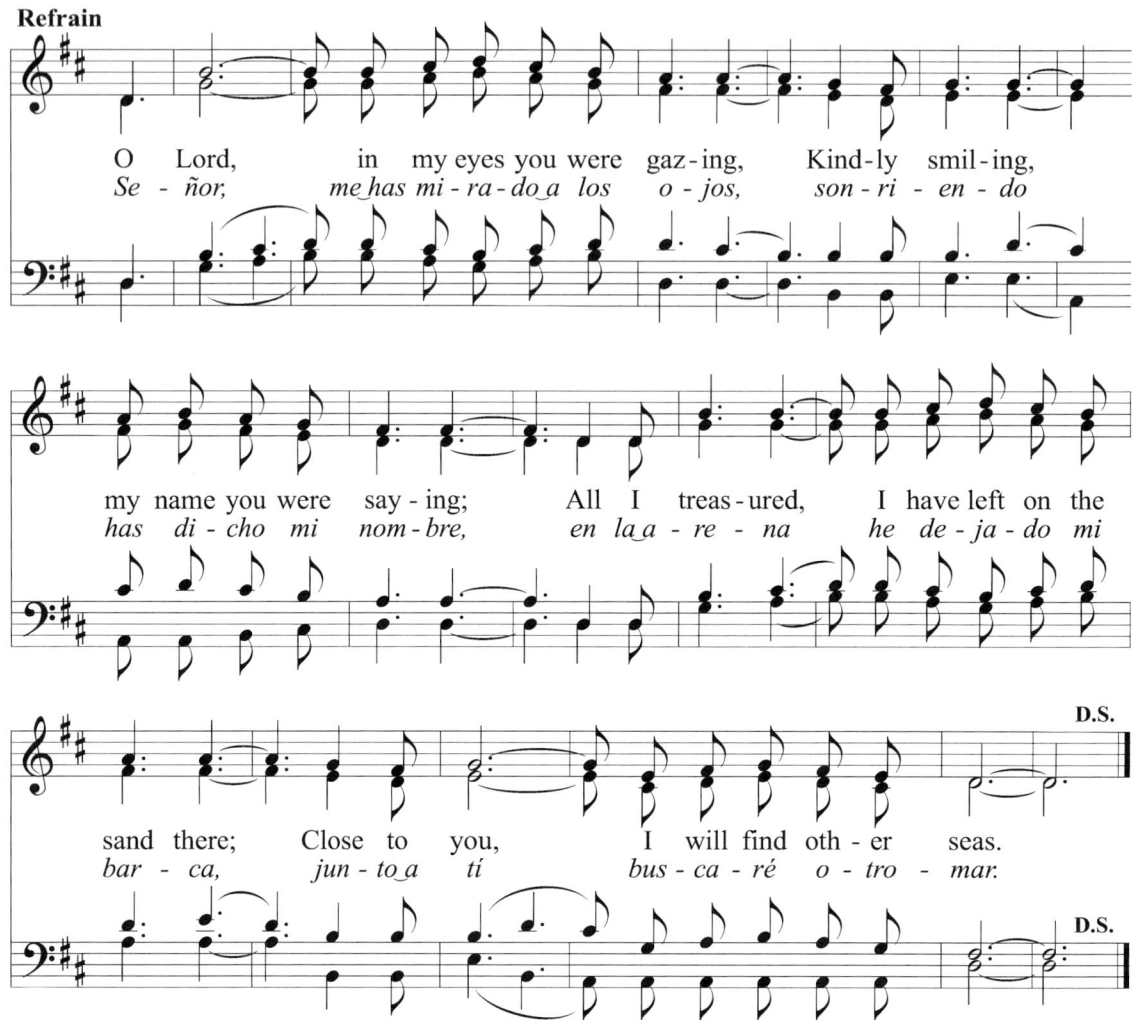

Lord, Who Throughout These Forty Days
224

Text: Claudia F. Hernaman, 1838–1898, alt. Music: ST. FLAVIAN, CM, *John's Day Psalter*, 1562; harm. based on the original faux-bourdon setting.
Descant: Christine Manderfeld, OSB, b. © 2009, the Sisters of Saint Benedict, St. Joseph, MN. Administered by Liturgical Press, Collegeville, MN. All rights reserved.

Lord, Whose Love in Humble Service

Descant (final verse):
4. Called from worship Forth in your great name we go, To children, youth and aged, Love in living deeds to show;

1. Lord, whose love in humble service Bore the weight of human need, Who did on the cross, forsaken, Show us mercy's perfect deed;
2. Still your children wander homeless; Still the hungry cry for bread; Still the captives long for freedom; Still in grief we mourn our dead.
3. As we worship, grant us vision, Till your love's revealing light, In its height and depth and greatness Dawns upon our human sight:
4. Called from worship into service, Forth in your great name we go, To the child, the youth, the aged, Love in living deeds to show;

226 Lord, You Give the Great Commission

227 Lord, Your Almighty Word

Text: John Marriott, 1780–1825. Music: ITALIAN HYMN, 66 4 666 4, Felice de Giardini, 1716–1796.
Descant: Christine Manderfeld, OSB, b. 1938, © 2009, the Sisters of Saint Benedict, St. Joseph, MN. Administered by Liturgical Press, Collegeville, MN. All rights reserved.

Love Divine, All Loves Excelling

228

Love Divine, All Loves Excelling, pg. 2

Text: Charles Wesley, 1707–1788. Music: HYFRYDOL, 87 87 D, Rowland H. Prichard, 1811–1887.
Descant: Christine Manderfeld, OSB, b. 1938, © 2009, the Sisters of Saint Benedict, St. Joseph, MN. Administered by Liturgical Press, Collegeville, MN. All rights reserved.

Magnificat / Luke 1:46-55   229

Text: Based on Luke 1:46–55; adapt. by James J. Chepponis, b. 1956. Music: James J. Chepponis, b. 1956.
Text and music: © 1980, GIA Publications, Inc. All rights reserved. Used with permission.

230 Make Us True Servants

Text: Susan G. Wente, b. 1952, © 1978, World Library Publications, 3708 River Road, Franklin Park, IL 60131. www.wlpmusic.com All rights reserved. Used with permission.
Music: SLANE, 10 10 9 10, Irish ballad melody; harm. David Evans, 1874–1948 © Oxford University Press. All rights reserved. Used with permission.
Descant: Christine Manderfeld, OSB, b. 1938, © 2009, the Sisters of Saint Benedict, St. Joseph, MN. Administered by Liturgical Press, Collegeville, MN. All rights reserved.

Maranatha, Come, pg. 2

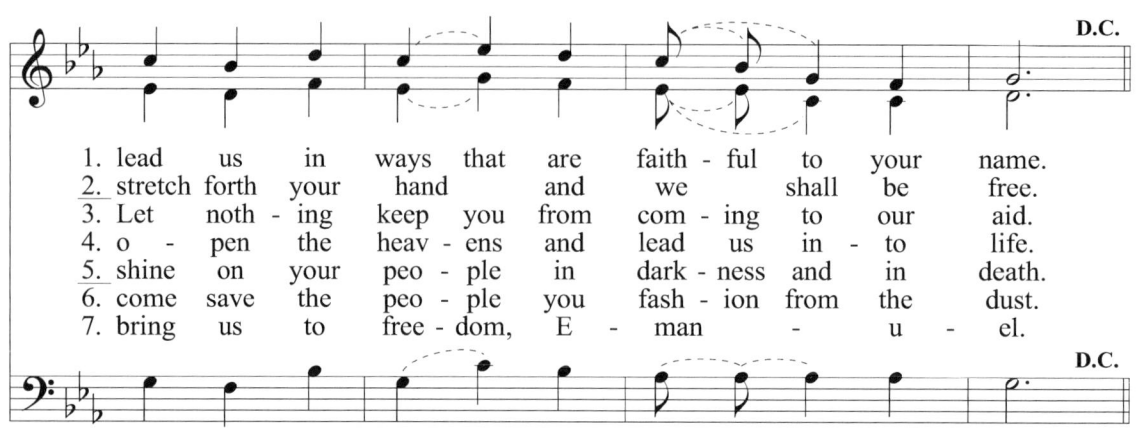

1. lead us in ways that are faith-ful to your name.
2. stretch forth your hand and we shall be free.
3. Let noth-ing keep you from com-ing to our aid.
4. o-pen the heav-ens and lead us in-to life.
5. shine on your peo-ple in dark-ness and in death.
6. come save the peo-ple you fash-ion from the dust.
7. bring us to free-dom, E-man-u-el.

Text: Based on the "O" Antiphons; adapt. by Francis Patrick O'Brien, b. 1958. Music: Francis Patrick O'Brien, b. 1958.
Text and music: © 1996, GIA Publications, Inc. All rights reserved. Used with permission.

232 Maranatha, Lord Messiah

Verses

1. Gra-cious God of Wis-dom, who hears your
2. Might-y Voice of Si-nai, whom Mos-es
3. Fra-grant Bud of Jes-se, whose bloom-ing
4. Da-vid's Key of Heav-en, un-lock us
5. Blaz-ing Sun of Jus-tice, the flame of
6. Sov-ereign of all Na-tions, our cor-ner-
7. Je-sus, be God with us, Em-man-u-

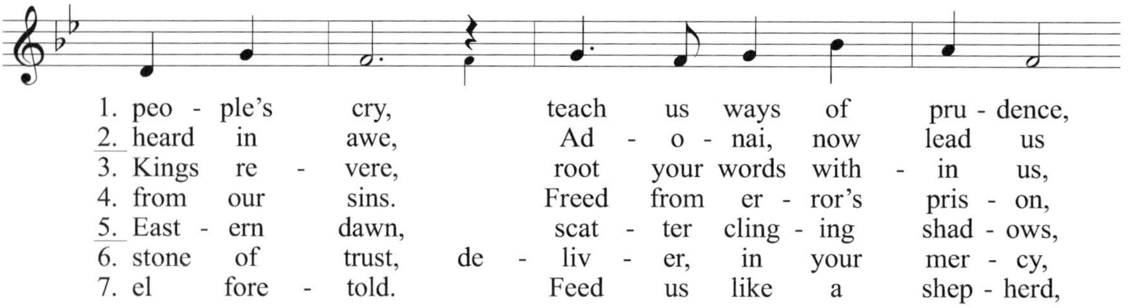

1. peo-ple's cry, teach us ways of pru-dence,
2. heard in awe, Ad-o-nai, now lead us
3. Kings re-vere, root your words with-in us,
4. from our sins. Freed from er-ror's pris-on,
5. East-ern dawn, scat-ter cling-ing shad-ows,
6. stone of trust, de-liv-er, in your mer-cy,
7. el fore-told. Feed us like a shep-herd,

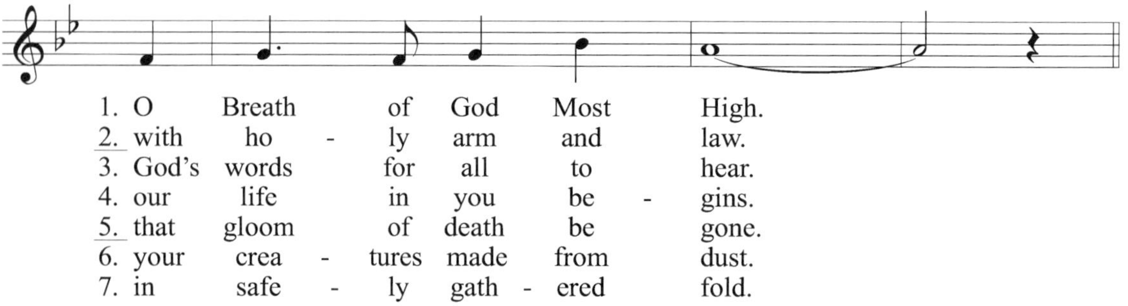

1. O Breath of God Most High.
2. with ho-ly arm and law.
3. God's words for all to hear.
4. our life in you be-gins.
5. that gloom of death be gone.
6. your crea-tures made from dust.
7. in safe-ly gath-ered fold.

Text: Based on the "O" Antiphons; adapt. by Kathy Powell, b. 1942. Music: Kathy Powell, b. 1942.
Text and music: © 1999, GIA Publications, Inc. All rights reserved. Used with permission.

Mary, Woman of the Promise

1. Mary, woman of the promise; Vessel of your people's dreams, Through your open, willing spirit Waters of God's goodness streamed.

2. Mary, song of holy wisdom, Sung before the world began, Faithful to the Word within, you Carried out God's wondrous plan.

3. Mary, morning star of justice; Mirror of the radiant light, In the shadows of life's journey, Be a beacon for our sight.

4. Mary, model of compassion; Wounded by your offspring's pain, When our hearts are torn by sorrow, Teach us how to love again.

5. Mary, woman of the Gospel; Humble home for treasured seed; Help us to be true disciples Bearing fruit in word and deed.

Text: Mary Frances Fleischaker, © 1988, Mary Frances Fleischaker, Selah Publishing Co., Inc., exclusive agent. All rights reserved. Used with permission.
Music: STUTTGART, 87 87, Christian Friedrich Witt, 1660–1716; adapt. and harm. William Henry Havergal, 1793–1870, alt.
Descant: Christine Manderfeld, OSB, © 2009, the Sisters of Saint Benedict, St. Joseph, MN. Administered by Liturgical Press, Collegeville, MN. All rights reserved.

May the Angels Lead You into Paradise 234

Text: *In paradisum; Rite of Funerals,* © 1970, ICEL.
Music: *Music for Rite of Funerals and Rite of Baptism for Children,* Howard Hughes, SM, b. 1930, © 1977, ICEL.
All rights reserved. Used with permission.

235   **Merciful Savior**

1. Merciful Savior, Lord of creation, Son of God and Son of Man! Jesus, we love you, serve and obey you, Light of the soul, our joy and peace.
2. Merciful Savior, King of the nations, Son of God and Son of Man! Glory and honor, praise, adoration, ever be yours from all mankind!

Text: Irwin Udulutsch, OFM, Cap, b. 1920, © 1959, 1977, Order of Saint Benedict, Collegeville, MN. Administered by Liturgical Press, Collegeville, MN. All rights reserved.
Music: ST. ELIZABETH, 11 8 10 8, melody from *Schlesische Volkslieder*, 1842; harm. Thomas Tertius Noble, 1867–1953.
Descant: Christine Manderfeld, OSB, b. 1938, © 2009, the Sisters of Saint Benedict, St. Joseph, MN. Administered by Liturgical Press, Collegeville, MN. All rights reserved.

Mercy, O God

236

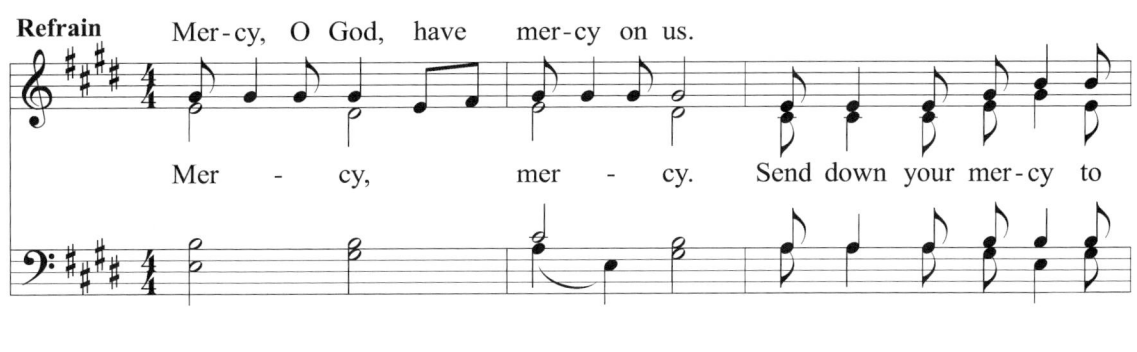

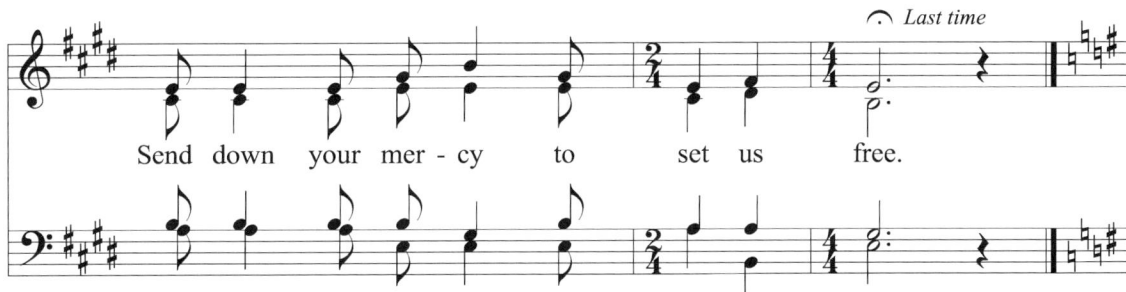

1. Gather the people, the children, the elders; come now and
2. Now is the hour, the day of salvation; now is the
3. Long is the journey and steep are the mountains, come now and
4. Wash us anew in your life-giving water; come quench the
5. Once lost in darkness you did not forsake us, but called us your
6. Wake, O sleeper awake from your slumber; rise from the

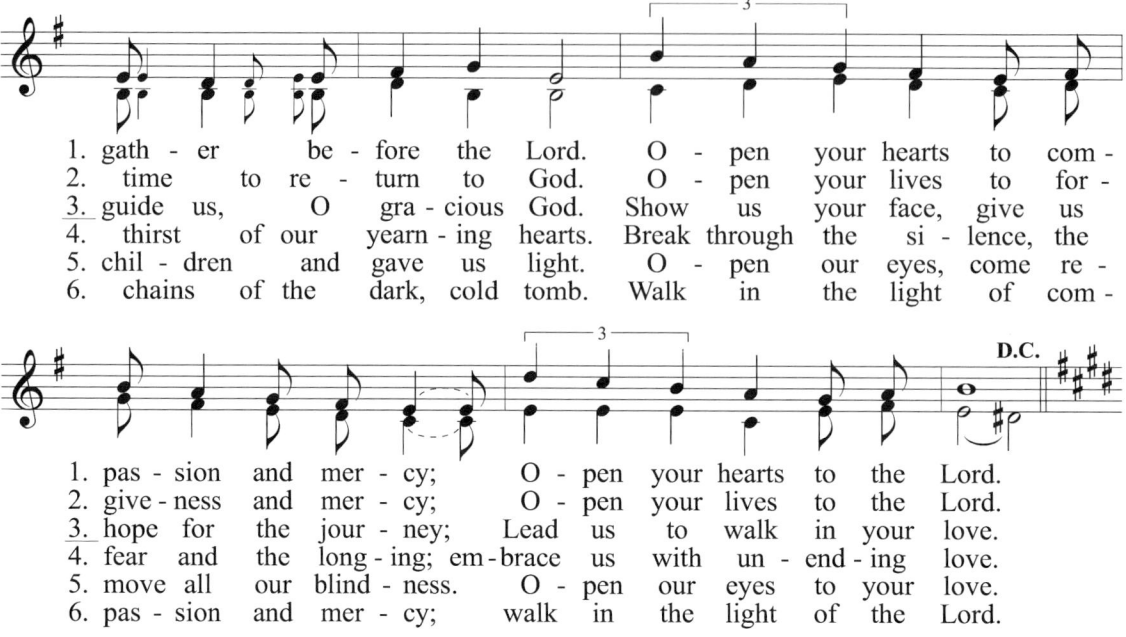

Mine Eyes Have Seen the Glory
(Battle Hymn of the Republic)

237

Text: Julia Ward Howe, 1819–1910. Music: BATTLE HYMN, 15 15 15 6 with refrain, John William Steffe, d. 1911, attr.

Morning Has Broken   238

Text: Eleanor Farjeon, 1881–1965, © 1957, Eleanor Farjeon, assigned to Harold Ober Associates, Inc. All rights reserved. Used with permission.
Music: BUNESSAN, 5 5 5 4 D; traditional Gaelic melody. Descant: Donald Busarow, © 1992, GIA Publications, Inc. All rights reserved. Used with permission.

Moved by the Gospel

Descant (final verse):
3. O Spirit, breathe among us here; inspire the work we do.

1. Moved by the Gospel, let us move with ev'ry gift and art.
2. Let weavers form from broken strands a tapestry of prayer.
3. O Spirit, breathe among us here; inspire the work we do.

3. May hands and voices, eye and ear attest to life made new.

1. The image of creative love indwells each human heart.
2. Let artists paint with skillful hands their joy, lament, and care.
3. May hands and voices, eye and ear attest to life made new.

3. In worship and in daily strife create among us still.

1. The Maker calls creation good, so let us now express
2. Then mime the story: Christ has come. With rev'rence dance the Word.
3. In worship and in daily strife create among us still.

Moved by the Gospel, pg. 2

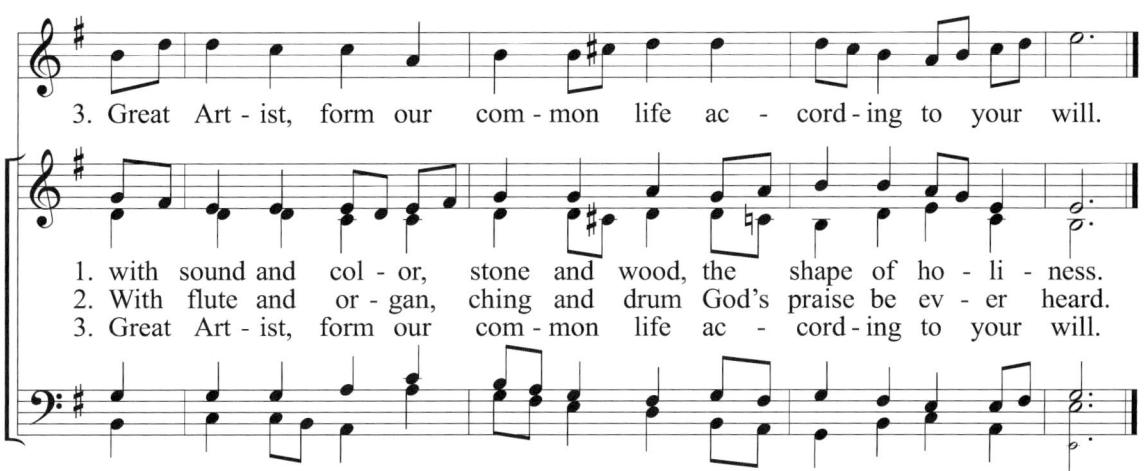

1. with sound and col-or, stone and wood, the shape of ho-li-ness.
2. With flute and or-gan, ching and drum God's praise be ev-er heard.
3. Great Art-ist, form our com-mon life ac-cord-ing to your will.

Text: Ruth Duck, b. 1947, © 1992, GIA Publications, Inc. All rights reserved. Used with permission.
Music: KINGSFOLD, CMD, English tune; harm. Ralph Vaughan Williams, 1872–1958.
Descant: Christine Manderfeld, OSB, b. 1938, © 2009, the Sisters of Saint Benedict, St. Joseph, MN. Administered by Liturgical Press, Collegeville, MN. All rights reserved.

240 My People, What Do I Require?

Text: Based on Micah 6:1-8; adapt. by Herman Stuempfle, Jr., 1923–2007, © 1992, 1997, GIA Publications, Inc. All rights reserved. Used with permission.
Music: LAND OF REST, CM, traditional American folk melody; harm. by Richard Proulx, b. 1937, © 1975, GIA Publications, Inc. All rights reserved. Used with permission.
Descant: Christine Manderfeld, OSB, b. 1938, © 2009, the Sisters of Saint Benedict, St. Joseph, MN. Administered by Liturgical Press, Collegeville, MN. All rights reserved.

My Shepherd Will Supply My Need   241

Text: Isaac Watts, 1674–1748, alt. Music: RESIGNATION, 86 86 D, *Southern Harmony*, 1835.
Descant: Christine Manderfeld, OSB, b. 1938, © 2009, the Sisters of Saint Benedict, St. Joseph, MN. Administered by Liturgical Press, Collegeville, MN. All rights reserved.

242 My Soul Gives Glory to the Lord

Text: *Magnificat anima mea*, tr. John T. Mueller, 1885–1967.
Music: O WALY, WALY, LM 88 88, English; Descant: Robert Hobby, © 1992, GIA Publications, Inc. All rights reserved. Used with permission.

My Soul in Stillness Waits 243

Text: Based on Psalm 95 and the "O" Antiphons; adapt. by Marty Haugen, b. 1950. Music: Marty Haugen, b. 1950.
Text and music: © 1982, GIA Publications, Inc. All rights reserved. Used with permission.

Night of Silence

244

1. Cold are the people, winter of life, We tremble in shadows this cold endless night, Frozen in the snow lie roses sleeping, Flowers that will echo the sunrise, Fire of hope is our only warmth, Weary, its flame will be dying soon.

2. Voice in the distance, call in the night, On wind you enfold us, you speak of the light, Gentle on the ear you whisper softly, Rumors of a dawn so embracing, Breathless love awaits darkened souls, Soon will we know of the morning.

3. Spirit among us, shine like the star, Your light that guides shepherds and kings from afar, Shimmer in the sky so empty, lonely, Rising in the warmth of the Son's love, Star unknowing of night and day, Spirit we wait for the loving Son.

"Night of Silence" was written to be sung simultaneously with "Silent Night." It is suggested that selected voices hum "Silent Night" while the remaining voices sing the final verse of "Night of Silence". Likewise, the song "Silent Night" may be sung by the choir and congregation as the instruments play "Night of Silence".

Text and music: Daniel Kantor, b. 1960, © 1984, GIA Publications, Inc. All rights reserved. Used with permission.

No Greater Love

245

Verse 3
3. You are my friends if you keep my com-mands; no long-er slaves but friends to me. All I heard from my Fa-ther, I have made known to you: Now I call you friends.

Verse 4
4. It was not you who chose me, it was I who chose you, chose you to go forth and bear fruit. Your fruit must en-dure, so you will re-ceive all you ask the Fa-ther in my name.

Text: Based on John 15; adapt. by Michael Joncas, b. 1951. Music: Michael Joncas, b. 1951.
Text and music: © 1988, GIA Publications, Inc. All rights reserved. Used with permission.

Now Bless the God of Israel
(Canticle of Zachary / Benedictus)

246

Now Bless the God of Israel (Canticle of Zachary / Benedictus), pg. 2

1. God has sworn to free us from a-larm, to save us
2. go be-fore to preach, to proph-e-sy, that all may
3. way to peace, that death shall reign no more. Sing prais-es

1. from the heav-y hand of all who wish us harm.
2. know the ten-der love, the grace of God most high.
3. to the Ho-ly One! O wor-ship and a-dore!

Text: *Benedictus*; Ruth Duck, b. 1947, © 1992, GIA Publications, Inc. All rights reserved. Used with permission.
Music: FOREST GREEN, 86 86 D, English; harm. by Ralph Vaughan Williams, 1872–1958.
Descant: Christine Manderfeld, OSB, b. 1938, © 2009, the Sisters of Saint Benedict, St. Joseph, MN. Administered by Liturgical Press, Collegeville, MN. All rights reserved.

247　　　　　　　　　　**Now Thank We All Our God**

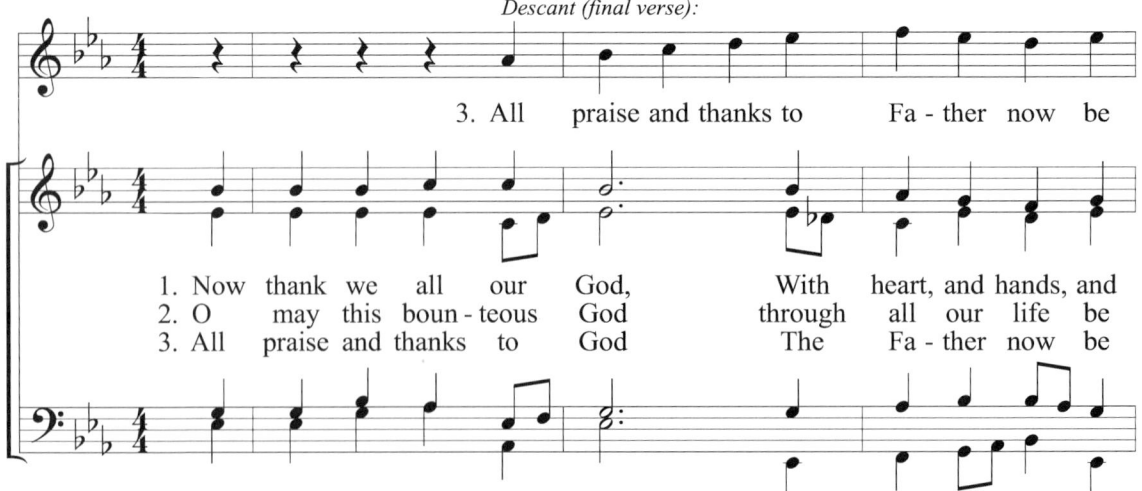

Descant (final verse):
3. All praise and thanks to Fa-ther now be

1. Now thank we all our God, With heart, and hands, and
2. O may this boun-teous God through all our life be
3. All praise and thanks to God The Fa-ther now be

Text: Martin Rinkart, 1586–1649; tr. Catherine Winkworth, 1827–1878, alt.
Music: NUN DANKET, 67 67 66 66, Johann Crüger, 1598–1662; harm. William Henry Monk, 1823–1889, alt. Felix Mendelssohn–Bartholdy, 1809–1847.
Descant: Christine Manderfeld, OSB, b. 1938, © 2009, the Sisters of Saint Benedict, St. Joseph, MN. Administered by Liturgical Press, Collegeville, MN. All rights reserved.

248 Now We Remain

We hold the death of the Lord deep in our hearts.

Living, now we remain with Jesus the Christ.
Living,

Verse 1

1. Once we were people afraid, lost in the night.
Then by your cross we were saved; Dead became living,
Life from your giving.

249 O Breathe on Me

Text: Edwin Hatch, 1835–1889, alt. Music: ST. COLUMBA, 87 87, traditional Irish hymn melody.
Descant: Christine Manderfeld, OSB, b. 1938, © 2009, the Sisters of Saint Benedict, St. Joseph, MN. Administered by Liturgical Press, Collegeville, MN. All rights reserved.

O Child of Promise, Come! 250

Descant (final verse):

5. O come, Messiah King, to reign in endless light, when heav'nly peace at last goes forth from Zion's holy height!

1. O Child of promise, come! O come, Emmanuel! Come, prince of peace, to David's throne; come, God, with us to dwell!
2. O come, anointed One, to show blind eyes your face! Good tidings to the poor announce; proclaim God's year of grace!
3. O Man of sorrows, come, despised and cast aside! O bear our griefs, and by your wounds redeem us from our pride!
4. O come, God's holy Lamb, to death be meekly led! O save the many by your blood, for sin so gladly shed!
5. O come, Messiah King, to reign in endless light, when heav'nly peace at last goes forth from Zion's holy height!

Text: James Quinn, SJ, b. 1919, ©James Quinn, SJ, Selah Publishing Co., Inc., North American agent. All rights reserved. Used with permission.
Music: FRANCONIA, 66 86, Johann B. Konig, 1691–1758, from his *Chorale;* adapt. and harm. by William Henry Havergal, 1793–1870.
Descant: Christine Manderfeld, OSB, b. 1938, © 2009, the Sisters of Saint Benedict, St. Joseph, MN. Administered by Liturgical Press, Collegeville, MN. All rights reserved.

251 O Christ Our True and Only Light

Text: Johann Heermann, 1585–1647; tr. Catherine Winkworth, 1827–1878.
Music: O WALY, WALY, LM 88 88, English; Descant: Robert Hobby, © 1992, GIA Publications, Inc. All rights reserved. Used with permission.

O Christ the Great Foundation

252

Descant (final verse):
4. This moment When he who once was dead

1. O Christ the great foundation On which your people stand
2. Baptized in one confession, One Church in all the earth,
3. Where tyrants' hold is tightened, Where strong devour the weak,
4. This is the moment glorious When he who once was dead

4. Shall lead his Church victorious, Their champion and their head.

1. To preach your true salvation In ev'ry age and land:
2. We bear our Lord's impression, The sign of second birth:
3. Where innocents are fright-ened The righteous fear to speak,
4. Shall lead his Church victorious, Their champion and their head.

4. The Lord of all creation his heav'nly kingdom brings,

1. Pour out your Holy Spirit To make us strong and pure,
2. One holy people gathered In love beyond our own,
3. There let your Church awaking Attack the pow'rs of sin
4. The Lord of all creation his heav'nly kingdom brings,

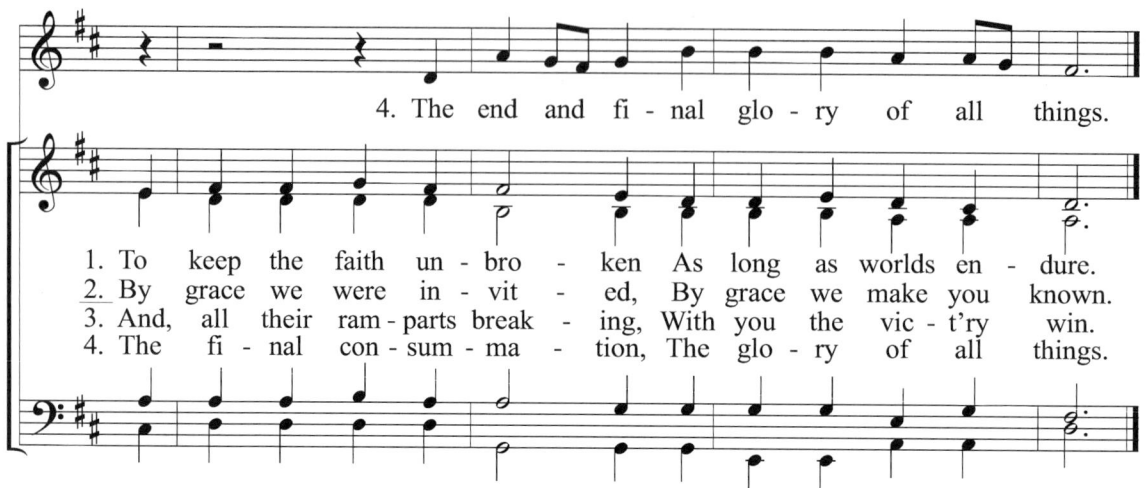

1. To keep the faith unbroken As long as worlds endure.
2. By grace we were invited, By grace we make you known.
3. And, all their ramparts breaking, With you the vic't'ry win.
4. The final consummation, The glory of all things.

Text: Timothy Tingfang Lew, 1891–1947, alt., © Christian Conference of Asia. All rights reserved. Used with permission.
Music: AURELIA, 76 76 D, Samuel S. Wesley, 1810–1876.
Descant: Christine Manderfeld, OSB, b. 1938, © 2009, the Sisters of Saint Benedict, St. Joseph, MN. Administered by Liturgical Press, Collegeville, MN. All rights reserved.

253   O Christ, What Can It Mean for Us

Descant (final verse):
4. You chose a humble human form and shunned the

1. O Christ, what can it mean for us to claim you
2. You came, the image of our God, to heal and
3. Though some would make their greatness felt and lord it
4. You chose a humble human form and shunned the

4. world's renown; you died for us upon a cross with

1. as our king? What royal face have you revealed whose
2. to forgive, to shed your blood for sinners' sake that
3. o - ver all, you said the first must be the last and
4. world's renown; you died for us upon a cross with

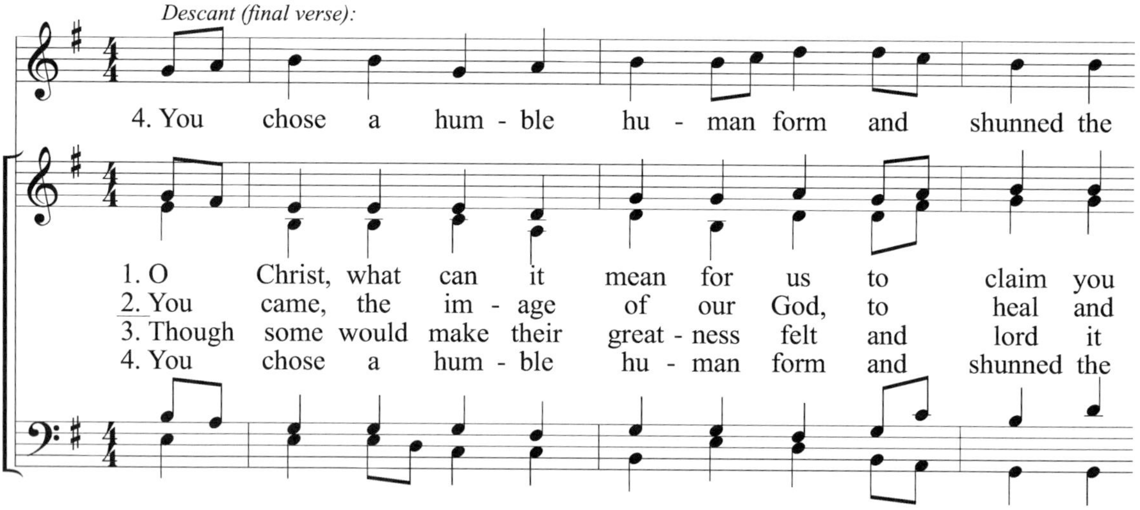

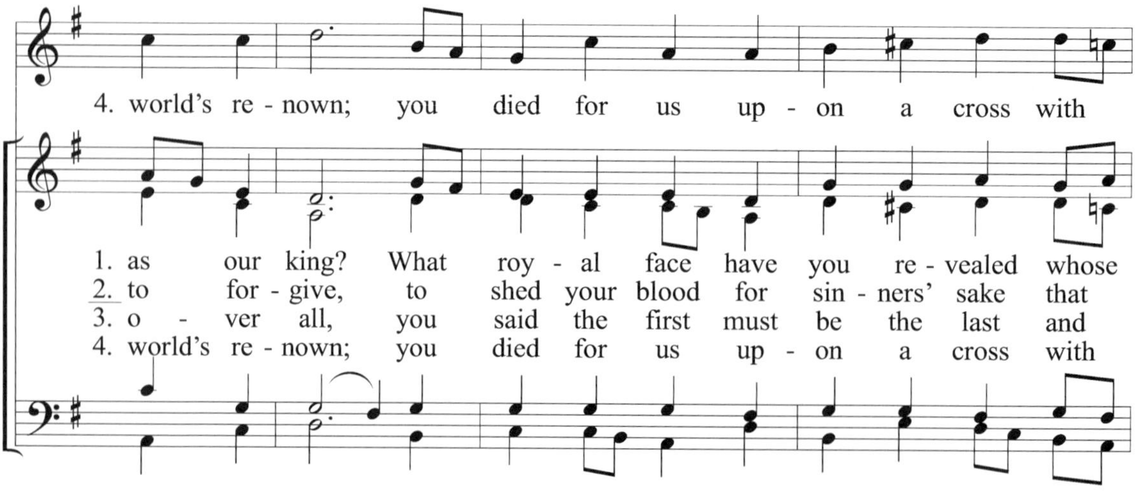

Text: Delores Dufner, OSB, b. 1939, © 2001, 2003, GIA Publications, Inc. All rights reserved. Used with permission.
Music: KINGSFOLD, CMD, English tune; harm. Ralph Vaughan Williams, 1872–1958.
Descant: Christine Manderfeld, OSB, b. 1938, © 2009, the Sisters of Saint Benedict, St. Joseph, MN. Administered by Liturgical Press, Collegeville, MN. All rights reserved.

254 O Come, Divine Messiah

O Come, Divine Messiah, pg. 2

Text: *Venez, divin Messie;* Abbé Simon-Joseph Pellegrin, 1663–1745; tr. S. Mary of St. Philip, 1877.
Music: VENEZ, DIVIN MESSIE, 7 8 7 6 with refrain; French Noël, 16th cent.;
harm. by Healey Willan, 1880–1968, © 1958, Ralph Jusko Publications, Inc., Willis Music Co. All rights reserved. Used with permission.

O Come, Little Children

O Come, Little Children, pg. 2

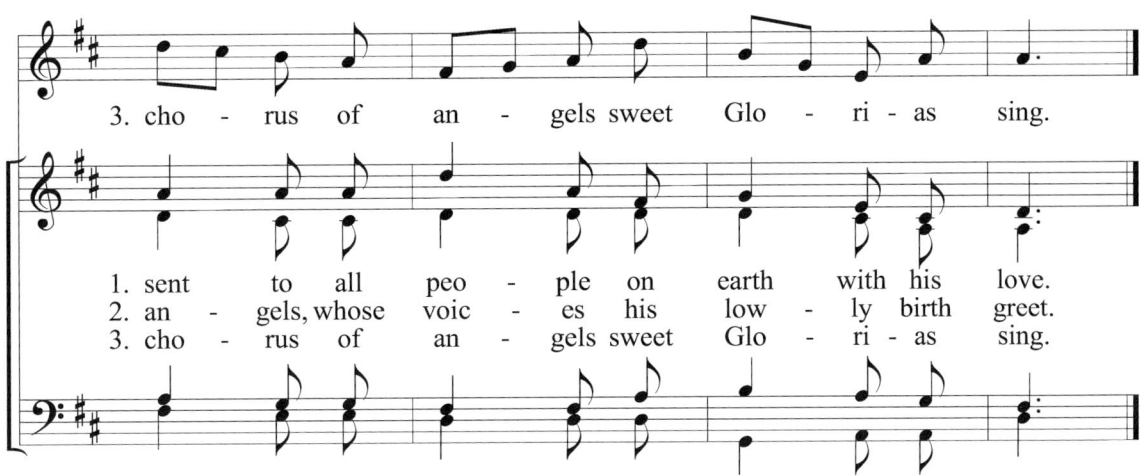

1. sent to all peo - ple on earth with his love.
2. an - gels, whose voic - es his low - ly birth greet.
3. cho - rus of an - gels sweet Glo - ri - as sing.

Text: Johann Christoph von Schmid, 1768–1854; tr. Melanie Schute, 1885–1922, alt.
Music: IHR KINDERLEIN, KOMMET, 11 11 11 11, Johann A. P. Schutz, 1747–1800; harm. by J. Alfred Schehl, 1882–1959, alt.
Arrangement: © 1958, Basilian Fathers, assigned to Ralph Jusko Publications, Inc., Willis Music Co. All rights reserved. Used with permission.
Descant: Christine Manderfeld, OSB, b. 1938, © 2009, the Sisters of Saint Benedict, St. Joseph, MN. Administered by Liturgical Press, Collegeville, MN. All rights reserved.

O Cross of Christ

Text: © Benedictine Nuns of Stanbrook Abbey. All rights reserved. Used with permission. Music: ST. FLAVIAN, CM, *John's Day Psalter,* 1562.
Descant: Christine Manderfeld, OSB, b. 1938, © 2009, the Sisters of Saint Benedict, St. Joseph, MN. Administered by Liturgical Press, Collegeville, MN. All rights reserved.

O Filii et Filiae / O Sons and Daughters

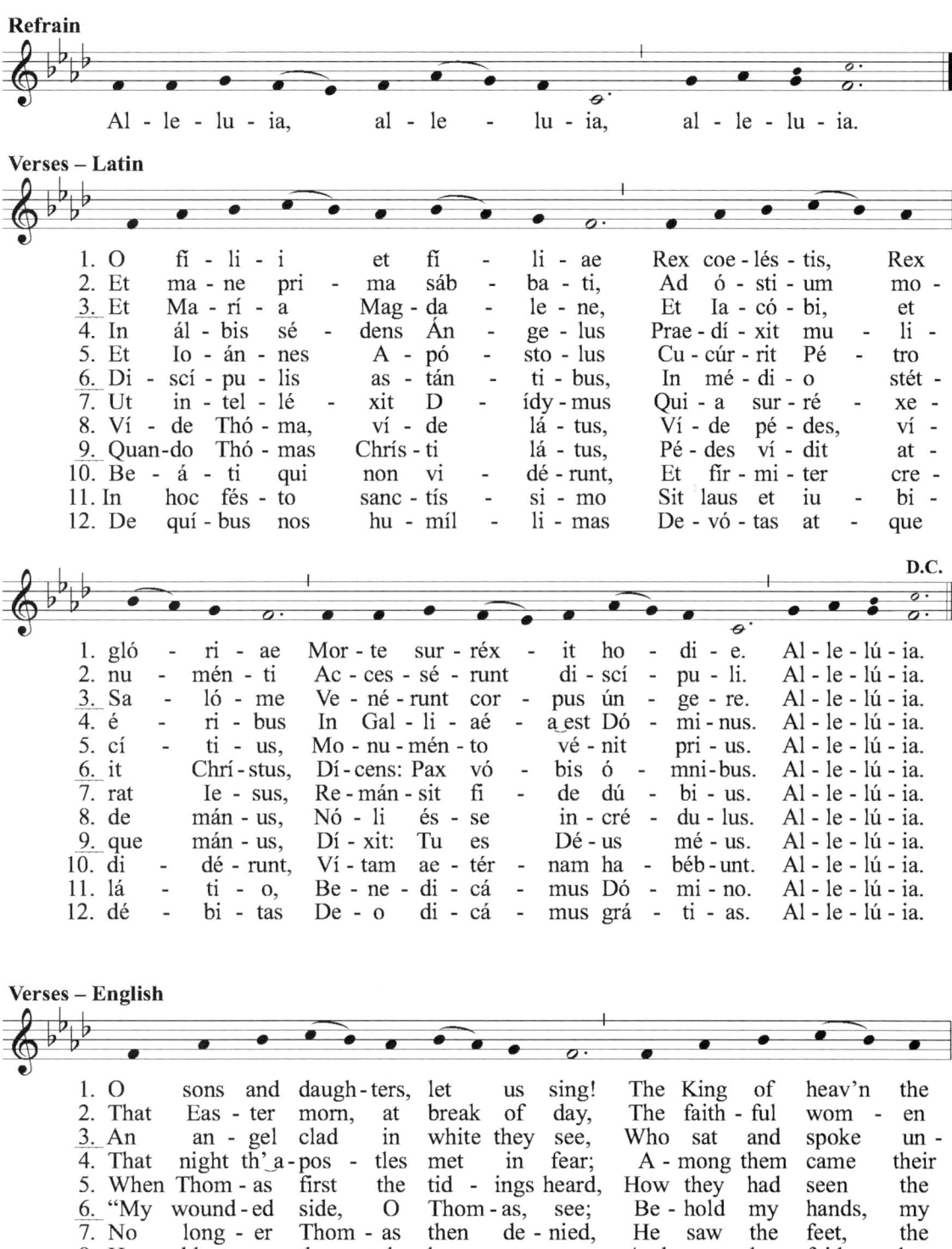

O Filii et Filiae / O Sons and Daughters, pg. 2

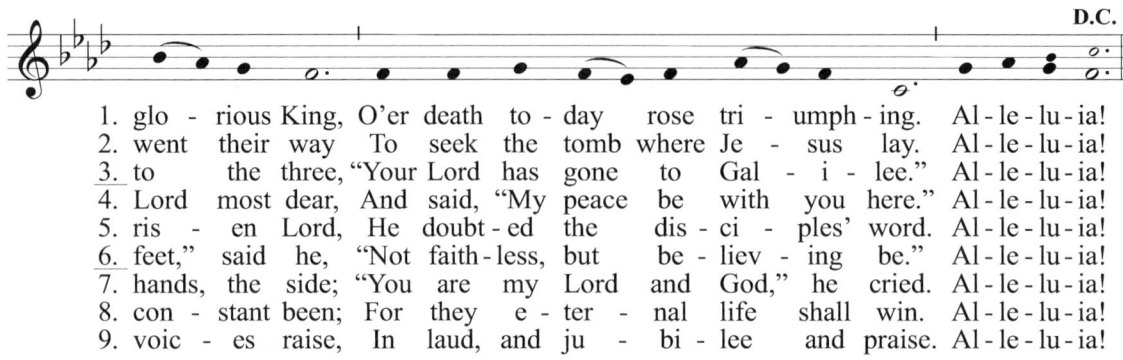

1. glo - rious King, O'er death to-day rose tri - umph-ing. Al-le-lu-ia!
2. went their way To seek the tomb where Je - sus lay. Al-le-lu-ia!
3. to the three, "Your Lord has gone to Gal - i - lee." Al-le-lu-ia!
4. Lord most dear, And said, "My peace be with you here." Al-le-lu-ia!
5. ris - en Lord, He doubt-ed the dis - ci - ples' word. Al-le-lu-ia!
6. feet," said he, "Not faith-less, but be - liev - ing be." Al-le-lu-ia!
7. hands, the side; "You are my Lord and God," he cried. Al-le-lu-ia!
8. con - stant been; For they e - ter - nal life shall win. Al-le-lu-ia!
9. voic - es raise, In laud, and ju - bi - lee and praise. Al-le-lu-ia!

Text: *O filii et filiae;* Jean Tisserand, d. 1494; tr. John Mason Neale, 1818–1866, alt. Music: O FILII ET FILIAE, 888 with refrain, Mode II.

258   O God, Almighty Father

Verses   *Descant (final verse):*

3. O God, the Ho - ly Spir - it, Who lives with - in our soul,

1. O God, al - might-y Fa - ther, Cre - a - tor of all things,
2. O Je - sus, Word in - car - nate, Re - deem - er most a - dored,
3. O God, the Ho - ly Spir - it, Who lives with - in our soul,

3. Send forth your light and lead us To our e - ter - nal goal.

1. The heav - ens stand in won - der, While earth your glo - ry sings.
2. All glo - ry, praise, and hon - or Be yours, O sov - 'reign Lord.
3. Send forth your light and lead us To our e - ter - nal goal.

O God, Almighty Father, pg. 2

Text: Anon.; tr. Irvin Udulutsch, OFM, Cap, b. 1920.
Music: GOTT VATER, SEI GEPRIESEN, 76 76 with refrain, *Limburg Gesangbuch,* 1838; harmonization by Mary Sylvestra, OSF.
Text and harmonization: © 1959, 1977, Order of Saint Benedict, Collegeville, MN. Administered by Liturgical Press, Collegeville, MN. All rights reserved.
Descant: James Chepponis, b. 1956, © 1980, GIA Publication, Inc. All rights reserved. Used with permission.

259   O God Beyond All Praising

Text: Michael Perry, 1942–1996, © 1982, Jubilate Hymns (admin. by Hope Publishing Co., Carol Stream, IL 60188). All rights reserved. Used with permission.
Music: THAXTED, 76 76 76 D, Gustav Holst, 1874–1934. Descant: Richard Proulx, © 1992, GIA Publications, Inc. All rights reserved. Used with permission.

O God, Our Help in Ages Past **260**

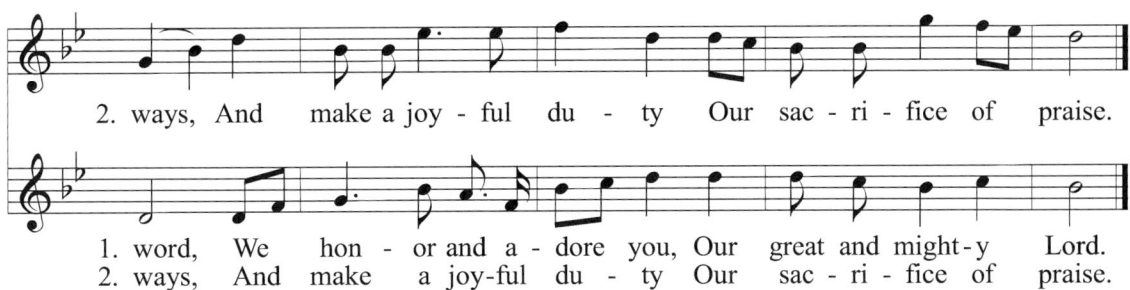

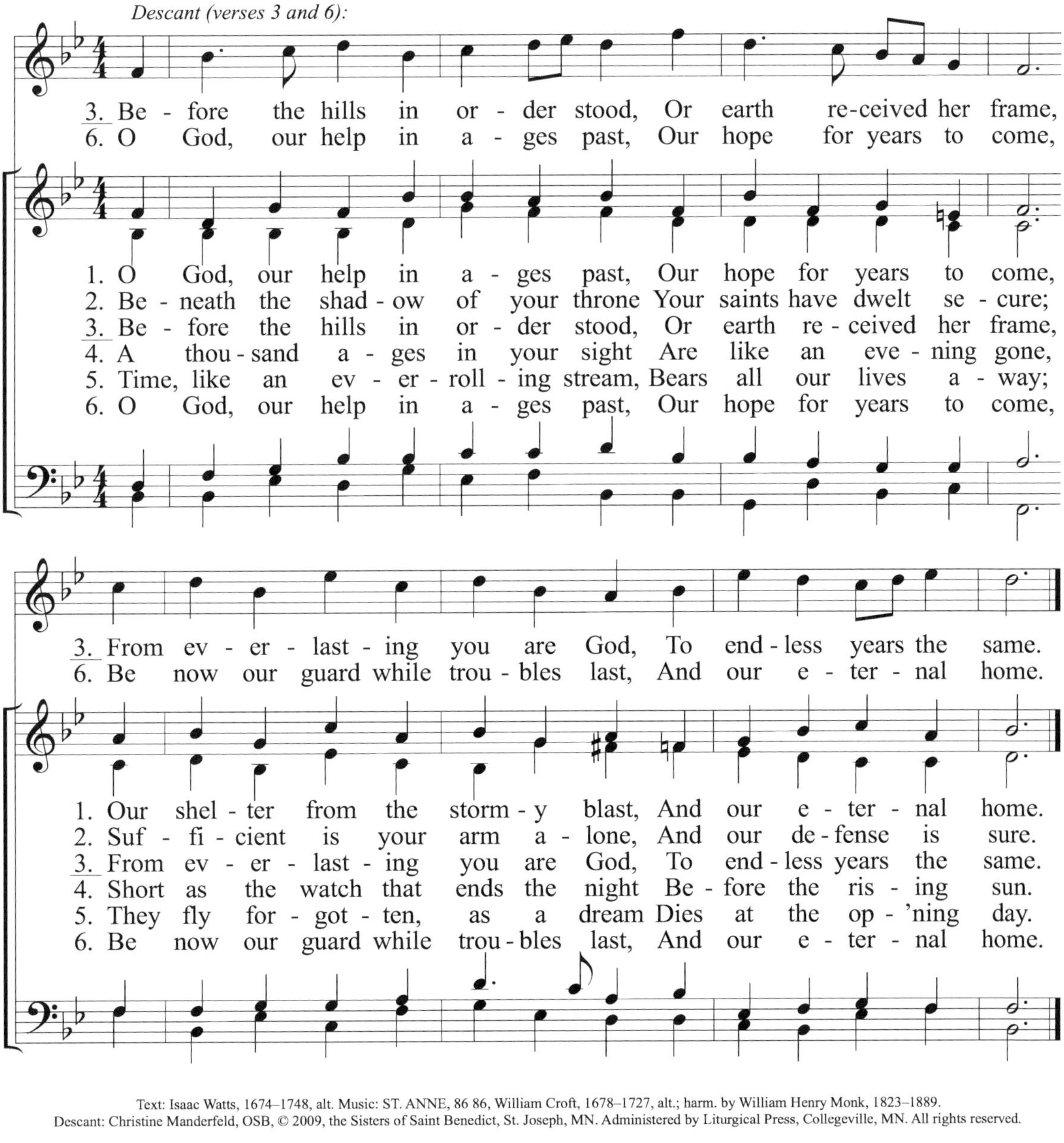

Text: Isaac Watts, 1674–1748, alt. Music: ST. ANNE, 86 86, William Croft, 1678–1727, alt.; harm. by William Henry Monk, 1823–1889.
Descant: Christine Manderfeld, OSB, © 2009, the Sisters of Saint Benedict, St. Joseph, MN. Administered by Liturgical Press, Collegeville, MN. All rights reserved.

O Holy Spirit, by Whose Breath, pg. 2

Text: *Veni, Creator Spiritus,* attr. to Rabanus Maurus, c. 776–856; tr. by John W. Grant, b. 1919, © John W. Grant. All rights reserved. Used with permission.
Music: LASST UNS ERFREUEN, LM 88 44 88 with alleluias, *Geistliche Kirchengesange,* Cologne, 1623.
Harmony: Christine Manderfeld, OSB, b. 1938, © 2009, the Sisters of Saint Benedict, St. Joseph, MN. Administered by Liturgical Press, Collegeville, MN. All rights reserved.
Descant: Eugene Martin Lindusky, 1924–2005, © Mary C. Lindusky. All rights reserved. Used with permission.

O King of Might and Splendor 263

1. O King of might and splendor, Creator most adored,
This sacrifice we render To thee as sov'reign Lord.
May these our gifts be pleasing Unto thy majesty.
Sinners from guilt releasing Who have offended thee.

2. Thy body thou hast given, Thy blood thou hast outpoured
That sin might be forgiven, O Jesus, loving Lord.
As now with love most tender Thy death we celebrate.
Our lives in self-surrender To thee we consecrate.

Text: Tr. A. Gregory Murray, OSB, 1905–1992, © Downside Abbey. All rights reserved. Used with permission.
Music: PASSION CHORALE, 76 76 D, Hans Leo Hassler, 1564–1612; harm. J. S. Bach, 1658–1750, adapt. Theophane Hytreck, OSF, 1915–1992.
Harmonization: © 1959, 1977, Order of Saint Benedict, Collegeville, MN. Administered by Liturgical Press, Collegeville, MN. All rights reserved.

264 O Little Town of Bethlehem

265 O Lord, Hear My Prayer

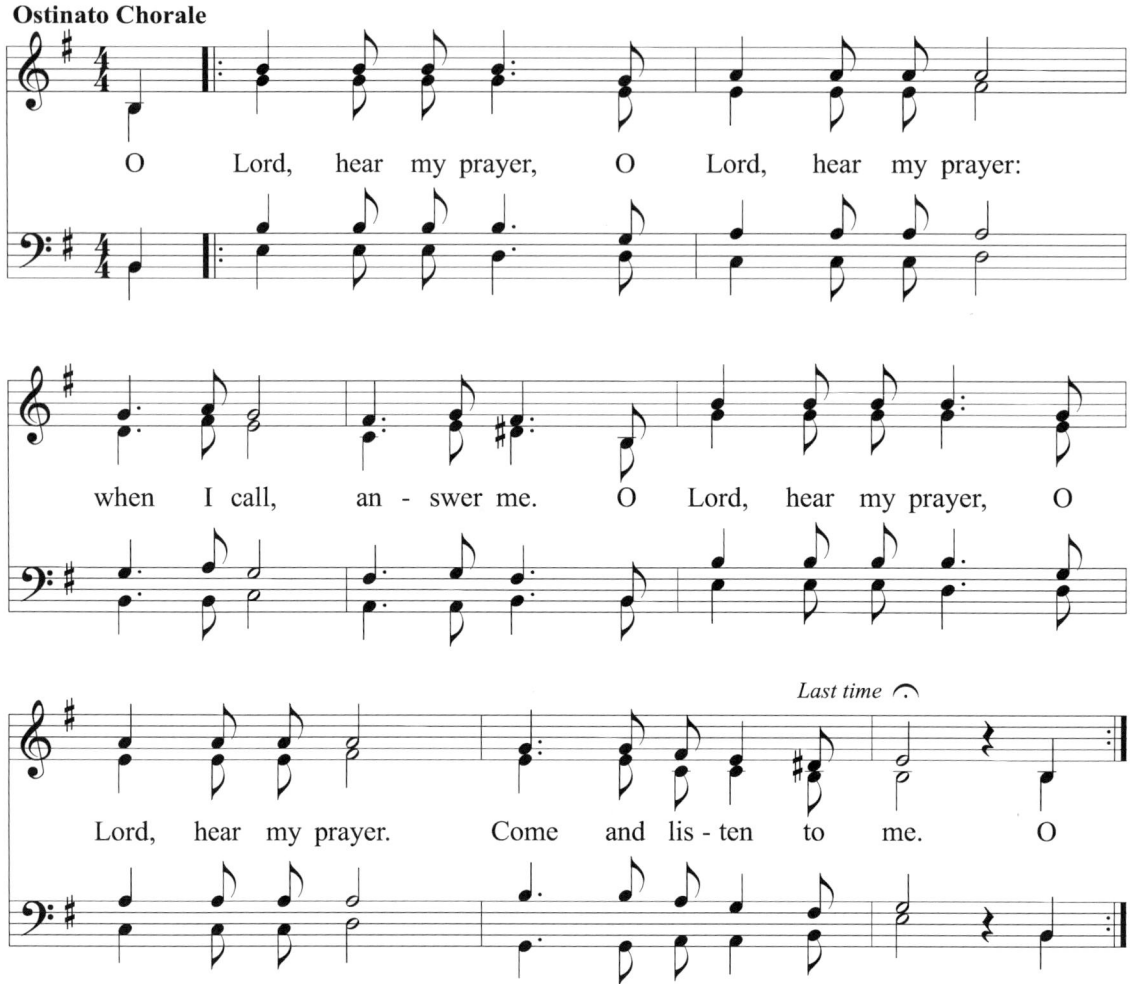

Text: Based on Psalm 102; adapt. by Taizé Community. Music: Jacques Berthier, 1923–1994.
Text and music: © 1982, Les Presses de Taizé, GIA Publications, Inc., North American agent. All rights reserved. Used with permission.

O Lord, I Am Not Worthy 266

1. O Lord, I am not worthy That thou should'st come to me,
   But speak the words of comfort, My spirit healed shall be.
2. O come, all you who labor In sorrow and in pain,
   Come, eat this Bread from heaven; Thy peace and strength regain.
3. O Jesus, we adore thee, Our Victim and our Priest,
   Whose precious Blood and Body Become our sacred feast.
4. O sacrament most holy, O sacrament divine!
   All praise and all thanksgiving Be ev-'ry moment thine.

Text: Vv. 1 & 4, anon.; vv. 2 & 3, Irvin Udulutsch, OFM, Cap, b. 1920, © 1959, 1977, Order of Saint Benedict, Collegeville, MN.
Administered by Liturgical Press, Collegeville, MN. All rights reserved.
Music: NON DIGNUS (CLARIBEL), 76 76, *Burns* traditional melody.

267 O Lord of Life

Text: Federick Lucian Hosmer, 1840–1929, alt. Music: GELOBT SEI GOTT, 888 with alleluias, Melchior Vulpius, 1560–1616.
Descant: Christine Manderfeld, OSB, b. 1938, © 2009, the Sisters of Saint Benedict, St. Joseph, MN. Administered by Liturgical Press, Collegeville, MN. All rights reserved.

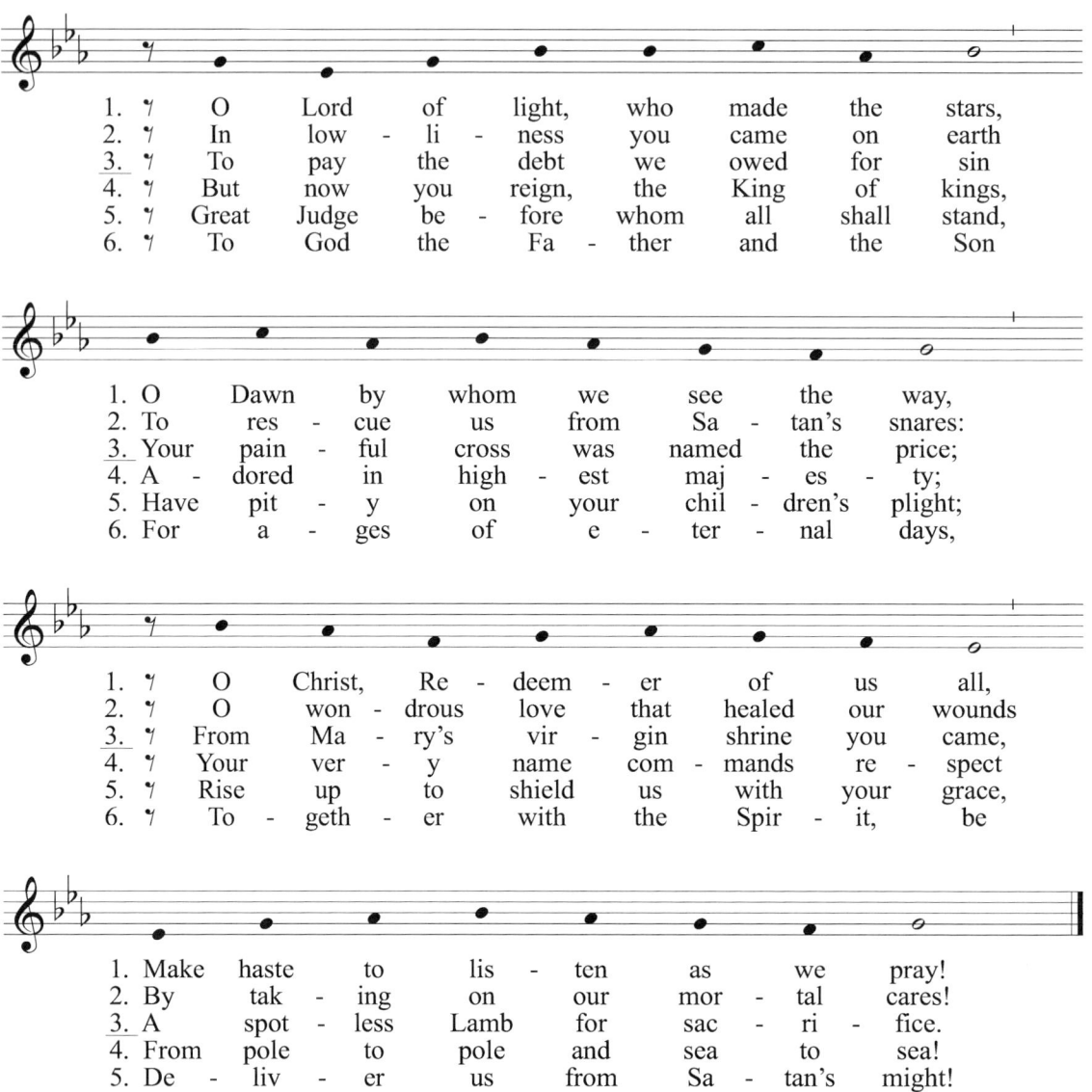

O Lowly Lamb of God Most High 269

1. O lowly Lamb of God most high, you clung not to divinity but laid aside your royal robes, embracing our humanity.
2. In all but sin like one of us, your body knew our ev'ry need. Lord, by your wounds we have been healed and by your death we have been freed.
3. A servant bowed by pain and scorn, you gave your life upon a tree. But from the tomb God raised you up and we now share your victory.
4. Let no one boast but in the cross, in Jesus Christ, the crucified, whose arms embrace the universe, whose love is faithful, deep and wide.

Text: Delores Dufner, OSB, b. 1939, © 1982, 2003, GIA Publications, Inc. All rights reserved. Used with permission.
Music: DEUS TUORUM MILITUM, *Grenoble Antiphoner*, 1753.
Descant: Christine Manderfeld, OSB, b. 1938, © 2009, the Sisters of Saint Benedict, St. Joseph, MN. Administered by Liturgical Press, Collegeville, MN. All rights reserved.

270 — O Mary, Our Mother

1. O Mary, our mother, to you do we come;
In all our afflictions, your love is our home.
Your heart is so gentle, so loving, so mild;
You will not reject any suppliant child.

2. O Mary, our mother, be gracious to all;
When burdened with sadness, to you do we call.
In sorrow, in darkness, O be at our side;
For you are our mother, our comfort and guide.

3. O Mary, our mother, so loving, so mild;
You love us as dearly as you loved your Child.
In life let us ever be faithful and true,
That death may but lead us to Jesus and you.

Text: *Maria zu lieben;* tr. Desmond A. Schmal, SJ, 1897–1958, alt. Music: PADERBORN (MARIA ZU LIEBEN), 11 11 11 11, *Gesangbuch,* 1765.

O Merciful Redeemer 271

O Merciful Redeemer, pg. 2

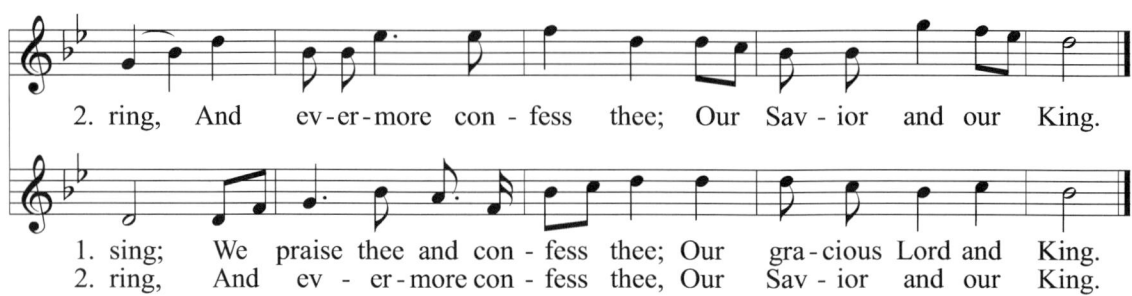

2. ring, And ev-er-more con-fess thee; Our Sav-ior and our King.

1. sing; We praise thee and con-fess thee; Our gra-cious Lord and King.
2. ring, And ev-er-more con-fess thee, Our Sav-ior and our King.

Text: Frances R. Havergal, 1836–1879, alt. Music: THAXTED, 76 76 76 D, Gustav Holst, 1874–1934.
Descant: Richard Proulx, © 1992, GIA Publications, Inc. All rights reserved. Used with permission.

272   O Merciful Redeemer, Hear

1. O mer - ci - ful Re - deem - er, hear;
2. Our hearts are o - pen, Lord, to thee
3. Our sins are great, our wills are weak,
4. O, grant most ho - ly Trin - i - ty,

1. In pit - y now in - cline your ear;
2. And know - ing our in - iq - ui - ty,
3. But your for - give - ness, Lord, we seek,
4. In un - di - vid - ed u - ni - ty,

1. Ac - cept the con - trite pray'rs we raise
2. Pour out on us your heal - ing grace,
3. And for the glo - ry of your name.
4. That these our ho - ly Lent - en days

1. In this our fast of for - ty days.
2. Re - store to life a fall - en race.
3. Do you our wound - ed souls re - claim.
4. In - crease our mer - it and your praise.

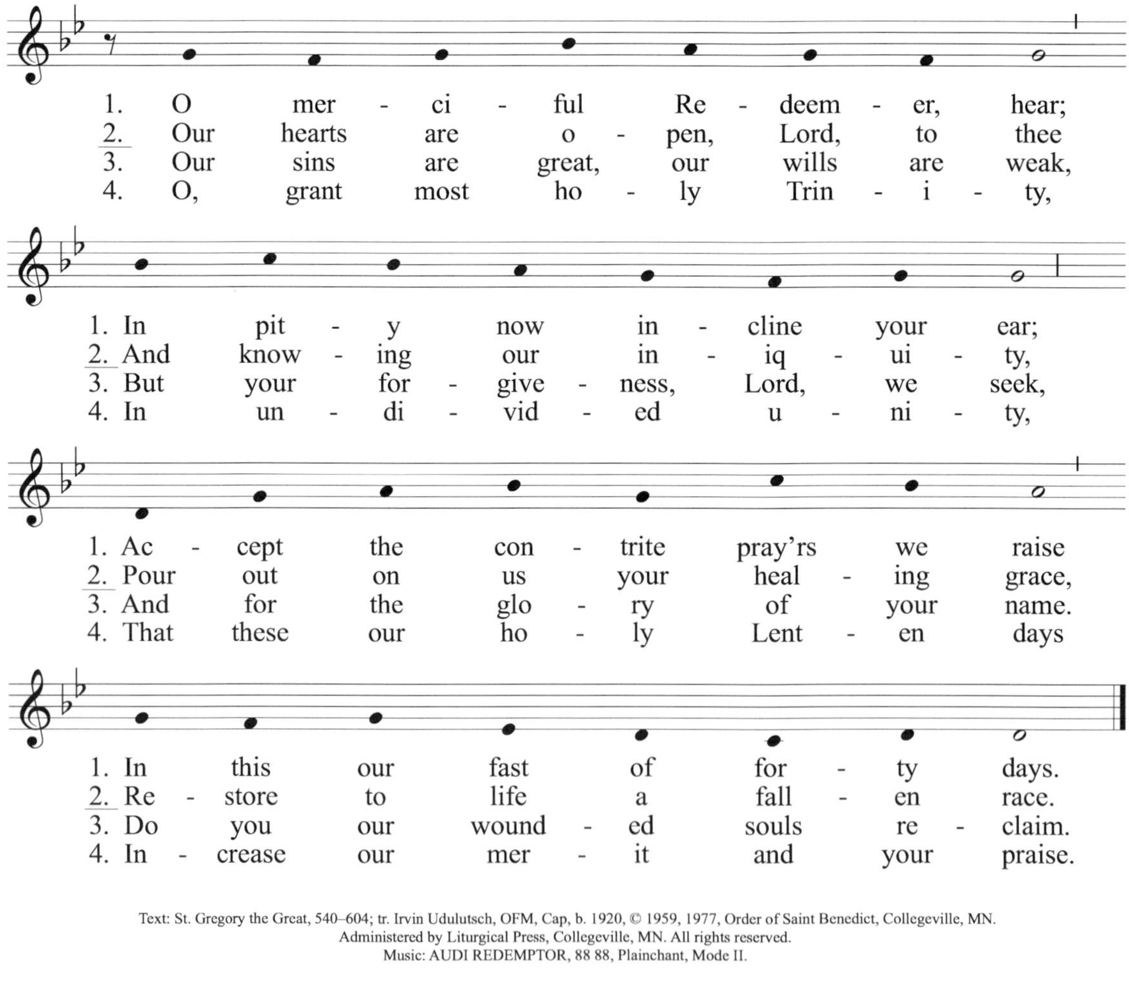

Text: St. Gregory the Great, 540–604; tr. Irvin Udulutsch, OFM, Cap, b. 1920, © 1959, 1977, Order of Saint Benedict, Collegeville, MN.
Administered by Liturgical Press, Collegeville, MN. All rights reserved.
Music: AUDI REDEMPTOR, 88 88, Plainchant, Mode II.

O Radiant Light

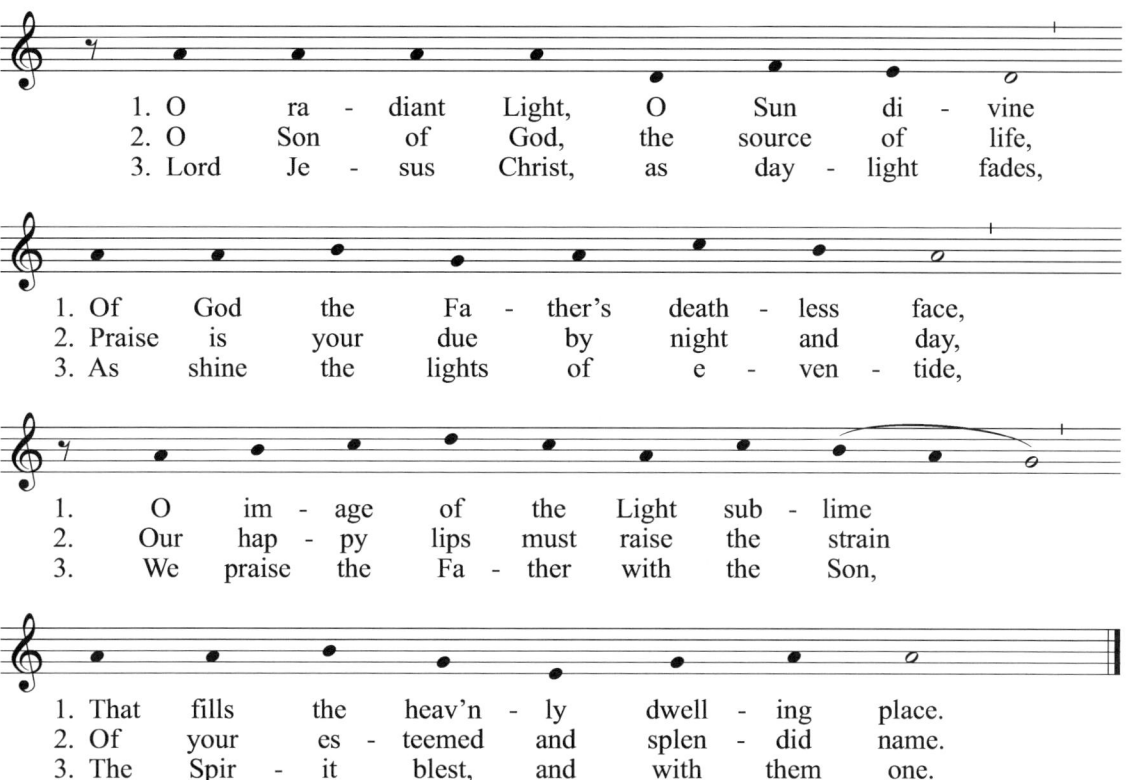

1. O radiant Light, O Sun divine
Of God the Father's deathless face,
O image of the Light sublime
That fills the heav'nly dwelling place.

2. O Son of God, the source of life,
Praise is your due by night and day,
Our happy lips must raise the strain
Of your esteemed and splendid name.

3. Lord Jesus Christ, as daylight fades,
As shine the lights of eventide,
We praise the Father with the Son,
The Spirit blest, and with them one.

Text: *Phos Hilaron,* Greek, c. 200; tr. by William George Storey, b. 1923, © William G. Storey. All rights reserved. Used with permission.
Music: JESU DULCIS MEMORIA, Plainchant, Mode I.

274   O Sacred Head Surrounded

1. O Sacred Head surrounded By crown of piercing thorn!
O bleeding Head, so wounded, Reviled and put to scorn!
The pow'r of death comes o'er you, The glow of life decays,
Yet angel hosts adore you, And tremble as they gaze.

2. I see your strength and vigor All fading in the strife,
And death with cruel rigor, Bereaving you of life;
O agony and dying! O love to sinners free!
Jesus, all grace supplying, O turn your face on me.

3. In this, your bitter passion, Good Shepherd, think of me
With your most sweet compassion, Unworthy though I be:
Beneath your cross abiding For ever would I rest,
In your dear love confiding, And with your presence blest.

Text: *Salve caput cruentatum;* ascr. to Bernard of Clairvaux, 1091–1153; tr. Henry Baker, 1821–1877.
Music: PASSION CHORALE, 76 76 D, Hans Leo Hassler, 1564–1612; harm. J. S. Bach, 1658–1750; adapt. Theophane Hytrek, OSF, 1915–1992.
Harmonization: © 1959, 1977, Order of Saint Benedict, Collegeville, MN. Administered by Liturgical Press, Collegeville, MN. All rights reserved.

O Salutaris / O Saving Victim

1. O salutáris hóstia, Quae caeli pandis óstium: Bella premunt hostília, Da robur fer auxílium.
2. Uni trinóque Dómino Sit sempitérna glória: Qui vitam sine término Nobis donet in pátria.

1. O Saving Victim, op'ning wide, The gate of heav'n to us below! Our foes press on from ev'ry side: Your aid supply, your strength bestow.
2. To your great name be endless praise, Immortal Godhead, One in Three; Grant us for endless length of days, In our true native land to be.

Text: St. Thomas Aquinas, 1227–1274; tr. Edward Caswall, 1814–1878. Music: DUGUET, 88 88, Abbé Duguet, c. 1767.

276 O Sanctissima / O Most Holy One

Text: Latin hymn, 18th cent.; tr. Charles W. Leland, CSB, © 1958, Basilian Fathers,
assigned 1958 to Ralph Jusko Publications, Inc., Willis Music Co. All rights reserved. Used with permission.
Music: SICILIAN MARINER'S, 10 7 10 7, traditional Sicilian melody, 18th cent.; acc. by Healey William, 1880–1968.

O Sun of Justice

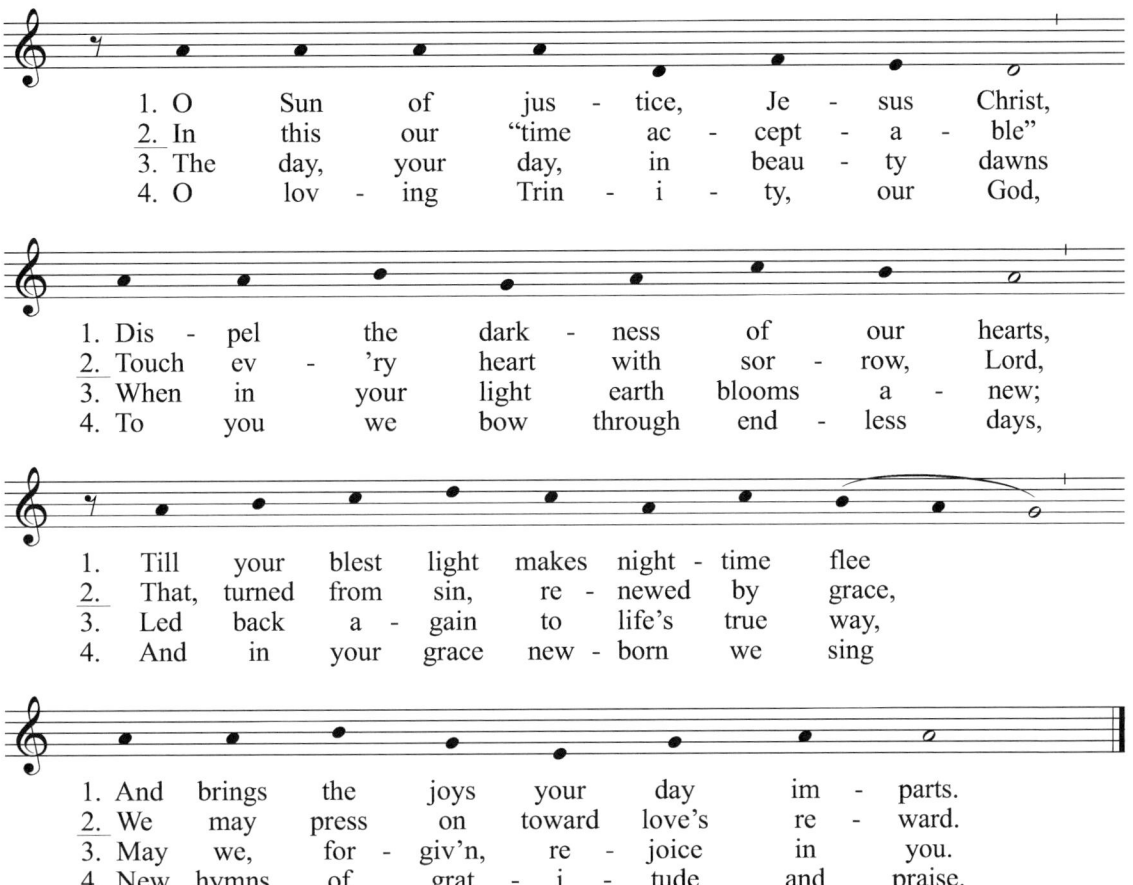

1. O Sun of justice, Jesus Christ,
Dispel the darkness of our hearts,
Till your blest light makes night-time flee
And brings the joys your day imparts.

2. In this our "time acceptable"
Touch ev'ry heart with sorrow, Lord,
That, turned from sin, renewed by grace,
We may press on toward love's reward.

3. The day, your day, in beauty dawns,
When in your light earth blooms anew;
Led back again to life's true way,
May we, forgiv'n, rejoice in you.

4. O loving Trinity, our God,
To you we bow through endless days,
And in your grace new-born we sing
New hymns of gratitude and praise.

Text: *Jam Christe sol justitiae*; Latin, 6th cent.; tr. Peter J. Scagnelli, b. 1949, © 1973, Peter J. Scagnelli. All rights reserved. Used with permission.
Music: JESU DULCIS MEMORIA, LM, Mode I.

278 — Of the Father's Love Begotten

1. Of the Father's love begotten, Ere the worlds began to be, He is Alpha and Omega, He the source the ending he, Of the things that are, that have been, And that future years shall see, Evermore and evermore.

2. Blessed was the day forever When the Virgin full of grace, By the Holy Ghost conceiving, Bore the Savior of our race, And the child, the world's Redeemer, First revealed his sacred face, Evermore and evermore.

3. This is he whom seers in old time Chanted of with one accord, Whom the voices of the prophets Promised in their faithful word; Now he shines, the long expected; Let creation praise the Lord, Evermore and evermore.

4. O ye heights of heav'n, adore him; Angel hosts, his praises sing; All dominions, bow before him, And extol our God and King; Let no tongue on earth be silent, Ev'ry voice in concert ring, Evermore and evermore.

5. Glory be to God the Father, Glory be to God the Son, Glory to the Holy Spirit, Persons three, yet Godhead One. Glory be from all creation While eternal ages run, Evermore and evermore. Amen.

Text: Marcus Aurelius Clemens Prudentius, 348–413, tr. John Mason Neale, 1818–1866, et al. Music: DIVINUM MYSTERIUM, 87 87 87 7; 12th c., Mode V.

On Emmaus' Journey 280

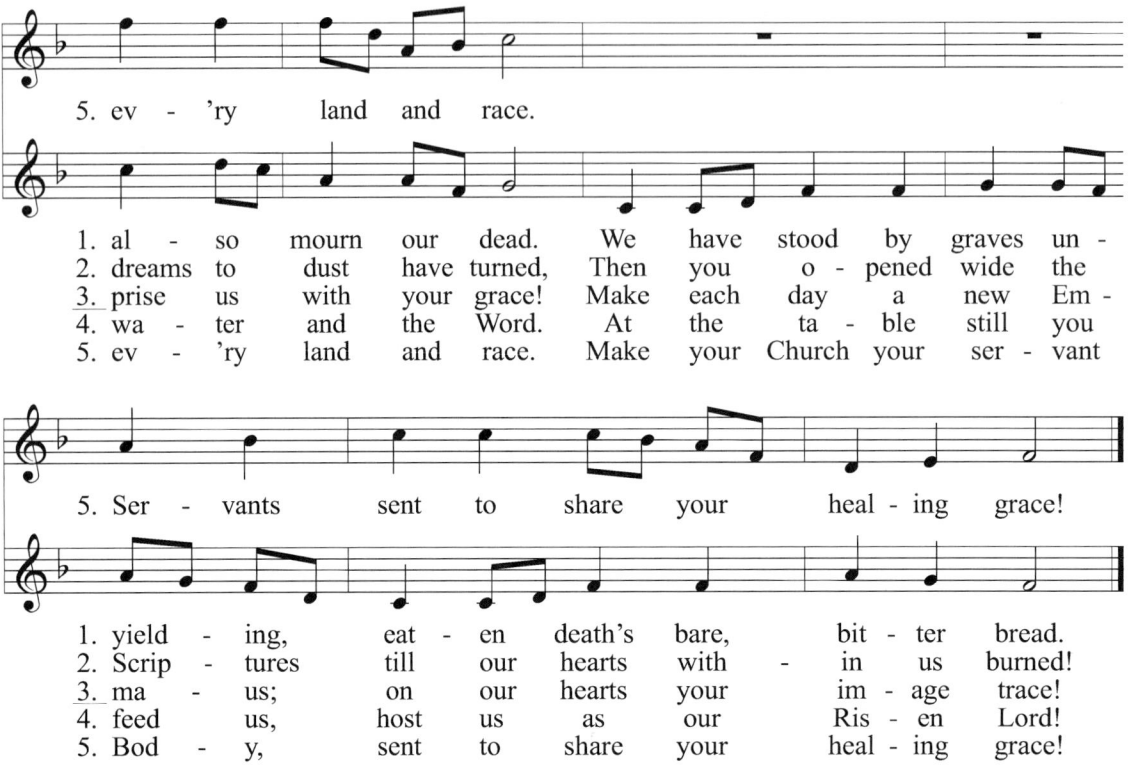

282 On Our Journey to the Kingdom

Text: Bernhardt Severin Ingemann, 1789–1862; tr. Sabine Baring-Gould, 1834–1924, alt.
Music: 87 87 D, Gerard Wojchowski, OSB, 1925–1997, © 1977, Order of Saint Benedict, Collegeville, MN.
Descant: Christine Manderfeld, OSB, b. 1938, © 2009, the Sisters of Saint Benedict, St. Joseph, MN.
Music and descant administered by Liturgical Press, Collegeville, MN. All rights reserved.

283 — On This Day, O Beautiful Mother

On This Day, O Beautiful Mother, pg. 2

Text: Anonymous. Music: BEAUTIFUL MOTHER, 77 77 with refrain, Louis Lambillotte, 1796–1855.

On This Day, the First of Days 285

1. On this day, the first of days, God the Father's name we praise; Who, creation's Lord and spring, Did the world from darkness bring.
2. On this day the eternal Son Over death his triumph won; On this day the Spirit came With his gifts of living flame.
3. Father, who did fashion all God-like by your loving call, Fill us with that love divine And our wills to yours incline.
4. Word made flesh, all hail to thee, Who from sin has set us free; And in you we die and rise Unto God in sacrifice.
5. Holy Spirit, you impart Gifts of love to ev'ry heart; Give us light and grace, we pray; Fill our hearts this holy day.
6. God the blessed Three-in-One, May your holy will be done; In your word our souls are blest, As with you this day we rest.

Text: Carcassonne Breviary, 1745; tr. Henry W. Baker, 1821–1877, alt.
Music: LÜBECK, 77 77, Johann A. Freylinghausen, 1670–1739; adapt. and harm. William Henry Havergal, 1793–1870, and William Henry Monk, 1823–1889.
Descant: Christine Manderfeld, OSB, b. 1938, © 2009, the Sisters of Saint Benedict, St. Joseph, MN. Administered by Liturgical Press, Collegeville, MN. All rights reserved.

286   Once in Royal David's City

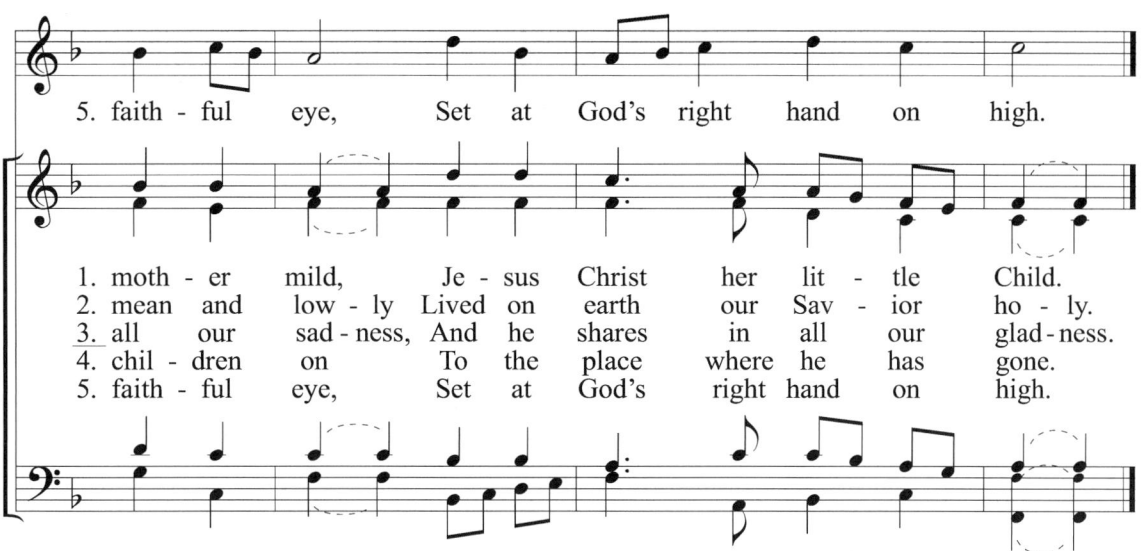

Text: Cecil Frances Alexander, 1818–1895, alt. Music: IRBY, 87 87 77, Henry John Gauntlett, 1805–1876.
Descant: Christine Manderfeld, OSB, © 2009, the Sisters of Saint Benedict, St. Joseph, MN. Administered by Liturgical Press, Collegeville, MN. All rights reserved.

One in Christ, We Meet Together 288

290 Pange Lingua / Hail Our Savior's Glorious Body

1. Pan - ge lín - gua glo - ri - ó - si,
2. No - bis da - tus, no - bis na - tus
3. In su - pré - mae no - cte coe - nae,
4. Ver - bum ca - ro, pa - nem ve - rum
5. Tan - tum er - go Sa - cra - mén - tum
6. Ge - ni - tó - ri, Ge - ni - tó - que

1. Hail our Sav - ior's glo - rious Bod - y,
2. To the Vir - gin, for our heal - ing,
3. On that pas - chal eve - ning see him
4. By his word the Word al - might - y
5. Come, a - dore this won - drous pres - ence;
6. Glo - ry be to God the Fa - ther,

1. Cór - po - ris my - sté - ri - um,
2. Ex in - tá - cta Vír - gi - ne,
3. Re - cúm - bens cum frá - tri - bus,
4. Ver - bo car - nem éf - fi - cit:
5. Ve - ne - ré - mur cér - nu - i:
6. Laus et ju - bi - lá - ti - o,

1. Which his Vir - gin Moth - er bore;
2. His own Son the Fa - ther sends;
3. With the cho - sen twelve re - cline,
4. Makes of bread his flesh in - deed;
5. Bow to Christ, the source of grace!
6. Praise to his co - e - qual Son,

1. San - gui - nís - que pre - ti - ó - si,
2. Et in mun - do con - ver - sá - tus,
3. Ob - ser - vá - ta le - ge ple - ne
4. Fít - que san - guis Chri - sti me - rum,
5. Et an - tí - quum do - cu - mén - tum
6. Sa - lus, ho - nor, vir - tus quo - que

1. Hail the Blood which, shed for sin - ners,
2. From the Fa - ther's love pro - ceed - ing
3. To the old law still o - be - dient
4. Wine be - comes his ver - y life - blood;
5. Here is kept the an - cient prom - ise
6. Ad - o - ra - tion to the Spir - it,

1. Quem in mundi pré - ti - um
2. Spar - so vér - bi sé - mi - ne,
3. Ci - bis in le - gá - li - bus,
4. Et si sen - sus dé - fi - cit,
5. No - vo ce - dat rí - tu - i:
6. Sit et be - ne - dí - cti - o:

1. Did a bro - ken world re - store;
2. Sow - er, seed and word de - scends;
3. In its feast of love di - vine;
4. Faith God's liv - ing Word must heed!
5. Of God's earth - ly dwell - ing place!
6. Bond of love, in God - head one!

1. Fru - ctus ven - tris ge - ne - ró - si
2. Su - i, mo - ras in - co - lá - tus
3. Ci - bum tur - bae du - o - dé - nae
4. Ad fir - mán - dum cor sin - cé - rum
5. Prae - stet fi - des sup - ple - mén - tum
6. Pro - ce - dén - ti ab u - tró - que

1. Hail the sac - ra - ment most ho - ly,
2. Won - drous life of Word in - car - nate
3. Love di - vine, the new law giv - ing,
4. Faith a - lone may safe - ly guide us
5. Sight is blind be - fore God's glo - ry,
6. Blest be God by all cre - a - tion

1. Rex ef - fú - dit gén - ti - um.
2. Mi - ro clau - sit ór - di - ne.
3. Se dat su - is má - ni - bus.
4. So - la fi - des súf - fi - cit.
5. Sén - su - um de - fé - ctu - i.
6. Com - par sit lau - dá - ti - o. A - men.

1. Flesh and Blood of Christ a - dore!
2. With his great - est won - der ends.
3. Gives him - self as bread and wine.
4. Where the sens - es can - not lead!
5. Faith a - lone may see his face!
6. Joy - ous - ly while a - ges run! A - men.

Text: *Pange lingua,* Thomas Aquinas, 1227–1274; tr. James Quinn, SJ, b. 1919,
© 1969, James Quinn, SJ, Selah Publishing Co., North American Agent. All rights reserved. Used with permission.
Music: PANGE LINGUA GLORIOSI, 87 87 87, Plainchant, Mode III.

291 Panis Angelicus / Jesus, Our Living Bread

Panis Angelicus / Jesus, Our Living Bread, pg. 2

Je - sus Christ, gift of joy and peace. A - men.

1. Pau - per, ser - vus et hú - mi - lis.
2. Ad lu - cem quám in há - bi - tas. A - men.
1. In peace, joy, love, and grat - i - tude.
2. Grant us rest, there, be - fore your sight. A - men.

Text: Saint Thomas Aquinas, OP, ca. 1225–1274; tr. by Jerome Siwek, © 1986, World Library Publications, 3708 River Road, Franklin Park, IL 60131. www.wlpmusic.com All rights reserved. Used with permission. Music: Louis Lambillotte, SJ, 1796–1855.
Descant: Christine Manderfeld, OSB, b. 1938, © 2009, the Sisters of Saint Benedict, St. Joseph, MN. Administered by Liturgical Press, Collegeville, MN. All rights reserved.

Parce Domine 292

Refrain

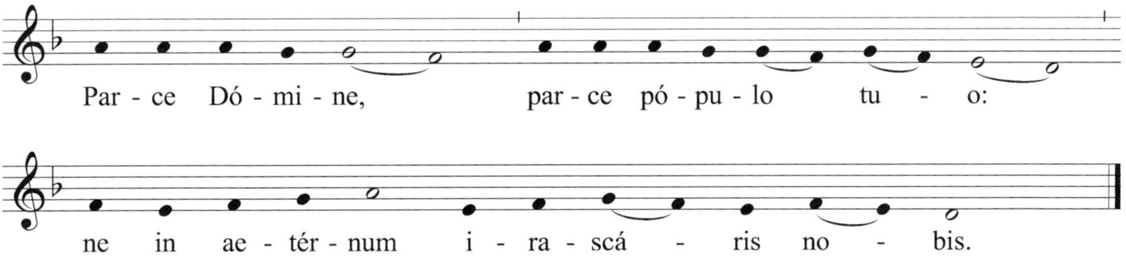

Par - ce Dó - mi - ne, par - ce pó - pu - lo tu - o:
ne in ae - tér - num i - ra - scá - ris no - bis.

Verses

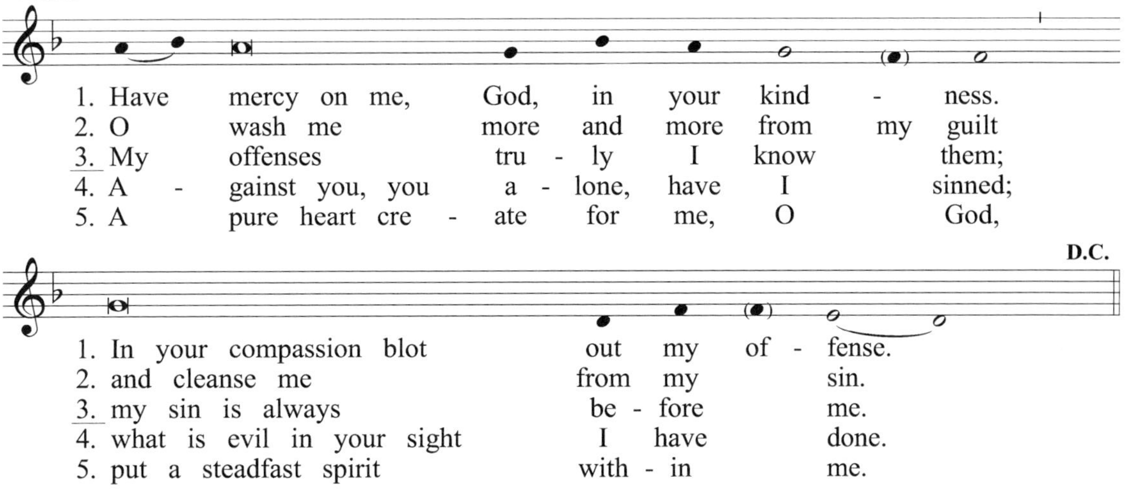

1. Have mercy on me, God, in your kind - ness.
2. O wash me more and more from my guilt
3. My offenses tru - ly I know them;
4. A - gainst you, you a - lone, have I sinned;
5. A pure heart cre - ate for me, O God,

D.C.

1. In your compassion blot out my of - fense.
2. and cleanse me from my sin.
3. my sin is always be - fore me.
4. what is evil in your sight I have done.
5. put a steadfast spirit with - in me.

Text: Joel 2:17, Psalm 51:3-6, 12; tr. The Grail, © 1963, The Grail, GIA Publications, Inc., North American agent.
All rights reserved. Used with permission. Music: PARCE DOMINE, Irregular; Mode I with Tonus Peregrinus.

293 People, Look East

People, Look East, pg. 2

Text: Eleanor Farjeon, 1881–1965, © 1957, Eleanor Farjeon, assigned to Harold Ober Associates, Inc. All rights reserved. Used with permission.
Music: BESANCON CAROL, 87 98 87, French carol; arr. by John Stainer, 1840–1901.
Descant: John Ferguson, © 1992, GIA Publications, Inc. All rights reserved. Used with permission.

294 Praise and Thanksgiving

Text: Albert F. Bayly, 1901–1984, © Oxford University Press. All rights reserved. Used with permission.
Music: BUNESSAN, 5 5 5 4 D; traditional Gaelic melody. Descant: Donald Busarow, © 1992, GIA Publications, Inc. All rights reserved. Used with permission.

Praise, My Soul, the King of Heaven
295

Praise, My Soul, the King of Heaven, pg. 2

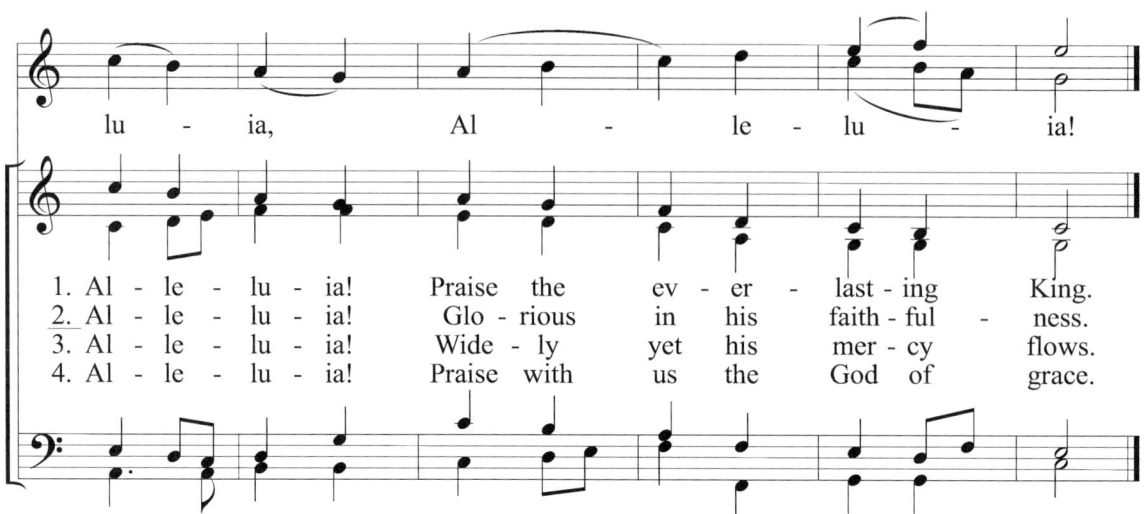

lu - ia, Al - le - lu - ia!

1. Al - le - lu - ia! Praise the ev - er - last - ing King.
2. Al - le - lu - ia! Glo - rious in his faith - ful - ness.
3. Al - le - lu - ia! Wide - ly yet his mer - cy flows.
4. Al - le - lu - ia! Praise with us the God of grace.

Text: Henry F. Lyte, 1793–1847, alt. Music: LAUDA ANIMA, 87 87 87, John Goss, 1800–1880.
Descant: Christine Manderfeld, OSB, b. 1938, © 2009, the Sisters of Saint Benedict, St. Joseph, MN. Administered by Liturgical Press, Collegeville, MN. All rights reserved.

296 Praise the Lord! Ye Heavens, Adore Him

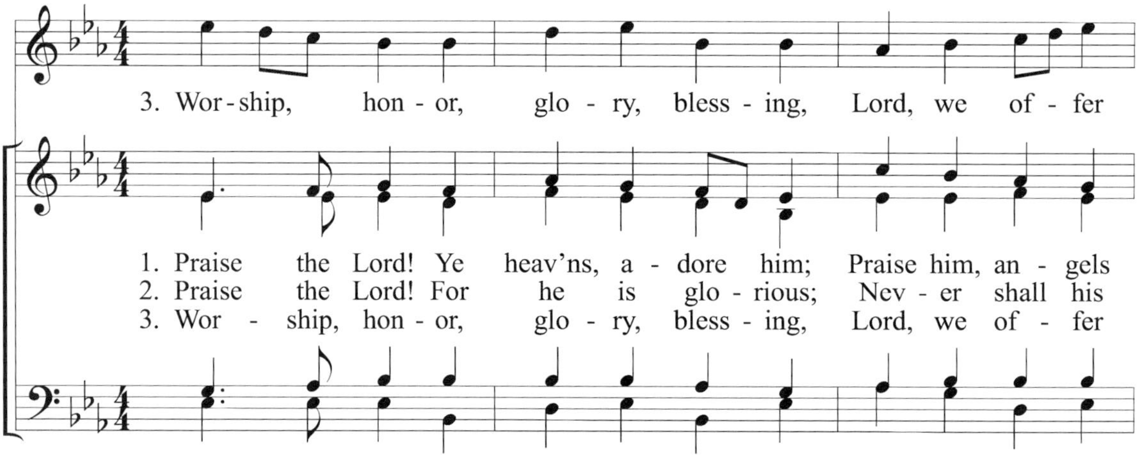

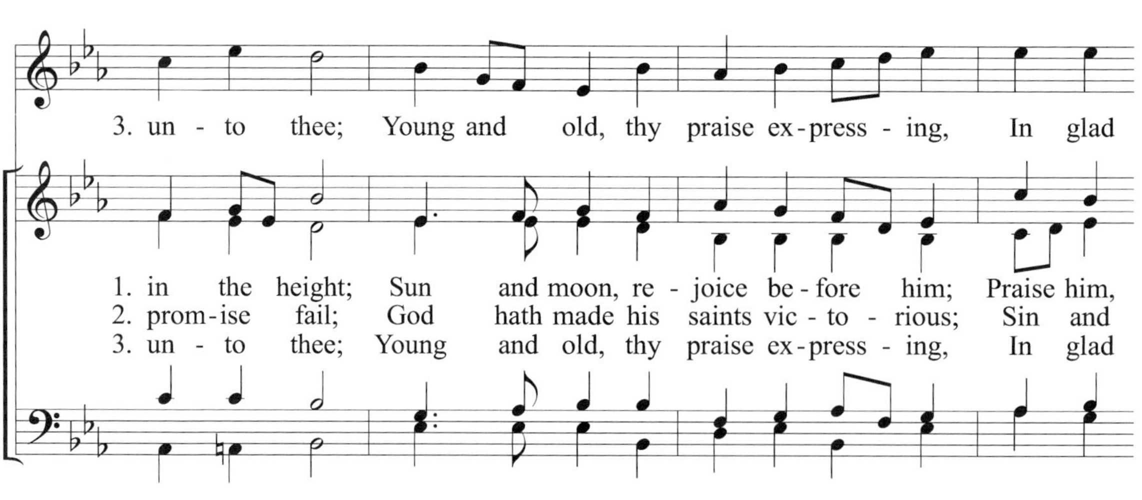

3. Wor - ship, hon - or, glo - ry, bless - ing, Lord, we of - fer

1. Praise the Lord! Ye heav'ns, a - dore him; Praise him, an - gels
2. Praise the Lord! For he is glo - rious; Nev - er shall his
3. Wor - ship, hon - or, glo - ry, bless - ing, Lord, we of - fer

3. un - to thee; Young and old, thy praise ex - press - ing, In glad

1. in the height; Sun and moon, re - joice be - fore him; Praise him,
2. prom - ise fail; God hath made his saints vic - to - rious; Sin and
3. un - to thee; Young and old, thy praise ex - press - ing, In glad

Praise the Lord! Ye Heavens, Adore Him, pg. 2

Text: From the Foundling Hospital collection, 1796, Thomas Coram, vv. 1 & 2; Edward Osler, 1798–1863, v. 3. Music: AUSTRIA, 87 87 D, Franz Josef Haydn, 1732–1809.
Descant: Christine Manderfeld, OSB, b. 1938, © 2009, the Sisters of Saint Benedict, St. Joseph, MN. Administered by Liturgical Press, Collegeville, MN. All rights reserved.

297   Praise to Our God, Creation's Lord

Text: Michael Kwatera, OSB, © 1991, Order of Saint Benedict, Collegeville, MN. Administered by Liturgical Press, Collegeville, MN. All rights reserved.
Music: OLD HUNDREDTH, LM, Louis Bourgeois, c. 1510–1561.
Descant: Christine Manderfeld, OSB, b. 1938, © 2009, the Sisters of Saint Benedict, St. Joseph, MN. Administered by Liturgical Press, Collegeville, MN. All rights reserved.

Praise to the Holiest in the Height 298

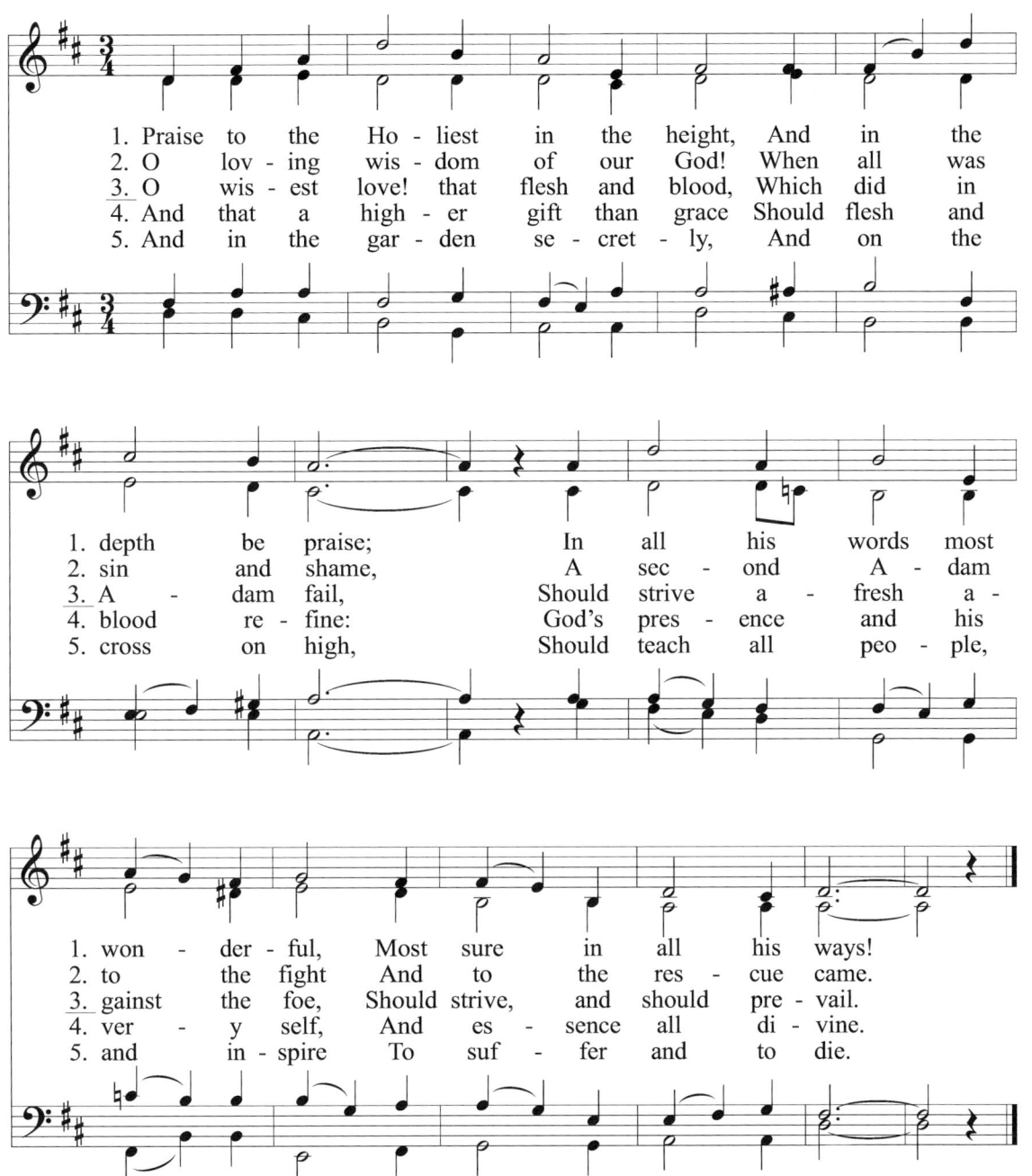

1. Praise to the Holiest in the height, And in the depth be praise; In all his words most wonderful, Most sure in all his ways!
2. O loving wisdom of our God! When all was sin and shame, A second Adam to the fight And to the rescue came.
3. O wisest love! that flesh and blood, Which did in Adam fail, Should strive afresh against the foe, Should strive, and should prevail.
4. And that a higher gift than grace Should flesh and blood refine: God's presence and his very self, And essence all divine.
5. And in the garden secretly, And on the cross on high, Should teach all people, and inspire To suffer and to die.

Text: John Henry Newman, 1801–1890, alt. Music: NEWMAN, 86 86, Richard Runciman Terry, 1865–1938.

299 Praise to the Lord, the Almighty

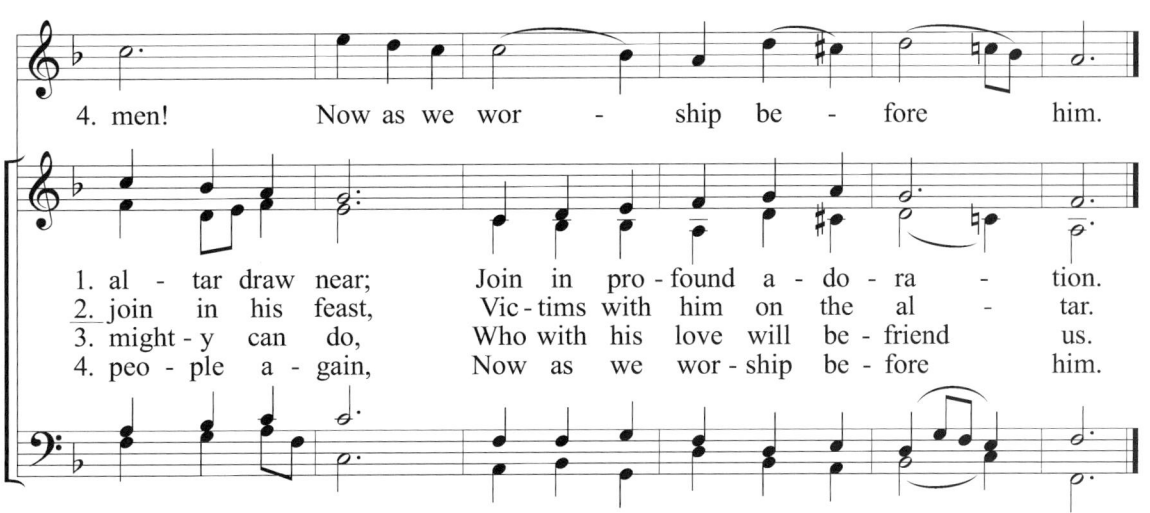

Text: Joachim Neander, 1650–1680; tr. Catherine Winkworth, 1827–1878, et al. Music: LOBE DEN HERREN, 14 14 4 7 8, *Erneuerten Gesangbuch*, 1665.
Descant: Hal Hopson, © 1979, GIA Publications, Inc. All rights reserved. Used with permission.

300 Prayer of Peace

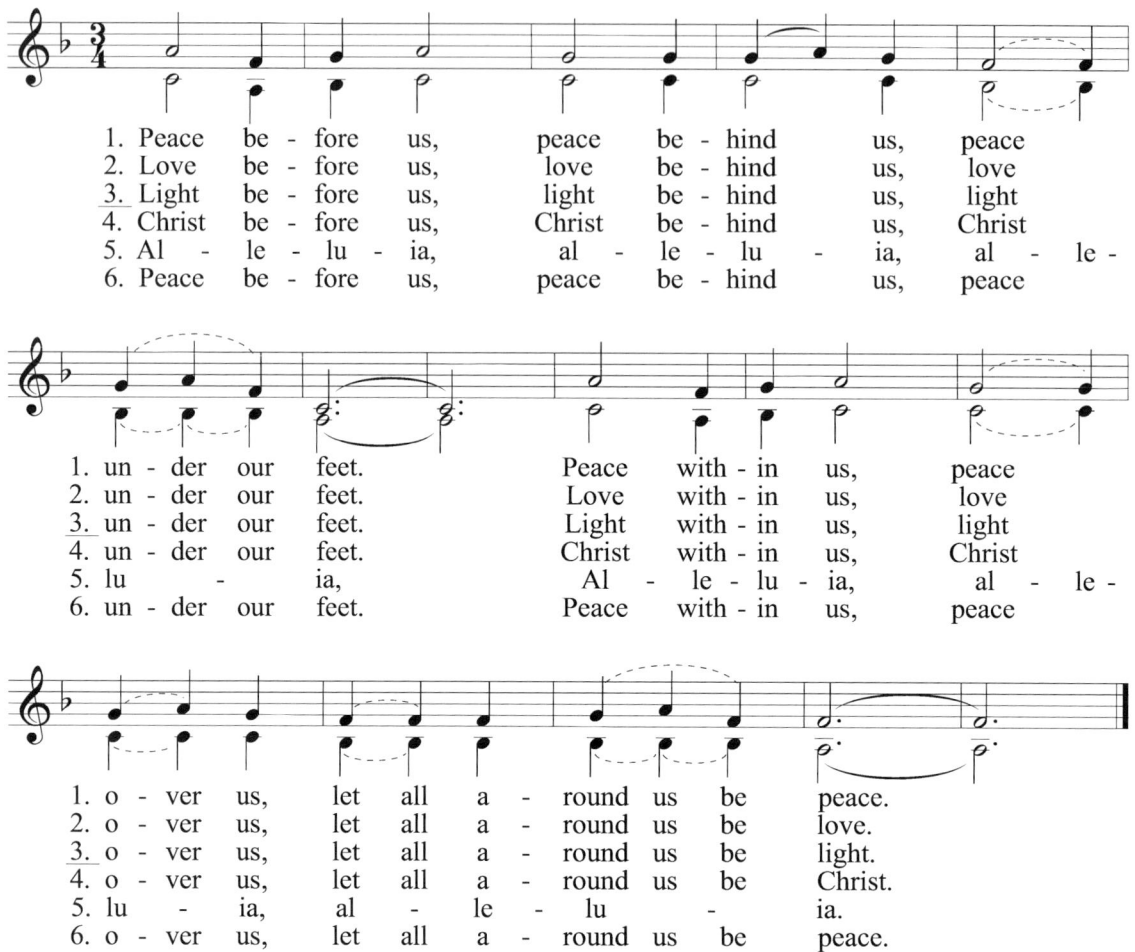

1. Peace before us, peace behind us, peace under our feet. Peace within us, peace over us, let all around us be peace.
2. Love before us, love behind us, love under our feet. Love within us, love over us, let all around us be love.
3. Light before us, light behind us, light under our feet. Light within us, light over us, let all around us be light.
4. Christ before us, Christ behind us, Christ under our feet. Christ within us, Christ over us, let all around us be Christ.
5. Alleluia, alleluia, alleluia, Alleluia, alleluia, alleluia.
6. Peace before us, peace behind us, peace within us, peace over us, let all around us be peace.

Text: Based on a Navajo prayer; adapt. by David Haas, b. 1957. Music: David Haas, b. 1957.
Text and music: © 1987, GIA Publications, Inc. All rights reserved. Used with permission.

Prepare a Room for Me

1. "Prepare a room for me, your Savior, Host and Priest, where I may gather you, my friends, to celebrate the feast."
2. "This room we have prepared; the Table now is set. We wait your promised presence, Lord, where we once more are met."
3. "Where even two or three have come the Meal to share, unseen, but living, loving still, I surely will be there!"
4. "Lord Christ, we seek the food your grace alone can give. We come with empty, hung'ring hearts that we may eat and live."
5. "My promise I will keep; your hunger will be fed, for in this Meal I offer you myself, the living Bread!"
6. "All thanks and praise to you, our Savior, Lord and Friend, that through this Loaf and Cup you share your love that has no end!"

Text: Herman G. Stuempfle, Jr., 1923–2007, © 2000, GIA Publications, Inc. All rights reserved. Used with permission.
Muisc: SWABIA, Johann M. Speiss, 1715–1772; adapt. by William H. Havergal, 1793–1870.
Descant: Christine Manderfeld, OSB, b. 1938, © 2009, the Sisters of Saint Benedict, St. Joseph, MN. Administered by Liturgical Press, Collegeville, MN. All rights reserved.

302 Psalm 16: You Will Show Me the Path of Life

Refrain
You will show me the path of life, you, my hope and my shelter;
In your presence is endless joy, at your side is my home forever.

Verses
1. Faithful God, I look to you, you alone my life and fortune,
2. From of old you are my heritage, you my wisdom and my safety,
3. So my heart shall sing for joy, in your arms I rest securely,

1. never shall I look to other gods, you shall be my one hope.
2. through the night you speak within my heart, silently you teach me.
3. you will not abandon me to death, you shall not desert me.

Text: Based on Psalm 16:1-2, 6-8, 9-10; adapt. by Marty Haugen, b. 1950. Music: Marty Haugen, b. 1950.
Text and music: © 1988, 1994, GIA Publications, Inc. All rights reserved. Used with permission.

Psalm 19: Lord, You Have the Words 303

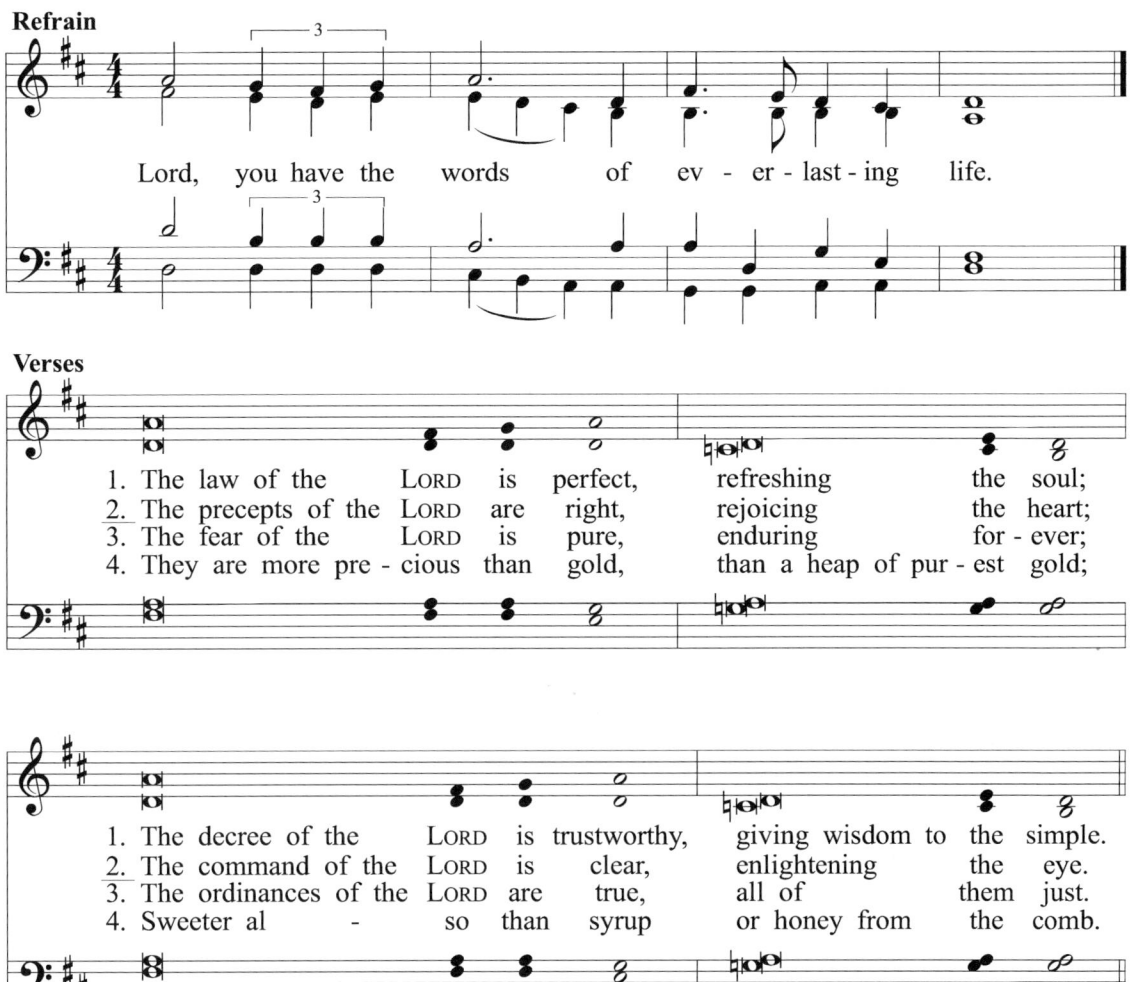

Text: Refrain—*Lectionary for Mass,* © 1968, 1981, 1997, ICEL; Psalm Verses—*New American Bible,* © 1970, 1997, 1998, CCD.
Music: Michel Guimont, © 1997, 1998, GIA Publications, Inc. All rights reserved. Used with permission.

304   Psalm 19: Lord, You Have the Words

Text: Based on Psalm 19:8, 9, 10, 11; adapt. by David Haas, b. 1957, © 1983, GIA Publications, Inc.; ref. trans., © 1969 ICEL. All rights reserved. Used with permission.
Music: David Haas, b. 1957, © 1983, GIA Publications, Inc. All rights reserved. Used with permission.

Psalm 22: My God, My God 305

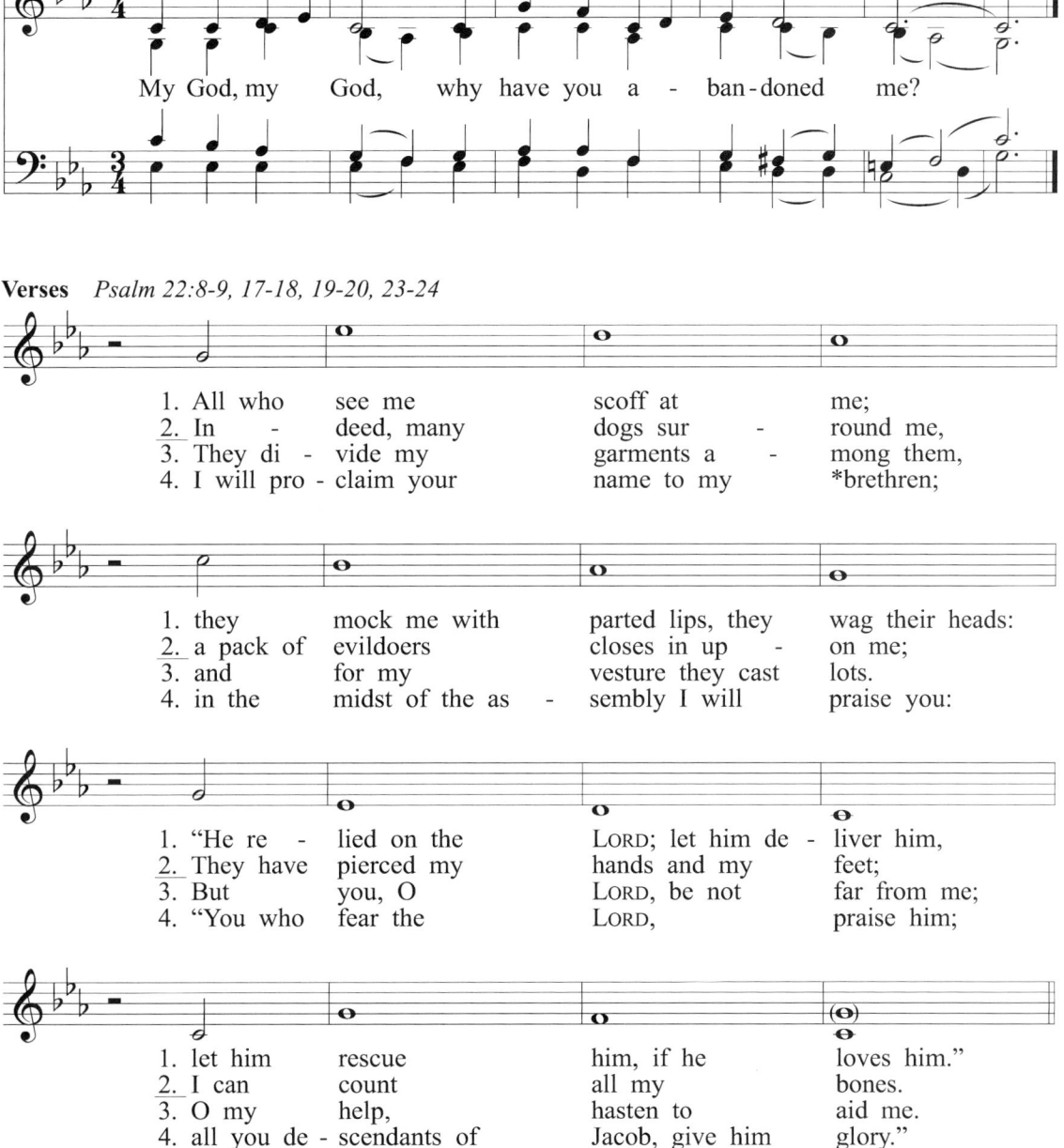

* alternate text: people

Text: antiphon–© 1968, 1981, 1997, International Committee on English in the Liturgy; verses–©1970, 1997, 1998, Confraternity of Christian Doctrine. All rights reserved.
Music: Jay F. Hunstiger, b. 1950, © 1990, Jay F. Hunstiger, administered by Liturgical Press, Collegeville, MN 56321. All rights reserved.

306 Psalm 22: My God, My God

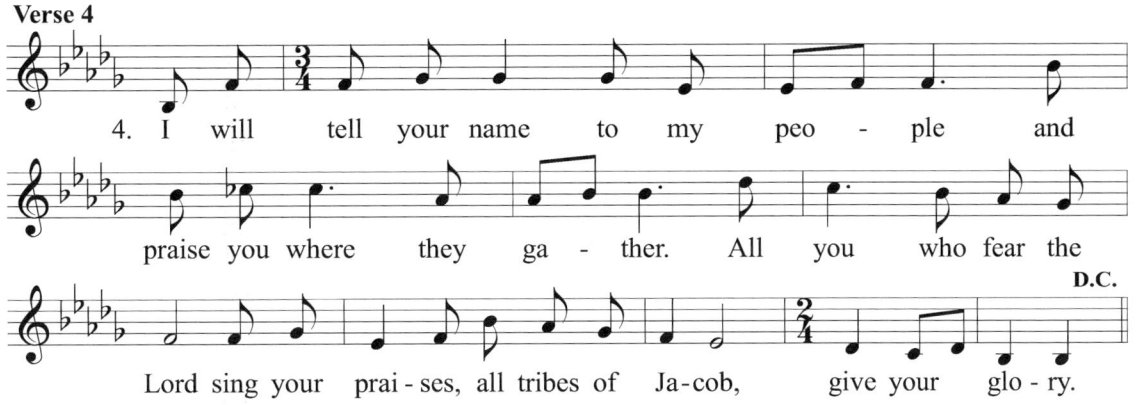

Text: antiphon © 1969, ICEL; verses © 1963, The Grail, GIA Publications, Inc., North American agent.
Music: Christopher Willcock, SJ, b. 1947, © 1977, 1990, Christopher Willcock, SJ. Published by OCP Publications.
All rights reserved. Used with permission.

307 Psalm 23: My Shepherd Is the Lord / The Lord Is My Shepherd

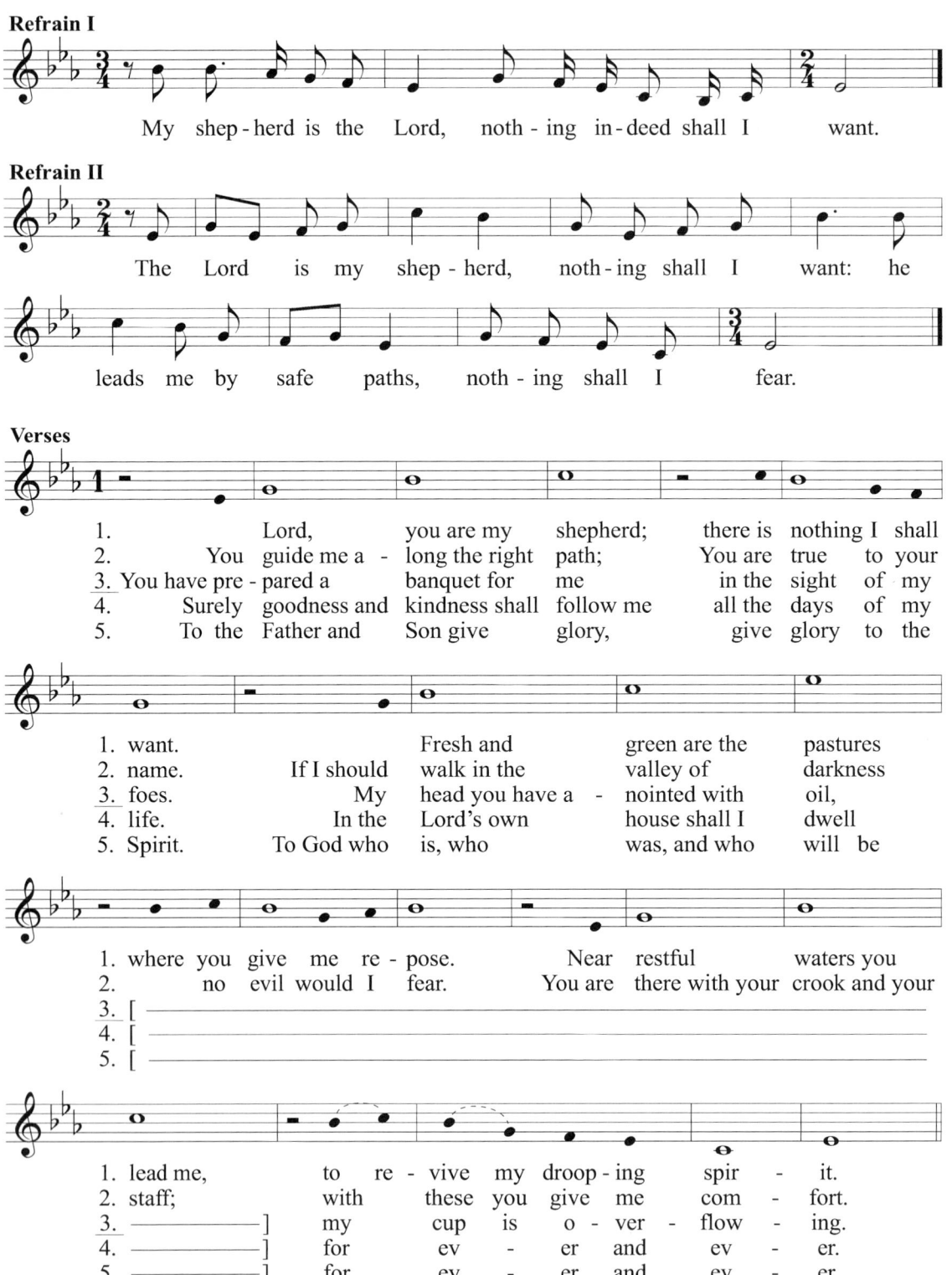

Text: Psalm 23; The Grail. Music: Joseph Gelineau, SJ, 1920–2008. Music: Refrain I—Joseph Gelineau, SJ, 1920–2008; Refrain II—A. Gregory Murray, OSB.
Text and music © 1963, The Grail, GIA Publications, Inc., North American agent. All rights reserved. Used with permission.

Psalm 23: Shepherd Me, O God 308

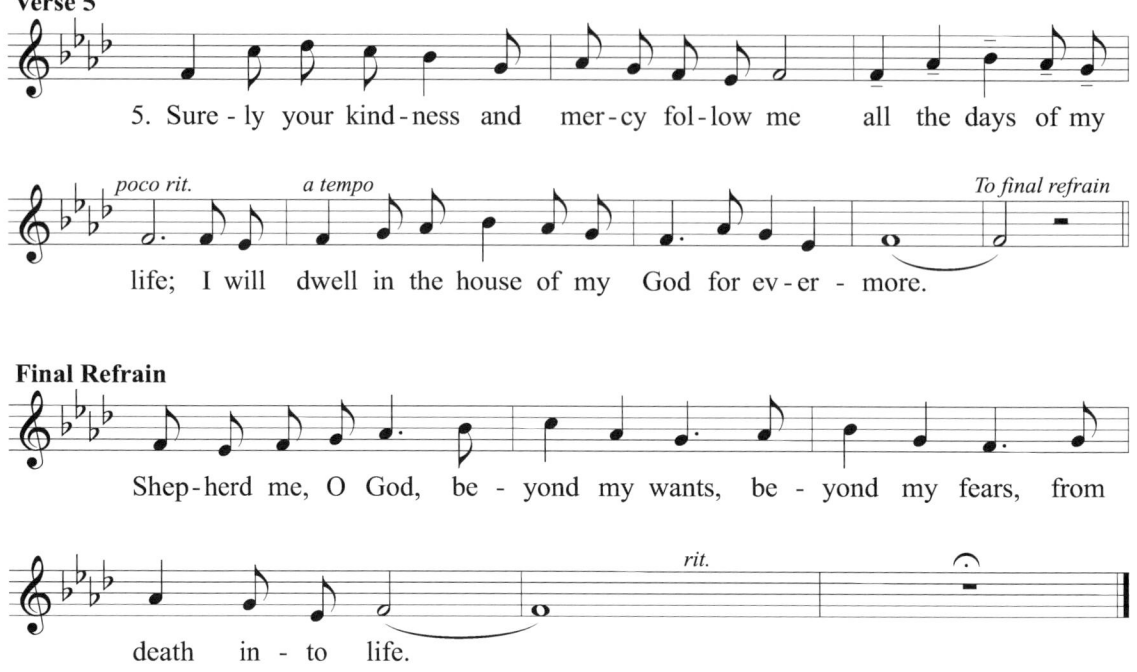

Psalm 25: To You, O Lord   309

Text: Based on Psalm 25:4-5, 8-9, 12-14; adapt. Marty Haugen, b. 1950, © 1982, GIA Publications, Inc.; refrain trans. © 1969, ICEL.
Music: Marty Haugen, b. 1950, © 1982, GIA Publications, Inc. All rights reserved. Used with permission.

Psalm 25: To You, O Lord

To you, O Lord, I lift my soul; to you, O Lord, I lift my soul.

Verse 1
1. O Lord, make me know your ways. O Lord, teach me your paths. Make me walk in your truth and teach me: for you are God my sav-ior.

Verse 2
2. The Lord is good and up-right, and shows the path to those who stray. The Lord guides the hum-ble in the right path, and teach-es God's way to the poor.

Verse 3
3. The Lord's ways are faith-ful-ness and love for those who keep God's will. The Lord's friend-ship is for those who are faith-ful, to them God's love has been re-vealed.

Text: antiphon © 1969, ICEL; verses © 1963, The Grail, GIA Publications, Inc., North American agent.
Music: Christopher Willcock, SJ, b. 1947, © 1977, 1990, Christopher Willcock, SJ. Published by OCP Publications.
All rights reserved. Used with permission.

Psalm 27: The Lord Is My Light 311

Text: Based on Psalm 27:1-2, 4, 13-14; adapt. by David Haas, b. 1957. Music: David Haas, b. 1957.
Text and music: © 1983, GIA Publications, Inc. All rights reserved. Used with permission.

Psalm 27: The Lord Is My Light

Text: antiphon © 1969, ICEL; verses © 1963, The Grail, GIA Publications, Inc., North American agent.
Music: Christopher Willcock, SJ, b. 1947, © 1977, 1990, Christopher Willcock, SJ. Published by OCP Publications.
All rights reserved. Used with permission.

313 Psalm 31: I Put My Life in Your Hands

Text: Based on Psalm 31:2, 6, 12-13, 15-16, 17; adapt. by Marty Haugen, b. 1950, © 1983, GIA Publications, Inc.; ref. trans. © 1969, ICEL.
Music: Marty Haugen, b. 1950, © 1983, 1994, GIA Publications, Inc.
All rights reserved. Used with permission.

Psalm 33: Let Your Mercy Be on Us / The Earth Is Full of the Goodness of God

314

Psalm 34: Taste and See

315

Ostinato Refrain

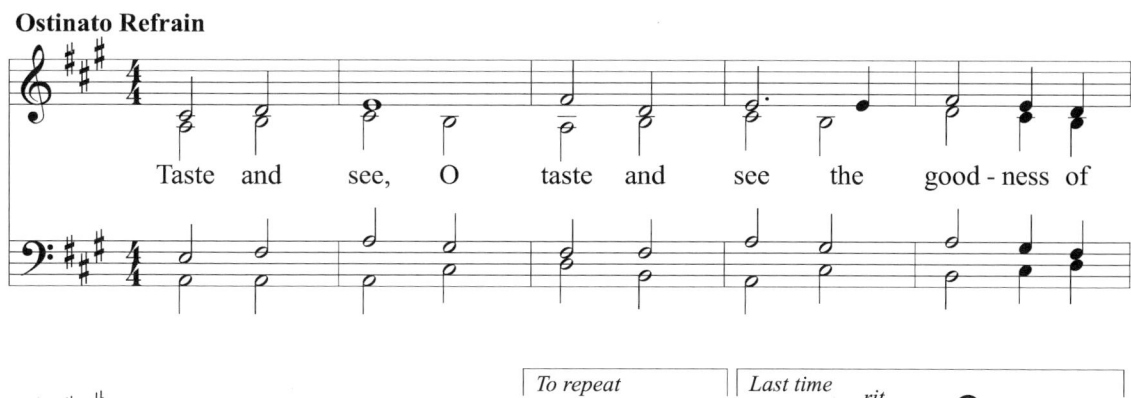

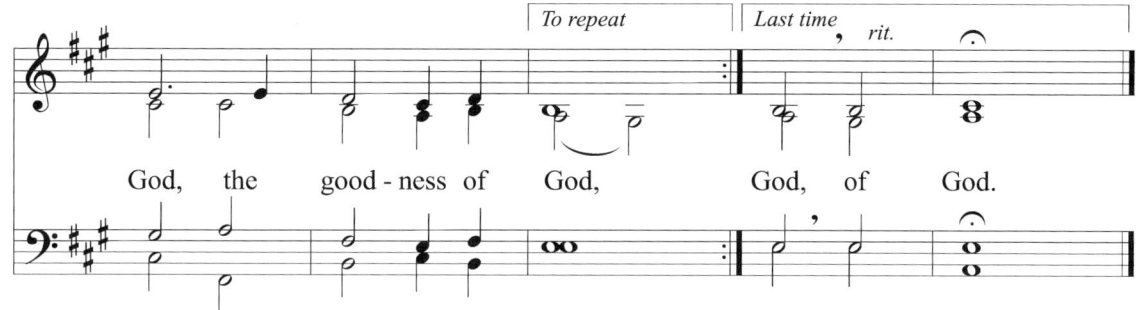

As the assembly continues to sing the Ostinato Refrain, the verses are sung by the cantor(s). If possible, verses should be alternated between two cantors (male and female), with both cantors singing Verse 7.

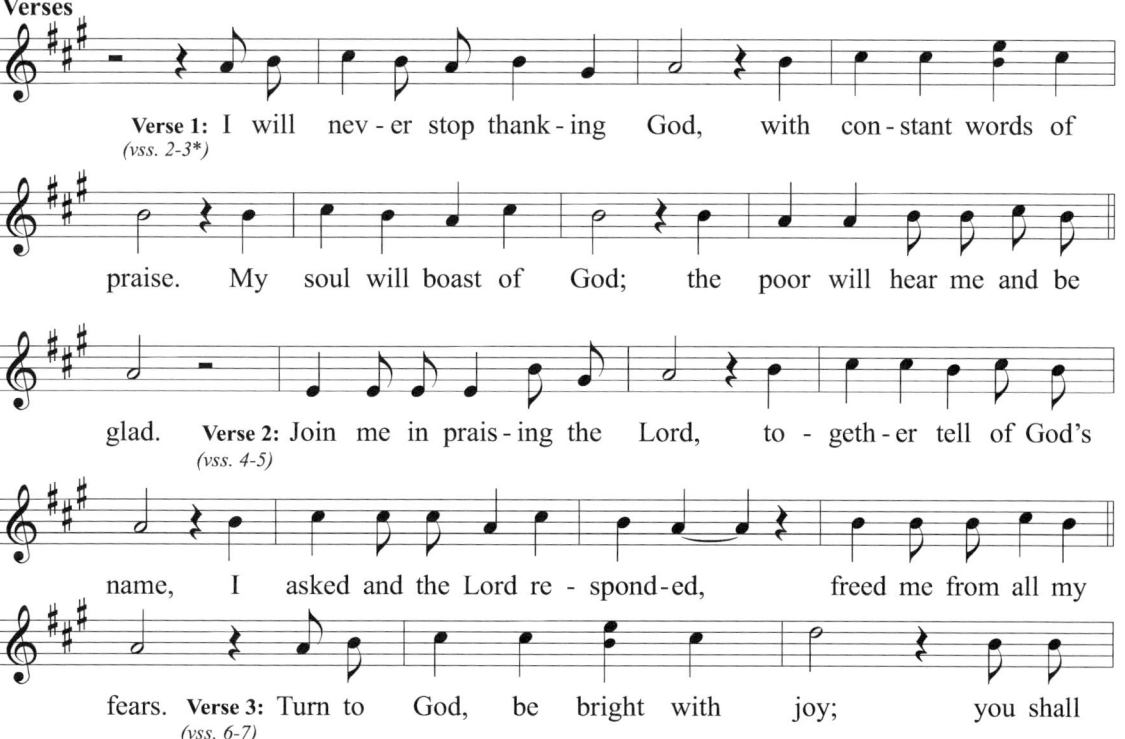

Psalm 34: Taste and See 316

Psalm 34: Taste and See, pg. 2

3. Look to God that you might be radiant with joy, and your faces free from all shame. The Lord hears the suffering souls, and saves them from all distress.

poco rit. D.C.

Text: Refrain—tr. © 1969, ICEL; Verses—based on Psalm 34, adapt. by Marty Haugen, b. 1950, © 1980, GIA Publications, Inc.
Music: Marty Haugen, b. 1950, © 1980, GIA Publications, Inc.
All rights reserved. Used with permission.

Psalm 34: Taste and See   317

Psalm 34: Taste and See, pg. 2

Verse 3

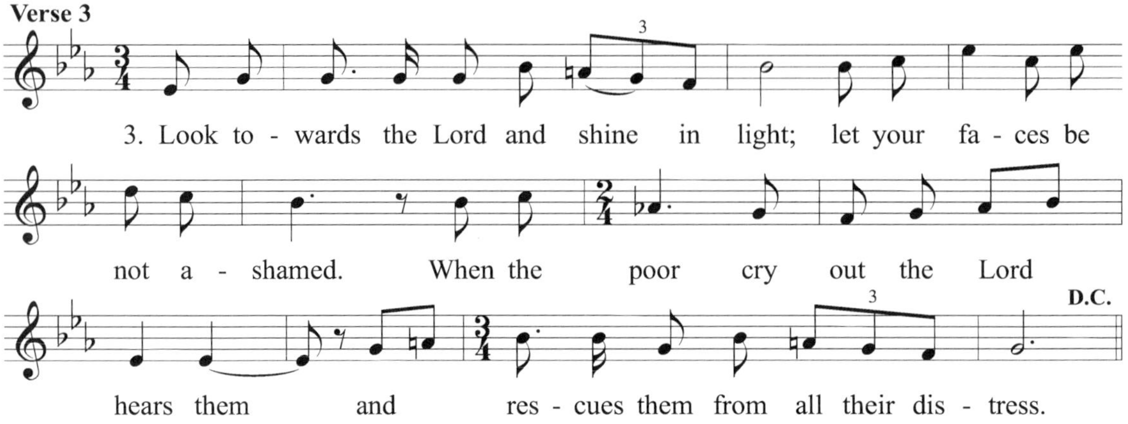

3. Look towards the Lord and shine in light; let your faces be not ashamed. When the poor cry out the Lord hears them and rescues them from all their distress. D.C.

Verse 4

4. The angel of the Lord is encamped around those who revere God. Taste and see that the Lord is good. They are happy who seek refuge in God. D.C.

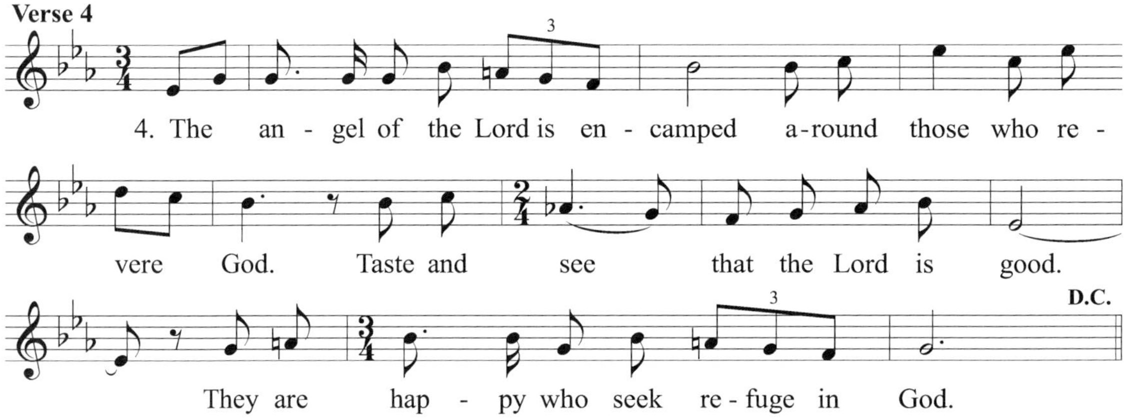

Text: antiphon © 1969, ICEL; verses © 1963, The Grail, GIA Publications, Inc., North American agent.
Music: Christopher Willcock, SJ, b. 1947, © 1977, 1990, Christopher Willcock, SJ. Published by OCP Publications.
All rights reserved. Used with permission.

318 Psalm 42: Like the Deer That Longs

Introduction (and optional interlude following each verse)

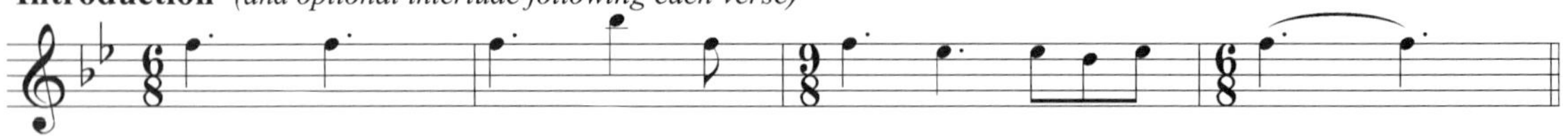

𝄋 Refrain

Like the deer that longs for running streams, my soul longs for you my God.

319 Psalm 51: Be Merciful, O Lord

320 Psalm 51: Be Merciful, O Lord

Text: Psalm 51:3-4, 5-6, 12-13, 14, 17. Music: Jay F. Hunstiger, b. 1950, © 1990, Jay F. Hunstiger, administered by Liturgical Press, Collegeville, MN 56321. All rights reserved.

Psalm 51: Be Merciful, O Lord

Psalm 51: Be Merciful, O Lord / Create in Me 322

Psalm 51: Be Merciful, O Lord / Create in Me, pg. 2

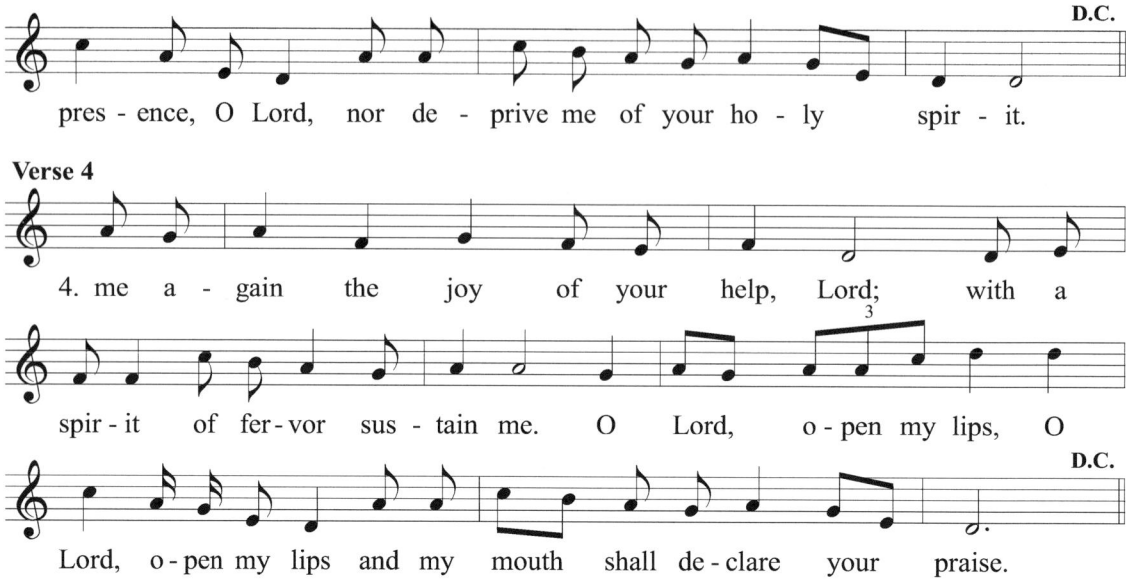

*The refrains may be sung in canon without the accompaniment.

Text: Psalm 51:3-4, 5-6, 12-13, 14, 17; © 1963, 1993, The Grail, GIA Publications, Inc., North American agent; refrain trans. © 1969, ICEL.
Music: Based on WONDROUS LOVE, Stephen Pishner, © 1998, GIA Publications, Inc. All rights reserved. Used with permission.

Psalm 63: My Soul Is Thirsting 323

Text: antiphon © 1969, ICEL; verses © 1963, The Grail, GIA Publications, Inc., North American agent.
Music: Christopher Willcock, SJ, b. 1947, © 1977, 1990, Christopher Willcock, SJ. Published by OCP Publications.
All rights reserved. Used with permission.

Psalm 63: My Soul Is Thirsting

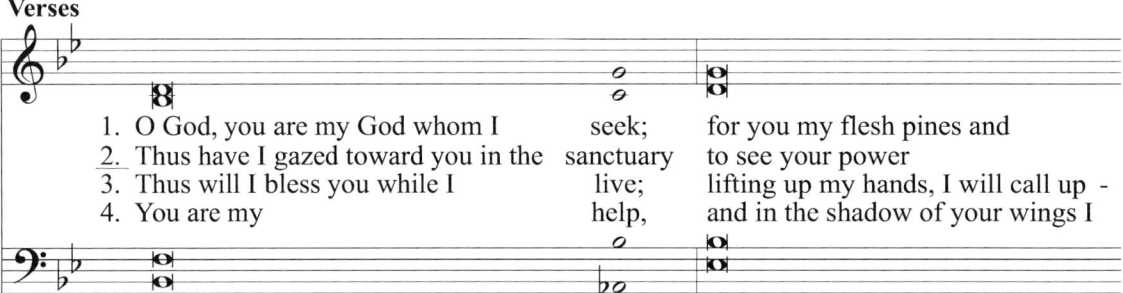

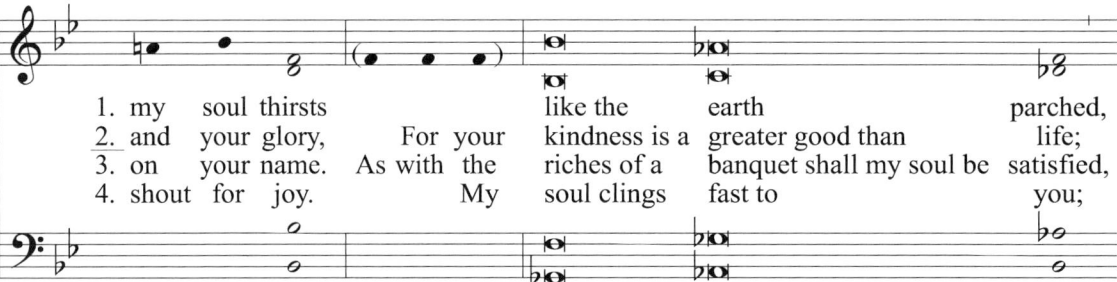

Text: Psalm 63:2, 3-4, 5-6, 8-9.
Music: Michel Guimont, © 1994, 1998, GIA Publications, Inc. All rights reserved. Used with permission.

Psalm 72: Justice Shall Flourish   325

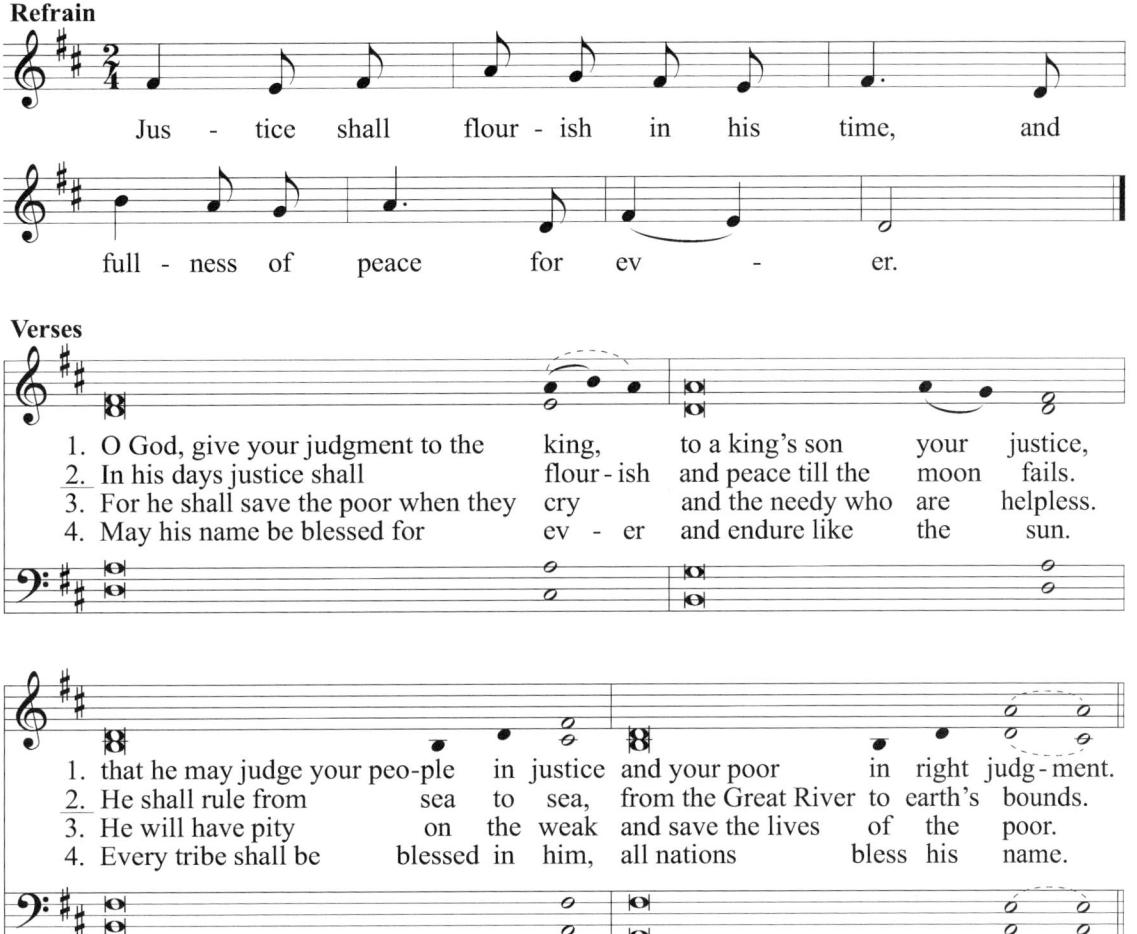

Text: Psalm 72, © 1963, 1993, The Grail, GIA Publications, Inc., North American agent; refrain trans. © 1969, ICEL.
Music: Michel Guimont, © 1995, GIA Publications, Inc.
All rights reserved. Used with permission.

326 Psalm 85: God Is Speaking Peace

Refrain *Descant:*
God is speaking peace, peace to faithful people.

Melody:
God is speaking peace, peace to faithful people.

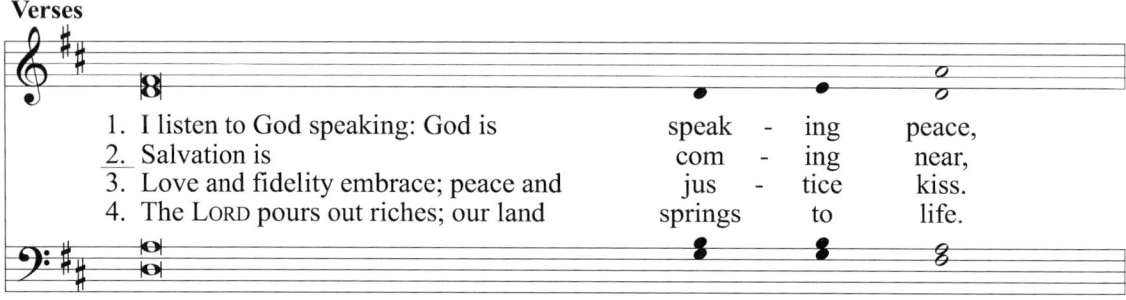

Verses
1. I listen to God speaking: God is speak - ing peace,
2. Salvation is com - ing near,
3. Love and fidelity embrace; peace and jus - tice kiss.
4. The Lord pours out riches; our land springs to life.

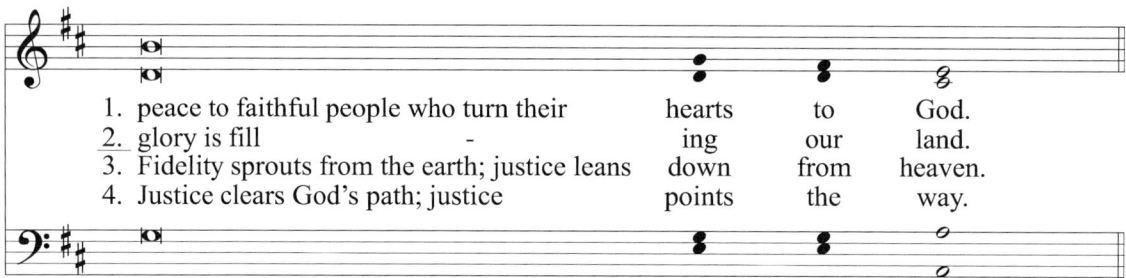

1. peace to faithful people who turn their hearts to God.
2. glory is fill - ing our land.
3. Fidelity sprouts from the earth; justice leans down from heaven.
4. Justice clears God's path; justice points the way.

Text: Psalm 85:9-10, 11-12, 13-14.
Music: Howard Hughes, b. 1930, from the *ICEL Liturgical Psalter Project,* © 1987, ICEL, Inc. All rights reserved. Used with permission.

Psalm 89: Forever I Will Sing

Text: Refrain—*Lectionary for Mass,* © 1969, 1981, ICEL; Verses—Psalm 89:2-3, 4-5, 16-17, 18-19, 27-29, The Grail, © 1963, 1993, The Grail.
Music: Refrain—J. Robert Carroll, © 1975, GIA Publications, Inc. Verses—Joseph Gelineau, SJ, 1920–2008, © 1963, 1993, The Grail.
GIA Publications, Inc., North American agent. All rights reserved. Used with permission.

Psalm 89: Forever I Will Sing 328

Verse 1
1. "With my chosen one I have made a covenant; I have sworn to David my servant: I will establish your dynasty forever and set up your throne through all ages."

Verse 2
2. Happy the people who acclaim such a God, who walk, O Lord, in the light of your face, who find their joy ev-'ry

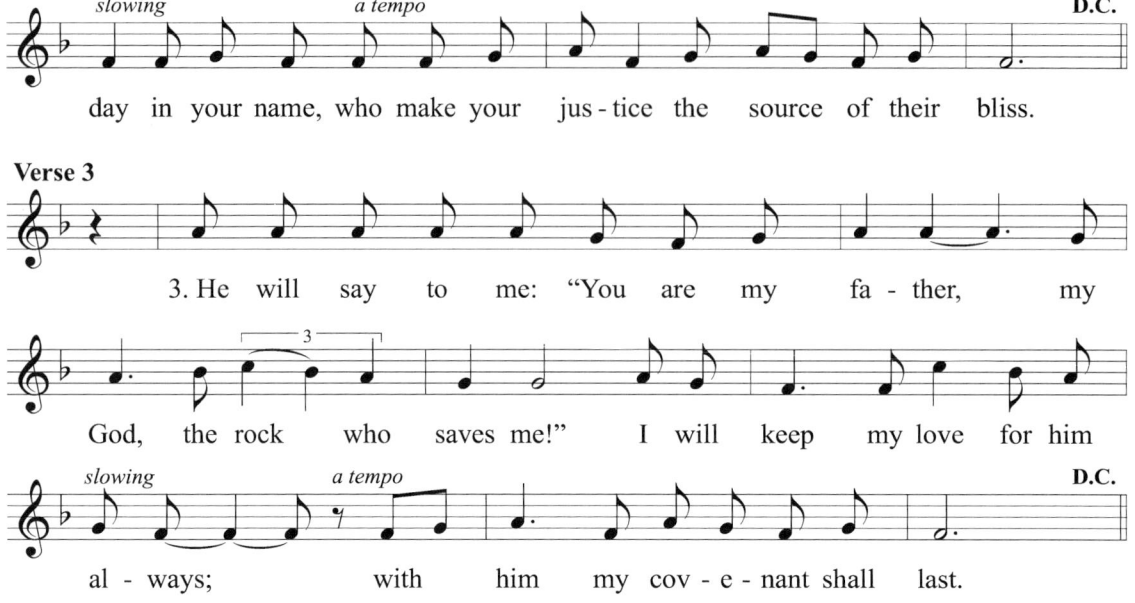

Psalm 91: Be with Me 329

Refrain
Be with me, Lord, when I am in trouble, be with me, Lord, I pray. pray.

Verse 1
1. You who dwell in the shelter of the Lord, Most High, who abide in the shadow of our God, say to the Lord: "My refuge and fortress, the God in whom I trust."

Verse 2
2. No evil shall befall you, no pain come near, for the angels stand close by your side,

Psalm 91: Be with Me, pg. 2

Text: Based on Psalm 91; adapt. by Marty Haugen, b. 1950. Music: Marty Haugen, b. 1950.
Text and music: © 1980, GIA Publications, Inc. All rights reserved. Used with permission.

Psalm 95: If Today You Hear the Voice of God / Let Us Come Before the Lord

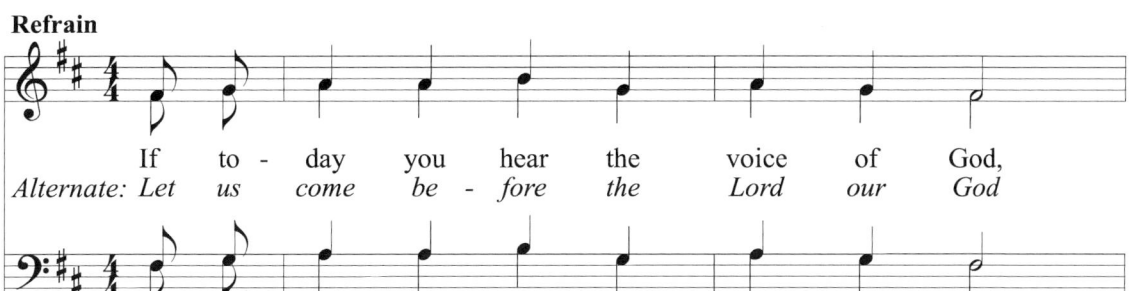

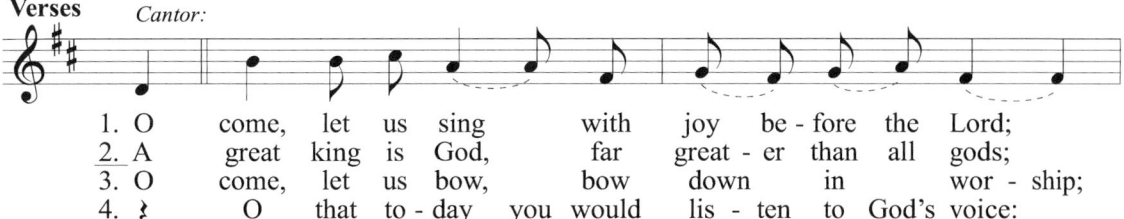

Psalm 95: If Today You Hear the Voice of God / Let Us Come Before the Lord, pg. 2

Text and music: James J. Chepponis, b. 1956, © 2004, GIA Publications, Inc. All rights reserved. Used with permission.

Psalm 96: Today Is Born Our Savior 331

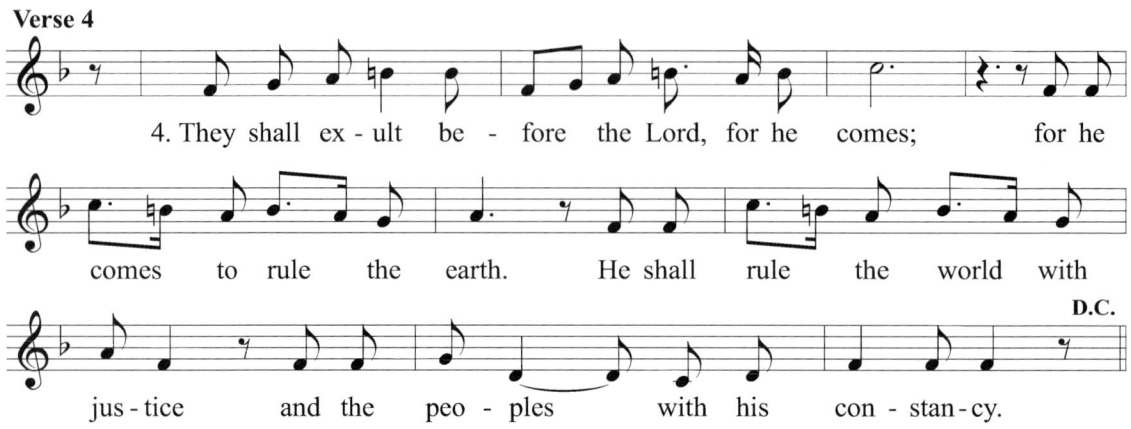

Psalm 96: Today Is Born Our Savior 332

Text: Refrain © 1969, 1991, ICEL. Verses—Psalm 96:1-2, 2-3, 11-12, 13, 14, © 1963, The Grail.
Music: Refrain—Richard Proulx, b. 1937. © 1986, GIA Publications, Inc. Verses—Joseph Gelineau, SJ, 1920–2008, © 1963, The Grail.
GIA Publications, Inc., North American agent. All rights reserved. Used with permission.

333 Psalm 98: All the Ends of the Earth

334 Psalm 98: All the Ends of the Earth

335 Psalm 98: All the Ends of the Earth / Sing a New Song to the Lord

Psalm 98: All the Ends of the Earth / Sing a New Song to the Lord, pg. 2

Final Refrain II *(following verse 5)*

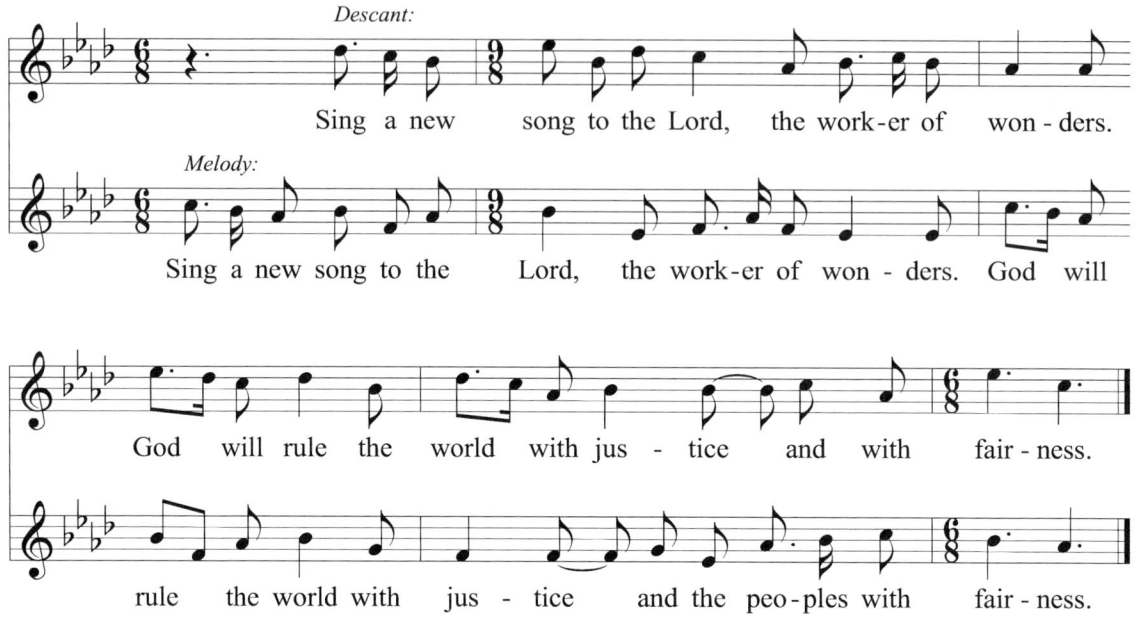

Text: antiphon © 1969, ICEL; verses © 1963, The Grail, GIA Publications, Inc., North American agent.
Music: Christopher Willcock, SJ, b. 1947, © 1977, 1990, Christopher Willcock, SJ. Published by OCP Publications.
All rights reserved. Used with permission.

336 Psalm 103: The Lord Is Kind and Merciful

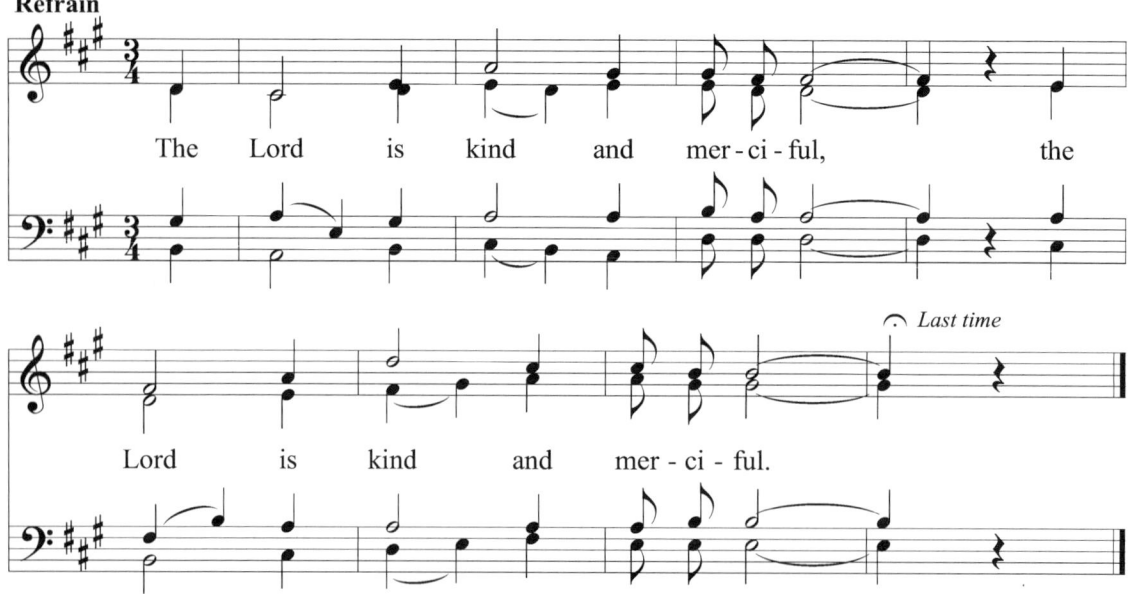

Psalm 103: The Lord Is Kind and Merciful, pg. 2

Text: Refrain—tr. © 1969, ICEL; Verses—based on Psalm 103; adapt. by Marty Haugen, b. 1950, © 1983, GIA Publications, Inc.
Music: Marty Haugen, b. 1950, © 1983, GIA Publications, Inc.
All rights reserved. Used with permission.

337   Psalm 104: Send Forth Your Spirit, O Lord

Text: Based on Psalm 104, adapt. by Steven C. Warner. Music: Steven C. Warner; Acc. by Steven C. Warner and Shirley Luttio.
Text and music: © 1996, World Library Publications, 3708 River Road, Franklin Park, IL 60131. www.wlpmusic.com All rights reserved. Used with permission.

Psalm 116: Our Blessing-Cup 338

Text: Based on Psalm 116:12-13, 15-16, 17-19; adapt. by Marty Haugen, b. 1950. Music: Marty Haugen, b. 1950,
© 1983, GIA Publications, Inc. All rights reserved. Used with permission.

339   Psalms 118, 47, 104: An Eastertime Psalm

Psalm 121: Our Help Is from the Lord 341

Psalm 121: Our Help Is from the Lord, pg. 2

Verse 3
3. God is your guard and pro-tec-tion; by your side God shall stand.
By day the sun shall not harm you, nor the moon in the night.

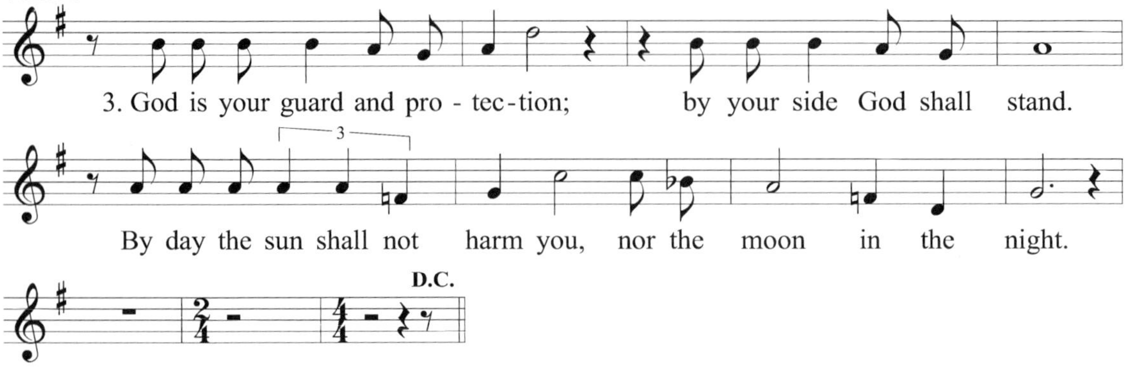

Verse 4
4. The Lord will shel-ter you from e-vil; God will guard your soul,
will guard your com-ing and your go-ing both now and for-ev-er more.

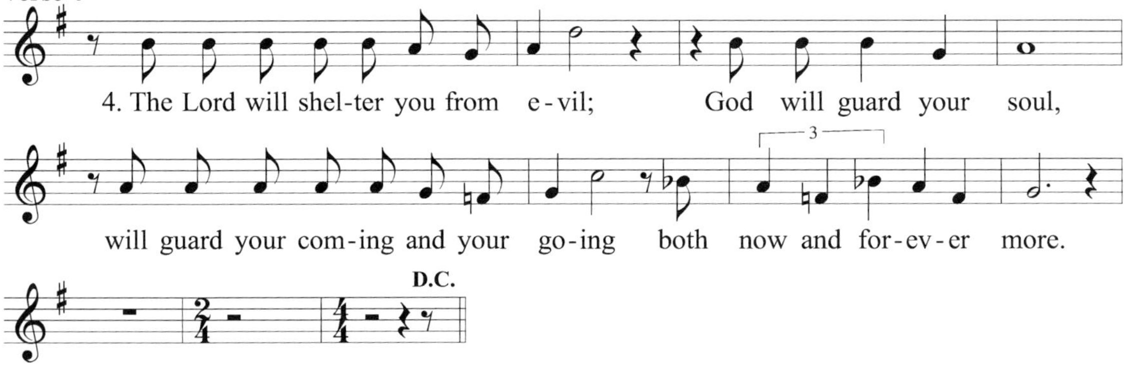

Text: Psalm 121, adapt. by Francis Patrick O'Brien, b. 1958; Music: Francis Patrick O'Brien, b. 1958, © 2001, GIA Publications, Inc. All rights reserved. Used with permission.

342 Psalm 122: Let Us Go Rejoicing

Refrain
Let us go re-joic-ing to the house of the Lord;
let us go re-joic-ing to the house of the Lord.

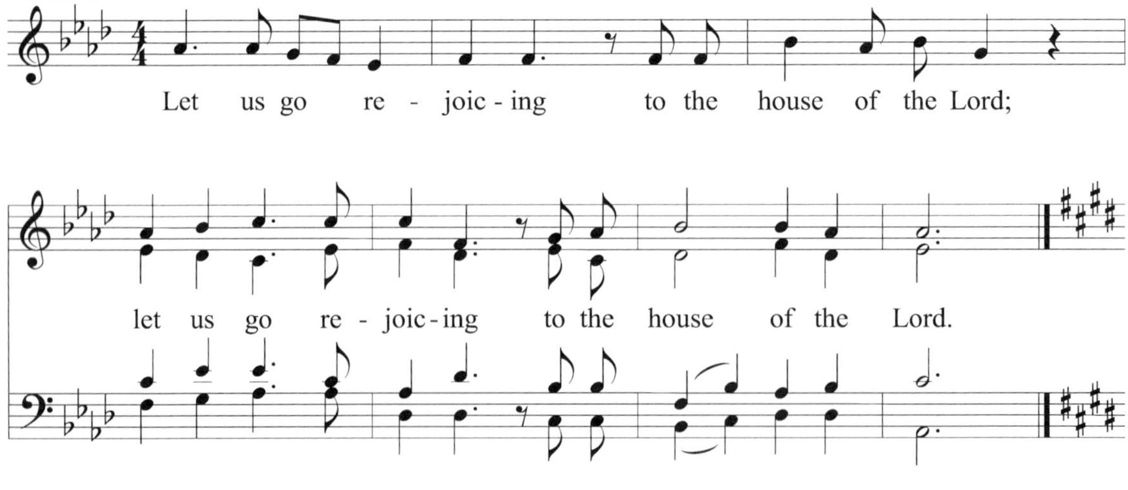

Psalm 122: Let Us Go Rejoicing, pg. 2

Text: antiphon © 1969, ICEL; verses © 1963, The Grail, GIA Publications, Inc., North American agent.
Music: Christopher Willcock, SJ, b. 1947, © 1977, 1990, Christopher Willcock, SJ. Published by OCP Publications.
All rights reserved. Used with permission.

Psalm 130: With the Lord There Is Mercy   344

Refrain
With the Lord there is mercy and fullness of redemption.

Verse 1
1. Out of the depths I cry to you, O Lord, Lord, hear my voice!
O let your ears be attentive to the voice of my pleading.

Verse 2
2. If you, O Lord, should mark our guilt, Lord, who would survive?
But with you is found forgiveness: for this we revere you.

Verse 3
3. My soul is waiting for the Lord I count on God's word.
My soul is longing for the Lord more than those who watch for daybreak.

Verse 4
4. Because with the Lord there is mercy and fullness of redemption,
Israel indeed God will redeem from all its iniquity.

Text: antiphon © 1969, ICEL; verses © 1963, The Grail, GIA Publications, Inc., North American agent.
Music: Christopher Willcock, SJ, b. 1947, © 1977, 1990, Christopher Willcock, SJ. Published by OCP Publications.
All rights reserved. Used with permission.

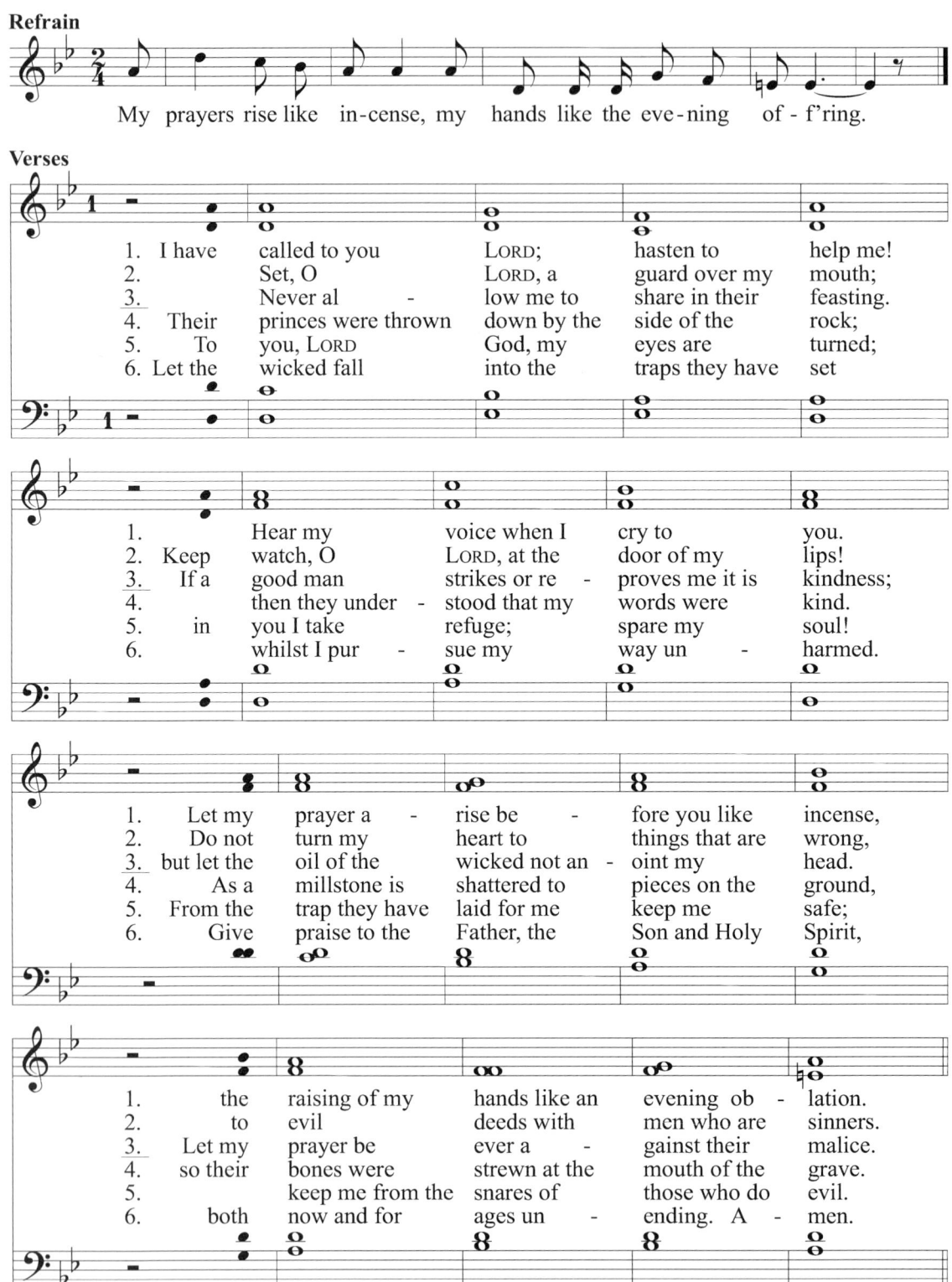

Psalm 145: I Will Praise Your Name 346

Psalm 145: I Will Praise Your Name

Psalm 146: I Will Praise the Lord 348

Psalm 147: Bless the Lord, My Soul 349

Text: Based on Psalm 147; adapt by Marty Haugen, b. 1950. Music: Marty Haugen, b. 1950.
Text and music: © 1987, GIA Publications, Inc. All rights reserved. Used with permission.

350 Puer Natus in Bethlehem / A Child Is Born in Bethlehem

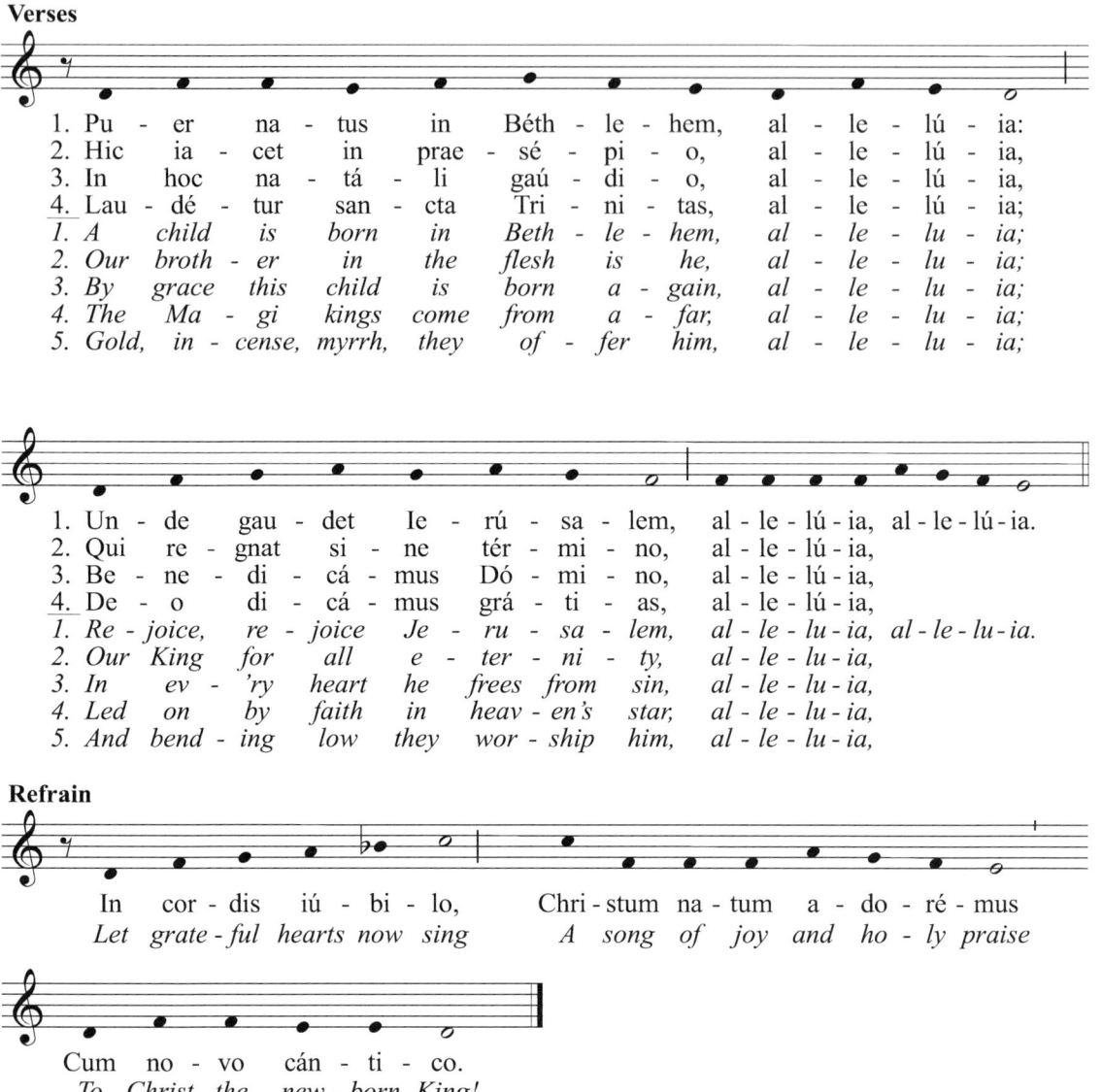

Text: *Puer natus,* 14th cent., tr. Irvin Udulutsch, OFM, Cap, b. 1920; English tr. © 1959, 1977, Order of Saint Benedict, Collegeville, MN. Administered by Liturgical Press, Collegeville, MN. All rights reserved.
Music: PUER NATUS, 88 with alleluias and refrain, Plainchant, Mode I.

Pues Si Vivimos / When We Are Living 351

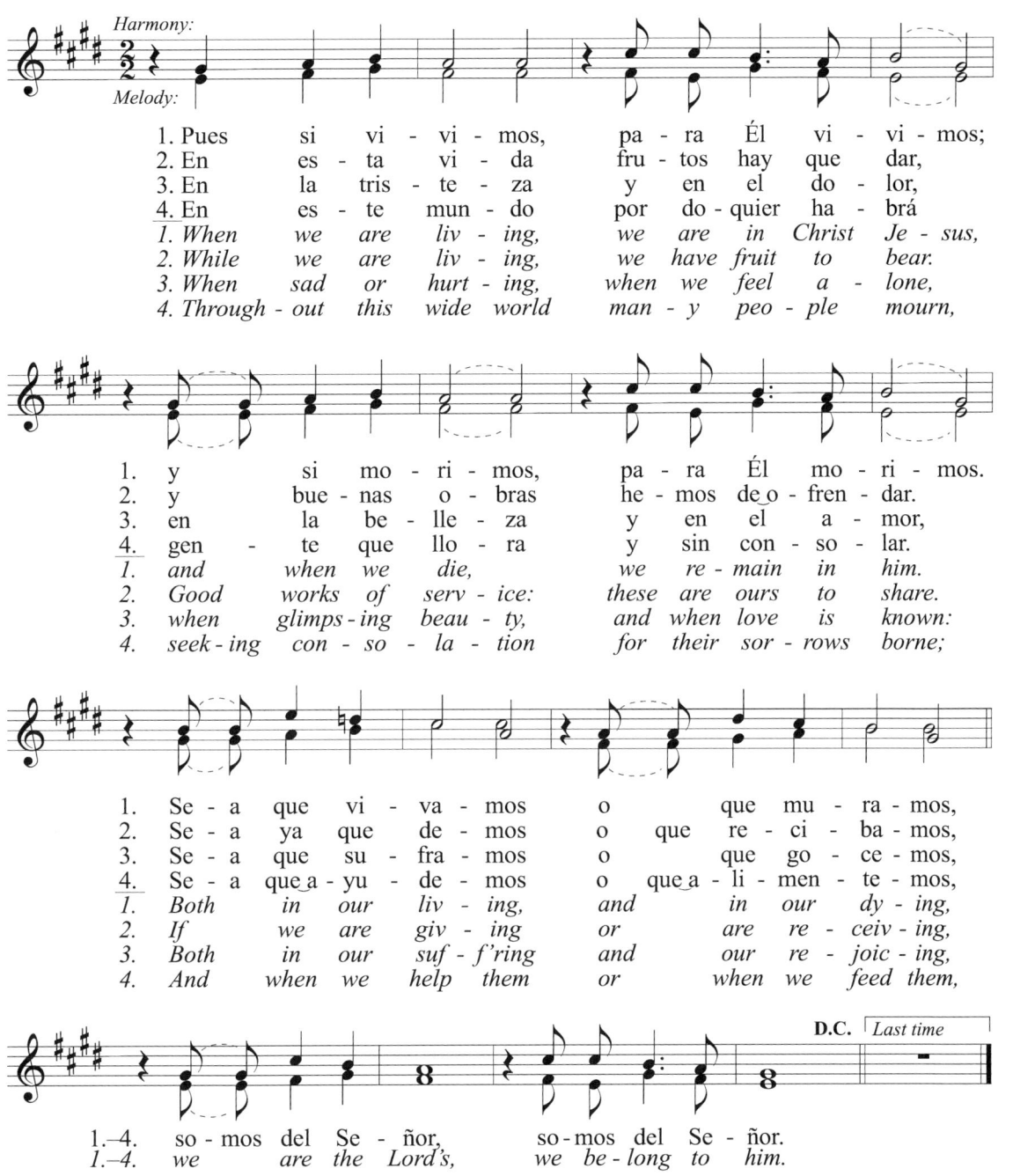

Text: v. 1, Romans 14:8; traditional Spanish; vv. 2-4, Robert Escamilla, © 1983, Abingdon Press (Administered by The Copyright Company, Nashville, TN); tr. Ron F. Krisman, b. 1946, © 2004, Abingdon Press (Administered by The Copyright Company, Nashville, TN). All rights reserved. International copyright secured. Used with permission.
Music: SOMOS DEL SEÑOR, irregular; traditional Spanish; arr. by Ron F. Krisman, b. 1946, © 2004, GIA Publications, Inc. All rights reserved. Used with permission.

352 Regina Caeli / O Queen of Heaven

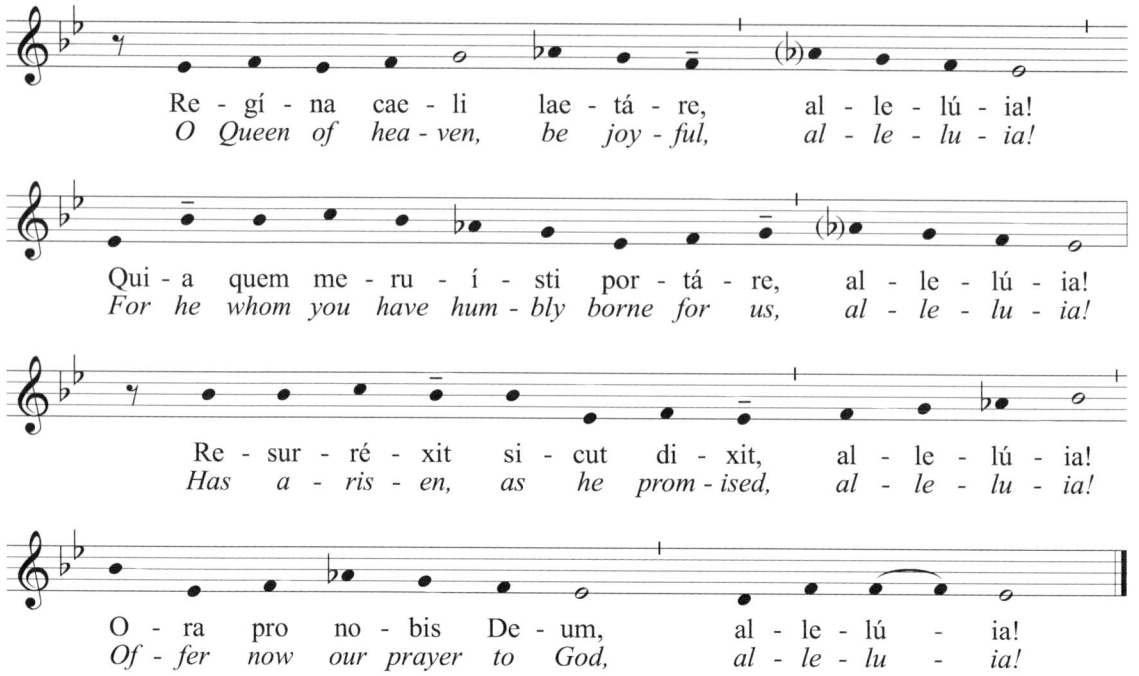

Re - gí - na cae - li lae - tá - re, al - le - lú - ia!
O   Queen of   hea - ven, be   joy - ful,   al - le - lu - ia!

Qui - a quem me - ru - í - sti por - tá - re, al - le - lú - ia!
For he whom you have hum - bly borne for us, al - le - lu - ia!

Re - sur - ré - xit si - cut di - xit, al - le - lú - ia!
Has a - ris - en, as he prom - ised, al - le - lu - ia!

O - ra pro no - bis De - um, al - le - lú - ia!
Of - fer now our prayer to God, al - le - lu - ia!

Text: *Regina Caeli*; tr. by Winfred Douglas, 1867–1944, alt.; tr. by Cecile Gertken, OSB, 1902–2001, © 1990, Sisters of Saint Benedict.
Published and administered by Liturgical Press, Collegeville, MN 56321. All rights reserved.
Music: Plainchant, Mode VI.

Rejoice, the Lord Is King! 353

1. Rejoice, the Lord is King! Your Lord and King adore!
2. The Lord, our Savior, reigns, The God of truth and love:
3. His kingdom cannot fail, He rules o'er earth and heav'n;
4. Rejoice in glorious hope! Our Lord the judge shall come

1. Rejoice, give thanks, and sing, And triumph evermore:
2. When he had purged our sins, He took his seat above:
3. The keys of death and hell Are to our Jesus giv'n:
4. And take his servants up To their eternal home:

Lift up your heart, lift up your voice! Rejoice, again I say, rejoice!

Text: Charles Wesley, 1707–1788. Music: DARWALL'S 148TH, 66 66 88, John Darwall, 1731–1789; acc. by William Henry Monk, 1823–1889, alt.
Descant: Sydney Hugo Nicholson, © 1972, *Hymns Ancient & Modern, Ltd.* All rights reserved. Used with permission.

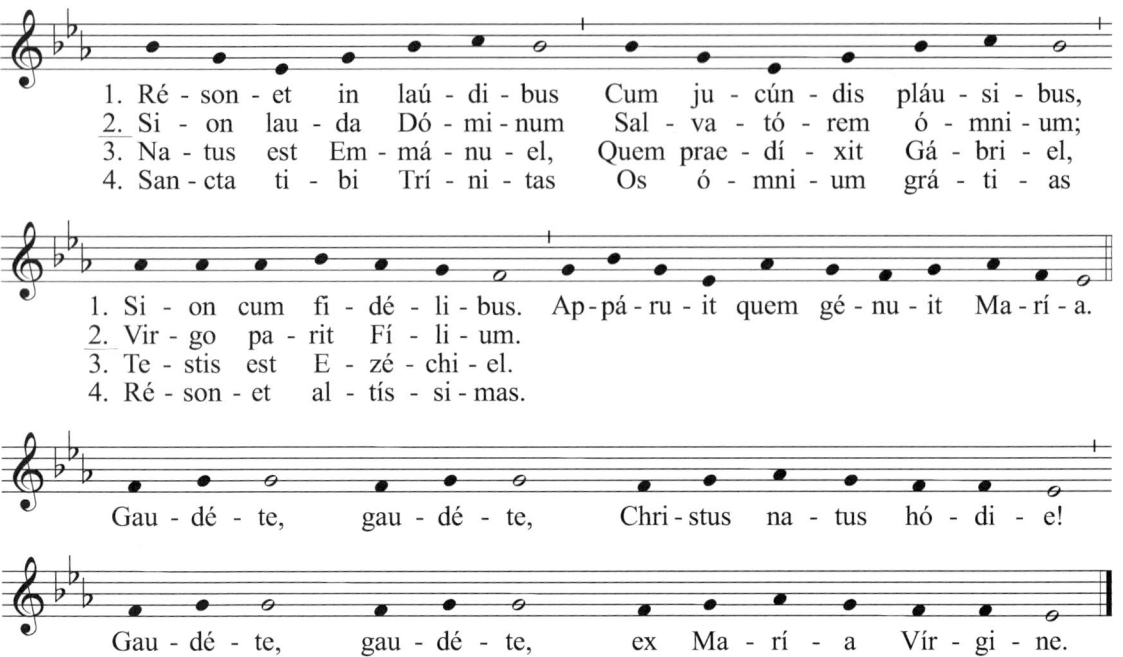

Return to God 355

*Soprano alone first time through repeated section, sopranos and tenors second time, all third time.

Text and music: Marty Haugen, b. 1950, © 1990, 1991, GIA Publications, Inc. All rights reserved. Used with permission.

Saints of God 356

1. Saints of God, come to his/her aid! Come to meet him/her, angels of the Lord.
2. May Christ who called you, take you home; May angels lead you to our parents' side!
3. Give eternal rest O Lord; And may your light shine on him/her, forever!

Refrain
Receive his/her soul and present him/her to God, present this soul to God most high.

Text: *Order of Christian Funerals;* para. by David Haas, b. 1957. Music: David Haas, b. 1957.
Text and music: © 1990, GIA Publications, Inc. All rights reserved. Used with permission.

Saints of God

Text: *Order of Christian Funerals*, © 1985, ICEL. Music: Steven R. Janco, b. 1961, © 1990, GIA Publications, Inc. All rights reserved. Used with permission.

Salve, Regina / Hail, Most Gracious Queen 358

Sal - ve, Re - gí - na, ma - ter mi - se - ri - cór - di - ae:
Hail, most gra - cious Queen, Moth - er of ten - der mer - cy,

Vi - ta dul - cé - do, et spes no - stra, sal - ve.
our con - so - la - tion and our hope, we greet you.

Ad te cla - má - mus, éx - su - les, fí - li - i He - vae.
To you do we cry, poor ban - ished de - scend - ants of Eve.

Ad te su - spi - rá - mus, ge - mén - tes et flén - tes
To you we make our prayer, sor - row - ing and weep - ing,

in hac la - cri - má - rum val - le. E - ia er - go, Ad - vo - cá - ta no - stra,
in this mourn - ful val - ley of tears. To you we come, most gra - cious Ad - vo - cate.

il - los tu - os mi - se - ri - cór - des ó - cu - los ad nos con - vér - te.
We call on you, be - seech - ing you to turn your eyes of mer - cy toward us.

Et Ie - sum, be - ne - dí - ctum fruc - tum ven - tris tu - i,
A - bove all, when the days of our ex - ile are end - ed,

no - bis post hoc ex - sí - li - um o - stén - de. O cle - mens,
show us the bless - ed fruit of your womb, Je - sus. O gen - tle,

O pi - a, O dul - cis Vir - go Ma - rí - a.
O lov - ing, O gra - cious, O Vir - gin Ma - ry.

Text: Latin ascr. to Hermanus Contractus of Reichenau, 1013–1054; tr. by Cecile Gertken, OSB, 1902–2001, © 1990, the Sisters of Saint Benedict, St. Joseph, MN.
Administered by Liturgical Press, Collegeville, MN. All rights reserved.
Music: SALVE REGINA, Plainchant, Mode V, Paris, 1643, Henri Du Mont, 1610–1684.

359 Savior of the Nations, Come

1. Savior of the nations, come, here among us make your home. All creation, heav'n and earth, groans until you come to birth.
2. Dew from heaven, gently come; bring our barren land to bloom. Melt our mountains, blessed rain; let proud hills be level plain.
3. Long-desired of ages past, show yourself to us at last; and from sin's captivity call us back and set us free.
4. Radiance of God's holy face, shine your love in this dark place. Splendor of God's glory bright, lead us to eternal light!

Text: Delores Dufner, OSB, b. 1939, © 1983, 2003, GIA Publications, Inc. All rights reserved. Used with permission.
Music: NUN KOMM DER HEIDEN HEILAND, 77 77, *Geistliche Gesangbüchlein,* Wittenberg, 1524; harm. by Melchior Vulpius, 1560–1615.
Descant: Christine Manderfeld, OSB, b. 1938, © 2009, the Sisters of Saint Benedict, St. Joseph, MN. Administered by Liturgical Press, Collegeville, MN. All rights reserved.

See Us, Lord, About Your Altar

360

1. See us, Lord, about your altar, Though so many, we are one; Many souls by love united In the heart of Christ, your Son.
2. Hear our prayers, O loving Father, Hear in them your Son, our Lord; Hear him speak our love and worship, As we sing with one accord.
3. Once were seen the blood and water, Now are seen but bread and wine; Once in human form he suffered, Now his form is but a sign.
4. Wheat and grape contain the meaning: Food and drink he is to all; One in him, we kneel, adoring, Gathered by his loving call.
5. Hear us yet; so much is needful In our frail, disordered life; Stay with us and tend our weakness, Till that day of no more strife.
6. Members of his Mystic Body Now we know our prayer is heard, Heard by you because your children Have received the eternal Word.

Text: John Greally, b. 1934, alt., © Burns & Oates, a Continuum imprint. All rights reserved. Used with permission.
Music: DRAKES BOUGHTON, 87 87, Edward William Elgar, 1857–1934.

Send Us Your Spirit, pg. 2

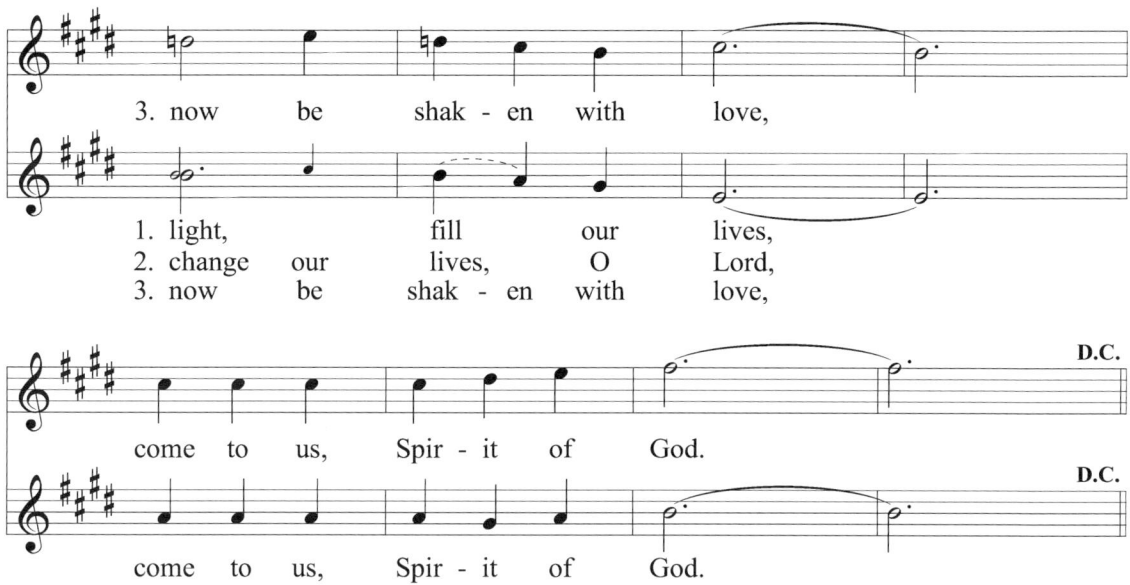

*May be sung in canon.

Text and music: David Haas, b. 1957, © 1981, 1982, 1987, GIA Publications, Inc. All rights reserved. Used with permission.

362 Shepherd of My Heart

1. My shepherd is the Lord, for nothing shall I want; green are the pastures where I'm led to repose. Near waters still and deep God will refresh my soul. I am led onward in ways true to the Name.
2. If I should walk one day into the vale of darkness, no evil shall I fear with God at my side. There with your crook and staff you give me strength and comfort; you spread a banquet in the sight of my foes.
3. You anoint my head with oil; my cup is overflowing; goodness and kindness crown the days of my life. Within the Lord's own house I dwell in peace for ever; within the house of God my soul is at rest.

Refrain: Guide me, O shepherd of my heart; lead me homeward through the

363 Shepherd of Souls

1. Shepherd of souls, refresh and bless Your chosen pilgrim flock With manna in the wilderness, With water from the rock.
2. We would not live by bread alone, But by your word of grace, In strength of which we travel on To our abiding place.
3. Be known to us in breaking bread, But do not then depart; Savior, abide with us, and spread Your table in our heart.
4. Lord, sup with us in love divine; Your Body and your Blood, That living bread, that heav'nly wine, Be our immortal food.

Text: James Montgomery, 1771–1854, vv. 1 & 2; anon. vv. 3 & 4. Music: ST. AGNES, 86 86, John Bacchus Dykes, 1823–1876.
Descant: Randall Sensmeier, © 1992, GIA Publications, Inc. All rights reserved. Used with permission.

Silent Night / Stille Nacht / Noche de Paz 364

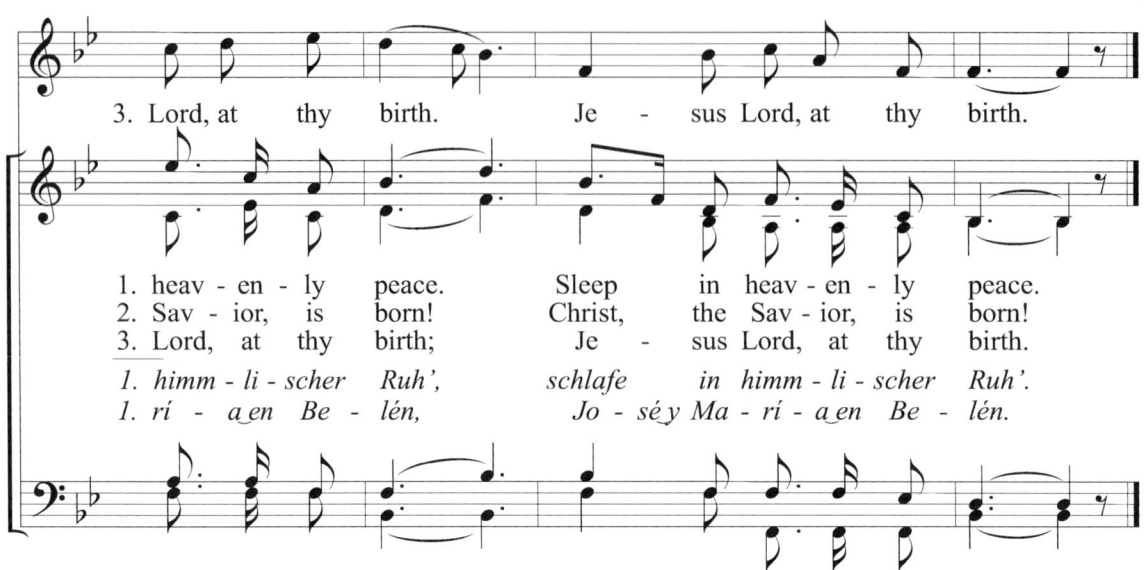

Text: Joseph Mohr, 1792–1848; English tr. John Freeman Young, 1820–1885; Español tr. Federico Fliedner, 1845–1901.
Music: STILLE NACHT, irregular, Franz Gruber, 1787–1863.
Descant: Christine Manderfeld, OSB, b. 1938, © 2009, the Sisters of Saint Benedict, St. Joseph, MN. Administered by Liturgical Press, Collegeville, MN. All rights reserved.

Sing a New Song to the Lord 365

Text: Timothy Dudley-Smith, b. 1926, © 1973, Hope Publishing Co., Carol Stream, IL 60188.
Melody: David G. Wilson, © 1973, Jubilate Hymns (admin. by Hope Publishing Co.). Descant: David Schelat, © 1992, GIA Publications, Inc.
All rights reserved. Used with permission.

366 Sing of Mary

Sing of Mary, pg. 2

* *Original text:* Though it drove him from her side, *adapted with permission.*

The arrangement in the accompaniment edition is in a higher key. The arrangement found here should be played when using the Soprano descant.

Text: Roland F. Palmer, SSJE, 1891–1985, © Estate of Roland F. Palmer. All rights reserved. Used with permission.
Music: PLEADING SAVIOR (SALTASH), 87 87 D; acc. Joshua Leavitt's *Christian Lyre,* 1830.
Descant: Randall Sensmeier, © 1992, GIA Publications, Inc. All rights reserved. Used with permission.

367   Sing Out, Earth and Skies

Verses (Cantor / All:)

1. Come, O God of all the earth: Come to us, O Righteous One;
2. Come, O God of wind and flame: Fill the earth with righteousness;
3. Come, O God of flashing light: Twinkling star and burning sun;
4. Come, O God of snow and rain: Shower down upon the earth;
5. Come, O Justice, Come, O Peace: Come and shape our hearts anew;

(Cantor / All:)

1. Come, and bring our love to birth: In the glory of your Son.
2. Teach us all to sing your name: May our lives your love confess.
3. God of day and God of night: In your light we all are one.
4. Come, O God of joy and pain: God of sorrow, God of mirth.
5. Come and make oppression cease: Bring us all to life in you.

Refrain

Sing out, earth and skies! Sing of the God who loves you!
Raise your joyful cries! Dance to the life around you!

Text: Marty Haugen, b. 1950. Music: SING OUT, 7 7 7 7 with refrain, Marty Haugen, b. 1950.
Text and music: © 1985, GIA Publications, Inc. All rights reserved. Used with permission.

Sing Praise to God Who Reigns Above 368

Sing Praise to God Who Reigns Above, pg. 2

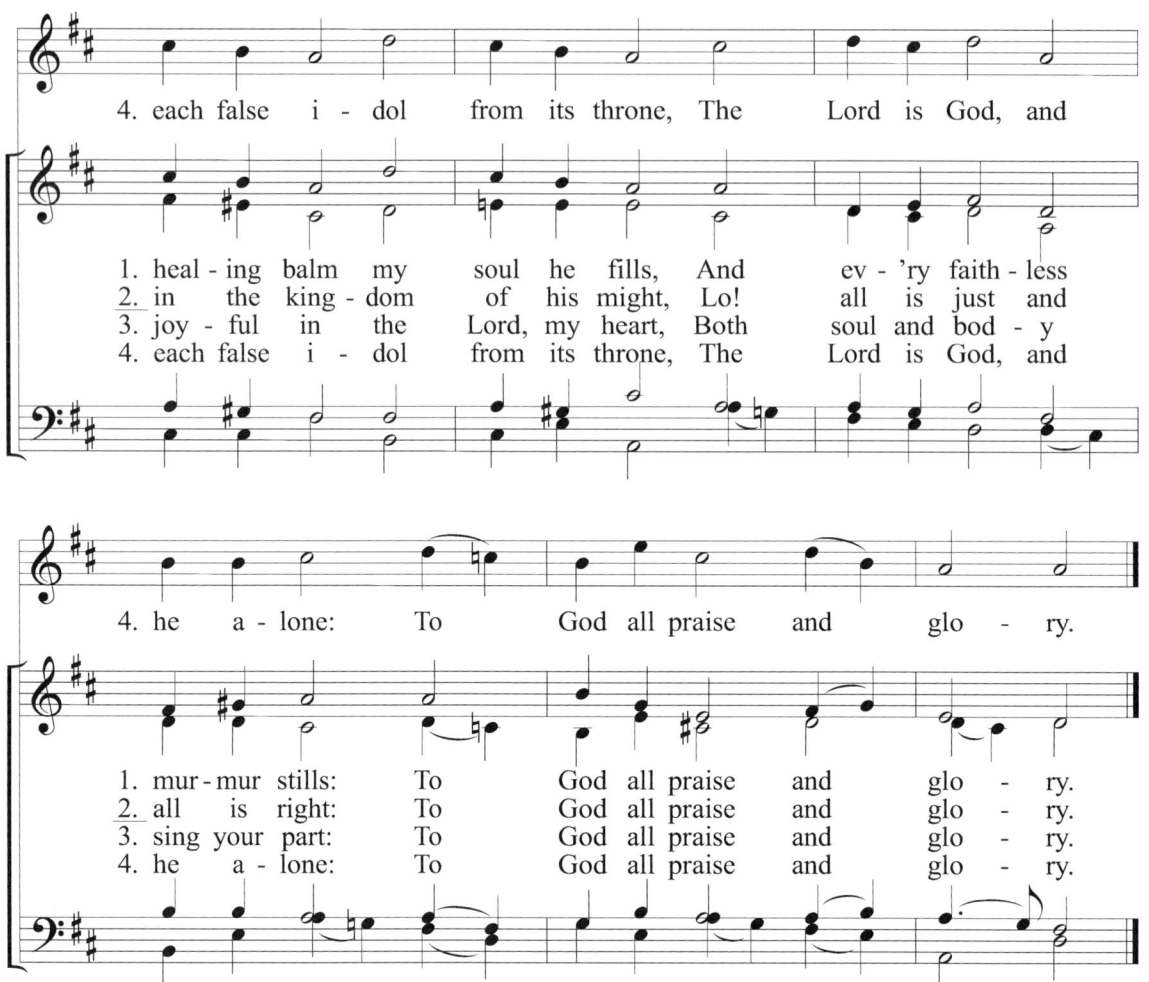

Text: *Sei Lob und Ehr' dem höchsten Gut;* Johann J. Schütz, 1640–1690; tr. by Frances E. Cox, 1812–1897.
Music: MIT FREUDEN ZART, 87 87 88 7; *Bohemian Brethren's Kirchengesänge,* 1566.
Descant: Christine Manderfeld, OSB, b. 1938, © 2009, the Sisters of Saint Benedict, St. Joseph, MN. Administered by Liturgical Press, Collegeville, MN. All rights reserved.

Sing We of the Blessed Mother 369

Sing We Triumphant Hymns of Praise 370

Sing We Triumphant Hymns of Praise, pg. 2

Text: The Venerable Bede, c. 673–735; tr. John David Chambers, 1805–1893; vv. 1, 2, & 4; Benjamin Webb, 1819–1885, v. 3.
Music: LASST UNS ERFREUEN, LM 88 44 88 with alleluias, *Geistliche Kirchengesange,* Cologne, 1623.
Harmony: Christine Manderfeld, OSB, b. 1938, © 2009, the Sisters of Saint Benedict, St. Joseph, MN. Administered by Liturgical Press, Collegeville, MN. All rights reserved.
Descant: Eugene Martin Lindusky, 1924–2005, © Mary C. Lindusky. All rights reserved. Used with permission.

Sing with All the Saints in Glory 371

Sing with All the Saints in Glory, pg. 2

Text: Based on 1 Corinthians 15:20; adapt. William Josiah Irons, 1812–1883, alt.
Music: HYMN TO JOY, 87 87 D, Ludwig van Beethoven, 1770–1827, adapt. Edward Hodges, 1796–1867.
Descant: Christine Manderfeld, OSB, b. 1938, © 2009, the Sisters of Saint Benedict, St. Joseph, MN. Administered by Liturgical Press, Collegeville, MN. All rights reserved.

Singers, Sing 372

1. Singers, sing, and trumpets, play! Christ has conquered death today. Join the endless hymn of praise; All creation, sing always: Alleluia. Alleluia, alleluia, alleluia!

2. Holy, holy risen Lord; Hear the song of life restored. You are our triumphant King, And your joyful people sing! Alleluia. Alleluia, alleluia, alleluia!

3. Angels, sing, and swell our hymn! Join with us, you seraphim. Christ has risen where he died; Walked among us glorified! Alleluia. Alleluia, alleluia, alleluia!

Text: Michael Gannon. Music: CHRIST IST ERSTANDEN, 77 77 4 with refrain; German, 12th cent.; arr. Paul M. Arbogast.
Text and arr.: © 1955, 1962, World Library Publications, 3708 River Road, Franklin Park, IL 60131. www.wlpmusic.com All rights reserved. Used with permission.

So You Must Do, pg. 2

1. hum-ble ser-vant he knelt at their feet.
2. they might share in his pas-sion and death.
3. you a wit-ness of what you must do."
4. you be will-ing to serve in my name."
5. love each oth-er as I have loved you."

done, so you must do." And he told them, "This is an ex-am-ple; just as I have done, so you must do."

Text: John 13:1-15, adapt. by Marty Haugen, b.1950. Music: Marty Haugen, b.1950.
Text and music: © 1998, GIA Publications, Inc. All rights reserved. Used with permission.

Song of Water 375

Song of Water, pg. 2

Text: Christopher Reicher, © 1980, Christopher Reicher. All rights reserved. Used with permission.
Music: LASST UNS ERFREUEN, LM 88 44 88 with alleluias, *Geistliche Kirchengesange,* Cologne, 1623.
Harmony: Christine Manderfeld, OSB, b. 1938, © 2009, the Sisters of Saint Benedict, St. Joseph, MN. Administered by Liturgical Press, Collegeville, MN. All rights reserved.
Descant: Eugene Martin Lindusky, 1924–2005, © Mary C. Lindusky. All rights reserved. Used with permission.

Song Over the Waters 376

Song Over the Waters, pg. 2

Verses

1. Come fill our waiting hearts with the spirit of
2. Give us a thirst for love, give us a hunger for
3. You are the breath of life, you are the hope of the
4. Come, open ev'ry heart, come now and wake us to

D.S.

1. Jesus, let us shine with your light and peace.
2. justice, make us one with the mind of Christ.
3. hopeless, come and fill us with light and peace.
4. wonder, make us vessels of light and peace.

Sprinkling Rite

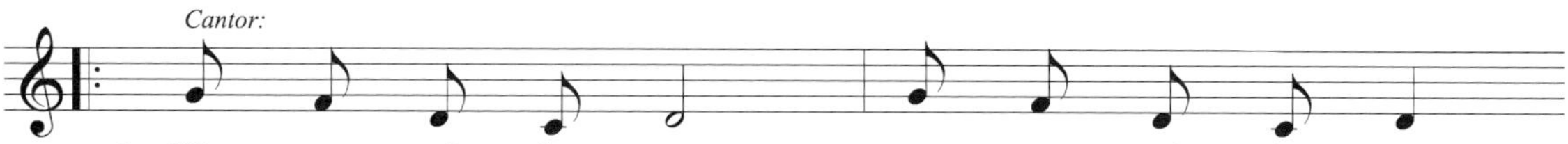

Cantor:

1. Waters of the sea, waters of the earth:
   Waters of the skies, waters of our birth:
2. Rivers of the earth, gentle flowing streams:
   Spirit of our hopes, spirit of our dreams:
3. Waters of the clouds, waters of the wind:
   Waters that will be, waters that have been:
4. Mighty blowing storms, gentle falling rains:
   Water for the vine, water for the grain:
5. You who give us life, you who give us breath:
   You beyond our fears, you beyond our death:
6. You who are the truth, you who are the way:
   You who give us light, lead us in the day:
7. Springing from the earth, dancing from the sky:
   Springing from our hearts, welling up within:
8. Spirit of all hope, spirit of all peace:
   Spirit of all joy, spirit of all life:

All:

Renew us!

Repeat as needed, then to refrain or verse

Text and music: Marty Haugen, b. 1950, © 1987, GIA Publications, Inc. All rights reserved. Used with permission.

Songs of Thankfulness and Praise 377

Soon and Very Soon

378

Text and music: Andraé Crouch, b. 1945, © 1976, Bud John Songs, Inc./Crouch Music/ASCAP.
All rights administered by EMI CMG Publishing. All rights reserved. Used with permission. International copyright secured.

Soul of My Savior   379

1. Soul of my Savior, sanctify my breast;
   Body of Christ, be thou my saving guest;
   Blood of my Savior, bathe me in thy tide,
   Wash me with water flowing from thy side.

2. Strength and protection may thy passion be;
   O Blessed Jesus, hear and answer me;
   Deep in thy wounds, Lord, hide and shelter me,
   So I shall never, never part from thee.

3. Guard and defend me from the foe malign;
   In death's dread moments make me only thine;
   Call me and bid me come to thee on high,
   Where I may praise thee with thy saints for aye.

Text: Pope John XXII, 1249–1334, attr.; tr. Edward Caswall, 1814–1878.
Music: ANIMA CHRISTI, 10 10 10 10, William J. Maher, SJ, 1823–1877.

380 Spirit Blowing through Creation

1. Spirit blowing through creation, Spirit burning in the skies, Let the hope of your salvation fill our eyes; God of splendor, God of glory, You who light the stars above, All the heavens tell the story of your love.

2. As you moved upon the waters, As you ride upon the wind, Move us all, your sons and daughters, deep within; As you shaped the hills and mountains, Formed the land and filled the deep, Let your hand renew and waken all who sleep.

3. Love that sends the rivers dancing, Love that waters all that lives, Love that heals and holds and rouses and forgives; You are hunger in the soul, You are food for all your creatures, In your hands the broken-hearted are made whole.

4. All the creatures you have fashioned, All that live and breathe in you, Find their hope in your compassion, strong and true; You, O Spirit of salvation, You alone, beneath, above, Come, renew your whole creation in your love.

Refrain
Spirit renewing the earth, renewing the

*Refrain may be sung after each verse by using this ending.

381 **Stand Firm in Faith**

Text: Delores Dufner, OSB, b. 1939, © 1983, 2003, GIA Publications, Inc. All rights reserved. Used with permission.
Music: SINE NOMINE, 10 10 10 with alleluias, Ralph Vaughan Williams, 1872–1958.
Descant: Michael Young, © 1979, GIA Publications, Inc. All rights reserved. Used with permission.

Stay Here and Keep Watch   382

Text: Based on Matthew 26, adapt. by the Taizé Community. Music: Jacques Berthier, 1923–1994.
Text and music: © 1984, Les Presses de Taizé, GIA Publications, Inc., North American agent. All rights reserved. Used with permission.

Stewards of Earth, pg. 2

1. Yet for this life it is our cher-ished home.
2. We hear the voice our faith can un-der-stand.
3. While earth gives glo-ry to cre-a-tion's Lord.

Text: Omer Westendorf, 1916–1997, © 1984, World Library Publications, 3708 River Road, Franklin Park, IL 60131. www.wlpmusic.com
All rights reserved. Used with permission.
Music: FINLANDIA 11 10 11 10 11 10, Jean Sibelius, 1856–1957.

Sub Tuum Praesidium / Under Your Protection   384

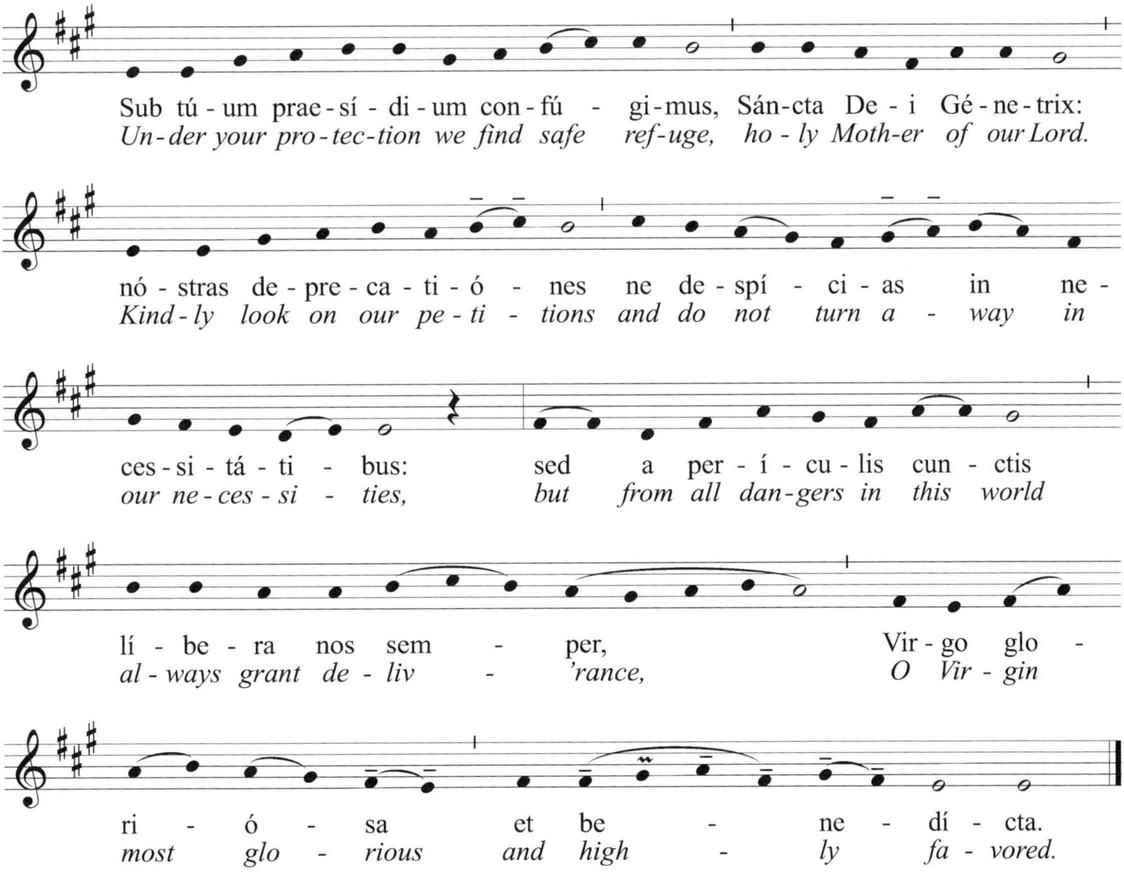

Sub tú-um prae-sí-di-um con-fú-gi-mus, Sán-cta De-i Gé-ne-trix:
Un-der your pro-tec-tion we find safe ref-uge, ho-ly Moth-er of our Lord.

nó-stras de-pre-ca-ti-ó-nes ne de-spí-ci-as in ne-
Kind-ly look on our pe-ti-tions and do not turn a-way in

ces-si-tá-ti-bus: sed a per-í-cu-lis cun-ctis
our ne-ces-si-ties, but from all dan-gers in this world

lí-be-ra nos sem-per, Vir-go glo-
al-ways grant de-liv-'rance, O Vir-gin

ri-ó-sa et be-ne-dí-cta.
most glo-rious and high-ly fa-vored.

Text: *Sub tuum praesidium*; tr. by Bartholomew Sayles, OSB, 1918–2006, and Cecile Gertken, OSB, 1902–2001, © 1987, Order of Saint Benedict, Collegeville, MN.
Administered by Liturgical Press, Collegeville, MN. All rights reserved.
Music: Plainchant, Mode VII.

385 Sweet Refreshment

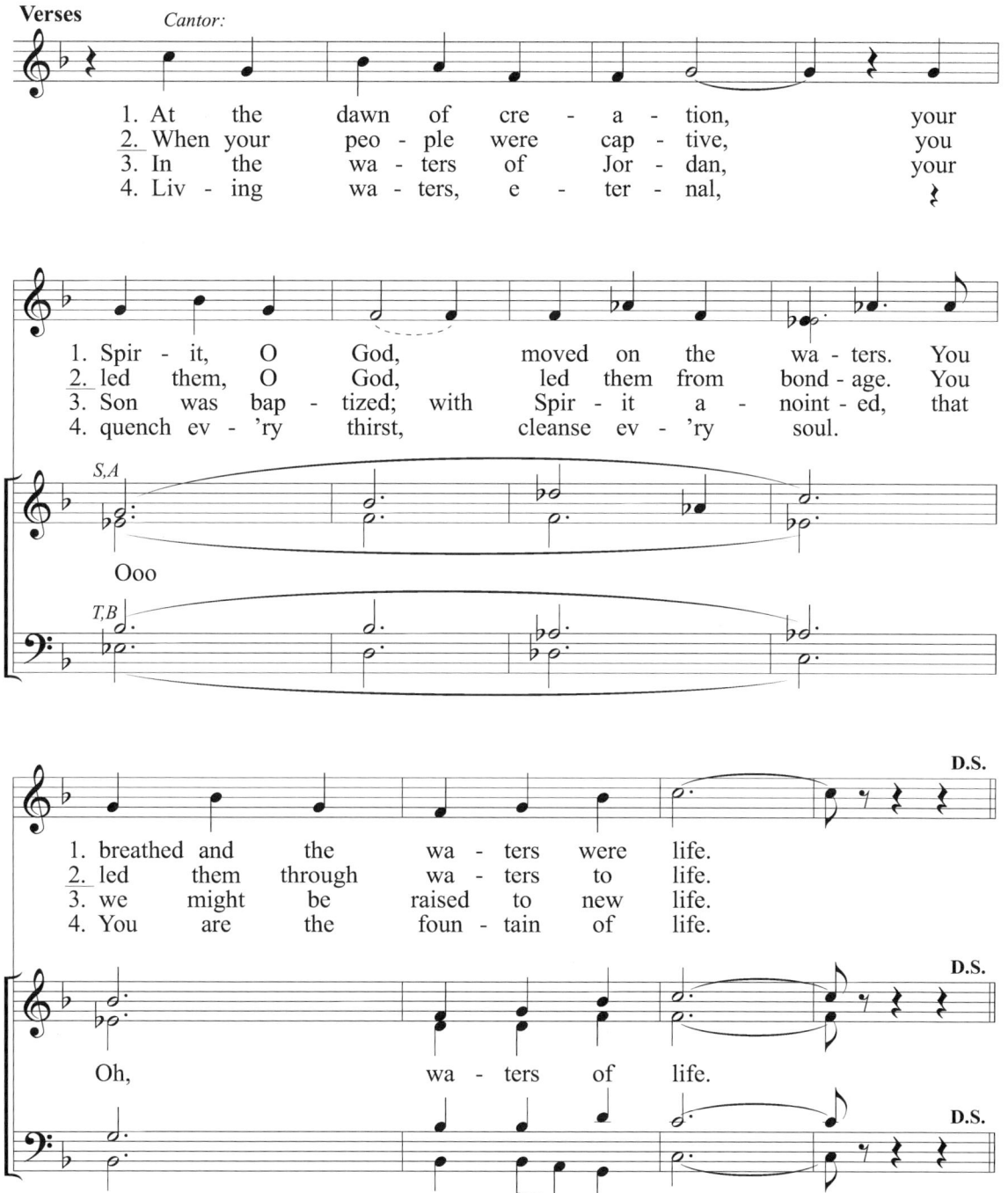

386 Take and Eat

Take and Eat, pg. 2

Text: Refrain—Michael Joncas, b. 1951, © 1989, GIA Publications, Inc.; Verses—James Quinn, SJ, b. 1919, © 1989, James Quinn, SJ, Selah Publishing Co., Inc., North American agent.
Music: Michael Joncas, b. 1951, © 1989, GIA Publications, Inc.
All rights reserved. Used with permission.

387 Take and Eat This Bread

Text and music: Francis Patrick O'Brien, b. 1958, © 1992, GIA Publications, Inc. All rights reserved. Used with permission.

Take, O Take Me as I Am 388

Ostinato Refrain

Text and music: John L. Bell, b. 1949, © 1995, The Iona Community, GIA Publications, Inc., North American agent.
Descant: Tony Alonso, b. 1980, © 2005, GIA Publications, Inc.
All rights reserved. Used with permission.

389 — Take Up Your Cross

1. Take up your cross, the Savior said, If you would my disciple be; Take up your cross with willing heart, And humbly follow after me.
2. Take up your cross, let not its weight Fill your weak spirit with alarm; His strength shall bear your spirit up, And brace your heart, and nerve your arm.
3. Take up your cross, heed not the shame, And let your foolish heart be still; The Lord for you accepted death Upon a cross, on Calv'ry's hill.
4. Take up your cross, then, in his strength, And calmly ev'ry danger brave: It guides you to a better home And leads to vict'ry o'er the grave.
5. Take up your cross, and follow Christ, Nor think till death to lay it down; For only those who bear the cross May hope to wear the glorious crown.

Text: Charles William Everest, 1814–1877. Music: BRESLAU, 88 88, Felix Mendelssohn-Bartholdy, 1809–1847, attr.

Tantum Ergo / Bowing Low 390

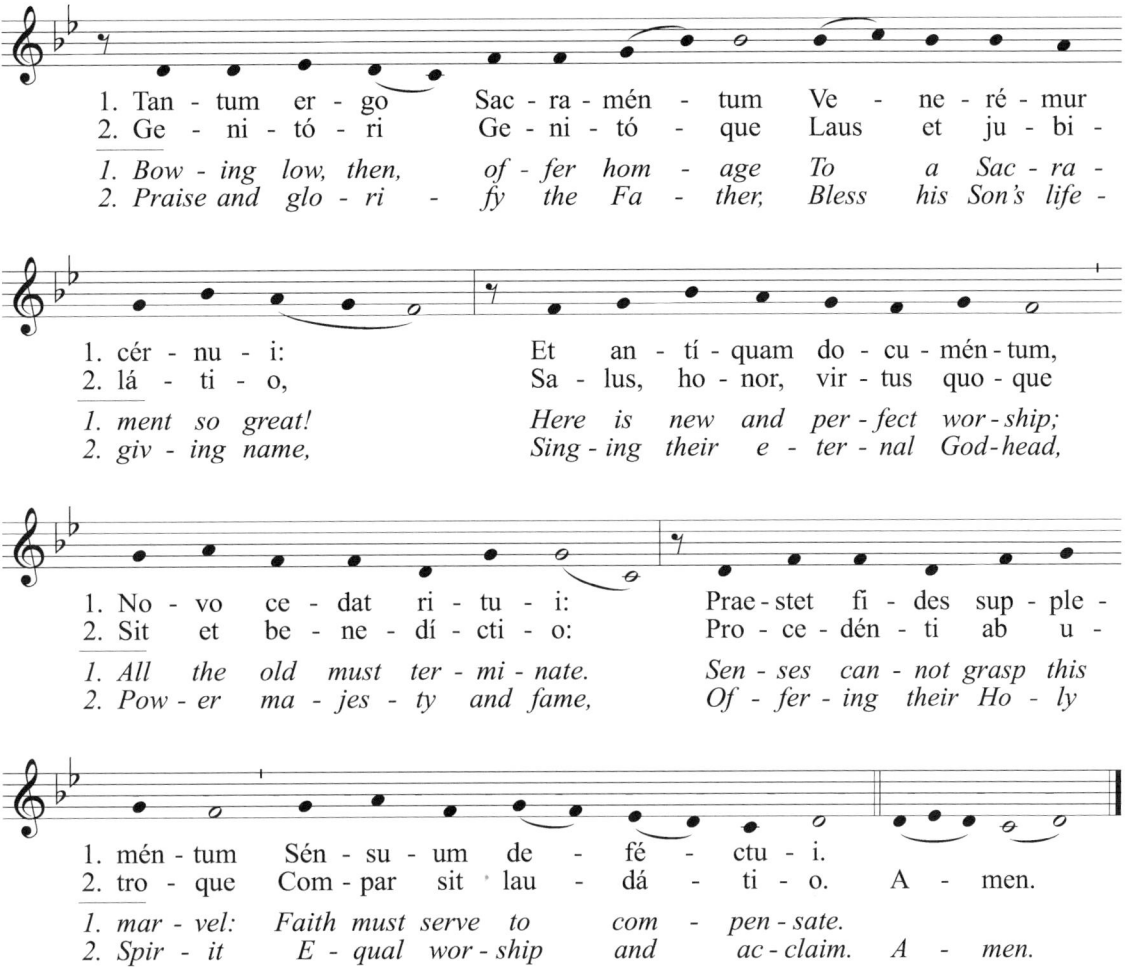

Text: St. Thomas Aquinas, 1227–1274; tr. Benedict Avery, 1919–2008, © 1959, 1977, Order of Saint Benedict, Collegeville, MN.
Administered by Liturgical Press, Collegeville, MN. All rights reserved.
Music: Plainchant Mode III.

391   **Taste and See**

Text: Based on Psalm 34; adapt. by James E. Moore, Jr., b. 1951. Music: James E. Moore, Jr., b. 1951.
Text and music: © 1983, GIA Publications, Inc. All rights reserved. Used with permission.

The Advent of Our God 393

1. The advent of our God With eager prayers we greet.
2. The everlasting Son Came down to make us free;
3. Daughter of Sion, rise To meet your lowly King;
4. As judge on clouds of light, He soon will come again,
5. Then evil flee away Before the rising dawn!
6. Praise to th' incarnate Son Who comes to set us free,

1. And singing, haste upon his road His coming reign to meet.
2. And he a servant's form put on To gain our liberty.
3. Nor let your faithless heart despise The peace he comes to bring.
4. His scattered people to unite, With them in heav'n to reign.
5. Let this old Adam day by day God's image still put on.
6. With Father, Spirit, ever one, To all eternity.

Text: Charles Coffin, 1676–1749; tr. John Chandler, 1806–1876, alt.
Music: FRANCONIA, 66 86, Johann B. Konig, 1691–1758; adapt. and harm. by William Henry Havergal, 1793–1870.
Descant: Christine Manderfeld, OSB, b. 1938, © 2009, the Sisters of Saint Benedict, St. Joseph, MN. Administered by Liturgical Press, Collegeville, MN. All rights reserved.

394 The Church of Christ in Every Age

1. The Church of Christ in ev-'ry age
   Be-set by change but Spir-it led,
   Must claim and test its her-i-tage
   And keep on ris-ing from the dead.

2. A-cross the world, a-cross the street,
   The vic-tims of in-jus-tice cry
   For shel-ter and for bread to eat,
   And nev-er live un-til they die.

3. Then let the ser-vant Church a-rise,
   A car-ing Church that longs to be
   A part-ner in Christ's sac-ri-fice,
   And clothed in Christ's hu-man-i-ty.

4. For he a-lone, whose blood was shed,
   Can cure the fe-ver in our blood,
   And teach us how to share our bread
   And feed the starv-ing mul-ti-tude.

5. We have no mis-sion but to serve
   In full o-be-dience to our Lord:
   To care for all, with-out re-serve,
   And spread his lib-er-at-ing Word.

Text: Fred Pratt Green, 1903–2000, © 1971, Hope Publishing Co., Carol Stream, IL 60188. All rights reserved. Used with permission.
Music: PROSPECT, 88 88; William Walker's *Southern Harmony*; arr. by Marty Haugen, b. 1950, © 1991, GIA Publications, Inc. All rights reserved. Used with permission.

The Church's One Foundation 395

The Church's One Foundation, pg. 2

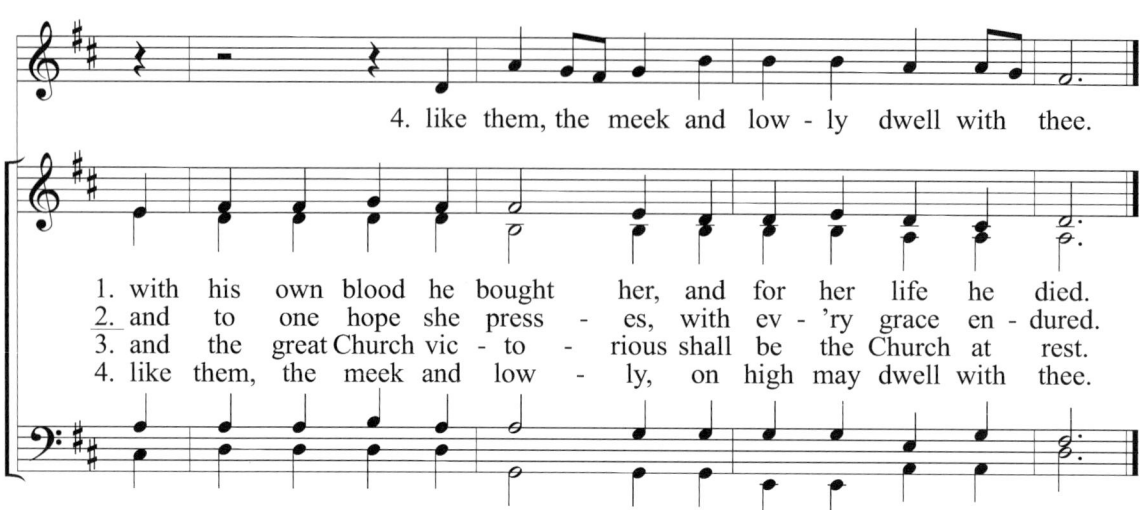

Text: Samuel John Stone, 1839–1900. Music: AURELIA, 76 76 D; Samuel Sebastian Wesley, 1810–1876.
Descant: Christine Manderfeld, OSB, b. 1938, © 2009, the Sisters of Saint Benedict, St. Joseph, MN. Administered by Liturgical Press, Collegeville, MN. All rights reserved.

The Cross of Jesus 396

The Day of Resurrection 397

The Day of Resurrection, pg. 2

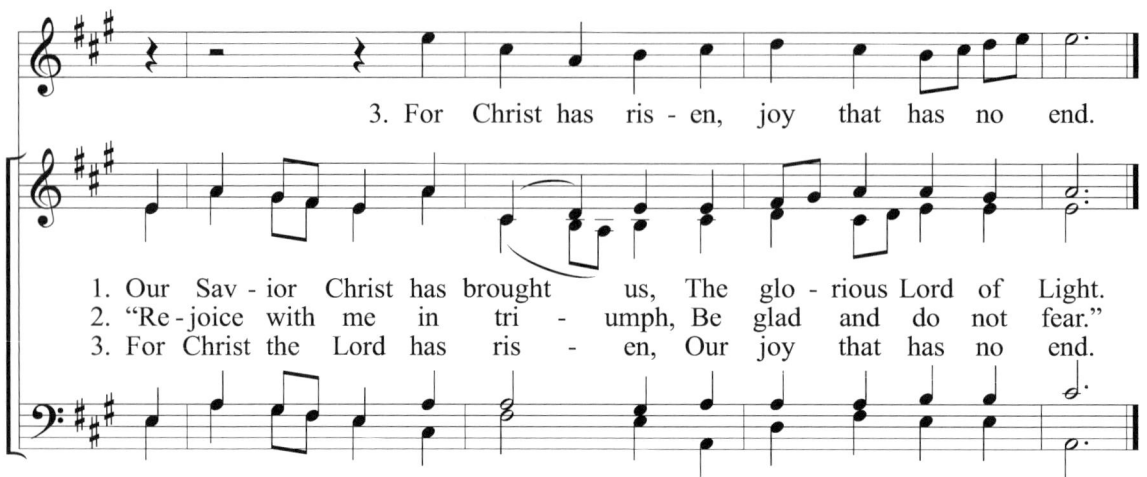

Text: St. John of Damascus, c. 675–749; tr. John Mason Neale, 1818–1866, alt. Music: ELLACOMBE, 76 76 D, *Würtemburg Gesangbuch,* 1784.
Descant: Christine Manderfeld, OSB, b. 1938, © 2009, the Sisters of Saint Benedict, St. Joseph, MN. Administered by Liturgical Press, Collegeville, MN. All rights reserved.

The First Nowell 398

The First Nowell, pg. 2

Text: English carol, 17th cent. Music: THE FIRST NOWELL, irregular with refrain, English carol; harm. by John Stainer, 1840–1901.
Descant: Christine Manderfeld, OSB, b. 1938, © 2009, the Sisters of Saint Benedict, St. Joseph, MN. Administered by Liturgical Press, Collegeville, MN. All rights reserved.

The Glory of These Forty Days   399

Text: *Clarum decus jejunii;* ascr. to Gregory the Great, c. 540–604; tr. Maurice F. Bell, 1862–1947.
Music: ERHALT UNS HERR, LM, Klug's *Geistliche Lieder,* 1543.
Descant: Randall Sensmeier, © 1992, GIA Publications, Inc. All rights reserved. Used with permission.

400 The God Whom Earth and Sea and Sky

1. The God whom earth and sea and sky Adore and laud and magnify, Whose might they own, whose praise they tell, In Mary's body deigned to dwell.
2. O Mother blest! the chosen shrine Wherein the Architect divine, Whose hand contains the earth and sky, Vouchsafed in hidden guise to lie.
3. Blest in the message Gabriel brought; Blest in the work the Spirit wrought; Most blest, to bring to human birth The long desired of all the earth.
4. O Lord, the Virgin-born, to thee Eternal praise and glory be, Whom with the Father we adore And Holy Spirit evermore.

Text: Anon., Latin, 11th cent.; tr. John Mason Neale, 1818–1866. Music: WAREHAM, 88 88, William Knapp, 1698–1768.
Descant: Sydney Hugo Nicholson, 1875–1987, © 1982, Royal School of Church Music. All rights reserved. Used with permission.

The King of Love — 401

402 — The King Shall Come

1. The King shall come when morning dawns And light triumphant breaks, When beauty gilds the eastern hills And life to joy awakes.
2. Not as of old a little child, To bear and fight and die, But crowned with glory like the sun That lights the morning sky.
3. Oh, brighter than the rising morn When Christ, victorious, rose And left the lonesome place of death, Despite the rage of foes.
4. Oh, brighter than that glorious morn Shall dawn upon our race The day when Christ in splendor comes, And we shall see his face.
5. The King shall come when morning dawns And light and beauty brings. Hail, Christ the Lord! Your people pray: Come quickly, King of kings.

Text: John Brownlie, alt. Music: MORNING SONG, 86 86, *Kentucky Harmony.*
Descant: Christine Manderfeld, OSB, b. 1938, © 2009, the Sisters of Saint Benedict, St. Joseph, MN. Administered by Liturgical Press, Collegeville, MN. All rights reserved.

The Reign of God 403

1. The reign of God like farmer's field, bears weeds along with wheat; the good and bad are intertwined till harvest is complete.
2. Like mustard tree, the reign of God from tiny seed will spread, till birds of ev'ry feather come to nest, and there be fed.
3. Though hidden now, the reign of God may yet, unnoticed, grow; from deep within it rises up, like yeast in swelling dough.
4. The reign of God is come in Christ; the reign of God is near. Ablaze among us, kindling hearts, the reign of God is here!

Text: Delores Dufner, OSB, b. 1939, © 1995, 2003, GIA Publications, Inc. All rights reserved. Used with permission.
Music: MCKEE, 86 86, African-American spiritual; adapt. Harry T. Burleigh, 1866–1949.
Descant: Christine Manderfeld, OSB, b. 1938, © 2009, the Sisters of Saint Benedict, St. Joseph, MN. Administered by Liturgical Press, Collegeville, MN. All rights reserved.

404 The Snow Lay on the Ground

Verses

1. The snow lay on the ground, the stars shone bright, When Christ our Lord was born on Christmas night. *To refrain*
2a. 'Twas Mary, daughter pure of holy Anne, that brought into this world the God made man. *To verse 2b*
2b. She laid Him in a stall at Bethlehem; The ass and oxen shared the roof with them. *To refrain*
3a. Saint Joseph, too, was by to tend the Child, To guard Him and protect His Mother mild. *To verse 3b*
3b. The Angels hover'd round and sang this song, Venite adoremus Dominum. *To refrain*
4a. And then that manger poor became a throne, For He whom Mary bore was God the Son. *To verse 4b*
4b. Oh, come, then, let us join the heav'nly host, To praise the Father, Son and Holy Ghost. *To refrain*

Refrain

Venite adoremus Dominum,
Venite adoremus Dominum.

Text: Old English carol. Music: VENITE, ADOREMUS, irregular with refrain.

The Song of the Trees 405

Verses

1. O sing to the Lord a song that's new, A song for the Lord of all. Proclaim his help each day that comes, His wondrous works and deeds.
2. Indeed he is worthy to be praised; All glory and might are his. An off'ring bring into his courts, His kingship there proclaim.
3. Let heaven exult and earth be glad, The sea thunder forth its praise. Let earth and all it bears rejoice Before the Lord who comes.
4. The presence of God is ev'rywhere, He comes now to rule the earth. With justice he will govern all, All people judge with truth.

Refrain

Let the trees of the woods all clap their hands, All

The Song of the Trees, pg. 2

Text: Based on Psalm 96, adapt. by Henry Bryan Hayes, OSB, b. 1920.
Music: SAYLOR'S CREEK, 97 86 with refrain, Henry Bryan Hayes, OSB, b. 1920.
Text and music: © 1981, Order of Saint Benedict, Collegeville, MN, administered by Liturgical Press, Collegeville, MN. All rights reserved.

406 The Strife Is O'er, the Battle Done

The Strife Is O'er, the Battle Done, pg. 2

Text: Anon.; tr. by Francis Pott, 1832–1909, alt.
Music: VICTORY, 888 with alleluias, Giovanni Pierluigi da Palestrina, c. 1525–1594; adapt. with alleluias, William Henry Monk, 1823–1889.
Descant: Randall Sensmeier, © 1992, GIA Publications, Inc. All rights reserved. Used with permission.

407   The Summons

The Summons, pg. 2

Text: John L. Bell, b. 1949, © 1987, Iona Community.
Music: KELVINGROVE, 7 6 7 6 777 6; Scottish traditional; descant © 1995, Wild Goose Resource Group, The Iona Community.
GIA Publications, Inc., North American agent. All rights reserved. Used with permission.

408 The Thirsty Cry for Water, Lord

1. The thirsty cry for water, Lord; the hungry plead for bread. And many long to rise again, where hope, cast down, lies dead.
2. The cup of water poured in love the pangs of thirst will still. The bread of earth you bid us share, the famished child can fill.
3. But help us also hear the cry of hung'ring, thirsting hearts for living water, bread of life your grace alone imparts.
4. And come to us, O risen Christ, our restless souls relieve; and satisfy our starving hearts that we may rise and live.

Text: Herman G. Stuempfle, Jr., 1923–2007, © 1994, 1997, GIA Publications, Inc. All rights reserved. Used with permission.
Music: LAND OF REST, CM, traditional American folk melody; harm. by Richard Proulx, b. 1937, © 1975, GIA Publications, Inc. All rights reserved. Used with permission.
Descant: Christine Manderfeld, OSB, b. 1938, © 2009, the Sisters of Saint Benedict, St. Joseph, MN. Administered by Liturgical Press, Collegeville, MN. All rights reserved.

The Time of Fulfillment   409

The Tomb Is Empty! 410

Text: Sylvia Dunstan, 1955–1993, © 1991, GIA Publications, Inc. All rights reserved. Used with permission.
Music: MCKEE, CM 86 86, African-American spiritual; adapt. Harry T. Burleigh, 1866–1949.
Descant: Christine Manderfeld, OSB, b. 1938, © 2009, the Sisters of Saint Benedict, St. Joseph, MN. Administered by Liturgical Press, Collegeville, MN. All rights reserved.

411 The Voice of God Speaks but of Peace

Verses

1. The voice of God speaks but of peace; Peace for all his friends,
2. Mercy and faithfulness have met, Justice and peace embraced.
3. The Lord shall bless our daily work; Earth shall yield its fruit.

1. For those who turn to him their heart, His help is always near.
2. God's love smiles up from earth below, His justice down from heav'n.
3. Justice shall march before the Lord, And peace behind his steps.

Refrain

Restore again our life, O Lord, May we rejoice in you!
Your mercy let us see, O Lord, Give us your saving help.

Text: Based on Psalm 85; adapt. by Henry Bryan Hayes, OSB, b. 1920. Music: SHALOM, 85 85 with refrain, Henry Bryan Hayes, OSB.
Text and music: © 1981, Order of Saint Benedict, administered by Liturgical Press, Collegeville, MN 56321. All rights reserved.

There Is a Balm in Gilead 412

Text: Based on Jeremiah 8:22. Music: BALM IN GILEAD, irregular with refrain, spiritual.
Descant: © 2009, Liturgical Press, Collegeville, MN 56321. All rights reserved.

413   There's a Wideness in God's Mercy

There's a Wideness in God's Mercy, pg. 2

Text: Frederick William Faber, 1814–1863, alt.
Music: 87 87 D, Gerard Wojchowski, OSB, 1925–1997, © 1977, Order of Saint Benedict, Collegeville, MN.
Descant: Christine Manderfeld, OSB, b. 1938, © 2009, the Sisters of Saint Benedict, St. Joseph, MN.
Music and descant administered by Liturgical Press, Collegeville, MN. All rights reserved.

414 This Day God Gives Me

Text: St. Patrick, 372–466; tr. James Quinn, SJ, b. 1919, © James Quinn, SJ, Selah Publishing Co., North American agent. All rights reserved. Used with permission.
Music: BUNESSAN, 5 5 5 4 D; traditional Gaelic melody. Descant: Donald Busarow, © 1992, GIA Publications, Inc. All rights reserved. Used with permission.

416 This Is My Song

1. This is my song, O God of all the nations,
A song of peace for lands afar and mine.
This is my home, the country where my heart is;
Here are my hopes, my dreams, my holy shrine;

2. My country's skies are bluer than the ocean,
And sunlight beams on cloverleaf and pine.
But other lands have sunlight too, and clover,
And skies are ev'rywhere as blue as mine.

3. This is my prayer, O Lord of all earth's kingdoms,
Thy kingdom come; on earth thy will be done.
Let Christ be lifted up till all shall serve him,
And hearts united learn to live as one.

This Is My Song, pg. 2

Text: Vv. 1 & 2 Lloyd Stone, v. 3 Georgia Harkness, © 1964, Lorenz Publishing Co. All rights reserved. International copyright secured. Used with permission.
Music: FINLANDIA 11 10 11 10 11 10, Jean Sibelius, 1856–1957.

417 This Is the Day

Text: Based on Psalm 118; adapt. by Paul F. Page. Music: Paul F. Page.
Text and music: © 1998, World Library Publications, 3708 River Road, Franklin Park, IL 60131. www.wlpmusic.com All rights reserved. Used with permission.

This Is the Feast of Victory (Festival Canticle) 418

Text: Based on Revelation 5; John W. Arthur, 1922–1980, © 1978, *Lutheran Book of Worship*, administered by Augsburg Fortress.
Music: FESTIVAL CANTICLE, irregular, Richard Hillert, b. 1923, © 1975, 1988, Richard Hillert.
All rights reserved. Used with permission.

419 Those Who Love and Those Who Labor

Text: Geoffrey Dearmer, 1893–1996, © Oxford University Press. All rights reserved. Used with permission.
Music: DOMHNACH TRIONOIDE, 87 87 D, Gaelic; harm. by Edward Currie.
Descant: Christine Manderfeld, OSB, b. 1938, © 2009, the Sisters of Saint Benedict, St. Joseph, MN. Administered by Liturgical Press, Collegeville, MN. All rights reserved.

420 Though We Are Many

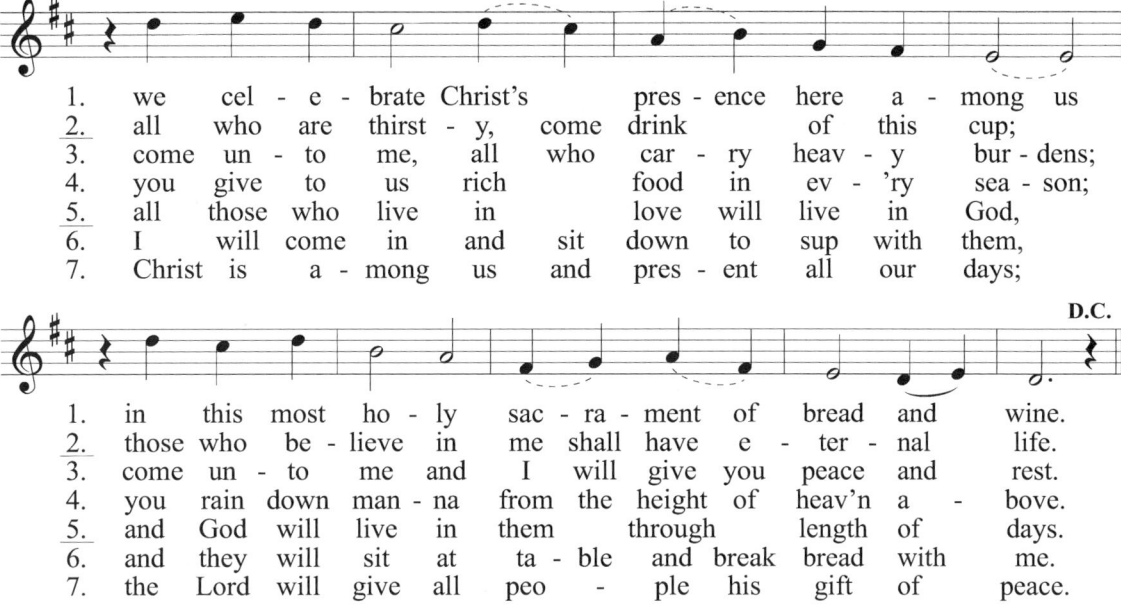

421 Throughout All Time

422 'Tis Good, Lord, to Be Here

1. 'Tis good, Lord, to be here! Your glory fills the night; Your face and garments, like the sun, Shine with un-bor-rowed light.
2. 'Tis good, Lord, to be here, Your beauty to behold, Where Moses and Elijah stand, Your messengers of old.
3. Fulfiller of the past! Promise of things to be! We hail your body glorified, And our redemption see.
4. 'Tis good, Lord, to be here! Yet we may not remain; But since you bid us leave the mount, Come with us to the plain.

Text: Joseph A. Robinson, 1858–1933, alt. Music: SWABIA, 66 86, Johann J. Speiss, 1715–1772; adapt. William H. Havergal, 1793–1870.
Descant: Christine Manderfeld, OSB, b. 1938, © 2009, the Sisters of Saint Benedict, St. Joseph, MN. Administered by Liturgical Press, Collegeville, MN. All rights reserved.

To Be Your Presence

423

Text: Delores Dufner, OSB, b. 1939, © 2000, 2003, GIA Publications, Inc. All rights reserved. Used with permission.
Music: ENGELBERG, 10 10 10 with alleluia; Charles V. Stanford, 1852–1924; harm. Robert Batastini, © 2000, GIA Publications, Inc. All rights reserved. Used with permission.
Descant: Christine Manderfeld, OSB, b. 1938, © 2009, the Sisters of Saint Benedict, St. Joseph, MN. Administered by Liturgical Press, Collegeville, MN. All rights reserved.

To Jesus Christ, Our Sovereign King   424

To Jesus Christ, Our Sovereign King, pg. 2

Text: Martin B. Hellrigel, 1890–1981, © 1941, assigned 1978 to Mrs. Irene C. Mueller. All rights reserved. Used with permission.
Music: ICH GLAUB AN GOTT, 87 87 with refrain; *Mainz Gesangbuch*, 1870;
harm. by Richard Proulx, b. 1937, © 1986, GIA Publications, Inc. All rights reserved. Used with permission.
Descant: Randall Sensmeier, © 1992, GIA Publications, Inc. All rights reserved. Used with permission.

425 Today We Have Gathered

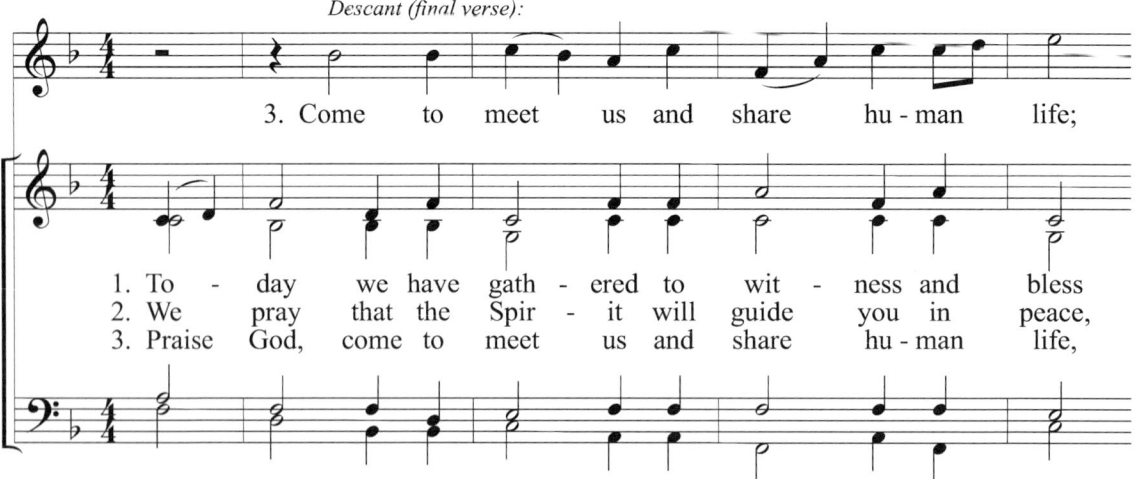

Text: Ruth Duck, b. 1947, © 1996, The Pilgrim Press. From *Circles of Care*. All rights reserved. Used with permission.
Music: FOUNDATION, 11 11 D, *The Sacred Harp*, 1844; arr. Russell Wollen, b. 1923.
Descant: Christine Manderfeld, OSB, b. 1938, © 2009, the Sisters of Saint Benedict, St. Joseph, MN. Administered by Liturgical Press, Collegeville, MN. All rights reserved.

426 Transform Us

1. Transform us as you, transfigured, Stood apart on Tabor's height. Lead us up our sacred mountains, Search us with revealing light. Lift us from where we have fallen, Full of questions, filled with fright.

2. Transform us as you, transfigured, Once spoke with those holy ones. We, surrounded by the witness Of those saints whose work is done, Live in this world as your Body, Chosen daughters, chosen sons.

3. Transform us as you, transfigured, Would not stay within a shrine. Keep us from our great temptation— Time and truth we quickly bind, Lead us down those daily pathways Where our love is not confined.

Text: Sylvia Dunstan, 1955–1993, © 1993 GIA Publications, Inc. All rights reserved. Used with permission.
Music: PICARDY, 87 87 87; French carol. Descant: Randall Sensmeier, © 1992 GIA Publications, Inc. All rights reserved. Used with permission.

Tree of Life 427

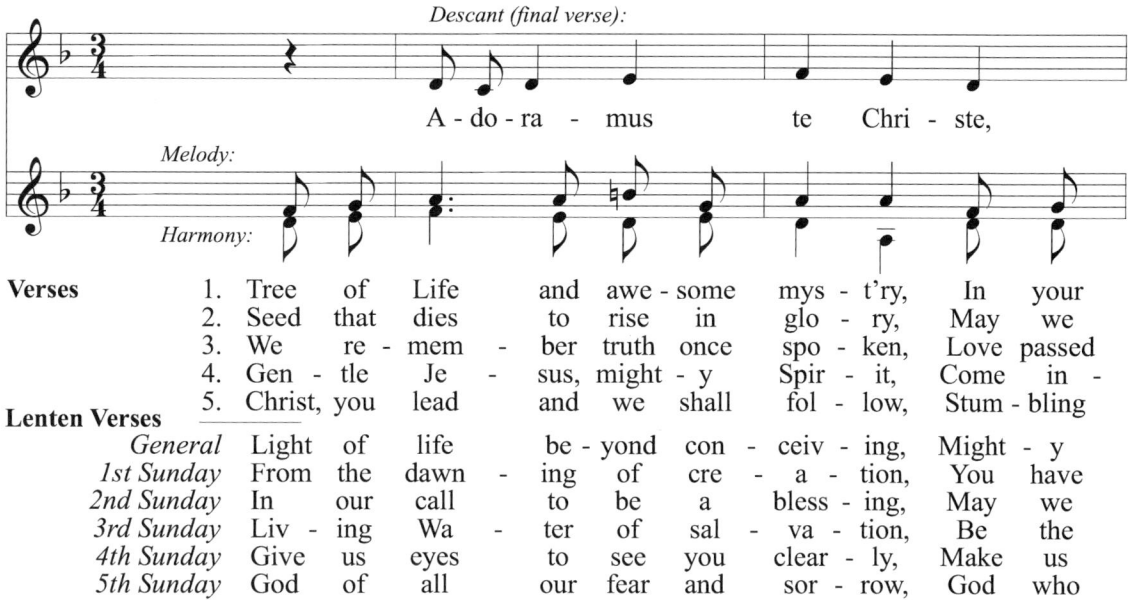

Verses
1. Tree of Life and awe-some mys-t'ry, In your
2. Seed that dies to rise in glo-ry, May we
3. We re-mem-ber truth once spo-ken, Love passed
4. Gen-tle Je-sus, might-y Spir-it, Come in-
5. Christ, you lead and we shall fol-low, Stum-bling

Lenten Verses
- *General* — Light of life be-yond con-ceiv-ing, Might-y
- *1st Sunday* — From the dawn-ing of cre-a-tion, You have
- *2nd Sunday* — In our call to be a bless-ing, May we
- *3rd Sunday* — Liv-ing Wa-ter of sal-va-tion, Be the
- *4th Sunday* — Give us eyes to see you clear-ly, Make us
- *5th Sunday* — God of all our fear and sor-row, God who

1. death we are re-born, Though you die in all of
2. see our-selves in you, If we learn to live your
3. on through act and word, Ev-'ry per-son lost and
4. flame our hearts a-new, We may all your joy in-
5. though our steps may be, One with you in joy and

- *Gen* — Spir-it of our Lord; Give new strength to our be-
- *1st* — loved us as your own; Stay with us through all temp-
- *2nd* — be a bless-ing true; May we live and die con-
- *3rd* — foun-tain of each soul; Spring-ing up in new cre-
- *4th* — chil-dren of your light; Give us hearts to live more
- *5th* — lives be-yond our death; Hold us close through each to-

Tree of Life, pg. 2

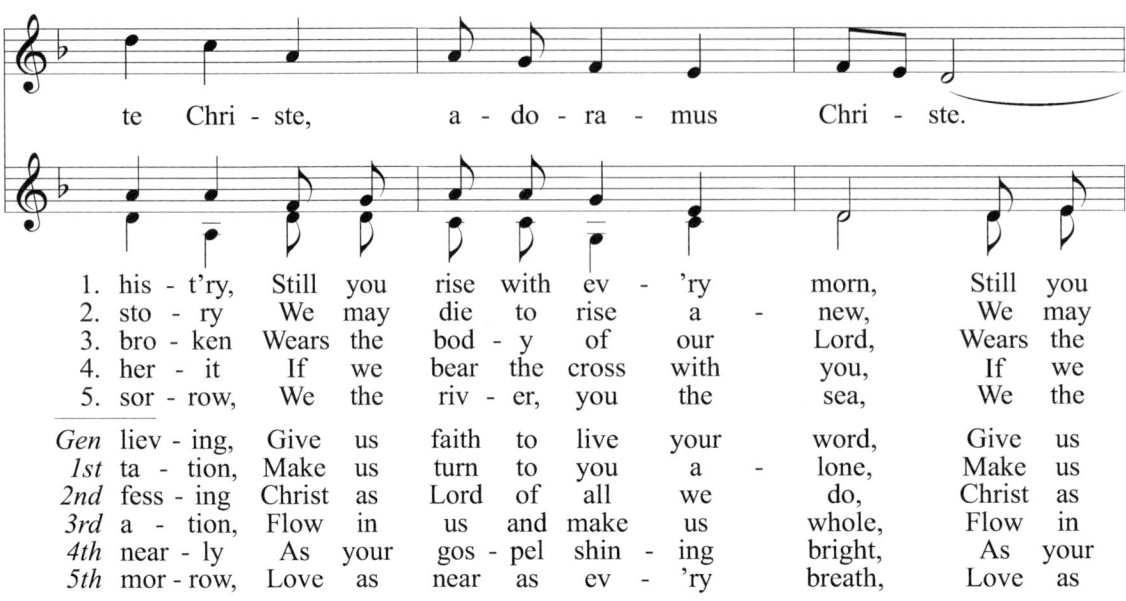

Text: Marty Haugen, b. 1950. Music: THOMAS, 8 7 8 77; Marty Haugen, b. 1950. Text and music: © 1984, GIA Publications, Inc. All rights reserved. Used with permission.

Ubi Caritas / Live in Charity 428

Refrain
U - bi ca - ri - tas et a - mor,
Live in char - i - ty and stead - fast love,
u - bi ca - ri - tas De - us i - bi est.
live in char - i - ty; God will dwell with you.

Verse 1
1. If I have the gift of prophecy, understanding all the mysteries there are, know-ing ev-'ry-thing; if I have faith in all its full-ness to move moun-tains, but have not love, I am noth-ing at all.

Verse 2
2. If I give ev'rything I have to feed the poor, and let them take my bod-y to be burned, but have not love, I gain noth-ing at all.

Text: Based on 1 Corinthians 13:2-8; adapt. by the Taizé Community, 1978. Music: Jacques Berthier, 1923–1994.
Text and music: © 1979, Les Presses de Taizé, GIA Publications, Inc., North American agent. All rights reserved. Used with permission.

Ubi Caritas / Where Charity and Love Are Found 429

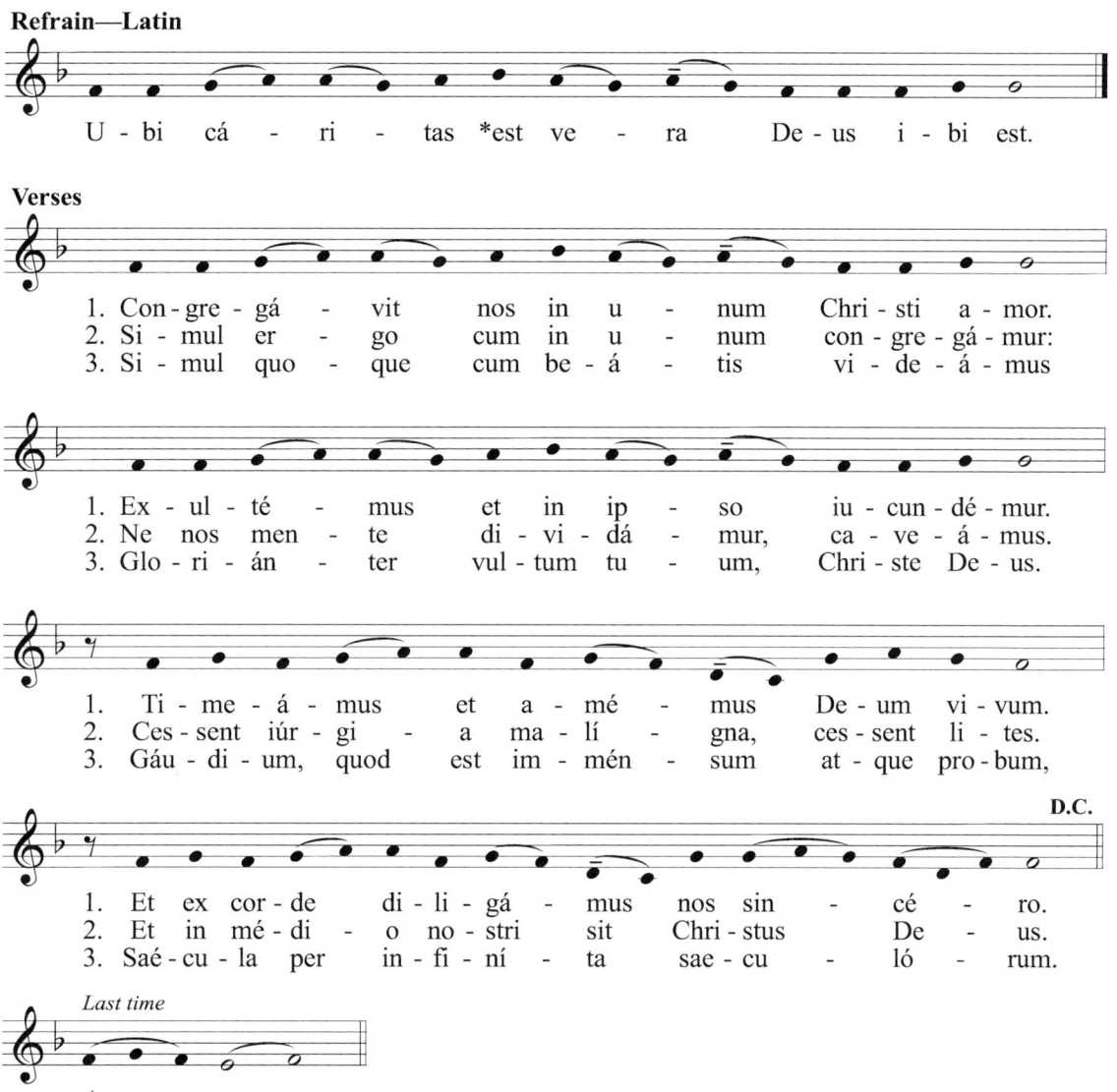

*Version taken from the 1973 edition of the *Roman Missal*. Previous editions of the *Missal* used "et amor."

Text: Anon. Music: UBI CARITAS, Plainchant, Mode VI.

Ubi Caritas / Where Charity and Love Are Found, pg. 2

Text: Anon. Music: UBI CARITAS, Plainchant, Mode VI.

Unseen God, Your Hand Has Guided 430

Text: Herman G. Stuempfle, Jr., 1923–2007, © 1998, 2000, GIA Publications, Inc. All rights reserved. Used with permission.
Music: STUTTGART, 87 87, Christian Friedrich Witt, 1660–1716; adapt. and harm. William Henry Havergal, 1793–1870, alt.
Descant: Christine Manderfeld, OSB, © 2009, the Sisters of Saint Benedict, St. Joseph, MN. Administered by Liturgical Press, Collegeville, MN. All rights reserved.

Veni Creator Spiritus

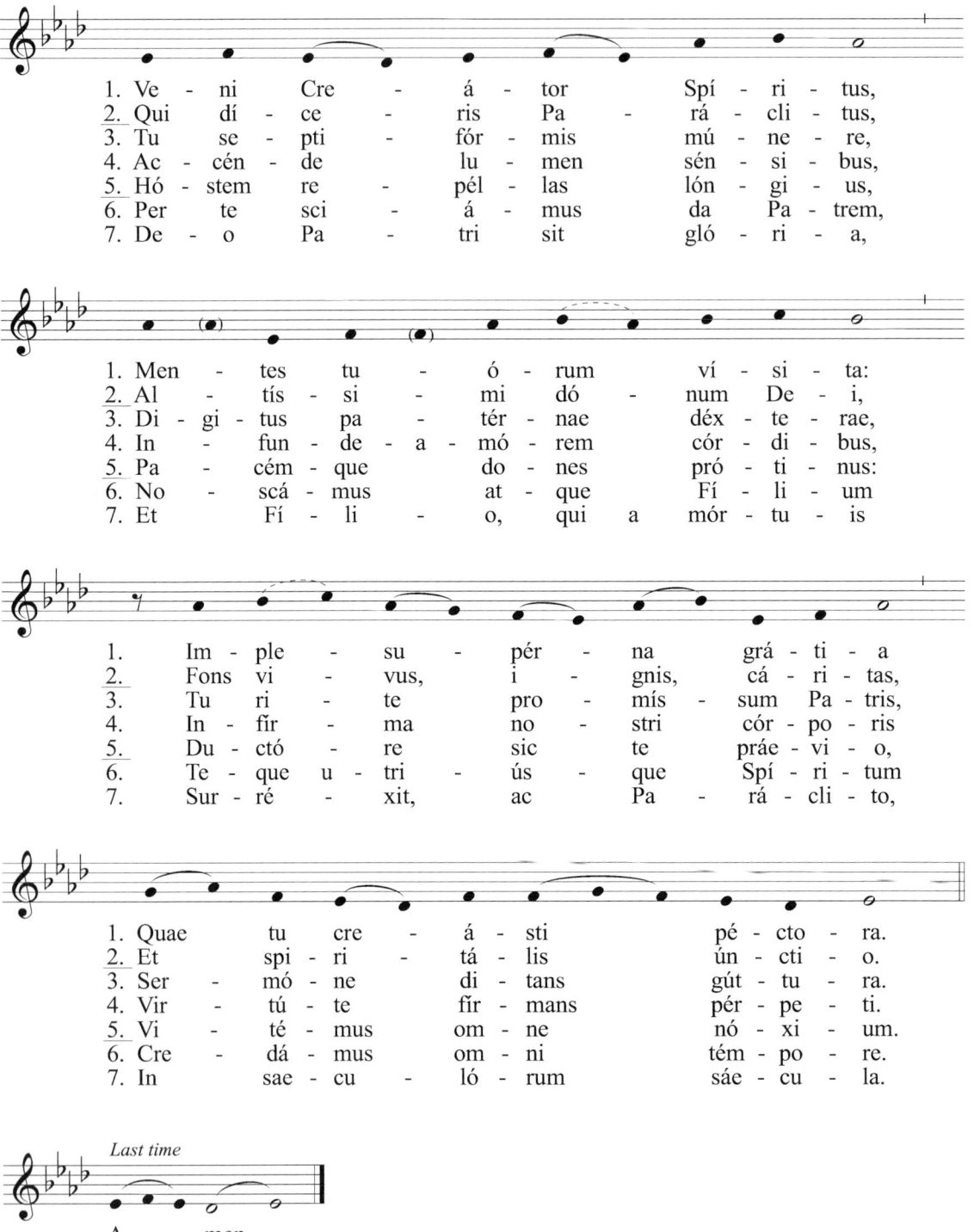

1. Veni Creátor Spíritus, Mentes tuórum vísita: Imple supérna grátia Quae tu creásti péctora.
2. Qui díceris Paráclitus, Altíssimi donum Dei, Fons vivus, ignis, cáritas, Et spiritális únctio.
3. Tu septifórmis múnere, Dígitus patérnae déxterae, Tu rite promíssum Patris, Sermóne ditans gúttura.
4. Accénde lumen sénsibus, Infúnde amórem córdibus, Infírma nostri córporis Virtúte firmans pérpeti.
5. Hóstem repéllas lóngius, Pacémque dones prótinus: Ductóre sic te práevio, Vitémus omne nóxium.
6. Per te sciámus da Patrem, Noscámus atque Fílium, Te que utriúsque Spíritum Credámus omni témpore.
7. Deo Patri sit glória, Et Fílio, qui a mórtuis Surréxit, ac Paráclito, In saeculórum saécula.

Last time
A - men.

Text: Attr. to Rabanus Maurus, 776–856. Music: VENI CREATOR SPIRITUS, LM; Mode VIII.

Veni, Lumen Cordium

432

Text: Stephen Langton, b. 1228. Music: Margaret Rizza, © 1997, Kevin Mayhew Ltd.
Administered and sub-published in North America by GIA Publications, Inc. All rights reserved. Used with permission.

Veni Sancte Spiritus

Ostinato Refrain

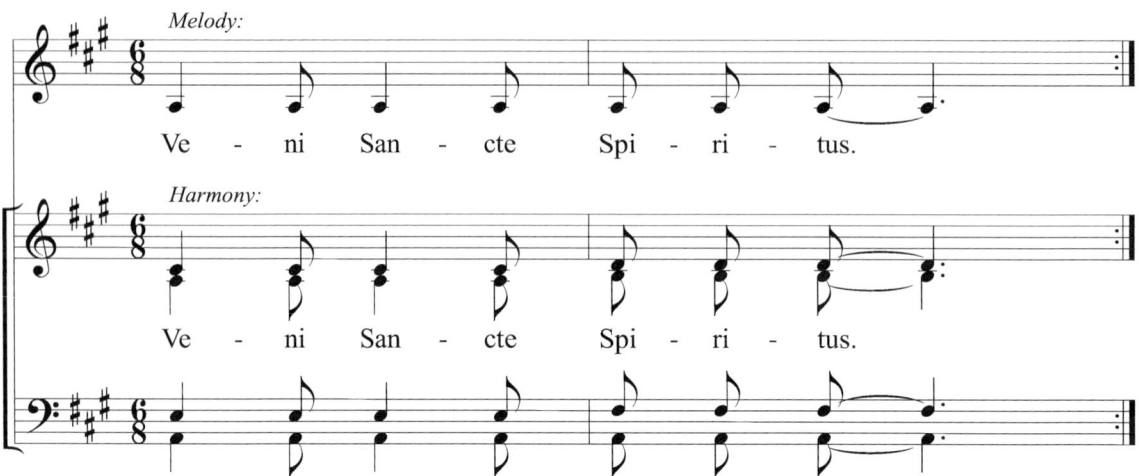

As the ostinato continues, vocal and instrumental verses are sung or played as desired with some space always left between the verses (after the cantor's "Veni Sancte Spiritus").

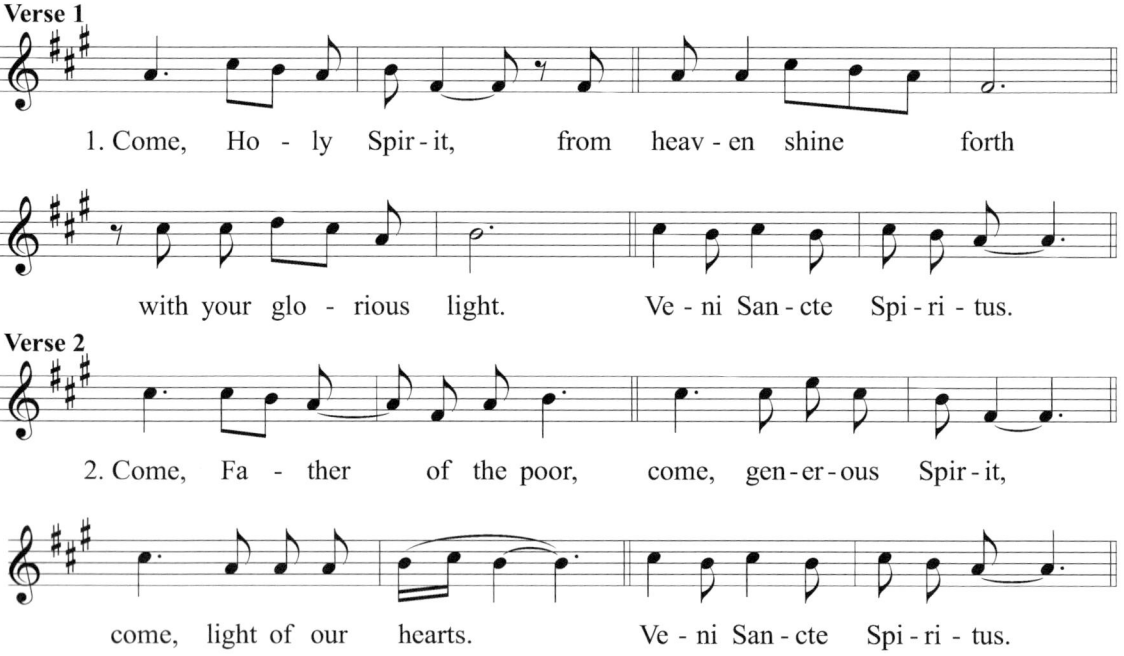

Text: *Come Holy Spirit;* Verses drawn from the Pentecost Sequence; Taizé Community, 1978. Music: Jacques Berthier, 1923–1994.
Text and music © 1979, Les Presses de Taizé, GIA Publications, Inc., North American agent. All rights reserved. Used with permission.

Veni, Sancte Spiritus / Sequence for Pentecost 434

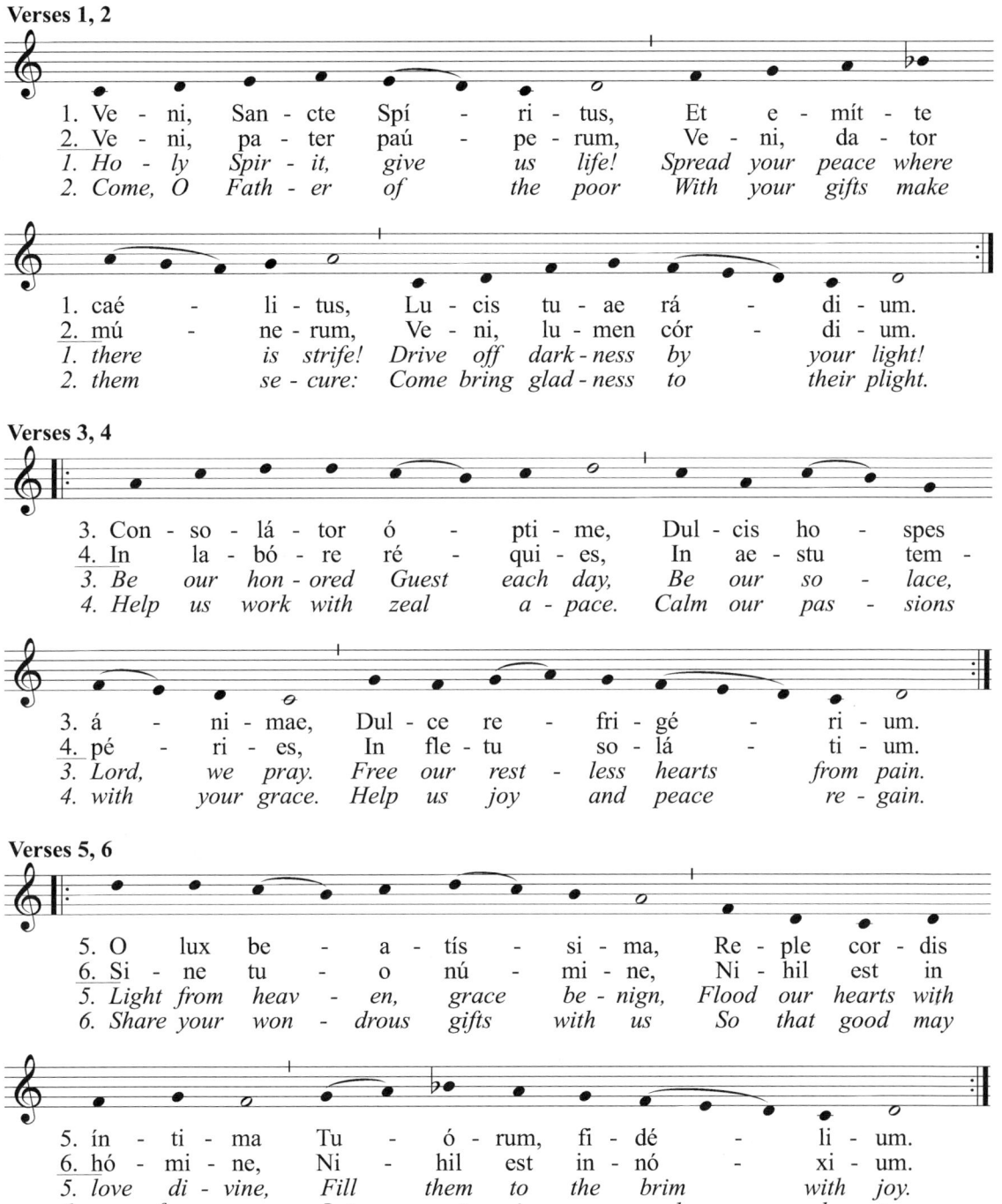

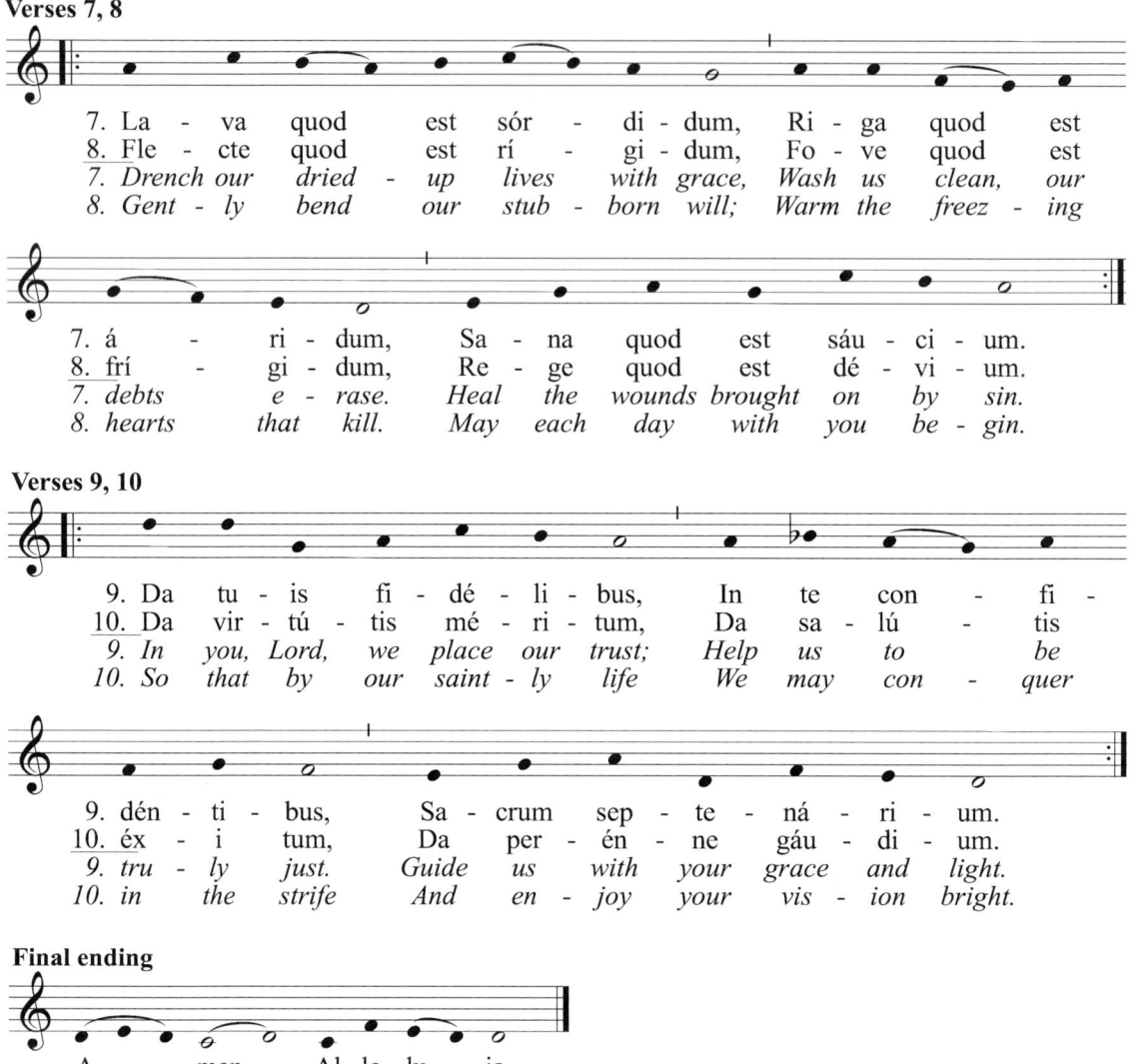

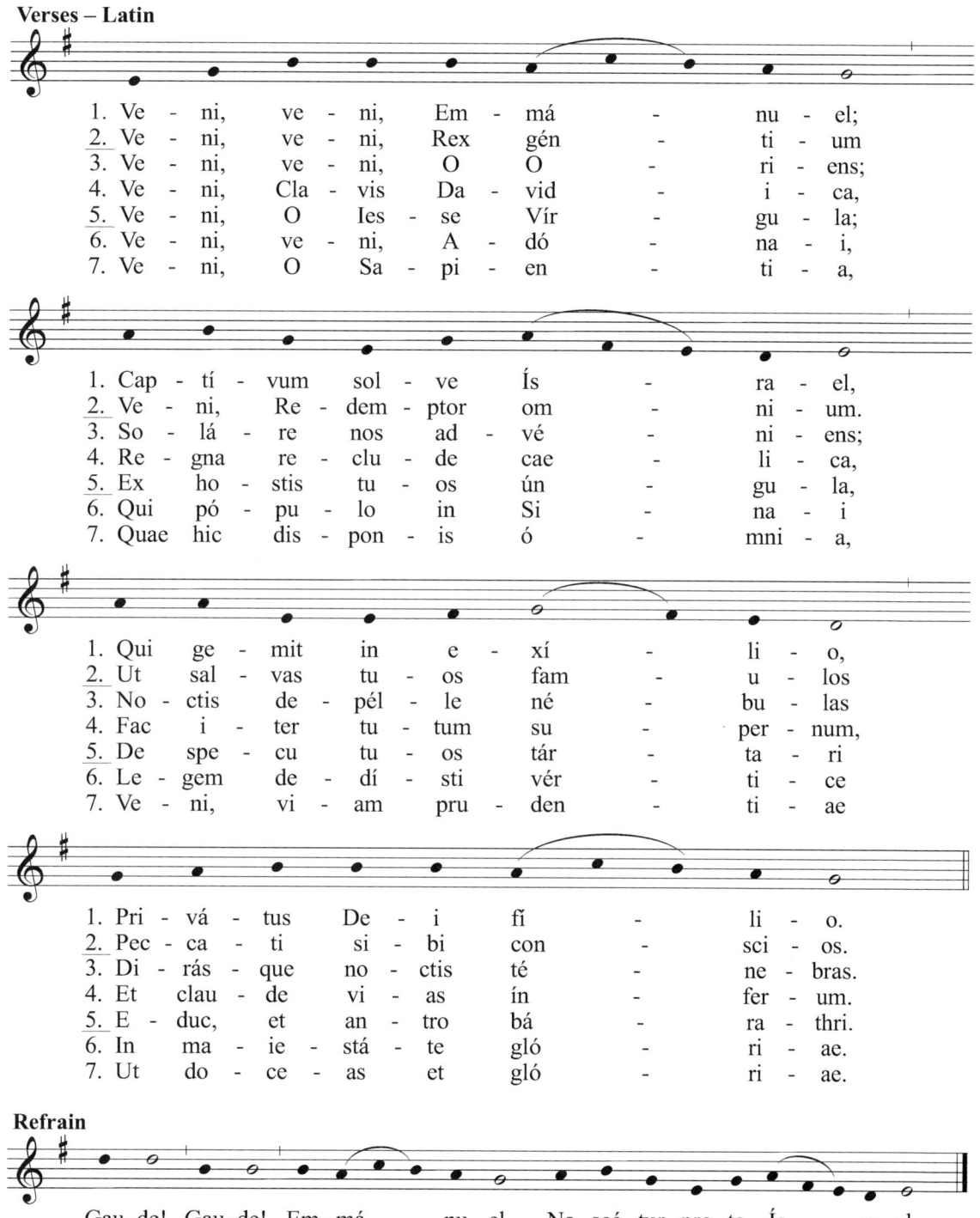

435 Veni, Veni, Emmanuel / O Come, O Come, Emmanuel

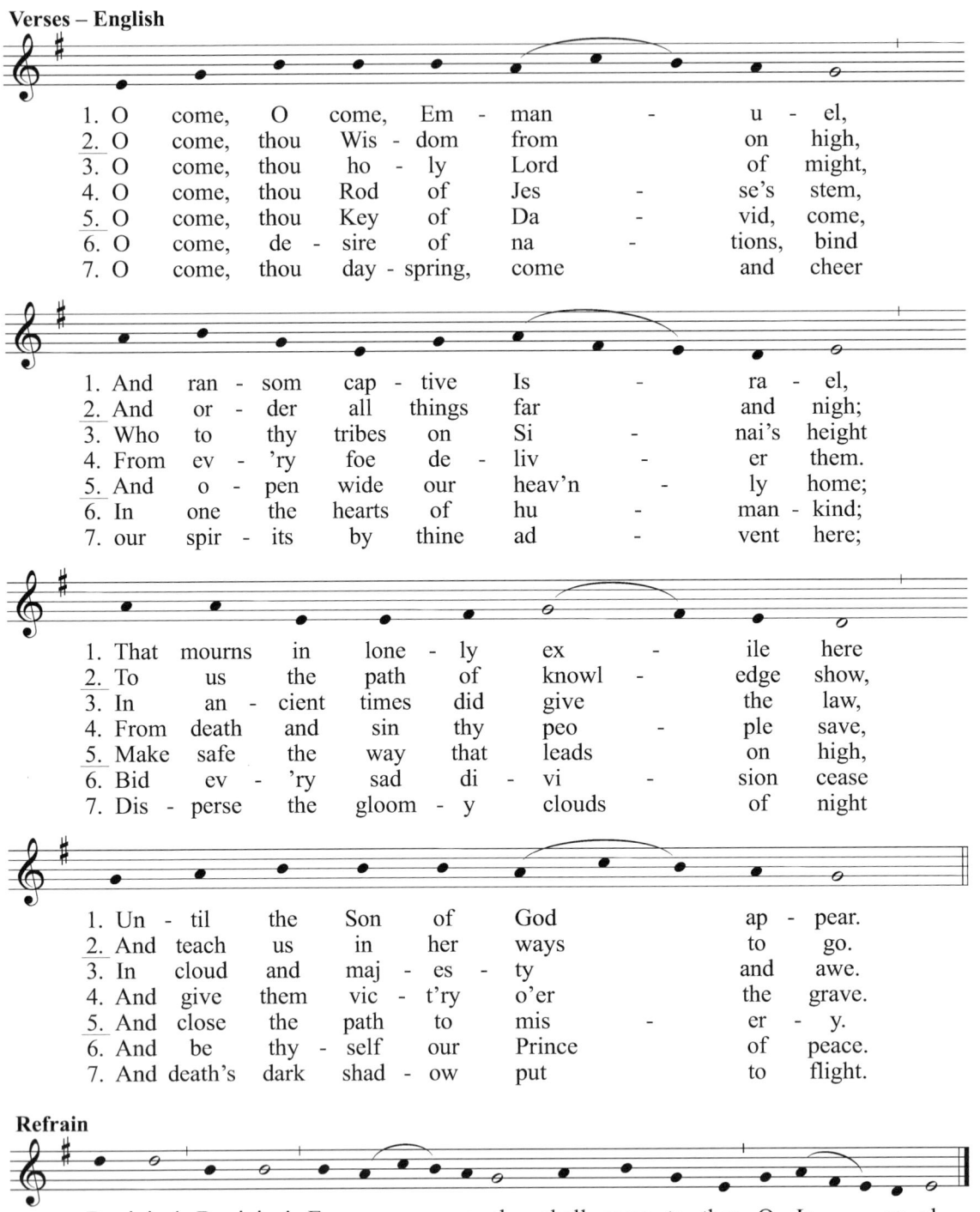

Victimae Paschali Laudes / Sequence for Easter 436

Verse 1

1. Víctimae Pascháli laudes immólent Christiáni.
1. Christians, to the Paschal victim offer your thankful praises!

Verses 2–3

2. Agnus rédemit óves: Christus ínnocens Pátri
3. Mors et vita duéllo conflixére mirándo:
2. A Lamb redeems the sheep: Christ who only is sinless,
3. Death and life have contended In that combat stupendous:

2. reconciliávit peccatóres.
3. dux vitae mórtuus regnat vivus.
2. reconciles sinners to the Father.
3. the Prince of life who dies, reigns immortal.

Verses 4–7

4. Dic nobis María, quid vidísti in via?
6. Angélicos testes, sudárium, et vestes.
4. Speak, Mary, declaring what you saw, wayfaring.
6. Bright angels attesting, shroud and napkin, resting.

5. Sepúlcrum Christi vivéntis,
7. Surréxit Christus spes mea:
5. "The tomb of Christ, who is living,
7. Yes, Christ my hope, is arisen:

5. et glóriam vidi resurgéntis:
7. praecédet suos in Galilaéam.
5. the glory of Jesus' resurrection;
7. To Galilee he goes before you."

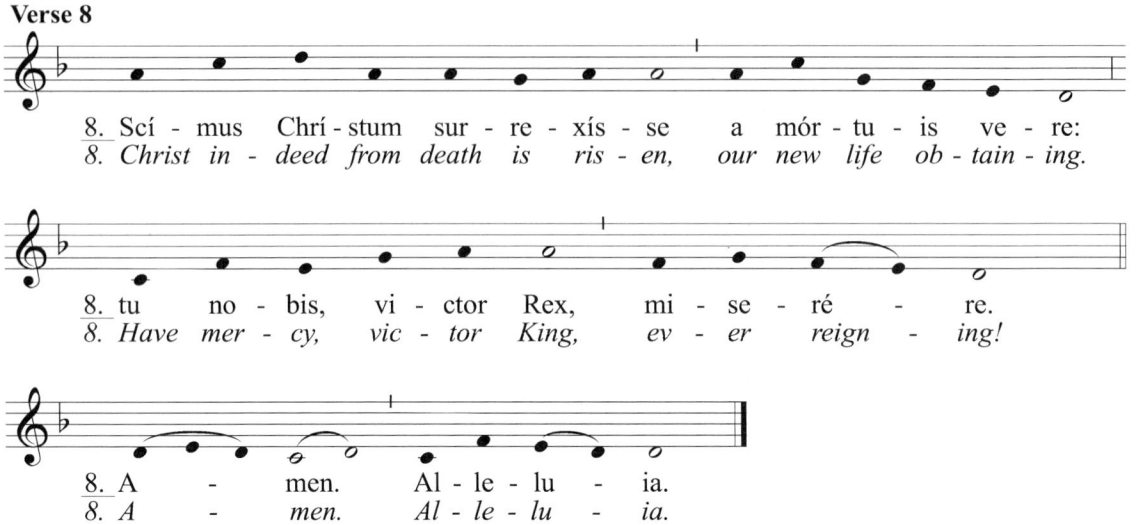

Text: Sequence for Easter, ascr. to Wipo of Burgundy, d. 1048; tr. by Joy Probst, © 1975, the Sisters of Saint Benedict, St. Joseph, MN.
Administered by Liturgical Press, Collegeville, MN. All rights reserved.
Music: VICTIMAE PASCHALI LAUDES, Plainchant, Mode I, ascr. to Wipo of Burgundy, d. 1048.

Wait for the Lord 437

*When verses are sung, the response should not be repeated as an ostinato, but the response and verses sung one following the other.

Text: Based on Isaiah 40; Philippians 4; Matthew 6–7; Taizé Community, 1984. Music: Jacques Berthier, 1923–1994.
Text and music: © 1984, Les Presses de Taizé, GIA Publications, Inc., North American agent. All rights reserved. Used with permission.

438 Wake, O Wake, and Sleep No Longer

Wake, O Wake, and Sleep No Longer, pg. 2

Text: *Wachet auf, ruft uns die Stimme,* Philipp Nicolai, 1556–1608; tr. and adapt. by Christopher Idle, b. 1938, © 1982, Hope Publishing Company. All rights reserved. Used with permission.
Music: WACHET AUF, irregular, melody, Hans Sach, 1494–1576; adapt. Philipp Nicolai; acc. by J. S. Bach, 1685–1750.
Descant: Christine Manderfeld, OSB, b. 1938, © 2009, the Sisters of Saint Benedict, St. Joseph, MN. Administered by Liturgical Press, Collegeville, MN. All rights reserved.

439 We Are Called

We Are Called, pg. 2

Text and music: David Haas, b. 1957; refrain arr. by Kate Cuddy, b. 1953. Text and music © 1988, GIA Publications, Inc. All rights reserved. Used with permission.

440 We Are Called to Tell the Story

We Are Called to Tell the Story, pg. 2

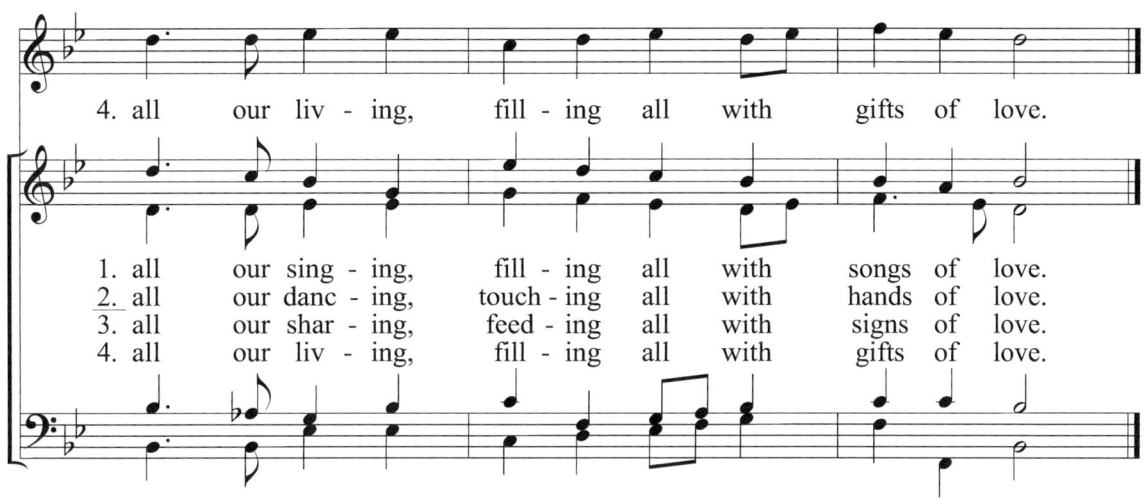

Text: Ruth Duck, b. 1947, © 1992, GIA Publications, Inc. All rights reserved. Used with permission.
Music: REGENT SQUARE, 87 87 87, Henry Smart, 1813–1879.
Descant: Delores Dufner, OSB, b. 1939, © 2009, the Sisters of Saint Benedict, St. Joseph, MN. Administered by Liturgical Press, Collegeville, MN. All rights reserved.

We Are Many Parts 441

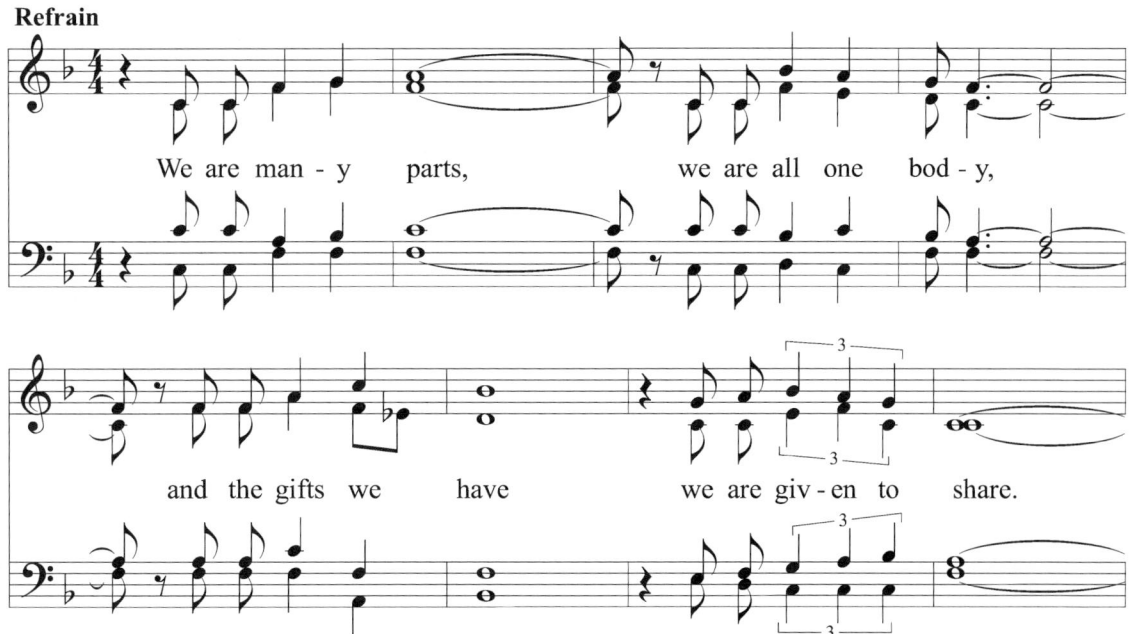

We Are Many Parts, pg. 2

We Are Your People   442

Text: Herman G. Stuempfle, Jr., 1923–2007, © 1994, World Library Publications, Inc., 3708 River Road, Franklin Park, IL 60131. www.wlpmusic.com
All rights reserved. Used with permission.
Music: SINE NOMINE, 10 10 10 with alleluias, Ralph Vaughan Williams, 1872–1958.
Descant: Michael Young, © 1979, GIA Publications, Inc. All rights reserved. Used with permission.

We Belong to Christ

444 We Come with Joy

Text: Delores Dufner, OSB, b. 1939, © 1994, 2003, GIA Publications, Inc. All rights reserved. Used with permission.
Music: FOREST GREEN, 86 86 D, English; harm. Ralph Vaughan Williams, 1872–1958.
Descant: Christine Manderfeld, OSB, b. 1938, © 2009, the Sisters of Saint Benedict, St. Joseph, MN. Administered by Liturgical Press, Collegeville, MN. All rights reserved.

445 We Gather Together

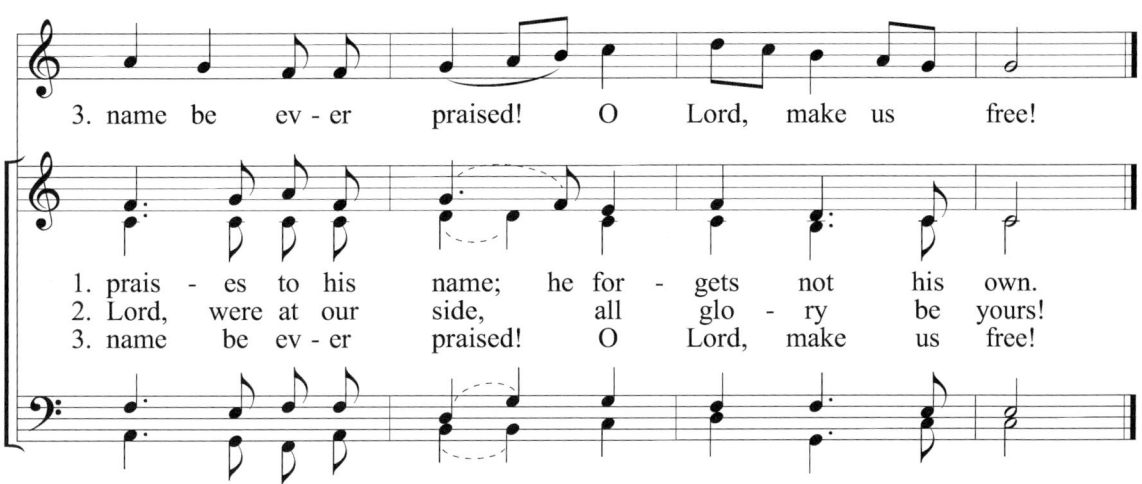

Text: *Wilt heden nu treden,* Netherlands folk hymn, tr. Theodore Baker, 1851–1934, alt.
Music: KREMSER, 12 11 12 11, Dutch traditional melody; arr. by Edward Kremser, 1838–1914.
Descant: Christine Manderfeld, OSB, b. 1938, © 2009, the Sisters of Saint Benedict, St. Joseph, MN. Administered by Liturgical Press, Collegeville, MN. All rights reserved.

446 We Glory in the Cross

1. We glory in the cross, in Christ, the crucified. In him we die to sin and self and in God's grace abide. We glory in the cross, in Christ, the risen Lord. In him we know the Spirit's life and pow'r of Gospel word.

2. The arms of Jesus' cross encompass all the earth; in this embrace we find our peace and in this death, new birth. We glory in the cross, salvation's shape and sign, the pledge of everlasting life, the span of God's design.

3. The folly of the cross is wisdom to the wise; for all who choose to die with Christ, with Christ will also rise. The myst'ry of God's plan unfolds on Jesus' cross: the blessings of abundant life are won by pain and loss.

4. The beauty of the cross is love revealed in death; with grateful lips we sing our praise, with mind and heart and breath. In joy we journey on, in hope of future bright; Christ Jesus walks the way with us through darkness into light.

Text: Delores Dufner, OSB, b. 1939, © 2002, 2003, GIA Publications, Inc. All rights reserved. Used with permission.
Music: TERRA BEATA, Franklin L. Sheppard, 1852–1930.

We Have Been Told

447

We Know That Christ Is Raised 448

Text: John Brownlow Geyer, b. 1932, alt. © John Geyer. All rights reserved. Used with permission.
Music: SINE NOMINE 10 10 10 with alleluias, Ralph Vaughan Williams, 1872–1958.
Descant: Michael Young, © 1979, GIA Publications, Inc. All rights reserved. Used with permission.

449   We Praise You, God / Te Deum

1. We praise you, God, we name you Lord. Eternal Father, earth adores, And heaven's choirs forever praise, Holy, holy, is our
2. Your majesty fills earth and sky. Apostles, prophets, martyrs join With all creation praising you. North and south and east and
3. Your glory, Father, has no end, Your true and only Son is love, The Holy Spirit pleads for us. Christ, you are our glorious
4. Becoming man to save us all, You did not scorn a virgin's womb, Destroying death triumphantly, Christ, you opened heaven's
5. You are enthroned at God's right hand, And we believe you come to judge. You shed your precious blood for us. Grant your servants grace and

We Praise You, God / Te Deum, pg. 2

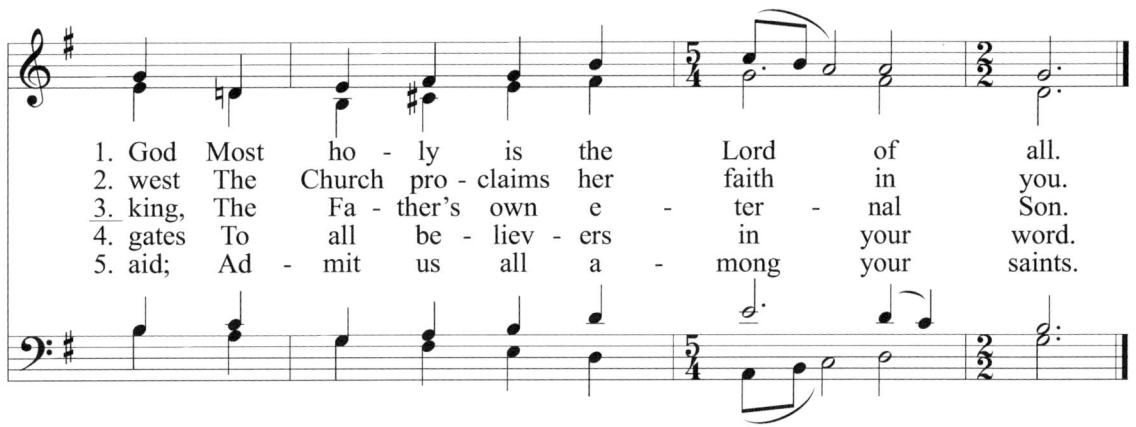

1. God Most ho - ly is the Lord of all.
2. west The Church pro - claims her faith in you.
3. king, The Fa - ther's own e - ter - nal Son.
4. gates To all be - liev - ers in your word.
5. aid; Ad - mit us all a - mong your saints.

Text: Based on the *Te Deum*, tr. Louis Blenkner, OSB, 1922–1993. Music: MONTANA, 888 78, Henry Bryan Hays, OSB, b. 1920.
Text and music: © 1981, Order of Saint Benedict, Collegeville, MN. Administered by Liturgical Press, Collegeville, MN. All rights reserved.

450 We Remember

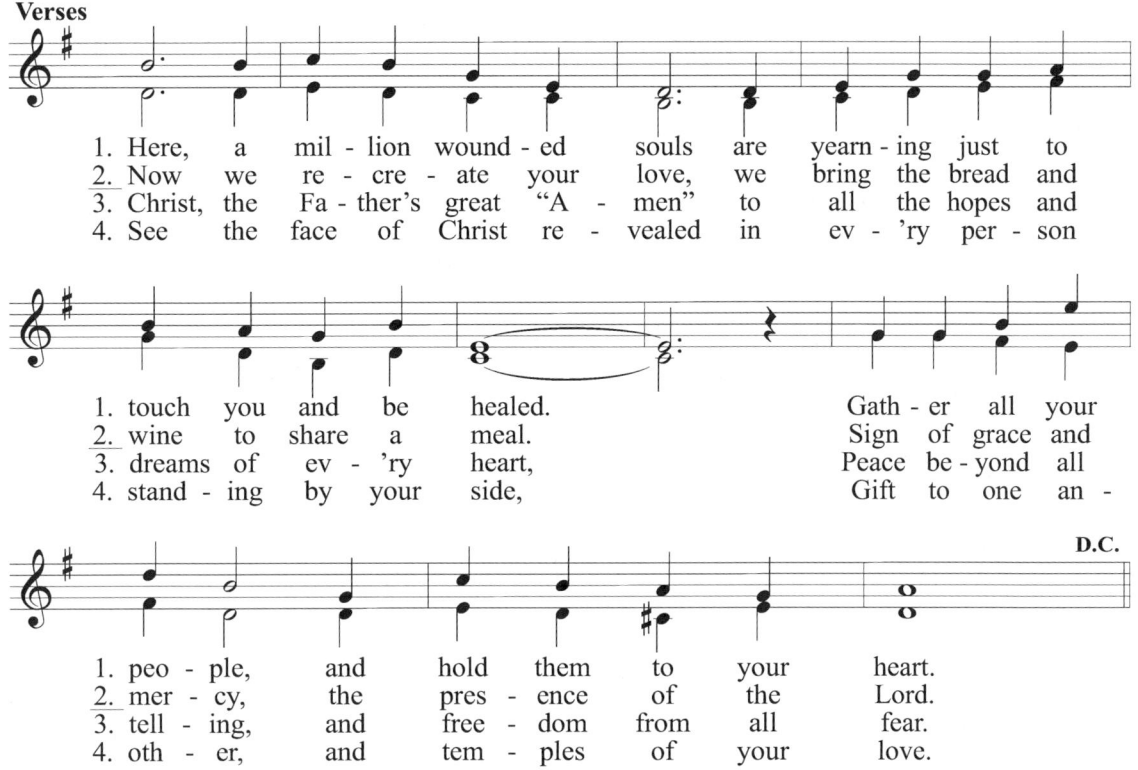

We Three Kings of Orient Are, pg. 2

Text: John Henry Hopkins, Jr., 1820–1891. Music: KINGS OF ORIENT, 88 44 6 with refrain, John Henry Hopkins, Jr., 1820–1981.
Descant: Christine Manderfeld, OSB, b. 1938, © 2009, the Sisters of Saint Benedict, St. Joseph, MN. Administered by Liturgical Press, Collegeville, MN. All rights reserved.

452 We Walk by Faith

1. We walk by faith, and not by sight; No gracious words we hear From him who spoke as none e'er spoke; But we believe him near.
2. We may not touch his hands and side, Nor follow where he trod; But in his promise we rejoice; And cry, "My Lord and God!"
3. Help then, O Lord, our unbelief; And may our faith abound, To call on you when you are near, And seek where you are found.
4. That, when our life of faith is done, In realms of clearer light We may behold you as you are, With full and endless sight.

Text: Henry Alford, 1810–1871, alt.
Music: DUNLAP'S CREEK, CM, Samuel McFarland, fl. 1816; harm. by Richard Proulx, b. 1937, © 1986, GIA Publications, Inc. All rights reserved. Used with permission.

We Walk by Faith   453

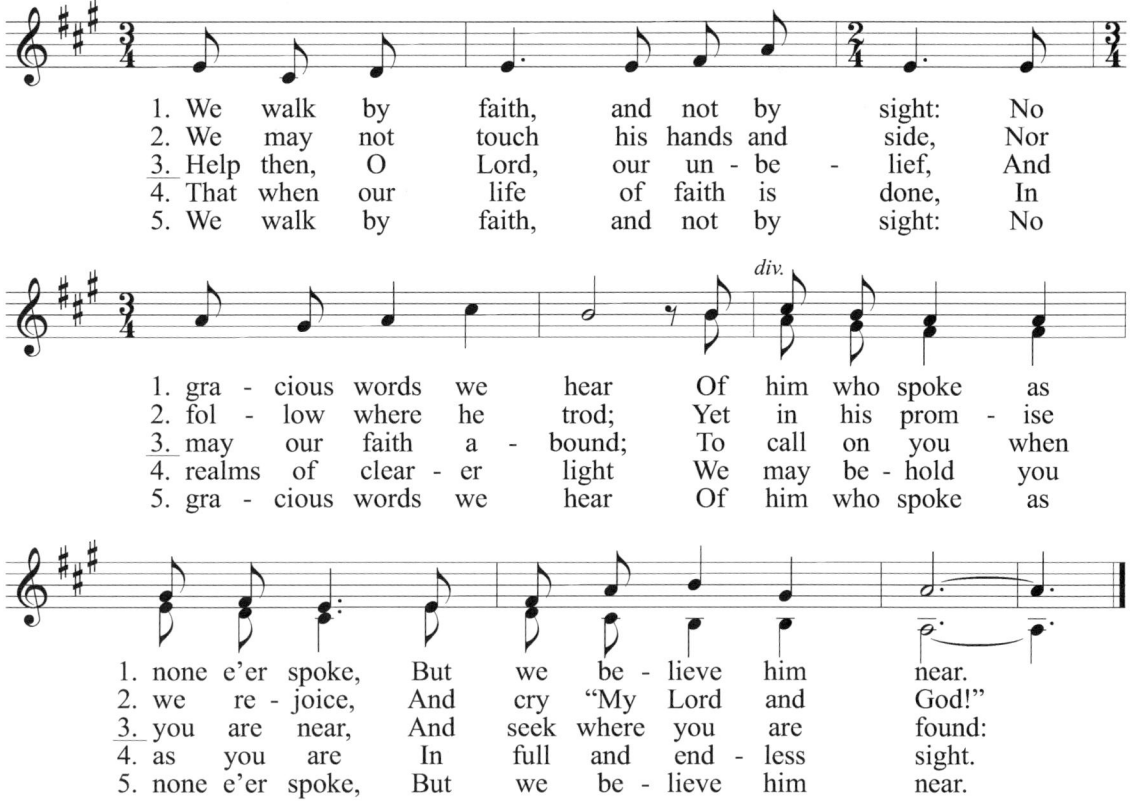

1. We walk by faith, and not by sight: No gracious words we hear Of him who spoke as none e'er spoke, But we believe him near.
2. We may not touch his hands and side, Nor follow where he trod; Yet in his promise we rejoice, And cry "My Lord and God!"
3. Help then, O Lord, our unbelief, And may our faith abound; To call on you when you are near, And seek where you are found:
4. That when our life of faith is done, In realms of clearer light We may behold you as you are In full and endless sight.
5. We walk by faith, and not by sight: No gracious words we hear Of him who spoke as none e'er spoke, But we believe him near.

Text: Henry Alford, 1810–1871, alt.
Music: SHANTI, CM; Marty Haugen, b. 1950, © 1984, GIA Publications, Inc. All rights reserved. Used with permission.

454 Were You There?

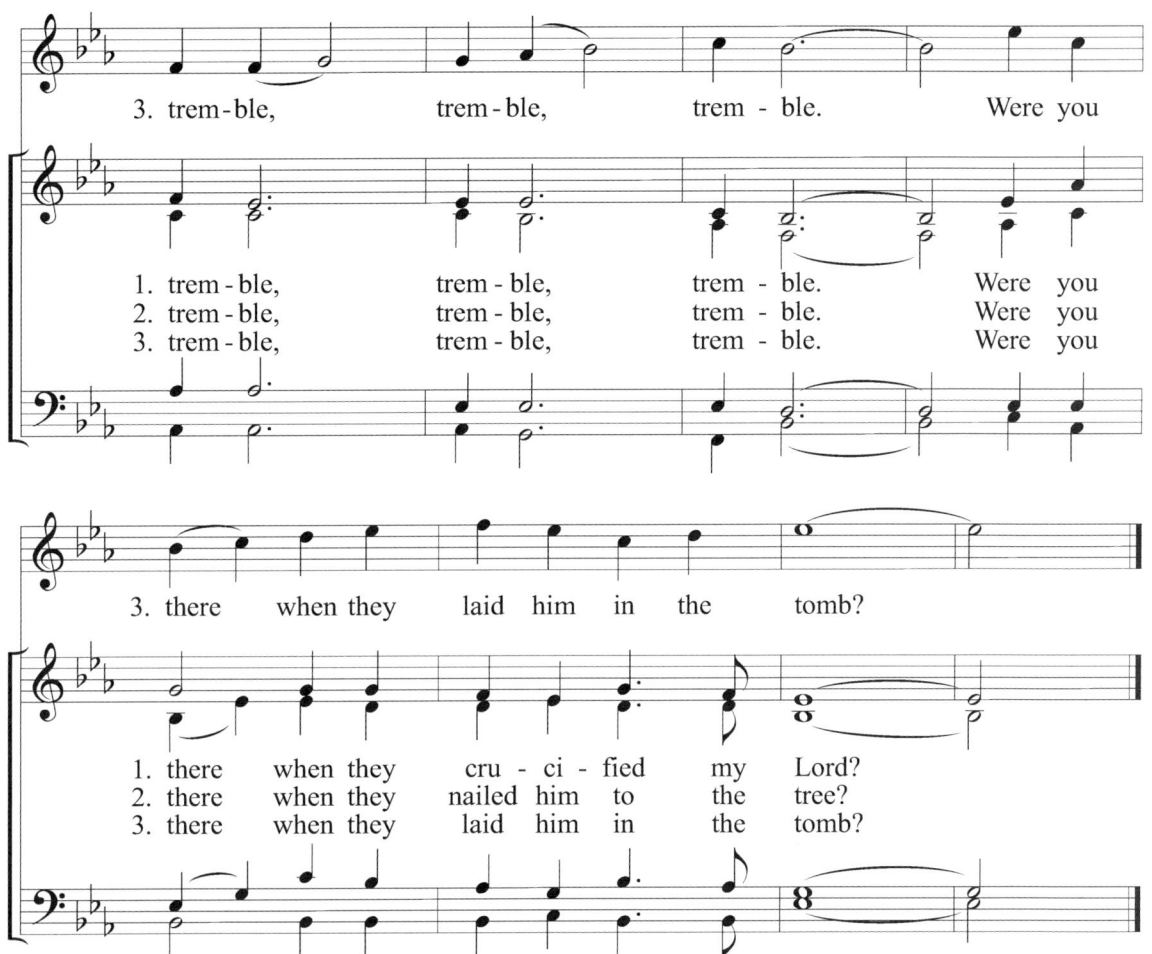

Text: African-American spiritual. Music: WERE YOU THERE, irregular, African-American spiritual.
Descant: John Ferguson, © 1992, GIA Publications, Inc. All rights reserved. Used with permission.

455 What Child Is This?

What Child Is This?, pg. 2

Text: William Chatterton Dix, 1837–1898. Music: GREENSLEEVES, 87 87 with refrain, English melody, 1580.
Descant: Christine Manderfeld, OSB, b. 1938, © 2009, the Sisters of Saint Benedict, St. Joseph, MN. Administered by Liturgical Press, Collegeville, MN. All rights reserved.

456 What Star Is This

Text: *Quem stella sole pulchrior*, Charles Coffin, 1676–1749; tr. by John Chandler, 1806–1876, alt.
Music: PUER NOBIS, LM; adapt. by Michael Praetorius, 1571–1621, adapt.; harm. George Woodward, 1843–1934.
Descant: Christine Manderfeld, OSB, b. 1938, © 2009, the Sisters of Saint Benedict, St. Joseph, MN. Administered by Liturgical Press, Collegeville, MN. All rights reserved.

What Wondrous Love Is This?   457

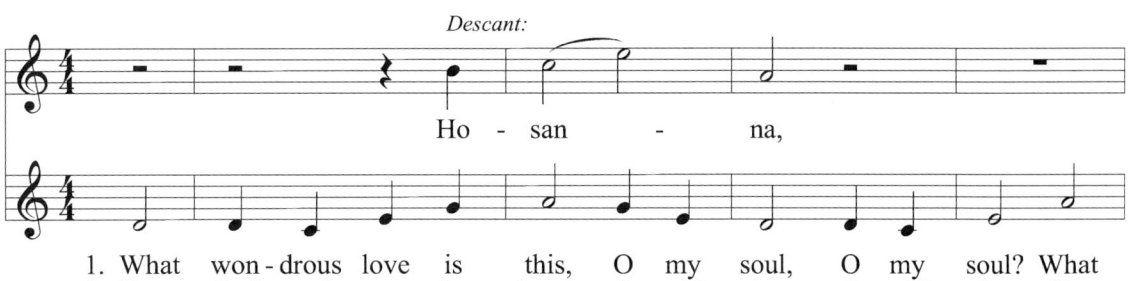

1. What wondrous love is this, O my soul, O my soul? What
2. To God and to the Lamb I will sing, I will sing; To
3. And when from death I'm free, I'll sing on, I'll sing on; And

1. wondrous love is this, O my soul? What wondrous love is
2. God and to the Lamb I will sing; To God and to the
3. when from death I'm free, I'll sing on; And when from death I'm

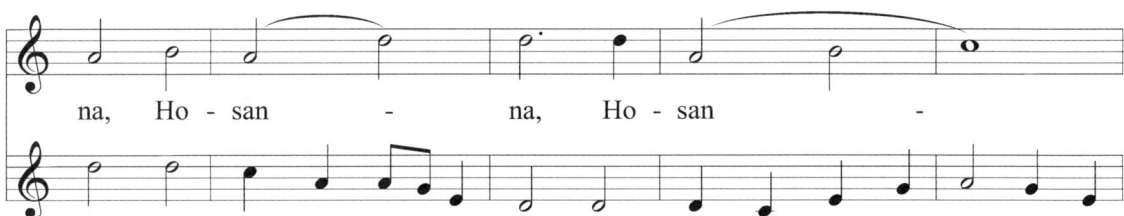

1. this That caused the Lord of bliss To bear the dreadful curse for my
2. Lamb Who is the great I AM, While millions join the theme, I will
3. free, I'll sing and joyful be, And through eternity I'll sing

1. soul, for my soul; To bear the dreadful curse for my soul?
2. sing, I will sing; While millions join the theme, I will sing.
3. on, I'll sing on! And through eternity, I'll sing on!

Text: Alexander Means, 1801–1853. Music: WONDROUS LOVE, 12 9 12 9, American folk hymn, c. 1835;
Descant: Christine Manderfeld, OSB, © 2009, the Sisters of Saint Benedict, St. Joseph, MN. Administered by Liturgical Press, Collegeville, MN. All rights reserved.

458 When from Bondage

1. When from bondage we are summoned out of darkness into light, we must go in hope and patience, walk by faith and not by sight. Let us throw off all that
2. When our God makes us a people, Jesus leads us by the hand through a lonely, barren desert to a great and glorious land.
3. At all stages of the journey God is with us, night and day, with compassion for our weakness ev-'ry step along the way.
4. We must not lose sight of Jesus, who accepted pain and loss, who, for joy of love unmeasured, dared embrace the shameful cross.
5. See the prize our God has promised: endless life with Christ the Lord. Now we fix our eyes on Jesus, walk by faith in Jesus' word.

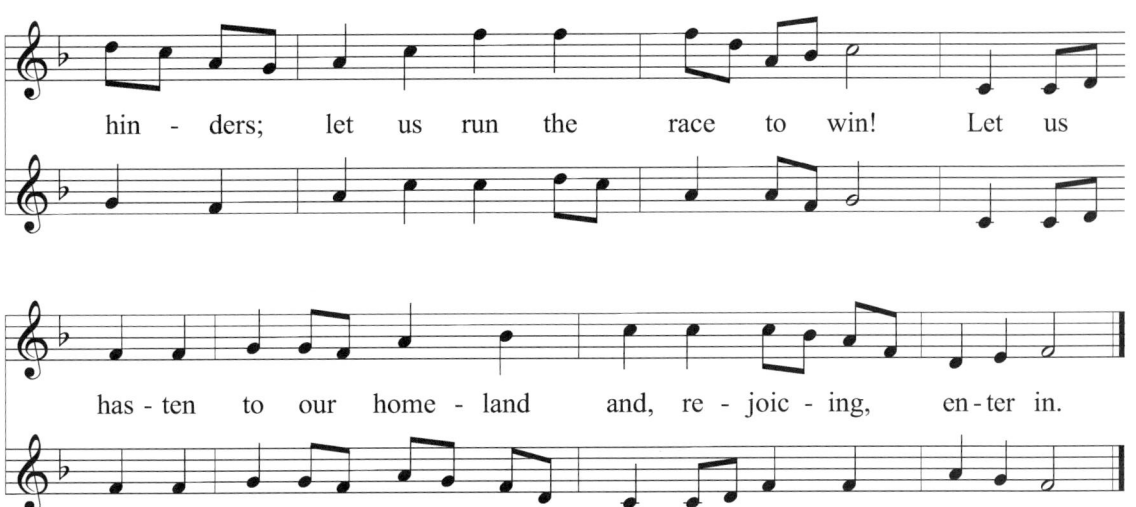

Text: Delores Dufner, OSB, b. 1939, © 1984, 2003, GIA Publications, Inc. All rights reserved. Used with permission.
Music: HOLY MANNA, 87 87 D, William Moore, *The Columbian Harmony,* 1825.
Descant: Robert Hobby, © 1992, GIA Publications, Inc. All rights reserved. Used with permission.

459 When in Our Music God Is Glorified

When in Our Music God Is Glorified, pg. 2

Verse 4 *Optional unaccompanied SATB verse*

Text: Fred Pratt Green, 1903–2000, © 1972, Hope Publishing Company. All rights reserved. Used with permission.
Music: ENGELBERG, 10 10 10 with alleluia; Charles V. Stanford, 1852–1924; harm. Robert Batastini, © 2000, GIA Publications, Inc. All rights reserved. Used with permission.
Descant: Christine Manderfeld, OSB, b. 1938, © 2009, the Sisters of Saint Benedict, St. Joseph, MN. Administered by Liturgical Press, Collegeville, MN. All rights reserved.

460 When John Baptized by Jordan's River

1. When John baptized by Jordan's river In faith and hope the people came, That John and Jordan might deliver Their troubled souls from sin and shame.
2. There as the Lord, baptized and praying, Rose from the stream, the sinless one, A voice was heard from heaven saying, "This is my own beloved Son."
3. O Son of Man, our nature sharing, In whose obedience all are blest, Savior, our sins and sorrow bearing, Hear us and grant us this request:

461 When Love Is Found

1. When love is found and hope comes home, Sing and be glad that two are one. When love explodes and fills the sky, Praise God and share our Maker's joy.
2. When love has flow'red in trust and care, Build both each day that love may dare To reach beyond home's warmth and light, To serve and strive for truth and right.
3. When love is tried as loved-ones change, Hold still to hope though all seems strange, Till ease returns and love grows wise Through list'ning ears and opened eyes.
4. When love is torn and trust betrayed, Pray strength to love till torments fade, Till lovers keep no score of wrong But hear through pain love's Easter song.
5. Praise God for love, praise God for life, In age or youth, in calm or strife. Lift up your hearts let love be fed Through death and life in broken bread.

Text: Brian Wren, b. 1936, © 1983, Hope Publishing Co., Carol Stream, IL 60188. All rights reserved. Used with permission.
Music: O WALY, WALY, LM 88 88, English; Descant: Robert Hobby, © 1992, GIA Publications, Inc. All rights reserved. Used with permission.

When Sorrow Turns Our Day to Night 462

Text: Michael Kwatera, OSB, b. 1950, © 2005, Order of Saint Benedict, Collegeville, MN. Administered by Liturgical Press, Collegeville, MN. All rights reserved.
Music: JERUSALEM, LMD; Charles H. H. Parry, 1848–1918; arr. by Richard Proulx, © 1986, GIA Publications, Inc. All rights reserved. Used with permission.

463 When the King Shall Come Again

When the King Shall Come Again, pg. 2

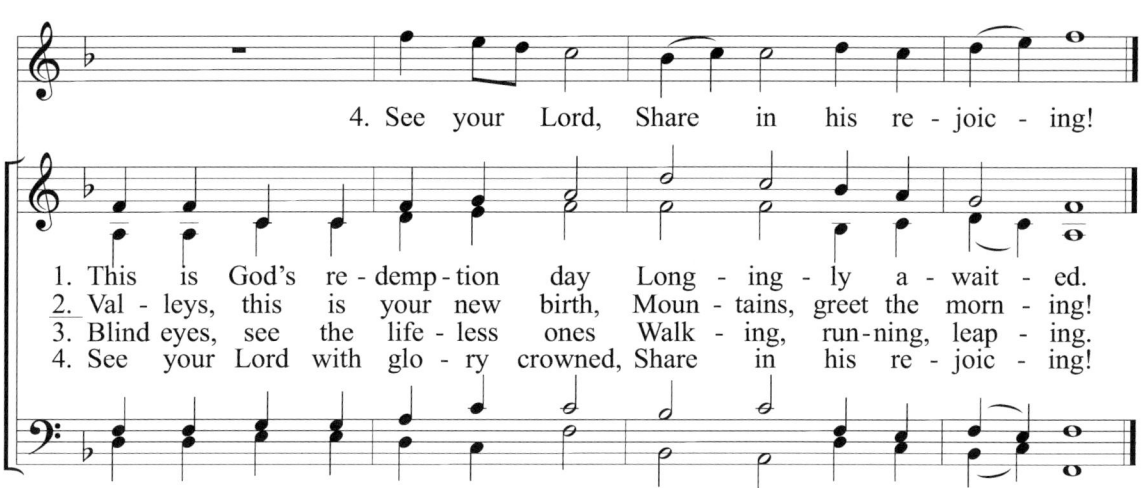

1. This is God's re-demp-tion day Long-ing-ly a-wait-ed.
2. Val-leys, this is your new birth, Moun-tains, greet the morn-ing!
3. Blind eyes, see the life-less ones Walk-ing, run-ning, leap-ing.
4. See your Lord with glo-ry crowned, Share in his re-joic-ing!

Text: Christopher Idle, b. 1938, © 1982, Jubilate Hymns, Ltd. All rights reserved. Administered by Hope Publishing Co., Carol Stream, IL 60188. Used with permission.
Music: GAUDEAMUS PARITER, 76 76 D, Johann Horn, c. 1495–1547.
Descant: Christine Manderfeld, OSB, b. 1938, © 2009, the Sisters of Saint Benedict, St. Joseph, MN. Administered by Liturgical Press, Collegeville, MN. All rights reserved.

464 Where Charity and Love Prevail

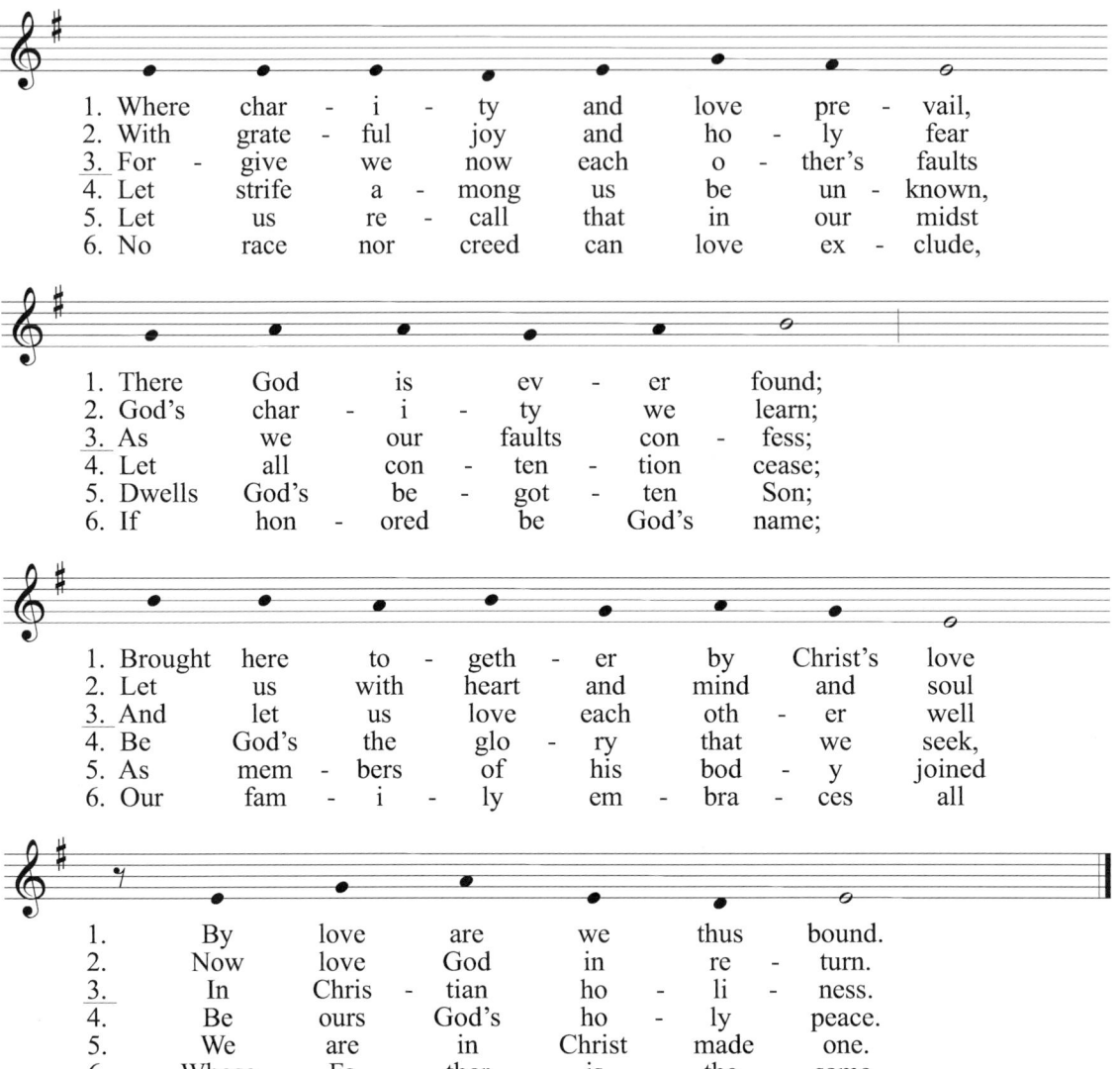

1. Where char-i-ty and love pre-vail,
There God is ev-er found;
Brought here to-geth-er by Christ's love
By love are we thus bound.

2. With grate-ful joy and ho-ly fear
God's char-i-ty we learn;
Let us with heart and mind and soul
Now love God in re-turn.

3. For-give we now each o-ther's faults
As we our faults con-fess;
And let us love each oth-er well
In Chris-tian ho-li-ness.

4. Let strife a-mong us be un-known,
Let all con-ten-tion cease;
Be God's the glo-ry that we seek,
Be ours God's ho-ly peace.

5. Let us re-call that in our midst
Dwells God's be-got-ten Son;
As mem-bers of his bod-y joined
We are in Christ made one.

6. No race nor creed can love ex-clude,
If hon-ored be God's name;
Our fam-i-ly em-bra-ces all
Whose Fa-ther is the same.

Text: Based on *Ubi caritas,* 9th cent., tr. Omer Westendorf, 1916–1997. Music: CHRISTIAN LOVE, CM 86 86, Paul Benoit, OSB, 1893–1979.
Text and music: © 1960, World Library Publications, 3708 River Road, Franklin Park, IL 60131. www.wlpmusic.com All rights reserved. Used with permission.

Where Your Treasure Is   465

Where Your Treasure Is, pg. 2

Text and music: Marty Haugen, b. 1950, © 2000, GIA Publications, Inc. All rights reserved. Used with permission.

While Shepherds Watched Their Flocks 466

1. While shepherds watched their flocks by night, All seated on the ground, The angel of the Lord came down, And glory shone around.
2. "Fear not," said he, for mighty dread Had seized their troubled mind; "Glad tidings of great joy I bring To you and humankind.
3. "To you in David's town this day Is born of David's line A Savior, who is Christ the Lord; And this shall be the sign:
4. "The heav'nly child you there shall find To human view displayed, All meanly wrapped in swaddling clothes And in a manger laid."
5. Thus spoke the seraph; and forthwith Appeared a shining throng Of angels praising God, who thus Addressed their joyful song:
6. "All glory be to God on high, And on the earth be peace: Good will henceforth from heav'n to all Begin and never cease."

Text: *New Version of the Psalms,* 1696; tr. Nahum Tate, 1652–1715, and Nicholas Brady, 1659–c. 1726.
Music: WINCHESTER OLD, 86 86, George Kirbye, c. 1560–1634, attr.

467 Who Calls You by Name

Text and music: David Haas, b. 1957, © 1988, GIA Publications, Inc. All rights reserved. Used with permission.

Who Can Measure Heaven and Earth? 468

Who Can Measure Heaven and Earth?, pg. 2

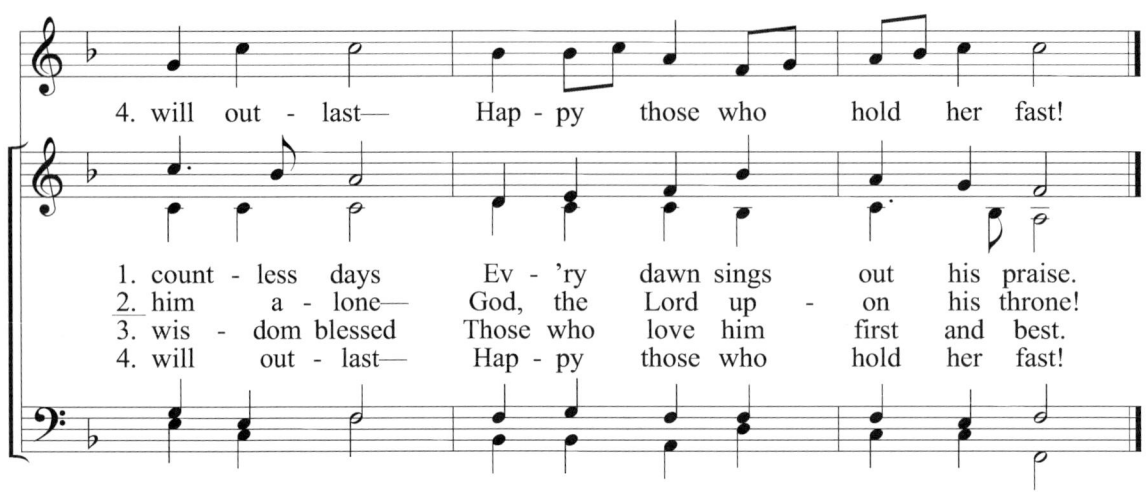

1. count - less days Ev - 'ry dawn sings out his praise.
2. him a - lone— God, the Lord up - on his throne!
3. wis - dom blessed Those who love him first and best.
4. will out - last— Hap - py those who hold her fast!

Text: Based on Ecclesiastes 1; adapt. by Christopher Idle, b. 1938, © 1982, Jubilate Hymns, Ltd. (admin. by Hope Publishing Co., Carol Stream, IL 60188). All rights reserved. Used with permission. Music: DIX, 77 77 77; arr. from Conrad Kocher, 1786–1872, by William H. Monk, 1823–1889.
Descant: Christine Manderfeld, OSB, b. 1938, © 2009, the Sisters of Saint Benedict, St. Joseph, MN. Administered by Liturgical Press, Collegeville, MN. All rights reserved.

469   With a Shepherd's Care

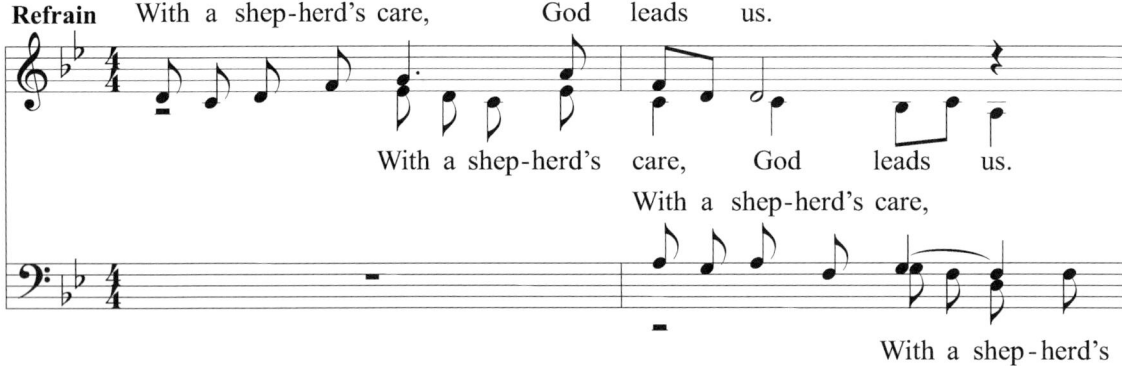

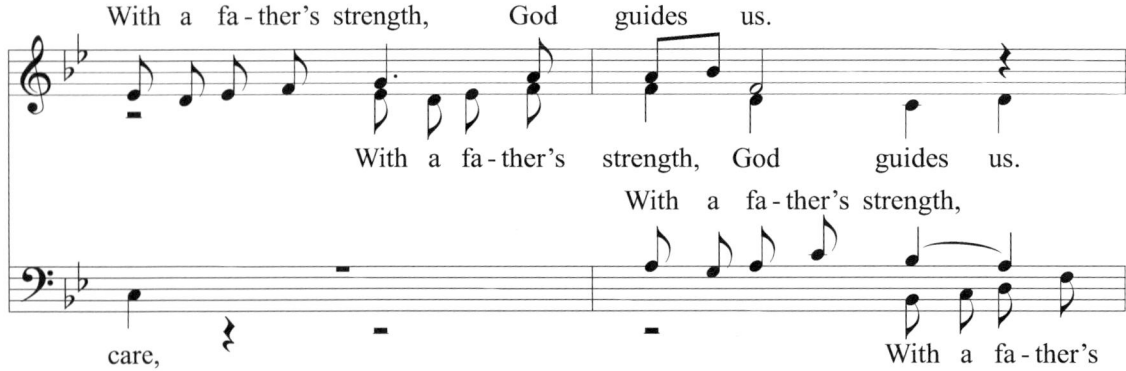

470 Within the Reign of God

471 Wood of the Cradle

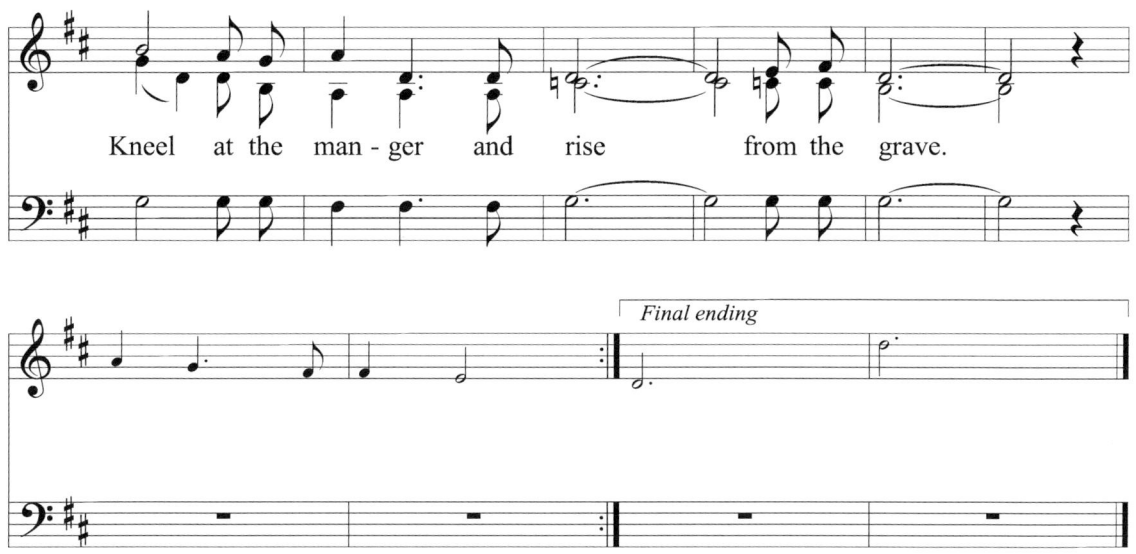

Text and music: Francis Patrick O'Brien, b. 1958, © 2002, GIA Publications, Inc. All rights reserved. Used with permission.

472 Word of God, Come Down on Earth

Descant (final verse):
4. Word that speaks God's tender love, One with God beyond all telling, Word that sends us from above, God the Spirit, with us dwelling, Word of truth, to

1. Word of God, come down on earth, Living rain from heav'n descending; Touch our hearts and bring to birth Faith and hope and love unending. Word almighty,
2. Word eternal, throned on high, Word that brought to life creation, Word that came from heav'n to die, Crucified for our salvation, Saving Word, the
3. Word that caused blind eyes to see, Speak and heal our mortal blindness; Deaf we are: our healer be; Loose our tongues to tell your kindness. Be our Word in
4. Word that speaks God's tender love, One with God beyond all telling, Word that sends us from above, God the Spirit, with us dwelling, Word of truth, to

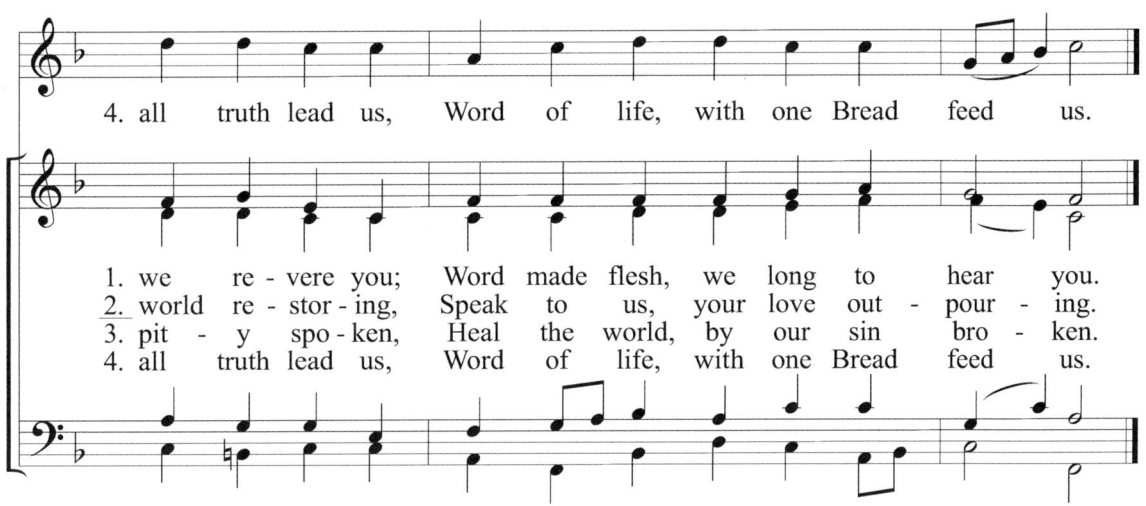

Text: James Quinn, SJ, b. 1919, © 1969, James Quinn, SJ, Selah Publishing Co., Inc., North American agent. All rights reserved. Used with permission.
Music: LIEBSTER JESU, 78 78 88, Johann R. Ahle, 1625–1673; arr. George H. Palmer, 1846–1926.
Descant: Christine Manderfeld, OSB, b. 1938, © 2009, the Sisters of Saint Benedict, St. Joseph, MN. Administered by Liturgical Press, Collegeville, MN. All rights reserved.

473 Ye Watchers and Ye Holy Ones

474 You Are All We Have

475　You Are God's Work of Art

Refrain
You are God's work of art, cre-at-ed in Je-sus the Christ.

Verse 1
1. You have been en-light-ened by the Lord.
Walk as chil-dren of the light. **D.C.**

Verse 2
2. Keep the flame of faith in your heart, and
may you meet him when he comes. **D.C.**

Verse 3
3. Bless-ed be our God, who
chose you in the light of Christ. **D.C.**

Text: Ephesians 1:4; 2:10, *Rite of Baptism,* adapt. by David Haas, b. 1957.
Music: David Haas, b. 1957, © 1988, GIA Publications, Inc. All rights reserved. Used with permission.

476　You Are Mine

Verses
1. I will come to you in the si-lence,
2. I am hope for all who are hope-less,
3. I am strength for all the des-pair-ing,
4. am the Word that leads all to free-dom, I

You Are My Shepherd, pg. 3

Text: Psalm 23, © 1963, 1986, 1993, The Grail, England. GIA Publications, Inc., North American agent. Music: David Haas, b. 1957, © 1999, GIA Publications, Inc.
All rights reserved. Used with permission.

479 You Call to Us, Lord Jesus

1. You call to us, Lord Jesus, As once in Galilee
You called to James and Andrew, "Come now and follow me."
They left their nets and followed, And did not look behind;

2. You came to preach deliv'rance, To set the captives free,
To heal the brokenhearted, To make the sightless see.
Your ministry of mercy And justice is our task;

3. You summon us to visions Of what this world can be,
Of hope and peace and freedom For all humanity.
For justice we will labor For ev'ry human soul

4. The path you bid us follow Is not an easy road,
And doubt or pain or conflict Will sometimes be our load.
Lord, grant us strength and courage To walk the way you trod,

Descant (final verse):
4. The path we follow, not an easy road,
And doubt or pain will sometimes be our load.
Lord, grant us strength to walk your way

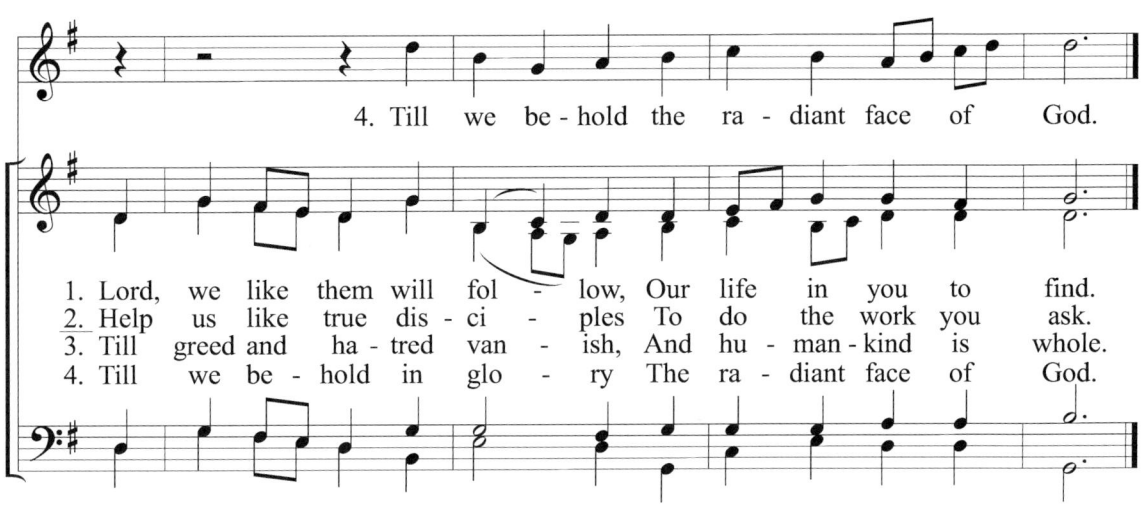

480   You Walk Along Our Shoreline

You Walk Along Our Shoreline, pg. 2

1. Then I will make you fishers But of the human soul."
2. Our boat a common shelter For all found by your grace.
3. To let your judgment heal us So that all may be one.

(Descant, v. 3): To let your healing make us all be one.

Text: Sylvia Dunstan, 1955–1993, © 1991, GIA Publications, Inc. All rights reserved. Used with permission.
Music: AURELIA, 76 76 D, Samuel Sebastian Wesley, 1810–1876.
Descant: Christine Manderfeld, OSB, b. 1938, © 2009, the Sisters of Saint Benedict, St. Joseph, MN. Administered by Liturgical Press, Collegeville, MN. All rights reserved.

Service and Ritual Music

481 Jubilation Mass: Kyrie

Jubilation Mass: Kyrie, pg. 2

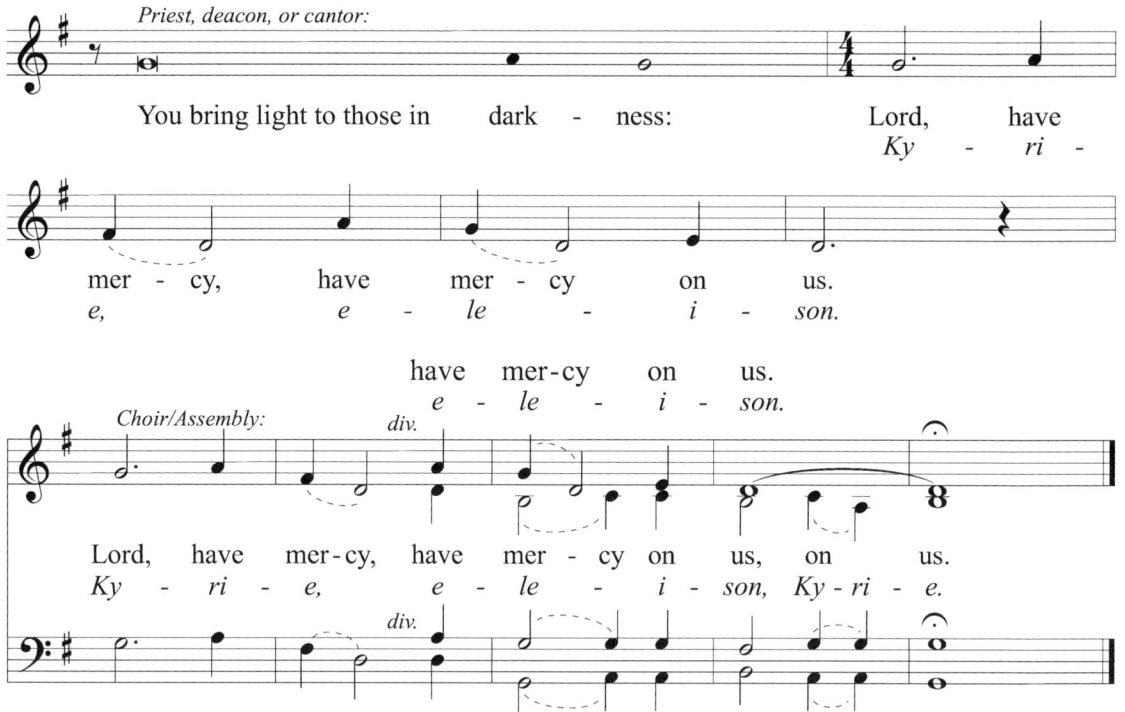

482 Jubilation Mass: Gloria

Jubilation Mass: Gloria, pg. 4

Music: *Jubilation Mass*, James J. Chepponis, b. 1956, © 1999, GIA Publications, Inc. All rights reserved. Used with permission.

483 Jubilation Mass: Gospel Acclamation

*Verses for each Sunday and feastday of the liturgical year are available from GIA in edition # G5045.

Music: *Jubilation Mass*, James J. Chepponis, b. 1956, © 1999, GIA Publications, Inc. All rights reserved. Used with permission.

Jubilation Mass: Sanctus 484

Jubilation Mass: Memorial Acclamation A 485

Music: *Jubilation Mass*, James J. Chepponis, b. 1956, © 1999, GIA Publications, Inc. All rights reserved. Used with permission.

486 Jubilation Mass: Memorial Acclamation B

Music: *Jubilation Mass*, James J. Chepponis, b. 1956, © 1999, GIA Publications, Inc. All rights reserved. Used with permission.

Jubilation Mass: Memorial Acclamation C 487

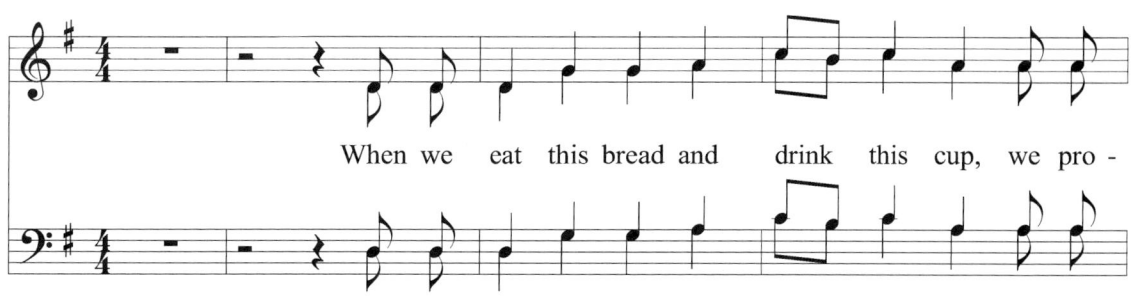

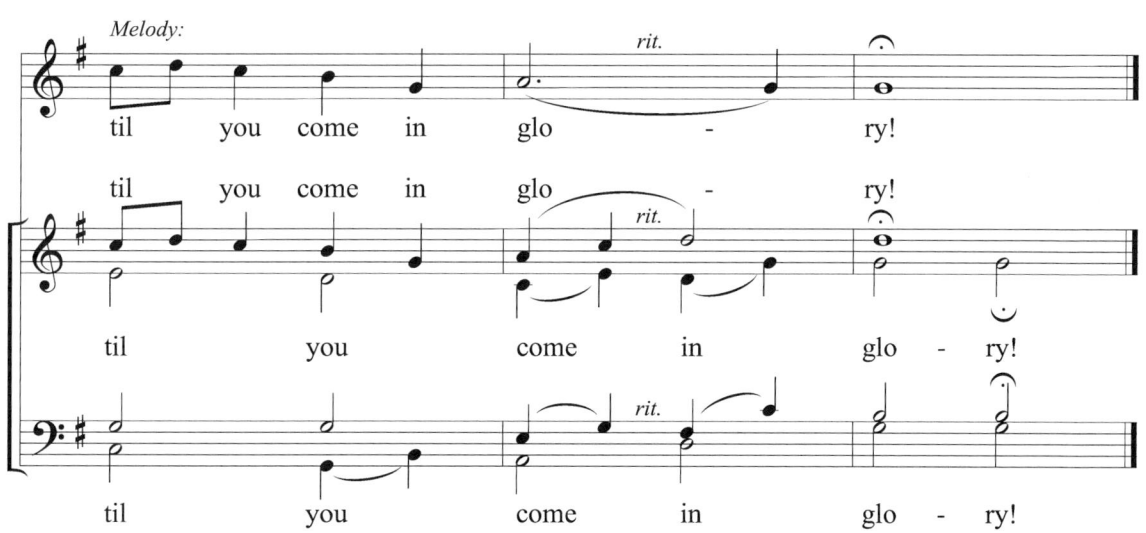

Music: *Jubilation Mass,* James J. Chepponis, b. 1956, © 1999, GIA Publications, Inc. All rights reserved. Used with permission.

488   **Jubilation Mass: Memorial Acclamation D**

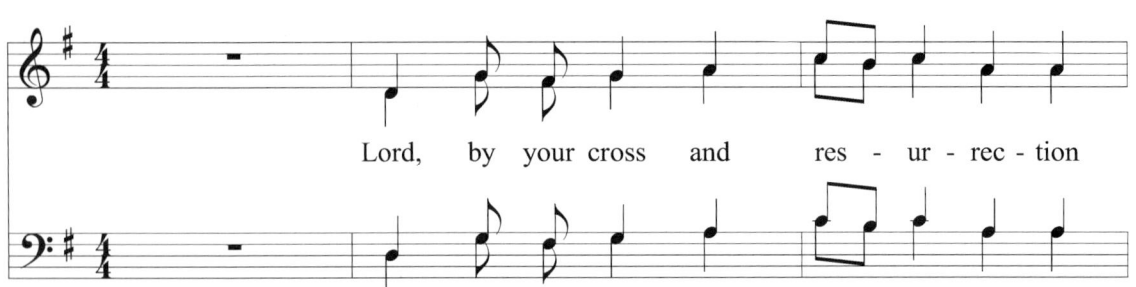
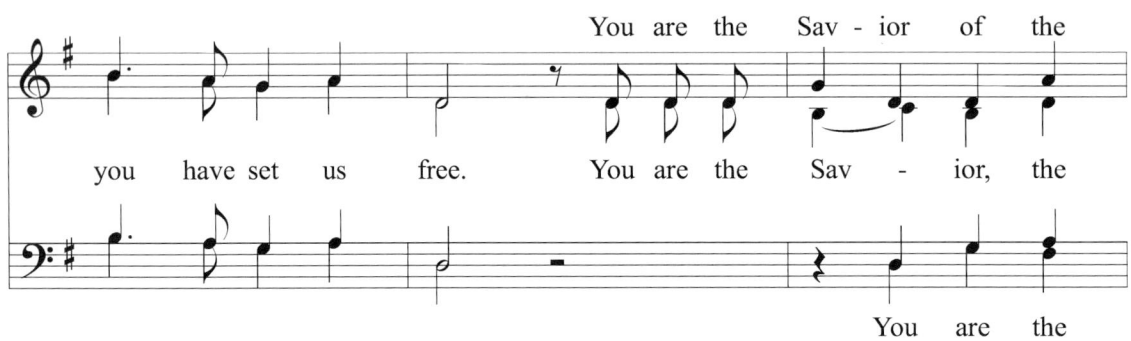
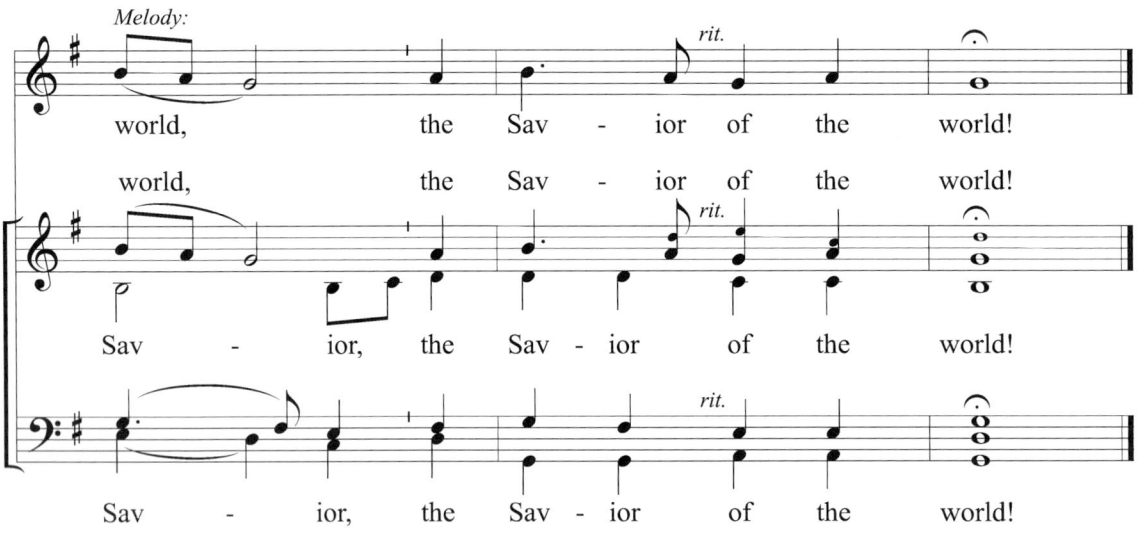

Music: *Jubilation Mass,* James J. Chepponis, b. 1956, © 1999, GIA Publications, Inc. All rights reserved. Used with permission.

Jubilation Mass: Amen 489

Music: *Jubilation Mass,* James J. Chepponis, b. 1956, © 1999, GIA Publications, Inc. All rights reserved. Used with permission.

490 Jubilation Mass: Agnus Dei

Lamb of God,* you take away the sins of the world, have mercy on us.
world, grant us peace, grant us peace.

* First and last trope is always "Lamb of God." Additional tropes may be chosen from the following:

ADVENT
Lord of light
Promised Savior
Son of Mary
King of glory
Root of Jesse

CHRISTMAS
Prince of peace
King of kings
Lord of lords
Christ the Lord
Light eternal

LENT
Source of mercy
Hope of sinners
Living water
Light in darkness
Life eternal

EASTER
Risen Lord
Paschal Lamb
King exalted
Gentle shepherd
Mighty victor

ORDINARY TIME
Bread of life
Saving cup
Word of God
Gift of love
Source of blessing
Mighty healer
Fruitful vine

Music: *Jubilation Mass*, James J. Chepponis, b. 1956, © 1999, GIA Publications, Inc. All rights reserved. Used with permission.

New Plainsong Mass: Sanctus 491

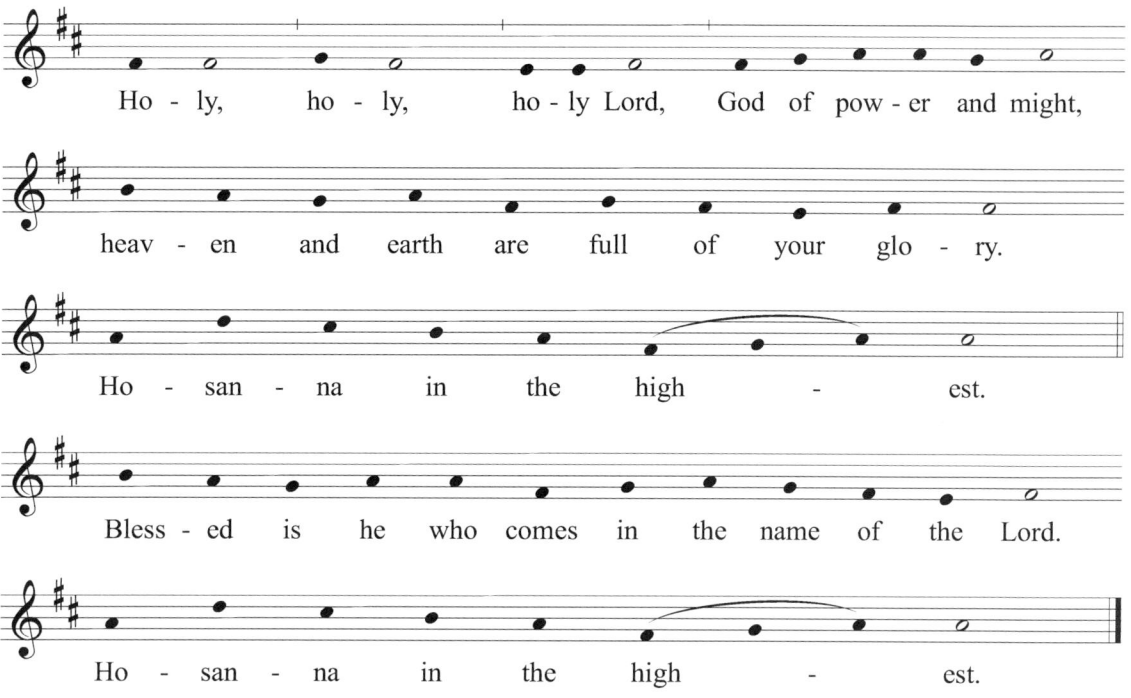

Holy, holy, holy Lord, God of power and might,
heaven and earth are full of your glory.
Hosanna in the highest.
Blessed is he who comes in the name of the Lord.
Hosanna in the highest.

Music: David Hurd, b. 1950, © 1980, GIA Publications, Inc. All rights reserved. Used with permission.

New Plainsong Mass: Memorial Acclamation 492

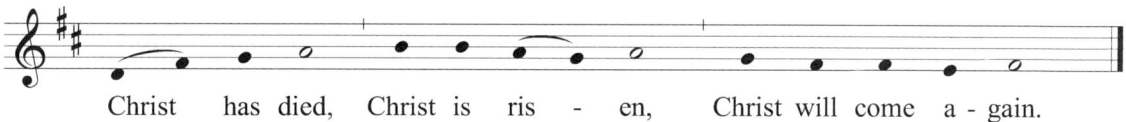

Christ has died, Christ is risen, Christ will come again.

Music: David Hurd, b. 1950, © 1980, GIA Publications, Inc. All rights reserved. Used with permission.

New Plainsong Mass: Amen 493

Amen, amen, amen.

Music: David Hurd, b. 1950, © 1980, GIA Publications, Inc. All rights reserved. Used with permission.

494 Mass of Creation: Kyrie

*May be sung over ostinato Kyrie, or in alternation with the Kyrie using the same accompaniment.

Music: *Mass of Creation,* Marty Haugen, b. 1950, © 1984, GIA Publications, Inc. All rights reserved. Used with permission.

Mass of Creation: Gloria 495

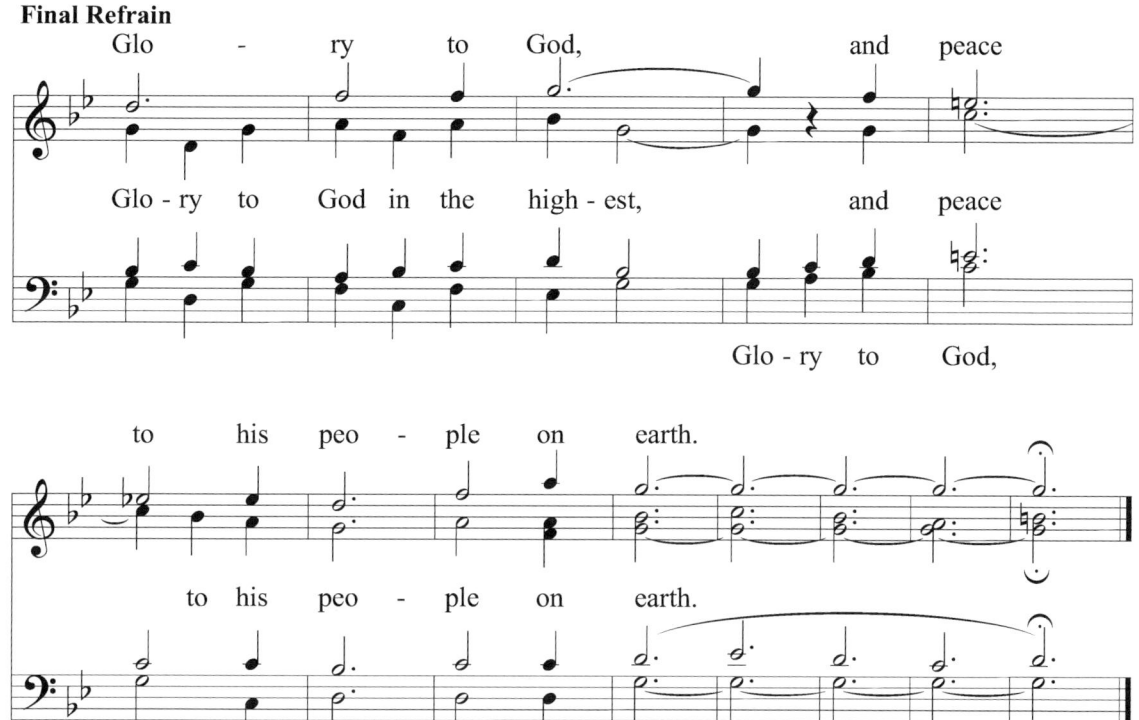

Music: *Mass of Creation,* Marty Haugen, b. 1950, © 1984, GIA Publications, Inc. All rights reserved. Used with permission.

496   Mass of Creation: Gospel Acclamation

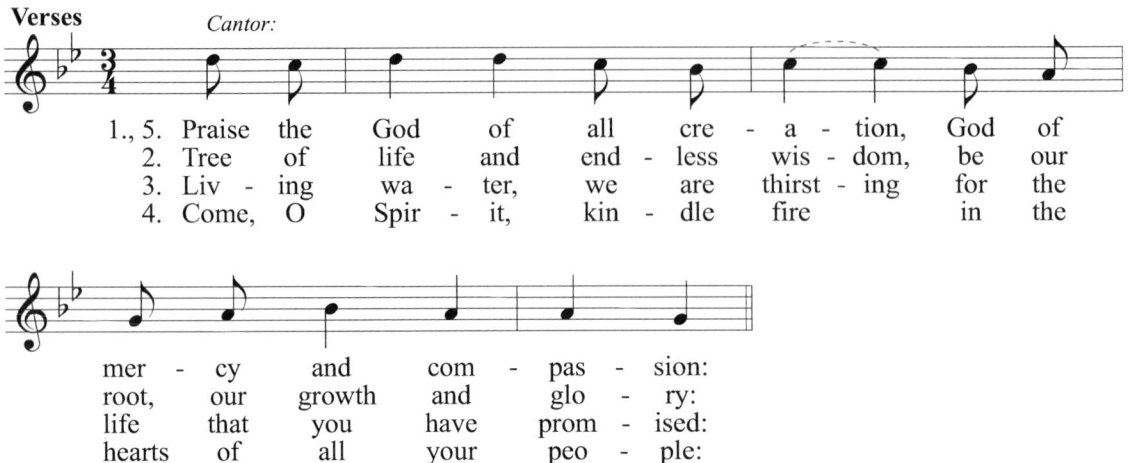

Alternate Verses:

Speak, O Lord, your servant listens, your's the word of life eternal:
To the humble and the lowly you reveal the Kingdom's myst'ry:
Praise the Word who lived among us, made us children of the Kingdom:
You are light, Lord, for our darkness, break upon our waiting spirits:
Gentle shepherd, you who know us, call us all into your presence:
Be our way, Lord, be our truth, Lord, be our hope of life eternal:
We who love you, seek your truth, Lord, come and make your home within us:
We shall watch, Lord, we shall pray, Lord, for we know not when you cometh:

Text and music: *Mass of Creation,* Marty Haugen, b. 1950, © 1984, GIA Publications, Inc. All rights reserved. Used with permission.

Mass of Creation: Lenten Gospel Acclamation 497

Text: Refrain © 1969, 1981, ICEL; verses by Marty Haugen, b. 1950, © 1984, GIA Publications, Inc. All rights reserved. Used with permission.
Music: *Mass of Creation,* Marty Haugen, b. 1950, © 1984, GIA Publications, Inc. All rights reserved. Used with permission.

498 Mass of Creation: Sanctus

Music: *Mass of Creation*, Marty Haugen, b. 1950, © 1984, GIA Publications, Inc. All rights reserved. Used with permission.

Mass of Creation: Memorial Acclamation A 499

Music: *Mass of Creation,* Marty Haugen, b. 1950, © 1984, GIA Publications, Inc. All rights reserved. Used with permission.

500 Mass of Creation: Memorial Acclamation B

Music: *Mass of Creation,* Marty Haugen, b. 1950, © 1984, GIA Publications, Inc. All rights reserved. Used with permission.

Mass of Creation: Memorial Acclamation C 501

Music: *Mass of Creation,* Marty Haugen, b. 1950, © 1984, GIA Publications, Inc. All rights reserved. Used with permission.

502 Mass of Creation: Memorial Acclamation D

Music: *Mass of Creation,* Marty Haugen, b. 1950, © 1984, GIA Publications, Inc. All rights reserved. Used with permission.

Mass of Creation: Doxology and Amen   503

Music: *Mass of Creation,* Marty Haugen, b. 1950, © 1984, GIA Publications, Inc. All rights reserved. Used with permission.

504 Mass of Creation: Agnus Dei

1. Je-sus, Lamb of God, you take a-way the sins of the
2. Je-sus, Bread of Life,
3. Je-sus, Prince of Peace,
Last time: Je-sus, Lamb of God,

world: have mer-cy on us.

world: grant us your peace.

Additional tropes:
4. Jesus, Word of God, . . .
5. Jesus, Tree of Life, . . .
6. Jesus, Lord of Lords, . . .
7. Jesus, King of Kings, . . .
8. Jesus, Fire of Love, . . .
9. Jesus, Bread of Peace, . . .
10. Jesus, Hope for All, . . .

Music: *Mass of Creation,* Marty Haugen, b. 1950, © 1984, GIA Publications, Inc. All rights reserved. Used with permission.

Mass of the Angels and Saints: Kyrie   505

Text and music: *Mass of the Angels and Saints,* Steven R. Janco, b. 1961, © 1996, GIA Publications, Inc. All rights reserved. Used with permission.

506 Mass of the Angels and Saints: Gloria

Mass of the Angels and Saints: Gospel Acclamation 507

*Verse – Option I: Additional verses are available from GIA in the *Mass of the Angels and Saints* collection # G4442.
**Verse Tone – Option II: Verses for each Sunday and Solemnity are available from GIA in *The Cantor's Book of Gospel Acclamations*, collection # G4987 or the text for the verse can be found in the appendix of this book.

Music: *Mass of the Angels and Saints*, Steven R. Janco, b. 1961, © 1996, GIA Publications, Inc. All rights reserved. Used with permission.

508 Mass of the Angels and Saints: Lenten Gospel Acclamation

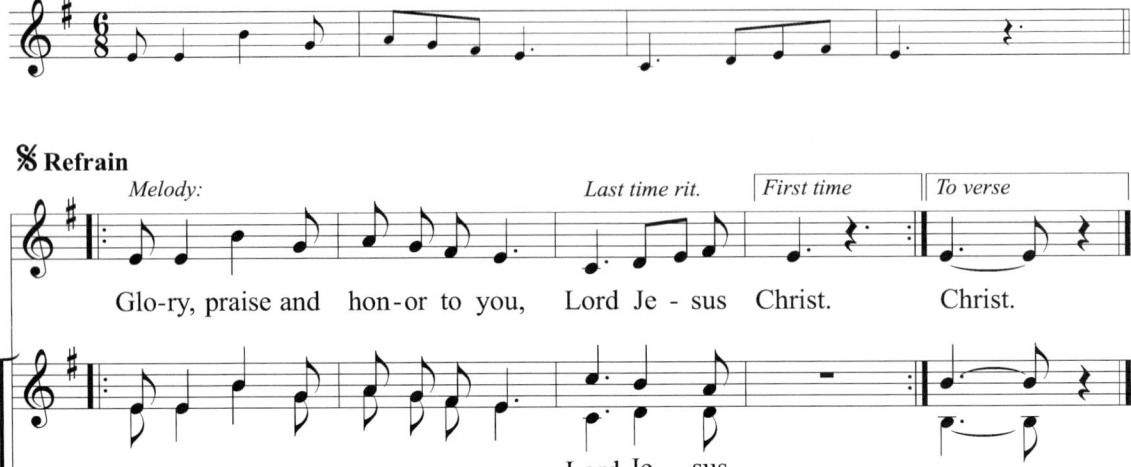

Verse text for Sundays and Solemnities can be found in the appendix of this book.
Verses for each Sunday in Lent are available from GIA in *The Cantor's Book of Gospel Acclamations,* collection # G4987.

Music: *Mass of the Angels and Saints,* Steven R. Janco, b. 1961, © 1996, GIA Publications, Inc. All rights reserved. Used with permission.

Mass of the Angels and Saints: Sanctus 509

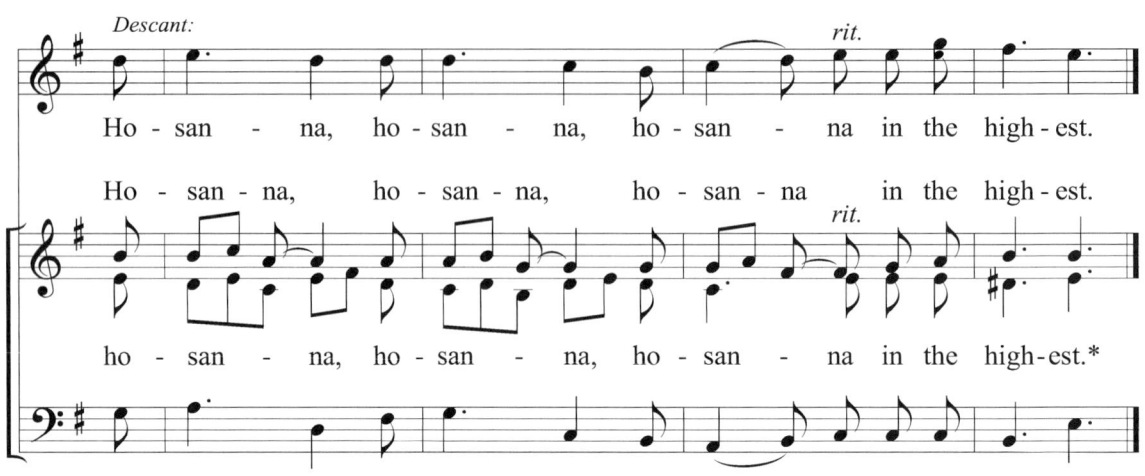

*The congregation's final note is the alto "E".

Music: *Mass of the Angels and Saints,* Steven R. Janco, b. 1961, © 1996, GIA Publications, Inc. All rights reserved. Used with permission.

510   Mass of the Angels and Saints: Memorial Acclamation A

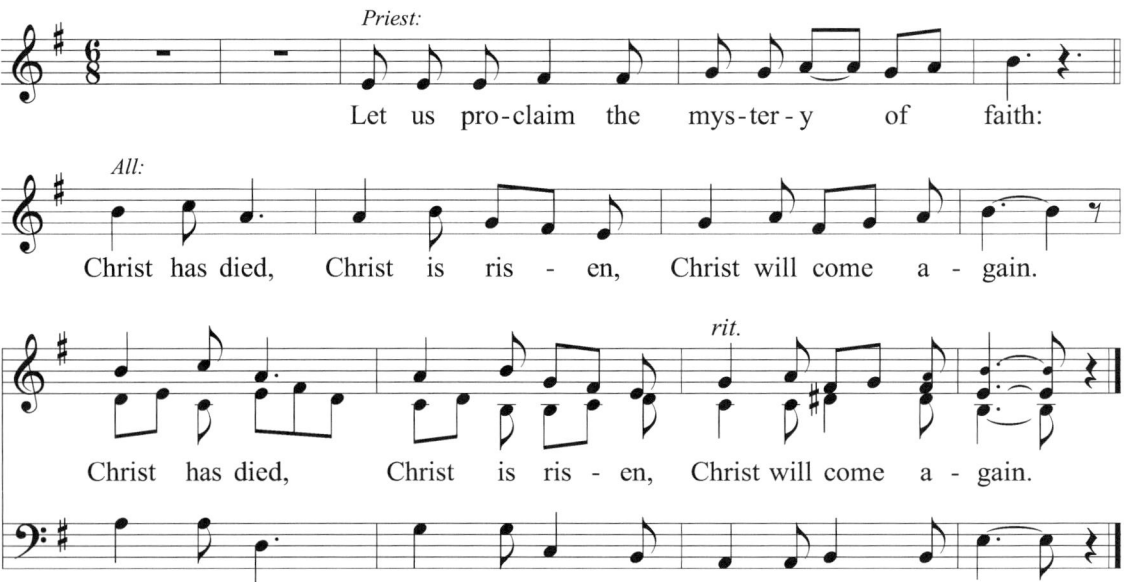

Music: *Mass of the Angels and Saints,* Steven R. Janco, b. 1961, © 1996, GIA Publications, Inc. All rights reserved. Used with permission.

Mass of the Angels and Saints: Memorial Acclamation B   511

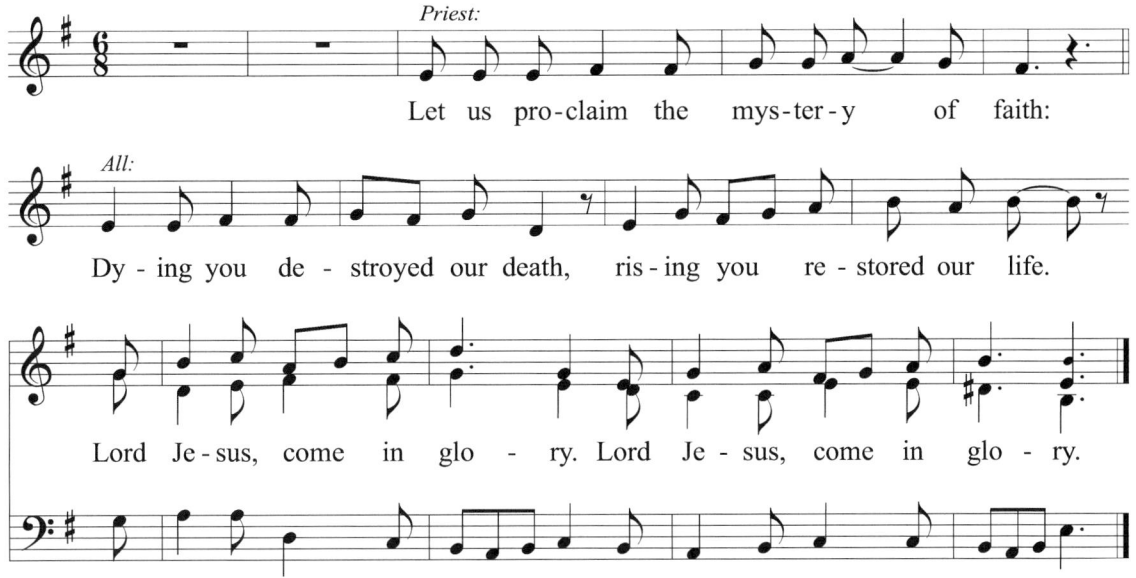

Mass of the Angels and Saints: Memorial Acclamation C   512

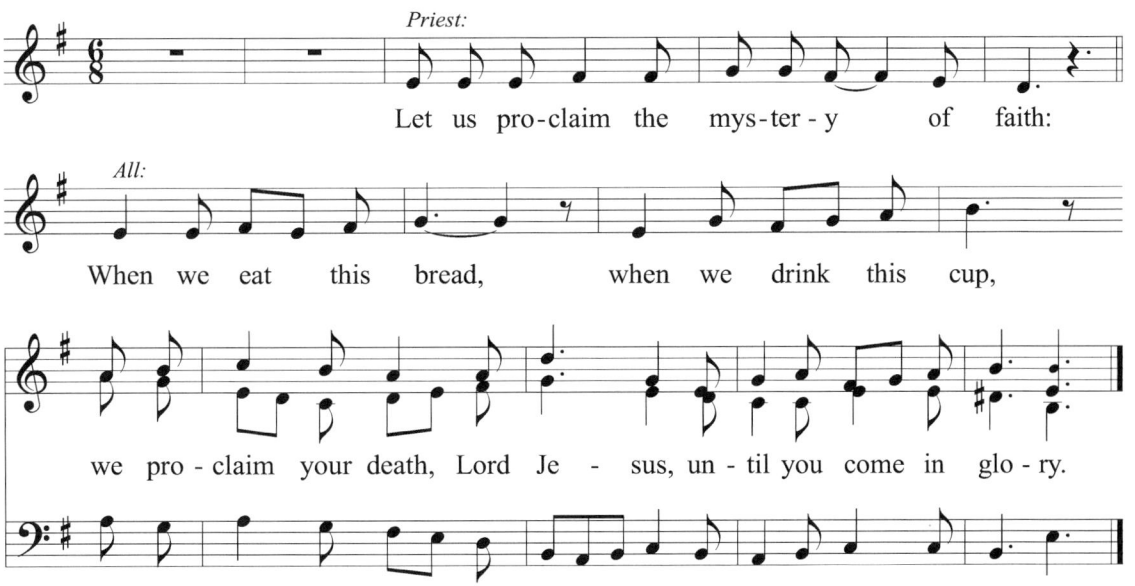

513 Mass of the Angels and Saints: Memorial Acclamation D

Music: *Mass of the Angels and Saints,* Steven R. Janco, b. 1961, © 1996, GIA Publications, Inc. All rights reserved. Used with permission.

Mass of the Angels and Saints: Doxology and Amen   514

Music: *Mass of the Angels and Saints,* Steven R. Janco, b. 1961, © 1996, GIA Publications, Inc. All rights reserved. Used with permission.

515 Mass of the Angels and Saints: Agnus Dei

Cantor or choir: Lamb of God, / Bread of Life, you take away the sins of the world:

All: have mercy on us. Have mercy on us.

Cantor or choir: Lamb of God, you take away the sins of the world:

All: grant us peace. Grant us peace. Grant us peace.

* First and last trope is always "Lamb of God." Additional tropes may be chosen from the following:

Advent	**Christmas**	**Lent**	**Easter**	**Ordinary Time**
Promise of God	Prince of peace	Mercy of God	Risen Lord	Saving Cup
Long-awaited Savior	Word made flesh	Healer of souls	Paschal Lamb	Hope of the poor
Rod of Jesse	Son of God	Refuge of sinners	Shepherd of all	Justice of God
Key of David	Light of the world	Tree of life	Dawn from on high	Lord of love
				King of kings

Text and music: *Mass of the Angels and Saints,* Steven R. Janco, b. 1961, © 1996, GIA Publications, Inc. All rights reserved. Used with permission.

Land of Rest Mass: Sanctus 516

Land of Rest Mass: Sanctus, pg. 2

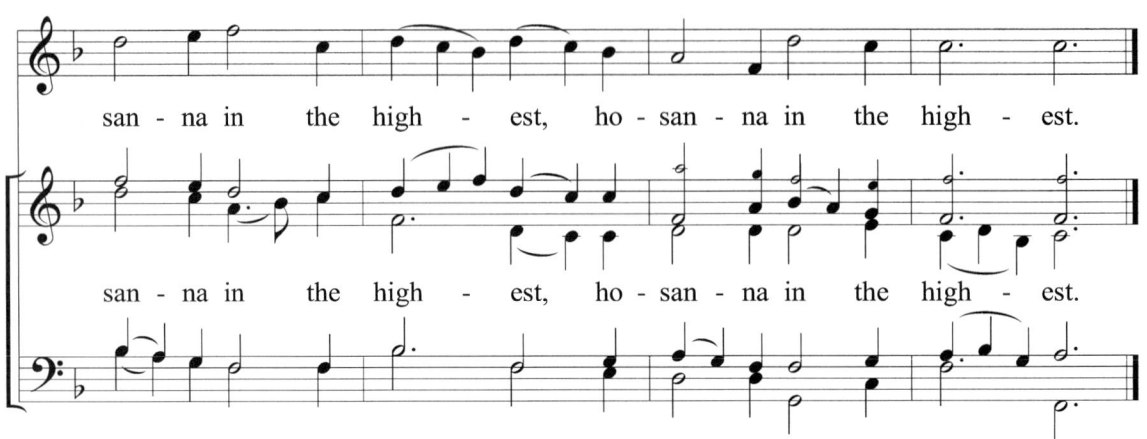

Melody: *Land of Rest;* adapt. by Marcia Pruner, © 1980, The Church Pension Fund. All rights reserved. Used with permission.
Choral arr.: Kelly Dobbs Mickus, © 2004, GIA Publications, Inc. All rights reserved. Used with permission.
Soprano harm.: Richard Proulx, © 1995, GIA Publications, Inc. All rights reserved. Used with permission.
Descant: Christine Manderfeld, OSB, b. 1938, © 2009, the Sisters of Saint Benedict, St. Joseph, MN. Administered by Liturgical Press, Collegeville, MN. All rights reserved.

Land of Rest Mass: Memorial Acclamation A 517

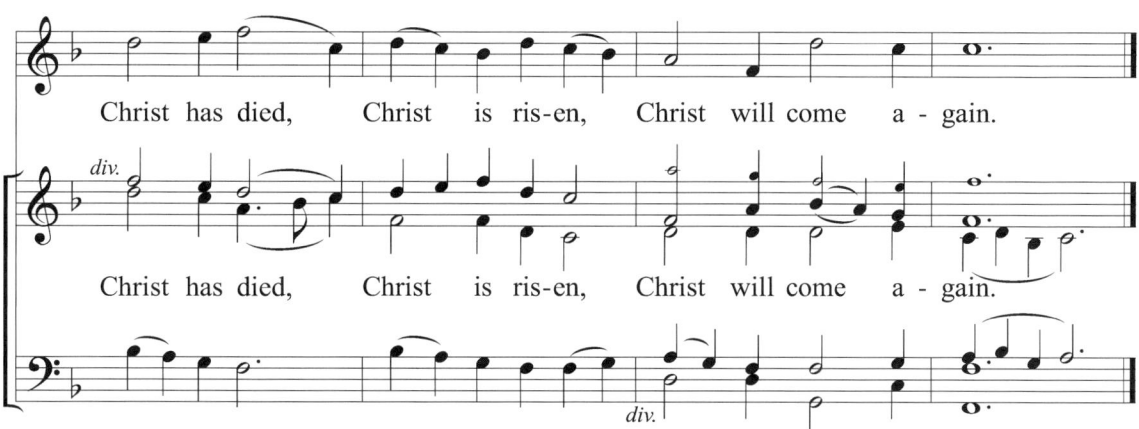

Music: *Land of Rest,* adapt. by Richard Proulx, © 1986, GIA Publications, Inc. All rights reserved. Used with permission.
Choral arr.: Kelly Dobbs Mickus, © 2004, GIA Publications, Inc. All rights reserved. Used with permission.
Soprano harm.: Richard Proulx, © 1995, GIA Publications, Inc. All rights reserved. Used with permission.
Descant: Christine Manderfeld, OSB, b. 1938, © 2009, the Sisters of Saint Benedict, St. Joseph, MN. Administered by Liturgical Press, Collegeville, MN. All rights reserved.

518 Land of Rest Mass: Memorial Acclamation D

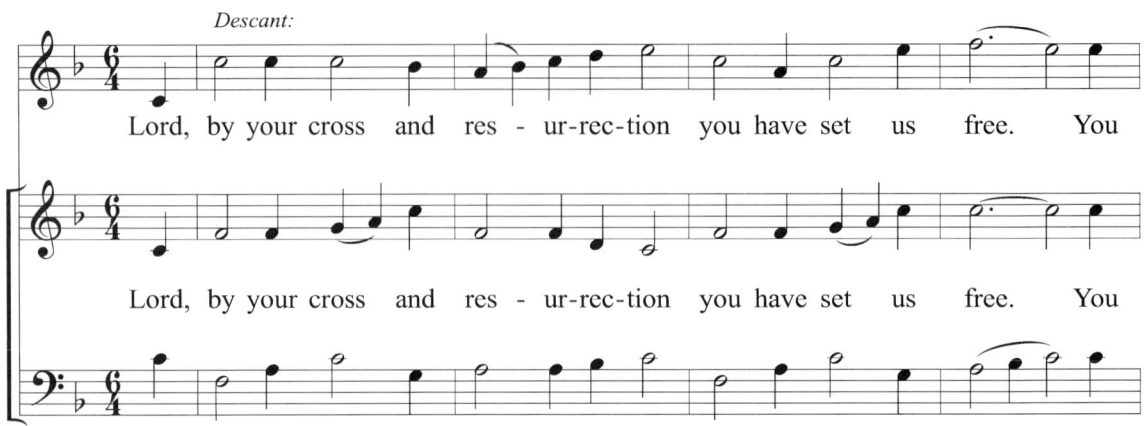

Music: *Land of Rest,* adapt. by Richard Proulx, © 1986, GIA Publications, Inc. All rights reserved. Used with permission.
Choral arr.: Kelly Dobbs Mickus, © 2004, GIA Publications, Inc. All rights reserved. Used with permission.
Soprano harm.: Richard Proulx, © 1995, GIA Publications, Inc. All rights reserved. Used with permission.
Descant: Christine Manderfeld, OSB, b. 1938, © 2009, the Sisters of Saint Benedict, St. Joseph, MN. Administered by Liturgical Press, Collegeville, MN. All rights reserved.

Land of Rest Mass: Amen   519

Music: *Land of Rest,* adapt. by Richard Proulx, © 1986, GIA Publications, Inc. All rights reserved. Used with permission.
Choral arr.: Kelly Dobbs Mickus, © 2004, GIA Publications, Inc. All rights reserved. Used with permission.
Soprano harm.: Richard Proulx, © 1995, GIA Publications, Inc. All rights reserved. Used with permission.
Descant: Christine Manderfeld, OSB, b. 1938, © 2009, the Sisters of Saint Benedict, St. Joseph, MN. Administered by Liturgical Press, Collegeville, MN. All rights reserved.

520 Land of Rest Mass: Agnus Dei

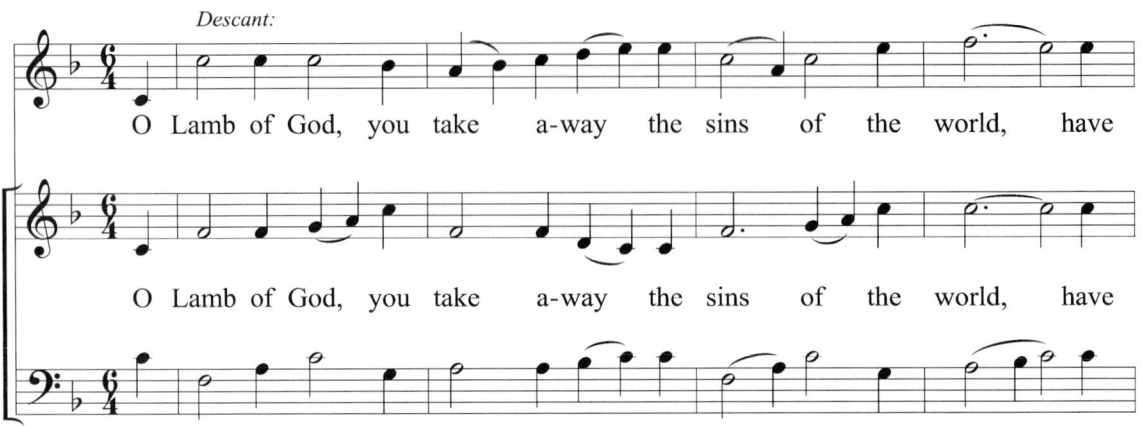

The acclamation is sung three times:
1: unison
2: add the choral arrangement
3: add the soprano harmony (cue size notes) and the descant

Music: *Land of Rest,* adapt. by Richard Proulx, © 1986, GIA Publications, Inc. All rights reserved. Used with permission.
Choral arr.: Kelly Dobbs Mickus, © 2004, GIA Publications, Inc. All rights reserved. Used with permission.
Soprano harm.: Richard Proulx, © 1995, GIA Publications, Inc. All rights reserved. Used with permission.
Descant: Christine Manderfeld, OSB, b. 1938, © 2009, the Sisters of Saint Benedict, St. Joseph, MN. Administered by Liturgical Press, Collegeville, MN. All rights reserved.

Community Mass: Sanctus 521

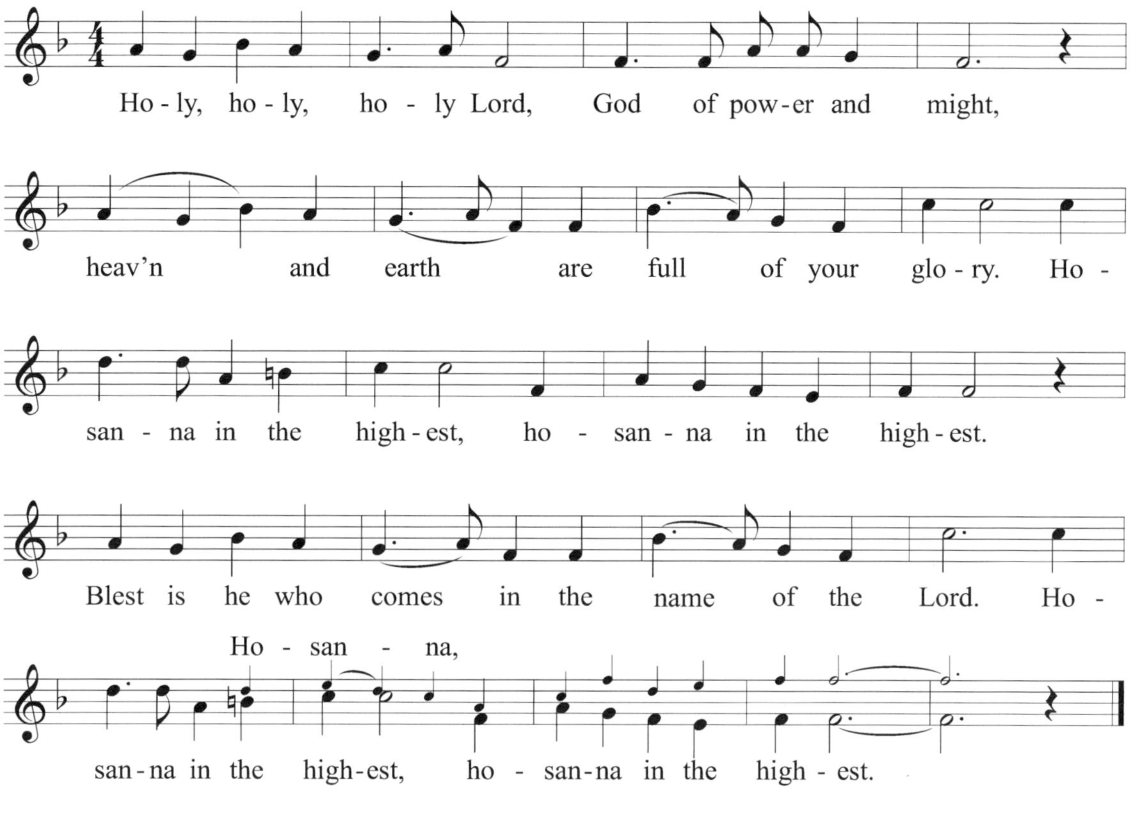

Ho-ly, ho-ly, ho-ly Lord, God of pow-er and might, heav'n and earth are full of your glo-ry. Ho-san-na in the high-est, ho-san-na in the high-est. Blest is he who comes in the name of the Lord. Ho-san-na, ho-san-na in the high-est, ho-san-na in the high-est.

Music: *A Community Mass,* Richard Proulx, b. 1937, © 1971, 1977, GIA Publications, Inc. All rights reserved. Used with permission.

Community Mass: Memorial Acclamation 522

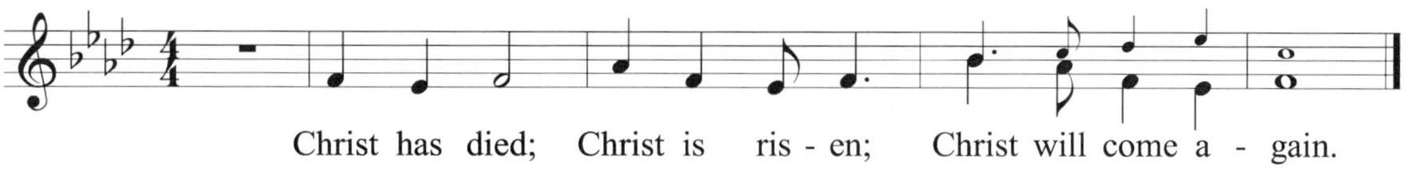

Christ has died; Christ is ris-en; Christ will come a-gain.

Music: *A Community Mass,* Richard Proulx, b. 1937, © 1971, 1977, GIA Publications, Inc. All rights reserved. Used with permission.

523   **Community Mass: Amen**

A - men, a - men, a - men.

Music: *A Community Mass,* Richard Proulx, b. 1937, © 1971, 1977, GIA Publications, Inc. All rights reserved. Used with permission.

524   **Community Mass: Agnus Dei**

Lamb of God, you take a-way the sins of the world: have mer-cy on us.

Lamb of God, you take a-way the sins of the world: grant us peace. grant us peace.

Music: *A Community Mass,* Richard Proulx, b. 1937, © 1971, 1977, GIA Publications, Inc. All rights reserved. Used with permission.

Saint Benedict Mass: Kyrie 525

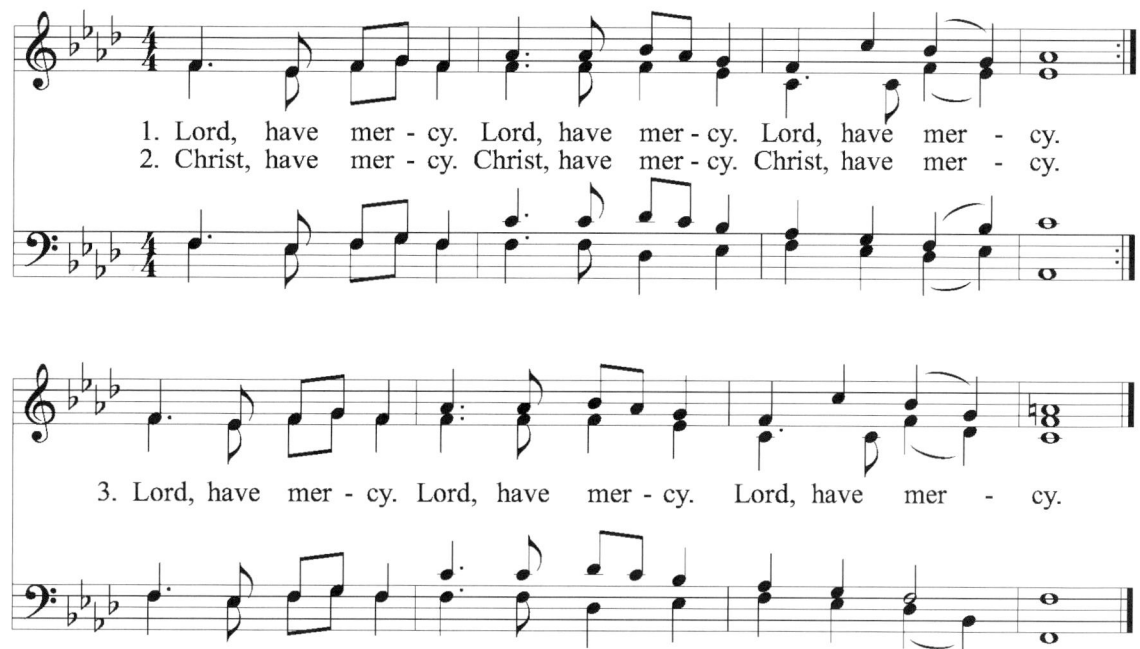

Music: *Saint Benedict Mass,* Robert LeBlanc, © 1991, Robert LeBlanc. All rights reserved. Used with permission.

526 **Saint Benedict Mass: Gloria**

527 Saint Benedict Mass: Gospel Acclamation

Verse text for Sundays and Solemnities can be found in the appendix of this book.

Music: *Saint Benedict Mass,* Robert LeBlanc, © 1991, Robert LeBlanc. All rights reserved. Used with permission.
Verse Tone: Jay F. Hunstiger, b. 1950, © 1990, Jay F. Hunstiger, administered by Liturgical Press, Collegeville, MN 56321. All rights reserved.

528 Saint Benedict Mass: Lenten Gospel Acclamation

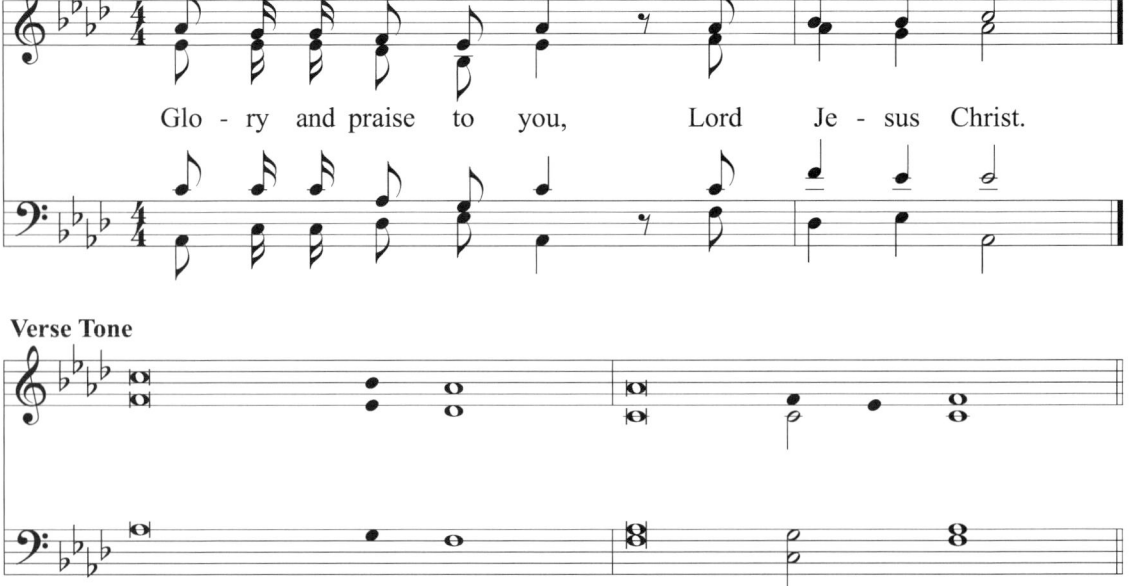

Verse text for Sundays and Solemnities can be found in the appendix of this book.

Music: *Saint Benedict Mass,* Robert LeBlanc, © 1991, Robert LeBlanc. All rights reserved. Used with permission.
Verse Tone: Jay F. Hunstiger, b. 1950, © 1990, Jay F. Hunstiger, administered by Liturgical Press, Collegeville, MN 56321. All rights reserved.

Saint Benedict Mass: Sanctus 529

Music: *Saint Benedict Mass,* Robert LeBlanc, © 1991, Robert LeBlanc. All rights reserved. Used with permission.

530   **Saint Benedict Mass: Memorial Acclamation**

Let us proclaim the mys-t'ry of our faith:
Christ has died, Christ is ris-en, Christ will come a-gain.

Music: *Saint Benedict Mass*, Robert LeBlanc, © 1991, Robert LeBlanc. All rights reserved. Used with permission.

531   **Saint Benedict Mass: Amen**

A - men, a - men, a - men.

Music: *Saint Benedict Mass*, Robert LeBlanc, © 1991, Robert LeBlanc. All rights reserved. Used with permission.

Saint Benedict Mass: Agnus Dei 532

Music: *Saint Benedict Mass,* Robert LeBlanc, © 1991, Robert LeBlanc. All rights reserved. Used with permission.

Cantus Missae: Asperges me

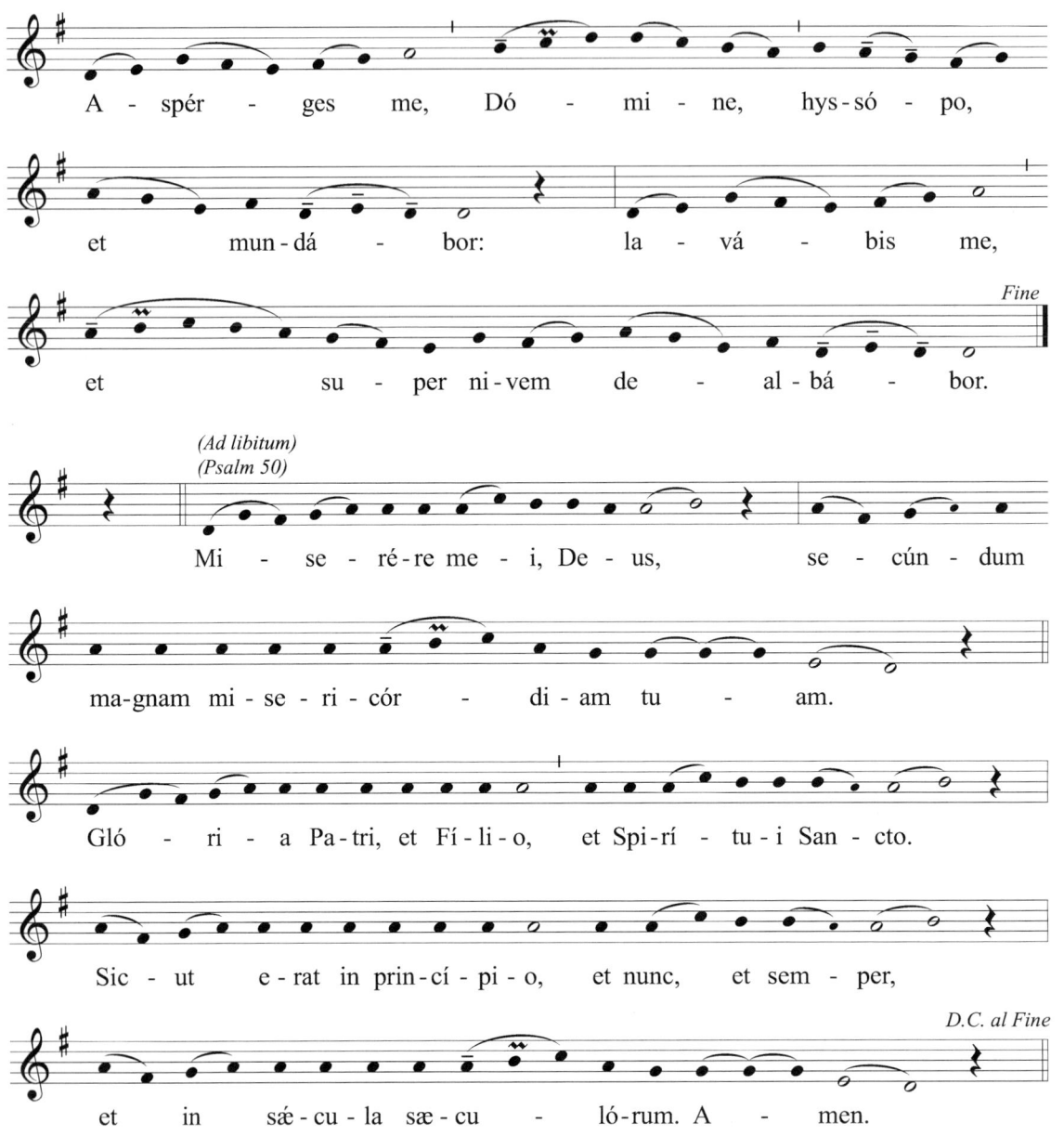

Text and music: *Graduale Romanum*, 1924.

Cantus Missae: Vidi Aquam 534

535 Cantus Missae: Kyrie I

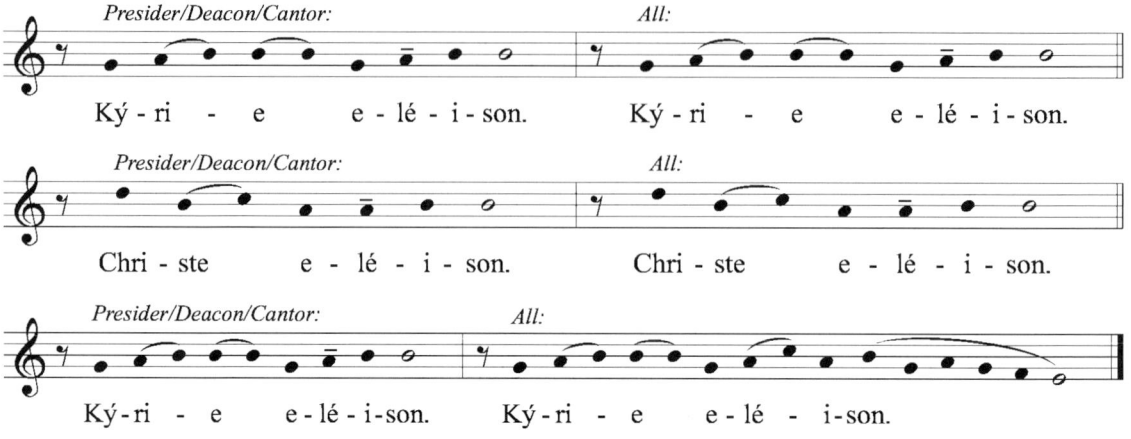

Text and music: Mass XVI, Mode III, from *Iubilate Deo*, Vatican Polyglot Press ed., 1974.

536 Cantus Missae: Kyrie II

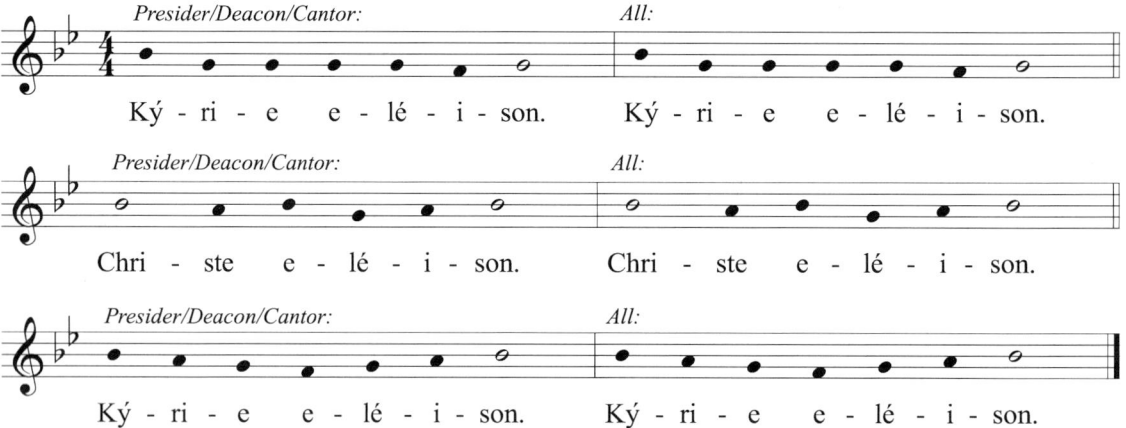

Music: *Litany of the Saints;* adapt. by Richard Proulx, © 1971, GIA Publications, Inc. All rights reserved. Used with permission.

Cantus Missae: Gloria 537

Cantus Missae: Gloria, pg. 2

Text and music: Mass VIII, Mode V, from *Iubilate Deo*, Vatican Polyglot Press ed., 1974.

Cantus Missae: Chants for the Liturgy of the Word

Response I to Reading *when there are two readings before the gospel*

Response II to Reading *or when there is only one reading before the gospel*

Gospel Acclamation

Introduction to the Gospel

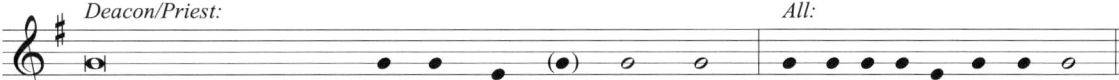

Conclusion to the Gospel

General Intercessions

Text and music: from *Iubilate Deo*, Vatican Polyglot Press ed., 1974.

539. Cantus Missae: Preface Dialogue

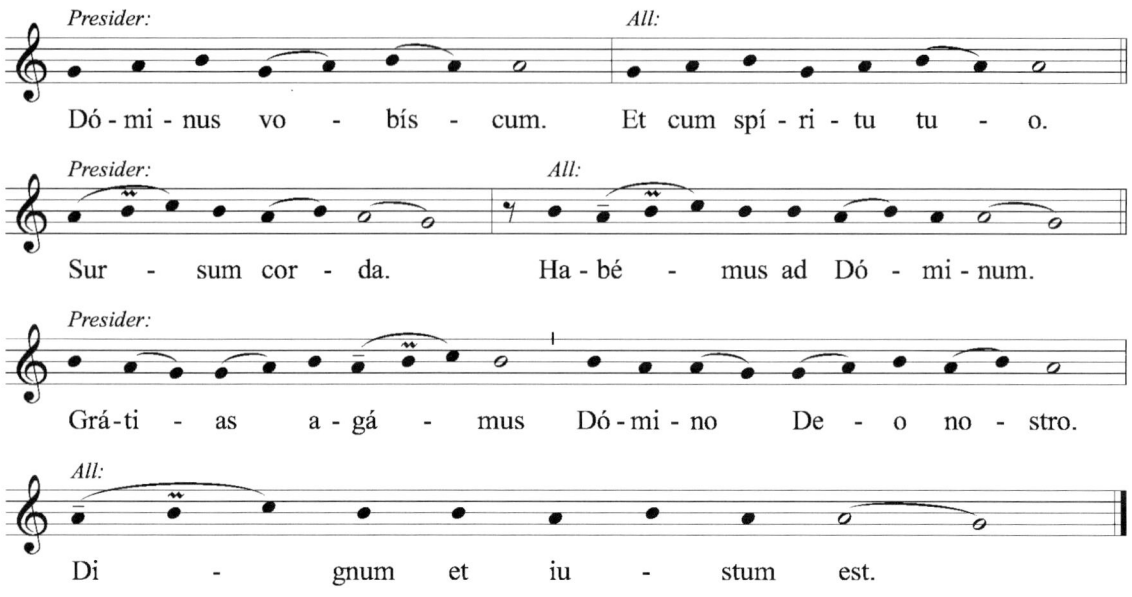

Presider: Dóminus vobíscum.
All: Et cum spíritu tuo.

Presider: Sursum corda.
All: Habémus ad Dóminum.

Presider: Grátias agámus Dómino Deo nostro.

All: Dignum et iustum est.

Text and music: from *Iubilate Deo*, Vatican Polyglot Press ed., 1974.

540. Cantus Missae: Sanctus

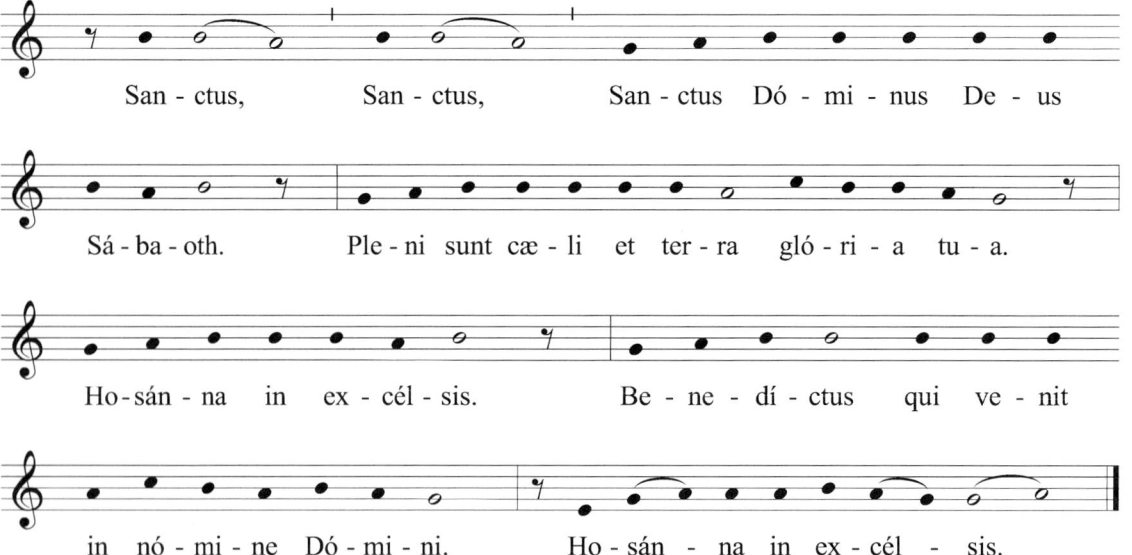

Sanctus, Sanctus, Sanctus Dóminus Deus Sábaoth. Pleni sunt cæli et terra glória tua. Hosánna in excélsis. Benedíctus qui venit in nómine Dómini. Hosánna in excélsis.

Text and music: Mass XVIII from *Iubilate Deo*, Vatican Polyglot Press ed., 1974.

Cantus Missae: Post Consecrationem — 541

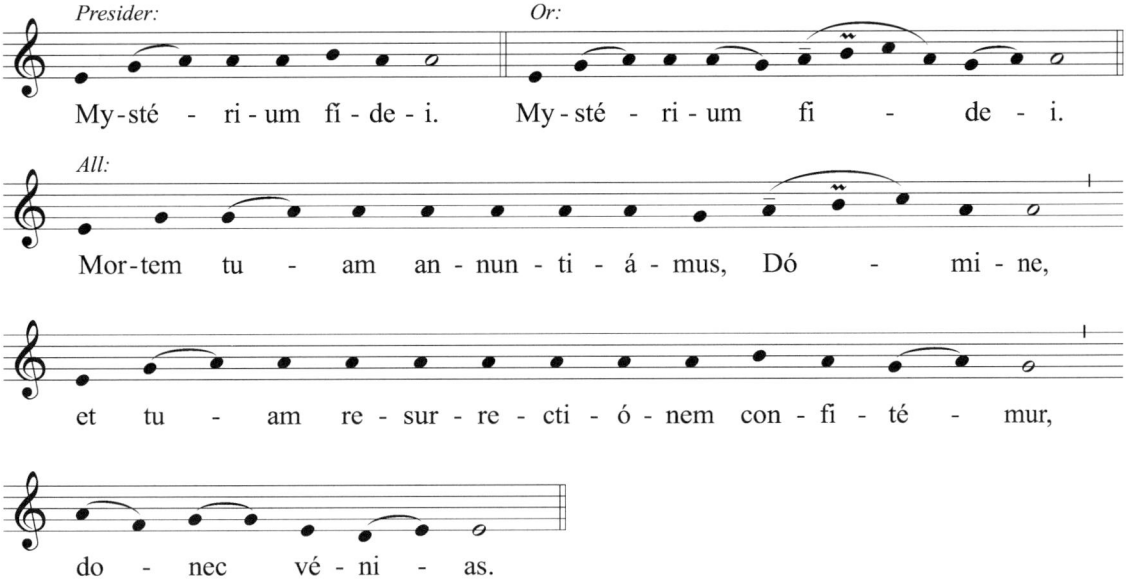

Text and music: from *Iubilate Deo*, Vatican Polyglot Press ed., 1974.

Cantus Missae: Amen — 542

Text and music: from *Iubilate Deo*, Vatican Polyglot Press ed., 1974.

Cantus Missae: Paer Noster

Cantus Missae: Paer Noster, pg. 2

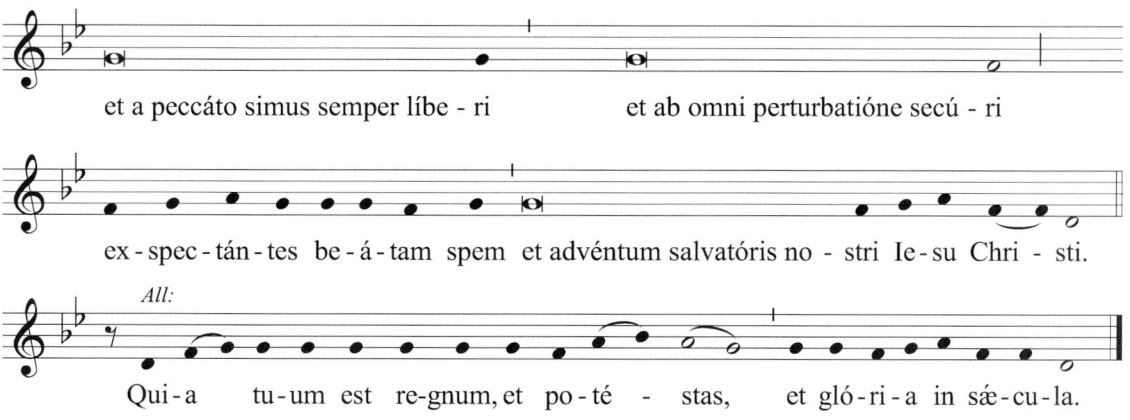

Text and music: from *Iubilate Deo*, Vatican Polyglot Press ed., 1974.

Cantus Missae: Agnus Dei 544

Text and music: Mass XVIII from *Iubilate Deo*, Vatican Polyglot Press ed., 1974.

545 Cantus Missae: Concluding Rite (Blessing & Dismissal)

Text and music: *Graduale Romanum*, 1979.

Sprinkling Rite: Springs of Water I 546

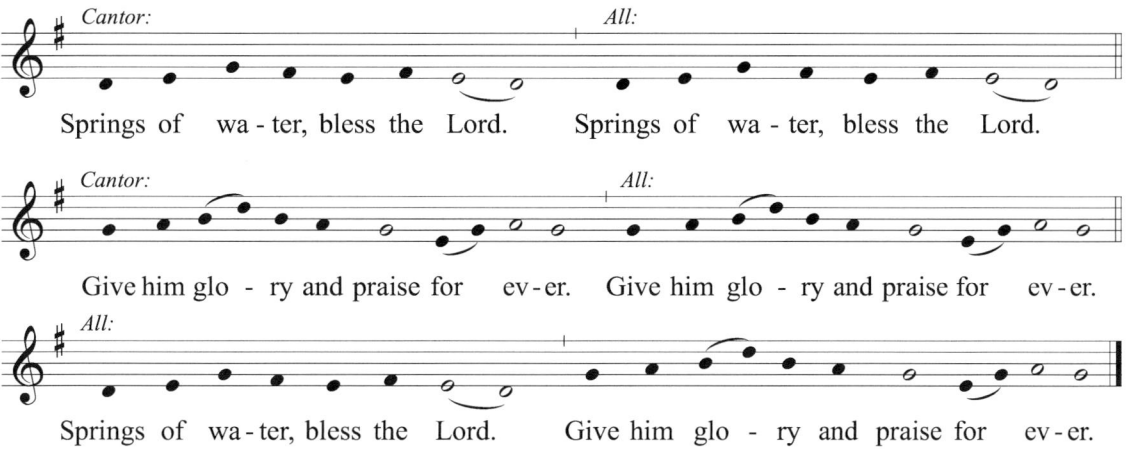

Text: *Blessing of Water,* © 1974, ICEL. Music: Richard Proulx, b. 1937, © 1985, GIA Publications, Inc. All rights reserved. Used with permission.

547 Sprinkling Rite: Springs of Water II

Text: *Vidi aquam* and Psalm 118; tr. and music by Eric Holland, 1960–1991, © 1986.
Published and administered by Liturgical Press, Collegeville, MN 56321. All rights reserved.

548 Lord, Have Mercy I

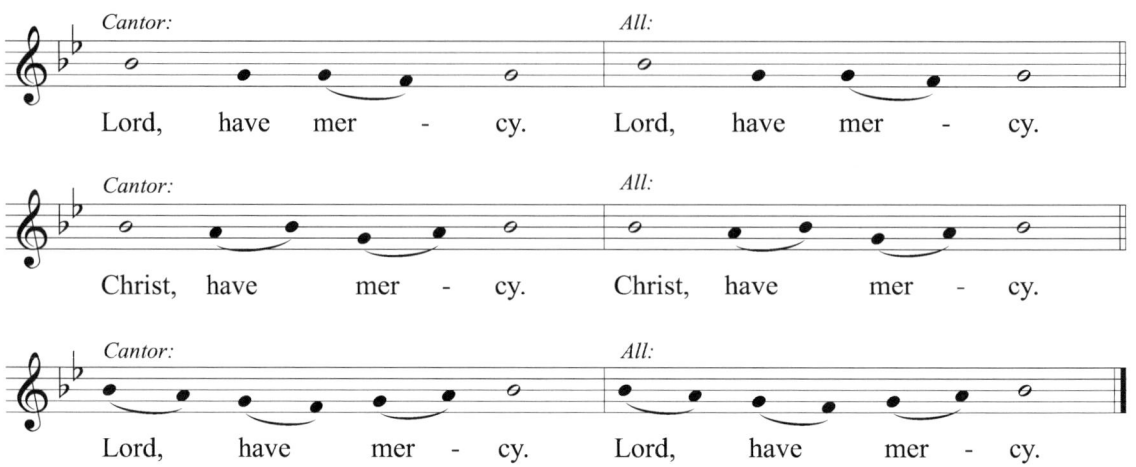

Lord, have mer - cy. Lord, have mer - cy.
Christ, have mer - cy. Christ, have mer - cy.
Lord, have mer - cy. Lord, have mer - cy.

Music: *Litany of the Saints;* adapt. by Richard Proulx, © 1971, GIA Publications, Inc. All rights reserved. Used with permission.

549 Lord, Have Mercy II

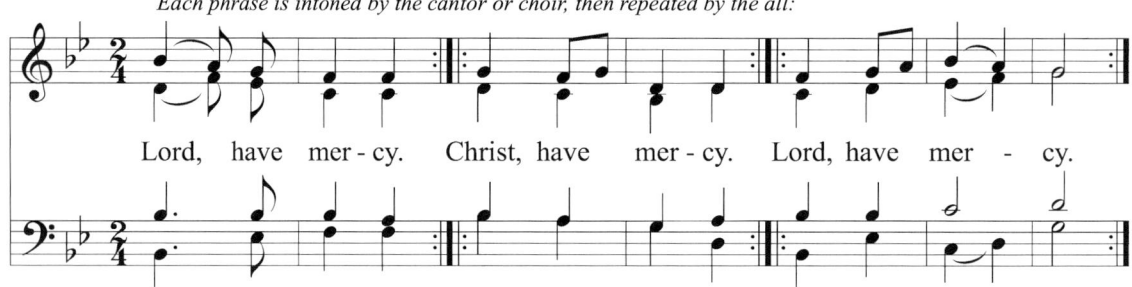

Each phrase is intoned by the cantor or choir, then repeated by the all:

Lord, have mer - cy. Christ, have mer - cy. Lord, have mer - cy.

Music: *Mass of the Good Shepherd,* Stephen Somerville, © 1976, Stephen Somerville. All rights reserved. Used with permission.

Gloria I (Melodic Gloria) 550

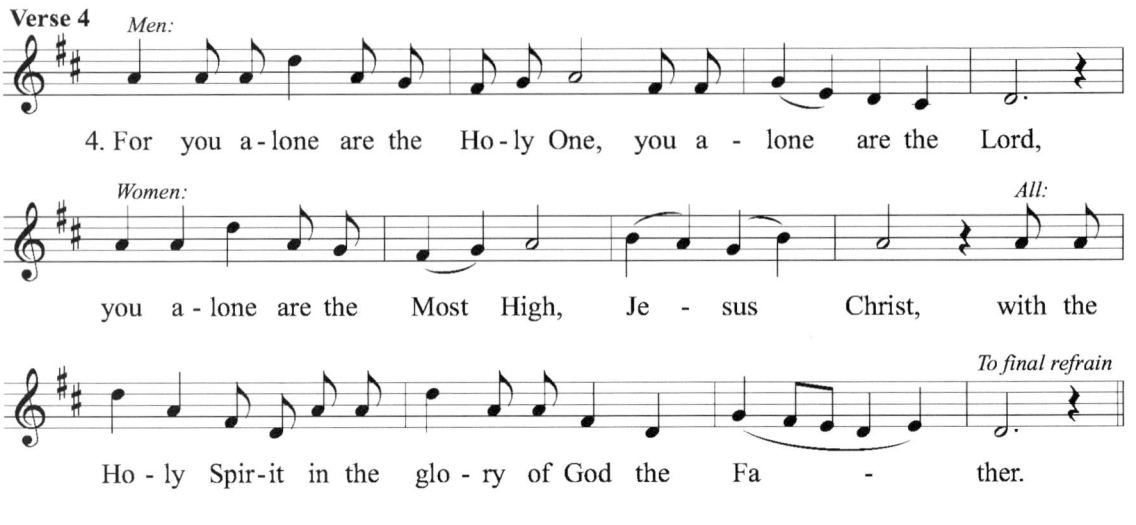

Gloria II (from the Mass of Hope) 551

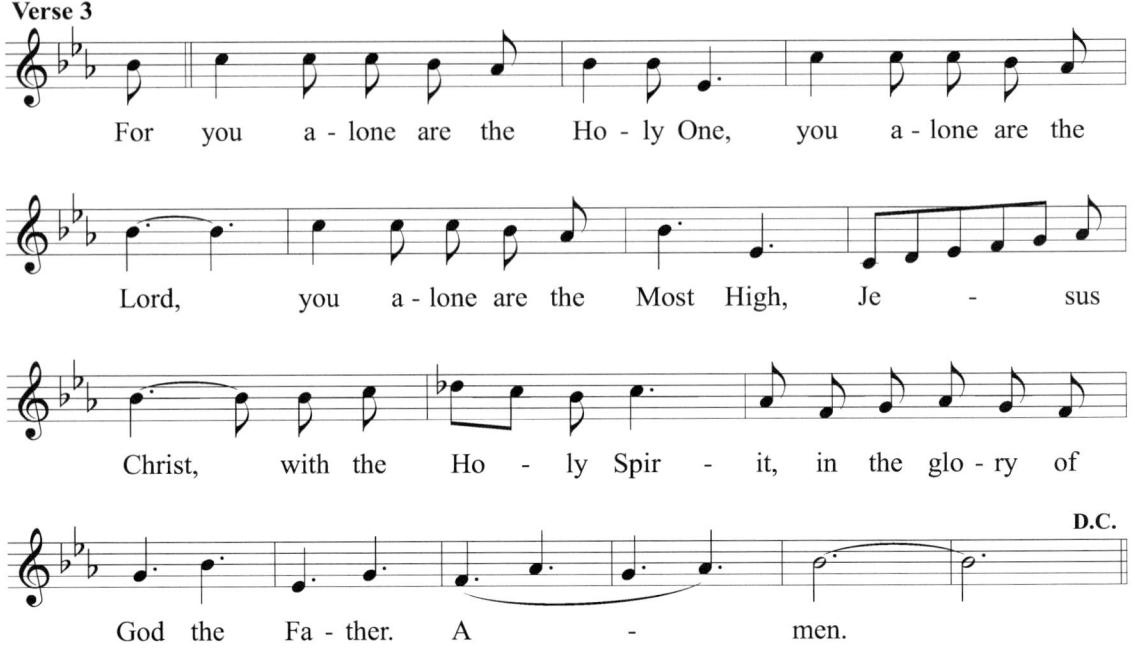

Gloria III (Congregational Mass) 552

Music: *Congregational Mass;* John Lee, © 1970, GIA Publications, Inc. All rights reserved. Used with permission.

553 — Gloria IV (A New Mass for Congregations)

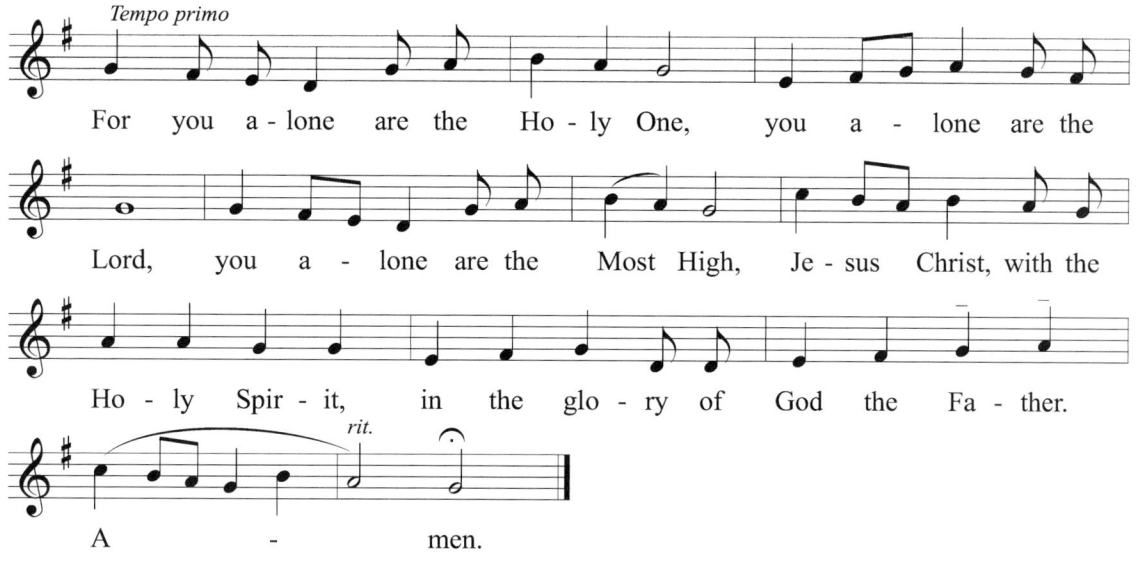

Gloria V

555　　　　　　　　　Gloria VI (Christmas Gloria)

Verse 1

1. Glo-ry to God in the high-est, and peace to his peo-ple on earth.

℘ Refrain

Glo - - - - ri-a in ex-cel-sis De - o, Glo - - - - ri-a in ex-cel-sis De - o.

Gloria VI (Christmas Gloria), pg. 3

Music: *Christmas Gloria,* Daniel W. Laginya, © 1986, GIA Publications, Inc. All rights reserved. Used with permission.
Final Descant: Christine Manderfeld, OSB, b. 1938, © 2009, the Sisters of Saint Benedict, St. Joseph, MN. Administered by Liturgical Press, Collegeville, MN. All rights reserved.

Gospel Acclamation I (Chant Mode VI) 556

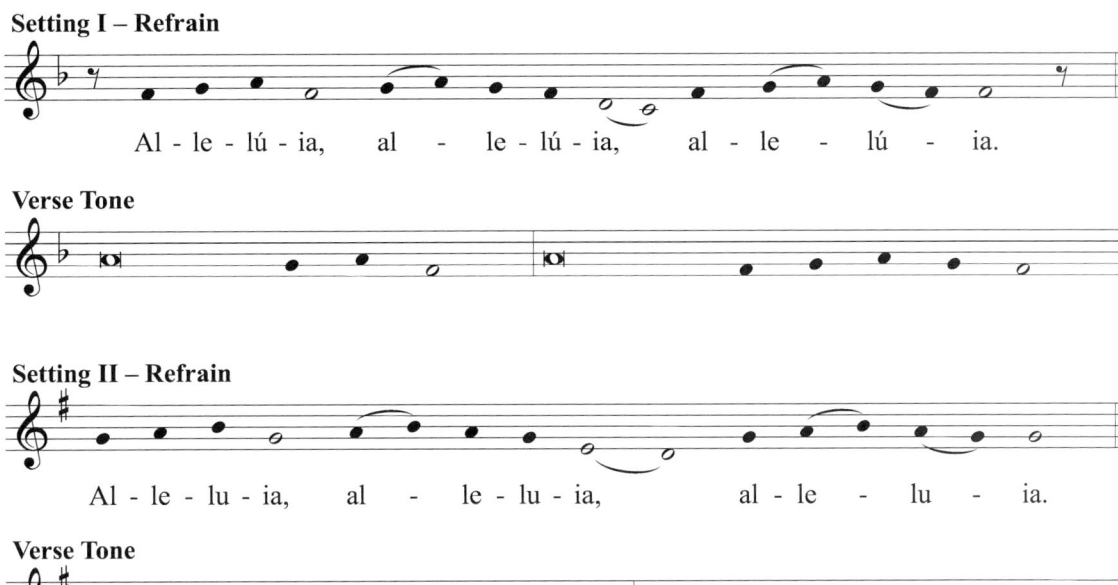

Verse text for Sundays and Solemnities can be found in the appendix of this book.

Verse Tone, Setting I: Musical adapt. by Bartholomew Sayles, OSB, 1918–2006, and Cecile Gertken, OSB, 1902–2001, © 1977, 1989, Order of Saint Benedict, Collegeville, MN. Administered by Liturgical Press, Collegeville, MN. All rights reserved.
Verse Tone, Setting II: Musical adapt. by Richard Proulx, b. 1937, © 1975, GIA Publications, Inc. All rights reserved. Used with permission.

557 Gospel Acclamation II

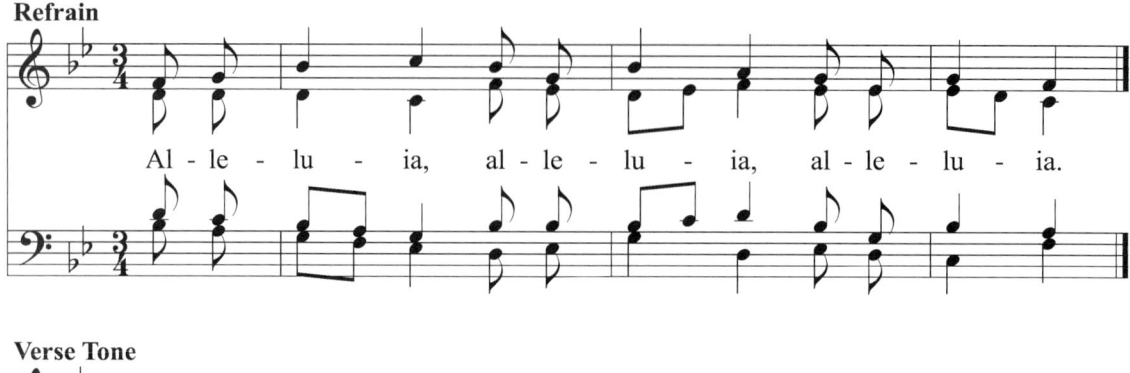

Verse text for Sundays and Solemnities can be found in the appendix of this book.

Music: Refrain–A. Gregory Murray, OSB, 1905–1992, © 1963, The Grail, GIA Publications, Inc., North American agent.
Verse Tone–Richard Proulx, b. 1937, © 1975, GIA Publications, Inc.
All rights reserved. Used with permission.

558 Gospel Acclamation III

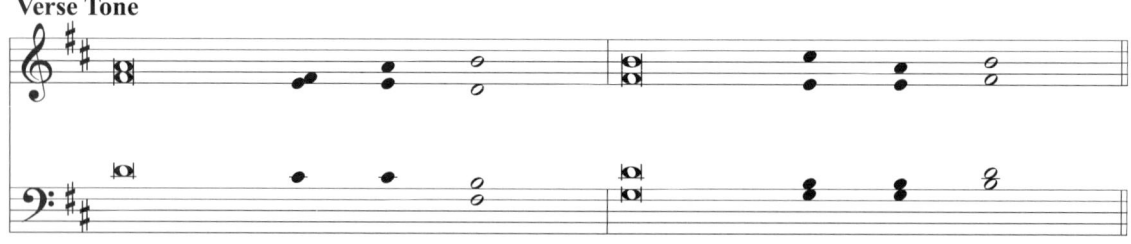

Verse text for Sundays and Solemnities can be found in the appendix of this book.

Music: Theophane Hytrek, OSF, 1915–1992, © 1981, International Committee on English in the Liturgy.
All rights reserved. Used with permission.

Gospel Acclamation IV 559

Verse text for Sundays and Solemnities can be found in the appendix of this book.

Music: Refrain–Fintan O'Carroll, d. 1977, © 1985, GIA Publications, Inc. Verse Tone–Robert J. Batastini, b. 1942, © 1998, GIA Publications, Inc.
All rights reserved. Used with permission.

560 Gospel Acclamation V (Festival Alleluia)

1. O Lord, open our hearts, to listen to the words of your Son, your Son.
2. If today you hear God's voice, O harden not your hearts, your hearts.
3. Your words give joy to my heart, your teaching is light to my eyes, my eyes.
4. Your word is a lamp for my feet, and a light on my path, my path.
5. Your word, O Lord, is truth; make us holy in the truth, the truth.
6. I hope in the Lord, I trust in God's word, God's word.
7. Whoever keeps the word of Christ grows perfect in the love of God, of God.

Music: *Festival Alleluia*, James J. Chepponis, b. 1956, © 1999, MorningStar Music Publishers. All rights reserved. Used with permission.

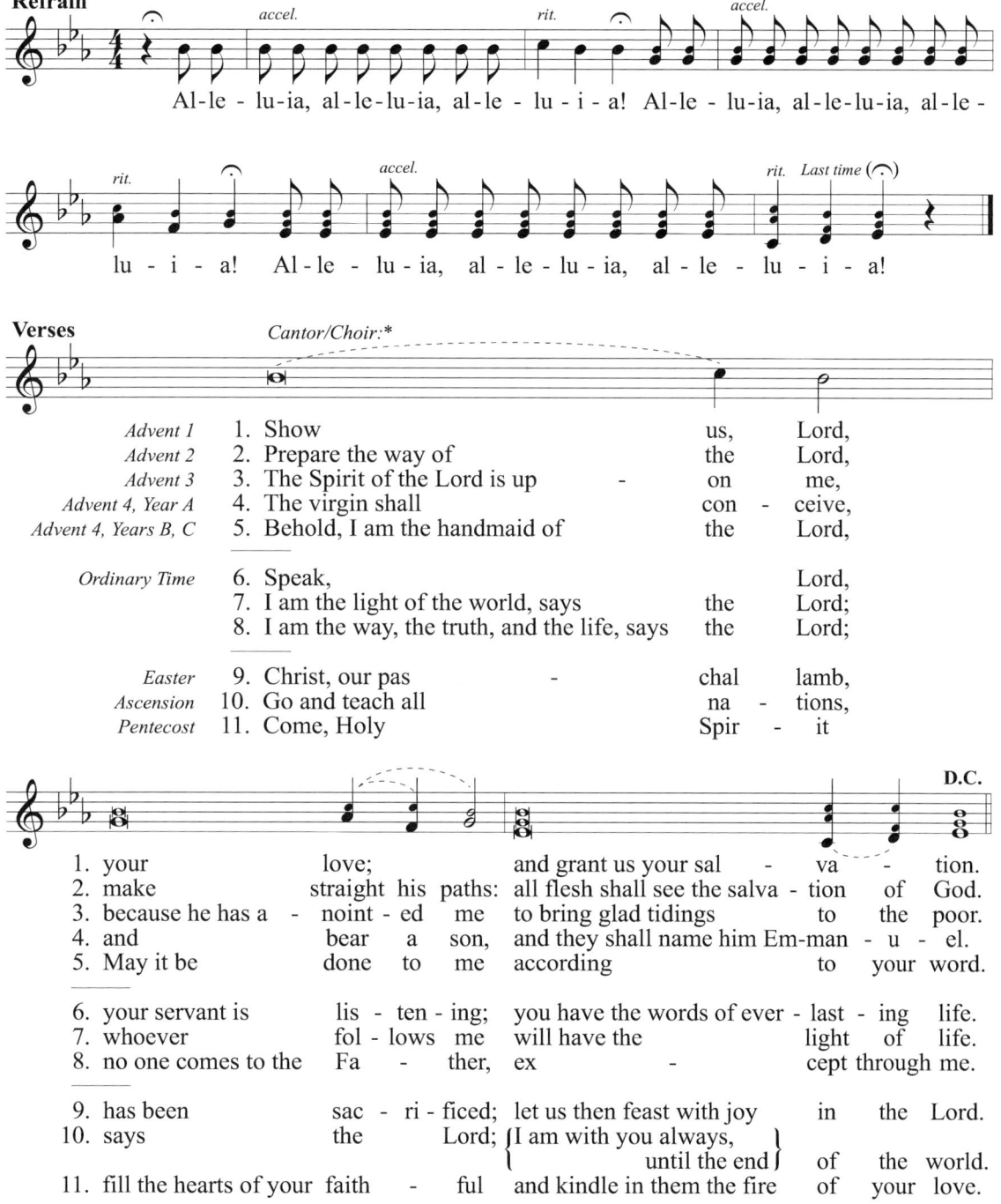

Gospel Acclamation VII

Al - le - lu - ia, al - le - lu - ia, al - le - lu - ia.

Verse Tone

Verse text for Sundays and Solemnities can be found in the appendix of this book.

Music: Refrain–GELOBT SEI GOTT, Melchior Vulpius, c. 1560–1616.
Verse Tone: Michel Guimont, © 1994, GIA Publications, Inc. All rights reserved. Used with permission.

Gospel Acclamation VIII 563

Verse text for Sundays and Solemnities can be found in the appendix of this book.

Music: Jay F. Hunstiger, b. 1950, © 1990, Jay F. Hunstiger, published and administered by Liturgical Press, Collegeville, MN 56321. All rights reserved.

564 Gospel Acclamation IX

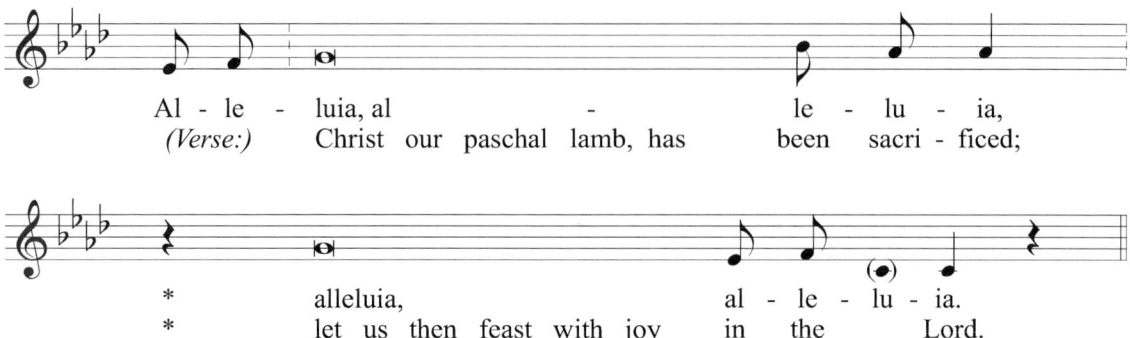

Verse text for Sundays and Solemnities can be found in the appendix of this book.

Musical adapt. by Bartholomew Sayles, OSB, 1918–2006, and Cecile Gertken, OSB, 1902–2001.
© 1977, 1989, Order of Saint Benedict, Collegeville, MN. Administered by Liturgical Press, Collegeville, MN. All rights reserved.

565 Gospel Acclamation X

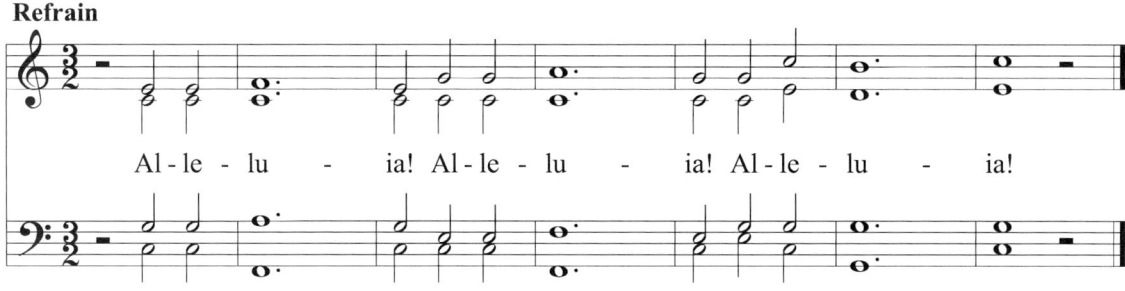

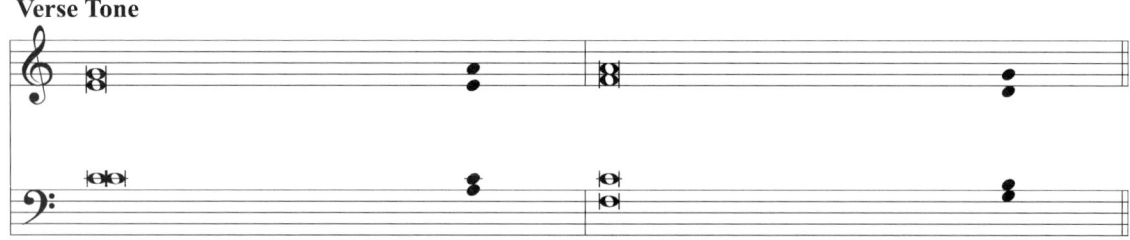

Verse text for Sundays and Solemnities can be found in the appendix of this book.

Music: Refrain–VICTORY, Giovannia da Palestrina, 1525–1594; adapt. by William H. Monk, 1823–1889.
Verse Tone–Howard Hughes, SM, b.1930, © 1973, GIA Publications, Inc. All rights reserved. Used with permission.

Gospel Acclamation XI (with verse for Easter) 566

Music: Gerard Farrell, OSB, 1919–2000, © 1959, 1977, Order of Saint Benedict, Collegeville, MN. Administered by Liturgical Press, Collegeville, MN. All rights reserved.

567 Gospel Acclamation / Lenten Gospel Acclamation
(from Mass for John Carroll)

*Verse sung during Lent.
Verse text for Sundays and Solemnities can be found in the appendix of this book.

Music: *Mass for John Carroll*, Michael Joncas, b. 1951, © 1990, GIA Publications, Inc. All rights reserved. Used with permission.

Lenten Gospel Acclamation I   568

Refrain
Praise to you, Lord Jesus, king of endless glory, Savior of the world, Savior of the world.

Verses
1. Turn to the Lord with all your heart, for the time of salvation is here.
2. We do not live by bread alone, but we live by the words of our God.
3. Follow the Lord in humbleness, that God's glory might shine from your hearts.
4. Out of the cloud a voice is heard saying: "Here is my voice in the world."
5. Give us the living water, that we never be thirsty again.
6. Jesus, the Light, is calling us, he will open the eyes of our soul.
7. "I am the resurrection and the life, if you live in me you live for all time.
8. Christ was obedient unto death, even death on the wood of the cross.

Text and music: Marty Haugen, b. 1950, © 1983, GIA Publications, Inc. All rights reserved. Used with permission.

Lenten Gospel Acclamation II

Praise to you, Lord Jesus Christ, king of endless glory.

Verse text for Sundays and Solemnities can be found in the appendix of this book.

Music: Refrain—Frank Schoen, © 1970, GIA Publications, Inc. Verse Tone—Robert J. Batastini, b. 1942, © 1998, GIA Publications, Inc.
All rights reserved. Used with permission.

Lenten Gospel Acclamation III   570

Verse text for Sundays and Solemnities can be found in the appendix of this book.

Music: Refrain–Donald Krubsack, b. 1964, © 2001, Donald Krubsack. Verse Tone–Chrysogonus Waddell, OCSO, © Gethsemani Abbey.
All rights reserved. Used with permission.

Lenten Gospel Acclamation IV

Verse text for Sundays and Solemnities can be found in the appendix of this book.

Music: Howard Hughes, © 1980, International Committee on English in the Liturgy. All rights reserved. Used with permission.

Lenten Gospel Acclamation V 572

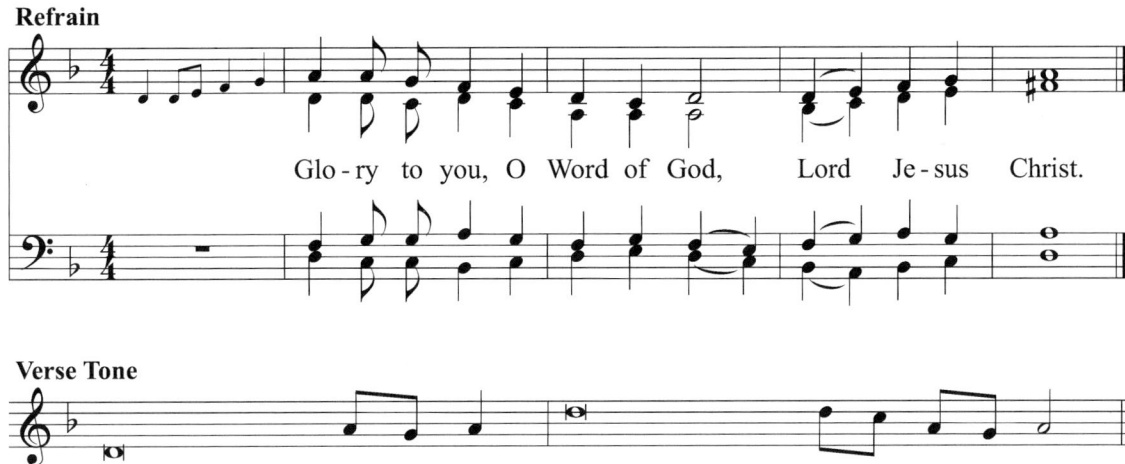

Glo-ry to you, O Word of God, Lord Jesus Christ.

Verse text for Sundays and Solemnities can be found in the appendix of this book.

Music: Richard Proulx, b. 1937, © 1975, GIA Publications, Inc. All rights reserved. Used with permission.

Lenten Gospel Acclamation VI 573

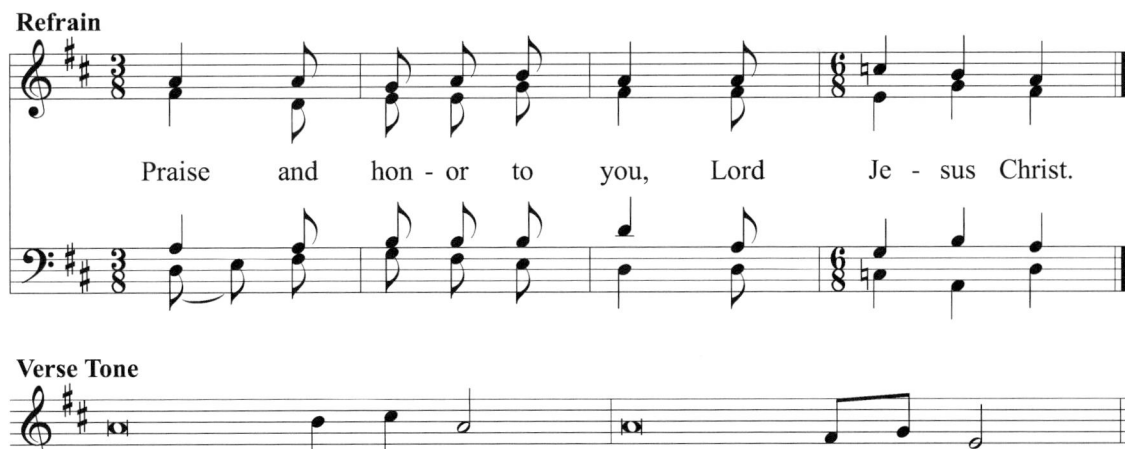

Praise and hon-or to you, Lord Jesus Christ.

Verse text for Sundays and Solemnities can be found in the appendix of this book.

Music: Refrain–Nicholas Doub, OSB, 1949–2002, © 2002, Order of Saint Benedict, Collegeville, MN. Administered by Liturgical Press, Collegeville, MN. All rights reserved.
Verse tone–Richard Proulx, b. 1937, © 1980, GIA Publications, Inc. All rights reserved. Used with permission.

574 Lenten Gospel Acclamation VII

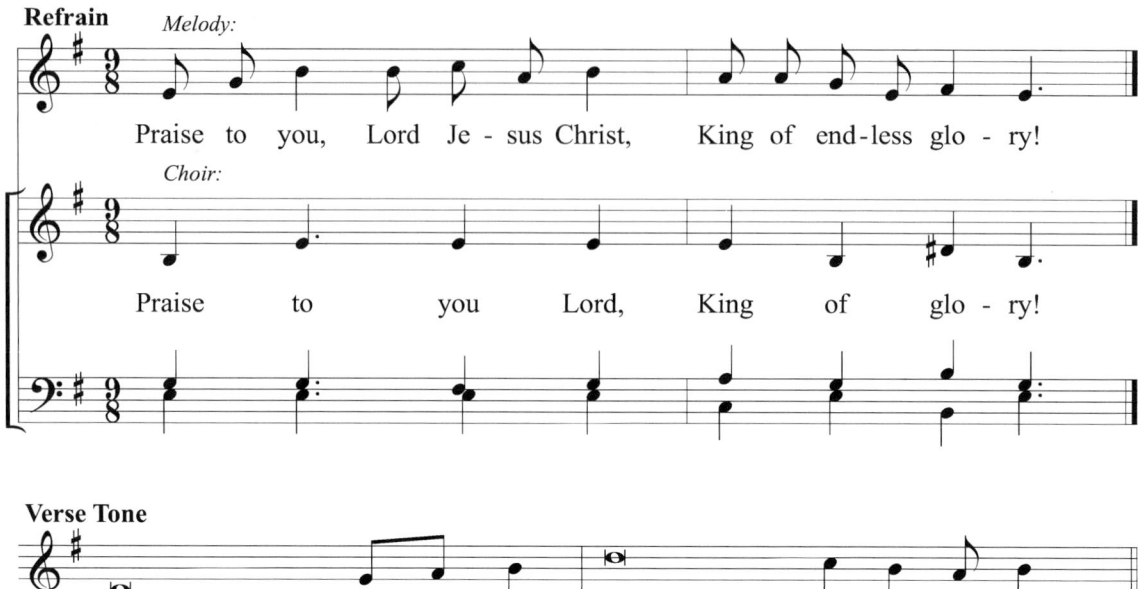

Verse text for Sundays and Solemnities can be found in the appendix of this book.

Music: Refrain–Nicholas Doub, OSB, 1949–2002, © 2002, Order of Saint Benedict, Collegeville, MN. Administered by Liturgical Press, Collegeville, MN. All rights reserved.
Verse tone–Richard Proulx, b. 1937, © 1975, GIA Publications, Inc. All rights reserved. Used with permission.

Lenten Gospel Acclamation VIII   575

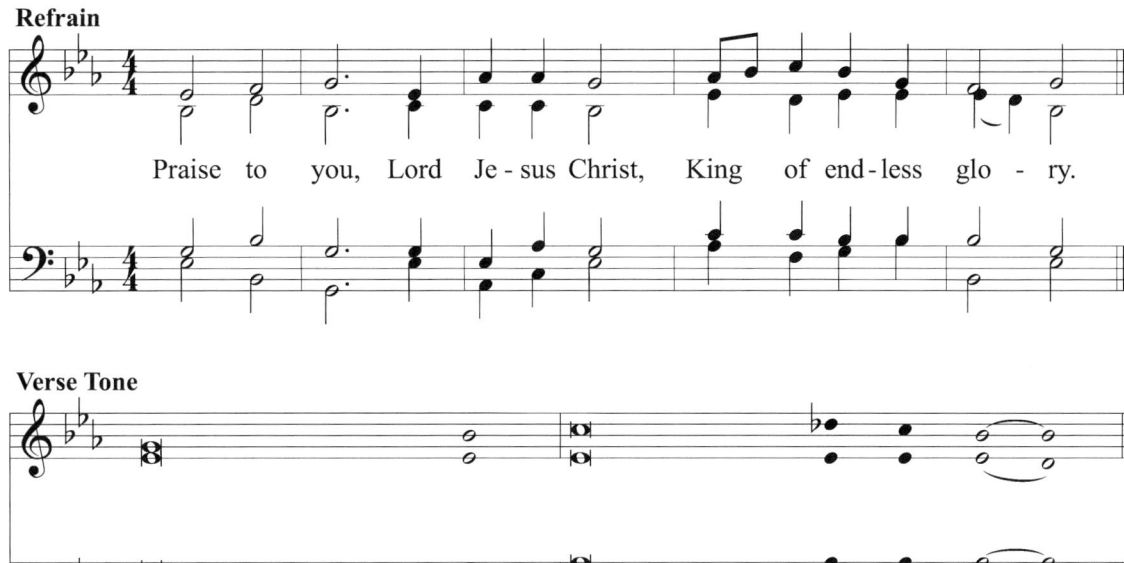

Praise to you, Lord Jesus Christ, King of endless glory.

Verse text for Sundays and Solemnities can be found in the appendix of this book.

Music: Refrain–Nicholas Doub, OSB, 1949–2002, © 2002, Order of Saint Benedict, Collegeville, MN. Administered by Liturgical Press, Collegeville, MN. All rights reserved.
Verse Tone: Michel Guimont, © 1994, 1998, GIA Publications, Inc. All rights reserved. Used with permission.

576   **Profession of Faith**

Presider
Do you believe in God, the Father Almighty, creator of heaven and earth?

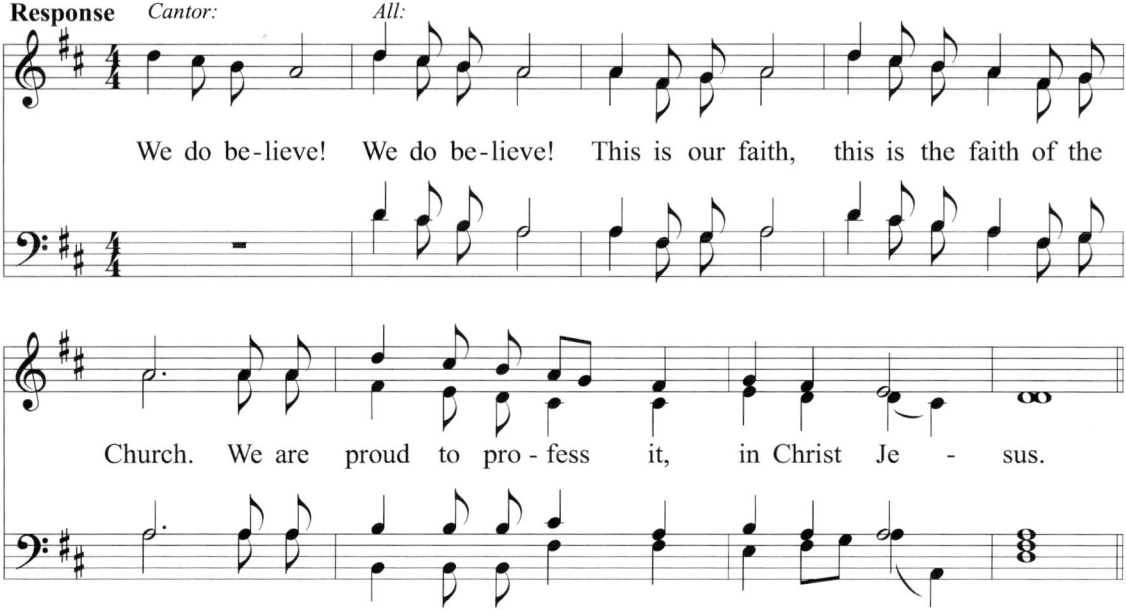

Presider
Do you believe in Jesus Christ, his only Son, our Lord, who was born of the Virgin Mary,
was crucified, died, and was buried, rose from the dead, and is now seated at the right hand of the Father?
Response by all

Presider
Do you believe in the Holy Spirit, the Holy Catholic Church, the communion of saints,
the forgiveness of sins, the resurrection of the body, and life everlasting?
Response by all

Presider
God, the all-powerful Father of our Lord Jesus Christ, has given us a new birth by water and the Holy Spirit,
and forgiven all our sins. May he also keep us faithful to our Lord Jesus Christ forever and ever.
Final Response by all

This setting is taken from the collection *Who Calls You By Name*, Volume 1, published by GIA Publications. The music collection includes sung verses for the presider and is available from the publisher, item number G-3193 (full score) and G-3193P (presider edition).

Text: *Renewal of Baptismal Promises*, © 1985, ICEL. Music: David Haas, b. 1957, © 1988, GIA Publications, Inc. All rights reserved. Used with permission.

This Is Our Faith   577

Refrain (Cantor/Choir:) This is our faith. (All:) This is our faith.
(Cantor/Choir:) This is the faith of the church. (All:) This is the faith of the church. (Cantor/Choir:) We are proud to pro-fess it in Je-sus Christ, our Lord. (All:) We are proud to pro-fess it in Je-sus Christ, our Lord.

Verse 1
1. Great is the mys-t'ry we pro-fess! Christ, re-vealed in the flesh; Christ, made just in the Spir-it; Christ, seen by the an-gels.

Verse 2
2. Great is the mys-t'ry we pro-fess! Christ, pro-claimed a-mong the na-tions; be-lieved through-out the world; Christ, ex-alt-ed in glo-ry.

Refrain text: *Rite of Baptism for Children,* © 1969, ICEL. All rights reserved. Verse text: Lucien Deiss, alt., © 1965, 1966, 1968, 1973. Music: Charles Gardner, © 2004.
Verse text and music *This Is Our Faith,* © World Library Publications, Inc., 3708 River Road, Franklin Park, IL 60131. www.wlpmusic.com
All rights reserved. Used with permission.

578 **General Intercessions I (Byzantine chant)**

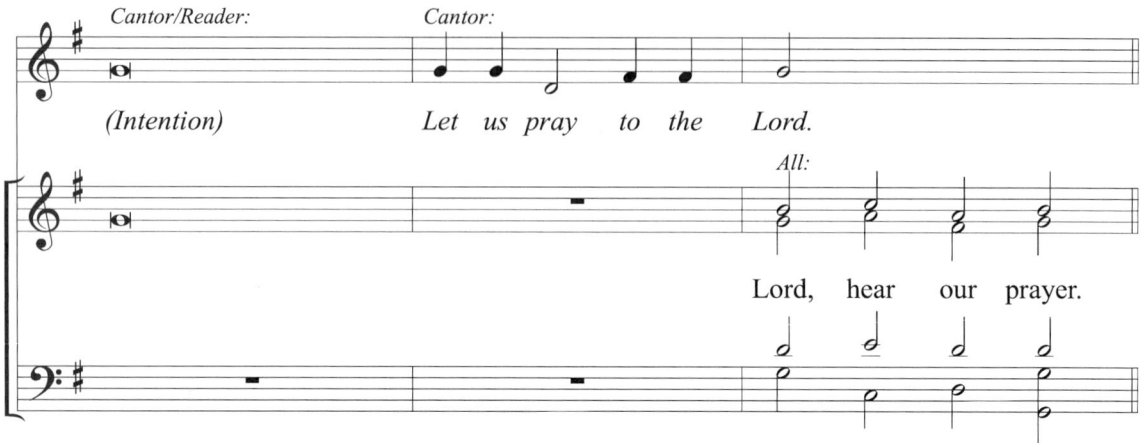

Music: Traditional Byzantine Chant.

579 **General Intercessions II**

Text and music: Paul Inwood, © 1997, Paul Inwood. All rights reserved. Published by Magnificat Music. Used with permission.

580 **General Intercessions III**

Text and music: Paul Inwood, © 1997, Paul Inwood. All rights reserved. Published by Magnificat Music. Used with permission.

General Intercessions IV 581

Text and music: Paul Inwood, © 1997, Paul Inwood. All rights reserved. Published by Magnificat Music. Used with permission.

General Intercessions V (Trilingual Intercessions) 582

Refrain

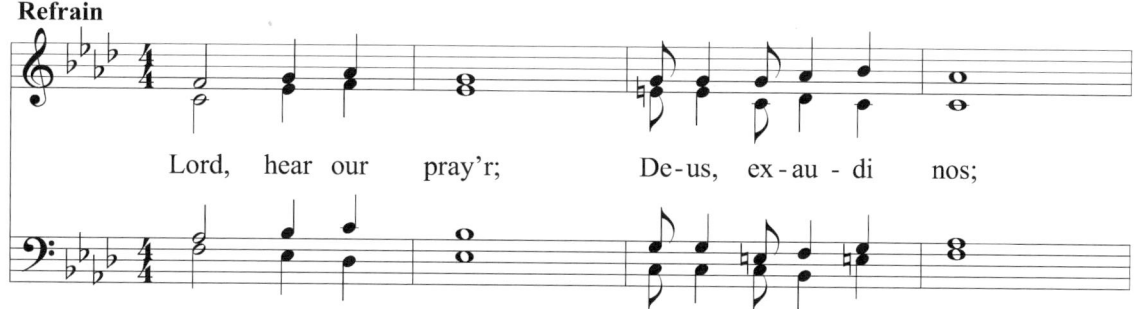

Intercession Tone

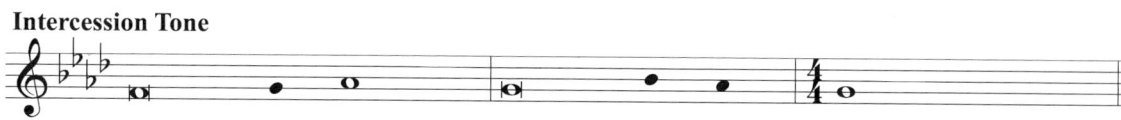

Text and music: *Trilingual Intercessions* by Michael Hay, © 1994, World Library Publications, 3708 River Road, Franklin Park, IL 60131. www.wlpmusic.com All rights reserved. Used with permission.

583 General Intercessions VI (Bilingual Intercessions: Te Rogamos, Óyenos / Lord, Hear Our Prayer)

Respuesta / Response

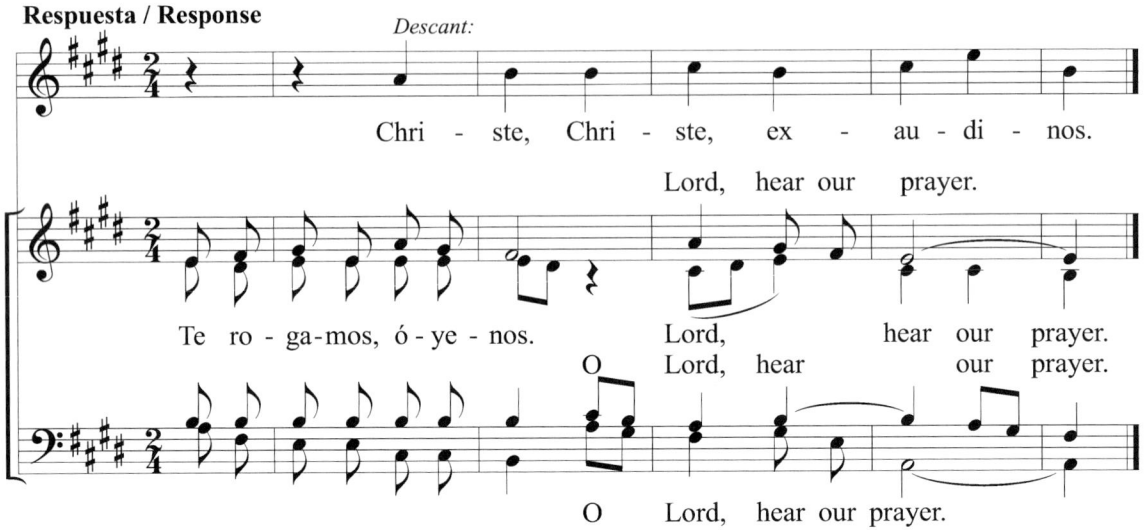

Christe, Christe, exaudinos.
Lord, hear our prayer.
Te rogamos, óyenos.
Lord, hear our prayer.
O Lord, hear our prayer.
O Lord, hear our prayer.

Tono Para Intercesiones / Tone For Intercessions

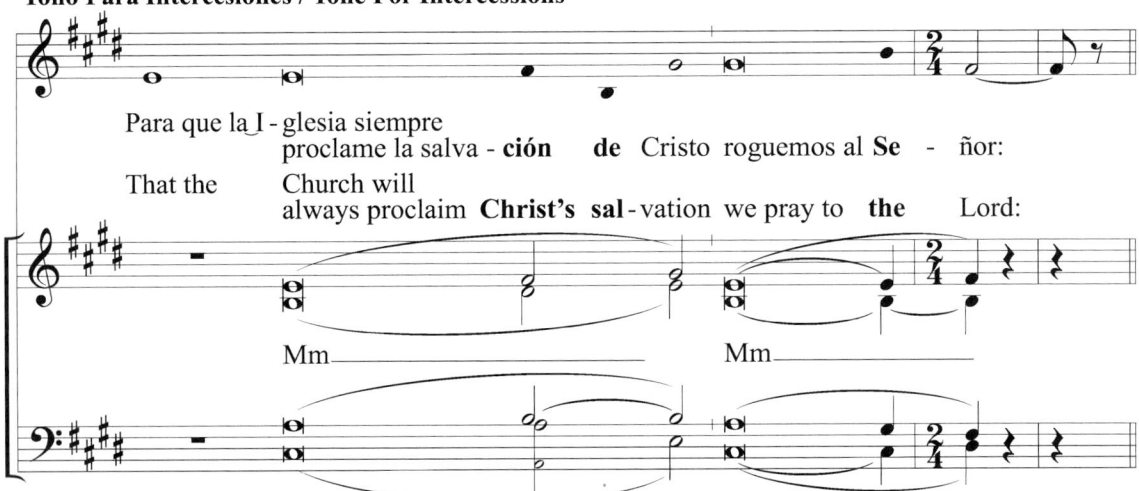

Para que la I-glesia siempre proclame la salva-ción de Cristo roguemos al Se-ñor:
That the Church will always proclaim Christ's sal-vation we pray to the Lord:
Mm— Mm—

INTERCESIONES SUGERIDAS / SUGGESTED INTERCESSIONS

Adviento / Advent
Para que la I- | glesia sea guiada por la Sa**bidu**ría | roguemos al **Se**ñor:
Para que el | fruto del tronco de Jesé embellezca **nuestras** vidas | roguemos al **Se**ñor:
Para que los | pobres encuentre al "Dios-con-nosotros" en nuestro **testi**monio | roguemos al **Se**ñor:
Para que los en- | fermos y los que sufren encuentren fortaleza **y con**suelo | roguemos al **Se**ñor:
Para que | nuestros fieles difuntos vivan en la Au**rora** eterna | roguemos al **Se**ñor:
Para que | nuestra invocación "Maranatha" sea escuchada **en el** cielo | roguemos al **Se**ñor:

That the | Church will be guid**ed in** Wisdom | we pray to **the** Lord:
That the | fruit of the tree of Jesse will be fruitful **to our** lives | we pray to **the** Lord:
That the | poor will find "God-with-us" **through our** witness | we pray to **the** Lord:
That the | sick and suffering will find strength and **conso**lation | we pray to **the** Lord:
That | those who have died will live to the ever**lasting** Dawn | we pray to **the** Lord:
That our | cry "Maranatha" will be **heard on** high | we pray to **the** Lord:

General Intercessions VI (Bilingual Intercessions: Te Rogamos, Óyenos / Lord, Hear Our Prayer), pg. 2

Tiempo de Navidad / Christmas Season
Para que la I- | glesia sea siempre la Palabra de Dios **hecha** carne | roguemos al **Se**ñor:
Para que la | gracia de esta estación Navideña nos traiga la paz **perdu**rable | roguemos al **Se**ñor:
Para que | nuestros líderes sean guiados por la humildad del nacimiento del **Salva**dor | roguemos al **Se**ñor:
Para que los que | sufren reciban la fortaleza del Príncipe **de la** Paz | roguemos al **Se**ñor:
Para que | nuestros queridos difuntos vivan en el **gozo** eterno | roguemos al **Se**ñor:
Para que | nuestro canto se una al **de los** ángeles | roguemos al **Se**ñor:

That the | Church will always be God's **Word made** flesh | we pray to **the** Lord:
That the | grace of this season will bring **lasting** peace | we pray to **the** Lord:
That our | leaders will be guided by the Savior's **humble** birth | we pray to **the** Lord:
That the | suffering will be strengthened by the **Prince of** Peace | we pray to **the** Lord:
That the | faithful departed will live to never-**ending** joy | we pray to **the** Lord:
That our | song will join the song **of the** angels | we pray to **the** Lord:

Cuaresma / Lent
Para que la I- | glesia sea verdaderamente una, santa, católica y **apo**stólica | roguemos al **Se**ñor:
Para que vol- | vamos nuestras vidas hacia la justicia y la paz del **Evan**gelio | roguemos al **Se**ñor:
Para que los Ele- | gidos crezcan más profundamente en oración y **santi**dad | roguemos al **Se**ñor:
Para que | los que sufren enfermedad espiritual, mental o corporal encuen**tren con**suelo| roguemos al **Se**ñor:
Para que | los que ya duermen en Cristo resuciten a la **paz** eterna | roguemos al **Se**ñor:
Para que | nuestras oraciones se unan a las **de los** santos | roguemos al **Se**ñor:

That the | Church may truly be one, holy, catholic, **apos**tolic | we pray to **the** Lord:
That our | lives may reflect Gospel jus**tice and** peace | we pray to **the** Lord:
That the E- | lect may grow deeper in **prayer and** holiness | we pray to **the** Lord:
That | those who are ill in spirit, mind, or body **may find** comfort | we pray to **the** Lord:
That all who | sleep in Christ may wake to ever**lasting** peace | we pray to **the** Lord:
That our | prayer may join the prayer **of the** saints | we pray to **the** Lord:

Tiempo de Pascua / Easter Season
Para que la I- | glesia viva una vida de testimonio a Cristo re**suci**tado | roguemos al **Se**ñor:
Para que | todos los que ejercen algún ministerio se renueven por la Re**surrec**ción | roguemos al **Se**ñor:
Para que | todos los que han sido bienvenidos a la Iglesia caminen **con gran** fe | roguemos al **Se**ñor:
Para que los en- | fermos de salud corporal, mental o espiritual encuentren ánimo en Cristo re**suci**tado | roguemos al **Se**ñor:
Para que el | gozo del misterio pascual llegue a todos nues**tros di**funtos | roguemos al **Se**ñor:
Para que | nuestro "aleluya" renueve y sostenga nuestra **fe Pas**cual | roguemos al **Se**ñor:

That the | Church will live in witness to the **risen** Christ | we pray to **the** Lord:
That | all who minister will be renewed by the **Resur**rection | we pray to **the** Lord:
That those | newly welcomed to the Church will **walk in** faith | we pray to **the** Lord:
That the | ill of body, mind, or spirit will take heart in the **risen** Christ | we pray to **the** Lord:
That the | joy of the paschal mystery will raise up all **who have** died | we pray to **the** Lord:
That our | "alleluia" will renew and sustain our **Easter** faith | we pray to **the** Lord:

Tiempo Ordinario / Ordinary Time
Se encuentra en la próxima página / Found on the next page

General Intercessions VI (Bilingual Intercessions: Te Rogamos, Óyenos / Lord, Hear Our Prayer), pg. 3

Tiempo Ordinario / Ordinary Time

Para que la_I- | glesia siempre proclame la salva**ción de** Cristo | roguemos al **Se**ñor:
Para que | todas las naciones y pueblos se unan **en la** paz | roguemos al **Se**ñor:
Para que | los que nos guían y gobiernan lo hagan con justicia **para** todos | roguemos al **Se**ñor:
Para que los en- | fermos y los oprimidos se liberen por nues**tros es**fuerzos | roguemos al **Se**ñor:
Para que los di- | funtos y los que sufren encuentren paz **y con**suelo | roguemos al **Se**ñor:
Para que | nuestras oraciones se unan en solidaridad con las que se elevan en todas **las na**ciones | roguemos al **Se**ñor:

That the | Church will always proclaim **Christ's sal**vation | we pray to **the** Lord:
That all | nations and peoples will be unit**ed in** peace | we pray to **the** Lord:
That | those who guide and govern us will do **so in** justice | we pray to **the** Lord:
That the | ill and oppressed will be raised by our out**reach and** care | we pray to **the** Lord:
That the de- | ceased and the sorrowing **will find** solace | we pray to **the** Lord:
That our | prayer will join prayers offered in **ev'ry** land | we pray to **the** Lord:

Text and music: *Te Rogamos, Óyenos/Lord, Hear Our Prayer,* Peter M. Kolar, b. 1973, © 2001, 2003,
World Library Publications, 3708 River Road, Franklin Park, IL 60131. www.wlpmusic.com All rights reserved. Used with permission.

Sanctus (Mass of the Good Shepherd) 584

Music: *Mass of the Good Shepherd,* Stephen Somerville, © 1976, Stephen Somerville. All rights reserved. Used with permission.

585 **Amen I**

Music: Traditional *Danish Amen.*

586 **Amen II**

Music: *Dresden Amen*, Johann G. Naumann, 1741–1801.

587 **Amen III**

Music: *Mass of Hope,* by Eugene Englert, b. 1931, © 1988, Eugene Englert. All rights reserved. Used with permission.

Lord's Prayer 588

Lord's Prayer (Gelineau), pg. 2

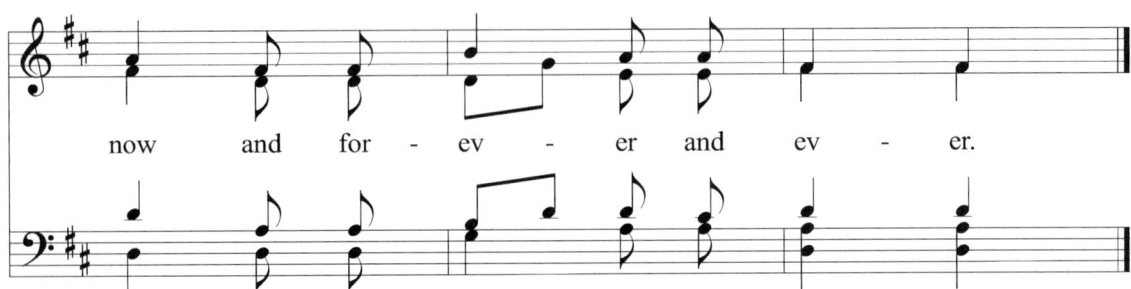

Music: © Joseph Gelineau, SJ, 1920–2008. All rights reserved. Used with permission.

589   **Agnus Dei I**

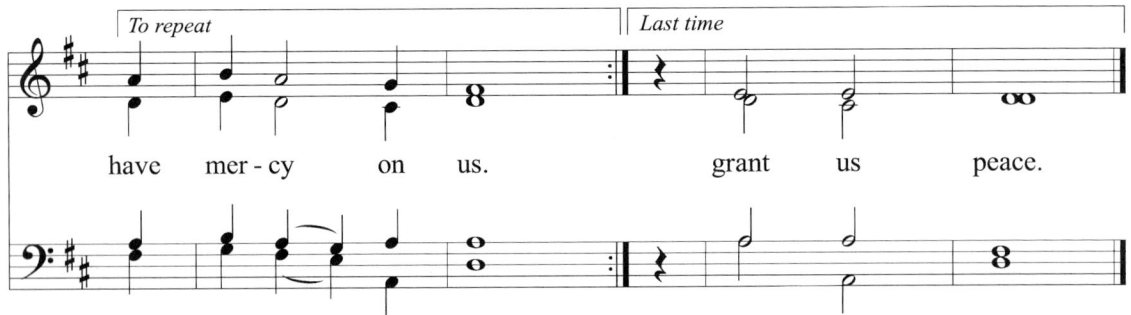

* First and last invocation is always "Lamb of God." Additional invocations may be chosen from the following:

Emmanuel	Bread of Life
Prince of peace	Lord Jesus Christ
Son of God	Lord of Love
Word made flesh	Christ the Lord
Paschal Lamb	King of kings

Music: *Holy Cross Mass*, David Clark Isele, © 1979, GIA Publications, Inc. All rights reserved. Used with permission.

Agnus Dei II 590

Music: *Lamb of God,* Richard Proulx, b. 1937, © 1975, GIA Publications, Inc. All rights reserved. Used with permission.

591 Acclamation I: Signing of the RCIA Candidates with the Cross

Acclamation I: Signing of the RCIA Candidates with the Cross, pg. 2

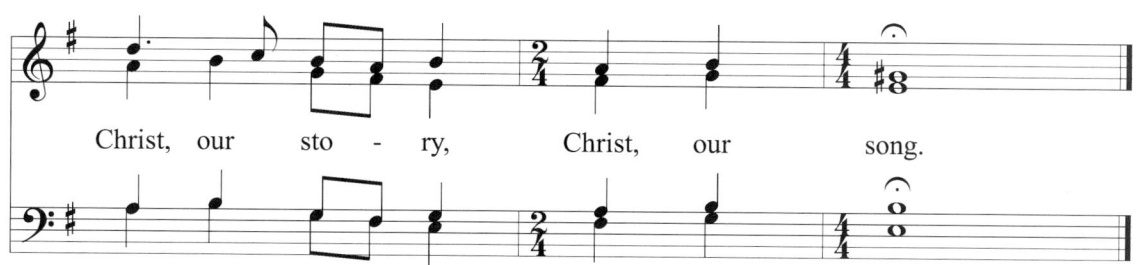

Christ, our story, Christ, our song.

Alternate Refrain

Glo-ry and praise to you, Lord Je-sus Christ! Christ!

Text: *In the Cross of Christ/Glory and Praise to You,*
Refrain–Marty Haugen, b. 1950, © 1997, GIA Publications, Inc.; Verses–From the *Rite of Christian Initiation of Adults,* tr. © 1985, ICEL.
Music: Marty Haugen, b. 1950, © 1997, GIA Publications, Inc.
All rights reserved. Used with permission.

592 Acclamation II: Dismissal of the Elect and Catechumens

Acclamation II: Dismissal of the Elect and Catechumens, pg. 2

Additional Verses

Verse 2 – *Ephesians 5:30*

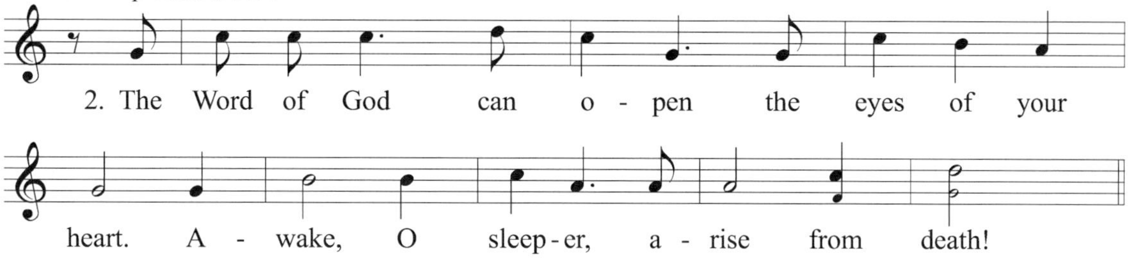

2. The Word of God can o-pen the eyes of your heart. A-wake, O sleep-er, a-rise from death!

Verse 3 – *John 4:14*

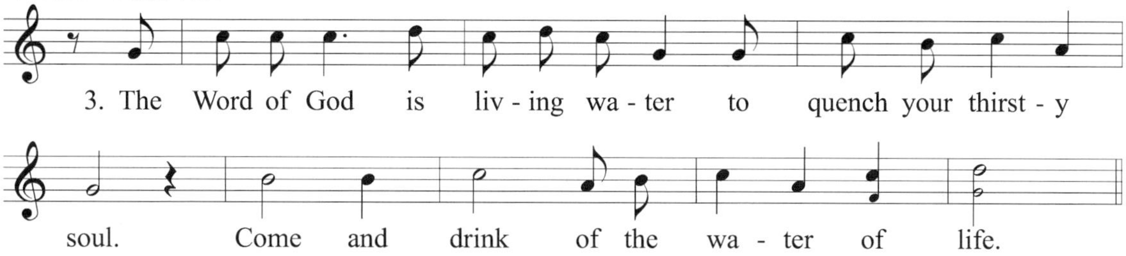

3. The Word of God is liv-ing wa-ter to quench your thirst-y soul. Come and drink of the wa-ter of life.

Verse 4 – *John 11:25*

4. The Word of God in Je-sus Christ is life be-yond all death. O-pen your heart to the Spir-it of God.

Text and music: *Go in Peace,* Marty Haugen, b. 1950, © 1997, GIA Publications, Inc. All rights reserved. Used with permission.

593 Acclamation III: Dismissal of the Elect and Catechumens

PRESIDER: My dear friends, this community sends you forth to reflect more deeply upon the Word of God which you have shared with us today. Be assured of our loving support and prayers for you. We look forward to the day when you will share fully in the Lord's table. Go in peace, and may the Lord remain with you always.

Presider's text: *Rite of Christian Initiation of Adults: Sending of the Catechumens for Election,* © 1988, United States Catholic Conference of Bishops, Washington, DC.
Acclamation text and music: *A Lamp for Our Feet,* David Haas, b. 1957, © 1991, GIA Publications, Inc.
All rights reserved. Used with permission.

Acclamation IV: Blessing of Water   594

Presider
God of all mercy, through these waters of baptism you have
filled us with new life as your very own children.

Response

Bless-ed are you, O God! Bless-ed are you, O God!

Presider
From all who are baptized in water and the Holy Spirit,
you have formed one people, united in your Son, Jesus Christ.
Response

Presider
You have set us free and filled our hearts with the Spirit of your love,
that we may live in your peace.
Response

Presider
You call those who have been baptized
to announce the Good News of Jesus Christ to people everywhere.
Response

Presider
You have called your children to this cleansing water and new birth,
that by sharing the faith of your Church they may have eternal life.
Bless this water in which they will be baptized.
We ask this in the name of Jesus the Lord.
Final Response

Final Response

A - men! A - men!

Note: This response is taken from the collection *Who Calls You By Name,* Volume 1, published by GIA Publications. The music collection includes sung verses for the presider and is available from the publisher, item number G-3193 (full score) and G-3193P (presider edition).

Music: David Haas, b. 1957, © 1988, GIA Publications, Inc. All rights reserved. Used with permission.

595 Acclamation V: Rite of Baptism

*May be sung in canon.

Text: *You Have Put on Christ,* © 1969, ICEL. Music: Howard Hughes, SM, b. 1930, © 1977, ICEL. All rights reserved. Used with permission.

Acclamation VI: Rite of Baptism 596

Text: *You Have Put on Christ,* © 1969, ICEL. Music: J. William Greene, © 1998, GIA Publications, Inc. All rights reserved. Used with permission.

597 Acclamation VII: Children's Liturgy of the Word Dismissal

PRESIDER: *(spoken over instrumental introduction)*
Dear children, please come forward.
You are about to go forth to hear the Word of God.
May your ears and hearts be open as you experience the stories of our faith.
We ask the Holy Spirit to guide you and your leader in the sharing of God's word.

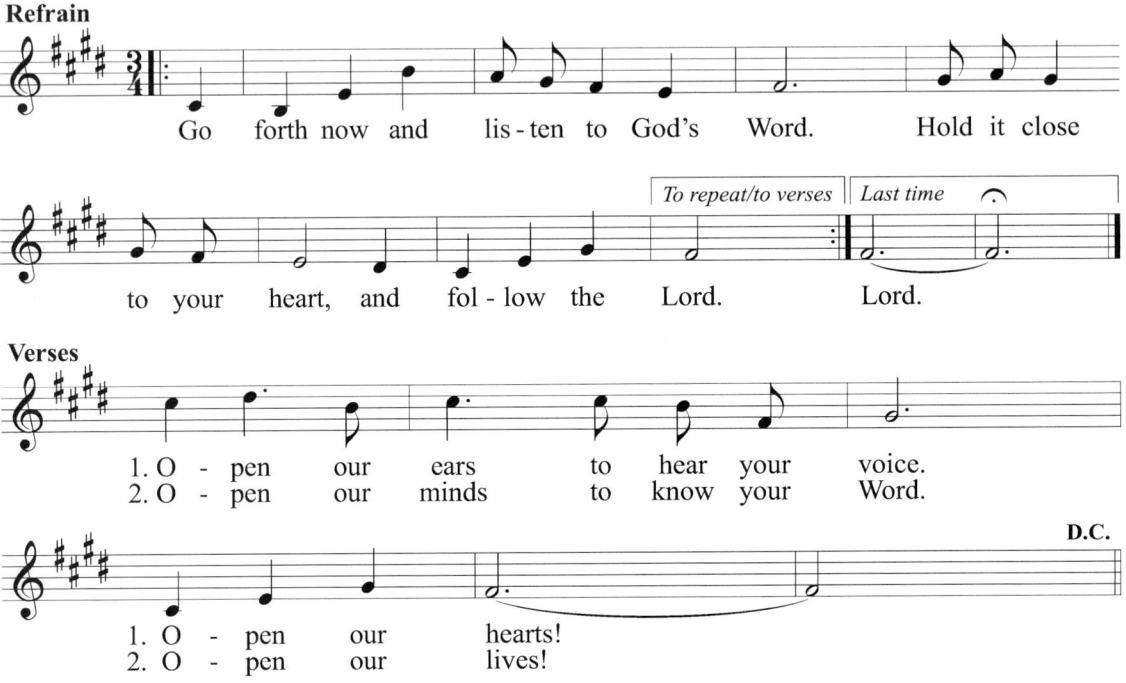

Refrain
Go forth now and listen to God's Word. Hold it close to your heart, and follow the Lord.

Verses
1. Open our ears to hear your voice. Open our hearts!
2. Open our minds to know your Word. Open our lives!

Text and music: *Listen to God's Word*, David Haas, b. 1957, © 1999, GIA Publications, Inc. All rights reserved. Used with permission.

Acclamation VIII:
Sending Forth Extraordinary Ministers of Holy Communion

598

PRESIDER: *(spoken over instrumental improvisation)*
All those who will be taking the eucharist to the sick and homebound, please come forward.

My friends, this community now sends you forth as our representatives to bring the Lord Jesus to our brothers
and sisters who cannot be with us, to those who are ill and in need of the Lord's gift of life and love.
We ask that you share with them the gift of God's Word that we have shared here today,
and by the gift of yourselves, assure them of our love and prayers.
Go now with the unity and support of this community—all of us one in Christ Jesus.

Text and music: *Go Forth in Peace,* David Haas, b. 1957, © 1999, GIA Publications, Inc. All rights reserved. Used with permission.

Acclamation IX: Community Blessing

May God bless and keep you, may God smile on you. May God show you kind-ness, fill you with peace. And may God bless you, Fa-ther, Son, and Spir-it; may you al-ways love and serve, filled with God's peace.

Text: Based on Numbers 6:24–26, adapt. by David Haas, b. 1957. Music: ADORO TE DEVOTE, adapt. by David Haas, b. 1957.
Text and music: *May God Bless and Keep You,* © 1997, GIA Publications, Inc. All rights reserved. Used with permission.

Publishers / Copyright Holders

To the many composers, authors, publishers, and copyright holders whose generous assistance and cooperation make this accompaniment edition possible, the publisher and editors are sincerely grateful. Every effort has been made to determine and acknowledge owners and administrators of copyrighted material. We regret any oversight that may have occurred and will correct such errors or omissions in future editions upon the receipt of written notification of them.

Permission to reproduce any of the copyrighted material contained in this publication must be obtained, in writing, from the copyright owner / administrator. Failure to do so is a violation of the U.S. Copyright Law. For ease in obtaining permissions, the following publisher / copyright holder information is provided:

Archdiocese of Philadelphia
222 North 17th Street
Philadelphia, PA 19103
215-587-3537

Augsburg Fortress
P.O. Box 1209
Minneapolis, MN 55440
800-421-0239

Celebration
P.O. Box 309
Aliquippa, PA 15001
724-375-1510

Church Pension Fund
445 Fifth Avenue
New York, NY 10016
800-223-6602

Concordia Publishing House
3558 South Jefferson Avenue
St. Louis, MO 63118
314-268-1000

Confraternity of Christian Doctrine, Inc.
3211 Fourth Street NE
Washington, DC 20017
202-541-3098

Continuum
11 York Road
London, England SE1 7NX
44 (0) 20 7922 0880

The Copyright Company
1025 16th Avenue South, #204
Nashville, TN 37212
615-321-1096

Downside Abbey
Stratton-on-the-Fosse
Radstock, Bath BA3 4RH
44-01761-235123

EMI Christian Music Pub.
101 Winners Circle
Brentwood, TN 37024
615-371-4412

Faber Music, Ltd.
3 Queen Square
London, England WC1N 3AU
44 (0)20-7833-7900

GIA Publications
7404 South Mason Avenue
Chicago, IL 60638
800-442-1358

Harold Ober Associates
425 Madison Avenue, 10th Floor
New York, NY 10017
212-759-8600

Hope Publishing Company
380 South Main Place
Carol Stream, IL 60188
800-323-1049

International Committee on English
in the Liturgy (ICEL)
1522 K Street NW, #1000
Washington, DC 20005
202-347-0800

Jan-Lee Music
P.O Box 111
Occidental, CA 95465
800-211-8454

Liturgical Press
Order of Saint Benedict
P.O. Box 7500
Collegeville, MN 56321
800-858-5450

The Lorenz Corporation
P.O. Box 802
Dayton, OH 45401-0802
937-228-6118

Manna Music, Inc.
35255 Brooten Road
Pacific City, OR 97135
503-965-6112

Morningstar Music Pub.
1727 Larkin Williams Road
Fenton, MO 63026
800-647-2117

OCP Publications
5536 NE Hassalo
Portland, OR 97213
800-548-8749

The Pilgrim Press
700 Prospect Avenue
Cleveland, OH 44115

Oxford University Press
198 Madison Avenue
New York, NY 10016
212-726-6048

Sacred Heart Monastery
1005 West 8th Street
Yankton, SD 57078
605-668-6000

Scripture in Song
1000 Cody Road
Mobile, AL 36695-3425
800-533-6912

Selah Publishing Company
4143 Brownsville Road, #2
Pittsburgh, PA 15227
800-852-6172

Sisters of Saint Benedict
104 Chapel Lane
Saint Joseph, MN 56374
320-363-7176

Society of the Sacred Heart
4389 West Pine Boulevard
St. Louis, MO 63108
(314) 652-1500

Stanbrook Abbey
Callow End
Worcester, WR2 4TD
44-01905-830209

Saint Vincent Archabbey
300 Fraser Purchase Road
Latrobe, PA 15650-2686
724-532-6600

Walton Music Corp.
935 Broad Street, #31
Bloomingdale, NJ 07003

Willis Music Company
7380 Industrial Road
Florence, KY 41042
800-354-9799

World Library Publications
3825 North Willow Road
Schiller Park, IL 60176
800-621-5197

Index of Gospel Acclamation Verses

ADVENT

1st Sunday of Advent
ABC Show us Lord, your love; and grant us your salvation.

2nd Sunday of Advent
ABC Prepare the way of the Lord, make straight his paths: all flesh shall see the salvation of God.

3rd Sunday of Advent
ABC The Spirit of the Lord is upon me, because he has anointed me to bring glad tidings to the poor.

4th Sunday of Advent,
A The Virgin shall conceive, and bear a son, and they shall name him Emmanuel.
BC Behold, I am the handmaid of the Lord. May it be done to me according to your word.

CHRISTMAS

Mass at the Vigil
ABC Tomorrow the wickedness of the earth will be destroyed: the Savior of the world will reign over us.

Mass at Midnight
ABC I proclaim to you good news of great joy: today a Savior is born for us, Christ the Lord.

Mass at Dawn
ABC Glory to God in the highest, and on earth peace to those on whom his favor rests.

Mass During the Day
ABC A holy day has dawned upon us. Come, you nations, and adore the Lord. For today a great light has come upon the earth.

Holy Family
ABC Let the peace of Christ control your hearts; let the word of Christ dwell in you richly.
B In the past God spoke to our ancestors through the prophets; in these last days, he has spoken to us through the Son.
C Open our hearts, O Lord, to listen to the words of your Son.

Mary, Mother of God
ABC In the past God spoke to our ancestors through the prophets; in these last days, he has spoken to us through the Son.

Epiphany
ABC We saw his star at its rising and have come to do him homage.

Baptism of the Lord
ABC The heavens were opened and the voice of the Father thundered: This is my beloved Son, listen to him.
B John saw Jesus approaching him, and said: Behold the Lamb of God who takes away the sin of the world.
C John said: One mightier than I is coming; he will baptize you with the Holy Spirit and with fire.

LENT

1st Sunday of Lent
ABC One does not live on bread alone, but on every word that comes forth from the mouth of God.

2nd Sunday of Lent
ABC From the shining cloud the Father's voice is heard: This is my beloved Son, hear him.

3rd Sunday of Lent
A Lord, you are truly the Savior of the world; give me living water, that I may never thirst again.
B God so loved the world that he gave his only Son, so that everyone who believes in him might have eternal life.
C Repent, says the Lord; the kingdom of heaven is at hand.

4th Sunday of Lent
A I am the light of the world, says the Lord; whoever follows me will have the light of life.
B God so loved the world that he gave his only Son, so everyone who believes in him might have eternal life.
C I will get up and go to my Father and shall say to him: Father, I have sinned against heaven and against you.

5th Sunday of Lent
A I am the resurrection and the life, says the Lord; whoever believes in me, whoever believes in me will never die.
B Whoever serves me must follow me, says the Lord; and where I am, there also will my servant be.
C Even now, says the Lord, return to me with your whole heart; for I am gracious and merciful.

Palm Sunday
ABC Christ became obedient to the point of death, even death on the cross. Because of this, God greatly exalted him and bestowed on him the name which is above every name.

Index of Gospel Acclamation Verses, pg. 2

EASTER TRIDUUM

Holy Thursday
ABC I give you a new commandment, says the Lord: love one another as I have loved you.

Good Friday
ABC Christ became obedient to the point of death, even death on the cross. Because of this, God greatly exalted him and bestowed on him the name which is above every name.

Easter Sunday
ABC Christ, our paschal lamb, has been sacrificed; let us then feast with joy in the Lord.

EASTER

2nd Sunday of Easter
ABC You believe in me, Thomas, because you have seen me, says the Lord; blessed are they who have not seen me, but still believe!

3rd Sunday of Easter
AB Lord Jesus, open the Scriptures to us; make our hearts burn while you speak to us.
C Christ is risen, creator of all; he has shown pity on all people.

4th Sunday of Easter
ABC I am the good shepherd, says the Lord; I know my sheep, and mine know me.

5th Sunday of Easter
A I am the way, the truth and the life, says the Lord; no one comes to the Father, except through me.
B Remain in me as I remain in you, says the Lord. Whoever remains in me will bear much fruit.
C I give you a new commandment, says the Lord: love one another as I have loved you.

Ascension
ABC Go and teach all nations, says the Lord; I am with you always, until the end of the world.

6th Sunday of Easter
ABC Whoever loves me will keep my word, says the Lord, and my Father will love him and we will come to him.

7th Sunday of Easter
ABC I will not leave you orphans, says the Lord. I will come back to you, and your hearts will rejoice.

Pentecost
ABC Come, Holy Spirit, fill the hearts of the faithful and kindle in them the fire of your love.

Most Holy Trinity
ABC Glory to the Father, the Son, and the Holy Spirit; to God who is, who was, and who is to come.

Most Holy Body and Blood of Christ
ABC I am the living bread that came down from heaven, says the Lord; whoever eats this bread will live forever.

Most Sacred Heart of Jesus
ABC Take my yoke upon you, says the Lord; and learn from me, for I am meek and humble of heart.
B God first loved us and sent his Son as expiation for our sins.
C I am the good shepherd, says the Lord, I know my sheep, and mine know me.

ORDINARY TIME

2nd Sunday in Ordinary Time
A The Word of God became flesh and dwelt among us. To those who accepted him, he gave power to become children of God.
B We have found the Messiah: Jesus Christ, who brings us truth and grace.
C God has called us through the Gospel to possess the glory of our Lord Jesus Christ.

3rd Sunday in Ordinary Time
A Jesus proclaimed the Gospel of the kingdom and cured every disease among the people.
B The kingdom of God is at hand. Repent and believe in the Gospel.
C The Lord sent me to bring glad tidings to the poor, and to proclaim liberty to captives.

4th Sunday in Ordinary Time
A Rejoice and be glad; your reward will be great in heaven.
B The people who sit in darkness have seen a great light; on those dwelling in a land overshadowed by death, light has arisen.
C The Lord sent me to bring glad tidings to the poor, to proclaim liberty to captives.

5th Sunday in Ordinary Time
A I am the light of the world, says the Lord; whoever follows me will have the light of life.
B Christ took away our infirmities and bore our diseases.

C Come after me and I will make you fishers of men.

6th Sunday in Ordinary Time
A Blessed are you, Father, Lord of heaven and earth; you have revealed to little ones the mysteries of the kingdom.
B A great prophet has arisen in our midst. God has visited his people.
C Rejoice and be glad; your reward will be great in heaven.

7th Sunday in Ordinary Time
A Whoever keeps the word of Christ, the love of God is truly perfected in him.
B The Lord sent me to bring glad tidings to the poor, and to proclaim liberty to captives.
C I give you a new commandment, says the Lord: love one another as I have loved you.

8th Sunday in Ordinary Time
A The word of God is living and effective; discerning reflections and thoughts of the heart.
B The Father willed to give us birth by the word of truth that we may be a kind of first-fruits of his creatures.
C Shine like lights in the world as you hold on to the word of life.

9th Sunday in Ordinary Time
A I am the vine, you are the branches, says the Lord; whoever remains in me and I in him will bear much fruit.
B Your word, O Lord, is truth; consecrate us in the truth.
C God so loved the world that he gave his only Son, so that everyone who believes in him might have eternal life.

10th Sunday in Ordinary Time
A The Lord sent me to bring glad tidings to the poor, and to proclaim liberty to captives.
B Now the ruler of this world will be driven out, says the Lord; and when I am lifted up from the earth, I will draw everyone to myself.
C A great prophet has risen in our midst, God has visited his people.

11th Sunday in Ordinary Time
A The kingdom of God is at hand. Repent and believe in the Gospel.
B The seed is the word of God, Christ is the sower. All who come to him will live forever.
C God loved us and sent his Son as expiation for our sins.

12th Sunday in Ordinary Time
A The Spirit of truth will testify to me, says the Lord; and you also will testify.
B A great prophet has risen in our midst, God has visited his people.
C My sheep hear my voice, says the Lord; I know them, and they follow me.

13th Sunday in Ordinary Time
A You are a chosen race, a royal priesthood, a holy nation; announce the praises of him who called you out of darkness into his wonderful light.
B Our Savior Jesus Christ destroyed death and brought life to light through the Gospel.
C Speak, Lord, your servant is listening; you have the words of everlasting life.

14th Sunday in Ordinary Time
A Blessed are you, O Father, Lord of heaven and earth; you have revealed to little ones the mysteries of the kingdom.
B The Spirit of the Lord is upon me, for he sent me to bring glad tidings to the poor.
C Let the peace of Christ control your hearts; let the word of Christ dwell in you richly.

15th Sunday in Ordinary Time
A The seed is the word of God, Christ is the sower. All who come to him will have life forever.
B May the Father of our Lord Jesus Christ enlighten the eyes of our hearts, that we may know what is the hope that belongs to our call.
C Your words, Lord, are Spirit and life; you have the words of everlasting life.

16th Sunday in Ordinary Time
A Blessed are you, Father, Lord of heaven and earth; you have revealed to little ones the mysteries of the kingdom.
B My sheep hear my voice, says the Lord; I know them, and they follow me.
C Blessed are they who have kept the word with a generous heart and yield a harvest through perseverance.

17th Sunday in Ordinary Time
A Blessed are you, Father, Lord of heaven and earth; you have revealed to little ones the mysteries of the kingdom.
B A great prophet has risen in our midst. God has visited his people.
C You have received a Spirit of adoption, through which we cry, Abba, Father.

Index of Gospel Acclamation Verses, pg. 4

18th Sunday in Ordinary Time
AB One does not live on bread alone, but on every word that comes forth from the mouth of God.
C Blessed are the poor in spirit, for theirs is the kingdom of heaven.

19th Sunday in Ordinary Time
A I wait for the Lord; my soul waits for his word.
B I am the living bread that came down from heaven, says the Lord; whoever eats this bread will live forever.
C Stay awake and be ready! For you do not know on what day the Son of Man will come.

20th Sunday in Ordinary Time
A Jesus proclaimed the Gospel of the kingdom and cured every disease among the people.
B Whoever eats my flesh and drinks my blood remains in me and I in him, says the Lord.
C My sheep hear my voice, says the Lord; I know them, and they follow me.

21st Sunday in Ordinary Time
A You are Peter and upon this rock I will build my Church and the gates of the netherworld shall not prevail against it.
B Your words, Lord, are Spirit and life; you have the words of everlasting life.
C I am the way, the truth and the life, says the Lord; no one comes to the Father, except through me.

22nd Sunday in Ordinary Time
A May the Father of our Lord Jesus Christ enlighten the eyes of our hearts, so that we may know what is the hope that belongs to our call.
B The Father willed to give us birth by the word of truth that we may be a kind of first-fruits of his creatures.
C Take my yoke upon you, says the Lord, and learn from me, for I am meek and humble of heart.

23rd Sunday in Ordinary Time
A God was reconciling the world to himself in Christ and entrusting to us the message of reconciliation.
B Jesus proclaimed the Gospel of the kingdom and cured every disease among the people.
C Let your face shine upon your servant; and teach me your laws.

24th Sunday in Ordinary Time
A I give you a new commandment, says the Lord: love one another as I have loved you.
B May I never boast except in the cross of our Lord through which the world has been crucified to me and I to the world.
C God was reconciling the world to himself in Christ and entrusting to us the message of reconciliation.

25th Sunday in Ordinary Time
A Open our hearts, O Lord, to listen to the words of your Son.
B God has called us through the Gospel to possess the glory of our Lord Jesus Christ.
C Though our Lord Jesus Christ was rich, he became poor, so that by his poverty you might become rich.

26th Sunday in Ordinary Time
A My sheep hear my voice, says the Lord; I know them, and they follow me.
B Your word, O Lord, is truth; consecrate us in the truth.
C Though our Lord Jesus Christ was rich, he became poor, so that by his poverty you might become rich.

27th Sunday in Ordinary Time
A I have chosen you from the world, says the Lord, to go and bear fruit that will remain.
B If we love one another, God remains in us and his love is brought to perfection in us.
C The word of the Lord remains forever. This is the word that has been proclaimed to you.

28th Sunday in Ordinary Time
A May the Father of our Lord Jesus Christ enlighten the eyes of our hearts, so that we may know what is the hope that belongs to our call.
B Blessed are the poor in spirit, for theirs is the kingdom of heaven.
C In all circumstances, give thanks, for this is the will of God for you in Christ Jesus.

29th Sunday in Ordinary Time
A Shine like lights in the world as you hold on to the word of life.
B The Son of Man came to serve and to give his life as a ransom for many.
C The word of God is living and effective, discerning reflections and thoughts of the heart.

30th Sunday in Ordinary Time
A Whoever loves me will keep my word, says the Lord, and my Father will love him and we will come to him.

Index of Gospel Acclamation Verses, pg. 5

B Our Savior Jesus Christ destroyed death and brought life to light through the Gospel.
C God was reconciling the world to himself in Christ, and entrusting to us the message of salvation.

31st Sunday in Ordinary Time
A You have but one Father in heaven and one master, the Christ.
B Whoever loves me will keep my word, says the Lord; and my Father will love him and we will come to him.
C God so loved the world that he gave his only Son, so that everyone who believes in him might have eternal life.

32nd Sunday in Ordinary Time
A Stay awake and be ready! For you do not know on what day your Lord will come.
B Blessed are the poor in spirit, for theirs is the kingdom of heaven.
C Jesus Christ is the first-born of the dead; to him be glory and power, forever and ever.

33rd Sunday in Ordinary Time
A Remain in me as I remain in you, says the Lord. Whoever remains in me bears much fruit.
B Be vigilant at all times and pray that you have the strength to stand before the Son of Man.
C Stand erect and raise your heads because your redemption is at hand.

Christ the King
ABC Blessed is he who comes in the name of the Lord! Blessed is the kingdom of our Father David that is to come.

SOLEMNITIES AND FEASTS OF THE LORD AND THE SAINTS

February 2: The Presentation of the Lord
A light of revelation to the Gentiles, and glory for your people Israel.

March 19: Saint Joseph
Blessed are those who dwell in your house, O Lord; they never cease to praise you.

March 25: The Annunciation of the Lord
The Word of God became flesh and made his dwelling among us; and we saw his glory.

June 24: Saint John the Baptist
Vigil: He came to testify to the light, to prepare a people fit for the Lord.
Day: You, child, will be called prophet of the Most High, for you will go before the Lord to prepare his way.

June 29: Saints Peter & Paul
Vigil: Lord, you know everything; you know that I love you.
Day: You are Peter and upon this rock I will build my Church, and the gates of the netherworld shall not prevail against it.

August 6: The Transfiguration of the Lord
This is my beloved Son, with whom I am well pleased; listen to him.

August 15: The Assumption
Vigil: Blessed are they who hear the word of God and observe it.
Day: Mary is taken up to heaven; a chorus of angels exults.

September 14: Exaltation of the Holy Cross
We adore you, O Christ, and we bless you, because by your Cross you have redeemed the world.

November 1: All Saints
Come to me, all you who labor and are burdened, and I will give you rest, says the Lord.

November 2: All Souls
I: Come, you who are blessed by my Father; inherit the kingdom prepared for you from the foundation of the world.
II: God so loved the world that he gave his only Son, that everyone who sees the Son and believes in him may have eternal life.
III: This is the will of my Father, says the Lord, that everyone who sees the Son and believes in him may have eternal life.
IV: I am the living bread that came down from heaven, says the Lord; whoever eats this bread will live forever.
V: I am the resurrection and the life, says the Lord; whoever believes in me will never die.

November 9: Lateran Basilica
I have chosen and consecrated this house, says the Lord, that my name may be there forever.

December 8: Immaculate Conception
Hail, Mary, full of grace, the Lord is with you; blessed are you among women.

Index of Tune Names

Tune	Page
ABBOTT'S LEIGH	226
ADESTE FIDELES	6
ADORO TE DEVOTE	8, 216
ALLE TAGE SING UND SAGE	94
AMERICA	24
ANIMA CHRISTI	379
ANTIOCH	201
AR HYD Y NOS	18, 95, 121
ASH GROVE	207
ATTENDE DOMINE	35
AU SANG QU'UN DIEU	139
AUDI REDEMPTOR	272
AURELIA	29, 75, 117, 252, 395, 480
AUSTRIA	296
AVE MARIA	36
AVE VERUM	39
AWAY IN A MANGER	41
BADZZE POZONOWIONA	284
BALM IN GILEAD	412
BATTLE HYMN	237
BEACH SPRING	85, 107, 120, 130, 134, 137, 138
BEAUTIFUL MOTHER	283
BESANCON CAROL	293
BICENTENNIAL	128
BOURGEOIS	90
BREAD OF LIFE	172
BRESLAU	389
BUNESSAN	42, 238, 294, 414
CAMROSE	56
CAROL	190
CHEREPONI	193
CHRIST IST ERSTANDEN	372
CHRISTIAN LOVE	464
COENA DOMINI	97
CONDITOR ALME SIDERUM	91, 268
CORONATION	16
CRUCIFER	212
DARWALL'S 148TH	353
DEUS TUORUM MILITUM	269
DIADEMATA	93
DIVINUM MYSTERIUM	278
DIX	31, 119, 468
DOMHNACH TRIONOIDE	419
DRAKES BOUGHTON	360
DUGUET	275
DUKE STREET	124, 176, 199
DUNLAP'S CREEK	452
EASTER HYMN	195
EIN' FESTE BURG	2, 72
ELKHORN TAVERN	222
ELLACOMBE	153, 397, 479
ENDLESS SONG	166
ENGELBERG	423, 459
ERHALT UNS HERR	10, 399
ES IST EIN ROS' ENTSPRUNGEN	214
FESTIVAL CANTICLE	418
FINLANDIA	383, 416
FOREST GREEN	178, 246, 444
FOUNDATION	105, 167, 425
FRANCONIA	52, 250, 393
FULDA MELODY	262
GAUDEAMUS PARITER	80, 88, 463
GELOBT SEI GOTT	67, 145, 267
GLORIA	27
GO TELL IT ON THE MOUNTAIN	131
GOD REST YOU MERRY	141
GOTT VATER SEI GEPRIESEN	258
GRAEFENBERG	219
GREENSLEEVES	455
GROSSER GOTT	161
HEINLEIN	123
HOLY ANTHEM	20
HOLY MANNA	19, 57, 280, 458
HOLY SPIRIT	77
HOUSTON	179
HYFRYDOL	21, 228, 288, 369
HYMN TO JOY	109, 143, 159, 202, 371
ICH GLAUB AN GOTT	424
IHR KINDERLEIN KOMMET	255
IN BABILONE	225
IN DULCI JUBILO	144
IRBY	286
ITALIAN HYMN	81, 227
JERUSALEM	462
JESU DULCIS MEMORIA	99, 273, 277
JESUS TOOK A TOWEL	200
JUST AS I AM	116
KELVINGROVE	407
KINGDOM	136
KINGS OF ORIENT	452
KINGSFOLD	47, 175, 239, 253
KREMSER	445
LAND OF REST	50, 82, 168, 173, 174, 192, 240, 408
LASST UNS ERFREUEN	1, 12, 209, 261, 370, 375, 473
LAUDA ANIMA	69, 71, 101, 295
LIEBSTER JESU	51, 472
LIVING GOD	177

Index of Tune Names, pg. 2

LLANFAIR	151
LOBE DEN HERREN	299
LOBT GOTT IN SEINEM HEILIGTUM	208
LOURDES	181
LÜBECK	285
MARIA ZU LIEBEN	270
MATERNA	25
MCKEE	183, 403, 410
MELITA	108
MENDELSSOHN	156
MERTON	155
MIT FREUDEN ZART	368
MONTANA	449
MORNING SONG	58, 122, 218, 402
NATIONAL HYMN	140
NETTLETON	30, 66, 73, 127, 142
NEW BRITAIN	23
NEWMAN	298
NICAEA	162
NOEL NOUVELET	98
NON DIGNUS	266
NUN DANKET	247
NUN KOMM DER HEIDEN HEILAND	115, 189, 359
O FILII ET FILIAE	104, 257
O WALY WALY	242, 251, 461
OLD HUNDREDTH	15, 17, 297, 374
PADERBORN	270
PANGE LINGUA GLORIOSI	290
PARCE DOMINE	292
PASSION CHORALE	263, 274, 289
PICARDY	206, 426
PLEADING SAVIOR	366
PROSPECT	28, 170, 171, 220, 394
PUER NATUS	350
PUER NOBIS	392, 415, 456
REGENT SQUARE	26, 194, 440
REGINA CAELI	43
REJOICE REJOICE	40
RENDEZ À DIEU	114, 460
RESIGNATION	241
RESONET IN LAUDIBUS	70
RICHARD'S SHOP	186
SALVE REGINA	358
SALVE REGINA COELITUM	149
SALVE FESTA DIES	152
SALZBURG	34, 377
SAYLOR'S CREEK	405
SHALOM	411
SHANTI	453
SICILIAN MARINER'S	276
SINE NOMINE	62, 118, 132, 381, 442, 448
SING OUT	367
SLANE	46, 133, 221, 230
SOMOS DEL SEÑOR	351
SOUTHWELL	157
ST. AGNES	363
ST. ANNE	260
ST. CATHERINE	113
ST. COLUMBA	249, 401
ST. DENIO	182
ST. ELIZABETH	112, 235
ST. FLAVIAN	125, 224, 256
ST. GEORGE'S WINDSOR	89, 150
ST. LOUIS	264
ST. THEODULPH	14, 55
ST. THOMAS	215
STABAT MATER	33
STILLE NACHT	364
STUEMPFLE	102
STUTTGART	84, 103, 146, 147, 148, 233, 430
SWABIA	301, 422
SWEET SACRAMENT	197
TE DEUM	161
TERRA BEATA	446
THAXTED	259, 271
THE CALL	79
THE FIRST NOWELL	398
THOMAS	427
TRURO	63, 213
TWO OAKS	11
UBI CARITAS	429
UNDE ET MEMORES	32
UNSER HERRSCHER	64, 158
VENEZ DIVIN MESSIE	254
VENI CREATOR SPIRITUS	431
VENI SANCTE SPIRITUS	434
VENI VENI EMMANUEL	435
VENITE ADOREMUS	404
VICTIMAE PASCHALI	68, 436
VICTORY	406
W ZLOBIE LEZY	188
WACHET AUF	438
WAREHAM	76, 400
WERE YOU THERE	454
WESTMINSTER ABBEY	65
WINCHESTER NEW	5, 281
WINCHESTER OLD	466
WONDROUS LOVE	457

Index of Metrical Tunes

Meter	Tunes
CM (86 86)	23, 50, 58, 82, 122, 125, 168, 173, 174, 183, 192, 201, 218, 219, 224, 240, 256, 260, 298, 363, 402, 403, 408, 410, 452, 453, 464, 466
CMD (86 86 D)	25, 47, 175, 178, 190, 222, 239, 241, 246, 253, 264, 444
LM (88 88)	5, 10, 15, 17, 28, 63, 76, 91, 99, 124, 170, 171, 176, 199, 208, 213, 220, 242, 251, 268, 269, 272, 273, 275, 277, 281, 297, 374, 389, 392, 394, 399, 400, 415, 431, 456, 461
LMD (88 88 D)	462
SM (66 86)	250
SMD (66 86 D)	93, 446
44 7 44 7 4444 7	188
5 5 5 4 D	42, 238, 294, 414
65 65 with refrain	181, 284
66 11 66 11 D	207
66 4 666 4	81, 227
66 66 88	353
66 77 78 55	144
66 86	52, 157, 301, 393, 422
664 6664	24
67 67 66 66	247
7 7 7 7 with refrain	283, 367
7 7 7 11	70
7 8 7 6 with refrain	254
76 76	266
76 76 D	14, 29, 55, 75, 80, 88, 117, 153, 252, 263, 274, 289, 395, 397, 463, 479, 480
76 76 with refrain	131, 258, 262
76 76 676	214
76 76 76 D	259, 271
76 76 777 6	407
76 76 86 with refrain	141
77 77	79, 115, 123, 189, 285, 359
77 77 with alleluias	151, 195
77 77 with refrain	27, 177
77 77 D	34, 68, 89, 150, 156, 377
77 77 4 with refrain	372
77 77 77	31, 119, 434, 468
78 78 77 77	161
78 78 88	51, 472
8 4 8 4 777 4 5	149
8 7 8 77	427
84 84 88 84	18, 95, 121
85 84 7	43
85 85 with refrain	411
86 86 with refrain	128
86 86 86	16
87 87	84, 103, 146, 147, 148, 155, 186, 233, 249, 360, 401, 430
87 87 D	19, 20, 21, 30, 56, 57, 66, 73, 85, 94, 107, 109, 120, 127, 130, 134, 137, 138, 139, 142, 143, 159, 202, 225, 226, 228, 280, 282, 288, 296, 366, 369, 371, 413, 419, 458
87 87 with refrain	166, 424, 455
87 87 66 66 7	2, 72
87 87 77	158, 286
87 87 77 88	90
87 87 87	26, 64, 65, 69, 71, 101, 194, 206, 215, 290, 295, 426, 440
87 87 87 7	278
87 87 88 7	368
87 98 87	293
88 with alleluias & refrain	350
88 44 6 with refrain	451
88 44 88 with alleluias	1, 12, 209, 261, 370, 375, 473
88 7	33
88 88 with alleluias	102
88 88 with refrain	197, 435
88 88 88	108, 113
88 888	77
888 6	116
888 78	449
888 with alleluias	67, 145, 267, 406
888 with refrain	257
9 6 8 6 8 7 10 with refrain	11
9 8 9 8 8 7 8 9	40
9 9 9 5	136
97 86 with refrain	405
98 98 D	114, 460
10 7 10 7	276
10 7 10 8 9 9 10 7	179
10 10	97
10 10 with refrain	212
10 10 9 10	46, 133, 221, 230
10 10 10 with alleluias	62, 104, 118, 132, 381, 423, 442, 448, 459
10 10 10 10	140, 379
10 10 10 10 with refrain	32
11 8 10 8	112, 235
11 10 10 11	98
11 10 11 10 11 10	383, 416
11 11 11 with refrain	35
11 11 11 11	41, 105, 167, 182, 255, 270, 425
11 12 12 10	162
12 9 12 12 9	457
12 11 12 11	445
14 14 4 7 8	299
15 15 15 6 with refrain	237
irregular	8, 36, 193, 200, 216, 292, 364, 418, 438, 454
irregular with refrain	6, 152, 172, 398, 404, 412

Liturgical Index

ADVENT

9	Advent Gathering Song: Come, Come Emmanuel
40	Awake! Awake, and Greet the New Morn
45	Be Patient, God's People
61	Christ, Be Our Light
79	Come, My Way, My Truth, My Life
84	Come, Thou Long Expected Savior
129	Come to Us
90	Comfort, Comfort, Ye My People
91	Conditor Alme Siderum
91	Creator of the Stars of Night
120	For the Coming of the Savior
136	God of All People
146	Gospel Responses for Advent – Year A
147	Gospel Responses for Advent – Year B
148	Gospel Responses for Advent – Year C
153	Hail to the Lord's Anointed
155	Hark! A Thrilling Voice Is Sounding
179	I Want to Walk as a Child of the Light
189	Infant Wrapped in God's Own Light
206	Let All Mortal Flesh Keep Silence
208	Let Desert Wasteland Now Rejoice
213	Lift Up Your Heads, You Mighty Gates
214	Lo, How a Rose E'er Blooming
217	Lord, Come
228	Love Divine, All Loves Excelling
229	Magnificat / Luke 1:46-55
231	Maranatha, Come
232	Maranatha, Lord Messiah
243	My Soul in Stillness Waits
250	O Child of Promise, Come!
254	O Come, Divine Messiah
435	O Come, O Come, Emmanuel
268	O Lord of Light
281	On Jordan's Bank
293	People, Look East
309	Psalm 25: To You, O Lord (Haugen)
310	Psalm 25: To You, O Lord (Willcock)
325	Psalm 72: Justice Shall Flourish
326	Psalm 85: God Is Speaking Peace
327	Psalm 89: Forever I Will Sing (Carroll)
328	Psalm 89: Forever I Will Sing (Haugen)
342	Psalm 122: Let Us Go Rejoicing
343	Psalm 126: The Lord Has Done Great Things
348	Psalm 146: I Will Praise the Lord
353	Rejoice, the Lord Is King
359	Savior of the Nations, Come
378	Soon and Very Soon
393	The Advent of Our God
400	The God Whom Earth and Sea and Sky
402	The King Shall Come
435	Veni, Veni, Emmanuel
437	Wait for the Lord
438	Wake, O Wake and Sleep No Longer
463	When the King Shall Come Again

CHRISTMAS

350	A Child Is Born in Bethlehem
6	Adeste Fideles
26	Angels, from the Realms of Glory
27	Angels We Have Heard on High
40	Awake! Awake, and Greet the New Morn
41	Away in a Manger
60	Child of Mercy
64	Christ Is Born
70	Christ Was Born on Christmas Day
129	Gift of God
131	Go Tell It on the Mountain
141	God Rest You Merry, Gentlemen
144	Good Christian Friends, Rejoice
156	Hark! The Herald Angels Sing
179	I Want to Walk as a Child of the Light
188	Infant Holy, Infant Lowly
189	Infant Wrapped in God's Own Light
190	It Came Upon the Midnight Clear
201	Joy to the World
206	Let All Mortal Flesh Keep Silence
213	Lift Up Your Heads, You Mighty Gates
214	Lo, How a Rose E'er Blooming
244	Night of Silence
364	Noche de Paz
6	O Come, All Ye Faithful
255	O Come, Little Children
264	O Little Town of Bethlehem
278	Of the Father's Love Begotten
286	Once in Royal David's City
331	Psalm 96: Today Is Born Our Savior (Hughes)
332	Psalm 96: Today Is Born Our Savior, Christ the Lord (Proulx)
333	Psalm 98: All the Ends of the Earth (Haas)
334	Psalm 98: All the Ends of the Earth (Trapp)
335	Psalm 98: All the Ends of the Earth (Willcock)
350	Puer Natus in Bethlehem
354	Resonet in Laudibus
359	Savior of the Nations, Come
364	Silent Night
364	Stille Nacht
398	The First Nowell
400	The God Whom Earth and Sea and Sky
404	The Snow Lay on the Ground
438	Wake, O Wake and Sleep No Longer
451	We Three Kings of Orient Are
455	What Child Is This?
456	What Star Is This
466	While Shepherds Watched Their Flocks
471	Wood of the Cradle

EPIPHANY

31	As with Gladness Men of Old
103	Earth Has Many a Noble City
107	Epiphany Carol
189	Infant Wrapped in God's Own Light

Liturgical Index, pg. 2

377	Songs of Thankfulness and Praise
398	The First Nowell
451	We Three Kings of Orient Are
455	What Child Is This?
456	What Star Is This

BAPTISM OF THE LORD
42	Baptized in Water
194	Jesus at the Jordan Baptized
460	When John Baptized by Jordan's River

LENT
593	A Lamp for Our Feet (RCIA Dismissal)
5	A Prayer for the Elect
10	Again We Keep This Solemn Fast
23	Amazing Grace
33	At the Cross Her Station Keeping
35	Attende, Domine
46	Be Thou My Vision
47	Beloved Son and Daughter Dear
48	Beneath the Tree of Life / En el Árbol de la Vida
65	Christ Is Made the Sure Foundation
85	Come to Me, All Pilgrims Thirsty
100	Dust and Ashes
48	En el Árbol de la Vida / Beneath the Tree of Life
122	Forgive Our Sins
123	Forty Days and Forty Nights
125	From Ashes to the Living Font
592	Go in Peace (RCIA Dismissal)
139	God of Mercy and Compassion
157	Have Mercy, Lord, on Us
35	Hear Our Entreaties, Lord
165	Hosea (Come Back to Me)
172	I Am the Bread of Life / Yo Soy el Pan de Vida
175	I Heard the Voice of Jesus Say
185	In the Cross of Christ
591	In the Cross of Christ (RCIA Signing)
186	In the Cross of Christ I Glory
191	Jerusalem, My Destiny
212	Lift High the Cross
218	Lord, Help Us Walk Your Servant Way
219	Lord Jesus, as We Turn from Sin
222	Lord, Teach Us How to Pray Aright
224	Lord, Who Throughout These Forty Days
236	Mercy, O God
240	My People, What Do I Require?
272	O Merciful Redeemer, Hear
277	O Sun of Justice
289	Our Father, We Have Wandered
292	Parce Domine
298	Praise to the Holiest in the Height
302	Psalm 16: You Will Show Me the Path of Life
303	Psalm 19: Lord, You Have the Words (Guimont)
304	Psalm 19: Lord, You Have the Words (Haas)
311	Psalm 27: The Lord Is My Light (Haas)
312	Psalm 27: The Lord Is My Light (Willcock)
314	Psalm 33: Let Your Mercy Be on Us
319	Psalm 51: Be Merciful, O Lord (Haugen)
320	Psalm 51: Be Merciful, O Lord (Hunstiger)
321	Psalm 51: Be Merciful, O Lord (Willcock)
329	Psalm 91: Be with Me (Haugen)
336	Psalm 103: The Lord Is Kind and Merciful (Haugen)
344	Psalm 130: With the Lord There Is Mercy
349	Psalm 147: Bless the Lord, My Soul
355	Return to God
389	Take Up Your Cross
396	The Cross of Jesus
399	The Glory of These Forty Days
408	The Thirsty Cry for Water, Lord
409	The Time of Fulfillment
411	The Voice of God Speaks but of Peace
413	There's a Wideness in God's Mercy
422	'Tis Good, Lord, to Be Here
426	Transform Us
427	Tree of Life
457	What Wondrous Love Is This?
458	When from Bondage
172	Yo Soy el Pan de Vida / I Am the Bread of Life

PALM SUNDAY
7	Adoramus te Christe
14	All Glory, Laud, and Honor
93	Crown Him with Many Crowns
164	Hosanna!
193	Jesu, Jesu, Fill Us with Your Love
198	Jesus, Remember Me
212	Lift High the Cross
213	Lift Up Your Heads, You Mighty Gates
274	O Sacred Head Surrounded
305	Psalm 22: My God, My God (Hunstiger)
306	Psalm 22: My God, My God (Willcock)
389	Take Up Your Cross
427	Tree of Life
454	Were You There?

HOLY THURSDAY
7	Adoramus te Christe
32	At That First Eucharist
48	Beneath the Tree of Life / En el Árbol de la Vida
74	Come and Eat This Bread
48	En el Árbol de la Vida / Beneath the Tree of Life
290	Hail Our Savior's Glorious Body
193	Jesu, Jesu, Fill Us with Your Love
198	Jesus, Remember Me
200	Jesus Took a Towel
212	Lift High the Cross
428	Live in Charity / Ubi Caritas
245	No Greater Love
248	Now We Remain
290	Pange Lingua
301	Prepare a Room for Me
338	Psalm 116: Our Blessing-Cup

Liturgical Index, pg. 3

373	So You Must Do
382	Stay Here and Keep Watch
428	Ubi Caritas / Live in Charity
429	Ubi Caritas / Where Charity and Love Are Found
447	We Have Been Told
450	We Remember
429	Where Charity and Love Are Found / Ubi Caritas
464	Where Charity and Love Prevail

GOOD FRIDAY
33	At the Cross Her Station Keeping
48	Beneath the Tree of Life / En el Árbol de la Vida
390	Bowing Low / Tantum Ergo
48	En el Árbol de la Vida / Beneath the Tree of Life
185	In the Cross of Christ
192	Jerusalem, My Happy Home
198	Jesus, Remember Me
212	Lift High the Cross
256	O Cross of Christ
274	O Sacred Head Surrounded
305	Psalm 22: My God, My God (Hunstiger)
306	Psalm 22: My God, My God (Willcock)
313	Psalm 31: I Put My Life in Your Hands
382	Stay Here and Keep Watch
390	Tantum Ergo / Bowing Low
446	We Glory in the Cross
454	Were You There?
457	What Wondrous Love Is This?

EASTER
1	A Hymn of Glory Let Us Sing
20	Alleluia! Alleluia! Let the Holy Anthem Rise
21	Alleluia! Sing to Jesus
34	At the Lamb's High Feast We Sing
43	Be Joyful, Mary
594	Blessing of Water
54	Bread of Life / Pan de Vida
63	Christ Is Alive
66	Christ Is Risen! Shout Hosanna!
67	Christ Is the King
68	Christ the Lord Is Risen Today
74	Come and Eat This Bread
82	Come, Sisters, Brothers, One in Faith
86	Come to Me and Live
88	Come, You Faithful, Raise the Strain
93	Crown Him with Many Crowns
98	Drinking Earth's Pure Water
102	Earth, Earth, Awake!
104	Easter Alleluia
109	Exsultet
418	Festival Canticle (This Is the Feast)
145	Good Christians All, Rejoice and Sing!
151	Hail the Day That Sees Him Rise
152	Hail Thee, Festival Day!
158	He Is Risen, He Is Risen

172	I Am the Bread of Life / Yo Soy el Pan de Vida
176	I Know That My Redeemer Lives
195	Jesus Christ Is Risen Today
196	Jesus Christ, Yesterday, Today and For Ever
204	Keep In Mind
206	Let All Mortal Flesh Keep Silence
209	Let Hymns of Joy to Grief Succeed
212	Lift High the Cross
226	Lord, You Give the Great Commission
238	Morning Has Broken
257	O Filii et Filiae
257	O Sons and Daughters
285	On This Day, the First of Days
576	Profession of Faith
577	This Is Our Faith
54	Pan de Vida / Bread of Life
339	Psalm 118: An Eastertime Psalm
340	Psalm 118: This is the Day
436	Sequence for Easter / Victimae Paschali Laudes
370	Sing We Triumphant Hymns of Praise
371	Sing with All the Saints in Glory
372	Singers, Sing
375	Song of Water
546	Sprinkling Rite: Springs of Water I (Proulx)
547	Sprinkling Rite: Springs of Water II (Holland)
381	Stand Firm in Faith
385	Sweet Refreshment
392	That Easter Day with Joy Was Bright
397	The Day of Resurrection
406	The Strife Is O'er, the Battle Done
410	The Tomb Is Empty
417	This Is the Day
418	This Is the Feast of Victory (Festival Canticle)
436	Victimae Paschali Laudes / Sequence for Easter
447	We Have Been Told
448	We Know That Christ Is Raised
450	We Remember
473	Ye Watches and Ye Holy Ones
172	Yo Soy el Pan de Vida / I Am the Bread of Life
595	You Have Put on Christ (Hughes)
596	You Have Put on Christ (Greene)

ASCENSION
16	All Hail the Power of Jesus' Name
20	Alleluia! Alleluia! Let the Holy Anthem Rise
21	Alleluia! Sing to Jesus
62	Christ, by Whose Death
63	Christ Is Alive
68	Christ the Lord Is Risen Today
71	Christ, You Formed the Church, Your Body
93	Crown Him with Many Crowns
132	Go to the World
151	Hail the Day That Sees Him Rise
152	Hail Thee, Festival Day!
226	Lord, You Give the Great Commission

339	Psalm 47: An Eastertime Psalm		
353	Rejoice, the Lord Is King		
436	Sequence for Easter / Victimae Paschali Laudes		
367	Sing Out, Earth and Skies		
370	Sing We Triumphant Hymns of Praise		
388	Take, O Take Me as I Am		
423	To Be Your Presence		
424	To Jesus Christ, Our Sovereign King		
436	Victimae Paschali Laudes / Sequence for Easter		

PENTECOST

57	Called and Gathered by the Spirit
62	Christ, by Whose Death
69	Christ, the Word Before Creation
71	Christ, You Formed the Church, Your Body
76	Come, Gracious Spirit, Heavenly Dove
77	Come, Holy Ghost, Creator Blest
80	Come, O Spirit
83	Come, Spirit, Come
115	Fire of God, Undying Flame
130	Go, Be Justice
152	Hail Thee, Festival Day!
163	Holy Spirit, Come to Us
239	Moved by the Gospel
249	O Breathe on Me
252	O Christ the Great Foundation
261	O Holy Spirit, by Whose Breath
337	Psalm 104: Send Forth Your Spirit, O Lord
339	Psalm 104: An Eastertime Psalm
361	Send Us Your Spirit
434	Sequence for Pentecost / Veni Sancte Spiritus
380	Spirit Blowing through Creation
388	Take, O Take Me as I Am
407	The Summons
423	To Be Your Presence
431	Veni Creator Spiritus
432	Veni, Lumen Cordium
433	Veni Sancte Spiritus
434	Veni Sancte Spiritus / Sequence for Pentecost
441	We Are Many Parts

MOST HOLY TRINITY

12	All Creatures of Our God and King
15	All Hail, Adored Trinity
65	Christ Is Made the Sure Foundation
81	Come, Our Almighty King
124	From All That Dwell Below the Skies
142	God, We Praise You!
161	Holy God, We Praise Thy Name
162	Holy, Holy, Holy!
171	How Wonderful the Three in One
227	Lord, Your Almighty Word
247	Now Thank We All Our God
258	O God, Almighty Father
285	On This Day, the First of Days

MOST HOLY BODY AND BLOOD OF CHRIST

8	Adoro Te Devote
19	All Who Hunger, Gather Gladly
32	At That First Eucharist
56	By Your Hand, You Feed Your People
58	Can God a Lavish Table Spread?
74	Come and Eat This Bread
97	Draw Near and Take the Body of Your Lord
105	Eat the Bread of Thanksgiving
106	Eat This Bread
128	Gift of Finest Wheat
130	Go, Be Justice
290	Hail Our Savior's Glorious Body / Pange Lingua
106	Jesus Christ, Bread of Life
291	Jesus, Our Living Bread / Panis Angelicus
211	Life-Giving Bread, Saving Cup
248	Now We Remain
287	One Bread We Bless and Share
290	Pange Lingua / Hail Our Savior's Glorious Body
291	Panis Angelicus / Jesus, Our Living Bread
338	Psalm 116: Our Blessing-Cup
349	Psalm 147: Bless the Lord, My Soul
360	See Us, Lord, About Your Altar
386	Take and Eat
387	Take and Eat This Bread
442	We Are Your People

CHRIST THE KING

14	All Glory, Laud, and Honor
16	All Hail the Power of Jesus' Name
21	Alleluia! Sing to Jesus
63	Christ Is Alive
67	Christ Is the King
68	Christ the Lord Is Risen Today
72	Christ's Church Shall Glory in His Power
78	Come, Let Us Sing for Joy
81	Come, Our Almighty King
93	Crown Him with Many Crowns
114	Father, We Thank Thee Who Hast Planted
418	Festival Canticle (This Is the Feast of Victory)
118	For All the Saints
142	God, We Praise You!
145	Good Christians All, Rejoice and Sing!
198	Jesus, Remember Me
199	Jesus Shall Reign
200	Jesus Took a Towel
213	Lift Up Your Heads, You Mighty Gates
252	O Christ the Great Foundation
253	O Christ, What Can It Mean for Us
269	O Lowly Lamb of God Most High
271	O Merciful Redeemer
295	Praise, My Soul, the King of Heaven
346	Psalm 145: I Will Praise Your Name (Haas)
347	Psalm 145: I Will Praise Your Name (Willcock)
353	Rejoice, the Lord Is King
378	Soon and Very Soon

Liturgical Index, pg. 5

402	The King Shall Come		385	Sweet Refreshment
418	This Is the Feast of Victory (Festival Canticle)		386	Take and Eat
424	To Jesus Christ, Our Sovereign King		388	Take, O Take Me as I Am
446	We Glory in the Cross		391	Taste and See
			401	The King of Love
			407	The Summons

CHRISTIAN INITIATION

593	A Lamp for Our Feet (RCIA Dismissal)		441	We Are Many Parts
5	A Prayer for the Elect		443	We Belong to Christ
12	All Creatures of Our God and King		447	We Have Been Told
21	Alleluia! Sing to Jesus		448	We Know That Christ Is Raised
23	Amazing Grace		452	We Walk by Faith (DUNLAP'S CREEK)
42	Baptized in Water		453	We Walk by Faith (SHANTI)
46	Be Thou My Vision		350	When We Are Living / Pues Si Vivimos
594	Blessing of Water		460	When John Baptized by Jordan's River
65	Christ Is Made the Sure Foundation		467	Who Calls You by Name
79	Come, My Way, My Truth, My Life		475	You Are God's Work of Art
88	Come, You Faithful, Raise the Strain		476	You Are Mine
104	Easter Alleluia		477	You Are My Shepherd
106	Eat This Bread		595	You Have Put on Christ (Hughes)
125	From Ashes to the Living Font		596	You Have Put on Christ (Greene)
591	Glory and Praise (RCIA Signing)			
592	Go in Peace (RCIA Dismissal)		**CONFIRMATION**	
174	I Come with Joy		3	A New Heaven and Earth
175	I Heard the Voice of Jesus Say		44	Be Not Afraid
186	In the Cross of Christ I Glory		57	Called and Gathered by the Spirit
591	In the Cross of Christ (RCIA Signing)		76	Come, Gracious Spirit, Heavenly Dove
191	Jerusalem, My Destiny		77	Come, Holy Ghost, Creator Blest
106	Jesus Christ, Bread of Life		80	Come, O Spirit
212	Lift High the Cross		83	Come, Spirit, Come
228	Love Divine, All Loves Excelling		115	Fire of God, Undying Flame
248	Now We Remain		126	Gather Us In
249	O Breathe on Me		132	Go to the World
252	O Christ the Great Foundation		152	Hail Thee, Festival Day!
282	On Our Journey to the Kingdom		163	Holy Spirit, Come to Us
576	Profession of Faith		226	Lord, You Give the Great Commission
577	This Is Our Faith		249	O Breathe on Me
302	Psalm 16: You Will Show Me the Path of Life		252	O Christ the Great Foundation
307	Psalm 23: My Shepherd Is the Lord		261	O Holy Spirit, by Whose Breath
307	Psalm 23: The Lord Is My Shepherd		337	Psalm 104: Send Forth Your Spirit, O Lord
308	Psalm 23: Shepherd Me, O God		339	Psalm 104: An Eastertime Psalm
311	Psalm 27: The Lord Is My Light (Haas)		361	Send Us Your Spirit
312	Psalm 27: The Lord Is My Light (Willcock)		434	Sequence for Pentecost / Veni Sancte Spiritus
315	Psalm 34: Taste and See (Chepponis)		380	Spirit Blowing through Creation
316	Psalm 34: Taste and See (Haugen)		388	Take, O Take Me as I Am
317	Psalm 34: Taste and See (Willcock)		389	Take Up Your Cross
318	Psalm 42: Like the Deer That Longs		407	The Summons
327	Psalm 89: Forever I Will Sing (Carroll)		423	To Be Your Presence
328	Psalm 89: Forever I Will Sing (Haugen)		431	Veni Creator Spiritus
330	Psalm 95: If Today You Hear the Voice of God		432	Veni, Lumen Cordium
337	Psalm 104: Send Forth Your Spirit, O Lord		433	Veni Sancte Spiritus
351	Pues Si Vivimos / When We Are Living		434	Veni Sancte Spiritus / Sequence for Pentecost
361	Send Us Your Spirit		439	We Are Called
367	Sing Out, Earth and Skies		442	We Are Your People
376	Song Over the Waters		443	We Belong to Christ
546	Springs of Water I (Proulx)		447	We Have Been Told
547	Springs of Water II (Holland)		476	You Are Mine

477	You Are My Shepherd		300	Prayer of Peace (Peace before Us)
478	You Are the Light of the World		301	Prepare a Room for Me

EUCHARIST

7	Adoramus te Christe		307	Psalm 23: My Shepherd Is the Lord
11	All Are Welcome		308	Psalm 23: Shepherd Me, O God
19	All Who Hunger, Gather Gladly		307	Psalm 23: The Lord Is My Shepherd
20	Alleluia! Alleluia! Let the Holy Anthem Rise		315	Psalm 34: Taste and See (Cheponis)
21	Alleluia! Sing to Jesus		316	Psalm 34: Taste and See (Haugen)
23	Amazing Grace		317	Psalm 34: Taste and See (Willcock)
28	Around This Table, Altar Blest		318	Psalm 42: Like the Deer That Longs
29	As Grain on Scattered Hillsides		323	Psalm 63: My Soul Is Thirsting (Willcock)
30	As We Gather at Your Table		324	Psalm 63: My Soul Is Thirsting (Guimont)
32	At That First Eucharist		336	Psalm 103: The Lord Is Kind and Merciful (Haugen)
39	Ave Verum Corpus		338	Psalm 116: Our Blessing-Cup
54	Bread of Life / Pan de Vida		346	Psalm 145: I Will Praise Your Name (Haas)
56	By Your Hand, You Feed Your People		347	Psalm 145: I Will Praise Your Name (Willcock)
58	Can God a Lavish Table Spread?		349	Psalm 147: Bless the Lord, My Soul
74	Come and Eat This Bread		360	See Us, Lord, About Your Altar
75	Come, Gather at the Table		363	Shepherd of Souls
79	Come, My Way, My Truth, My Life		373	So You Must Do
86	Come to Me and Live		382	Stay Here and Keep Watch
87	Come to the Banquet		386	Take and Eat
97	Draw Near and Take the Body of Your Lord		387	Take and Eat This Bread
104	Easter Alleluia		391	Taste and See
105	Eat the Bread of Thanksgiving		401	The King of Love
106	Eat This Bread		420	Though We Are Many
114	Father, We Thank Thee Who Hast Planted		428	Ubi Caritas / Live in Charity
126	Gather Us In		429	Ubi Caritas / Where Charity and Love Are Found
128	Gift of Finest Wheat		440	We Are Called to Tell the Story
130	Go, Be Justice		441	We Are Many Parts
132	Go to the World		443	We Belong to Christ
134	God Is Here! As We His People		444	We Come with Joy
290	Hail Our Savior's Glorious Body / Pange Lingua		447	We Have Been Told
172	I Am the Bread of Life / Yo Soy el Pan de Vida		450	We Remember
174	I Come with Joy		452	We Walk by Faith (DUNLAP'S CREEK)
175	I Heard the Voice of Jesus Say		453	We Walk by Faith (SHANTI)
177	I Received the Living God		429	Where Charity and Love Are Found / Ubi Caritas
179	I Want to Walk as a Child of the Light		464	Where Charity and Love Prevail
193	Jesu, Jesu, Fill Us with Your Love		469	With a Shepherd's Care
106	Jesus Christ, Bread of Life		470	Within the Reign of God
291	Jesus, Our Living Bread / Panis Angelicus		172	Yo Soy el Pan de Vida / I Am the Bread of Life
206	Let All Mortal Flesh Keep Silence			

MARRIAGE

211	Life-Giving Bread, Saving Cup		4	A Nuptial Blessing
428	Live in Charity / Ubi Caritas		79	Come, My Way, My Truth, My Life
215	Lord, Accept the Gifts We Offer		133	God in the Planning
248	Now We Remain		135	God Is Love
257	O Filii et Filiae / O Sons and Daughters		143	God, You Made the Earth and Heavens
263	O King of Might and Splendor		159	Hear Us Now, Our God and Father
257	O Sons and Daughters / O Filii et Filiae		228	Love Divine, All Loves Excelling
280	On Emmaus' Journey		245	No Greater Love
284	On This Day of Sharing		247	Now Thank We All Our God
287	One Bread We Bless and Share		315	Psalm 34: Taste and See (Cheponis)
54	Pan de Vida / Bread of Life		316	Psalm 34: Taste and See (Haugen)
290	Pange Lingua / Hail Our Savior's Glorious Body		317	Psalm 34: Taste and See (Willcock)
291	Panis Angelicus / Jesus, Our Living Bread		336	Psalm 103: The Lord Is Kind and Merciful (Haugen)
			341	Psalm 121: Our Help Is from the Lord

342	Psalm 122: Let Us Go Rejoicing	413	There's a Wideness in God's Mercy
346	Psalm 145: I Will Praise Your Name (Haas)	437	Wait for the Lord
347	Psalm 145: I Will Praise Your Name (Willcock)	457	What Wondrous Love Is This?
415	This Day Is Filled with Love so Bright	458	When from Bondage
425	Today We Have Gathered	462	When Sorrow Turns Our Day to Night
428	Ubi Caritas / Live in Charity	351	When We Are Living / Pues Si Vivimos
430	Unseen God, Your Hand Has Guided	469	With a Shepherd's Care
447	We Have Been Told	474	You Are All We Have
461	When Love Is Found	476	You Are Mine
464	Where Charity and Love Prevail	477	You Are My Shepherd

PASTORAL CARE OF THE SICK

FUNERAL

23	Amazing Grace	12	All Creatures of Our God and King
44	Be Not Afraid	20	Alleluia! Alleluia! Let the Holy Anthem Rise
53	Blest Are They	21	Alleluia! Sing to Jesus
79	Come, My Way, My Truth, My Life	23	Amazing Grace
111	Eye Has Not Seen	44	Be Not Afraid
154	Hands of Healing	53	Blest Are They
167	How Firm a Foundation	55	By All Your Saints Still Striving
170	How Lovely Is Your Dwelling Place	68	Christ the Lord Is Risen Today
175	I Heard the Voice of Jesus Say	79	Come, My Way, My Truth, My Life
177	I Received the Living God	93	Crown Him with Many Crowns
221	Lord of All Hopefulness	95	Day is Done
241	My Shepherd Will Supply My Need	101	Dwellers in the Holy City
251	O Christ Our True and Only Light	104	Easter Alleluia
259	O God Beyond All Praising	106	Eat This Bread
262	O Jesus, We Adore Thee	111	Eye Has Not Seen
265	O Lord, Hear My Prayer	118	For All the Saints
279	On Eagle's Wings	138	God of Love
302	Psalm 16: You Will Show Me the Path of Life	167	How Firm a Foundation
305	Psalm 22: My God, My God (Hunstiger)	169	How Great Thou Art
306	Psalm 22: My God, My God (Willcock)	170	How Lovely Is Your Dwelling Place
307	Psalm 23: My Shepherd Is the Lord	172	I Am the Bread of Life / Yo Soy el Pan de Vida
308	Psalm 23: Shepherd Me, O God	173	I Call You to My Father's House
307	Psalm 23: The Lord Is My Shepherd	175	I Heard the Voice of Jesus Say
309	Psalm 25: To You, O Lord (Haugen)	176	I Know That My Redeemer Lives
310	Psalm 25: To You, O Lord (Willcock)	177	I Received the Living God
313	Psalm 31: I Put My Life in Your Hands	179	I Want to Walk as a Child of the Light
314	Psalm 33: Let Your Mercy Be on Us	180	I Will Be the Vine
315	Psalm 34: Taste and See (Chepponis)	184	In Paradisum / May Choirs of Angels
316	Psalm 34: Taste and See (Haugen)	191	Jerusalem, My Destiny
317	Psalm 34: Taste and See (Willcock)	192	Jerusalem, My Happy Home
318	Psalm 42: Like the Deer That Longs	106	Jesus Christ, Bread of Life
323	Psalm 63: My Soul Is Thirsting (Willcock)	195	Jesus Christ Is Risen Today
324	Psalm 63: My Soul Is Thirsting (Guimont)	198	Jesus, Remember Me
336	Psalm 103: The Lord Is Kind and Merciful (Haugen)	202	Joyful, Joyful, We Adore Thee
341	Psalm 121: Our Help Is from the Lord	204	Keep In Mind
349	Psalm 147: Bless the Lord, My Soul	221	Lord of All Hopefulness
351	Pues Si Vivimos / When We Are Living	225	Lord, Whose Love in Humble Service
362	Shepherd of My Heart	184	May Choirs of Angels / In Paradisum
363	Shepherd of Souls	234	May the Angels Lead You into Paradise
382	Stay Here and Keep Watch	241	My Shepherd Will Supply My Need
389	Take Up Your Cross	243	My Soul in Stillness Waits
391	Taste and See	260	O God, Our Help in Ages Past
401	The King of Love	265	O Lord, Hear My Prayer
412	There Is a Balm in Gilead	267	O Lord of Life

279	On Eagle's Wings	175	I Heard the Voice of Jesus Say
302	Psalm 16: You Will Show Me the Path of Life	191	Jerusalem, My Destiny
307	Psalm 23: My Shepherd Is the Lord	202	Joyful, Joyful, We Adore Thee
308	Psalm 23: Shepherd Me, O God	219	Lord Jesus, as We Turn from Sin
307	Psalm 23: The Lord Is My Shepherd	222	Lord, Teach Us How to Pray Aright
309	Psalm 25: To You, O Lord (Haugen)	240	My People, What Do I Require?
310	Psalm 25: To You, O Lord (Willcock)	241	My Shepherd Will Supply My Need
311	Psalm 27: The Lord Is My Light (Haas)	251	O Christ Our True and Only Light
312	Psalm 27: The Lord Is My Light (Willcock)	265	O Lord, Hear My Prayer
318	Psalm 42: Like the Deer That Longs	289	Our Father, We Have Wandered
323	Psalm 63: My Soul Is Thirsting (Willcock)	300	Prayer of Peace (Peace before Us)
324	Psalm 63: My Soul Is Thirsting (Guimont)	302	Psalm 16: You Will Show Me the Path of Life
336	Psalm 103: The Lord Is Kind and Merciful (Haugen)	305	Psalm 22: My God, My God (Hunstiger)
342	Psalm 122: Let Us Go Rejoicing	306	Psalm 22: My God, My God (Willcock)
344	Psalm 130: With the Lord There Is Mercy	309	Psalm 25: To You, O Lord (Haugen)
351	Pues Si Vivimos / When We Are Living	310	Psalm 25: To You, O Lord (Willcock)
356	Saints of God (Haas)	313	Psalm 31: I Put My Life in Your Hands
357	Saints of God (Janco)	314	Psalm 33: Let Your Mercy Be on Us
363	Shepherd of Souls	319	Psalm 51: Be Merciful, O Lord (Haugen)
371	Sing with All the Saints in Glory	320	Psalm 51: Be Merciful, O Lord (Hunstiger)
374	Song of Farewell	321	Psalm 51: Be Merciful, O Lord (Willcock)
378	Soon and Very Soon	322	Psalm 51: Be Merciful, O Lord / Create in Me
381	Stand Firm in Faith	329	Psalm 91: Be with Me
386	Take and Eat	336	Psalm 103: The Lord Is Kind and Merciful (Haugen)
391	Taste and See	344	Psalm 130: With the Lord There Is Mercy
397	The Day of Resurrection	345	Psalm 141: My Prayers Rise Like Incense
401	The King of Love	349	Psalm 147: Bless the Lord, My Soul
406	The Strife Is O'er, the Battle Done	355	Return to God
412	There Is a Balm in Gilead	388	Take, O Take Me as I Am
424	To Jesus Christ, Our Sovereign King	401	The King of Love
447	We Have Been Told	411	The Voice of God Speaks but of Peace
452	We Walk by Faith (DUNLAP'S CREEK)	412	There Is a Balm in Gilead
453	We Walk by Faith (SHANTI)	413	There's a Wideness in God's Mercy
457	What Wondrous Love Is This?	457	What Wondrous Love Is This?
351	When We Are Living / Pues Si Vivimos	458	When from Bondage
172	Yo Soy el Pan de Vida / I Am the Bread of Life	469	With a Shepherd's Care
476	You Are Mine	476	You Are Mine
477	You Are My Shepherd		

RECONCILIATION / PENANCE

BLESSED VIRGIN MARY

23	Amazing Grace	22	Alma Redemptoris Mater / O Gracious Mother
30	As We Gather at Your Table	33	At the Cross Her Station Keeping
35	Attende, Domine / Hear Our Entreaties, Lord	36	Ave Maria
52	Blest Are the Pure in Heart	37	Ave Maria, God Is with You
165	Come Back to Me (Hosea)	38	Ave, Regina Caelorum / Queen of the Heavens, We Greet You
79	Come, My Way, My Truth, My Life	43	Be Joyful, Mary
91	Conditor Alme Siderum / Creator of the Stars of Night	94	Daily, Daily Sing to Mary
91	Creator of the Stars of Night / Conditor Alme Siderum	117	For All the Faithful Women
100	Dust and Ashes	149	Hail, Holy Queen Enthroned Above
125	From Ashes to the Living Font	358	Hail, Most Gracious Queen / Salve, Regina
139	God of Mercy and Compassion	181	Immaculate Mary
157	Have Mercy, Lord, on Us	214	Lo, How a Rose E'er Blooming
35	Hear Our Entreaties, Lord / Attende, Domine	229	Magnificat / Luke 1:46-55
165	Hosea (Come Back to Me)	233	Mary, Woman of the Promise
167	How Firm a Foundation	242	My Soul Gives Glory to the Lord
		22	O Gracious Mother / Alma Redemptoris Mater

270	O Mary, Our Mother	262	O Jesus, We Adore Thee
276	O Most Holy One / O Sanctissima	266	O Lord, I Am Not Worthy
352	O Queen of Heaven / Regina Caeli	276	O Most Holy One / O Sanctissima
276	O Sanctissima / O Most Holy One	275	O Salutaris / O Saving Victim
278	Of the Father's Love Begotten	276	O Sanctissima / O Most Holy One
283	On This Day, O Beautiful Mother	275	O Saving Victim / O Salutaris
38	Queen of the Heavens, We Greet You / Ave, Regina Caelorum	290	Pange Lingua / Hail Our Savior's Glorious Body
352	Regina Caeli / O Queen of Heaven	291	Panis Angelicus / Jesus, Our Living Bread
358	Salve, Regina / Hail, Most Gracious Queen	379	Soul of My Savior
366	Sing of Mary	390	Tantum Ergo / Bowing Low
369	Sing We of the Blessed Mother		
384	Sub Tuum Praesidium / Under Your Protection		
400	The God Whom Earth and Sea and Sky		
384	Under Your Protection / Sub Tuum Praesidium		

NATIONAL

24	America (My Country, 'Tis of Thee)
25	America the Beautiful
237	Battle Hymn of the Republic (Mine Eyes Have Seen the Glory)
108	Eternal Father, Strong to Save
140	God of Our Fathers
237	Mine Eyes Have Seen the Glory (Battle Hymn of the Republic)
24	My Country, 'Tis of Thee (America)
416	This Is My Song

EUCHARISTIC DEVOTION

390	Bowing Low / Tantum Ergo
290	Hail Our Savior's Glorious Body / Pange Lingua
197	Jesus, My Lord, My God, My All
291	Jesus, Our Living Bread / Panis Angelicus
216	Lord and God, Devoutly You I Now Adore

Index of Service Music

MASS SETTINGS

Jubilation Mass by James Chepponis
481 Kyrie
482 Gloria
483 Gospel Acclamation
484 Sanctus
485 Memorial Acclamation A
486 Memorial Acclamation B
487 Memorial Acclamation C
488 Memorial Acclamation D
489 Amen
490 Agnus Dei

New Plainsong Mass by David Hurd
491 Sanctus
492 Memorial Acclamation
493 Amen

Mass of Creation by Marty Haugen
494 Kyrie
495 Gloria
496 Gospel Acclamation
497 Lenten Gospel Acclamation
498 Sanctus
499 Memorial Acclamation A
500 Memorial Acclamation B
501 Memorial Acclamation C
502 Memorial Acclamation D
503 Doxology and Amen
504 Agnus Dei

Mass of the Angels and Saints by Steven Janco
505 Kyrie
506 Gloria
507 Gospel Acclamation
508 Lenten Gospel Acclamation
509 Sanctus
510 Memorial Acclamation A
511 Memorial Acclamation B
512 Memorial Acclamation C
513 Memorial Acclamation D
514 Doxology and Amen
515 Agnus Dei

Land of Rest Acclamations by Richard Proulx
516 Sanctus
517 Memorial Acclamation A
518 Memorial Acclamation D
519 Amen
520 Agnus Dei

Community Mass by Richard Proulx
521 Sanctus
522 Memorial Acclamation
523 Amen
524 Agnus Dei

Saint Benedict Mass by Robert LeBlanc
525 Kyrie
526 Gloria
527 Gospel Acclamation
528 Lenten Gospel Acclamation
529 Sanctus
530 Memorial Acclamation
531 Amen
532 Agnus Dei

Cantus Missae–Chant Mass
533 Asperges me
534 Vidi Aquam
535 Kyrie I
536 Kyrie II
537 Gloria
538 Chants for the Liturgy of the Word
539 Preface Dialogue
540 Sanctus
541 Post Consecrationem
542 Amen
543 Pater Noster
544 Agnus Dei
545 Concluding Rite

SERVICE AND RITUAL MUSIC

546 Sprinkling Rite: Springs of Water I (Proulx)
547 Sprinkling Rite: Springs of Water II (Holland)
548 Lord, Have Mercy I (Proulx)
549 Lord, Have Mercy II (Somerville)
550 Gloria I (Melodic Gloria)
551 Gloria II (Mass of Hope)
552 Gloria III (Congregational Mass)
553 Gloria IV (A New Mass for Congregations)
554 Gloria V (Colgan)
555 Gloria VI (Christmas Gloria)
597 Children's Liturgy of the Word Dismissal (Listen to God's Word)
556 Gospel Acclamation I (Chant Mode VI)
557 Gospel Acclamation II (Murray)
558 Gospel Acclamation III (Hytrek)
559 Gospel Acclamation IV (O'Carroll)
560 Gospel Acclamation V (Festival Alleluia)
561 Gospel Acclamation VI (Traditional Byzantine Chant)
562 Gospel Acclamation VII (Gelobt sei gott)
563 Gospel Acclamation VIII (Hunstiger)
564 Gospel Acclamation IX (Sayles/Gertken)
565 Gospel Acclamation X (Victory)
566 Gospel Acclamation XII (with verse for Easter)
567 Gospel Acclamation / Lenten Gospel Acclamation (Mass for John Carroll)
568 Lenten Gospel Acclamation I (Haugen)
569 Lenten Gospel Acclamation II (Schoen)
570 Lenten Gospel Acclamation III (Krubsack)
571 Lenten Gospel Acclamation IV (Hughes)

Index of Service Music, pg. 2

572	Lenten Gospel Acclamation V (Proulx)	579	General Intercessions II (Inwood)
573	Lenten Gospel Acclamation VI (Doub)	580	General Intercessions III (Inwood)
574	Lenten Gospel Acclamation VII (Doub)	581	General Intercessions IV (Inwood)
575	Lenten Gospel Acclamation VIII (Doub)	582	General Intercessions V (Trilingual Intercessions)
591	Signing of the RCIA Candidates with the Cross (In the Cross of Christ / Glory and Praise)	583	General Intercessions VI (Bilingual Intercessions: Te Rogamos, Óyenos / Lord, Hear Our Prayer)
592	Dismissal of the Elect and Catechumens (Go in Peace)	584	Sanctus (Mass of the Good Shepherd)
		585	Amen I (Danish)
593	Dismissal of the Elect and Catechumens (A Lamp for Our Feet)	586	Amen II (Dresden)
		587	Amen III (Englert)
576	Profession of Faith	588	Lord's Prayer (Gelineau)
577	This Is Our Faith	589	Agnus Dei I (Holy Cross Mass)
594	Blessing of Water	590	Agnus Dei II (Proulx)
595	Rite of Baptism (You Have Put on Christ)	598	Sending Forth Extraordinary Ministers of Holy Communion (Go Forth in Peace)
596	Rite of Baptism (You Have Put on Christ)		
578	General Intercessions I (Byzantine chant)	599	Community Blessing (May God Bless and Keep You)

Index of First Lines and Common Titles

A

350	A Child Is Born in Bethlehem / Puer Natus in Bethlehem
1	A Hymn of Glory Let Us Sing
2	A Mighty Fortress Is Our God
3	A New Heaven and Earth
4	A Nuptial Blessing
5	A Prayer for the Elect
6	Adeste Fideles / O Come, All Ye Faithful
7	Adoramus te Christe
8	Adoro Te Devote
9	Advent Gathering Song: Come, Come Emmanuel
10	Again We Keep This Solemn Fast
11	All Are Welcome
12	All Creatures of Our God and King
13	All Glory Is Yours
14	All Glory, Laud, and Honor
15	All Hail, Adored Trinity
16	All Hail the Power of Jesus' Name
17	All People That on Earth Do Dwell
383	All praise to you
333	All the Ends of the Earth (Haas)
334	All the Ends of the Earth (Trapp)
335	All the Ends of the Earth (Willcock)
18	All the Wonder That Surrounds Us
19	All Who Hunger, Gather Gladly
20	Alleluia! Alleluia! Let the Holy Anthem Rise
21	Alleluia! Sing to Jesus
22	Alma Redemptoris Mater / O Gracious Mother
23	Amazing Grace
24	America (My Country, 'Tis of Thee)
25	America the Beautiful
339	An Eastertime Psalm
26	Angels, from the Realms of Glory
27	Angels We Have Heard on High
28	Around This Table, Altar Blest
29	As Grain on Scattered Hillsides
30	As We Gather at Your Table
31	As with Gladness Men of Old
32	At That First Eucharist
33	At the Cross Her Station Keeping
34	At the Lamb's High Feast We Sing
146	At your coming, Christ, in glory
35	Attende, Domine / Hear Our Entreaties, Lord
36	Ave Maria
37	Ave Maria, God Is with You
38	Ave, Regina Caelorum / Queen of the Heavens, We Greet You
39	Ave Verum Corpus
40	Awake! Awake, and Greet the New Morn
41	Away in a Manger

B

42	Baptized in Water
237	Battle Hymn of the Republic
43	Be Joyful, Mary
44	Be Not Afraid
45	Be Patient, God's People
319	Be Merciful, O Lord (Haugen)
320	Be Merciful, O Lord (Hunstiger)
322	Be Merciful, O Lord (Pishner)
321	Be Merciful, O Lord (Willcock)
46	Be Thou My Vision
329	Be with Me
47	Beloved Son and Daughter Dear
48	Beneath the Tree of Life / En el Árbol de la Vida
246	Benedictus (Canticle of Zachary)
49	Bless the Lord
349	Bless the Lord, My Soul
467	Blessed be God, O blessed be God
50	Blessed Be the God of Israel
51	Blessed Jesus, at Thy Word
52	Blest Are the Pure in Heart
53	Blest Are They
390	Bowing Low / Tantum Ergo
54	Bread of Life / Pan de Vida
55	By All Your Saints Still Striving
56	By Your Hand, You Feed Your People

C

57	Called and Gathered by the Spirit
58	Can God a Lavish Table Spread?
59	Canticle of the Sun
246	Canticle of Zachary (Benedictus)
60	Child of Mercy
61	Christ, Be Our Light
62	Christ, by Whose Death
63	Christ Is Alive
64	Christ Is Born
65	Christ Is Made the Sure Foundation
66	Christ Is Risen! Shout Hosanna!
67	Christ Is the King
68	Christ the Lord Is Risen Today
69	Christ, the Word Before Creation
70	Christ Was Born on Christmas Day
71	Christ, You Formed the Church, Your Body
72	Christ's Church Shall Glory in His Power
73	Church of God, Elect and Glorious
244	Cold are the people
74	Come and Eat This Bread
92	Come and Fill / Confitemini Domino
165	Come Back to Me
9	Come, Come Emmanuel
75	Come, Gather at the Table
76	Come, Gracious Spirit, Heavenly Dove
77	Come, Holy Ghost, Creator Blest
78	Come, Let Us Sing for Joy
439	Come, live in the light
79	Come, My Way, My Truth, My Life
470	Come now, the feast is spread

Index of First Lines and Common Titles, pg. 4

367	Come, O God of all the earth
80	Come, O Spirit
81	Come, Our Almighty King
82	Come, Sisters, Brothers, One in Faith
83	Come, Spirit, Come
374	Come to his/her aid
84	Come, Thou Long Expected Savior
85	Come to Me, All Pilgrims Thirsty
86	Come to Me and Live
87	Come to the Banquet
385	Come to the water
129	Come to Us
88	Come, You Faithful, Raise the Strain
89	Come, You Thankful People, Come
90	Comfort, Comfort, Ye My People
91	Conditor Alme Siderum / Creator of the Stars of Night
92	Confitemini Domino / Come and Fill
322	Create in Me
91	Creator of the Stars of Night / Conditor Alme Siderum
93	Crown Him with Many Crowns

D
94	Daily, Daily Sing to Mary
95	Day is Done
96	Dona Nobis Pacem
97	Draw Near and Take the Body of Your Lord
98	Drinking Earth's Pure Water
375	Droplets of water bright with light
99	Dulcis Iesu Memoria / O Jesus, Joy of Loving Hearts
100	Dust and Ashes
101	Dwellers in the Holy City

E
102	Earth, Earth, Awake!
103	Earth Has Many a Noble City
104	Easter Alleluia
105	Eat the Bread of Thanksgiving
106	Eat This Bread / Jesus Christ, Bread of Life
48	En el Árbol de la Vida / Beneath the Tree of Life
107	Epiphany Carol
108	Eternal Father, Strong to Save
107	Every nation sees the glory
109	Exsultet
110	Exultate, Justi
111	Eye Has Not Seen

F
112	Fairest Lord Jesus
113	Faith of Our Fathers
114	Father, We Thank Thee Who Hast Planted
418	Festival Canticle
115	Fire of God, Undying Flame
116	For All the Blessings of the Year
117	For All the Faithful Women
118	For All the Saints
327	Forever I Will Sing (Carroll)
328	Forever I Will Sing (Haugen)
119	For the Beauty of the Earth
120	For the Coming of the Savior
121	For the Fruits of All Creation
147	For the time of your returning
243	For you, O Lord, my soul in stillness waits
122	Forgive Our Sins
123	Forty Days and Forty Nights
477	Fresh and green are the pastures
124	From All That Dwell Below the Skies
125	From Ashes to the Living Font

G
126	Gather Us In
127	Gathered Now
128	Gift of Finest Wheat
129	Gift of God
130	Go, Be Justice
131	Go Tell It on the Mountain
132	Go to the World
133	God in the Planning
134	God Is Here! As We His People
135	God Is Love
326	God Is Speaking Peace
339	God Mounts His Throne
136	God of All People
137	God of Day and God of Darkness
138	God of Love
139	God of Mercy and Compassion
140	God of Our Fathers
141	God Rest You Merry, Gentlemen
142	God, We Praise You!
376	God, you have moved upon the waters
143	God, You Made the Earth and Heavens
144	Good Christian Friends, Rejoice
145	Good Christians All, Rejoice and Sing!
146	Gospel Responses for Advent – Year A
147	Gospel Responses for Advent – Year B
148	Gospel Responses for Advent – Year C
362	Guide me, O shepherd of my heart
232	Gracious God of Wisdom

H
149	Hail, Holy Queen Enthroned Above
358	Hail, Most Gracious Queen / Salve, Regina
290	Hail Our Savior's Glorious Body / Pange Lingua
150	Hail, Redeemer, King Most Blest
151	Hail the Day That Sees Him Rise
152	Hail Thee, Festival Day!
153	Hail to the Lord's Anointed
154	Hands of Healing

Index of First Lines and Common Titles, pg. 4

155	Hark! A Thrilling Voice Is Sounding	99	Jesu Dulcis Memoria / O Jesus, Joy of Loving Hearts
156	Hark! The Herald Angels Sing	193	Jesu, Jesu, Fill Us with Your Love
157	Have Mercy, Lord, on Us	194	Jesus at the Jordan Baptized
158	He Is Risen, He Is Risen	106	Jesus Christ, Bread of Life / Eat This Bread
35	Hear Our Entreaties, Lord / Attende, Domine	195	Jesus Christ Is Risen Today
159	Hear Us Now, Our God and Father	196	Jesus Christ, Yesterday, Today and For Ever
160	Here I Am, Lord	197	Jesus, My Lord, My God, My All
126	Here in this place	291	Jesus, Our Living Bread / Panis Angelicus
161	Holy God, We Praise Thy Name	373	Jesus, our teacher and our Lord
162	Holy, Holy, Holy!	198	Jesus, Remember Me
163	Holy Spirit, Come to Us	199	Jesus Shall Reign
164	Hosanna!	200	Jesus Took a Towel
165	Hosea (Come Back to Me)	148	Jesus, when you come in glory
166	How Can I Keep from Singing?	201	Joy to the World
167	How Firm a Foundation	202	Joyful, Joyful, We Adore Thee
168	How Good It Is	203	Jubilate Servite (Jubilate Deo)
169	How Great Thou Art	325	Justice Shall Flourish
170	How Lovely Is Your Dwelling Place		
171	How Wonderful the Three in One		

K

204	Keep In Mind

I

172	I Am the Bread of Life / Yo Soy el Pan de Vida
173	I Call You to My Father's House
174	I Come with Joy
191	I have fixed my eyes
175	I Heard the Voice of Jesus Say
176	I Know That My Redeemer Lives
313	I Put My Life in Your Hands
177	I Received the Living God
178	I Sing the Almighty Power of God
160	I, the Lord of sea and sky
179	I Want to Walk as a Child of the Light
180	I Will Be the Vine
476	I will come to you in the silence
348	I Will Praise the Lord
346	I Will Praise Your Name (Haas)
347	I Will Praise Your Name (Willcock)
421	I will sing forever to you, my God
330	If Today You Hear the Voice of God
181	Immaculate Mary
182	Immortal, Invisible, God Only Wise
99	Iesu Dulcis Memoria / O Jesus, Joy of Loving Hearts
183	In Christ There Is No East or West
184	In Paradisum / May Choirs of Angels
185	In the Cross of Christ
186	In the Cross of Christ I Glory
187	In the Lord I'll Be Ever Thankful
188	Infant Holy, Infant Lowly
189	Infant Wrapped in God's Own Light
190	It Came Upon the Midnight Clear

L

205	Laudate Dominum
206	Let All Mortal Flesh Keep Silence
207	Let All Things Now Living
208	Let Desert Wasteland Now Rejoice
209	Let Hymns of Joy to Grief Succeed
154	Let our hands be hands of healing
210	Let There Be Peace on Earth
11	Let us build a house
330	Let Us Come Before the Lord
342	Let Us Go Rejoicing
314	Let Your Mercy Be on Us
211	Life-Giving Bread, Saving Cup
212	Lift High the Cross
213	Lift Up Your Heads, You Mighty Gates
318	Like the Deer That Longs
428	Live in Charity / Ubi Caritas
214	Lo, How a Rose E'er Blooming
61	Longing for light
215	Lord, Accept the Gifts We Offer
216	Lord and God, Devoutly You I Now Adore
217	Lord, Come
218	Lord, Help Us Walk Your Servant Way
219	Lord Jesus, as We Turn from Sin
217	Lord, let us turn to you
220	Lord, Make Us Servants of Your Peace
221	Lord of All Hopefulness
339	Lord, Send Out Your Spirit
222	Lord, Teach Us How to Pray Aright
223	Lord, When You Came / Pescador de Hombres
224	Lord, Who Throughout These Forty Days
225	Lord, Whose Love in Humble Service
226	Lord, You Give the Great Commission

J

191	Jerusalem, My Destiny
192	Jerusalem, My Happy Home

Index of First Lines and Common Titles, pg. 4

303	Lord, You Have the Words (Guimont)	256	O Cross of Christ
304	Lord, You Have the Words (Haas)	257	O Filii et Filiae / O Sons and Daughters
227	Lord, Your Almighty Word	258	O God, Almighty Father
228	Love Divine, All Loves Excelling	259	O God Beyond All Praising
		260	O God, Our Help in Ages Past
		22	O Gracious Mother / Alma Redemptoris Mater

M

229	Magnificat / Luke 1:46-55	261	O Holy Spirit, by Whose Breath
230	Make Us True Servants	99	O Jesus, Joy of Loving Hearts / Dulcis Iesu Memoria
231	Maranatha, Come	262	O Jesus, We Adore Thee
232	Maranatha, Lord Messiah	263	O King of Might and Splendor
233	Mary, Woman of the Promise	264	O Little Town of Bethlehem
184	May Choirs of Angels	265	O Lord, Hear My Prayer
4	May God bless you, hold and keep you	266	O Lord, I Am Not Worthy
234	May the Angels Lead You into Paradise	169	O Lord my God
235	Merciful Savior	267	O Lord of Life
236	Mercy, O God	268	O Lord of Light
237	Mine Eyes Have Seen the Glory (Battle Hymn of the Republic)	269	O Lowly Lamb of God Most High
238	Morning Has Broken	270	O Mary, Our Mother
239	Moved by the Gospel	271	O Merciful Redeemer
24	My country, 'tis of thee	272	O Merciful Redeemer, Hear
305	My God, My God (Hunstiger)	276	O Most Holy One / O Sanctissima
306	My God, My God (Willcock)	273	O Radiant Light
166	My life flows on in endless song	352	O Queen of Heaven / Regina Caeli
240	My People, What Do I Require?	274	O Sacred Head Surrounded
345	My Prayers Rise Like Incense	275	O Salutaris / O Saving Victim
307	My Shepherd Is the Lord	276	O Sanctissima / O Most Holy One
241	My Shepherd Will Supply My Need	275	O Saving Victim / O Salutaris
242	My Soul Gives Glory to the Lord	257	O Sons and Daughters / O Filii et Filiae
243	My Soul in Stillness Waits	277	O Sun of Justice
323	My Soul Is Thirsting (Willcock)	278	Of the Father's Love Begotten
324	My Soul Is Thirsting (Guimont)	279	On Eagle's Wings
		280	On Emmaus' Journey
		281	On Jordan's Bank
		282	On Our Journey to the Kingdom
		283	On This Day, O Beautiful Mother
		284	On This Day of Sharing

N

244	Night of Silence	285	On This Day, the First of Days
245	No Greater Love	286	Once in Royal David's City
364	Noche de Paz / Silent Night / Stille Nacht	287	One Bread We Bless and Share
246	Now Bless the God of Israel (Canticle of Zachary / Benedictus)	288	One in Christ, We Meet Together
		338	Our Blessing-Cup
247	Now Thank We All Our God	289	Our Father, We Have Wandered
248	Now We Remain	341	Our Help Is from the Lord

O

P

25	O beautiful for spacious skies	54	Pan de Vida / Bread of Life
249	O Breathe on Me	290	Pange Lingua / Hail Our Savior's Glorious Body
250	O Child of Promise, Come!	291	Panis Angelicus / Jesus, Our Living Bread
251	O Christ Our True and Only Light	292	Parce Domine
252	O Christ the Great Foundation	300	Peace before us
253	O Christ, What Can It Mean for Us	293	People, Look East
6	O Come, All Ye Faithful / Adeste Fideles	223	Pescador de Hombres / Lord, When You Came
254	O Come, Divine Messiah	294	Praise and Thanksgiving
255	O Come, Little Children	17	Praise God from Whom All Blessings Flow
435	O Come, O Come, Emmanuel / Veni, Veni, Emmanuel	295	Praise, My Soul, the King of Heaven

Index of First Lines and Common Titles, pg. 4

296	Praise the Lord! Ye Heavens, Adore Him
297	Praise to Our God, Creation's Lord
298	Praise to the Holiest in the Height
299	Praise to the Lord, the Almighty
300	Prayer of Peace (Peace before Us)
301	Prepare a Room for Me
229	Proclaim the greatness of God
302	Psalm 16: You Will Show Me the Path of Life
303	Psalm 19: Lord, You Have the Words (Guimont)
304	Psalm 19: Lord, You Have the Words (Haas)
305	Psalm 22: My God, My God (Hunstiger)
306	Psalm 22: My God, My God (Willcock)
307	Psalm 23: My Shepherd Is the Lord / The Lord Is My Shepherd
308	Psalm 23: Shepherd Me, O God
309	Psalm 25: To You, O Lord (Haugen)
310	Psalm 25: To You, O Lord (Willcock)
311	Psalm 27: The Lord Is My Light (Haas)
312	Psalm 27: The Lord Is My Light (Willcock)
313	Psalm 31: I Put My Life in Your Hands
314	Psalm 33: Let Your Mercy Be on Us / The Earth Is Full of the Goodness of God
315	Psalm 34: Taste and See (Chepponis)
316	Psalm 34: Taste and See (Haugen)
317	Psalm 34: Taste and See (Willcock)
318	Psalm 42: Like the Deer That Longs
319	Psalm 51: Be Merciful, O Lord (Haugen)
320	Psalm 51: Be Merciful, O Lord (Hunstiger)
321	Psalm 51: Be Merciful, O Lord (Willcock)
322	Psalm 51: Be Merciful, O Lord / Create in Me
323	Psalm 63: My Soul Is Thirsting (Willcock)
324	Psalm 63: My Soul Is Thirsting (Guimont)
325	Psalm 72: Justice Shall Flourish
326	Psalm 85: God Is Speaking Peace
327	Psalm 89: Forever I Will Sing (Carroll)
328	Psalm 89: Forever I Will Sing (Haugen)
329	Psalm 91: Be with Me
330	Psalm 95: If Today You Hear the Voice of God / Let Us Come Before the Lord
331	Psalm 96: Today Is Born Our Savior (Hughes)
332	Psalm 96: Today Is Born Our Savior (Proulx)
333	Psalm 98: All the Ends of the Earth (Haas)
334	Psalm 98: All the Ends of the Earth (Trapp)
335	Psalm 98: All the Ends of the Earth / Sing a New Song to the Lord
336	Psalm 103: The Lord Is Kind and Merciful
337	Psalm 104: Send Forth Your Spirit, O Lord
338	Psalm 116: Our Blessing-Cup
339	Psalms 118, 47, 104: An Eastertime Psalm
340	Psalm 118: This is the Day
341	Psalm 121: Our Help Is from the Lord
342	Psalm 122: Let Us Go Rejoicing
343	Psalm 126: The Lord Has Done Great Things
344	Psalm 130: With the Lord There Is Mercy
345	Psalm 141: My Prayers Rise Like Incense
346	Psalm 145: I Will Praise Your Name (Haas)
347	Psalm 145: I Will Praise Your Name (Willcock)
348	Psalm 146: I Will Praise the Lord
349	Psalm 147: Bless the Lord, My Soul
350	Puer Natus in Bethlehem / A Child Is Born in Bethlehem
351	Pues Si Vivimos / When We Are Living

Q
38	Queen of the Heavens, We Greet You / Ave, Regina Caelorum

R
352	Regina Caeli / O Queen of Heaven
353	Rejoice, the Lord Is King
354	Resonet in Laudibus
355	Return to God

S
356	Saints of God (Haas)
357	Saints of God (Janco)
358	Salve, Regina / Hail, Most Gracious Queen
359	Savior of the Nations, Come
360	See Us, Lord, About Your Altar
337	Send Forth Your Spirit, O Lord
361	Send Us Your Spirit
436	Sequence for Easter / Victimae Paschali Laudes
434	Sequence for Pentecost / Veni Sancte Spiritus
308	Shepherd Me, O God
362	Shepherd of My Heart
363	Shepherd of Souls
364	Silent Night / Stille Nacht / Noche de Paz
365	Sing a New Song to the Lord (Dudley-Smith)
335	Sing a New Song to the Lord (Willcock)
366	Sing of Mary
367	Sing Out, Earth and Skies
368	Sing Praise to God Who Reigns Above
369	Sing We of the Blessed Mother
370	Sing We Triumphant Hymns of Praise
371	Sing with All the Saints in Glory
372	Singers, Sing
373	So You Must Do
374	Song of Farewell
375	Song of Water
376	Song Over the Waters
377	Songs of Thankfulness and Praise
378	Soon and Very Soon
379	Soul of My Savior
109	Sound salvation's mighty trumpet!
380	Spirit Blowing through Creation
3	Spirit of God, come burn in your people
381	Stand Firm in Faith
382	Stay Here and Keep Watch
383	Stewards of Earth

Index of First Lines and Common Titles, pg. 4

364	Stille Nacht / Noche de Paz / Silent Night
384	Sub Tuum Praesidium / Under Your Protection
385	Sweet Refreshment

T

386	Take and Eat
387	Take and Eat This Bread
388	Take, O Take Me as I Am
389	Take Up Your Cross
390	Tantum Ergo / Bowing Low
315	Taste and See (Chepponis)
316	Taste and See (Haugen)
391	Taste and See (Moore)
317	Taste and See (Willcock)
449	Te Deum / We Praise You, God
392	That Easter Day with Joy Was Bright
393	The Advent of Our God
394	The Church of Christ in Every Age
395	The Church's One Foundation
396	The Cross of Jesus
397	The Day of Resurrection
314	The Earth Is Full of the Goodness of God
398	The First Nowell
399	The Glory of These Forty Days
400	The God Whom Earth and Sea and Sky
59	The heavens are telling the glory of God
401	The King of Love
402	The King Shall Come
343	The Lord Has Done Great Things
336	The Lord Is Kind and Merciful
311	The Lord Is My Light (Haas)
312	The Lord Is My Light (Willcock)
307	The Lord Is My Shepherd
403	The Reign of God
404	The Snow Lay on the Ground
405	The Song of the Trees
406	The Strife Is O'er, the Battle Done
407	The Summons
408	The Thirsty Cry for Water, Lord
409	The Time of Fulfillment
410	The Tomb Is Empty
411	The Voice of God Speaks but of Peace
412	There Is a Balm in Gilead
245	There is no greater love
413	There's a Wideness in God's Mercy
414	This Day God Gives Me
415	This Day Is Filled with Love so Bright
339	This Is the Day (Chepponis)
340	This is the Day (Willcock)
416	This Is My Song
417	This Is the Day
418	This Is the Feast of Victory (Festival Canticle)
419	Those Who Love and Those Who Labor
420	Though We Are Many
421	Throughout All Time
422	'Tis Good, Lord, to Be Here
423	To Be Your Presence
424	To Jesus Christ, Our Sovereign King
13	To you, O God, all glory be
309	To You, O Lord (Haugen)
310	To You, O Lord (Willcock)
331	Today Is Born Our Savior (Hughes)
332	Today Is Born Our Savior (Proulx)
425	Today We Have Gathered
426	Transform Us
427	Tree of Life

U

428	Ubi Caritas / Live in Charity
429	Ubi Caritas / Where Charity and Love Are Found
384	Under Your Protection / Sub Tuum Praesidium
430	Unseen God, Your Hand Has Guided

V

431	Veni Creator Spiritus
432	Veni, Lumen Cordium
433	Veni Sancte Spiritus
434	Veni Sancte Spiritus / Sequence for Pentecost
435	Veni, Veni, Emmanuel / O Come, O Come, Emmanuel
436	Victimae Paschali Laudes / Sequence for Easter

W

437	Wait for the Lord
438	Wake, O Wake and Sleep No Longer
439	We Are Called
440	We Are Called to Tell the Story
441	We Are Many Parts
442	We Are Your People
443	We Belong to Christ
444	We Come with Joy
445	We Gather Together
446	We Glory in the Cross
447	We Have Been Told
248	We hold the death of the Lord
448	We Know That Christ Is Raised
5	We praise and thank you, Lord, this day
449	We Praise You, God / Te Deum
450	We Remember
451	We Three Kings of Orient Are
452	We Walk by Faith (DUNLAP'S CREEK)
453	We Walk by Faith (SHANTI)
454	Were You There?
455	What Child Is This?
456	What Star Is This
457	What Wondrous Love Is This?
458	When from Bondage
459	When In Our Music God Is Glorified
460	When John Baptized by Jordan's River

Index of First Lines and Common Titles, pg. 5

461	When Love Is Found	471	Wood of the Cradle
462	When Sorrow Turns Our Day to Night	472	Word of God, Come Down on Earth
463	When the King Shall Come Again	473	Ye Watches and Ye Holy Ones
351	When We Are Living / Pues Si Vivimos	172	Yo Soy el Pan de Vida / I Am the Bread of Life
429	Where Charity and Love Are Found / Ubi Caritas	474	You Are All We Have
464	Where Charity and Love Prevail	475	You Are God's Work of Art
465	Where Your Treasure Is	476	You Are Mine
466	While Shepherds Watched Their Flocks	477	You Are My Shepherd
467	Who Calls You by Name	478	You Are the Light of the World
468	Who Can Measure Heaven and Earth?	479	You Call to Us, Lord Jesus
280	Who are you who walk in sorrow	128	You satisfy the hungry heart
407	Will you come and follow me	44	You shall cross the barren desert
469	With a Shepherd's Care	480	You Walk Along Our Shoreline
344	With the Lord There Is Mercy	279	You who dwell in the shelter of the Lord
470	Within the Reign of God	302	You Will Show Me the Path of Life